MASTER GUIDE
for Passing the Respiratory Care Credentialing Exams
Fourth Edition

RICK MEYER, MS, RRT
Professor
Director of Clinical Education
Department of Respiratory Therapy
Mt. San Antonio College
Walnut, California

Education Coordinator
Cardiorespiratory Department
Pomona Valley Hospital Medical Center
Pomona, California

With contributions by:

TERRANCE M. KRIDER, BS, RRT
Professor and Chair
Health Science Division
Department of Respiratory Therapy
Mt. San Antonio College
Walnut, California

WILLIAM A. SYVERTSEN, MS, RRT
Instructor
Business Division
Fresno City College
Fresno, California

Prentice Hall Health
Upper Saddle River, NJ 07458

Library of Congress Cataloging-in-Publication Data

Meyer, Rick, 1945–
    Master guide for passing the respiratory care credentialing exams / Rick Meyer, with contributions by Terrance M. Krider and William A. Syvertsen. — 4th ed.
      p. cm.
    Includes bibliographical references and index.
    ISBN 0-444-50074-X
    1. Respiratory therapy—Outlines, syllabi, etc. 2. Respiratory therapy—Examinations, questions, etc. I. Krider, Terrance M. II. Syvertsen, Willam A. III. Krider, Terrance M. Master guide for passing the respiratory care credentialing exams. IV. Title.
    [DNLM: 1. Respiratory Therapy—Examination Questions. 2. Respiratory Therapy—instrumentation—Examination Questions. WB 18.2 M613m 2000]
    RC735 I5 K75 2000
    615.8'36'076—dc21

                                                                                                                      99-043212

Acquisitions Editor: Mark Cohen
Director of Manufacturing & Production: Bruce Johnson
Manufacturing Buyer: Ilene Sanford
Managing Editor: Pat Walsh
Production Liaison: Larry Hayden IV
Editorial Assistant: Melissa Kerian
Full Service Production/Formatting: BookMasters, Inc.
Creative Director: Marianne Frasco
Cover Design Coordinator: Maria Guglielmo
Cover Design: Karen Salzbach
Marketing Manager: Tiffany Price
Printer/Binder: R. R. Donnelley & Sons, Harrisburg, VA

© 2000 by Prentice-Hall, Inc.
Upper Saddle River, New Jersey 07458

All rights reserved. No part of this book may be
reproduced, in any forma or by any means,
without permission in writing from the publisher.

This review text is specifically designed to present information to guide the reader in preparing for respiratory care certification examinations. The author and publisher have made a conscientious effort to assure accuracy, completeness, and compatibility with the standards generally accepted for information presented at the time of publication. Nevertheless, as new information becomes available as a result of research and experience, changes in respiratory care practice become necessary. Also, certification examinations may vary from offering to offering. The reader is advised that the author and publisher cannot be responsible for any errors or omissions arising from new information, interpretations, or changes in the scope of the examination.

Printed in the United States of America

10 9 8 7 6 5 4 3 2 1

ISBN 0-13-013832-0

Prentice-Hall International (UK) Limited, *London*
Prentice-Hall of Australia Pty. Limited, *Sydney*
Prentice-Hall Canada Inc., *Toronto*
Prentice-Hall Hispanoamericana, S. A., *Mexico*
Prentice-Hall of India Private Limited, *New Delhi*
Prentice-Hall Japan, Inc., *Tokyo*
Prentice-Hall (Singapore) Pte. Ltd.
Editora Prentice-Hall do Brasil, Ltda., *Rio de Janeiro*

To Bill and Terry

To Bill, whose foresight, friendship, leadership, and vision led to the creation of this project, and who is responsible for the structure of this current version.

To Terry, whose wonderful depth of knowledge in this field led to the formation of the original content sections, and who served as an excellent consultant and reference for this edition.

The fond memories were truly in the chase and continuing the flame provides the comfort of closure.

Thank you!

Contents

PREFACE vii

CHAPTER 1 Improving Your Credentialing Exam Results 1

SECTION I DATA 15

CHAPTER 2 Patient Assessment 17
CHAPTER 3 Bedside Respiratory Monitoring 41
CHAPTER 4 Pulmonary Laboratory 58
CHAPTER 5 Clinical Laboratory 79
CHAPTER 6 Bedside Hemodynamic Monitoring 91
CHAPTER 7 Radiographic Monitoring 106
CHAPTER 8 Other Assessments and Diagnostic Testing 117
CHAPTER 9 Perinatal/Neonatal Assessment 127
CHAPTER 10 Analyze Data and Determine Plan 133

SECTION II EQUIPMENT 157

CHAPTER 11 Resuscitation Devices 159
CHAPTER 12 Oxygen Delivery Devices 177
CHAPTER 13 Aerosol Generators and Humidification Equipment 197
CHAPTER 14 Respiratory Support Equipment 208
CHAPTER 15 Ventilator Systems and Support Accessories 228
CHAPTER 16 Monitoring, Analyzing, and Testing Devices 254
CHAPTER 17 Sterilization 277

SECTION III THERAPY 287

CHAPTER 18 Removal of Bronchopulmonary Secretions 289
CHAPTER 19 Respiratory Pharmacologic Agents 308

CHAPTER 20	Ensuring Adequate Ventilation	344
CHAPTER 21	Mechanical Ventilation of Adults	353
CHAPTER 22	Mechanical Ventilation of Neonates	399
CHAPTER 23	Monitoring of Blood Gases	412
CHAPTER 24	Achieving Adequate Oxygenation	424
CHAPTER 25	Cardiovascular Monitoring	441
CHAPTER 26	Cardiopulmonary Resuscitation	453
CHAPTER 27	Pulmonary Rehabilitation and Home Care	469
CHAPTER 28	Assistance with Special Procedures	476
CHAPTER 29	Record Maintenance and Documentation	492

SECTION IV Self-Assessment 499

| CHAPTER 30 | Certified Respiratory Therapist (CRT) Self-Assessment Examination | 503 |
| CHAPTER 31 | Registered Respiratory Therapist (RRT) Self-Assessment Examination | 521 |

SELF-ASSESSMENT ANSWER KEY 535

ASSESSMENT QUESTIONS 537

INDEX 541

Preface

Nothing succeeds like success.
French Proverb, 1854

Since the first edition of *Master Guide* was published in 1984, thousands of respiratory therapists have used this book to successfully complete their national credentialing exams. I believe you will find this fourth edition of *Master Guide* an excellent tool that will help you to pass both the state and national exams, and provide the content necessary to address your strengths and weaknesses as a respiratory therapist. *Master Guide*, 4th Edition, is ideal for the educator, whose program curriculum is evaluated and needs to meet current national guidelines. In addition, the format is quite useful toward the production of questions for both student exams and as a reference guide for item writing. Finally, *Master Guide*, 4th Edition, may serve as a useful reference for physicians, nurses, and other allied health practitioners who desire a concise review of current developments in the practice of respiratory care.

As with previous editions, *Master Guide* offers to the exam candidate the first publication that actually discusses the specific content areas that are assessed on all three national board examinations. Since the third edition of *Master Guide* was offered in 1994, there have been several changes in the national examination process that warrant a new edition. In 1998, the National Board for Respiratory Care, Inc. (NBRC)[1] published new examination matrices and content outlines for the revised Certification Examination for Entry Level Respiratory Therapists (CRT), and the Written Registry and Clinical Simulation Examinations for Advanced Respiratory Therapists (RRT).[2] These matrices are a direct result of a national job analysis conducted in 1997 and impact the examination processes beginning in July and December 1999.

The fourth edition of *Master Guide* not only addresses these new examination matrices, but also includes several improvements over the third edition. The three major content sections (data, equipment, and therapy) have been expanded to accommodate the new matrix material. New graphics have been included to add clarity to the section describing ventilator waveforms. Self-assessment questions have been inserted at the end of each chapter, with all the correct answers identified at the end of Section IV.

The mock board exams (CRT/RRT) in chapters 30 and 31 have been rewritten to parallel the format of the national exams. The references at the end of each chapter have been updated and furnish a descriptive review of other sources of information needed for more in-depth analysis beyond this text. No attempt has been made in *Master Guide,* 4th Edition, to be exhaustive in the areas covered, but simply to provide you with the essential information to successfully pass the examinations.

Within this text you will find referenced material that identifies the content areas assessed on all three national examinations for both certification and registry. *Master Guide,* 4th Edition, focuses on the three main areas assessed on all NBRC examinations.

> SECTION I: DATA includes collecting and applying clinical information, and evaluating the effectiveness of a respiratory care plan.
>
> SECTION II: EQUIPMENT discusses equipment operation, function, troubleshooting, selection, and sterilization procedures in the clinical setting.
>
> SECTION III: THERAPY emphasizes a review of the therapeutic application of clinical management, assisting the physician with clinical procedures, and monitoring of the patient's response to the therapy.

Special assistance was provided by Bud Spearman, MS RRT, for which I am extremely grateful. Without Bud's wise counsel and recommendations this volume would not have been produced. I am also grateful to Mark Cohen, Acquisitions Editor at Prentice-Hall, who enthusiastically and successfully handled the reins of this production. I would also like to express special gratitude to Gary Gugelchuk, Ph.D., who patiently and with meticulous attention to detail, proofread the entire volume. Finally, I would like to acknowledge the many valuable suggestions I received from successful users of the first, second, and third editions of *Master Guide.*

Rick Meyer, MS, RRT
April 1999

References

1. As with previous editions, readers should understand that *Master Guide,* 4th Edition, does not necessarily express the views held by the NBRC and does not in any way reflect sponsorship or sanctioning of this text by the NBRC.
2. Revised Content Outlines, National Board for Respiratory Care Inc., 1998.

Preface

How to Use Your Master Guide

To get maximum benefit from your *Master Guide*, I recommend that you begin by joining the Five Percent Club. Make the commitment to excellence by signing and dating the pledge found at the end of Chapter 1. Ask a friend or relative to act as your supporting witness by signing the pledge with you.

If you desire additional information beyond that offered in the text, utilize the references listed at the end of each chapter. These references will direct you to common sources available to most hospital and school libraries, where additional information may be obtained.

Success on the NBRC board exams relies on two prerequisites:

- Knowing the areas assessed on the exams that are your strengths.
- Knowing the areas assessed on the exams that are your **weaknesses**.

First, go through each section, one chapter at a time, to get an idea of what areas are covered on the exam. By going through each chapter, you will discover topics in which you need more information **(weak areas)**. Once you find out what your weak areas are, **study those.** Then study the self-assessment questions at the end of each chapter, paying particular attention to understanding why distractors that are incorrect are attractive to you. Why did you pick them?

Next, upon completion of your review of the three major sections (data, equipment, and therapy), take the self-assessment test (Section IV) to monitor your own retention and understanding of the material for your specific examination. Once weak areas on the self-assessment exam are analyzed, refer back to the appropriate pages in the text that are identified on the answer sheet. If the information there isn't enough to clarify the concept, go to the references. If you know what areas you are weak in, and make those areas your strengths, you will pass the exam you are sitting for. Pretty simple really.

Finally, keep *Master Guide*, 4th Edition, in your possession for ready reference during your workday. As a clinical situation arises, refer to the extensive index and read how the actual clinical situation associates with the examination process. It is this conscientious blending of academics and clinical experiences that will most effectively prepare you for the successful completion of the Respiratory Care Credentialing Exams.

Chapter 1

Improving Your Credentialing Exam Results

The respiratory care credentialing process requires you, as an aspiring respiratory therapist, to demonstrate your mastery of key clinical skills and their underlying theoretical foundation. **Master Guide** is designed to help reinforce your command of the facts and principles of respiratory care by guiding you step-by-step through a thorough review of each topic tested on the credentialing examinations.

The Entry-Level Certification Examination

Graduating therapists and technicians must pass a 140-item multiple choice Entry Level Certification Examination with a scaled score of 75 percent or greater in order to become certified by the National Board for Respiratory Care (NBRC). The exam candidate is allowed three hours (180 minutes) to complete the 140 questions, which is an average of 1.28 minutes, or just under 78 seconds, per question.

The Advanced Practitioner Examination

To be registered by the NBRC, registry-eligible candidates must first pass a 100-item multiple choice exam, and then successfully work through a second exam consisting of ten clinical simulations.

Multiple-Choice Exams

A scaled score of 70 percent is required for successful completion of the exam. The exam candidate is allotted two hours (120 minutes) to complete the 100 questions on the Written Registry exam. This allotment permits an average of 1.38 minutes or 83 seconds per question.

Clinical Simulations

Achieving the minimal pass level (MPL) requirements for the ten clinical simulations involves demonstrating both decision-making and information-gathering skills.

> **TABLE 1-1:** Scoring Rationale for Clinical Simulation Exams
>
> +3 Very important or critical for appropriate care of the patient. Essential to do in order to resolve the problem.
>
> +2 Strongly recommended for appropriate care of the patient.
>
> +1 Helpful and facilitative for appropriate care of the patient.
>
> 0 Optional/noncontributory at this stage of problem. Does not help or harm the patient and does not contribute to the resolution of the problem.
>
> −1 Not helpful but mildly detrimental for care of the patient and does not help to resolve the problem.
>
> −2 Very inappropriate and harmful to the patient and does not lead to resolution of the problem.
>
> −3 Very harmful and damaging to the patient and does not lead to resolution of the problem.

Candidates have four hours (twenty minutes per problem) to solve ten situational patient management cases. All simulations use latent image response sheets on which data appear after being marked with a special latent image pen. Starting in 2000 all NBRC examinations will be administered via computer, thus ending the latent image mechanism.[1] All options are scored on a +3 to −3 scale using the rationale listed in Table 1-1.

How the Examinations Are Validated

All national credentialing exams are validated for reliability. The exams themselves are tested to assure that the questions accurately measure the knowledge and problem-solving ability required of a registered respiratory therapist at the designated level. Although the questions themselves may vary from exam to exam, the same content areas are always tested, and the level of difficulty is consistent. Thus, a group of candidates sitting for the Entry Level Exam in Florida in July, and another group sitting for the Entry Level Exam in California in December, can be assured that the two exams are closely matched in terms of overall knowledge, skills tested, and the degree of difficulty.

Becoming Familiar with the Exam

The new NBRC Entry Level and Advanced Practitioner exams have changed according to the new matrix (published August 1998).[2] Test items have been deleted from the Data and Equipment sections, and questions have been added to the Therapeutic Pro-

Chapter 1: Improving Your Credentialing Exam Results

cedures section. Both examinations have become more job related, with many items based on clinical application. Overall the number of recall items has decreased, while the overall number of application and analysis-level questions has increased. The NBRC has moved away from testing for basic knowledge, with the majority of items relating to actual evaluation of data and administration of clinical procedure.

Many candidates clearly fail because they are inadequately prepared to sit for an examination that requires the transfer of theory into practice. Taking the first steps toward passing the exam involves working to achieve mastery over the subject matter, becoming thoroughly familiar with the kinds of questions contained in the exam. The questions administered by the NBRC are not misleading or tricky items, they just require conceptual understanding. Overall superficial knowledge is not enough. The exam candidate must have an excellent working knowledge of both theory and clinical application if they are to succeed.

The credentialing process is intimidating, and candidates are likely to be subject to pre-examination jitters. When it comes time to study for the exam, some candidates may not know how to get started. This lack of focus tends to be so disheartening that they may feel defeated before they even begin. Refuse to allow the exam process to intimidate you. Remember that the best way to overcome your anxiety is to be confident that you have mastered the subject matter.

Study Skills

Studying sample questions can make you aware of your potential deficiencies in content matter. As you complete reading the content areas for the CRT, take the 140-question self-assessment exam immediately. Set a three-hour time limit, and see how long it takes to complete the exam. After you complete reading the content areas for the RRT exam, take the 100-question self-assessment exam immediately. Set a two-hour time limit, and see how long it takes to complete the exam. This practice will allow you to relate to exactly how the real exams will be administered. Analysis of your self-assessment exam results will help you diagnose and address your strengths and weaknesses. If you can answer a question correctly, and know why each distractor is incorrect, then you can be reassured that you have a basic understanding of that fact or skill. However, if you miss a question, return to the pertinent section and reread the content carefully. If after a thorough review, you still feel uncertain about your grasp of the facts and ideas, use the references at the end of the chapter to guide you to an expanded discussion.

Multiple-Choice Questions

Multiple-choice questions are used to test simple knowledge and theoretical understanding. Questions are composed of an item stem, the correct option, and the distractors. You are required to choose the correct answer from among four alternative responses. Read the stem statement first. It allows the candidate to break down the question and find out what it is really asking.

Stem Statements

The stem statement tells what to evaluate among the choices available, and may be in the format of a complete or incomplete statement.[3] The item stem is designed to provide all the information you need to choose the proper selection from among the options. After reading the stem statement, try and answer the question prior to viewing the different responses.

Examples:

Complete statement:
What is the most frequently used ventilator for administering IPPB therapy?

Incomplete statement:
The most frequently used ventilator for IPPB administration is

Carefully reading the stem statement is crucial. Many candidates develop mental fatigue as they progress through the exam and do not concentrate on reading the question. Careless reading may result in your skipping essential information, or misinterpreting the question altogether. The resulting confusion can cause you to linger indecisively over the choices and waste valuable time. You may find words used in the stem statement that are also used in one of the responses. Many times these words can be a clue to the correct answer.

Negative item stems can be confusing even to the most practiced reader, and many anxious candidates completely miss the use of them. Negative words like "**NOT**, **EXCEPT**, **NEVER**, or **LEAST**" are emphasized by the use of either boldface, underline, and/or capital letters.

Example:

Which of the following is **NOT** a correct statement when classifying electric ventilators?

Correct or Keyed Options

The correct or keyed option directs you to choose either the correct answer or the best answer from a list of provided options. In the correct answer form, one response is correct, whereas the other options are definitely incorrect.

Example: (one correct answer only)

Which of the following represents normal pulmonary capillary wedge pressure?

* A. 5–12 mmHg
  B. 6–15 mmHg
  C. 7–18 mmHg
  D. 8–21 mmHg

In the best answer version, more than one option may be partially correct.

Example: (best answer only)

Hazards of the intubation process include

   I. damage to the teeth and jaw
  II. damage to the vocal cords
 III. rupture of the trachea

    A. I only
* B. I and II only
    C. I, II, and III
    D. II only

The use of specific determiners such as *all, never, always,* and other all-inclusive terms are more likely to be found in incorrect options. *"None of the above"* and *"All of the above"* are weak distractors and are incorrect.[4]

Distractor Options

The distractor options are incorrect alternatives that nevertheless may seem plausible to candidates who have not completely mastered the concepts being tested. The distractor usually is appealing to candidates with some idea about the facts but without a secure grasp of the underlying principles. Distractors may be presented as incomplete but related ideas, common misconceptions, procedural mistakes, or predictable errors, and may appear to make distinctions so fine as to appear inconsequential.[5] Distractors that appear longer than the other options available are many times the correct response, because they need to provide more information to make the distractor plausible.

To Guess or Not to Guess

Multiple-choice items do encourage guessing. Many test-wise candidates pick the second distractor, B, if they have no idea which option is correct. This technique applies only to single response items, however, where statistically B does show up as the correct response more often than A, C, or D. Therefore, if you are going to guess you may as well pick the distractor with the greatest odds of being correct.

Multiple-choice items with numerical values frequently contain a high and a low value that can be eliminated straightaway. Thus, when in doubt concerning which option is correct, you often can narrow the choices by eliminating the high and low values and thus increase your chances of selecting the correct option.

Example:

Hypokalemia causes cardiac arrhythmias and reduced skeletal muscle contraction. This will not occur as long as serum potassium levels remain above

    A. 1.0 mEq/L (low range)
    B. 1.5 mEq/L
* C. 3.0 mEq/L
    D. 4.5 mEq/L (high range)

Difficulty Levels

The cognitive level of the content tested determines that the candidates who answer the questions correctly do so because they have mastered the information. Multiple-choice questions can test simple knowledge and comprehension as well as analysis and application.[6]

Recall Items. Recall items usually are reserved for simple knowledge type questions where the candidate recalls previously learned information. Determining the correct response requires neither analysis, nor understanding, nor judgment.

Example:

The normal V/Q ratio is

  A. very high
  B. very low
  C. 8.0
* D. 0.8

Application Items. Application items require you to analyze a limited amount of data, and apply your understanding appropriately to specified clinical situations. Such questions require more than simply recalling information, but do not call for complex problem solving.

Example:

An infant delivered by caesarian section at 26 weeks of gestation has nasal flaring, retraction, and expiratory grunting. The chest x-ray shows a ground glass appearance. On the basis of this information, the infant's difficulty is most likely a result of

  A. prenatal hypoxia
  B. bronchopulmonary dysplasia
  C. pulmonary edema
* D. infant respiratory distress syndrome

Analysis Level Items. Analysis level items require you to break down information into its component parts, and examine the relationships between the parts in order to make appropriate judgments. In such items you will have to make calculations or use your problem-solving skills, or both.

Example:

An 80-Kg, 35-year-old male is breathing at a respiratory rate of 30 breaths/minute with a tidal volume of 800 ml. ABG results show: $FIO_2 = 0.21$, $pH = 7.45$, $SaO_2 = 97\%$, $PaCO_2 = 35$ mmHg, $HCO_3 = 24$ mEq/L, $Hb = 14.5$ grams, and a $PaO_2 = 98$ mmHg. On the basis of this information, which of the following studies is most likely to show ABNORMAL results?

Chapter 1: Improving Your Credentialing Exam Results 7

   * A. V_D/V_T
     B. Q_S/Q_T
     C. Arterial oxygen content
     D. Closing volume

Item Responses

The item response may be structured in one of three basic formats: one-response, multiple true-false question, or situational set.

One Response Items. One-response items consist of a stem statement, a series of four distractors, and one correct response. Even if you cannot understand the question at all, you have a 25 percent chance (1 out of 4) of selecting the correct response. If you can eliminate any distractor, you increase your odds of answering the question correctly.

Example: (one response correct)

<u>Pseudomonas</u> is found in a patient's sputum culture. You would recommend that the patient be treated with

  * A. polymyxin B
    B. amphotericin B
    C. ampicillin
    D. penicillin

Multiple True-False Items. Multiple true-false items consist of a stem statement, a series of three to five true or false statements, and five optional choices, with one response being correct. You must respond correctly with the complete set of correct choices or no credit will be given.

Example: (more than one option may be correct)

Oxygen content is a measurement of

    I. oxygen dissolved in plasma
   II. hemoglobin per 100 ml of blood
  III. oxygen attached to hemoglobin
  IV. affinity of oxygen that is combined with hemoglobin
   V. the maximum amount of oxygen that is combined with blood

    A. I, II, and IV only
 * B. I and III only
    C. II, III, and IV only
    D. II, IV, and V only

As you answer each statement TRUE or FALSE, one distractor generally can be eliminated. In this example, number I is true, which means distractors C and D are incorrect because number I is not mentioned. Thus, in this example by answering one true-false statement, you can reject two distractors and increase your odds of arriving at the correct answer.

Test-wise candidates may pick the third distractor, C, if they have no idea which choice is correct. In multiple true-false items, C shows up statistically as the correct response more often than A, B, or D. Again, if you are going to guess, you may as well pick the distractor with the greatest odds of being correct.

Situational Set Items. Situational set items require candidates to solve a clinical problem. The stem statement is a brief description of a scenario in which you are provided with a succession of facts. The stem is followed by a series of one-item responses or multiple true-false questions.

> **Example: (three questions relate to the following scenario)**

A 150-lb. male enters the emergency room complaining of progressive inspiratory chest pain and dyspnea on exertion for the past 24 hours. Examination shows bilateral, basilar, bronchial breath sounds with coarse rales, and dullness to percussion in both bases. Which of the following statements best defines the assessment?

  A. Massive bilateral pneumothorax
  B. Emphysema
* C. Consolidation in bases
  D. Pleural effusion

Room air blood gases are taken with the following results: pH = 7.56, PaO_2 = 55, $PaCO_2$ = 25, B.E. = +2. These results are compatible with

  A. metabolic acidosis
  B. respiratory acidosis
  C. metabolic alkalosis
* D. respiratory alkalosis

The patient is placed on 40% oxygen and there is no change in the PaO_2. The most likely cause is

  A. ventilation in excess of perfusion
* B. perfusion without ventilation
  C. hypoventilation
  D. thickening of the alveolar capillary membrane

Clinical Simulation Questions

Clinical simulation exams are intended to assess clinical judgment by stressing interpretative, management, diagnostic, and therapeutic skills, including deciding when to delay and when to act promptly. Each simulation is structured so that you must gather pertinent laboratory, clinical, and physical detail, in order to identify and analyze the situation and make a treatment recommendation.

Clinical simulation items are divided into three sections: scenario, information gathering, and decision making.

Chapter 1: Improving Your Credentialing Exam Results

Scenario. The scenario is the stem statement in which the simulation's opening scene occurs. It is designed to help you begin analyzing the problem.

Example: (each simulation has a unique scenario)

You are a respiratory therapist in a 250-bed community hospital working the NOC shift. An ambulance arrives with an automobile accident victim in respiratory distress. The ER physician is involved with another emergency and insists that you begin immediate assessment of the patient for critical therapeutic needs. You approximate the patient at 5′10″ in height and weighing 150 lbs.

Information Gathering. The information gathering section gives you the opportunity to select the information necessary to make a logical clinical judgment. You are instructed to gather the facts applicable to the case presented. It is important not to gather too much information. Just select the essential data. Do not try guessing on this part of the exam.

Example:

Upon your arrival in the emergency room, you proceed to evaluate the patient's condition. Which of the following would you evaluate?

Select as Many as You Consider Indicated in This Section

Options		Latent Responses	Score
A-1.	General appearance	Distressed and cyanotic	(+1)
A-2.	Accessory muscle activity	Present	(+1)
A-3.	Sternal retractions	None	(+2)
A-4.	Asymmetrical chest movement	Yes, paradoxical on right	(+2)
A-5.	Capillary refill	Good	(−1)
A-6.	Urinary output	650 ml upon catheterization	(+2)
A-7.	Neck veins	Distended	(+2)
A-8.	Ocular pressure	Normal	(−2)
A-9.	Pedal edema	None	(0)
A-10.	Deep pain response	Present	(−2)
A-11.	Color of urine	Dark, gross blood	(+2)
A-12.	Babinski reflex	Absent	(0)
A-13.	Respiratory rate/pattern	30/min and shallow	(+2)
A-14.	Pulse	110/minute	(+2)
A-15.	Cardiac output	Not done	(−2)
A-16.	Intracranial pressure	Not done	(−2)
A-17.	Hamman's Sign	Negative	(−1)
A-18.	Chest X-ray	Blunting of the R costophrenic angle; hyperlucency along R thoracic border	(+2)

NOTE: In this section, you are given a list of data concerning the patient's physical condition. The latent responses and score identified are samples only. The latent response will show up only after being marked by a latent image pen. The score is only included here to serve as a guide, and will not be seen on an actual exam.

Regardless of how many options you chose your score for this section will differ from the scores of other candidates. It is possible to choose options that will leave you with a negative score.

Choosing options A-1, A-2, A-3, A-13, and A-14 would score +8. On the other hand, choosing options A-1, A-2, A-3, A-10, A-15, and A-16 would score −1. Options A-5, A-8, A-10, A-15, and A-16 are scored negatively because, at this stage in the simulation, it would either be too time consuming or too costly to acquire the optional information.

Decision Making. Your performance in the decision-making section is a direct reflection of your ability to interpret and synthesize previously obtained data in order to make the appropriate decision and resolve the problem. In general, you must select a single correct response. You need to be aware, however, that you may be required to select as many options as you believe relevant.

This section is composed of five options. Do not try to guess the right answer. Decide on the optimal therapy before reviewing the provided options. After analyzing each option carefully, select the option that most closely approximates the therapy you already have chosen as optimal.

Example:

The results of the ABG drawn in the ER are as follows: pH = 7.47, PCO_2 = 34, and PO_2 = 54. The ER physician determined that the internal and thoracic trauma required surgical intervention. Now, 4 hours later, the patient returns to the ICU, anesthetized, intubated, and being manually ventilated via an undetermined FIO_2. The ICU resident asks for your recommendations regarding the patient's management.

NOTE: You should decide the method and parameters for mechanical support of ventilation following the physician's request for recommendations. Remember that these questions require you to demonstrate appropriate decision-making skills based on your prior assessment of the patient's condition.

Making the correct decision at this point would yield a score of +2 (C-1). Note that by guessing, it is feasible to obtain a net score of −4. Be warned, however, that once any part of a latent response is exposed, you are assessed that score. Be careful to use the latent image marker only *after* your decision has been made.

Choose Only One Unless You Are Directed to "Make Another Selection"

Options	Latent Response	Score
C-1. FIO_2 of 1.0, Vt of 700 ml, back-up rate of 12/minute, assist-control, volume cycled ventilator	Done—End of problem	(+2)

Chapter 1: Improving Your Credentialing Exam Results 11

    C-2. FIO_2 of 0.3, Vt of 400 ml, f of 20/minute, controlled, volume ventilator   Make another selection   (−2)

    C-3. FIO_2 of 1.0, Vt of 1200 ml, f of 8/minute, assist-control, pressure cycled ventilator   Make another selection   (−2)

    C-4. FIO_2 of 0.6, Vt of 900 ml, f of 12/minute, control, pressure ventilator   Make another selection   (−2)

Joining the 5 Percent Club

The majority of candidates failing the national Respiratory Care credentialing exams come within 5 percent of the minimum passing score. It is well documented that both success and failure are the result of habits. Give yourself the benefit of cultivating habits that work to your greatest advantage. By following the attitude and preparation tips given here, you will gain the edge you need to overcome the 5 percent barrier and excel.

    First, make the **COMMITMENT TO EXCELLENCE.** Candidates passing theses exams are people who rise to the top in any occupation, and they get there because they have superior attitudes and a great work ethic.

Test Tips:

Look to see whether any part of the stem statement is included in the distractor. If it is, it can help guide you to the correct response.

Attitude Tips:

1. Imagine yourself as already successfully passing the exam, before you take it.
2. Act as if you already are credentialed, as opposed to only starting to act that way the day you take the exam.
3. Always expect the best, always. If you expect the worst you may get exactly what you expect. Expect to pass!
4. Use action, not procrastination to cure fear and gain confidence. Procrastination will keep you from attaining your goal.

Preparation Tips:

1. Start preparing now! Avoid the procrastination trap.
2. Designate a study place! Find a quiet place where you can concentrate without interruptions from friends, family, telephone, television, or radio. The location should be conducive to studying, with good lighting, ventilation, and easy access to reference material.

3. Budget your time! Planning a realistic time schedule actually will save you time and increase your efficiency. Once the schedule is written, post it in conspicuous places and follow it.

4. Use this **MASTER GUIDE,** which explains the content areas assessed on the credentialing exams as a guide. Once you have completely studied **MASTER GUIDE,** then take the self-assessment exams at the back. Use your responses to determine the areas requiring further study.

5. Practice reading and evaluating the question. It has been said that a person can score 5 percent better on any exam simply by reading the question; just another reason to join the 5 percent club.

6. After completing your individual study of **MASTER GUIDE,** consider scheduling some time for reviewing with a study group if you can hook up with one. Multiple input can enhance learning quickly.

7. Get plenty of rest the night prior to the exam to help ensure that your mental capabilities will be at their best during the exam.

8. Become familiar with the location of the exam. Leave home early enough to get to the exam location in plenty of time to find a parking place, and go to the restroom. Nothing can build up stress faster than to be caught in a traffic jam while your precious test time ticks away.

9. Don't allow yourself to become confused during the exam. Start at the beginning of the exam and move through to the end. Do not use the mark and skip method. Pick the response you think is best, answer each question, and move on. If you are unsure of your response and would like to reconsider if time permits, make a light mark off to the side. If you have time to come back do so. Remember, a question left unanswered is a definite miss.

10. The only person who can stop you from reaching your goal is you yourself. Believe in yourself and your abilities. If you have used **MASTER GUIDE** as it was intended, then you have worked hard and prepared well. Give the exam your best effort, and you will succeed. Concentrate on reading the stem statement carefully, analyzing the options, and making the correct choice. Finally, make the commitment to excellence and prepare yourself for success.

COMMITMENT TO EXCELLENCE

On this _____ day of , _____, ____, I _____, do
      (date)   (month)   (year)   (name)

hereby make the commitment to accept the challenge and do whatever it takes to proudly become a member of the 5 Percent Club. By my signature, I am indicating my willingness to faithfully follow the membership requirements of the 5 Percent Club. I also understand that as a member, I will be eligible for the 5 Percent edge on the upcoming Respiratory Care credentialing exam.

_____   _____

Signature   Witness

References

1. *AARC Times,* Vol. 23, Issue 2, February 1999.
2. The National Board for Respiratory Care, Inc. *Revised Content Outlines,* July 1998.
3. Clegg, V. L., and Cashin, W. E., *Improving Multiple-Choice Tests,* Center for Faculty and Development, Kansas State University, 1986.
4. Neufeld, V. R., and Norman, G. R., *Assessing Clinical Competence,* Springer Publishing Company, 1985.
5. Vitale, Barbara A., and Nugent, Patricia M., *Test Success,* F. A. Davis Company, 1996.
6. Kemp, J. E., Morrison, G. R., and Ross, S. M., *Designing Effective Instruction,* 2nd ed., Prentice-Hall, 1998.

Section I:

Data

Setting

In any patient care setting the respiratory therapist reviews existing clinical data, collects additional data, and recommends obtaining more pertinent data. The therapist evaluates and interprets all data to determine the appropriateness of the prescribed respiratory care, and participates in the development of the respiratory care plan.

Chapters within this section include:

    2. Patient Assessment

    3. Bedside Respiratory Monitoring

    4. Pulmonary Laboratory

    5. Clinical Laboratory

    6. Bedside Hemodynamic Monitoring

    7. Radiographic Monitoring

    8. Other Assessments and Diagnostic Testing

    9. Perinatal/Neonatal Assessment

   10. Analyze Data and Determine Plan

Chapter 2

Patient Assessment

The Respiratory Therapist must "**master**" four clinical areas to accomplish more than superficial clinical experience.[1]

1. physical examination of the chest
2. interpretation of portable chest X-rays
3. application and interpretation of bedside pulmonary function testing
4. interpretation of arterial blood gases

I. Patient history, physical examination, current vital signs, admission and current respiratory care orders, progress notes

A. The patient history and current vital signs are important to monitor for obtaining baseline data.

B. In the patient's chart, review the personal history (occupation, smoking, and family), medical history (pulmonary disease), progress notes, physicians' orders, lab and chest X-ray data, previous respiratory care orders, past response to similar therapy, trends, etc.

C. Assessment of body temperature, respiratory rates, pulse rate, and blood pressure are the most commonly performed clinical measurements.[2]

   1. No single temperature level can be considered normal, however measurements of many normal patients range between 97–99 degrees Fahrenheit, or 98.6 degrees F (37 degrees Centigrade).[3]

      a. Elevations in temperature increase oxygen consumption (normal $\dot{V}O_2$ is 250 ml/min.) and carbon dioxide production (normal $\dot{V}CO_2$ is 200 ml/min.).

      b. Elevations in temperature signify infection, environmental overheating, CNS damage, myocardial infarction, collagen vascular disease, occult or overt malignancy, or atelectasis.

2. Pulse should be monitored for the following reasons.
   a. Normal heart rate is 60–100 beats per minute. Refer to Table 2-1.
   b. The strength of the pulse will give an indication of systemic pressures (e.g., a bounding pulse may be present in hypertension).
   c. Certain arrhythmias may be assessed during palpation of the pulse (e.g., PVCs, sinus arrhythmias, etc.).
   d. Tachycardia is the first clinical sign of hypoxemia.
3. Normal respiratory rate in adults is between 14–20/minute, with an occasional sigh.[4]
   a. Ventilation is the mechanical movement of air into and out of the lung in a cyclic fashion.
   b. Respiration is the exchange of O_2 and CO_2 in the lung and at the body cell.
4. The respiratory rate in infants and children has a greater range and is more responsive to diseases, exercise, and emotion.[4] The respiratory rate ranges as follows:
   a. Newborn: 30–80 breaths per minute
   b. Early childhood: 20–40 breaths per minute
   c. Late childhood: 15–25 breaths per minute
   d. Adult levels: reached during mid-teens

D. Progress notes should include the following items.
   1. The name and proper identification of the patient
   2. The type of therapy administered (to include date, time, frequency of therapy, medication, and any ventilatory data)
   3. An assessment as to the benefit and tolerance of the therapy
   4. Any additional information regarding the patient's clinical status and/or information relevant to coordinating patient care (scheduling, avoiding conflicts, sequencing therapy, or problems that occurred during the given therapy)

TABLE 2-1: Causes of Change in Pulse Rate

Change	Conditions
Increase	Hypoxemia, fever, pain, anxiety, hypotension, drugs (sympathomimetics), septicemia w/o fever, thyrotoxicosis, anemia
Decrease	Heart block, vagal stimulation, sedation, hypothermia, hypothyroidism

E. Drawing a line through the mistake, writing "ERROR," and then initialing it should correct mistakes in the progress notes.
F. Problem-oriented medical record (POMR) is a method of recording patient care that is clear and logical, and is an acceptable format to document care. Information relative to each problem is frequently written in the SOAP format.
  1. "S" Subjective information is obtained regarding the problem or symptoms as the patients express it.
  2. "O" Objective information of clinical findings or astute observations is obtained if related to the patient's problem.
  3. "A" Assessment, diagnosis, impression, or change in condition is identified after both the subjective and objective data have been analyzed and synthesized.
  4. "P" Plan or proposed solution(s) for the identified problem is/are finally made. The therapeutic objective(s) should be addressed.
G. A corresponding request should be placed on the order sheet prior to initiating changes to the patient care plan as described in the doctor's progress notes.
H. Documenting information in the patient's chart provides the necessary data to effectively communicate the patient's clinical status to appropriate members of the health care team.
I. Legally, documentation of any care given means that care was rendered; whereas lack of documentation means that care was not given.[23]

II. Assess patient's overall cardiopulmonary status by *inspection* to determine:

A. General appearance
  1. The first cardinal rule of physical exam is take the time necessary to observe the patient.[1]
  2. Immediate life-threatening abnormalities are usually apparent from initial observations (e.g., choking, occluded airway, copious secretions, ventilator disconnect, etc.).
B. Muscle wasting
  1. There are several causes of muscular atrophy.[6]
     a. It is a normal occurrence of aging.
     b. Generalized muscle wasting diseases include malignancy, tuberculosis or other chronic diseases, diabetes mellitus, thyrotoxicosis, Cushing's disease, and Addison's disease.
     c. Disuse atrophy may occur as a result from fractured bones and immobilization or casting, or ankylosing joint disease.
     d. Lower motor neuron lesions with flaccid paralysis may result from disc disease, cord tumor, poliomyelitis, amyotrophic lateral sclerosis, meningitis, or trauma.

2. There may be several causes of muscle weakness.[6]
    a. Congenital disorders: muscular dystrophies
    b. Infections: viral, bacterial, and parasitic
    c. Toxic: alcohol, corticosteroids, botulism, and heroin
    d. Metabolic: hyper/hypothyroidism, hypokalemia, diabetes mellitus, myasthenia gravis, and hyperaldosteronism
    e. Immune/idiopathic: scleroderma, systemic lupus erythema, rheumatoid arthritis, and sarcoidosis
    f. Traumatic: exercise, injury, and seizure
    g. Neoplastic: carcinomatous myopathies
C. Venous distension
    1. Jugular venous pressure greater than 3 cm above the level of the sternal angle (junction of the body of the sternum and the manubrium) with the head of the bed elevated 45° is abnormal.[4]
    2. Neck vein distension may be seen in congestive heart failure, right-sided heart failure associated with increases in pulmonary vascular resistance, constrictive pericarditis, or superior vena cava obstruction.
D. Peripheral edema
    1. It is an accumulation of fluid in the peripheral tissues.
    2. There are several causes of edema formation.[6]
        a. Increased hydrostatic pressure in the vascular space
            (1) increased volume: CHF, renal failure, certain hormones (corticosteroids, estrogens), and certain drugs (indomethacin, sodium-rich compounds)
            (2) increased mechanical pressure: venous thrombosis, venous compression (tumor, scar, fibrosis), portal hypertension, pericardial constriction, prolonged standing
        b. Decreased oncotic pressure in the vascular space: hyponatremia, nephrotic syndrome, starvation, and protein loss
        c. Tissue or vascular damage: vasculitis, allergy, trauma, burns, ischemia, and infection
        d. Other: myxedema, lymphedema, and prolonged increased intrathoracic pressures from continuous mechanical ventilation
E. Flushing
    1. It is a transient redness of the face and neck.
    2. Certain diseases (carcinoid tumor), ingestion of certain drugs or other substances (atropine), heat, emotional factors, or physical exertion may cause it.[7]
F. Capillary refill
    1. Compressing the fingernail and monitoring the amount of time in which blood flow returns assesses this cardiopulmonary aspect.
    2. Capillary refill is slow when cardiac output is reduced and digital perfusion is slow.

Chapter 2: Patient Assessment

3. Normal capillary refill time should take less than 3 seconds.[8]
4. It is important to monitor in peripheral vascular disease.
5. There is slightly more movement of fluid into the interstitial spaces than is re-absorbed into the capillary. Refer to Table 2-2.
6. The net filtration of fluid movement is balanced by fluid removal from the interstitial space by the lymphatic vessels and is returned to the general circulation via the thoracic duct.

G. Diaphoresis
1. It is a profuse perspiration that may be caused by anxiety.
2. A cold, "clammy" sweat may be associated with an acutely decreased cardiac output found with an acute myocardial infarction.[6]
3. Diaphoresis is caused by intense sympathetic nervous system discharge.
   a. Intense vasoconstriction occurs in an attempt to maintain blood pressure and makes the skin cold.
   b. Sweat glands are also under sympathetic control and are strongly stimulated at the same time, making the skin feel "clammy."

H. Digital clubbing
1. It is the painless, non-tender enlargement of the terminal phalanges, with loss of the cuticular angle (greater than 180°).
2. The specific etiology is unknown, but is probably related to increased blood flow through multiple arteriovenous shunts in the distal phalanges, with resultant tissue hypoxemia.[6]

TABLE 2-2: Fluid Movement in the Tissues

Mean forces tending to move fluid out of the capillary	
Mean capillary pressure	17 mmHg
Negative interstitial fluid pressure	7 mmHg
Interstitial fluid colloid osmotic pressure	+4.5 mmHg
Total Outward Force =	28.5 mmHg
Mean force tending to move fluid inward (colloid osmotic pressure)	−28.0 mmHg
Net Outward Force =	0.5 mmHg

Ref. 3:238

3. Causes of clubbing in adults include: pulmonary disease (75–85%); cardiac disorders (10–15%); liver or gastrointestinal disorders (10%); and miscellaneous (5%).
4. Associated causes in children include: cystic fibrosis, bronchiectasis, empyema, and congenital heart disease.

I. Cyanosis
   1. Cyanosis is a bluish discoloration of the nailbeds and mucus membranes that occurs when the capillary content of reduced Hb exceeds 5 gm/100 ml.[9]
   2. It is an unreliable clinical sign, except when combined with other physical data.
   3. Conditions with severe hypoxia that may exist without the presence of cyanosis include: reduced circulating hemoglobin (anemia), abnormal hemoglobin (carboxyhemoglobin), systemic vasodilatation with rapid blood flow, or abnormal pigmentation.
   4. Central cyanosis is generalized and associated with arterial oxygen desaturation (congenital heart defects with right to left shunts, pulmonary arteriovenous fistulas, and advanced pulmonary disease with hypoxemia).[6]
   5. Peripheral cyanosis (acrocyanosis) results from a reduction in systemic blood flow, usually from decreases in cardiac output or obstructive peripheral arterial disease.

J. Chest configuration[4]
   1. Normal infant: it is circular in shape on cross section.
   2. Normal adult: the ratio of anterior-posterior to lateral diameter ranges from 1:2 to 1:1.4.
   3. Geriatrics: there is a slight increase in anterior posterior diameter.
   4. There are several pathological deformities of the chest.
      a. Barrel chest: associated with COPD and normal aging (the A-P to lateral ratio approaches 1:1)
      b. Funnel chest (pectus excavatum): depression of the lower portion of the sternum (NOTE: compression of the heart and great vessels may cause murmurs.)
      c. Pigeon chest (pectus carinatum): the sternum is displaced anteriorly
      d. Thoracic kyphoscoliosis: dorsolateral curvature of the spine and distortion of the underlying lungs may create difficulties in interpretation of the lung findings

K. Evidence of diaphragmatic movement[1]
   1. The diaphragm is the major muscle of ventilation, and accounts for approximately 60% of the normal tidal volume.
   2. It consists of two muscular hemidiaphragms (domes).
   3. Innervation arises from the cervical vertebrae (C3-5), which give rise to the phrenic nerve.
   4. Contraction of the diaphragm pulls the domes down.

Chapter 2: Patient Assessment

5. The diaphragm is the most common target for improvement during pulmonary rehabilitation.
6. Evidence of movement is determined by inspection or palpation of the abdomen, or by percussion of the posterior thorax.
7. The diaphragm should move at least 3 cm with maximum effort.

L. Breathing pattern
   1. Eupnea is a normal breathing pattern.
   2. Bradypnea is slower than normal breathing.
   3. Tachypnea is faster than normal breathing.
   4. Apnea is the cessation of breathing.
      a. It may occur as a result of cardiac arrest, CNS trauma, drug overdose, satisfaction of the hypoxic drive mechanism (CO_2 narcosis), etc.
      b. Refer to sections on sleep apnea in chapters 8 and 10.
   5. Hyperventilation is an increased rate and depth of breathing resulting in an increase in alveolar ventilation ($\dot{V}_A$) and a decrease in PCO_2.[9]
      a. $\dot{V}_A$ may increase in proportion to $\dot{V}CO_2$ (i.e., exercise, hyperthyroidism, hypermetabolism, etc.).
      b. $\dot{V}_A$ may increase out of proportion to $\dot{V}CO_2$ by several mechanisms.
         (1) chemoreceptor stimulation: arterial hypoxemia, metabolic acidosis, and hypotension
         (2) stimulation of pulmonary receptors: pneumonia, pulmonary embolism, asthma, and pulmonary fibrosis
         (3) anxiety neurosis
         (4) pharmaceutical agents: theophylline, salicylates, catecholamines, and progesterone
         (5) miscellaneous: fever, head injury, and hepatic failure
   6. Cheyne-Stokes breathing is an abnormal breathing pattern characterized by alternating periods of apnea with gradually increasing and decreasing the rate and depth of respiration.
      a. It is commonly found in patients with a diffuse loss of cortical function or with chronic heart failure.
      b. It may also be found in normal patients in the early stages of slow-wave sleep or at high altitudes.[10]
      c. It commonly is a physiologic phenomenon in premature infants due to an immature respiratory center formation or the incomplete elimination of lung fluids.
   7. Kussmaul's is a deep, rapid and regular breathing pattern or hyperpnea. Diabetic ketoacidosis is the classic cause.
   8. Biot's is an irregular-breathing pattern in which deep and shallow breaths occur at random and are interspersed with long and short pauses.

a. It results from either compression, trauma, or hemorrhage to the medulla, meningitis, or poliomyelitis.

b. The normal response to CO_2 is also depressed.

9. Oligopnea is a slow respiratory rate due to either respiratory center depression or some form of respiratory muscle impedance.

M. Accessory muscle activity
1. Intercostal muscles are two layers of muscle fibers connecting the ribs.
    a. Nerves arising from the thoracic vertebrae (T1-11) innervate them.
    b. External intercostal contraction elevates the anterior end of each rib in an upward and outward direction, thus increasing the A-P diameter.
    c. Internal intercostal contraction pulls the ribs down and in, and is used in forceful expiration.
    d. Neither plays a major role in resting ventilation.
2. Accessory muscles elevate and stabilize the chest wall to increase thoracic cavity size. They include the following: scalene, sternocleidomastoids, trapezius, and pectoralis muscles.
    a. When used to assist ventilation, there is a reversal of usage between the muscle origin and insertion.
    b. These muscles are not normally active during resting ventilation.
    c. They are used in active ventilation (e.g., exercise), in the presence of increased airway resistance, or by panic-stricken patients with COPD (inefficient).
    d. Their use is less cost effective in terms of the O_2 requirements necessary to sustain ventilation than is use of the diaphragm.
3. Expiratory muscles: expiration is usually passive.
    a. Abdominal muscles playing a major part in active expiration include the external obliques, rectus abdominous, internal obliques, and transverse abdominous muscles.
    b. Nerves from the thoracic and lumbar vertebrae T6-L1 innervate these muscles.
    c. Contraction of these muscles depresses the lower ribs, flexes the trunk, and forces the diaphragm upward.
4. Under maximum effort, the respiratory muscles may use up to 50% of the available O_2 in the blood.

N. Asymmetrical chest movement
1. Asymmetrical chest movement creates inefficient ventilation that results in an increased work of breathing.
2. Flail chest: multiple consecutive rib fractures create an instability in the chest wall. It may cause severe respiratory embarrassment when the unstable area

moves inward during inspiration (paradoxical breathing). It is frequently associated with an underlying pulmonary contusion.
   3. Improper tube placement: selective ventilation of the right lung will lead to overinflation of the right and corresponding underventilation of the left lung.
   4. Unilateral pneumothorax: there is an expansion of the unaffected side unless a tension pneumothorax is present.
   5. Atelectasis: there is less expansion on the affected side and compensatory hyperinflation on the unaffected side.
   6. Rib deformities: either congenital or traumatic changes may create asymmetry.
   7. Occlusion of a bronchus due to aspiration creates less expansion on the affected side.
O. Intercostal and/or sternal retractions
   1. These result from increased inspiratory efforts to meet ventilatory needs and reflect the use of accessory muscles.
   2. Occurrence is prominent in the neonate with respiratory distress due to an increased chest wall compliance.
   3. They may be caused by either airway obstruction (tongue or foreign body in the upper airway) or changes in the lung parenchyma (hyaline membranes, mucus, etc).
   4. Supraclavicular and intercostal retractions, marked increased use of accessory muscles of ventilation, along with an inability to speak and agitation, would indicate the presence of an acute upper airway obstruction.
P. Nasal flaring
   1. Flaring of the alae nasi is a common sign of respiratory distress in the newborn.
   2. Marked flaring will generally coincide with a seesaw movement of the upper chest, lower chest and sternal retractions, and expiratory grunting.
Q. Grunting
   1. Grunting is an audible sound heard most frequently in an infant during the expiratory phase of respiration.
   2. While exhaling, the infant performs a Valsalva maneuver in an attempt to maintain an increased end-expiratory airway pressure, thus preventing alveolar and airway collapse secondary to their noncompliant lungs.
R. Transillumination of chest[10]
   1. A fiberoptic probe is useful in the diagnosis of pneumothorax in infants.
   2. The probe is placed on both sides of the chest. If either side transilluminates more than the other, the possibility of abnormal air in the chest exists.
   3. A confirming chest radiograph should be obtained prior to needle aspiration or chest tube placement.
   4. Normal lungs transmit a uniform circle of light called a "halo" (halo sign).

S. Character/quality of cough[2]
1. The cough is one of the most frequent complaints of patients with pulmonary disease, and is the most vital factor in sputum management.
2. A cough is initiated by inflammatory, chemical, mechanical, or thermal stimulation of the cough receptors.[11]
3. A viral respiratory infection is the most frequent cause of cough.[2]
4. There are several factors that may impair a patient's ability to cough.
   a. Muscular weakness: neurological disease, musculoskeletal disease, trauma, and prolonged ventilator management
   b. Tracheal or laryngeal stenosis from intubation
   c. Inflammation of the upper airways
   d. Pain from trauma or surgery
   e. Drugs (sedatives, morphine)
   f. Structural abnormalities (bronchiectasis, tracheomalacia)
5. There are several terms that may be used to describe coughing.[8]
   a. Barking: croup, epiglottal disease, and influenza
   b. Hoarse: laryngitis, laryngotracheal bronchitis, pressure on the recurrent laryngeal nerve, mediastinal tumor, aortic aneurysm
   c. Stridor: tracheal or main stem bronchial obstruction, croup, and epiglottitis
   d. Wheezy: bronchospasm, asthma, and cystic fibrosis
   e. Dry: viral infection, irritant gas inhalation, interstitial lung disease, tumor, pleural effusion, and radiation therapy
   f. Chronic productive: bronchiectasis, chronic bronchitis, lung abscess, asthma, and tuberculosis
   g. Inadequate: debility, weakness, drugs, pain, and poor effort
   h. Paroxysmal: aspiration, asthma
6. An ineffective cough is usually high-pitched and originates high in the airway.
7. Huff coughing (Forced Expiratory Technique, FET), or use of expiratory accessory muscles without vocal cord closure, has been found to be a superior technique in patients with COPD.
8. The indications for a directed cough, a deliberate maneuver that is taught, supervised, and monitored, include:
   a. Aid in the removal of retained secretions from central airways
   b. Atelectasis
   c. Prophylaxis against postoperative pulmonary complications
   d. Routine part of bronchial hygiene in patients with cystic fibrosis, bronchiectasis, chronic bronchitis, necrotizing pulmonary infection, or spinal cord injury

Chapter 2: Patient Assessment

  e. As an integral part of other bronchial hygiene therapies such as postural drainage, positive expiratory pressure therapy, and incentive spirometry
  f. Obtain sputum specimens for diagnostic analysis
 9. The hazards and/or complications of directed cough maneuvers (forced expiratory technique or manually assisted coughs) may include:
  a. Reduced coronary artery perfusion
  b. Reduced cerebral perfusion
  c. Incontinence
  d. Fatigue
  e. Headache
  f. Paresthesia or numbness
  g. Bronchospasm
  h. Muscular damage or discomfort
  i. Spontaneous pneumothorax, pneumomediastinum, subcutaneous emphysema
  j. Cough paroxysms
  k. Chest pain
  l. Rib or costochondral junction fracture
  m. Incisional pain, evisceration
  n. Anorexia, vomiting, and retching
  o. Visual disturbances including retinal hemorrhage
  p. Central line displacement
  q. Gastroesophageal reflux

T. Amount and characteristics of sputum
 1. The patient should be asked to demonstrate the effectiveness of their cough.
 2. A nonproductive cough, in the presence of audible secretions, may be the result of poor positioning, exhaustion from frequent coughing attempts, improper cough techniques, or pain due to inadequate splinting of an abdominal wound.
 3. Parameters to note include: volume produced per time period, consistency and viscosity, presence or absence of purulence, odor, and presence or absence of blood.
 4. The gross appearance of sputum may be used as a helpful guide as to the pulmonary problem. Refer to Table 2-3.[2]
 5. Sputum containing *Pseudomonas* sp. or anaerobic organisms has a particularly putrid odor.
 6. Curschmann's spirals are casts of small airways that may be seen along with the clear mucoid sputum of bronchial asthma.[12]
 7. Bronchodilators may create pink tinged sputum.

TABLE 2-3: Gross Appearance of Sputum

Disease	Mucoid*	Muco-Purulent	Purulent§	Fetid	Bloody	Frothy
Bronchitis						
Acute		X	X		X	
Chronic	X	X				
Pneumonia			X		X	
Pulmonary edema					X	X
Bronchiectasis			X	X	X	
Tuberculosis					X	
Lung cancer					X	
Asthma	X					
Cystic fibrosis		X		X		

*white or clear; §yellow or green

III. Assess patient's overall cardiopulmonary status by *palpation* to determine:

A. Heart rate, rhythm, and force
   1. Note the rate, rhythm (regular or irregular) and force.
   2. Pulses utilized for palpation include the radial for general clinical monitoring, and the carotid and femoral pulses primarily for cardiac arrest monitoring.
   3. The index finger should be used and not the thumb, which has a palpable pulse of its own.
B. Asymmetrical chest movements
   1. Normal chest expansion depends on the patient size.
      a. Normal thumb excursion posteriorly moves an equal distance of approximately 3–5 centimeters during a deep inhalation.[5]
      b. A restrictive problem exists if there is less than 3 centimeters excursion.
   2. A lag or impairment of the thoracic movement would suggest an underlying disease in the lung or pleura, such as:[4]
      a. Chronic fibrotic disease
      b. Pleural effusion

Chapter 2: Patient Assessment

       c. Lobar pneumonia

       d. Tenderness, pleural pain with associated splinting

       e. Unilateral bronchial obstruction

    3. Palpation of accessory muscles may be done to ascertain their use.

C. Secretions in the airway

    1. Solid material and fluids transmit vibrations better than a gas.

    2. Secretions in the large airways may cause turbulence and vibrations that may be felt on deep breathing.

D. Tactile fremitus

    1. It is a vibration transmitted through the bronchopulmonary system to the chest wall that is perceptible by palpation while a patient speaks "one, two, three," or "ninety-nine."[4]

    2. An increased tactile fremitus may be noticeable during palpation near large bronchi, and in the presence of lung consolidation.

    3. Air passage through airways containing thick secretions may produce vibrations referred to as rhonchial fremitus. These may clear if the patient produces an effective cough.[5]

    4. A decreased tactile fremitus may be caused from a pneumothorax, pleural effusion, or emphysema.

E. Crepitus

    1. Palpation of the external thoracic cage would be useful in detecting the presence of fractured ribs, lymph node enlargement, enlargement of the thyroid, or costochondritis (Tietze's Syndrome).

    2. Subcutaneous emphysema may be palpated. It is often the first observed clinical indication of barotrauma in patients on airway pressure therapy.[1]

F. Tracheal deviation

    1. Palpation of the area above the sternal notch may identify a deviation or shift of the mediastinum.

    2. Tracheal deviation may be caused from several sources.

       a. Tumors or masses in the neck or mediastinum

       b. Abnormal pleural conditions (e.g., pneumothorax)

       c. Pulmonary disease (e.g., unilateral atelectasis)

G. Endotracheal tube placement[2]

    1. A Sellick maneuver should be performed prior to orally intubating a patient with depressed levels of consciousness (especially those with recent food ingestion or intestinal obstruction).

2. Pressure is applied to the cricoid cartilage to compress the esophagus and prevent any gastric contents from being regurgitated and aspirated during the intubation procedure.

IV. Assess patient's overall cardiopulmonary status by *percussion* to determine:

A. Diaphragmatic excursion[9]
   1. While the patient is either sitting or standing, the chest wall may be percussed to determine the extent of excursion of the diaphragm. Normal excursion is 4–6 cm with a deep ventilatory pattern.
   2. Unequal excursion of the hemidiaphragms could indicate several conditions.
      a. Diaphragmatic paralysis: encephalitis, poliomyelitis, tetanus, motor neuron disease, trauma, and compression tumor
      b. Adhesions from past infections: tuberculosis, empyema, and pneumonia
      c. Miscellaneous conditions: aortic aneurysm, pulmonary infarction, congenital anomalies, and substernal thyroid
   3. Bilateral loss of diaphragmatic functions are a result of the following conditions.
      a. Anatomical conditions: congenital absence, rupture
      b. Myelo and myopathies: amyotrophic lateral sclerosis, poliomyelitis, and systemic lupus erythematosus
      c. Peripheral neuropathies: Guillain-Barrè syndrome, surgery, closed chest trauma, alcoholic neuropathy
B. Areas of altered resonance
   1. In making clinical judgments, it is important to compare the symmetry between corresponding lung fields or sides.
   2. The normal lung is resonant, whereas the diseased lung is more apt to be dull to percussion (except in abnormal collection of gas).
   3. Hyperresonance is present in emphysema and with a pneumothorax.
   4. Dullness to percussion may be noted with pleural effusion, lung consolidation, pleural thickening, and carcinoma.
   5. Kronig's Isthmus
      a. This is a normal 4-6 cm band of resonance at the lung apices.
      b. Dullness or flatness to percussion may indicate:
         (1) apical consolidation
         (2) the presence of a tumor (Pancoast)
         (3) tuberculosis
   6. Dullness should be present to percussion over the heart and liver.

Chapter 2: Patient Assessment

V. **Assess patient's overall cardiopulmonary status by *auscultation* to determine presence of:**

A. Bilateral normal breath sounds
   1. They have a characteristic quality that varies according to chest area over which they are heard. Refer to Table 2-4.
   2. Bronchial and bronchovesicular breath sounds may be heard abnormally over consolidated areas with a patent bronchial tree (i.e., in pneumonia, pulmonary edema, atelectasis, and extensive pulmonary fibrosis).
   3. Breath sounds are useful in identifying lung lobes for pulmonary drainage.

B. Increased, decreased, absent, or unequal breath sounds
   1. Normal vesicular sounds are accentuated in children and patients with thin chest walls.
   2. Decreased or absent breath sounds are present in the following conditions.[11]
      a. Increased thickness of the chest wall (fat or muscle)
      b. Decreased airflow to a lung segment (tumor, mucosal edema, mucus plugs, foreign bodies, and apnea)
      c. Hyperinflation of the lung (exacerbations of asthma, and emphysema)
      d. Separation of the lung and chest wall with air or fluid (pleural effusion and/or thickening, and pneumothorax)
   3. Unequal breath sounds may occur from any unilateral condition (e.g., bronchial intubation, pleural effusion, pneumonia, etc.).

TABLE 2-4: Normal Breath Sounds

Type	Location	Description	I:E Relationship
Tracheal	over trachea	loud, harsh, & tubular	I greater than E, with pause
Bronchial	major central airways	hollow & tubular	E greater than I, with pause
Broncho-vesicular	major central airways	breezy & tubular	I = E, with no pause
Vesicular	chest, except trachea and bronchi	crisp & breezy	I greater than E, with no pause

4. Several older terms are still occasionally used to designate increased voice transmission from the presence of the same processes that cause bronchial breathing (consolidation, atelectasis, and extensive parenchymal fibrosis).
    a. Bronchophony is the increase in the intensity and clarity of the spoken voice.
    b. Egophony is the sound of "ay" on auscultation when the patient speaks "ee."
    c. Whispered pectoriloquy is an unusually clear transmission of the whispered voice.
5. Vocal fremitus is the change in the quality and intensity of the sound on auscultation.
    a. An increased vocal fremitus may be caused by consolidation in the presence of an open airway.
    b. Decreased vocal fremitus is noticeable in emphysema, pneumothorax, obstructed bronchus, and when the voice is decreased.

C. Rhonchi or rales (crackles)
  1. Adventitious breath sounds indicate some abnormality in the pulmonary parenchyma or airways and are not found in normal people.
  2. Recent studies on lung sounds recommend the terms *crackles* and *wheezes* rather than *rales* and *rhonchi*.[2]
  3. Rales or crackles[2]
      a. They are the most common abnormal sound heard on auscultation.
      b. It is the sound of air entry into small airways or alveoli containing fluid.
      c. They are discontinuous sounds heard predominately on inspiration.
      d. The presence of early inspiratory crackles indicates obstructive airway diseases or severe heart failure; late inspiratory crackles indicate either mild heart failure, interstitial fibrosis, or pneumonia.[1]
      e. Course crackles (bubbling rales or course crepitations) may be clinically associated with pulmonary edema or resolving pneumonia.
      f. Fine crackles (fine crepitations) are most often heard in interstitial fibrosis.
      g. They seldom clear following coughing.

D. Wheeze
  1. They indicate narrowing of the airways or intraluminal obstruction caused by the presence of secretions, bronchospasm, airway collapse and/or narrowing. This type of wheezing is also called sibilant rhonchi or high-pitched wheezes.
  2. Increased air turbulence produces a rumbling sound; a high velocity airflow through restricted air passages (i.e., asthma) may produce a sound that is musical in quality.
  3. They are more pronounced during expiration in COPD, but can be present during both inspiration and expiration as continuous sounds.[11]

Chapter 2: Patient Assessment

      4. The low-pitched wheeze (rhonchus or sonorous rhonchus) is clinically heard in the presence of sputum production.
      5. They often will clear on coughing.
- E. Stridor
  1. It is a croup-like or specialized type of wheeze that is heard during inspiration.
  2. The presence of stridor indicates large airway obstruction due to laryngotracheobronchitis, foreign body aspiration, laryngeal tumors, or tracheomalacia.
  3. It may be present following traumatic extubation resulting in vocal cord damage.
- F. Friction rub
  1. It is a loud grating discontinuous sound like creaky shoe leather, that is unaffected by a cough.
  2. The sound is heard during both inspiration and expiration and in synchronization with the breathing pattern, and indicates the presence of inflamed visceral and/or parietal pleura (pleurisy).
  3. Causes of a friction rub include tuberculosis, primary or metastatic carcinoma, pulmonary infarction, and pneumonia.
- G. Heart sounds[4]
  1. These are lower pitched sounds than breath sounds.
     a. S_1: It is produced by closure of the atrioventricular valves (primarily the mitral). It is loudest in the left 5th interspace just medial to the midclavicular line.
     b. S_2: It is produced by closure of the two semilunar valves.
        (1) S_2A: Closure of the aortic valve is loudest at the right 2nd interspace close to the sternum.
        (2) S_2P: Closure of the pulmonic valve is heard normally in the left 2nd interspace close to the sternum.
  2. Murmur: It is a benign or pathologic auscultatory sound heard during systole or diastole, and is produced by vibrations of the ventricular walls, the heart valves, or the walls of blood vessels.[13]
     a. Systolic murmurs begin with or after the first heart sound and end at or before the second sound.
     b. Diastolic murmurs begin with or after the second heart sound and end before the first sound.
     c. Continuous murmurs begin during systole and continue without pause through the second sound.
  3. Bruits are abnormal sounds that are associated with increased risk of stroke. They are heard when the stethoscope is placed over an artery. The abnormal sound comes from an obstruction or partial obstruction in the artery being auscultatated.
  4. Heart sounds are best heard utilizing the bell side of the stethoscope.

H. Dysrhythmias
   1. They may be noted by the presence of irregularities in the heart rate.
   2. Identifying the origin of arrhythmia is accomplished with an ECG.
I. Blood pressure[4]
   1. During auscultation of the brachial artery for blood pressure determination, the cuff should be inflated to about 30 mmHg above the level at which the radial pulse disappears.
   2. The pressure from the sphygmomanometer should be reduced at a rate of about 3 mmHg per second.
   3. Caution should be taken while monitoring a hypertensive patient because there may be a silent interval part way between systolic and diastolic pressures (auscultatory gap). If it is not recognized, a serious underestimation of systolic or overestimation of diastolic pressures may result.
   4. Pressure differences of greater than 10 mmHg between right and left arms suggest arterial compression or obstruction.

VI. Interview patient

A. Understanding an illness can come from several sources, the most important of which are the patients themselves.[4]
B. Level of consciousness
   1. Impaired consciousness implies dysfunction of the cerebral hemispheres, the upper brain stem, or both areas.
   2. Somnolence
      a. It is a state of sleepiness or unnatural drowsiness.
      b. It may occur with patients that retain CO_2 by satisfying their hypoxic drive, or with a drug overdose.
   3. Confusion
      a. It is expressed by mental slowness, inattentiveness, dulled perception of the environment, or incoherence in thinking.
      b. Hypoxic patients may be in a confused state.
   4. Stupor
      a. The patient will have marked reduction in mental and physical ability, marked slowness and reduction in response to commands or "stimuli," but usually retains preservation of the reflexes.
      b. This state may be caused by electrolyte imbalance or drug intoxication.
   5. Coma
      a. This state is an unresponsiveness to stimuli, or absence of most reflexes.

Chapter 2: Patient Assessment

      b. Causes of coma include cerebral vascular accidents, cerebral trauma, drugs or toxins, infections, tumors, hypoxemia, diabetes, hepatic failure, etc.

C. Orientation to time, place and person
1. Through orientation of time and place, one can monitor the cognitive functions of mental status.
2. The state of patient cooperation is dependent on the level of consciousness and the emotional state.

D. Emotional state[7]
1. Fear is a normal emotional response to consciously recognized and external sources of danger.
   a. Alarm, apprehension, or disquiet manifests it.
   b. Informing the patient is one of the best ways to alleviate fears.
2. Anger is an emotional agitation of no specified intensity that is aroused by great displeasure.
   a. Frequently anger will be a result of the self-denial process, i.e., an unwillingness to accept the current situation.
   b. Associated hyperventilation from an emotionally charged encounter may stimulate bronchospasm.
3. Euphoria may be defined as bodily comfort, a well being, or the absence of pain or distress. Three types of euphoria include:
   a. Psychological: a self-induced feeling of wellness
   b. Pharmacological: drug-induced feeling of wellness
   c. Terminal: a calmness resulting from acceptance of the terminal condition and that death is near
4. Denial is a defense mechanism in which the existence of intolerable actions, ideas, wishes, impulses and affects are unconsciously denied.[7]
5. Depression is expressed as a dejected mood sometimes associated with guilt feelings and somatic preoccupations, often of delusional proportions.
6. Delirium is a mental disturbance marked by illusions, hallucinations, cerebral excitement, and/or physical restlessness and incoherence.
   a. It may be caused by drugs, alcohol, fever, metabolic disorders (hypo- or hyperglycemia), head injury, edema, meningitis, or cerebral infarction.

E. Ability to cooperate
1. Subjective information regarding the patient may be obtained from the patient, family, friend, or other health care professionals.
2. There are several factors to consider prior to a patient interview, which encourage patient cooperation.
   a. Make sure a proper introduction is made at the beginning of the interview.
   b. Provide for privacy and avoid interruptions.

c. Remember that the patient is hospitalized because he or she is sick (i.e., hypoxemia is known to lead to irritability).
d. Listen and show genuine interest in the patient's needs, wants, and desires.
e. Begin the interview with a few casual and friendly comments to put the patient at ease. Once this is done, then focus in on relevant data.
f. Occasionally personality conflicts do exist. If this is the case, attempt to employ the services of a co-worker.
3. A poor level of cooperation may be due to a number of factors.
a. Medications: sedatives
b. Hypoxemia: irritability and anxiety
c. Language difficulties
d. Fear and apprehension
4. Performing tasks on command indicate the patient's ability to cooperate and follow instructions.
5. Almost all spirometric tests for pulmonary function are effort dependent.
a. Tests that are not effort dependent still rely on patient cooperation with the procedure for results.[14]
b. Patient apprehension or lack of understanding may affect vital signs as well as patient cooperation, and therefore, affect the test results.
F. Dyspnea and/or orthopnea
1. Dyspnea is the patient's subjective complaint of difficulty in breathing.
a. It may be observed by movement of the upper extremities in patients relying on accessory muscles.
b. It is a sensitive and reliable indicator that work of breathing has changed.[1]
2. Pulmonary causes of dyspnea include obstructive and restrictive lung diseases. Refer to Table 4-7.
3. There are several nonpulmonary causes of dyspnea.[11]
a. Heart disease: left ventricular failure from any cause, aortic or mitral stenosis or insufficiency, congenital defects, or cardiomyopathies
b. High cardiac output states: hyperthyroidism, beriberi, or peripheral arteriovenous shunts
c. Others: anemia, high altitude, obesity, anxiety, excessive exercise, febrile states, or deconditioning
4. The following classification system may be used to describe the degree of dyspnea in objective terms.[15]
a. GRADE I   normal, becomes breathless only after unusual exertion
b. GRADE II   can walk at normal speed on level surface, but becomes breathless going up hills or stairs
c. GRADE III can walk slowly on level surface, but becomes breathless at normal speed

Chapter 2: Patient Assessment

      d. GRADE IV cannot walk one block even at slow speed without becoming breathless

      e. GRADE V becomes breathless from simple activities such as shaving or dressing

  5. PND or paroxysmal nocturnal dyspnea is a form of respiratory distress related to posture (especially while supine at night) that is usually attributed to congestive heart failure with pulmonary edema.[7]

  6. Orthopnea is a difficulty in breathing except in the upright position.

      a. Either severe lung disease, congestive heart failure, or a combination of both may cause it.

      b. Patients will frequently state that they must use 2–3 pillows to minimize any breathing difficulty during sleep.

  7. Platypnea is a difficulty in breathing when sitting up. It may be noticed in the postoperative pneumonectomy patient.

G. Exercise tolerance and activities of daily living

  1. Dyspnea is a normal condition following exercise, but a sudden increase or a sudden decrease in tolerance for exercise is an important finding commonly found in patients with respiratory disease.[2]

  2. Activities of daily living (ADL) information should be obtained in order to determine the extent of shortness of breath. For example, does the patient get short of breath while shaving, dressing, eating, etc?

  3. As exercise is performed regularly, the patient will usually gain an increased tolerance for dyspnea, have improved appetite, and demonstrate an increased physical capability, with resultant improvement in quality of life.[2]

  4. As a result of reconditioning exercise training, several physiological adaptations should occur.

      a. Lower heart rate

      b. Lower systolic blood pressure

      c. Decreased blood flow through working muscles, while maintaining muscular oxygen consumption

      d. Increase in skeletal blood flow

      e. Improvement in MVV

  5. The goal of therapy is to modify activities to consume less oxygen and become more energy efficient.[2]

H. Physical environment, social support systems, nutritional status

  1. A physical environment inquiry may reveal any of the following conditions.

      a. Presence of allergens or other irritants (animal danders, mold, smoke, dust, fumes, chemicals, or air pollutants)

      b. Exercise patterns

c. Personal hygiene

  d. Occupation considerations (i.e., exposure to asbestos, fumes, or chemicals)

2. Social support systems generally include the patient's family and friends. There are several other factors to identify.

  a. Hobbies

  b. Who does the housework, and is a vacuum or broom used

  c. Personal habits

3. Nutritional status may be determined by assessment of the following considerations.

  a. Usual meal times

  b. Types and amounts of food eaten

  c. Amount of water intake per day

  d. Alcohol use

  e. Constipation/diarrhea problems

4. A smoking history should be obtained due to the strong relationship between smoking and chronic pulmonary disease.

  a. Cigarettes are recorded in "pack-years."

    (1) One pack-year is equal to the number of packs per day multiplied by the number of years smoked.

    (2) Either one of the following combinations may acquire a 50 pack-year history:

      (a) 2 packs per day for 25 years

      (b) 1 pack per day for 50 years

    (3) The beginning and quitting age of smoking should also be noted.

  b. Smoking pipes, cigars, marijuana, or using chewing tobacco are recorded in the amount of daily usage.

I. Assess patient's learning needs

The initial patient interview should focus on identifying the characteristic symptoms of respiratory disease and the gathering of pertinent details.[2]

1. The ability to listen carefully is both an art and a vital clinical skill.

2. A skilled interviewer will assess the patient's level of education and familiarity with their disease process, and choose the appropriate terminology.

References

1. Shapiro, B. A., *Clinical Application of Respiratory Care*, 4th ed., Yearbook Medical Publishers, 1991.

2. Burton, G. G., Hodgkin, J. E., and Ward, J. J., *Respiratory Care: A Guide to Clinical Practice*, 4th ed., J. B. Lippincott, 1997.

Chapter 2: Patient Assessment

3. Guyton, A. C., *Textbook of Medical Physiology*, 9th ed., W. B. Saunders, 1999.
4. Bates, B., *A Guide to Physical Examination and History Taking*, 5th ed., J. B. Lippincott, 1991.
5. Scanlon, C. L., Wilkins, R. L., and Stoller, J. K. *Egan's Fundamentals of Respiratory Therapy*, 7th ed., Mosby, 1999.
6. Judge, R. D., Zuidema, G. D., and Fitzgerald, F. T., *Clinical Diagnosis*, 4th ed., Little, Brown and Company, 1982.
7. *Mosby's Medical, Nursing, & Allied Health Dictionary*, 4th ed., Mosby, 1994.
8. Wilkins, R. L., Sheldon, R. L., and Krider, S. J., *Clinical Assessment in Respiratory Care*, Mosby, 1995.
9. Guenter, C. A., and Welch, M. H., *Pulmonary Medicine*, 2nd ed., J. B. Lippincott, 1982.
10. Alone, C. A., and Hill, T. V., *Respiratory Care of the Newborn and Child*, 2nd ed., Lippincott, 1997.
11. Glauser, F. L., *Signs and Symptoms in Pulmonary Medicine*, J. B. Lippincott, 1983.
12. Netter, F. H., *Respiratory System*, Vol. 7, CIBA Collection of Medical Illustrations, 1979.
13. Goldberger, E., *Essentials of Clinical Cardiology*, J. B. Lippincott, 1990.
14. Eubanks, D. H., and Bone, R. C., *Comprehensive Respiratory Care*, 2nd ed., Mosby, 1990.
15. Epstein, J., and Gaines, J., *Clinical Respiratory Care of the Adult Patient*, R. J. Brady Co., 1983.

Assessment Questions

1. Upon review of the patient's chart, the respiratory therapist finds that the physician has changed the respiratory care plan. The respiratory therapist should:
   A. Initiate the physician's changes at once
   B. Check for an identical physician's order changing the plan
   C. Initiate the physician's changes at once and carefully assess the patient
   D. Carefully assess the patient and then initiate the changes immediately

2. Tactile fremitus would be increased in which of the following conditions?
   A. A patient with an open pneumothorax
   B. A patient in pulmonary edema
   C. A patient with a closed pneumothorax
   D. A patient with a pleural effusion

3. Using a fiberoptic probe to transilluminate an infant's chest, one side transilluminates more that the other side, which can indicate:
   A. The infant is in pulmonary edema
   B. The infant has a pleural effusion
   C. A need to begin CPR
   D. The infant has a pneumothorax

4. Which of the following symptoms would be present in a patient exhibiting acute respiratory distress?
   I. Intercostal retractions
   II. Increased respiratory rate
   III. Nasal flaring
   IV. Use of accessory muscles
   A. I only
   B. I and II only

C. I, II and III only
   D. I, II, III and IV

5. An extremely fatigued patient presents in the emergency room with increased respiratory rate and jugular venous distension. This would indicate on assessment:
   I. That the patient may be in congestive heart failure
   II. That the patient may have increased vascular resistance
   III. That the patient may have atelectasis
   IV. That the patient may have pneumonia
   A. I and II only
   B. I, III and IV only
   C. II and III only
   D. III and IV only

6. When auscultating the carotid artery of a patient, an obstruction in the artery is heard, leading the therapist to believe the sounds are:
   A. Egophony
   B. Bruits
   C. Murmurs
   D. Pectoriloquy

7. A patient who exhibits an elevated left hemidiaphragm along with decreased left diaphragmatic excursion would indicate:
   I. The patient's left hemidiaphragm is paralyzed
   II. The patient has left-sided atelectasis
   III. The patient has an enlarged liver
   A. I and II only
   B. I, II and III
   C. II and III only
   D. III only

8. When documenting sputum production by a patient, which of the following should be charted?
   I. Amount
   II. Color
   III. Consistency
   IV. Odor
   A. I and II only
   B. I, II and III only
   C. I, II, III and IV
   D. I, III and IV only

9. Upon receiving an order for MDI aerosol therapy the therapist should first:
   A. Review the patient's chart
   B. Ask the patient if they have used an MDI before
   C. Explain the procedure to the patient
   D. Ask if the patient has been instructed in how to use an MDI

Chapter 3

Bedside Respiratory Monitoring

I. Respiratory rate. Items to note include the following:

A. Greater than 30 breaths per minute indicate an unacceptable level of increased work of breathing.

B. The mode of ventilation: Is the patient breathing spontaneously, or if on a ventilator, is he on control, assist-control, IMV, etc.?

C. The normal adult rate is 12–20/minute. Women tend to breathe more rapidly than men do.

D. Any alterations in breathing may be due to hypoxemia, metabolic disturbance, altered neurogenic input, anxiety, drugs, or any of the disorders listed under E.

E. Tachypnea may be caused by a number of disorders.[1]
   1. Pulmonary: found in both obstructive (emphysema, chronic bronchitis, asthma, and less common in bronchiectasis, cystic fibrosis) and restrictive (interstitial fibrosis, pulmonary edema, neuromuscular disorders, carcinomas, pneumonia, acute pulmonary embolism, etc.) diseases
   2. Cardiovascular: decreased cardiac output, right heart failure, cardiac defects, or shock
   3. Metabolic: methemoglobinemia, drugs, primary metabolic acidosis, fever, or thyrotoxicosis
   4. Mechanical or traumatic: brain trauma, tracheal obstruction, and abdominal distension
   5. Miscellaneous: amniotic fluid embolus, cirrhosis, collagen vascular disease, high altitude residency, anxiety, drugs

II. Tidal volume

A. It is the average amount of exhaled gas per breath over a minute.

$TV = \dot{V}_E/f$ Reported tidal volumes should be an average value obtained from the exhaled minute volume divided by the frequency.

B. Normal V_T is 6–7 ml/Kg of ideal body weight for a spontaneously breathing individual.
C. 10–15 ml/Kg of ideal body weight is utilized for continuous ventilatory support.
D. A spirometer or ventilometer (respirometer) is utilized to obtain the tidal volume. There are several requirements for the effective use of a bedside spirometer.[2]
   1. It should be simple for the patient to perform.
   2. It should be reliable to distinguish normal from abnormal patterns.
   3. It should be portable.
   4. It should provide for at least FVC, FEV_1, and PEF.
   5. There should be proper patient instruction.
   6. The data should be taken from the best of three efforts of the same test.
E. Visual estimation is generally inaccurate.
F. Hypopnea (volumes less than 300 ml) or hyperpnea (volumes greater than 700 ml) are abnormal and require further evaluation.
G. A decreased tidal volume usually is secondary to three primary conditions:
   1. Restrictive pulmonary disease
   2. Central nervous system depression
   3. Decreased ventilatory reserve

III. Minute volume[2]

A. $\dot{V}_E$ is the total amount of gas exhaled in one minute.
B. The normal $\dot{V}_E$ is 4–8 liters/minute.
C. Determination of minute volume is the best index of ventilation when used in conjunction with blood gas values. Refer to Equation 3-1.

EQUATION 3-1: Calculation of Minute Volume

Minute Volume $(\dot{V}_E)$ = Tidal Volume (V_T) × Frequency (f)

EXAMPLE: Determine the $\dot{V}_E$ given a V_T of 500 ml and f of 15/minute.

$$\dot{V}_E = V_T \times f$$
$$\dot{V}_E = 500 \times 15$$
$$\dot{V}_E = 7500 \text{ ml or } 7.5 \text{ L}$$

Chapter 3: Bedside Respiratory Monitoring

D. Minute volume is important to monitor in considering O_2 therapy and estimating the work of breathing.

E. Absolute values for $\dot{V}_E$ are not necessarily indicative of alveolar hyperventilation or hypoventilation.

F. Minute volume may be increased due to hypoxia, hypercapnia, acidosis, low compliance, or exercise.

G. Minute volume may be decreased due to hyperoxia, hypocapnia, rest, or alkalosis.

IV. Alveolar ventilation

A. The volume of fresh gas entering the respiratory gas exchange units each minute is the alveolar ventilation ($\dot{V}_A$).

B. V_A can be determined as follows (note: although V_D is not easy to measure, allowing 1 ml per pound of ideal body weight may approximate its value):

$$V_E = V_D + V_A$$

C. The PCO_2 is the best indicator of alveolar ventilation.

D. The alveolar PCO_2 can be approximated by monitoring the end-tidal carbon dioxide partial pressure ($P_{ET}CO_2$), or it may be deduced from the arterial PCO_2.

E. For monitoring $P_{ET}CO_2$, refer to the section on capnography.

F. Because rapid carbon dioxide equilibration occurs between alveolar gas and pulmonary capillary blood, the $PaCO_2$ can be used as an accurate estimate of the adequacy of alveolar ventilation.

G. Alveolar ventilation is inversely proportional to the $PaCO_2$ as demonstrated here:

$$PaCO_2 = \frac{1}{V_A}$$

H. If alveolar ventilation is halved, the $PaCO_2$ will double.

I. The most efficient way to increase alveolar ventilation during continuous mechanical ventilation is to increase the tidal volume delivered to the patient.

V. I:E ratio

A. The I:E ratio must be appropriate to ensure cardiovascular stability.

B. Because exhalation is usually passive and airways are narrower, a longer time is required than for inhalation.

C. A normal I:E ratio is 1:2.

D. In chronic obstructive pulmonary disease, the expiratory time is increased and the ratio is extended (e.g., 1:5).

E. The ratio between inspiratory and expiratory times on a mechanical ventilator should be individualized, especially when an inflation hold is used.

F. The longer the expiratory time, the lower will be the mean airway pressure during continuous mechanical ventilation.

G. The inspiratory time (T_I) should be 0.5–1.5 seconds with tidal volumes of 10–20 ml/Kg for minimal variations in mean inspiratory airway pressures.

H. The expiratory phase is primarily effected in the presence of tachypnea.

VI. Maximum inspiratory pressure[2]

A. Both maximum inspiratory and expiratory pressures are excellent indicators of restrictive lung diseases due to neuromuscular disorders.

B. The maximum inspiratory pressure (MIP) is a spontaneous inspiratory maneuver that is performed with a manometer attached to an occluded airway with monitoring of inspiratory efforts for 10–20 seconds.

C. MIP has also been referred to as negative inspiratory force.

D. An average normal maximum inspiratory pressure is about 100 cmH$_2$O for men and 70 cmH$_2$O for women. The lower limit of normal range is approximately 65% of the predicted value.[2]

E. A reduction in MIP indicates diaphragmatic weakness (inspiratory muscles).

F. The MIP maneuver may be used for several reasons:
 1. As a suitable substitute for the FVC in estimating ventilatory reserve, i.e., in Guillain-Barrè Syndrome
 2. To assess postoperatively the patient's ability to breathe adequately after anesthesia
 3. To assess ventilatory ability in the unresponsive, comatose, or obtunded patient

G. It serves as an index of the muscular power needed to provide a VC of approximately 15 ml/Kg. A maximum inspiratory pressure of greater than −20 cmH$_2$O pressure indicates this level in 20 seconds.

H. Weaning is likely to be successful if the MIP is greater than −30 cmH$_2$0.

VII. Maximum expiratory pressure

A. Like the MIP, the maximum expiratory force or pressure (MEP) maneuver is physiologically similar to the FVC, but may be a more sensitive indicator of neuromuscular failure than the FVC.[3]

B. The MEP, like the MIP, is useful in assessing patients prior to weaning from a continuous mechanical ventilator.

C. An average normal maximum expiratory pressure for adults is about 200 cmH$_2$O for men and 140 cmH$_2$O for women. The lower limit of normal range is approximately 65% of the predicted value.[2]

Chapter 3: Bedside Respiratory Monitoring

VIII. Vital capacity[2]

A. The work of breathing increases as the portion of the VC utilized for the tidal volume increases.

B. A previously healthy adult requires a minimal vital capacity of 15 ml/Kg to assure an effective cough and to adequately ventilate.

C. The simplest method of measuring diaphragmatic function is to measure the VC and the maximum static inspiratory pressure.[2]

D. Postoperatively, VC, along with other lung volumes, is decreased.

IX. Forced vital capacity

A. The FVC represents the maximal amount of gas exhaled after a maximal inspiration, and is approximately 80% of the TLC.

B. Normal values range from only 3 seconds in normal children to more than 30 seconds in adults with emphysema.[2]

C. It represents the maximum volume available to the patient for ventilation under conditions of stress.

D. A previously healthy adult requires a minimum of 15 ml/Kg to assure an effective cough and adequately deep breath.[2]

E. An FVC equal to or less than 10 ml/Kg may not allow the patient to maintain adequate spontaneous ventilation for a prolonged period.

F. It is a gross indicator of ventilatory reserve.[2]

G. The procedure must be explained fully to the patient to obtain accuracy.

X. Timed forced expiratory volumes[2]

A. FEV_T is related to the FVC and expressed as a percentage of the actual FVC. Refer to Table 4-2.

B. The FEV_1 is the most reproducible pulmonary function parameter when airway obstruction is present.

C. A normal FEV_1/FVC is greater than 70%, which decreases with age.

D. Due to aging alone, the FEV_1 normally decreases about 30 ml/yr. after age 30. The FEV_1 in cigarette smokers with COPD decreases about 60–120 ml/yr.

XI. Peak flow

A. The peak expiratory flow (PEF) is the maximum flow attainable at any time during the FVC maneuver.

B. It is an index for evaluation of therapeutic maneuvers to control bronchospasm, i.e., and pre- and post-bronchodilator effectiveness.

C. Surveys the initial blast of the FVC maneuver.

D. Not a good indicator of obstruction.[4]

XII. Airway resistance

A. Airway resistance (R_{aw}) is defined as the ratio between the driving pressure responsible for gas movement and the flow of gas as follows:[4]

$$R_{aw} = \Delta P/V$$

B. There are several factors that effect the resistance to airway gas flow: pattern of flow (laminar, turbulent, or tracheobronchial); physical characteristics of the inhaled gas; and the size, shape, and caliber of the airways.

C. Normal airway resistance ranges from approximately 0.5 to 2.5 cmH$_2$O/L/sec.[4]
   1. A normal adult breathing through an 8.0 mm endotracheal tube will experience about 4–6 cmH$_2$O higher resistance.
   2. If the R_{aw} increases by 10–15 cmH$_2$O/L/sec in an intubated patient with otherwise normal lungs, suspect any of the following: increased secretions, bronchospasm, pulmonary vascular congestion, or partial occlusion of the artificial airway.

D. One of the major concerns in clinical care is the potential for artificial airways to increase the resistance to gas flow.[2]
   1. Under laminar conditions, the pressure drop down a straight tube follows Poiseuille's Law, where the pressure gradient (ΔP) is linearly related to the flow (V), tube length (L), and viscosity (μ) but inversely proportional to the fourth power of the radius (r). Refer to Chapter 18 for example.
   2. Reynolds Number is a dimensionless number that predicts whether gas flow is laminar or turbulent (laminar if <2300 and turbulent if >2500).
   3. Because patients seldom breathe at constant gas flows, the Womersley number predicts turbulent flow during oscillatory patterns.

E. Clinical application of Poiseuille's Law indicates the following:
   1. To maintain stable ventilation in the presence of narrowing airways, greater driving pressure may be needed.
   2. A small change in airway caliber can effect a tremendous change in the amount of gas flowing through an airway.
   3. Under conditions of laminar flow, the driving pressure is linearly proportional to the gas flow times a constant related to gas viscosity, tube length, and radius.

F. Airway obstruction may occur at any point in the airway.[4]

Chapter 3: Bedside Respiratory Monitoring

1. Upper airway obstruction occurs above the glottis, which includes the larynx, oropharynx, and nasopharynx.
2. Lower airway obstruction occurs below the vocal cord in the trachea, main stem bronchi, or conducting airways.
3. The airway obstruction may be partial with mild increases in airway resistance and work of breathing to complete obstruction with no airflow.
4. Although artificial airways may be used to relieve airway obstruction, they all increase airway resistance above normal.

G. IPPB alone does not decrease airway resistance, but may be beneficial if it is used as a vehicle for delivering bronchodilators.[5]

H. Chest physical therapy has been shown to increase airway resistance, particularly in patients with reactive airways (which may be reversed with the administration of bronchodilators).[4]

XIII. Lung compliance

A. Lung compliance (C_L) is the measure of volume (liters of air) change per unit of pressure change (cmH_2O).
B. It is the inverse of elasticity.
C. Static compliance (C_{st}) is measured during a period of no flow (inspiratory pause) and reflects the compliance of the lung and chest wall.
D. Dynamic compliance (C_{dyn}) takes into consideration the compliance of ventilator tubing, the pressures needed to overcome artificial airway resistance, the airways of the lung, and the compliance of the lung and chest.
E. Effective compliance (C_{eff}) is a close approximation of the total compliance of the lungs and chest wall of a patient on a mechanical ventilator.[4]
   1. Normal values range 60–100 ml/cmH_2O.
   2. Low values may be indicative of diseases of lung parenchyma (pneumonia, pulmonary edema, and pulmonary fibrosis), or any chronic disease with a fibrotic component.
   3. A rapid drop in C_{eff} may be noted in acute pulmonary changes such as atelectasis, pulmonary edema, or lung compression due to a tension pneumothorax.
   4. When C_{eff} is less than 25–30 ml/cmH_2O, weaning from a ventilatory support will be difficult.
F. The relative changes in compliance curves can be used to assess the possible causes for hypoxemia.[2]
   1. A rightward shift of the dynamic curve, without a similar shift in the static curve, would suggest an airway process such as bronchospasm, retained secretions, or insertion of an endotracheal tube with a smaller internal diameter.

2. A shift in both dynamic and static compliance curves to the right is seen in main stem bronchus intubation, increased fluid in the lung (pulmonary edema, pneumonia), collapse of the lung (atelectasis), tension pneumothorax, or large pleural effusion.

G. Certain ventilatory patterns develop when lung compliance decreases and airway resistance increases.
 1. When C_L decreases, the patient's respiratory rate generally increases while the tidal volume decreases.[6]
  a. This breathing pattern is commonly seen in restrictive lung disorders such as pneumonia, pulmonary edema, or adult respiratory distress syndrome.
  b. This pattern is also commonly seen during the early stages of an acute asthmatic attack with hyperinflated alveoli.
 2. With a severe increase in airway resistance, the patient's breathing rate will generally decrease while the tidal volume increases. This breathing pattern is commonly seen in obstructive pulmonary diseases, especially in the advanced stages (e.g., chronic bronchitis, emphysema, bronchiectasis, asthma, and cystic fibrosis).

XIV. Lung mechanics

A. The importance of monitoring ventilatory mechanics is based on knowledge that excessive work of breathing can lead to fatigue of respiratory muscles, leading to:
 1. Respiratory failure
 2. Exacerbation of an existing insufficiency due to other causes
B. The average total work of breathing for normal patients is about 0.073 kg-m/L or 0.73 j/L.[4]
 1. Patients with obstructive or restrictive lung disease may exhibit two to three times this value at rest.
 2. At higher minute ventilations, there will be marked increases in work, especially in the compromised patient.
 3. Maintenance of adequate spontaneous ventilation is difficult when work of breathing exceeds 0.2 kg-m/L or 2.0 j/L.
C. Bedside analysis of lung mechanics may be accomplished in three primary ways.
 1. Physical assessment (refer to Chapter 2)
 2. Direct assessment utilizing pressure-volume curves (refer to pressure, flow, volume wave forms)
 3. Indirect assessment by obtaining peak airway pressure
D. Symbols used to represent measurements of mechanics of breathing may be found in Table 3-1.[4]

Chapter 3: Bedside Respiratory Monitoring

TABLE 3-1: Mechanics of Breathing Symbols

Symbol	Definition
P_{bs}	pressure at the body surface (P_B)
P_{aw}	pressure at any point along the airways
P_{ao}	pressure at the airway opening
P_{pl}	pleural pressure
P_{alv}	alveolar pressure
P_L	transpulmonary pressure ($P_{alv} - P_{pl}$)
P_W	transthoracic pressure ($P_{pl} - P_{bs}$)
P_{rs}	transrespiratory pressure ($P_{alv} - P_{bs}$, or $P_L + P_W$)

E. The greatest source of airway resistance in most ventilated patients is from the endotracheal tube. Airway resistance and work of breathing increase exponentially as smaller-sized tubes are used.[2]

F. Note discussion under airway resistance and lung compliance.

XV. Pressure, flow, volume waveforms[7]

A. Modern technology permits the obtaining of pressure, flow, and volume waveforms for graphical analysis.

B. Comparison of these waveforms over time provides an easily interpreted graphic portrayal of changing lung mechanics.

C. The pressure (P_{AW}), flow (V), and volume (V_T) wave forms for mechanical and spontaneous breaths are distinctly different (refer to Figure 3-1).

D. The pattern of pressure, flow, and volume delivery to a patient is referred to as the "mode" of ventilatory support, with each mode having its own characteristic graphics.

E. The graphic pattern for controlled mechanical ventilation (CMV) is determined by the clinician (volume cycled with fixed I:E ratio). The P_{AW} is dependent upon the patient's lung compliance and airway's resistance. Refer to Figure 3-2.

F. The Assist CMV mode permits patient cycling, with the tidal volume and flow rate for the mechanical breath being clinician set. If the patient becomes apneic, the graphic appears like the CMV mode. Refer to Figure 3-3.

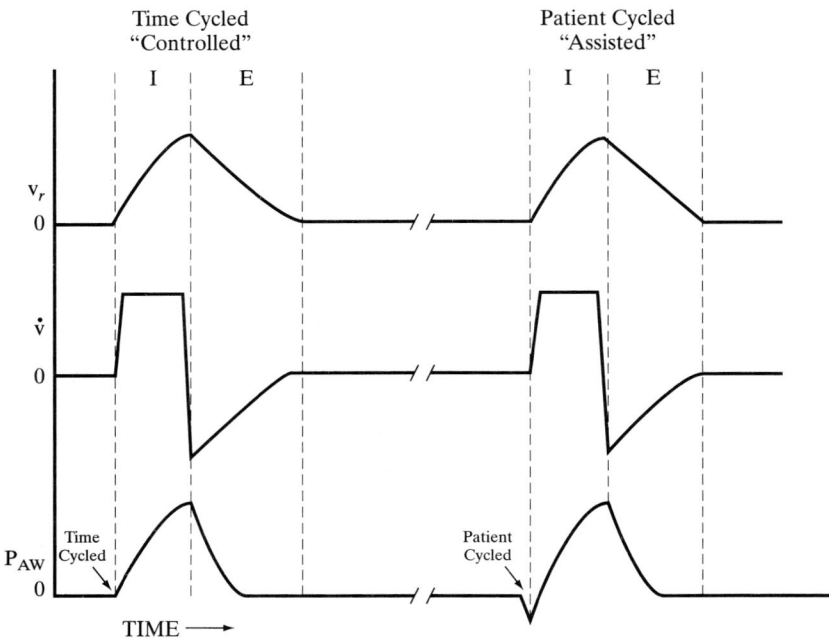

FIGURE 3-1: Volume, Flow, Pressure Graphics. Source: Figures 3-1 through 3-6 are taken from MacIntyre, N. R., *Graphical Analysis of Flow, Pressure, and Volume during Mechanical Ventilation.* Bear Medical Systems, 1991. Used with permission.

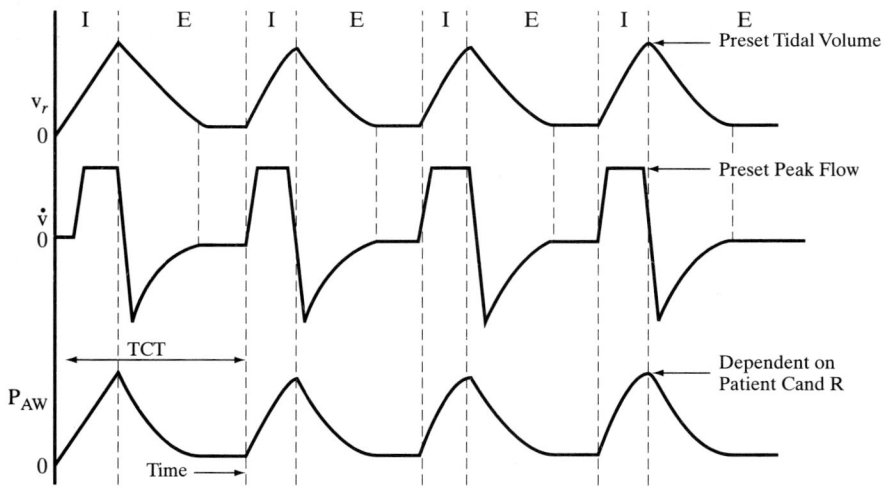

FIGURE 3-2: Controlled Mechanical Ventilation Graphics

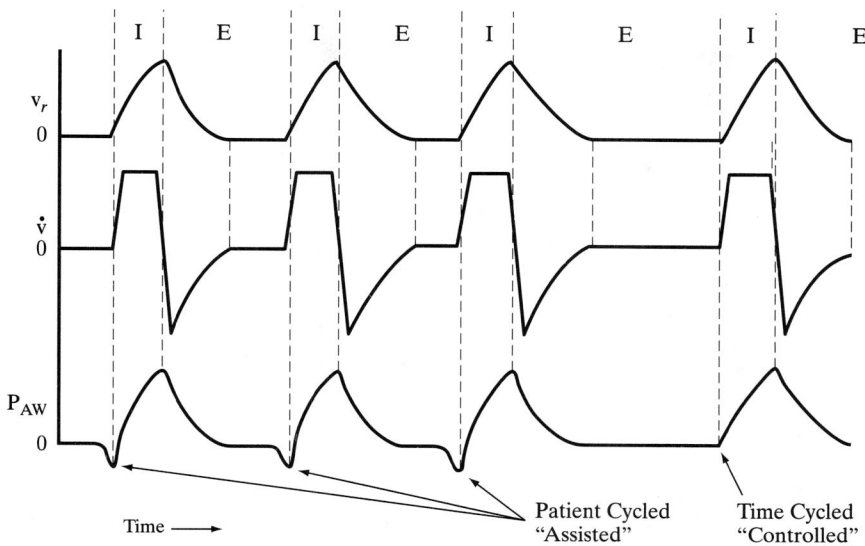

FIGURE 3-3: Assist CMV Graphics

G. Synchronized intermittent mandatory ventilation (SIMV) is a mode in which both mechanical and spontaneous breaths occur, with the mechanical breaths being clinician set.
   1. The mechanical breaths may be either patient or time cycled.
   2. Spontaneous breaths will vary dependent upon the patient's effort.
   3. The mechanical breaths are synchronized with the patient's first inspiratory effort in each preset time period, provided the assist sensitivity is set appropriately.
   4. Refer to Figure 3-4.
H. Intermittent mandatory ventilation (IMV) is similar to SIMV with the exception that the mechanical breath is delivered at regular intervals without regard to the patient's inspiratory effort. Refer to Figure 3-5.
I. Continuous positive airway pressure (CPAP) maintains a constant P_{AW} throughout a spontaneous breathing cycle. The pattern of breathing, peak flow, and tidal volume of each breath is determined solely by the patient. Refer to Figure 3-6.

XVI. Pulse oximetry[8]

A. Pulse oximetry is a noninvasive monitoring procedure, requiring minimal training, and allows the oxygen saturation (SaO_2) to be obtained and updated quickly.
B. The major disadvantage of pulse oximetry is that it does not detect changes in alveolar ventilation or acid-base status as does analysis of arterial blood.

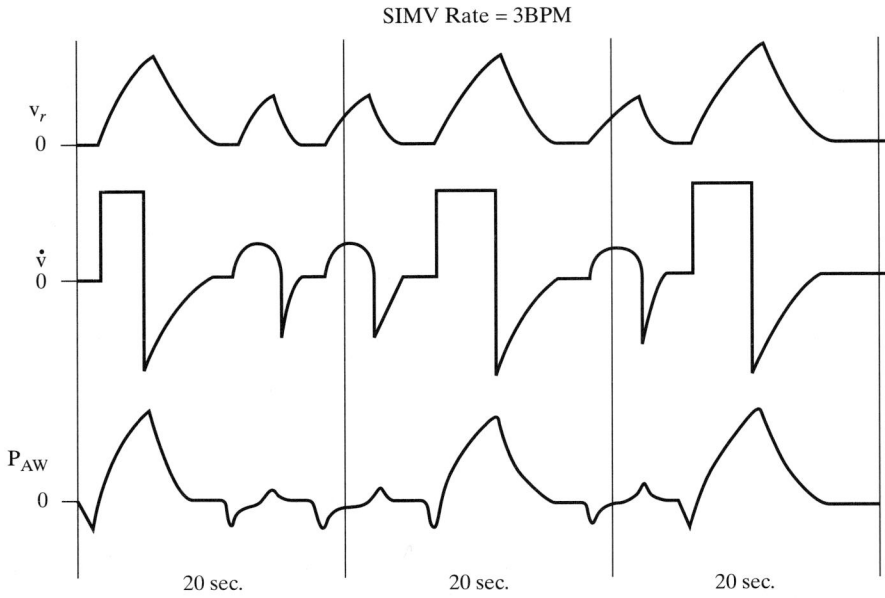

FIGURE 3-4: Synchronized Intermittent Mandatory Ventilation Graphics

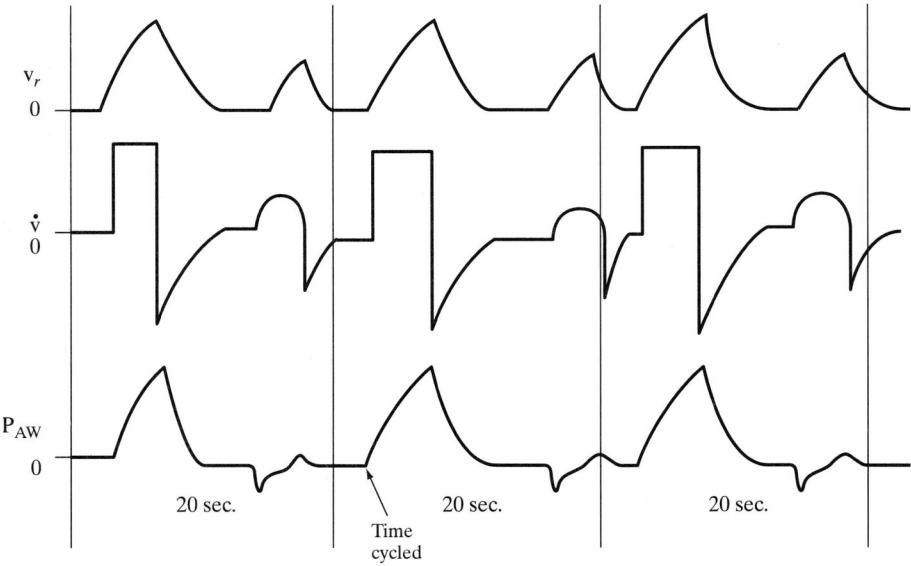

FIGURE 3-5: Intermittent Mandatory Ventilation Graphics

Chapter 3: Bedside Respiratory Monitoring

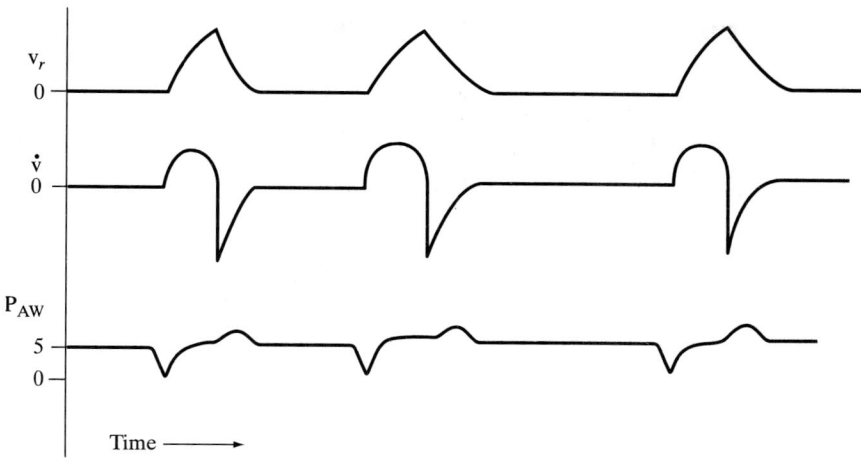

FIGURE 3-6: Continuous Positive Airway Pressure Graphics

C. Pulse oximeters transmit infrared and red light via light-emitting diodes (LEDs), which is partially absorbed in the pulsating vascular bed of a finger, ear, or nose.

D. SaO_2 is determined from the ratio of infrared to red light absorbed.

E. NOTE: If either large quantities of methemoglobin (MetHb) or carboxyhemoglobin (COHb) are present, true oxygen saturation will be lower than recorded values.

F. Pulse oximetry is an important adjunct to patient care, and its use reduces the number of arterial blood gas samples required.

G. The O_2-Hb dissociation curve demonstrates the relationship between PaO_2 and SaO_2.

H. Pulse oximetry is also utilized to document the following:
 1. Nocturnal hypoxemia during sleep
 2. Exercise-induced hypoxemia during maximal exercise testing
 3. The benefits of pursed-lip breathing, paced exercise, and relaxation techniques in patients with COPD
 4. Oxygenation status during procedures such as bronchoscopy
 5. Monitoring of vascular blood flow in transplanted digits
 6. Assessment of collateral circulation prior to arterial cannulation

XVII. Transcutaneous O_2/CO_2[8]

A. Transcutaneous monitoring permits noninvasive estimations of PO_2 and PCO_2 provided on a continuous versus an intermittent basis.

B. The PO_2 (Clark) and PCO_2 (Severinghaus pH) electrodes may be combined into a single sensor.

C. There is a high correlation between PaO_2 and $PtcO_2$ in the stable patient with good cardiac output and fluid balance.
   1. However, with peripheral vasoconstriction (e.g., shock), cutaneous blood flow is also minimized, rendering accurate estimations of PaO_2 difficult.
   2. Because of this, transcutaneous measurements of PO_2 should be reserved to patients with a stable hemodynamic system.
D. An accurate $PtcCO_2$ is also dependent upon adequate blood flow.
   1. The heating of the sensor increases the metabolic rate, causing the $PtcCO_2$ reading to be higher than arterial PCO_2.
   2. Obtaining $PtcCO_2$ is useful to analyze ventilatory changes.
E. Clinical application for transcutaneous monitors includes: [5]
   1. Continuous noninvasive method for rapidly identifying shock and hypoxia
   2. Substituting for repetitive arterial blood gas punctures in hemodynamically stable patients after obtaining a stabilized baseline
   3. Monitoring O_2 and CO_2 during transport or exercise testing

XVIII. Capnography[2]

A. A capnograph records the proportion of carbon dioxide in expired air.
B. With relatively normal lungs, the $P_{ET}CO_2$ (end-tidal CO_2) correlates with the $PaCO_2$.
C. Capnography may be used in clinical medicine for monitoring, regulating, or verifying the following:
   1. The adequacy of mechanical ventilation
   2. Airflow for polysomnography or apnea detection
   3. Hyperventilation in craniocerebral trauma
   4. Cardiopulmonary resuscitation
   5. Steady-state before respiratory calorimetry
   6. Anesthesia (disconnects, tube position, hypoventilation, etc.)
D. It may be used to supplement auscultation as a means of determining proper tube placement.[4]

XIX. Dead space to tidal volume ratio (V_D/V_T)[2]

A. The physiologic dead space (V_D) is the volume of the lungs that is ventilated but not perfused by the pulmonary capillary blood flow (wasted ventilation).
B. It is subdivided into two main components.
   1. Anatomic dead space (V_{Danat}) is comprised of the conducting airways and is roughly equal to the ideal body weight in pounds.

Chapter 3: Bedside Respiratory Monitoring

  a. It is larger in men than in women.
  b. It increases with increasing tidal volume caused by exercise or diseases that increase the FRC (i.e., COPD, bronchiectasis, etc.).
  c. It decreases with asthma or other obstructive diseases of the bronchi.
 2. Alveolar dead space (V_{Dalv}) includes all nonperfused alveoli. Because a direct measurement is difficult to collect without the contamination of anatomic gas, the physiologic dead space is generally calculated as follows:[9]

$$V_{Danat} + V_{Dalv} = V_{Dphys}$$

C. Determination of the V_D/V_T may be accomplished by several mechanisms.
 1. Laboratory determination utilizes a single breath analysis (Fowler's Method).
  a. This value may be obtained by a modification of the Bohr equation.
  b. The patient takes a single inhalation of 100% O_2.
  c. The exhaled graphic measurement of N_2% and volume is measured and plotted by an X-Y recorder.
  d. The V_{Danat} is calculated from the manipulation of the actual exhaled N_2%–Volume tracing.
 2. Clinical bedside assessment requires obtaining a well-mixed exhaled gas sample, while obtaining an arterial blood gas sample concurrently. The formula to calculate V_D/V_T is found in Equation 3-2.

D. A normal V_D/V_T is 0.2–0.4 and increases gradually with age.

E. The V_D/V_T ratio is a good index of the ventilation/blood flow ratio because all CO_2 in the expired gas comes from perfused alveoli.

F. Conventional weaning criteria have established a V_D/V_T of 0.6 as maximally acceptable. An increased V_D/V_T (greater than 0.6) indicates inefficient air movement, and would make it quite difficult to successfully wean a patient from a continuous mechanical ventilator.

EQUATION 3-2: **The Bohr Equation for Dead Space Calculation**

$$V_D/V_T = \frac{PaCO_2 - P_ECO_2}{PaCO_2}$$

Example: Find V_D/V_T where $PaCO_2$ is 40 mmHg and P_ECO_2 is 30 mmHg.

$$V_D/V_T = (40 - 30)/40 = 0.25$$

Note: This indicates that 25% of the tidal volume is wasted ventilation (physiologic dead space).

References

1. Glauser, F. L., *Signs and Symptoms in Pulmonary Medicine,* J. B. Lippincott, 1983.
2. Ruppel, G., *Manual of Pulmonary Function Testing,* 7th ed., Mosby, 1998.
3. Burton, G. G., Hodgkin, J. E., and Ward, J. J., *Respiratory Care: A Guide to Clinical Practice,* 4th ed., Lippincott, 1997.
4. Scanlon, C. L., Wilkins, R. L., and Stoller, J. K., *Egan's Fundamentals of Respiratory Care,* 7th ed., Mosby, 1999.
5. Eubanks, D. H., and Bone, R. C., *Comprehensive Respiratory Care,* 2nd ed., Mosby, 1990.
6. Des Jardins, T., *Clinical Manifestations of Respiratory Disease,* 3rd ed., Year Book Medical Publishers, Inc., 1997.
7. MacIntyre, N. R., *Graphical Analysis of Flow, Pressure, and Volume During Mechanical Ventilation,* Bear Medical Systems, Inc., 1991.
8. Kacmarek, R. M., et al., *Monitoring in Respiratory Care,* Mosby, 1993.
9. West, J. B., *Respiratory Physiology—The essentials,* 4th ed., Lippincott, Williams and Wilkins Co., 1994.

Assessment Questions

1. A patient running a high fever would exhibit which of the following?

    A. Increased pulse rate
    B. Decreased respiratory rate
    C. Decreased V_D/V_T ratio
    D. Decreased oxygen consumption

2. A carpet layer trapped in a burning building is transported by ambulance to the emergency room. The patient is receiving oxygen by simple mask at 5 liters per minute, and the pulse oximeter is reading $SaO_2 = 94\%$. You would expect the reading on the pulse oximeter to be:

    A. Erroneously low
    B. Erroneously high
    C. Accurate
    D. Unable to be read due to high levels of CO

3. A 160 lb. male patient displaying a tidal volume of 750 ml and a respiratory rate of 18 breaths per minute would have a minute volume of:

    A. 9.65 L/min.
    B. 10.8 L/min.
    C. 11.45 L/min.
    D. 13.5 L/min.

4. The alveolar minute volume displayed in the preceding question (3) is equal to:

    A. 9.65 L/min.
    B. 10.8 L/min.
    C. 11.45 L/min.
    D. 13.5 L/min.

5. A patient is being treated with IPPB every hour for carbon dioxide retention. The IPPB machine spends 2.3 seconds in inspiration each breath, with the total ventilatory cycle lasting seven seconds. What is the I:E ratio?

    A. 1:1.5
    B. 1:2.0
    C. 1:2.5
    D. 1:3.0

6. The patient's respiratory rate in the preceding question (5) would be approximately:

Chapter 3: Bedside Respiratory Monitoring

    A. 12/BPM
    B. 11/BPM
    C. 10/BPM
    D. 9/BPM

7. A well-conditioned athlete is undergoing an exercise test on a treadmill, which of the following would you expect to decrease?

    A. V_D/V_T
    B. A/a gradient
    C. PaO_2
    D. pH

8. A patient has just been intubated and the physician wants to verify tube placement, you would provide the physician with a

    A. Calorimeter
    B. Capnometer
    C. Cartharometer
    D. Co-oximeter

9. Transcutaneous measurements will not correlate well with arterial values under which of the following conditions?

    I. Cutaneous vasoconstriction secondary to low cardiac output
    II. Hypothermia
    III. Changes in blood flow
    IV. Increased intrapleural pressure

    A. I and II only
    B. I, II and III only
    C. III and IV
    D. IV only

Chapter 4

Pulmonary Laboratory

I. Pulmonary function values

A. There are several uses of pulmonary function tests:[1]
   1. Screening for pulmonary diseases
   2. Preoperative evaluation for baseline assessment
   3. Assessment of disease progression
   4. Assist in the determination of pulmonary disability
   5. Modify the therapeutic approach to patient care
B. For lung volumes and capacities, refer to Table 4-1.
C. For flow rate terminology, refer to Table 4-2.
D. From a FVC maneuver one can obtain the following volumes and/or capacities: VC, FVC, and flow rates for FEV_1, FEV_3, the $FEF_{200-1200}$, and $FEF_{25-75\%}$.
E. Spirometry before and/or after bronchodilator
   1. It is primarily used to measure the degree of reversibility of airway obstruction.
   2. The reversibility of airway obstruction following the use of a bronchodilator is considered significant if flow rates increase 15–20%, or as follows:[2]
      a. FVC increases greater than 10%
      b. FEV_1 increases by 200 ml or 15% of baseline
      c. FEF_{25-75} increases 20%
   3. The type of bronchodilator drug generally used is a $beta_2$ sympathomimetic, although the specific drug is not standardized between labs.
   4. Bronchodilators are frequently given in the clinical setting even though no response is documented in the laboratory, because prolonged exposure might be required for clinical benefit.
F. Reliability of the tests is a function of the reproducibility and consistency of repeated tests, and the absence of communication barriers, anxiety, and/or pain in the patient being tested.

Chapter 4: Pulmonary Laboratory

TABLE 4-1: Lung Volumes and Capacities

Capacities	Volumes
(TLC) Total Lung	(IRV) Inspiratory Reserve
(VC) Vital	(TV) Tidal
(IC) Inspiratory	(ERV) Expiratory Reserve
(FRC) Functional Residual	(RV) Residual

$$TLC = IRV + TV + ERV + RV$$

$$VC = IC + ERV$$

$$FRC = ERV + RV$$

TABLE 4-2: Flow Rate Definitions

FVC	forced vital capacity; the maximum amount of gas that can be forcefully exhaled following a maximum inspiration.
FEV_1	forced expired volume at 1 second; the maximum amount of gas that can be exhaled during the first 1 second of a forced vital capacity maneuver. FEV_3 is the amount exhaled in 3 seconds.
$FEF_{200-1200}$	forced expiratory flow between the first 200 ml of volume and the next 1000 ml of volume. It is the average of the expiratory flow during the early phase of exhalation. It can also be referred to as the maximum expiratory flow rate (MEFR). It is effort dependent.
FEF_{25-75}	forced expiratory flow 25–75%, is the average expiratory flow rate during the middle 50% of exhalation. It can also be referred to as the maximal mid-expiratory flow rate (MMEFR). It is the least effort dependent and is useful in identifying smaller airway obstruction.
MVV	maximum voluntary ventilation; the maximum amount of gas that can be moved in 1 minute. It is also referred to as the maximum breathing capacity (MBC).
PEF	peak expiratory flow rate; the maximum flow rate during the forced vital capacity.
PIF	peak inspiratory flow rate; the fastest flow rate during a maximum inspiratory effort.

G. The actual values should be monitored and not just the percentage of predicted values. Refer to Table 4-3.
H. FRC by helium dilution
   1. This test utilizes a closed circuit with the patient breathing a gas mixture containing 10% helium, and oxygen added to maintain volume. The gas mixture is rebreathed through a CO_2 absorber until equilibration occurs (generally less than 7 minutes).
   2. The patient is connected into the system at FRC, or resting lung level.
   3. Immediately after equilibration, the patient is instructed to perform a vital capacity maneuver in order that expiratory reserve volume, inspiratory capacity, and vital capacity can be used to calculate residual volume and total lung capacity.
   4. Both initial and final He concentrations are obtained and used to calculate the FRC as follows:

$$\text{FRC} = \frac{\% \text{ He(initial)} - \% \text{ He(final)}}{\% \text{ He(final)}} \times \text{initial volume}$$

   5. In some labs, oxygen is added to the system equal to the rate of its use, or consumption.[3]
   6. There are several factors to consider during the test.
      a. The system must be leak free.
      b. The blower speed should be adjusted for adequate mixing without creating an iatrogenic PEEP effect.

TABLE 4-3: Pulmonary Function Abnormalities

Function	Normal %	Obstructive	Restrictive	Combined
FVC	±20	N or ↓	↓	↓
FEV_1	±20	N or ↓	↓	↓
FEV_1/FVC	75	↓	N or ↑	↓
FEF_{25-75}	±20	↓	↑, N or ↓	↓
TLC	±20	N or ↑	↓	↑
RV/TLC	25–40	↑	N	↑
D_LCO		N or ↓	N or ↓	N or ↓
MVV	±20	↓	N	↓

Chapter 4: Pulmonary Laboratory

   c. There must be an accurate volume determined for the system.
   d. A correction must be made to account for the mechanical dead space.
   e. Duplicate measurements should agree within 90–160 ml.[3]
 7. The obtained value must be converted to body temperature and pressure under saturated conditions (BTPS).
 8. This method may be used to obtain FRC, RV and TLC, which is unobtainable on spirometry.

I. Nitrogen washout
 1. This method utilizes an open-circuit to determine the FRC, RV, and TLC.
 2. The method is based on the assumption that the concentration of nitrogen in the lungs is in equilibrium with the surrounding atmosphere (approximately 78%).
 3. The patient breathes 100% oxygen in an attempt to "washout" the nitrogen from the lungs.
 4. The exhaled gas is collected into a spirometer or bellows and the nitrogen concentration is measured.
 5. The FRC is calculated as follows:

$$FRC = \frac{\% \ N_{2 \ Final} \times Expired \ Volume}{\% \ N_{2 \ Alveolar}}$$

 6. A normal nondiseased lung can generally be washed out in 7 minutes or less.
 7. Considerations in washing out the lungs of a patient with COPD may include incomplete washout due to extensive bullous disease, absorption atelectasis, or satisfaction of the hypoxic drive mechanism from inhalation of 100% O_2.
 8. Patients with unequal or poor distribution of ventilation will take much longer to washout. As a result, the alveolar N_2 concentration at the end of the test may serve as a rough index of the distribution of ventilation.
 9. The FRC is corrected for BTPS conditions and for any nitrogen excretion (nitrogen absorbed from the blood during the washout process).

J. Total lung capacity (other methods of obtaining TLC)
 1. Body plethysmography
   a. Body plethysmography measures thoracic gas volume (V_{TG}), whether in communication with open airways or trapped within the thorax. Utilizing Boyle's Gas Law does this. Refer to Table 4-4.
   b. This test measures a change in lung volume that occurs while a patient sits and breathes inside a closed container.
   c. The value obtained is actually the thoracic gas volume (V_{TG}) whether it is in ventilatory communication with the atmosphere or not.

> **TABLE 4-4:** Boyle's Gas Law
>
> $P_1V_1 = P_2V_2$ where,
>
> P_1 = the original pressure in the plethysmograph, which is usually atmospheric or 760 mmHg
>
> V_1 = the original volume within the plethysmograph less the volume displaced by the patient
>
> P_2 = the new pressure in the plethysmograph as a result of an inspiratory effort by the patient
>
> V_2 = the new volume in the plethysmograph, which is a calculated value

   d. If the V_{TG} measurement of FRC is larger than the FRC measured by either the helium dilution or the nitrogen washout method, then generally severe emphysema or a closed pneumothorax exists.
   e. When dilution tests extend beyond 7 minutes, the results for FRC determinations approach the V_{TG} figures.[2]
   2. TLC determined radiographically, or CXR planimetry
      a. Radiological estimation of TLC requires a standard posterior-anterior and lateral chest film.[2]
      b. A planimeter is used to approximate the volume after the lung areas have been divided into specified segments.
      c. Radiological determination of TLC correlates well with plethysmography in normal and obstructed patients. This technique may be more accurate than dilution methods in moderate to severe obstruction.
K. Raw (airway resistance) is the pressure difference to move a volume of gas measured in $cmH_2O/L/sec$. The normal value range is 0.6–2.4 $cmH_2O/L/sec$ measured at flow rates of 0.5 L/sec. It may increase up to three times normal in asthma.[2]
   1. Approximately 90% of the change in pressure caused by frictional resistance to airflow occurs in the nose, mouth, and large airways.
   2. Only about 10% of the total resistance to gas flow are attributable to smaller airways less than 2 mm in diameter.[1]
L. Lung compliance[2]
   1. C (compliance) is a volume change per unit pressure change and is a measurement of the distensibility of the lung in L/cmH_2O.

Chapter 4: Pulmonary Laboratory

2. Normal lung compliance (C_L) of 0.2 L/cmH$_2$O plus normal thoracic compliance (C_T) of 0.2 L/cmH$_2$O equals a total compliance (C_{LT}) of 0.1 cmH$_2$O.[2]
3. The average compliance (C_L) in the normal adult is 0.2 L/cmH$_2$O, and 0.006 L/cmH$_2$O in the neonate.
4. C_L varies with the volume of the lungs at FRC. The specific compliance is obtained by dividing the C_L by the FRC. By this comparison of compliance at a specified lung volume, the specific compliance (C_S) of both the adult and the neonate are similar (refer to Table 4-5).
5. The frequency dependence of compliance is expressed as (C_{dyn}/C_{st}) × 100. Normal patients will exhibit similar values for compliance during both dynamic (C_{dyn}) and static (C_{st}) conditions.
   a. Values less than 80% is a finding consistent with airway disease.
   b. This test is considered a sensitive indicator of small airway obstruction.[1]

M. CV (closing volume) is the lung volume at which airway closure begins, expressed as a percentage of the vital capacity. Normal values are dependent upon age and sex. In normal young people the CV is approximately 10% of the VC.[4]

N. Diffusing capacity[2]
  1. D_LCO is the diffusing capacity of carbon monoxide across the lung. This evaluates the lung's gas exchange mechanism in ml/min/mmHg, and the ability to diffuse across the alveolar capillary membrane.
  2. Normal values range 17–25 ml/min/mmHg, depending on the technique of steady state or single breath test.[2]
  3. The most common agent used is 0.2–0.3% carbon monoxide (it combines with hemoglobin 210 times more strongly than oxygen).
  4. There are several methods used to determine the D_LCO.
      a. During the single breath technique (modified Krogh), the patient inspires 0.3% CO and 10% helium with the remainder consisting of 21% O_2 and N_2.

TABLE 4-5: Specific Compliance Comparisons

Value	Adult	Neonate
FRC	2400 ml	75 ml
C_L	0.2 L/cmH$_2$O	0.006 L/cmH$_2$O
C_S	0.8 L/cmH$_2$O/L	0.8 /cmH$_2$O/L

After breath holding for ten seconds, an end tidal sampler analyzes the exhaled gas for CO.
   b. In the steady state technique (Filey), the patient breathes a gas mixture of 0.1–0.2% CO in air for 5–6 minutes. During the final two minutes of the study, the expired gas is collected in a Douglas bag and analyzed for CO, CO_2, and O_2. An arterial blood gas is drawn for analysis of the $PaCO_2$.
   c. Other methods for the determination of the D_LCO include end-tidal CO determination, the assumed V_D technique, mixed venous PCO_2 technique, rebreathing technique, equilibration-washout method, fractional CO uptake, and membrane diffusion coefficient and capillary blood technique.
5. All of the methods used to measure the D_LCO do so according to the following equation:

$$D_LCO = \frac{\text{ml CO transferred/min.}}{\text{mean}P_ACO - \text{mean }P_CCO}$$

6. The normal value for D_LCO for adult males is 25 ml/min/mmHg (single breath and STPD). Values for females are slightly less.
7. The D_LCO can increase two or three times normal with exercise. Refer to Table 4-6.
8. Diffusing capacity tests are useful for evaluation and follow up of various clinical conditions:
   a. Parenchymal lung diseases associated with dusts, drug reactions, or sarcoidosis
   b. Emphysema and cystic fibrosis
   c. Differentiating among chronic bronchitis, emphysema, and asthma in patients with obstructive pulmonary patterns
   d. Pulmonary involvement in systemic diseases (e.g., rheumatoid arthritis, systemic lupus erythematosus)
   e. Cardiovascular diseases (e.g., primary pulmonary hypertension, pulmonary edema, acute or recurrent thromboembolism)

TABLE 4-6: Conditions That May Influence D_LCO

Change	Conditions
Increase	exercise, polycythemia, increased pulmonary capillary blood volume, supine position
Decrease	pulmonary emboli, pulmonary fibrosis, lung resection, emphysema, anemia, decreased Hct and Hb

Chapter 4: Pulmonary Laboratory

- f. Effects of chemotherapy agents, or other pharmacologic agents know to induce pulmonary dysfunction
- g. Hemorrhagic disorders
- h. Prediction of arterial desaturation during exercise in COPD
- i. Quantification of disability associated with interstitial lung disease.

O. Maximum voluntary ventilation (MVV) is also called the maximum breathing capacity (MBC).[2]
  1. This value is obtained by having the patient perform maximum breathing for 10–15 seconds. The results are then extrapolated to one minute.
  2. It is useful in measuring the status of the respiratory muscles, compliance of the lung-thorax system, and the resistance offered.
  3. It is a test with limitations because the maneuver exaggerates air trapping and exertion of the respiratory muscles.
  4. It is decreased in obstructive diseases.
  5. It may be normal in some patients with restrictive lung disease, as limitation of thoracic expansion does not in most cases impede the respiratory muscles.

P. Flow volume loops ($\dot{V}/V$)
  1. The flow-volume curve is the graphic analysis of the flow generated during an FVC maneuver (inspiratory and expiratory), versus the volume change.[2]
  2. The flow is recorded in liters per second and the volume in liters.
  3. From a flow/volume loop one can obtain the following flows, volumes, and/or capacities: VC, TV, IRV, FVC, and flow rates for PIF, PEF, and $FEF_x\%$.
  4. They are believed by many to be the most efficient test for early detection of obstruction in the small airways (less than 2–3 mm).
  5. The peak flows are effort dependent.
  6. The interpretation is based primarily on the downslope of the curve, which is effort independent.
     a. As the lung volume is reduced, the flow declines, but it is the maximum flow for that particular lung volume.
     b. A high degree of patient cooperation is not necessary to obtain a satisfactory tracing.
  7. A limitation of flow results from the dynamic compression of the airways.
  8. The shape of the loop may be used to differentiate between restrictive and obstructive lung disease.
  9. The flow/volume curve may also be utilized to obtain the $\dot{V}$ max50 and the Viso $\dot{V}$.
  10. $\dot{V}$max50 (maximum flow at 50% of the VC) is a test that also superimposes flow-volume loops obtained while the patient breathes first room air, and then a He/O_2 mixture.

a. It compares flow rates of the forced vital capacity at 50% of the vital capacity.
b. The test appears to be uninfluenced by the lung elastic properties and thus seems to be specific for small airway caliber because the flow in the smaller airways is dependent on gas viscosity, and not as much on the gas density dependence of the larger airways.
c. In normal patients, the maximum flow decreases linearly with volume over most of the VC.
d. In obstructive patients, there is a greater decrease in the $\dot{V}max50$ so that the flow-volume curve appears "scooped-out."
e. There is good correlation with FEF_{25-75} and decreases in the $\dot{V}max50$ in patients with obstructive lung disease.

11. Viso$\dot{V}$ (isoflow volume point) consists of a flow-volume loop obtained during a forced inspiratory and forced expiratory maneuver while the patient is breathing room air, and then superimposing on the tracing a flow-volume loop done while having the patient breathe a mixture of He and O_2.
    a. The resulting value identifies the amount of VC that remains in the lung when gas flow becomes independent of gas density.
    b. The Viso$\dot{V}$ is the volume at which the flows are equal, and it is expressed as a percentage (%) of the FVC.
    c. The Viso$\dot{V}$ is larger in small airway disease.
    d. Viso$\dot{V}$ is one of the most sensitive indicators of small airway obstruction.
    e. A normal test will show equal flows between 10–20% of the vital capacity for patients 20–50 years of age.[2]

12. The expiratory part (upward deflection) of the curve is more useful in distinguishing between restrictive and obstructive components.

13. The inspiratory part (downward deflection) is more helpful in differentiating extrathoracic and intrathoracic airway obstruction.

Q. Bronchoprovocation
1. Bronchial challenge testing provides information about airway hyperreactivity. A spirometer or body plethysmograph is used to test the airway following exposure to a provocative agent with the FEV_1 being the most reliable index of hypersensitive airways in the suspected asthma patient.
2. The challenge consists of having a patient inhale increasing doses of methacholine, producing bonchoconstriction. The dose that produces a 20% reduction in FEV_1 is termed the provocative dose, or $PD_{20\%}$, and confirms a diagnosis of asthma.[2]
3. Aerosolization of histamine may be administered for the same purpose as previously described. A positive response to the test is determined by the FEV_1. Again, a $PD_{20\%}$, confirms a diagnosis of asthma.

TABLE 4-7: Types of Pulmonary Disease

Obstructive

Emphysema	Chronic Bronchitis	Bronchial Asthma
Bronchiectasis	Cystic Fibrosis	Asthmatic Bronchitis
	Tracheobronchomalacia	

Restrictive

Intrapulmonic	**Thoracic**	**Abdominal**
Pneumonia	Kyphoscoliosis	Abdominal Surgery
Pulmonary Edema	Multiple Rib Fractures	Ascites
Sarcoidosis	Rheumatoid Spondylitis	Peritonitis
Vascular Congestion	Thoracic Surgery	Severe Obesity
Reduced Surfactant	Pleural Effusion	Pregnancy
Pneumoconiosis	Pneumothorax	
Interstitial Fibrosis		

Respiratory Center Depression	**Neuromuscular Defects**
Narcotics	Poliomyelitis
Barbiturates	Myasthenia Gravis
Anesthesia	Guillain-Barrè
Brain Stem Trauma	Tetanus
	Drugs

II. Pulmonary disease may be classified as either obstructive or restrictive in nature. Refer to Table 4-7.

A. In obstructive diseases, pay particular attention to the monitoring of the flow rates.

B. In restrictive diseases, monitor the lung volumes.

III. Blood gas results are used to determine the oxygenation and acid-base status.

A. Normal values are identified in Table 4-8.
 1. pH is the negative logarithm of the H^+ concentration.

TABLE 4-8: Normal Blood Gas Values

Value	Arterial Range	Arterial Mean	Venous
pH	7.35–7.45	7.40	7.35
PCO_2	35–45	40 torr	46 torr
PO_2	age, position, and altitude dependent*	40 torr	
SaO_2	≥96%		70–75%
HCO_3^-	22–26	24 mEq/L	
BE	±2	0 mEq/L	

*Refer to Table 4-10 for predicted PO_2.

    a. It indicates the degree of acidosis or alkalosis (acidemia or alkalemia) in the body.

    b. The presence of a normal pH does not rule out an acid-base disturbance (i.e., a fully compensated acid-base disorder will have a normal pH).

    c. The normal ratio of $HCO_3^-/PCO_2 \times 0.03$ is 20:1. Refer to Table 4-9.

2. $PaCO_2$ is the partial pressure of carbon dioxide in the arterial blood.

    a. It is the respiratory component of acid-base conditions.

    b. It is the best indicator of alveolar ventilation:

$$PaCO_2 \simeq VCO_2/V_A$$

    c. Alveolar hypoventilation may be defined as a $PaCO_2$ greater than 45 torr.

    d. Alveolar hyperventilation may defined as a $PaCO_2$ less than 35 torr.

    e. Alveolar hypoventilation and hyperventilation are not synonymous with overall hypoventilation and hyperventilation, i.e., an increased $\dot{V}_E$ may be present with an increased $PaCO_2$ due to increased V_D/V_T.

3. PaO_2 is the partial pressure of oxygen in arterial blood.

    a. This value normally decreases with age as a result of an increasing $\dot{V}/\dot{Q}$ imbalance with normal aging (the predicted PaO_2 is approximately $100 - 1/3$ the age). Refer to Table 4-10.

    b. PaO_2 is usually lower when the patient is supine than when upright due to a change in ventilation to perfusion ($\dot{V}/\dot{Q}$) matching.

Chapter 4: Pulmonary Laboratory

TABLE 4-9: pH Relationships

pH = pK* + log HCO_3/$PaCO_2$ × 0.03

pH is approximately equal to the following relationships:

1. HCO_3^-/$PaCO_2$**
2. metabolic component/respiratory component
3. base/acid
4. kidney/lung

*Dissociation constant is the pH of 6.1 where roughly one-half of the H_2CO_3/HCO_3^- buffering system is ionized into H^+ and HCO_3^- and the other half remains unionized as H_2CO_3.

**The normal ratio of HCO_3^-/(PCO_2 × 0.03) is 20:1, and yields a pH of 7.4.

TABLE 4-10: Predicted PaO_2 as a Function of Age[5]

Years	PaO_2 (±5)
10	100 torr
20	95
30	90
40	85
50	80
60	75
70	70

Note: There is approximately a 5 mmHg (torr) decrease in PaO_2 for each 10 year increase in age. Modification of work by Sorbini.

c. $\dot{V}/\dot{Q}$ in the apices is approximately 3.3, while in the bases it is 0.63.
d. The average $\dot{V}/\dot{Q}$ ratio is 0.8, and is determined by dividing the amount of ventilation by the perfusion as follows.[4]

$$\dot{V}/\dot{Q} = 4\ L/m\ /\ 5\ L/m = 0.8$$

e. Hypoxemia is a deficient oxygenation of the blood.
f. Hypoxia is a deficient oxygenation of the tissue.

4. HCO_3^- is the bicarbonate within the plasma.
   a. It is primarily the metabolic component, BUT it is influenced by the respiratory system as seen in the following hydration equation:

   $$CO_2 + H_2O \longleftrightarrow H_2CO_3 \longleftrightarrow H^+ + HCO_3^-$$

   b. The preceding reaction occurs rather slowly in the plasma, but is speeded up in the erythrocyte and in the renal tubular cell by the presence of carbonic anhydrase.[6]
   c. H_2CO_3/HCO_3 is the main physiologic buffer system in the body. Other buffers include hemoglobin, phosphate, and proteins.
   d. Standard bicarbonate is the plasma bicarbonate concentration when the blood has been equilibrated at a PCO_2 of 40 torr (an in vivo measurement). It has a normal value of 22–26 mEq/L.
   e. T_{40} is an in vitro measurement of the buffering system that also excludes respiratory system interference.

5. BE is the base excess/deficit, which reflects either an increase or decrease in the buffer base.
   a. Buffer base is the total value of the buffering system that includes bicarbonate, hemoglobin, plasma proteins, and phosphates. Refer to Table 5-2.
   b. This value allows one to look strictly at the metabolic component, eliminating the respiratory component.
   c. A deviation of base in the extracellular fluids of greater than 2 mEq/L means either acid has been removed or base added.

6. SaO_2 is the saturation of hemoglobin by oxygen in the arterial blood.
   a. The oxyhemoglobin (O_2-Hb) dissociation curve shows the relationship between PaO_2 and SaO_2.
   b. The flat part of the O_2-Hb dissociation curve is an advantage in the lung (the hemoglobin will adequately saturate despite wide deviations in PO_2 above 60 mmHg).
   c. The steep part of the curve has an advantage at the tissue level (tissue O_2 consumption facilitates Hb unloading of O_2).
   d. The shape of the curve determines the loading and unloading ability of hemoglobin for O_2. Refer to Table 4-11.
   e. The PaO_2 is a more sensitive indicator of mild hypoxemia than the SaO_2.

Chapter 4: Pulmonary Laboratory

TABLE 4-11: Factors That Shift the O_2-Hb Dissociation Curve

Left Shift	Right Shift
alkalosis	acidosis
hypocapnia	hypercapnia
hypothermia	fever
decreased 2,3 DPG	increased 2,3 DPG
certain congenital hemoglobinopathies	certain congenital hemoglobinopathies
fetal hemoglobin	
carboxyhemoglobin	

    f. P_{50} is a method of expressing the position of the oxyhemoglobin dissociation curve. The PaO_2 at 50% saturation, a pH of 7.40, and temperature of 37 degrees C is normally 26–28 mmHg.

7. O_2 content is the actual amount of oxygen present in blood in ml of O_2/100 ml of whole blood expressed in vol%, or deciliter (dl).[7]

    a. This factor is more important than PaO_2 or SaO_2 for monitoring because it is the amount available to the tissues (assuming a normal cardiac output).

    b. The normal value is about 20 vol% (refer to Equation 4-1).

EQUATION 4-1: Calculation of O_2 Content

$$O_2 \text{ content} = Hb \times SaO_2 \times 1.34^* + PaO_2 \times 0.003^{**}$$

Example: given a Hb of 15 gm%, a SaO_2 of 95% and a PaO_2 of 100 mmHg, calculate the O_2 content:

$$[O_2] = (15 \times 0.95 \times 1.34) + (100 \times 0.003)$$
$$[O_2] = 19.4 \text{ vol\%}$$

*The factor equal to the maximum amount of O_2 that each gram of hemoglobin is capable of holding. Some use 1.39.

**Solubility coefficient of O_2 in plasma, at 37°C, and equal to the amount of O_2 dissolving per mmHg (volume%).

c. Deviations in the amount of Hb have a more significant impact on O_2 content than the PaO_2.
8. A-a Do_2
   a. The alveolar-arterial oxygen gradient, also referred to as $P(A-a)O_2$, assesses the difficulty with which oxygen moves across the alveolar-capillary membrane, from the alveolus to the arterial blood. Refer to Equation 4-2.
   b. Normally, the A-a Do_2 is less than 15 mmHg on room air, and may rise up to 30 mmHg on 100% O_2.[3]
   c. On account of the PaO_2 decreasing with age, the $P(A-a)O_2$ increases with age. It increases approximately 4 mmHg for every increase of 10 years of age.[3]
   d. As oxygen gas exchange is hindered in diseased lungs, the $P(A-a)O_2$ increases.
   e. Pathologic reasons for a widening gradient include $\dot{V}/\dot{Q}$ mismatching, intrapulmonary shunting, or wasted ventilation. Refer to Table 4-18.
   f. Following administration of 100% O_2, for every 15–20 mmHg increase in the gradient, there is approximately a 1% shunt.[8]

B. Blood gas interpretation
   1. Both oxygenation and acid-base disturbance should be assessed.
   2. Oxygenation: concern must be for the O_2 content available and not just the PaO_2.
      a. Predicted PaO_2 is a function of age (refer to Table 4-10).
      b. Suggested guidelines for consistently applying the terms MILD, MODERATE, and SEVERE hypoxemia to any given patient's PaO_2 are given in Table 4-12.
      c. To correct for alveolar hyper/hypoventilation, adjust the predicted PaO_2 by a factor of 1.5 times the difference between the actual $PaCO_2$ and a normal $PaCO_2$ of 40 mmHg, which represents normal alveolar ventilation.

EQUATION 4-2:   Calculation of $P(A-a)O_2$

$$P(A-a)O_2 = PAO_2 - PaO_2 =$$
$$[FIO_2(P_B - 47) - PaCO_2 \times 1.25^*] - PaO_2$$

where * = metabolic factor

Example: calculate the $P(A-a)O_2$ given a PaO_2 of 90 mmHg, $PaCO_2$ of 40 mmHg, and P_B of 760 mmHg, when the patient is breathing room air.

$$PAO_2 = [0.21 (760 - 47)] - (40 \times 1.25) = 100$$
$$P(A-a)O_2 = 100 - 90, \text{ or } 10 \text{ mmHg}$$

Chapter 4: Pulmonary Laboratory

TABLE 4-12: Classification of Hypoxemic Interpretation

Hypoxemia	# of Torr Less than Predicted PaO_2
Mild	0–10 torr
Moderate	10–20 torr
Severe	more than 20 torr

*Correction must be made for deviations in $PaCO_2$.

3. Acid-base determination: interpretation may be described in up to four words. Refer to Table 4-13 for interpretation possibilities. In each step, only the selected words may be utilized.
   a. STEP 1: pH determination
      (1) Acidosis: where pH is less than 7.40

      Note: may be caused by either an increased PCO_2 or decreased BE or HCO_3^-

      (2) Alkalosis: where pH is greater than 7.40

      Note: may be caused by either a decreased PCO_2 or increased BE or HCO_3^-

      (3) Normal: pH equals 7.35–7.45 with BOTH PCO_2 and HCO_3^- within normal limits

TABLE 4-13: Acid-Base Interpretation Possibilities

Fully Partially	Compensated (Uncompensated)*	Respiratory Metabolic Combined	Acidosis Alkalosis Normal
4	3	2	1

STEPS

Note: Only one possible response may be used per space; determine the interpretation by completing Steps 1–4 (right to left), but read the interpretation from left to right (4–1).

*Leave steps three and four blank.

b. STEP 2: Identification of the primary component (refer to Table 4-9)
   (1) Respiratory: PCO_2 is the primary problem or component
   (2) Metabolic: base or HCO_3^- is the primary problem or component
   (3) Combined: both PCO_2 and HCO_3^- or bases are primary components
c. STEP 3: Identification of the secondary component or compensation (refer to Table 4-14)
   (1) Compensated: the secondary component has changed in response to the primary component
   (2) Uncompensated: the secondary component is still within normal limits (NOTE: in this case, step 4 is eliminated)
d. STEP 4: Determination of extent of compensation if present
   (1) Fully: the secondary component has offset the primary component so that the pH is still within normal limits (frequently seen in chronic conditions)
   (2) Partially: the secondary component has changed in response to the primary component BUT the pH is still outside of the normal limits of 7.35–7.45

C. The acid-base status is obtained by monitoring the pH, PCO_2, HCO_3^- and/or the BE. Refer to Tables 4-13, 4-14, and 4-15.
D. Symptoms associated with acid-base disturbances are found in Table 4-16.
E. The causes of acid-base disturbances may be found in Table 4-17.
F. Oxygenation status is obtained by monitoring PaO_2, SaO_2, Hb, and cardiac output.
  1. Tachycardia secondary to shortness of breath is the first clinical indication of hypoxemia. Other clinical signs and symptoms include the following, which are listed in order of increasing severity:
     a. Tachycardia
     b. Tachypnea
     c. Hypertension
     d. Cyanosis

TABLE 4-14: Acid-Base Compensation

Primary Problem	Secondary Compensation	Manifestations
Respiratory acidosis	Metabolic alkalosis	↑ HCO_3^-; ↑ BE
Respiratory alkalosis	Metabolic acidosis	↓ HCO_3^-; ↓ BE
Metabolic acidosis	Respiratory alkalosis	↓ $PaCO_2$
Metabolic alkalosis	Respiratory acidosis	↑ $PaCO_2$

Chapter 4: Pulmonary Laboratory

TABLE 4-15: Acid-Base Interpretation Example

Given a pH of 7.36, PaCO$_2$ of 33 mmHg, HCO$_3^-$ of 18 mEq/L, and base of −6, the interpretation would be derived as follows:

$$\frac{\text{Fully}}{4} \bigg| \frac{\text{Compensated}}{3} \bigg| \frac{\text{Metabolic}}{2} \bigg| \frac{\text{Acidosis}}{1}$$

Step 1: The pH is either normal or acidic. Normal is ruled out, however, because all values are not normal.
Step 2: The acidosis is caused by a decreased metabolic component.
Step 3: The body compensates for a metabolic acidosis by creating a respiratory alkalosis, which is manifested by a decreased PCO$_2$.
Step 4: The pH is within normal limits, hence there is full compensation. Note that full compensation will occur when normal (step 1) is ruled out.

---

    e. Confusion
    f. Metabolic acidosis
    g. Bradycardia
    h. Hypotension
    i. Coma
2. The four primary causes of hypoxemia are listed in Table 4-18.
3. Most clinicians feel that an F$_I$O$_2$ less than 0.5 will not lead to oxygen toxicity.

TABLE 4-16: Symptoms Associated with Acid-Base Disturbances

Disturbance	Symptoms
Acidosis	headache, mental slowness, asterixis, confusion, drowsiness, nausea, vomiting, Kussmaul's respiration
Alkalosis	dizziness, paresthesia, muscle weakness or spasm, carpopedal spasm, tetany, sweating, arrhythmias

TABLE 4-17: Causes of Acid-Base Disturbances

Respiratory Acidosis
Overall hypoventilation
COPD
Pulmonary edema (severe)

Respiratory Alkalosis
Neurogenic hyperventilation
Interstitial disease
Pulmonary embolism
Acute asthma
Hyperventilation syndrome

Metabolic Acidosis
Increased metabolic formation of acids
Exogenous addition of acids
Loss of bicarbonate
Exogenous administration of Diamox

Metabolic Alkalosis
Loss of hydrogen ion
Exogenous bicarbonate
Diuresis
Electrolyte imbalance

TABLE 4-18: Causes of Hypoxemia

Cause	$P(A-a)O_2$	$P_aO_2 + P_aCO_2$*
Overall Hypoventilation	normal	110–130 mmHg
V̇/Q̇ Mismatch	increased	less than 110
Diffusion Defect	increased	less than 110
Shunt	increased	less than 110

*Note: Value is obtained by adding P_aO_2 and P_aCO_2 together with the patient breathing room air. A value greater than 130 indicates either lab error, or delivery of supplemental O_2.

Chapter 4: Pulmonary Laboratory

References

1. Scanlon, C. L., Wilkins, R. L., and Stoller, J. K., *Egan's Fundamentals of Respiratory Care,* 7th ed., Mosby, 1999.
2. Ruppel, G., *Manual of Pulmonary Function Testing,* 7th ed., Mosby, 1998.
3. Burton, G. G., Hodgkin, J. E., and Ward, J. J., *Respiratory Care: A Guide to Clinical Practice,* 4th ed., Lippincott, 1997.
4. Fishman, A. P., *Assessment of Pulmonary Function,* McGraw-Hill, 1980.
5. Sorbini, C., et al., "Arterial Oxygen Tensions in Relation to Age in Healthy Subjects," *Respiration,* Vol. 25, No. 3, 1968.
6. West, J. B., *Respiratory Physiology: The essentials,* 4th ed., Lippincott, Williams and Wilkins Co., 1991.
7. Shapiro, B. A., Peruzzi, R. W. T., *Clinical Application of Blood Gases,* 5th ed., Yearbook Medical Publishers, 1994.
8. Kacmarek, R. M., Mack, C. W., and Dimas, S., *The Essentials of Respiratory Therapy,* 2nd ed., Yearbook Medical Publishers, 1985.

Assessment Questions

1. Which of the following would you expect to be consistent in a patient with obstructive pulmonary disease?
   I. Increased expiratory flows
   II. Decreased expiratory flows
   III. Decreased lung volumes
   A. I only
   B. I and III only
   C. II only
   D. II and III only

2. Normal residual volume is approximately which of the following?
   A. 25% of VC
   B. 25% of TLC
   C. 33% of VC
   D. 33% of TLC

3. As long as peak expiratory flow is inscribed early in the forced exhalation at high volume, the maneuver best indicates:
   A. Restriction in the large airways
   B. Obstruction in the large airways
   C. Restriction in the small airways
   D. Obstruction in the small airways

4. Which of the following statements apply to bronchoprovocation testing?
   I. Methacholine is commonly used as a bronchoprovocation agent
   II. Histamine is commonly used as a bronchoprovocation agent
   III. Used to diagnose the occult bronchial asthmatic
   A. I only
   B. I and II only
   C. I, II and III
   D. I and III only

5. The respiratory therapist directs a patient to take a deep inspiration and exhale as quickly as possible. This maneuver will measure:
   A. Peak expiratory flow
   B. FEF 25–75%
   C. Vital Capacity
   D. FEV_1

6. A patient receiving mechanical ventilation is having a static compliance check. Tidal

volume = 1000ml, plateau pressure = 25 cmH$_2$O, peak pressure = 35cmH$_2$O. What is the calculated static compliance?

A. 30 ml/cmH$_2$O
B. 40 ml/cmH$_2$O
C. 50 ml/cmH$_2$O
D. 60 ml/cmH$_2$O

7. A 32-year-old woman presents in the emergency room after being found slumped over the wheel unconscious in an automobile. Classify the results of the ABG: pH = 7.28, PaO$_2$ = 60mmHg, HCO$_3^-$ = 33mEq/L, PaCO$_2$ = 70mmHg, BE = +5.

A. Partially compensated metabolic acidosis
B. Patially compensated respiratory acidosis
C. Fully compensated respiratory acidosis
D. Fully compensated metabolic acidosis

8. Calculate the oxygen content for a patient with the following values: PaO$_2$ = 96 mmHg, Hb = 11gm%, SaO$_2$ = 97%.

A. 14.2 vol%
B. 14.6 vol%
C. 15.2 vol %
D. 15.8 vol %

9. An abnormal A/a gradient is the result of:
   I. $\dot{V}$/Q mismatch
   II. Difussion defect
   III. Shunt
   IV. Respiratory quotient

A. I II, III and IV
B. I, II and III only
C. II, III and IV only
D. III only

Chapter 5

Clinical Laboratory

I. Complete blood count

A. Blood is a heterogeneous substance comprised of cellular components (red blood cells or RBC; white blood cells or WBC; and platelets) and a fluid (plasma).

B. The RBC (erythrocyte) is formed in the red bone marrow (a process called erythropoiesis).
   1. The RBC is covered by a semi-permeable membrane that permits swelling and rupture (hemolysis) in the presence of a hypotonic solution (less than 0.9% NaCl), or shriveling (crenation) if exposed to a hypertonic fluid (greater than 0.9% NaCl).[1]
   2. The normal range for RBC is higher in males than in females.
      a. Males: 4.8–6.0 million RBC/mm^3
      b. Females: 4.1–5.1 million RBC/mm^3
   3. Hematocrit is the ratio of the number of RBC to the volume of plasma.[2]
      a. Average male hematocrit is 44–54 volumes per 100 ml of whole blood (47%).
      b. Average female hematocrit is 37–47 volumes per 100 ml of whole blood (42%).
      c. Normally, hemoglobin is about one-third the hematocrit.

C. Hemoglobin (Hb) is the oxygen-carrying pigment and major solute contained within the erythrocyte (RBC). It is also one of the major buffering mechanisms for hydrogen ions, which is accomplished by the hydration of carbon dioxide within the RBC.
   1. The normal amount Hb varies according to sex, and is expressed as Gm% (grams of Hb per 100 ml of blood (or deciliter).
      a. Men: 13–16 Gm%
      b. Women: 12–13 Gm%
   2. Hb activity in the lung
      a. There is a loading of O_2 and an unloading of CO_2.

      b. Each gram of Hb is capable of carrying 1.34 ml of oxygen. More recent studies utilizing hemolyzed blood suggest that a factor of 1.39 is more valid.[3]
  3. Hb activity in the tissues
      a. Bohr effect: An increased PCO_2 and decreased pH facilitates the unloading of O_2 in the tissues.
      b. Haldane effect: The unloading of O_2 facilitates the binding of CO_2.
  4. Pathological conditions related to hemoglobin include:
      a. Anemia is a reduction below normal in the number of erythrocytes, in the quantity of hemoglobin, or in the volume of packed red cells. It has a significant effect on the O_2 content.[4]
      b. Polycythemia is an increase in the total red cell mass of the body. It may be a compensatory mechanism of chronic obstructive pulmonary disease.[4]
      c. Carboxyhemoglobinemia occurs following the exposure to carbon monoxide, which binds to Hb approximately 210 times more strongly than O_2 and tends to shift the O_2/Hb curve leftward. Carboxyhemoglobin saturations greater than 50% are known to produce central nervous system dysfunction and death. Co-oximetry is used to analyze the proportion of Hb being bound by CO.
      d. Sulfhemoglobinemia may occur following exposure to the gas hydrogen sulfide and it's binding to the hemoglobin. Like CO poisoning, it occupies O_2 carrying sites.
      e. Methemoglobinemia occurs as either a congenital defect in the hemoglobin, or the result of exposure to various toxic substances. The conversion of ferrous iron to the ferric form destroys the O_2 carrying capacity of the hemoglobin.
      f. Fetal hemoglobin is produced during fetal development and has a greater affinity for O_2 than that of the adult form, which allows saturations of 80–90% at the severely low fetal arterial PO_2 values of 30–35 torr.
D. WBC, or white blood cell count indicates the number of mobile units of the body's protective system.[5]
  1. The normal range of leukocytes is between 5,000 to 10,000 mm^3.
  2. The differential count identifies the percentages of the total white blood cell count of which each white blood cell type comprises. Refer to Table 5-1.
  3. Granulocytes are formed in bone marrow.
      a. Neutrophils are increased in acute infection, neoplastic diseases of the bone marrow, diabetic ketosis, and digitalis poisoning; decreased in acute leukemia and overwhelming bacterial infections.
      b. Eosinophils are frequently elevated during an allergic reaction and in eosinophilic leukemia; they are decreased with steroid therapy.
      c. Basophils are increased in acute severe infections and basophilic leukemia.

TABLE 5-1: Normal Values for Differential Leukocyte Count

Cell Type	Percentage
Granulocytes (Polys) polymorphonuclear	
neutrophils	50–75%
eosinophils	2–4%
basophils	0.5%
Monocytes	3–8%
Lymphocytes	20–40%
Platelets	$3 \times 10^5/mm^3$

4. Monocytes and lymphocytes are formed in the lymph nodes and transported to the site of infection. The lymphocytes form more monocytes.
   a. Monocytes are increased in chronic bacterial diseases and monocytic leukemia.
   b. Lymphocytes are increased in viral diseases, whooping cough, chronic infections, infectious mononucleosis, thyrotoxicosis, and chronic lymphocytic leukemia; decreased in Hodgkin's disease, steroid therapy, and whole body irradiation.
5. Granulocytes and monocytes ingest invading organisms by phagocytosis.
6. Platelets are fractured large white blood cells or megalokaryocytes that activate the blood clotting mechanism. They are increased after trauma or surgery, massive hemorrhage, or polycythemia; decreased in thrombocytopenic purpura, lupus erythematosus, and following massive blood transfusions.

II. Electrolytes are substances that dissociate into ions and are capable of conducting electricity. Ions consist of an atom or group of atoms with a positive or negative electrical charge. Electrolyte variations from normal can cause some drastic changes in bodily functions. Refer to Table 5-2 for normal values and Table 5-3 for causes of electrolyte disturbances.

A. Na^+: Sodium, the chief cation in the extracellular fluid, plays an important part in the regulation of acid-base balance, protecting the body against excessive fluid loss, and preserving the normal function of muscle tissues.[5]

B. K^+: Potassium, the major cation of the intracellular fluid, influences acid-base balance, osmotic pressure and electrical membrane potential in all muscle cells, including respiratory muscle function.

TABLE 5-2: Normal Electrolyte Values

	Electrolyte	Value (mEq/L)
Cations	Na^+ (sodium)	136–145
	K^+ (potassium)	3.5–5.5
	Ca^{++} (calcium)	4.5–5.5
	Mg^{++} (magnesium)	1.5–3.0
Anions	Cl^- (chloride)	98–106
	HCO_3^- (bicarbonate)	24–33
	HPO_4^- (phosphate)	1.2–3.0
	SO_4^- (sulfate)	0.3–1.5
	protein	14.6–19.4

TABLE 5-3: Causes of Electrolyte Disturbances[1]

Disturbance	Causes
Hyponatremia	A decrease in sodium may result from starvation, diarrhea, diuretics, CHF without treatment, malabsorption syndrome, burns and exudate, acute and chronic renal failure, adrenal insufficiency, vomiting, or severe hemorrhage.
Hypernatremia	An increased sodium may be caused by diabetes insipidus, primary aldosteronism, or dehydration.
Hypokalemia	A decrease in potassium may result from vomiting, GI suction, diarrhea, aldosteronism, steroid therapy, or certain diuretics (furosemide, diuril, diamox, edecrin, or mannitol).
Hyperkalemia	An increased potassium may be caused by excess K^+ ingestion, tissue trauma, acute renal failure, Addison's Disease, adrenal insufficiency, acidosis, rapid transfusion of a large volume of bank blood, or certain diuretics (aldactone, triamterene, or diazides).

Chapter 5: Clinical Laboratory

C. Ca^{++}: Calcium, the most abundant cation in the body, is vital to the transmission of nerve impulses, respiratory muscle function, maintenance of cardiac and skeletal muscle contractility, and preservation of efficient blood clotting.

D. Mg^{++}: Magnesium is an abundant intracellular cation that is a vital coenzyme in the metabolism of carbohydrates, lipids and proteins, and energy production. It is also of importance in respiratory muscle function.

E. Cl$^-$: Chloride, the most abundant anion of the extracellular fluid, has the main function of preserving electrolyte neutrality by counter-balancing the positive ionic charge of sodium. It therefore effects acid-base balance and osmotic pressure.

F. HCO$_3^-$: The total CO$_2$ consists of a combination of dissolved CO$_2$ gas, bicarbonate ion, and carbonic acid. It reflects the body's ability to control pH.

G. HPO$_4^-$: Phosphate is essential to respiratory muscle function, bone formation, energy storage and liberation, carbohydrate and lipid metabolism, and serum pH regulation.

H. SO$_4^-$: It is one of the miscellaneous ions that constitute the anion gap (sum of phosphates, sulfates, organic acids and proteins). It is important in both intra- and extracellular buffering.[5]

I. Proteins: They serve as a source for rapid tissue replacement, maintenance of osmotic pressure, buffering of pH, transportation of other blood constituents, and act as immunologic agents, coagulation factors, and contribute to the body's nitrogen needs.

J. Cardiac arrhythmias occur with electrolyte deficiencies.

K. The anion gap is the difference between the commonly measured cations and anions.[6]

L. The normal anion gap is 8–12 mmol/l, and is useful is discriminating between different causes of metabolic acidosis.[7]

   1. In order to calculate the anion gap, subtract the serum chloride and bicarbonate from the serum sodium.

   $$\text{Anion gap} = [\text{Na}^+ - (\text{Cl}^- + \text{HCO}_3^-)]$$

   2. Elevation in the anion gap will occur when fixed acids are produced (lactic acidosis) or added to the blood (poisoning), resulting in metabolic acidosis.

III. Blood chemistries

A. Glucose is the principal source of energy for living organisms and is monitored for high (hyperglycemia) or low (hypoglycemia) values. Insulin makes glucose available to the tissues (normal is 65–106 mg/dl).

B. Blood urea nitrogen (BUN) is the chief product of protein metabolism, formed in the liver and transported by the blood to the kidney for excretion in the urine. If elevated it is most commonly related to kidney disease (normal is 6–20 mg/dl).

C. Creatinine is the metabolic end product of energy released from phosphocreatine, the skeletal muscle energy compound. Breakdown of muscle cells elevates blood levels, which if remain elevated, indicate kidney disease (normal is 2.5–2.7 gm/24 hr).

D. The blood chemistries (enzymes) are used to validate tissue death.

E. Serum glutamic oxaloacetic transaminase (SGOT) is an enzyme that acts as a catalyst in amino acid metabolism during glycolysis and is found primarily in the heart and liver. Cellular death elevates SGOT (normal is 6–30 units/L).

F. Lactic dehydrogenase (LDH) is an enzyme that acts as a catalyst of carbohydrate metabolism and is found primarily in kidney, liver, heart and skeletal muscles, and in red blood cells. Damage to these tissues elevates LDH (normal is 0–110 units/L).

G. Creatine phosphokinase (CPK) is an enzyme that acts as a catalyst in the energy production process found in skeletal muscle, heart, and brain. Cellular death releases CPK from these tissues (normal is 0–95 units/L).

H. Cholesterol, a substance found in animal fats, is transported from the liver through the bloodstream, to cells throughout the body, by three types of lipoproteins: HDL (high density lipoprotein); LDL (low density lipoprotein); or VLDL (very low density lipoprotein). High levels of LDL and/or VLDL have been linked to certain diseases, particularly arteriosclerosis (normal is 150–230 mg/dl).

I. Triglycerides are fat-related compounds from excess carbohydrates (normal is 35–165 mg/dl). They are also associated with coronary artery disease.

IV. Sputum culture, sensitivity, and/or gram stain

A. Sputum cultures are the most common method used to diagnose the etiology of lower respiratory tract infections.

B. Expectorated sputum is unsuitable for culture of anaerobes because they do not survive in the presence of oxygen. If anaerobe collection is desired, a needle aspirate should be used.

C. The technique guidelines for collecting sputum include:[3]
   1. Have the patient brush his teeth and rinse his mouth for the early morning collection of the specimen (before breakfast).
   2. Have the patient perform a deep vigorous cough.
   3. Have the patient immediately expectorate into a sterile container. The container should have a fixative solution only if the collection is for tumor cells, and not for bacterial growth.
   4. Transport the specimen immediately to the lab.
   5. Discard the specimen if it contains primarily saliva.

D. There are several methods of obtaining the specimen.

Chapter 5: Clinical Laboratory

1. Sputum induction may be accomplished by administering a 5% sterile saline solution via an ultrasonic nebulizer, or IPPB machine.
2. Endotracheal tube suctioning using a Lukens's trap is generally done in the intensive care units.
3. Transtracheal aspiration through the cricoid cartilage, bronchoscopic aspiration via bronchoscopy, and transthoracic collection via a needle aspiration may be utilized for obtaining anaerobic cultures.

E. It is worth noting that many physicians recognize that sputum cultures may be of little value, unless the presence of an unusual organism is suspected.

F. Samples should be immediately transported to the lab. Several results may occur from delays in analysis.
   1. Deformation and rupture of polymorphonuclear leukocytes may occur.
   2. Bacteria may multiply, especially the gram negative bacilli.
   3. The pH can become more acidic, which will tend to kill the pH sensitive microorganisms (i.e., gram positive cocci).

G. Gram's stain is the most commonly used staining process for the microscopic identification of bacteria.
   1. Gram positive microorganisms appear blue on stain.
   2. Gram negative microorganisms appear red.

H. Acid fast stain is used for determination of the tubercle bacillus.
   1. Acid fast microorganisms appear red with staining.
   2. Nonacid fast microorganisms appear blue.

I. The important microorganisms to be aware of include:
   1. Gram negative bacilli: *Pseudomonas aeruginosa, Klebsiella, Haemophilus influenza, Escherichia coli, Serratia marcesans, Proteus*
   2. Gram positive bacilli: *Clostridium botulinum, C. tetani*
   3. Gram negative cocci: *Neisseria meningitides*
   4. Gram positive cocci: *Staphylococcus aureus, Streptococcus, Diplococcus pneumoniae*
   5. Acid fast bacillus: *Mycobacterium tuberculosis*

J. Lab reports include type and relative numbers of organisms that may be used as immediate guides for therapy.

K. Pathology may be noted from sputum samples.
   1. Sputum may contain some cellular debris in bronchopulmonary illness.
   2. In bronchogenic carcinoma, tumor cells may be present, which may be identified from sputum cytology.
   3. In acute infection, polymorphonuclear cells are present in large numbers. Refer to Table 5-1.

L. Patients who are without pulmonary disease and have no history of smoking have sterile lungs below the carina.

M. Sensitivity determination of the microbial growth, using small antibiotic impregnated disks in the culture medium, may be useful in selecting the appropriate antibiotic.

V. **Culture, sensitivity, and/or Gram's stain results from blood and other body fluids (pleural fluid, urine, etc)**

A. Blood
  1. The advent of the acquired immunodeficiency syndrome (AIDS) has increased the awareness of the health care practitioner to the importance of proper handling of blood and other body fluids.
  2. Two or more viruses can cause viral hepatitis, which is characterized by inflammation of the liver.[8]
     a. Hepatitis A enters the body by ingestion of infected water or food, or the fecal-oral route.
        (1) It spreads through the bloodstream to the parenchymal cells of the liver.
        (2) The virus is detectable in the blood and feces during the week prior to the appearance of dark urine.
        (3) The incubation period is about four weeks.
     b. Hepatitis B (also known as serum hepatitis) enters the body by artificial inoculation of human serum.
        (1) The incubation period ranges from six weeks to six months.
        (2) Blood is the most consistently efficient vehicle of transmission of hepatitis B.
        (3) It is a major nosocomial problem and blood precautions should be used constantly (refer to Chapter 17).
  3. Some of the more common contagious diseases that may be transmitted via the blood include: hepatitis B, cytomegalovirus (CMV), and human immunodeficiency virus (HIV).

B. Pleural fluids
  1. The types of pleural abnormalities include:
     a. Hemothorax: abnormal collection of blood within the thorax where the erythrocytes are greater than 5,000–10,000 per ml.
     b. Empyema: accumulation of pus within the pleural space.
     c. Chylothorax: the presence of effused chyle (milky substance from the intestinal lymphatics) in the thorax.
     d. Serous fluid (refer to Table 5-4)
        (1) Transudate: a fluid substance with low content of protein, cells, or solid materials; primarily lymphocytes.

TABLE 5-4: Specific Etiologies of Pleural Effusions[10]

Transudates	Exudates
congestive heart failure	tuberculosis
constrictive pericarditis	neoplasms
overexpanded fluid volume	pulmonary embolus
cirrhosis with ascites	connective tissue disease
	pancreatitis
Infections	subdiaphragmatic abscess
bacterial empyema	
tuberculosis	**Trauma**
fungi	hemothorax
parasites	chylothorax
viruses and mycoplasma	esophageal rupture

      (2) Exudate: composed of cells that escaped from blood vessels as a result of inflammation; the content is high in protein, cells or solid materials derived from the cell; leukocytes are greater than 1,000/ul.[9]
   e. Pneumothorax: an abnormal collection of air in the thorax that may be either spontaneous or traumatic in origin.
2. A fluid line is usually seen on chest X-ray when an effusion is present.
3. Thoracentesis: it is a surgical puncture of the thorax for fluid removal.
   a. CAUTION: A sudden rapid loss of fluid may cause rapid shifting of the mediastinum, bradycardia, rapid onset of pulmonary edema, and/or cardiac arrest.
   b. Analysis of the fluid is done for protein content, cellular morphology, and bacteriology.
   c. When drainage is less than approximately 75 ml/day and is serous, chest tubes may be removed if chest expansion is confirmed via X-ray.
4. Character of pleural fluid [9]
   a. Low glucose levels are associated with empyema, carcinoma, tuberculosis, rheumatoid and lupus pleurisy.
   b. Elevated amylase may indicate acute pancreatitis, esophageal rupture, or primary or metastatic carcinoma of the lung.

c. Low pleural pH (less than 7.3) has been found in empyema, esophageal rupture, rheumatoid pleurisy, and tuberculosis. This data is useful for differentiating uncomplicated parapneumonic effusions from empyemas.
d. Cytology is positive in 50–60% of the patients with documented carcinoma of the pleura.
e. AFB (acid-fast bacilli) smears are positive in 20% of the patients with tuberculosis pleurisy.

C. Urine
1. Urinary samples are obtained to monitor metabolic status, screen for kidney disease, screen for substance abuse, or assess the presence or absence of an urinary tract infection.
2. The concentration of urine is monitored by the specific gravity to determine the presence of either dehydration or overhydration.
3. Proteinuria (presence of protein in the urine) reflects the presence of renal disease.
4. Glucosuria (presence of glucose in the urine) most commonly indicates diabetes. It may also be found in renal disease.
5. The presence of bilirubin indicates an obstruction to the outflow of bile from the liver.
6. Hematuria (presence of blood in the urine) may be caused by a number of kidney, urethra, or bladder disturbances (trauma, infection, drugs, or cancer).
7. Dark urine is a LATER symptom of a hepatitis A infection.[8]

D. Although HIV has been isolated from blood, vaginal secretions, semen, saliva, tears, urine, cerebrospinal fluid, breast milk, and amniotic fluid, transmission of HIV has been linked only to blood, semen, vaginal secretions, and possibly breast milk.[3]

E. Diseases requiring blood and body-fluid precautions include AIDS, hepatitis B, hepatitis (non-A, non-B), yellow fever, Colorado tick fever, leptospirosis, malaria, and primary or secondary syphilis with skin and mucous membrane lesions.[11]

F. Refer to Chapter 17 for a discussion on universal precautions.

VI. Coagulation studies

A. Prothrombin time (PT) is used to identify plasma coagulation defects caused by a low activity level of factors I, II, V, VII, and X. The test is a measure of time required to create a clot.
1. A prolonged prothrombin time indicates factor deficiencies leading to increased bleeding.
2. Normal PT 12–15 seconds

B. Platelet count reflects the number of platelets circulating in the blood ready to respond to injury. The major role of the platelet is to form a plug so clotting factors can repair the injury.
   1. Normal platelet count is 200,000–400,000/mm^3.
   2. Low values exhibit bleeding disorders, while high values lead to the formation of thrombus.[9]

References

1. Kacmarek, R. M., Mack, C. W., and Dimas, S., *The Essentials of Respiratory Therapy, 2nd ed.*, Yearbook Medical Publishers, 1985.
2. Eubanks, D. H., and Bone, R. C., *Comprehensive Respiratory Care, 2nd ed.*, Mosby, 1990.
3. Burton, G. G., Hodgkin, J. E., and Ward, J. J., *Respiratory Care: A Guide to Clinical Practice, 4th ed.*, Lippincott, 1997.
4. *Mosby's Medical, Nursing, & Allied Health Dictionary, 4th ed.*, Mosby, 1994.
5. Guyton, A. C., *Textbook of Medical Physiology, 9th ed.*, W. B. Saunders, 1999.
6. Shapiro, B. A., *Clinical Application of Respiratory Care, 4th ed.*, Yearbook Medical Publishers, 1991.
7. Parsons, P. E., and Heffner, J. E., *Pulmonary/Respiratory Therapy Secrets*, Hanley & Belfus Inc., 1997.
8. Henry, J., "Contagious Diseases and Universal Precautions," *Master Modules*, Vol. II, No. 2, Education Resource Consortium, Inc., 1992.
9. Lehmann, C. A., *Saunders Manual of Clinical Laboratory Science*, W. B. Saunders Co., 1998.
10. Guenter, C. A., and Welch, M. H., *Pulmonary Medicine, 2nd ed.*, Lippincott, 1982.
11. Scanlon, C. L., Wilkins, R. L., and Stoller, J. K., *Egan's Fundamentals of Respiratory Therapy, 7th ed.*, Mosby, 1999.

Assessment Questions

1. The test used to measure a patient's blood clotting ability is

   A. Differential count
   B. Prothrombin time
   C. Bleeding time
   D. Complete blood count (CBC)

2. Neutrophilia is commonly found in patients suffering from

   A. Pneumonia
   B. Cystic fibrosis
   C. Pulmonary edema
   D. Pulmonary fibrosis

3. Of the listed electrolytes, which one has the greatest effect upon muscle function?

   A. Calcium
   B. Magnesium

C. Potassium
D. Sodium

4. In which of the following conditions would a sputum culture be beneficial?

   A. Pleural effusion
   B. Pulmonary edema
   C. Pneumonia
   D. Pneumothorax

5. Of the listed electrolytes, which one has the greatest effect upon water balance?

   A. Calcium
   B. Magnesium
   C. Potassium
   D. Sodium

6. The normal range for the anion gap is:

   A. 4–7 mmol/l
   B. 8–12 mmol/l
   C. 13–15 mmol/l
   D. 16–20 mmol/l

7. A decrease in potassium (hypokalemia) may result from which of the following?

   I. Vomiting
   II. G.I. suction
   III. Diarrhea

   A. I and II only
   B. I, II and III
   C. I and III only
   D. III only

8. When attempting a thoracentesis, removing the pleural fluid too rapidly can result in which of the following?

   I. Bradycardia
   II. Pulmonary edema
   III. Mediastinal shift
   IV. Cardiac arrest

   A. I, II, III and IV
   B. II, III and IV only
   C. III and IV only
   D. IV only

9. SGOT, LDH, and CPK are

   A. Fat-related compounds related to coronary artery disease
   B. Lipoproteins that are linked with arteriosclerosis
   C. Enzymes that are used to validate tissue death
   D. Proteins leading to excessive urine excretion

Chapter 6

Bedside Hemodynamic Monitoring

I. **Blood pressure is the force or pressure exerted against walls of arteries, usually 120/80 mmHg.**[1]

A. Systolic: The normal range is 90–150 mmHg. The first sound is heard as blood escapes past the point of cuff occlusion and is related to the highest degree of force as the left ventricle contracts. An increase implies an increase in resistance of the arterial tree. A decrease indicates a drop in the conducting system resistance.

B. Diastolic: The normal range is 70–90 mmHg. A muffling of the arterial sound represents the lowest degree of force as the heart rests. An increase in pressure is consistent with an increase in peripheral vascular resistance. A decrease in pressure is found with loss of resistance, myocardial weakness, or an incompetent aortic valve.

C. Pulse pressure: It is the difference between systolic and diastolic pressures. It is normally 35–40 mmHg (120–80).

D. Mean arterial pressure (MAP): The normal averages between 80–100 mmHg. It is the average pressure tending to push blood through the systemic circulatory system. Refer to Equation 6-1.

E. Hypertension exists when the blood pressure is persistently above 140/90 mmHg, and may cause:[1]
   1. Central nervous system abnormalities (i.e., headaches, blurred vision, and confusion)
   2. Uremia
   3. Congestive heart failure
   4. Cerebral hemorrhage leading to stroke.

F. Hypotension occurs when blood pressure is less than 95/60 mmHg.
   1. It may occur as a result of blood loss, peripheral dilation, or left ventricular failure.
   2. Perfusion to the vital organs is decreased and oxygen delivery is impaired.

> **EQUATION 6-1: Calculation of Map[2]**
>
> $$MAP = \frac{(\text{Systolic Pressure}) + (2 \times \text{Diastolic Pressure})}{3}$$
>
> **Example:** given a BP of 122/80, the MAP would be
>
> $$MAP = \frac{(122) + (2 \times 80)}{3}$$
>
> $$MAP = \frac{282}{3} = 94 \text{ mmHg}$$

II. Cardiac output

A. Cardiac output (CO) is the product of heart rate and stroke volume.
   1. Normal stroke volume is between 60 to 130 ml per beat.
   2. With a normal rate of 60 to 100 per minute, the normal cardiac output is approximately 4–8 liters per minute.
   3. Cardiac output may increase to 25–30 L/M with exercise.
B. The cardiac output is dependent upon several factors.
   1. The contractile strength of the heart
   2. The peripheral vascular resistance
   3. The amount of venous return
C. There are three primary factors that affect the amount of blood returned to the heart, and consequently cardiac output.[3]
   1. Changes in circulating volume
   2. Changes in the distribution of the blood volume
   3. Atrial contraction
D. Clinical signs of inadequate CO may include hypotension, cool extremities, absent or weak pulses, reduced urinary output, or coma.
E. There are several methods used to measure cardiac output.
   1. Fick method: relies on the measurement of the uptake of oxygen by blood flowing through the lungs under a steady state. Refer to Equation 6-2.
   2. Indicator-dilution method: after the injection of a given amount of indicator (i.e., indocyanine green, 5% DW, radioactive albumin), the flow through the vessel is proportional to the reciprocal of the area under the curve that plots concentration against time.

Chapter 6: Bedside Hemodynamic Monitoring

EQUATION 6-2:   Fick Equation for Determining Cardiac Output

$$\dot{V}O_2 = \dot{Q}_t (CaO_2 - C\bar{v}O_2)$$

$$\text{rearranged } \dot{Q}_t = \frac{\dot{V}O_2}{CaO_2 - C\bar{v}O_2}$$

Example: Given an O_2 consumption of 250 ml/min, a CaO_2 of 20* vol%, and a $C\bar{v}O_2$ of 15 vol%, calculate CO:

$$\dot{Q}_t = \frac{250}{20 - 15} \times 100$$

$$\dot{Q}_t = 5000 \text{ ml/min, or } 5 \text{ L/m}$$

*vol% is equal to the amount of O_2 in 100 ml.

---

3. Thermodilution technique: injection of an aliquot of cold saline (colder than blood) into the right atrium, with the temperature change measured via a thermistor in the pulmonary artery. As cardiac output varies at different points during the respiratory cycle, convention dictates CO be measured at the end of expiration. The calculation of cardiac output from the input data is accomplished with an attached computer.

F. $C(a-v)O_2$ is also known as the arterial-venous oxygen difference (gradient).
   1. Under normal conditions, there is approximately a 5 vol% difference between arterial content (CaO_2) and mixed venous content ($C\bar{v}O_2$).
   2. Cardiac output can be estimated by using the arterial-venous O_2 gradient.
   3. The hypoxemic patient who is able to adequately increase blood flow (cardiac output) will still have an arterial-venous O_2 difference of approximately 5 vol% or less.
   4. If cardiac decompensation occurs and cardiac output drops, the gradient will increase, due to more oxygen being extracted per 100 ml of blood.
   5. Refer to Table 6-1 for conditions that may alter the cardiac output.

G. Several parameters of cardiac function can be evaluated by ventricular volume measurements.[4]
   1. Stroke volume (SV)
   2. Ventricular work
   3. End-diastolic volume (EDV)
   4. End-systolic volume (ESV)
   5. Left ventricular myocardial mass

TABLE 6-1: Conditions Altering Cardiac Output[4]

Change	Conditions
Increase	anemia, exercise, hyperthyroidism, obesity, beriberi, polycythemia, pregnancy
Decrease	cardiac tamponade, cardiogenic shock, constrictive pericarditis, undernutrition, hypertension

H. Stroke volume may be determined as follows:
$$SV = EDV - ESV$$
I. Ejection fraction (EF) expresses the stroke volume as a fraction of the ventricular volume at the beginning of contraction.
   1. Normal EF is approximately 67 ± 8.
   2. EF may be calculated as follows:
   $$EF = \frac{SV}{EDV}$$
   3. An increased EF may be indicative of any of the following.
       a. Stronger myocardial contraction
       b. Hypertrophied ventricles
       c. Mitral insufficiency
       d. Pharmacological intervention (i.e., nitroglycerin)
   4. Myocardial ischemia is the most common cause of a reduced EF.
J. The cardiac index is the cardiac output divided by the body surface area (this compensates for the changes in cardiac output due to variations in body size).
K. Cardiac index is highest at 10 years of age and decreases with age.[3]

III. Shunt studies ($\dot{Q}s/\dot{Q}t$)[5]

A. Shunt is a measurement of the fraction of cardiac output that traverses the pulmonary system without participating in gas exchange. It is recorded as a percentage of the total capillary blood flow.
B. It is generally referred to as a right-to-left intrapulmonary shunt. Less than 5% of the normal cardiac output is shunted.

Chapter 6: Bedside Hemodynamic Monitoring

C. Equation 6-3 shows the relationship of shunted cardiac output to total cardiac output as derived from the Fick equation.

D. Increased shunt values are generally indicative of reduced ventilation in relationship to the perfusion ($\dot{V}/\dot{Q}$ imbalance).
   1. Abnormal right-to-left shunts may develop into certain types of chronic pulmonary diseases (i.e., bronchiectasis) and may occur in some forms of congenital heart disease.[1]
   2. A physiologic right-to-left shunt occurs when part of the cardiac output perfuses underventilated alveoli, such as in pulmonary edema, pneumonia, and atelectasis.
   3. Low $\dot{V}/\dot{Q}$ ratios (poor ventilation in relation to perfusion) account for most clinical cases of hypoxemia.

E. The most common causes of increased shunting include the following conditions.
   1. Acute disease patterns such as atelectasis
   2. Secretions (particularly while intubated and receiving continuous mechanical ventilation)
   3. Aspiration of particulate matter

F. The subject is allowed to breathe 100% O_2 for at least 20 minutes at atmospheric pressure so that the nitrogen (N_2) is washed out of the alveoli and the hemoglobin is as saturated as possible. This test may be contraindicated in patients breathing on a hypoxic drive.

G. There are two methods of calculation:
   1. The modified shunt equation is accurate only when the hemoglobin is completely saturated. Its use requires the sampling of arterial and mixed venous

---

EQUATION 6-3:   The Classic Shunt Equation (Fick Derivation)

$$\dot{Q}s/\dot{Q}t = \frac{CcO_2 - CaO_2}{CcO_2 - C\bar{v}O_2}$$

where, CcO_2 = the end-pulmonary capillary O_2 content

CaO_2 = the arterial O_2 content

$C\bar{v}O_2$ = the mixed venous O_2 content

$\dot{Q}s$ = the portion of the cardiac output that does not exchange with the cardiac output

$\dot{Q}_t$ = the total cardiac output

blood (from a right heart catheter) as well as calculation of the alveolar to arterial O_2 gradient. Its use should be reserved for the hemodynamically stable patient. Refer to Equation 6-4.
2. Bedside calculation (rule of thumb) of the shunt can be obtained by having the patient breathe 100% O_2 for 20 minutes. Upon sampling of the arterial blood, for every 100 mmHg the PaO_2 is less than 550–600 mmHg, there is approximately a 5% shunt.[6]
   a. Utilizing the data from the Equation 6-4 example, the bedside calculation of the shunt would be as follows:

$$\frac{(600 - 300)}{100} \times 5 = 15\% \quad \text{OR} \quad \frac{(550 - 300)}{100} \times 5 = 12.5\%$$

H. Everyone normally has a 2–4% physiologic shunt.
I. CAUTION: Because breathing 100% O_2 washes the nitrogen out of the alveoli, alveolar collapse (absorption atelectasis) may result and lead to shunt values that include the original shunt and the created "nitrogen shunt."

IV. Pulmonary artery pressure

A. The Swan-Ganz flow-directed balloon-tipped catheter is most commonly used for pulmonary artery (PAP) and pulmonary capillary wedge (PCWP) pressure monitoring.
   1. Frequently this catheter is inserted under fluoroscopy, although is not necessary, as long as pressure waveforms are being monitored.
   2. The catheter is inserted through the basilic vein into the right side of the heart, and allowed to float through the right ventricle into the pulmonary artery.

EQUATION 6-4: The Modified Shunt Equation

$$\dot{Q}s/\dot{Q}t = \frac{P(A - a)O_2 \times 0.003}{C(a - v)O_2 + [P(A - a)O_2 \times 0.003]}$$

Example: calculate the percent of intrapulmonary shunting given an A-a gradient of 300 mmHg, and an a-v O_2 difference of 6.0 vol%.

$$\dot{Q}s/\dot{Q}t = \frac{(300) \times (0.003)}{6 + [(300)(0.003)]}$$

$$= \frac{0.9}{6.9} = .13 = 13\%$$

3. The balloon is deflated during both insertion and monitoring of the pulmonary artery pressure.
4. Generally the catheter should be changed after 5–7 days in order to minimize complications.[6]

B. There are several hazards associated with the use of a Swan-Ganz catheter.[6]
1. Clotting and infection
2. Perforation of the pulmonary artery and subsequent hemoptysis
3. Cardiac arrhythmias
4. Pneumothorax and hemopneumothorax
5. Balloon rupture

C. The normal pulmonary artery pressure (PAP) is about 25/8, with a mean = 15 mmHg.

D. The pressure waveform from this measurement reflects some of the high pressure of the right ventricle from behind and some of the left atrial pressure across the pulmonary circulation in front of the catheter tip.

E. The catheter may also be used for obtaining mixed venous blood samples in determining cardiac output. Refer to Equation 6-2.

F. An increase in the PAP may indicate an increase in pulmonary vascular resistance, body fluids, or left ventricular failure, pulmonary embolism, diffuse sclerosis of the lungs, or atelectasis.[7]

G. Elevations in the pulmonary artery pressure may occur in the following conditions.[3]
1. Pulmonary artery constriction (hypoxia, acidosis, pulmonary vascular disease, hyaline membrane disease), with an increased pulmonary vascular resistance
2. Constriction around the heart
3. Increased intrathoracic pressure
4. Mitral valve stenosis
5. Left heart failure

H. Falling pressures within the heart and pulmonary circuit frequently are the result of intravascular volume depletion (hemorrhage, shock, etc).

I. PAP, PCWP, and cardiac output are usually normal in adult respiratory distress syndrome, but may serve as a guide to therapy if abnormal.[6]

V. Pulmonary capillary wedge pressure

A. The normal pulmonary capillary wedge pressure (PCWP) is approximately 6–12 mmHg.

B. The PCWP is obtained by momentarily inflating the balloon (wedging the catheter in the pulmonary arterioles) and obtaining the pressure downstream. It represents the left atrial pressure across the pulmonary circulation.

C. This measurement can be used as an indirect indicator of left atrial pressure and filling pressure in the left ventricle.
D. It is a more reliable guide to fluid therapy than monitoring of the CVP.
E. It is helpful in diagnosing pulmonary embolism where the PAP and CVP are elevated, while the PCWP is normal.
F. Because PCWP closely reflects the left atrial pressures under most conditions, use of the Swan-Ganz catheter can be used to distinguish cardiac from pulmonary conditions.[6]
   1. Myocardial infarction complicated by shock
   2. Respiratory failure complicated by myocardial failure
   3. Acute respiratory distress syndrome in the adult
   4. Combined cardiopulmonary failure
   5. Septic shock
   6. Fluid overload VS cardiogenic shock
   7. Post-cardiac surgery
   8. Situations where pulmonary arterial blood is needed for various calculations (cardiac output and shunt fraction)

VI. Central venous pressure

A. Central venous pressure (CVP) is the pressure in the large veins within the body, and normally is about 8–12 cmH$_2$O.
B. It represents the pressure in the systemic veins as well as the resistance in the right atrium.
C. It gives a clear indication of the function of the right heart. Refer to Table 6-2.
D. Serial measurements are indicated for replacement of fluid volume, and evaluation of the patient's fluid and cardiovascular status.

VII. Insertion of central monitoring lines

A. The CVP is classically obtained by placing the tip of a catheter at the junction of the superior vena cava and the right atrium.
B. This catheter is inserted through the body surface directly into a peripheral vein (antecubital, internal jugular, or subclavian), and advanced until the tip is in the superior vena cava.
C. CVP readings may be normal even in the presence of pulmonary and left heart abnormalities, because the tricuspid valve isolates right atrial pressures from the rest of the pulmonary circulation.
D. Increased thoracic pressures as a result of mechanical ventilation will result in a variable effect depending upon the catheter tip location.

Chapter 6: Bedside Hemodynamic Monitoring

TABLE 6-2: Clinical Deviations from Normal CVP

Increased	pulmonary edema, congestive heart failure, fluid overload, cardiac tamponade, excessive PEEP, hypoxic pulmonary vasoconstriction, pulmonary valvular stenosis, pulmonary embolism, myocardial infarction
Decreased	hypovolemic shock, peripheral vasodilatation, spontaneous inspiration, leaks in the pressure line

1. If the tip of the CVP line is placed in the right atrium, increased intrathoracic pressures will decrease CVP.
2. If the tip is placed within the vena cava, and somewhat removed from the right atrium, it is quite possible that increased intrathoracic pressures will lead to an increased CVP.
3. As a result, monitoring the trends is of utmost importance.

VIII. Insertion of arterial lines

A. Placement of an intra-arterial catheter is indicated when multiple arterial blood samples are required.
B. Arterial lines are also useful in measuring systemic blood pressure. To accomplish this, a pressure transducer must be connected to the system.
C. The radial site is usually the site of choice, because it is close to the surface, it has collateral circulation, and is relatively easy to cannulate.
D. Prior to cannulation, an Allen's test should be performed.
E. The brachial artery is the alternate site if either the radial sites are unavailable, or the Allen's test fails.
F. The complication rate with indwelling arterial lines increases as the length of use increases. Complications may include any of the following:
  1. Clotting
  2. Endothelial trauma
  3. Thromboembolism
  4. Infection

G. A plastic infusion bag (with heparin) wrapped in a sphygmomanometer cuff inflated above arterial blood pressure is used to permit continual infusion and minimize thrombus formation.

H. An arterial line should only remain in place as long as it is medically necessary for a critically ill patient.

IX. Mixed venous sampling

A. $P_{\bar{v}}O_2$: mixed venous PO_2; the normal value is 35–40 mmHg.
   1. This value is the best overall indicator of the adequacy of tissue oxygenation.
   2. A value of less than 35 mmHg for $P\bar{\ }O_2$ indicates that tissue oxygen delivery is inadequate.
   3. Optimal PEEP is indicated by the highest $P\bar{\ }O_2$, except for patients in shock.

B. A true mixed sample can only be obtained by sampling the pulmonary artery blood.

C. The tissues retain normally only 25% of the oxygen in arterial blood. If oxygen extraction remains constant as cardiac output decreases, the mixed venous PO_2 will decrease.[3]

D. Decreases in $P\bar{\ }O_2$ may be caused from any of the following conditions.[3]
   1. Low cardiac output
   2. Anemia
   3. PaO_2 of less than 70 mmHg
   4. "Affinity" hypoxia (low $P\bar{\ }O_2$ with increased SvO_2%)

E. Increases in $P\bar{\ }O_2$ may be caused from any of the following conditions.[3]
   1. Poor sampling technique
   2. Left-to-right shunt
   3. Septic shock
   4. Increased cardiac output
   5. Cyanide poisoning

X. Hemodynamic changes may be noted in different clinical conditions.[1]

A. Based on clinically derived information, it is possible to differentiate between various common conditions. Refer to Table 6-3.

B. Quantitative analysis should always complement and refine, but never replace the traditional techniques of patient assessment.

Chapter 6: Bedside Hemodynamic Monitoring

TABLE 6-3: Hemodynamic Changes In Various Clinical Conditions[8]

Condition	MAP	CO	CVP	PAP	PAWP
ARDS	↑/↓	↑/↓	↑	↑/↓	N/↓
Dehydration	↓	N/↓	↓	N/↓	↓
Left-Sided Heart Failure	N/↓	↓	↑	↑	↑
Pulmonary Hypertension	N	N	↑	↑	N
Septic Shock	↓	↑	↓	N/↓	N/↓

XI. Electrocardiogram

A. The ECG graphically displays the cardiac cycle. Refer to Table 6-4.

B. ECG paper and time elements: each 1 mm small square is equivalent to 0.04 seconds horizontally and measures voltage vertically. Each large square (5 mm) is the equivalent of 0.2 seconds.

C. There are two manual methods to determine the rate.
  1. If the rate is greater than 60/min and the rhythm is regular, locate an "R" wave that falls on a heavy black line and memorize the triplicates "300-150-100" and "75-60-50." Where the next "R" falls determines the rate.

TABLE 6-4: Cardiac Cycle of the ECG

ECG Tracing	Cardiac Activity
P wave	atrial depolarization
QRS complex	ventricular depolarization
T wave	ventricular repolarization

Note: The atria are repolarized during ventricular depolarization so that any wave that might be seen is normally buried within the QRS complex.

2. If the rate is less than 60/min OR the rhythm is irregular, count the number of complete cardiac cycles in a 6-second strip and multiply by 10 for the rate.
D. An ECG allows for the evaluation of both myocardial rate and electrical patterns. There are several rate disorders. Refer to Table 2-1.
   1. Bradycardia: rate less than 60 beats per minute
   2. Tachycardia: rate between 100–150 beats per minute; the first clinical sign of hypoxemia
   3. Normal sinus: consistent regular P-QRS-T complexes
   4. Sinus arrhythmia: an irregular rhythm with normal P-QRS-T complexes
   5. Atrial fibrillation: no clearly defined P waves; irregular rhythm with normal QRS complex
   6. Premature ventricular contraction (PVC): premature beats; no P wave; wide, distorted QRS
   7. Sinus arrest: pause in a normal rhythm that does not return to the same time sequencing
   8. Paroxysmal atrial tachycardia (PAT): normal wave sequence at a rate of 150–250 beats per minute; the P waves may not appear
   9. Paroxysmal ventricular tachycardia: series of PVC-like complexes with a rate of 150–250 per minute
   10. Atrial flutter: continuous rapid succession of identical P waves that appear saw-toothed
   11. Ventricular fibrillation: totally erratic electrical activity with no well-defined complexes
E. There are other ECG abnormalities that require attention.
   1. Symmetrically inverted "T" waves represent myocardial ischemia.
   2. Inverted "T" waves in the chest leads indicate left ventricular hypertrophy.
   3. Flattened "T" waves are observed in hypokalemia.
   4. "ST" segment elevation indicates either acute or recent myocardial injury.
   5. "ST" depression may be observed in certain conditions.
      a. Pulmonary infarction
      b. Digitalis
      c. Subendocardial infarction
      d. Positive Master's Test (exercising a patient with suspected coronary ischemia)
   6. "Q" waves indicate myocardial infarction or pulmonary infarction if observed in lead III.
   7. Wide "QRS" complex may be observed in increasing potassium levels (hyperkalemia).

Chapter 6: Bedside Hemodynamic Monitoring

8. "U" waves (upward deflection of the ECG following a flattened "T" wave) will appear and increase in prominence with decreasing potassium levels (hypokalemia).

F. Abnormalities may be late manifestations of respiratory, electrolyte, and/or acid-base disturbances.

XII. Fluid balance (intake and output)

A. The average normal adult ingests from 1500–3000 ml of water per day.

B. The total body water is between 50–70% of the total body weight.

C. The normal adult urinary output is approximately 30 ml/hour or 0.5 ml/kg/hr. The normal child's output is approximately 1.0/ml/kg/hr.[3]

D. A minimum of 1800 ml of fluid should be ingested daily by the average normal healthy adult.

E. Urinary output is one of the best indicators of the adequacy of both cardiac output and arterial pressure.

F. Over extended periods of time, the urinary output should equal the fluid intake.

G. A decrease in the urine output may be noticed in the following conditions.
   1. Inadequate kidney perfusion (decreased cardiac output, increased intrathoracic pressures, hypovolemia, dehydration)
   2. During positive pressure ventilation, increased ADH (antidiuretic hormone) production from hemorrhage, pain, anxiety, and certain drugs (morphine, tranquilizers, and some anesthetics)[3]

H. An increase in urine output may be a result of the following conditions.
   1. Use of diuretics
   2. Overhydration
   3. Decreased ADH production from alcohol, diabetes insipidus, hypothalamus tumor

I. Monitoring for intake and output is done by either actual volume measurement, or by monitoring weight gain or loss.

References

1. Scanlon, C. L., Wilkins, R. L., and Stoller, J. K., *Egan's Fundamentals of Respiratory Therapy*, 7th ed., Mosby, 1999.
2. Kacmarek, R. M., Mack, C. W., and Dimas, S., *The Essentials of Respiratory Therapy*, 2nd ed., Yearbook Medical Publishers, 1985.
3. Wilkins, R. L., Sheldon, R. L., and Krider, S. J., *Clinical Assessment in Respiratory Care*, 3rd ed, Mosby, 1995.

4. Goldberger, E., *Essentials of Clinical Cardiology,* Lippincott, 1990.
5. Ruppel, G., *Manual of Pulmonary Function Testing,* 7th ed., Mosby, 1998.
6. Burton, G. G., Hodgkin, J. E., and Ward, J. J., *Respiratory Care: A Guide to Clinical Practice,* 4th ed., Lippincott, 1997.
7. Guyton, A. C., *Textbook of Medical Physiology,* 9th ed., W. B. Saunders, 1999.
8. Martin, L., *Pulmonary Physiology in Clinical Practice: The Essentials for Patient Care and Evaluation,* Mosby, 1987.

Assessment Questions

1. Measurement of cardiac output by the thermodilution technique requires that the injectate be administered
   A. At the beginning of inspiration
   B. At the end of inspiration
   C. At the beginning of expiration
   D. At the end of expiration

2. The numerical value for central venous pressure (CVP) represents or indicates which of the following?
   I. Right atrial pressure
   II. Right ventricular pressure
   III. Fluid status
   IV. Left ventricular end diastolic pressure
   A. I and II only
   B. I, II and III only
   C. III and IV only
   D. IV only

3. In the adult, the normal range for cardiac output at rest is:
   A. 3–4 L/min.
   B. 4–8 L/min.
   C. 8–10 L/min.
   D. 10–12 L/min.

4. Which of the following values can be measured with the pulmonary artery catheter?
   I. Pulmonary artery (systolic, diastolic, and mean) pressure
   II. Pulmonary artery wedge pressure
   III. Cardiac output
   IV. Mixed-venous blood parameters
   A. I and II only
   B. I, II, III and IV
   C. II and III only
   D. IV only

5. Which of the following is considered to be the most common complication of radial artery catheter monitoring?
   A. Infection
   B. Hematoma
   C. Embolization
   D. Thrombosis

6. When observing an ECG, which of the following waveforms represent ventricular repolarization?
   A. P wave
   B. Q wave
   C. R wave
   D. T wave

7. A pulmonary artery catheter (Swan-Gantz) is being inserted into a patient with normal hemodynamics. Which of the following pressures would provide the best information that the catheter has entered the pulmonary artery?
   A. 120/80 mmHg
   B. 60/30 mmHg
   C. 25/8 mmHg
   D. 10/8 mmHg

8. ECG monitoring can be used to detect which of the following?

I. Hypoxemia
II. Peripheral perfusion
III. Conduction disturbances
IV. Oxygen toxicity

A. I, II and III only
B. I and III only
C. II and IV only
D. III and IV only

9. A P-R interval that is prolonged (> 0.24 sec) could indicate:

A. Normal sinus rhythm
B. Bradycardia
C. Heart block
D. Tachycardia

Chapter 7

Radiographic Monitoring

I. Chest X-rays

A. The clinician is usually forced to use portable A-P views.

B. The further an object is from the film the larger it will appear.

C. The densities range from radiopaque (impedes the passage of X-rays) to radiolucent (permits passage).
   1. Gas density is the most radiolucent and appears black on X-ray, following development. Its presence represents either normal or pathologic air in the thorax (i.e., emphysema or pneumothorax).
   2. Fat density appears less radiolucent than gas.
   3. Water density is the most common radiopaque-type density observed on X-ray. It normally represents the mediastinum, heart, great vessels, and the diaphragm. Atelectasis, CHF, pneumonia, and effusions are pathologic water densities.
   4. Metal density is the most radiopaque and appears white on the X-ray. Bony structures are normal examples, calcified lesions are pathologic. Barium the contrast media is second to metal.

D. Underexposed films appear more radiopaque and therefore the lung fields appear more consolidated.

E. Different degrees of inspiration effect the chest appearance (expiratory films are more radiopaque than inspiratory films due to the lung tissue being closer together).

F. A consistent pattern should be used in reading films.
   1. Examine the bony structures and surrounding tissues.
   2. Examine the heart shadow and mediastinum.
   3. Examine the tracheobronchial tree and the lung parenchyma.

G. The right hemidiaphragm is normally higher than the left.

H. The left hilum is normally higher than the right (97% incidence).

Chapter 7: Radiographic Monitoring

I. Vascular markings appear like fine white strings fanning out.
J. Techniques for locating pathologic densities include:
1. Silhouette sign: a similar density that is in anatomic contact with a structure will obliterate the border of that structure (e.g., a right middle lobe consolidation will obliterate the right heart border, whereas the border will be seen in a right lower lobe consolidation).
   a. Anterior structures in the chest include the right and left heart borders, and the ascending aorta.
   b. Posterior structures in the chest include the aortic knob and descending aorta.
   c. This sign is of particular importance in helping to identify the involved bronchopulmonary segment prior to performing postural drainage.
   d. Refer to Table 7-1 for a listing of the lung segments and their relative positions within the chest.

TABLE 7-1: Relative Anatomic Positions of Lung Segments

Right Lung	Left Lung
Upper Lobes	
1. Apical (M)	1–3. Apical-posterior (P)
2. Anterior (A)	2. Anterior (A)
3. Posterior (P)	4. Superior lingula (A)
	5. Inferior lingula (A)
Middle Lobe	
4. Lateral (A)	
5. Medial (M)	
Lower Lobes	
6. Superior (M)	6. Superior (M)
7. Medial basal (M)	7–8. Anterior-medial basal (M)
8. Anterior basal (M)	9. Lateral basal (P)
9. Lateral basal (P)	10. Posterior basal (P)
10. Posterior basal (P)	

Key (refers to anatomic plane): A = anterior P = posterior M = medial
Note: Numbers refer to recognized segmental numbers.

2. Air bronchogram sign: air-filled bronchi surrounded by consolidated tissue will be visible (normally airways are not visible as the airways are filled with air, are surrounded by air, and have thin walls).
   a. Visualization of this sign indicates the presence of a pulmonary lesion, and therefore excludes a pleural or mediastinal abnormality.
   b. This sign may be observed in pneumonia, pulmonary edema, pulmonary infarcts, and certain chronic lung lesions.
   c. It is also useful in recognizing endotracheal tube placement.
K. There are several radiographic views.
   1. Posterior-anterior (PA) is the general clinic view.
   2. Anterior-posterior (AP) is the usual clinical view. (Note that the heart will appear slightly larger because it is further from the film.)
   3. Lateral views are useful for observing mediastinal lesions and retrosternal air (e.g., found in COPD).
   4. Obliques are circumferential views of the thorax, useful in differentiating between parenchymal and mediastinal lesions.
   5. Apical lordotic views are angled AP views of the thorax, useful in obtaining improved views of the lung apices (i.e., for tuberculosis).
   6. Lateral decubitus X-ray is taken while the patient is lying on either the right or left side. Its use is for detecting the presence of free pleural fluid or fluid entrapped within thoracic cavities.
   7. Expiratory films are useful for observing any discrepancies in diaphragmatic excursions, air trapping, or the presence of a small pneumothorax.
L. Chest X-rays are used primarily to establish the existence of:
   1. Atelectasis: lung collapse that appears radiopaque
   2. Pneumonia: inflammation of the lungs with consolidation that appears radiopaque on film
   3. Pneumothorax: an accumulation of gas in the pleural space that appears radiolucent
   4. Mediastinal shifts: a movement from the normal position of the mediastinum, either away from an area of hyperinflation or towards an area of consolidation or collapse
M. Radiographic changes in diffuse obstructive airway disease may be fairly subtle or very obvious.[1] These changes may include the following:
   1. Hyperinflation: depression of the diaphragms, generalized increased translucency of the lung fields, blunting of the costophrenic angles, and an increase in retrosternal airspace (on lateral view)
   2. Air-trapping: as evidenced by comparing end-inspiratory and end-expiratory roentgenograms

3. Diminution or loss of interstitial tissue and pulmonary vessels: most apparent if bullae are present
4. Increased lung markings: often referred to as "dirty lung," most likely caused by bronchial wall inflammation or peribronchial fibrosis

N. X-rays are useful to detect disease processes, display the pattern of an abnormality, or monitor the progression of disease.

O. There are several radiographic techniques.
1. Roentgenography is photography by means of X-rays.
2. Tomography is body section roentgenography and is useful for determining the exact location of a lesion by taking "slices" of the body for viewing.
3. Computed tomographic scans (CT) provides cross-sectional tomographs of the body structure at multiple levels.[1]
    a. It is useful in detecting the presence and determining the size of, shape, location, and radiodensity of mediastinal masses.
    b. It is also useful to help differentiate pleural from parenchymal masses, detect pulmonary nodules and subpleural lesions not visible from standard X-rays, and show bone and thoracic wall lesions.
4. Bronchography is obtained following the instillation of a radiopaque substance into the tracheobronchial tree. This technique is diagnostic for bronchiectasis.
5. Angiography is the injection of a radiopaque medium into the pulmonary vascular tree to determine the status of the pulmonary circulation.
6. Fluoroscopy is dynamic roentgenography used frequently in the placement of a flotation type catheter into the pulmonary circulation.
7. Radioactive ventilation scans view the lung field following the inhalation of a radioactive gas (xenon) in order to determine the distribution of ventilation. The lung perfusion scan is the most popular method of defining pulmonary embolism.
8. Magnetic resonance imaging (MRI) produces images similar to CT although the processes are quite different.[1]
    a. CT tends to be superior in imaging most intrapulmonary disorders.
    b. MRI is of particular value in the study of mediastinal vascular disorders (i.e., aneurysm).
9. Ultrasonography is an excellent tool for visualization of heart structure and function. Ultrasound has also been used as a needle guide for thoracentesis.

II. Inspection of chest X-ray to determine the presence of or changes in the following:

A. Patency and size of major airways
1. The average adult trachea is 11–13 centimeters in length, and supported by about 20 C-shaped cartilages.

2. Bifurcation of the trachea is located at the level of the fourth thoracic vertebrae.[2]
3. At the bifurcation, the angle of the right main stem bronchus is less acute, causing a more direct vertical passage than the left.[3]
4. Foreign objects (peanuts, pins, etc.) are more likely to lodge in the right main stem bronchus.
5. The trachea is normally positioned to the side opposite of the aortic arch.
6. The vertical spinous processes should go down the middle of the air column. Deviations might indicate:
   a. Film rotation
   b. Unilateral lung inflation (bronchial intubation)
   c. Tension pneumothorax
   d. Pulmonary fibrosis
7. A tapering or reduction in size of the major airways, particularly at bifurcations, might indicate the presence of bronchogenic carcinoma.
8. A difference in widths between the trachea and vertebral column may be indicative of tracheobronchomegaly.[4]

B. Endotracheal or tracheostomy tube
   1. During intubation, there is a greater tendency towards right main stem bronchus intubation, because the right main stem bronchus angles away from the trachea less sharply than the left.
   2. With the mandible in the neutral position (aligned with C-5), the radiopaque marking on the endotracheal tube tip should be equal to or greater than 2 centimeters above the carina, as seen on X-ray. One source recommends 3–7 cm above the carina.[4]
   3. The tip of the tube should be inserted approximately 5 centimeters beyond the vocal cords.
   4. A chest X-ray should be taken to confirm tube placement after the tube has been secured in place.[2]
   5. Right main stem bronchial intubation usually results in the rapid development of left lung atelectasis.

C. Endotracheal or tracheostomy tube cuff hyperinflation
   1. Evidence of cuff hyperinflation and resulting tracheal damage prior to extubation include:
      a. Difficulty in sealing the trachea with the cuff
      b. Evidence of tracheal dilatation on X-ray
   2. Long-term cuff hyperinflation may lead to the following:
      a. Tracheomalacia: softening of the cartilaginous rings, which may result in tracheal collapse during inspiration
      b. Tracheal stenosis: a narrowing of the tracheal wall due to fibrous scarring

Chapter 7: Radiographic Monitoring

      c. Tracheoesophageal fistula: an abnormal communication between the trachea and the esophagus

      d. Tracheoinnominate fistula: an abnormal communication between the trachea and the innominate artery

  3. Tracheoesophageal fistulae have an incidence between 1–5% with use of either tube. Diagnosis is made by:

      a. History of recurrent aspiration

      b. Abdominal distension

      c. Direct examination by bronchoscopy

  4. Tracheoinnominate fistula is a rare complication.

      a. It is a life threatening condition.

      b. Diagnosis is made by noticing a pulsating tube prior to hemorrhage.

      c. Surgical intervention is required, with only about a 25% survival rate, even when proper procedures are taken.[4]

D. Chest tubes[1]

  1. Chest tubes should be of optimal size to drain both blood and air (usually a No. 24 or 28 French).

  2. The standard position for insertion is the midaxillary line in about the fourth or fifth interspace. The placement depends on whether the patient has a pneumothorax (anterior), hemopneumothorax (posterior), or a tension pneumothorax.

  3. When the tube is inserted, it is directed toward the apex of the lung.

  4. A radiopaque line on the chest tube identifies its position when a follow-up chest film is obtained.

E. Pneumothorax or subcutaneous emphysema

  1. Pneumothorax is the presence of air within the pleural cavity.

      a. Air can gain access to the pleural space through the chest wall, diaphragm, mediastinum, or lung via the visceral pleura (may be referred to as pulmonary barotrauma).

      b. It may be traumatic, iatrogenic, or spontaneous in origin.

      c. X-ray recognition of a pneumothorax is dependent upon the degree of collapse, and the state of the collapse, as well as the uninvolved lung.[5]

      d. Visible on X-ray is a "hairline" linear shadow with a lack of vascular markings in the affected area.

      e. A small pneumothorax is more prominent on expiratory films because the lung tissues are closer together.

  2. Subcutaneous emphysema is an indicator that pulmonary air is leaking.

      a. It shows as multiple linear lucencies representing air within the subcutaneous tissues.

b. It is most commonly due to alveolar rupture with air dissection of the mediastinum, which results in air escape into the neck tissues.
   c. It is the most reliable physical finding of traumatic pneumothorax.[5]
F. Hyperinflation
   1. The following are considered X-ray evidence of pulmonary hyperinflation:
      a. Flattened diaphragms with more than 7 anterior ribs showing
      b. The presence of retrosternal airspace
      c. The loss of peripheral vascular markings
      d. A proportionally narrower mediastinum
G. Consolidation and/or atelectasis
   1. Consolidation of part or all of the lung due to loss of volume will appear radiopaque on X-ray.
   2. Pathological conditions that exhibit a water density include CHF, pneumonia, atelectasis, fibrosis, carcinoma, adult respiratory distress syndrome, etc.
   3. Atelectasis may be caused by:
      a. Bronchial obstruction: extratracheal compression from tumors or enlarged lymph nodes, endobronchial disease (bronchogenic carcinoma), inflammation, or an intrabronchial mass such as a foreign body, mucus plug, or blood
      b. Cicatrization: scar tissue formation (i.e., tuberculosis)
      c. Absorption of high levels of oxygen during either diagnostic testing or therapeutic procedures with concomitant washout of alveolar nitrogen.
   4. Other radiographic signs of atelectasis include the following:
      a. Elevation of the hemidiaphragm on the affected side
      b. A decrease in the rib interspace size over the affected side
      c. A tracheal, hilar, or mediastinal shift toward the affected area
H. Pulmonary edema
   1. The characteristic edema appearance on chest film is a fluffy alveolar pattern (butterfly) with possible air bronchograms.
   2. If the edema is cardiac in origin, the following X-ray signs should be present.
      a. Cardiac enlargement
      b. Increased vascularity
      c. Kerley "B" lines (short, linear densities at the lung parenchyma), which indicate pulmonary venous hypertension or pulmonary lymphatic obstruction
   3. Noncardiogenic pulmonary edema presents with the following signs on X-ray.
      a. A normal cardiac silhouette
      b. Absence of Kerley "B" lines

Chapter 7: Radiographic Monitoring

4. The most reliable way to differentiate cardiogenic from noncardiogenic pulmonary edema is with measurement of the pulmonary capillary wedge pressure. If the PCWP is normal, then the edema is noncardiogenic in origin.

I. Swan-Ganz, pacemaker, CVP, and other catheters
   1. All catheters or electrical lines inserted invasively are radiopaque, and therefore will appear white on X-ray.
   2. The radiopaque feature of the catheter provides easy identification of its placement.
   3. The most common view during insertion is AP.
   4. Either insertion under fluoroscopy (dynamic conditions) or bedside monitoring (i.e., viewing pressure waveforms) with a follow-up X-ray facilitates placement.
   5. Accidental lung puncture is possible during catheter insertion and placement. Because of this risk, radiographic confirmation (chest X-ray, fluoroscopy) is required.
      a. If this occurs, lung collapse with an increase in the radiopacity will occur.
      b. If fluids are being administered (blood placement, total parenteral nutrition) via the catheter, they would end up in the chest cavity, and would also appear radiopaque.

J. Foreign bodies
   1. The patient history is important in properly identifying the substance that was aspirated.
   2. Radiopaque objects may include screws, coins, safety pins, bottle caps, etc.
   3. While nonradiopaque objects themselves are not usually visible, the tissue responses to the presence of the foreign body may be seen on chest X-ray. These can be divided into two categories: (1) vegetable; and (2) nonvegetable (i.e., plastic).
   4. Aspirated foreign bodies are usually found in larger upper airways.
   5. A lateral view may be useful in distinguishing the presence of an upper airway foreign body.

K. Hemidiaphragms
   1. They present as a water density. The right diaphragm is continuous with the liver. The left diaphragm is superior to the gastric air bubble.
   2. The right hemidiaphragm is usually elevated one interspace higher than the left due to the liver underneath.
   3. In checking for diaphragmatic position, it is important to monitor the costophrenic angles. Blunting would indicate the presence of pleural fluid.
   4. On chest X-ray, the diaphragms should be checked for the presence of scalloping or herniation that might indicate lung hyperinflation.

L. Pleural fluid
   1. Free pleural fluid has a ground glass appearance in the upright chest, through which lung markings can be seen near the medial margins. The upper margin usually forms a meniscus (curvature) at the lateral chest wall.
   2. The presence of pleural fluid is indicated by a loss of acuity (less sharp) of the costophrenic angle in the upright film. This usually takes 300 ml or more of pleural fluid accumulation.
   3. Smaller amounts of free pleural fluid (less than 300 ml) may be revealed on a lateral decubitus chest film.
   4. Residual effects of pleural fluid accumulation may include pleural thickening and/or fibrotic changes.
M. Mediastinal shift
   1. Mediastinal shifts can occur as a result of a pneumothorax, bronchial obstruction and atelectasis, unilateral hyperinflation, pleural effusion, or tumor with concomitant consolidation.
   2. In the presence of a tension pneumothorax, the mediastinum will be shifted away from the involved side.

III. Upper airway X-rays

A. These X-rays are especially useful in verifying the presence of a suspected foreign body aspiration (i.e., acute respiratory distress in the child).

B. If cervical spine trauma exists, an upper airway X-ray will show the location and extent (i.e., C_4 fracture may lead to diaphragmatic paralysis).

C. The presence of cervical ribs may be noted on X-ray with the thoracic outlet syndrome.

D. An upper airway X-ray is used to differentiate between supraglottic and subglottic ("steeple sign") inflammatory processes of epiglottitis and croup respectively.[1]

IV. Inspect lateral neck X-ray to determine the presence of:

A. Epiglottitis
   1. Epiglottitis is a supraglottic condition.
   2. A lateral neck X-ray is particularly valuable in the evaluation of patients with stridor.[6]
   3. A swollen epiglottis will often be visible on the lateral film in patients with epiglottitis.

B. Croup
   1. Subglottic edema, as found in croup, is more easily identified with a posterior-anterior film.[6]

Chapter 7: Radiographic Monitoring

2. Tomography is rarely of use to evaluate the airways of children, but can be helpful in selected circumstances (e.g., lesions).

References

1. Burton, G. G., Hodgkin, J. E., and Ward, J. J., *Respiratory Care: A Guide to Clinical Practice, 4th ed.,* Lippincott, 1997.
2. Netter, F. H., *Respiratory System,* Vol. 7, CIBA Collection of Medical Illustrations, 1979.
3. Eubanks, D. H., and Bone, R. C., *Comprehensive Respiratory Care, 2nd ed.,* Mosby, 1990.
4. Scanlon, C. L., Wilkins, R. L., and Stoller, J. K., *Egan's Fundamentals of Respiratory Therapy, 7th ed.,* Mosby, 1999.
5. Shibel, E. M., and Moser, K. M., *Respiratory Emergencies,* Mosby, 1977.
6. Alone, C. A., and Hill, T. V., *Respiratory Care of the Newborn and Child, 2nd ed.,* Lippincott, 1997.

Assessment Questions

1. What lung diseases are associated with increased radiographic density (lungs are too white or opaque)?
    I. Edema
    II. Pneumonia
    III. COPD
    IV. Sarcoidosis
    A. I and II only
    B. I, II and IV only
    C. III only
    D. IV only

2. Pulmonary embolism is normally best defined by a:
    A. A/P chest X-ray
    B. Lung scan
    C. Bronchography
    D. Fluoroscopy

3. Chest X-ray can confirm the correct placement of an endotracheal tube if the tip is approximately how many centimeters above the carina?
    A. 0–1 cm
    B. 2–3 cm
    C. 3–6 cm
    D. 6–8 cm

4. In order for a chest X-ray to detect a pneumothorax, it would need to reveal the following:
    I. Absence of lung markings on the affected side
    II. Flattened diaphragm on the affected side
    III. Mediastinal shift toward the unaffected side
    IV. Blunting of the costophrenic angle on the unaffected side
    A. I and IV only
    B. I, II and III only
    C. III and IV only
    D. IV only

5. Which of the following would have the greatest radiopacity?

A. Barium
   B. Body fluid
   C. Silhouette sign
   D. Fat

6. Upon viewing a A/P chest X-ray, the radiologist observes that the anterior-posterior chest diameter is larger than the transverse chest diameter. This finding would indicate:
   A. The observation is normal
   B. An obstructive disorder
   C. A restrictive disorder
   D. The observation is not clinically significant

7. When the lung fields appear well aerated or black on the X-ray, their appearance could be best described as:
   A. Reticulogranular
   B. Lucent
   C. Opaque
   D. A silhouette

8. The radiographic technique used to guide the needle when performing transthoracic needle biopsy (TNB) is related to which of the following?
   A. Fluoroscopy
   B. Angiography
   C. Computerized tomography
   D. Lung scan

9. Which of the following are radiographic signs of atelectasis?
   I. Mediastinal shift towards the unaffected side
   II. Hemidiaphragm elevation
   III. Increased radiopacity
   A. I only
   B. I, II and III only
   C. II and III only
   D. III only

Chapter 8

Other Assessments and Diagnostic Testing

I. Metabolic studies ($\dot{V}O_2$, $\dot{V}CO_2$, nutrition)

A. The metabolic rate of the body tissues, along with the balance of protein, fat, and carbohydrates, dictates the amount of oxygen required, the amount of carbon dioxide produced, and consequently the nutritional requirements.

B. The respiratory quotient is the ratio of carbon dioxide produced to oxygen consumed as follows:

$$RQ = \frac{\dot{V}CO_2}{\dot{V}O_2} \quad \text{normally,} \quad \frac{200}{250} = 0.8$$

C. One of the most useful aspects of monitoring the RQ is to determine the type of food group (fats, carbohydrates, or protein) that is being metabolized for energy.
   1. Normally, a RQ of 0.8–0.85 indicates a mixed metabolic pattern, or protein source.
   2. A decreased RQ (0.7) indicates that fats are the predominate energy source.
   3. An increased RQ (1.0) indicates that carbohydrates are the main energy source.

D. Because carbon dioxide is a direct by-product of carbohydrate metabolism, a patient being fed primarily a diet of glucose (carbohydrate) produces more CO_2. Consequently, the work of breathing is increased in order to increase the effective alveolar minute volume, which could cause a serious impairment when trying to wean patients who retain CO_2.

E. Lipids or fats have been reported to cause hypoxemia and reduce the diffusion capacity (D_LCO).[1]

F. Looking strictly at the RQ can be misleading, because patients with sepsis and injury (normal nutrition) respond differently to high glucose loads than do patients who are nutritionally depleted.

G. Nutritionally speaking, the oxygen uptake ($\dot{V}O_2$) indicates the energy requirement of the patient.[2]

H. There are obligatory energy and protein losses in severe illness and trauma, whether accidental or planned.[3]
I. There are several results of malnourishment.[3]
   1. Impaired wound healing
   2. Compromised immune status
   3. Increased morbidity and mortality
J. A semi-starved state can decrease the hypoxic drive and render a patient less sensitive to the need for more oxygen.[4]

II. Ventilation/perfusion scan data

A. Inhaled xenon and injected technetium, xenon, or radioactive iodinated serum albumin may be observed on lung scans to determine the relationship of ventilation to perfusion.
B. Ventilation and perfusion ($\dot{V}/\dot{Q}$) lung scans are usually compared to chest X-rays to diagnose different types of pulmonary disease.
   1. A $\dot{V}/\dot{Q}$ scan is most useful in diagnosing pulmonary emboli, because the chest X-ray usually appears normal.
   2. The mismatching of $\dot{V}/\dot{Q}$ seen in COPD is readily observed on a lung scan, whereas the chest X-ray may appear normal.
   3. Patients with pneumonia may show regional infiltrates on chest X-ray with matching $\dot{V}/\dot{Q}$ seen on the lung scan.
C. Pulmonary scanning is useful in measuring the volume and spatial distribution of ventilation.
D. Xenon inhalation is useful in detecting uneven distribution of ventilation from air trapping.
E. $\dot{V}/\dot{Q}$ scanning of patients with bullous emphysema is useful, particularly in identifying the patient who will benefit from surgical removal.

III. Exercise/stress testing

A. Exercise testing allows for evaluation of the heart and lungs under conditions of increased metabolic demand. This testing is done so abnormalities not readily defined in terms of decreased flows, volumes, or diffusing capacities may by quantified.
B. The measured parameters are assessed in relation to the workload performed (exercise level).
C. Although previously confined to research laboratories, cardiopulmonary exercise testing is now being used for the following:[5]
   1. To measure a patient's ability to perform work (disability evaluation)

Chapter 8: Other Assessments and Diagnostic Testing

2. To measure the cardiovascular fitness for vigorous sports (maximal oxygen uptake)
3. To differentiate between pulmonary and cardiac causes of dyspnea
4. To determine the need for and the amount of ambulatory oxygen
5. To assist in developing a safe exercise program for patients with cardiopulmonary disease
6. To predict the morbidity of lung resection.

D. In patients with a chief complaint of dyspnea on exertion, the following items indicate the importance of performing an exercise study.[6]
   1. Determine the presence and nature of ventilatory limitations to work.
   2. Determine the presence and nature of cardiac limitations to work.
   3. Assess the extent of conditioning or deconditioning.
   4. Determine maximum tolerable workloads and safe levels of daily exercise.
   5. Quantify the extent of disability for rehabilitation purposes.
   6. Evaluate the effect of preventive, therapeutic, and rehabilitative programs.

E. Exercise testing is indicated in ascertaining fitness to engage in vigorous physical activity in the healthy individual.

F. The best overall indicator of cardiopulmonary health and physical fitness is the patient's maximum oxygen uptake ($\dot{V}O_2max$).

G. There are two methods of varying exercise work loads that are generally used.[6]
   1. Treadmill
      a. The workload is adjusted by changing the belt speed, the slope (percent grade), or both.
      b. The actual work performed is a function of the mechanical adjustments as well as the weight of the subject.
      c. The advantages of using a treadmill are that it elicits walking, jogging, or running, which are familiar forms of exercise, and that maximal levels of exercise can be easily attained.
   2. Bicycle ergometer
      a. The workload is adjusted by altering the resistance to pedaling.
      b. The advantages to using a bicycle ergometer are that the workload can be changed rather rapidly, can be precisely quantified, and is independent of the weight of the subject.

H. Exercise testing may be divided into two main categories.[6]
   1. Progressive multistage tests examine the effects of increasing workloads on various cardiopulmonary parameters.
      a. This approach is frequently used to determine a maximum tolerable workload and to establish trends for the various exercise parameters measured.

b. The workload is increased at predetermined workload levels.
  (1) The uses of short intervals (1–3 minutes) are acceptable if the primary objective is to determine the maximum tolerable workload.
  (2) Longer intervals (4–6 minutes) may result in a steady state (relatively constant gas exchange, ventilation, and cardiovascular response).
 2. Steady state tests: these tests assess the parameters of cardiopulmonary function specifically under conditions of constant metabolic demand.
  a. This approach is useful to assess the effectiveness of various therapies or pharmacologic agents on exercise ability.
  b. This test is designed to evaluate specific parameters at submaximal levels.
I. Basic measurements taken during exercise testing include the following.[5]
 1. Heart rate, blood pressure, oxygen saturation, and ECG
 2. Minute ventilation ($\dot{V}_E$)
 3. Frequency of breathing
 4. An estimate of the patient's work rate
  a. Work: expressed in kilopond-meters (KPM), which is the work of moving a 1 kg mass a vertical distance of 1 m against the force of gravity[6]
  b. Power: expressed in KPM per minute, or watts
  c. Energy: expressed in $\dot{V}O_2$ at STPD, or in multiples of the resting O_2 uptake or METS
J. Equipment of use during an exercise test includes the following:[5]
 1. Treadmill or calibrated bicycle ergometer
 2. Cardiac monitor
 3. Pulse oximeter
 4. For noninvasive oxygen uptake measurement add a low-resistance breathing valve, mixing chamber, pneumotach, and an oxygen analyzer.
K. In a healthy young adult, and under normal conditions, the following changes occur during exercise.[6]
 1. The $\dot{V}_E$ increases throughout the exercise.
 2. The V_D/V_T rapidly decreases initially, and then continues to decrease at a slower rate.
 3. The $\dot{V}CO_2$ steadily increases, and increases at a faster rate at higher levels of exercise (at the anaerobic threshold).
 4. The respiratory exchange ratio ($\dot{V}CO_2/\dot{V}O_2$) has a steady rise until the final stages of exercise when there is a rapid increase.

IV. Co-oximetry; interpret results

A. A co-oximeter may be used to measure the Hb concentration, as well as the amount of abnormal hemoglobin.

B. Its use is preferable to that of calculations because it directly measures the actual saturation. Other methods assume the absence of conditions, such as the presence of carbon monoxide, which may alter the O_2/Hb relationship.[7]
C. It will simultaneously analyze reduced hemoglobin, oxyhemoglobin, carboxyhemoglobin and methemoglobin, and report the sum as total hemoglobin (gm%).
D. The co-oximeter calculates a fractional oxyhemoglobin saturation, which is the product of dividing the amount of oxyhemoglobin by the total oxyhemoglobin, deoxyhemoglobin, carboxyhemoglobin, and methemoglobin, and then expressing it as a percentage.
E. The device (spectrophotometer) accepts a small amount of whole blood, and then dilutes and hemolyzes the cells.
F. Different wavelengths of light are passed through the sample.
   1. The amounts of the different types of hemoglobin are determined by application of Beer's Law.
   2. Beer's Law states that the intensity of a light ray is inversely proportional to the depth of a liquid through which the light ray is transmitted. It is concluded that the absorption is dependent upon the number of molecules in the path of the light ray.
G. The presence of carboxyhemoglobin is a double threat to the oxygenation of the patient.
   1. It shifts the O_2/Hb dissociation curve to the left, which manifests by creating a tighter binding of the O_2 by the hemoglobin.
   2. It binds to the hemoglobin 200–250 times more strongly than does O_2.
H. Elevated levels of carboxyhemoglobin generally indicate that the patient has been smoking.
   1. Pathologic levels may be seen in toll bridge attendants, and most often in firefighters.
   2. Higher than normal levels have also been noted in patients exposed to secondhand smoke.
I. The principle of laboratory oximetry has been adapted for continuous noninvasive monitoring of hemoglobin in the clinical setting.[8] Refer to pulse oximetry in Chapter 3.

V. Sleep studies

A. Sleep apnea syndrome is the lack of air flow for more than 10 seconds, occurring just after falling asleep, and again during REM sleep.
   1. Obstructive sleep apnea occurs in men more often than women (8:1). It is often associated with obesity (Pickwickian), or some deformity of the upper airway.
      a. Even though there is no airflow, the inspiratory muscles continue to contract, generating large subatmospheric pressures and distorting the chest wall.

b. Several factors increase the risk of obstructive sleep apnea.[8]
   (1) obesity (particularly in men)
   (2) alcohol
   (3) irregular work shift
   (4) COPD
   (5) large tonsils
   (6) craniofacial deformities
   (7) macroglossia
   (8) hypothyroidism
   (9) chest wall deformities
   (10) tranquilizers (especially when added to other risk factors)
   (11) drug addiction
2. In central sleep apnea, all signs of respiratory activity stop.
   a. It is predominantly a CNS disorder, either associated with narcolepsy, respiratory center damage, or "Ondine's Curse."
   b. Central sleep apnea is present if the apnea occurs simultaneously with the absence of abdominal or chest wall movement.
3. Mixed sleep apnea is initially a central problem, but turns into obstructive apnea as the first resuming inspiratory efforts are frustrated by upper airway closure.

B. Sleep comes in two distinctively different types:[9]
1. Nonrapid eye movement (NREM) or quiet sleep
   a. NREM sleep occurs first in normal sleepers and consists of different stages.
      (1) Stage 1: a light stage from which the sleeper is easily aroused, usually occurring within 10–20 minutes upon reclining in bed.
      (2) Stage 2: occurs after 5–10 minutes of Stage 1 sleep and is recognized by evidence of sleep spindles and K complexes on the EEG.
      (3) Approximately 30–45 minutes after the onset of sleep, the healthy sleeper will enter the deeper stages of sleep (stages 3 and 4), also known as delta sleep.
   b. Younger people will experience longer periods of delta sleep as compared to the elderly person.
   c. Respiratory drive is decreased during NREM due to the loss of the stimulatory effect of wakefulness on breathing.
   d. Brief periods of apnea may occur during the onset of stages 1 and 2.
2. Rapid eye movement (REM) or active sleep
   a. The first episode of REM typically occurs about 90 minutes after the onset of NREM sleep.

Chapter 8: Other Assessments and Diagnostic Testing

      b. Dreaming occurs during REM sleep.

      c. Most REM episodes continue for 10–20 minutes before the sleeper cycles back to NREM sleep.

      d. The drive to breathe is irregular during REM sleep and may result in short periods of hypopnea and central apnea in the healthy sleeper.

C. Refer to discussion of clinical abnormalities regarding sleep apnea in Chapter 10.

D. Apnea monitoring

  1. Polysomnography is utilized for accurate diagnosis of sleep-disordered breathing.[5]

  2. Apneic episodes are quite common in preterm infants (approximately 50% of infants whose birth weights are less than 1500 g.)[5]

  3. Impedance pneumography is a measurement of the resistance (impedance) change due to respiratory activity. A pneumo belt containing two electrodes (one for each side of the chest) is placed on the chest at the nipple line. A low voltage current is sent from the monitor to the electrode, encountering electrical impedance that changes with respiratory motion.

  4. The impedance monitor contains a microprocessor that calculates the respiratory rate and alarm circumstances (apnea). Respiratory rate is not breath-to-breath, but an average of the number of breaths the patient takes over a period of time (usually 10–15 sec).[10]

VI. Bronchoscopy

A. The most common indication for bronchoscopy is an abnormal chest X-ray.[5]

B. Bronchoscopy may be used for both diagnostic and therapeutic purposes.

  1. Diagnostic uses include biopsy, obtaining sputum samples for lab testing, location of hemoptysis, and quantification of structural airway changes (granulomas, stenosis, fistulas, tears, etc.).

  2. Therapeutic uses may include removal of foreign bodies, aspiration of secretions (mucus, hemoptysis), endotracheal intubation, laser therapy, and endobronchial surgery.

C. Flexible fiberoptic bronchoscopy (FFB) is one of the most definitive diagnostic tools for lung cancer, and is able to allow inspection of the trachea, bronchi, lobar bronchi, and segmental bronchi to the fourth division.[8]

D. There is a much lower risk of pneumothorax with FFB than with transthoracic biopsy. Refer to Table 8-1.

E. Contraindications to bronchoscopy include the following.[5]

  1. Hypoxemia that is unresponsive to medical management or oxygen supplementation

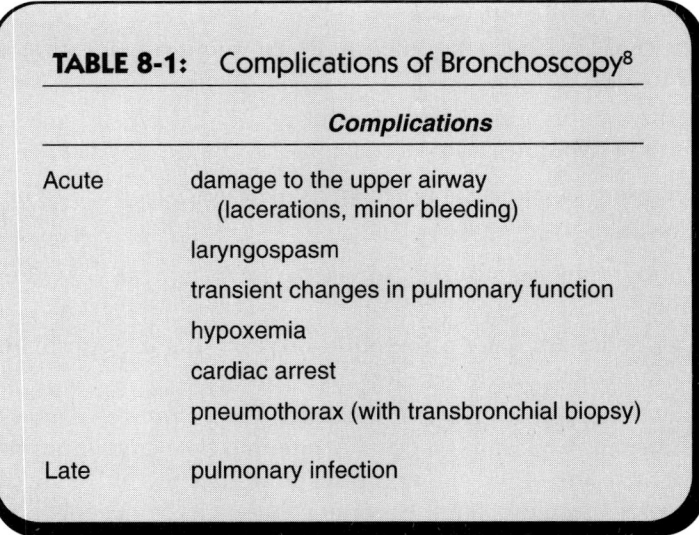

2. Hypercapnia that is unresponsive to medical management or mechanical ventilation
3. Cardiovascular instability such as hypotension, uncontrolled angina, myocardial infarction, or life-threatening arrhythmias
4. Asthma
5. Patients that are unable to cooperate with the procedure

F. Rigid bronchoscopy is used for removal of foreign bodies, bronchoscopic laser therapy, and dilatation of tracheobronchial strictures.[11]

G. A flexible bronchoscope may be passed through the rigid scope to reach more distant airways.

H. Fluoroscopy has had success with diagnostic maneuvers to direct biopsy brush, needle, and forceps to specific areas.[5]

VII. Intracranial pressure monitoring[12]

A. Monitoring of intracranial pressure (ICP) is essential, as increased ICP is unable to be judged clinically. Sites for monitoring include the epidural, ventricular, subarachnoid, and subdural spaces.

B. The most popular method is to drill a burr hole in the skull and insert a screw to communicate with the subarachnoid space. An arterial pressure transducer is connected to the screw, and is able to generate an electrical signal that is converted to waveforms allowing observation of peak intercranial pressures.

C. Normal ICP is less than 15 mmHg, but is capable of rising to pressures of 60–80 mmHg.

References

1. Branson, R. D., and Hurst, J. M., "Nutrition and Respiratory Function: Food for Thought," *Respiratory Care,* Vol. 33, 1988.
2. Guyton, A. C., *Textbook of Medical Physiology, 9th ed.,* W. B. Saunders, 1999.
3. Bartlett, R. H., Whitehouse, W. M., and Turcotte, J. G., *Life Support Systems in Intensive Care,* Yearbook Medical Publishers, 1984.
4. Doekel, R. C., et al., "Clinical semi-starvation: depression of hypoxic ventilatory response," *N Eng J Med,* Vol. 295, pg. 358, 1976.
5. Burton, G. G., Hodgkin, J. E., and Ward, J. J., *Respiratory Care: A Guide to Clinical Practice, 4th ed.,* Lippincott, 1997.
6. Ruppel, G., *Manual of Pulmonary Function Testing, 7th ed.,* Mosby, 1998.
7. Epstein, J., and Gaines, J., *Clinical Respiratory Care of the Adult Patient,* R. J. Brady Co., 1983.
8. Scanlon, C. L., Wilkins, R. L., and Stoller, J. K., *Egan's Fundamentals of Respiratory Therapy, 7th ed.,* Mosby, 1999.
9. Wilkins, R., and Parks, T., "Causes and Care of Sleep Apnea," *Master Modules,* Vol. II, No. 3, Education Resource Consortium, Inc., 1994.
10. Alone, C. A., and Hill, T. V., *Respiratory Care of the Newborn and Child, 2nd ed.,* Lippincott, 1997.
11. Parsons, P. E., and Heffner, J. E., *Pulmonary/Respiratory Therapy Secrets,* Hanley & Belfus Inc., 1997.
12. Ripe, J. M., et al, *Procedures and Techniques in Intensive Care Medicine,* Little Brown and Co., 1995.

Assessment Questions

1. A patient on a pure carbohydrate diet would have an RQ value of:

   A. .65
   B. .8
   C. .95
   D. 1.00

2. On a stress test, the best indicator of physical fitness is the patient's

   A. PaO_2
   B. $\dot{V}O_2$ max
   C. SaO_2
   D. $PaCO_2$

3. When determining the nutritional status of a patient about to be weaned from a mechanical ventilator, which of the following would indicate malnourishment?

   I. Reduced response to hypoxemia
   II. Compromised immune status
   III. Impaired wound healing

   A. I and II only
   B. I, II and III
   C. II and III only
   D. III only

4. Which of the following is affiliated with sleep apnea?
   I. Decreased cardiac output
   II. Decreased heart rate
   III. Decreased SaO$_2$
   A. I and II only
   B. I, II and III
   C. II and III only
   D. III only

5. How long must ventilation stop on an adult during sleep to be considered an apneic event?
   A. 3 seconds
   B. 7 seconds
   C. 10 seconds
   D. 12 seconds

6. What contributes to the obstruction of sleep apnea?
   I. Obesity
   II. Upper airway tumors
   III. Snoring
   A. I and II only
   B. I, II and III
   C. II and III only
   D. III only

7. Currently the most popular method of treating obstructive sleep apnea is by:
   A. Administration of 100% oxygen
   B. BiPAP
   C. Mechanical ventilation
   D. Nasal CPAP

8. Which airways are accessible to the flexible fiberoptic bronchoscope?
   I. Trachea
   II. Bronchi
   III. Lobar bronchi
   IV. 3rd division segmental bronchi
   A. I only
   B. I and II only
   C. I, II and III only
   D. I, II, III and IV

9. The most popular therapeutic use for bronchoscopy is:
   A. Laser surgery
   B. Removal of foreign bodies
   C. Removal of secretions
   D. Anesthetize vocal cords

Chapter 9

Perinatal/Neonatal Assessment

I. Perinatal history and data

A. There are several factors that affect neonatal mortality and morbidity.[1]
  1. Maternal factors
     a. Labor and delivery drugs: inhaled (N_2O) and local anesthetics, parental medications (narcotics)
     b. Cardiopulmonary problems: hypotension, hypoxia, uterine artery vasoconstriction, cardiopulmonary disease, anemia, hypocalcemia, and hypoglycemia
     c. Infection, through exposure to rubella, herpes, cytomegalovirus, HIV, and toxoplasmosis
     d. Labor: abnormal presentations, dysfunctional uterine activity, traumatic delivery, cephalopelvic disproportion, and intrauterine obstetric manipulations
     e. Uteroplacental factors: abruptio placenta, placenta previa, postmaturity, toxemia of pregnancy, diabetes mellitus
     f. Miscellaneous factors: drug addiction, radiation exposure, cigarette smoking, emotional stress
  2. Fetal factors
     a. Umbilical cord compression
     b. Prematurity
     c. Congenital abnormalities
     d. Multiple pregnancy
     e. Meconium staining
     f. Neonatal hypothermia

B. There are anatomic and physiologic differences between neonates and adults.
  1. The neonatal larynx is more cephalad (at the level of the 4th cervical vertebrae versus the 6th in the adult).
  2. The epiglottis is U-shaped, longer, and stiffer in the neonate.

3. The cricoid ring is the narrowest point in the neonate's larynx, versus the glottis in the adult.
4. The tracheobronchial angle is more obtuse (120°) and bilaterally equal. This angle becomes more acute with age.
5. The tongue is proportionately larger in the neonate.
6. The FRC is closer to the RV in the neonate (RV/TLC of 0.33) than the adult (RV/TLC of 0.2).
7. Fetal hemoglobin has a greater affinity for oxygen, which means at any PaO_2 fetal hemoglobin will be more saturated than adult hemoglobin. This is the same as a left shift in the curve.
8. Newborn pulmonary arterial blood pressure nearly equals the systemic arterial blood pressure.
9. The neonate is an obligatory nose-breather, and has a higher breathing frequency and smaller tidal exchange than the adult.
10. Neonates meet increased metabolic demand by increasing respiratory rate greater than tidal volume, thereby maintaining minimal muscular work.
11. The term infant has more plantar creases and deeper creases than in utero. At 32 weeks gestation there are only one or two creases, where the entire sole is covered by 40 weeks gestation. Post-term infants soles have much deeper creases.[2]

II. APGAR scores

A. A clinical assessment of the cardiopulmonary status is made at one minute with another assessment made at five minutes to determine prognosis in terms of neurologic development and survival in later life.

B. Refer to Table 9-1 for the APGAR scoring system.

TABLE 9-1: APGAR Scoring System

Signs	0	1	2
A: Appearance	Blue, pale	Body pink, blue extremities	Completely pink
P: Pulse	Absent	Slow, <100/min	Over 100/min
G: Grimace	No response	Grimace	Cry
A: Activity	Limp	Some flexion of extremities	Active motion
R: Respiration	Absent	Slow, irregular	Good, crying

Chapter 9: Perinatal/Neonatal Assessment

C. Depending on the total scores, the infant is classified as follows:
 1. Normal infant: an APGAR score of 7–10.
 2. Moderately depressed: APGAR score of 4–6.
 3. Severely depressed: an APGAR score of 0–3.
D. The initial stimulus to breathe comes from the resultant hypoxia during the birthing process; where gas exchange is performed primarily by the placenta. This process also leads to hypercapnia, which results in respiratory acidosis, thus stimulating the infant to take their first breath upon birth.

III. Gestational age

A. Normal gestation is 38–42 weeks (number of weeks from the first day of the mother's last menstrual period until delivery of the infant). Infants born prior to 38 weeks are considered preterm, and infants born after 42 weeks are considered postterm.
 1. Normal Full-Term Infant: The infant has had a normal prenatal history, normal physical examination, and is considered to be appropriate for gestational age (approximately 19" in length, and 2.7 Kg in weight).
 2. Low Birth Weight Infant: The infant weighs less than 2,500 grams, and may be either premature or small for gestational age.
 3. Premature Infant: The true premature infant is born before the 38th gestational week and is low birth weight.
 4. Small for Gestational Age: These infants weigh less than the 10th percentile, regardless of the gestational age.
 5. Large for Gestational Age: This infant's weight is above the 90th percentile.
B. The Ballard[4] scales include six different physical and six different neurologic signs based on physical maturity that determine gestational age assessment. Since the most critical factor for neonatal survival is fetal lung maturation, an accurate assessment of gestational age is required. There are three phases of lung development.
 1. Glandular phase (conception to 16 weeks): bronchial divisions are established; and life support is impossible.
 2. Canalicular phase (16–24 weeks): there is vascularization and formation of respiratory portions (life support possible).
 3. Alveolar phase (24th week to postpartum): the alveoli delineate; surfactant is present at 28th week; extrauterine life becomes possible; alveoli continue to proliferate throughout childhood.
C. Dubowitz[1]
 1. The assessment of gestational age is important as the degree of prematurity will predict the severity of respiratory distress syndrome, even though marked signs may not be immediately present at birth.

2. A modification of the standard Dubowitz scoring system for gestational age assesses skin texture, plantar creases, breast size, ear firmness, nail length, lens vascularization, and skin color.
   a. Infant may present totally cyanotic, or very pale or gray.
   b. Infant may present with cyanotic feet and hands while the body is pink (acrocyanosis).
3. Each of the listed categories is weighted from 0–4 points with the higher value representing greater maturity or age.
4. The gestational age is approximated based on the total score as follows: 0 = 25 weeks, 5 = 29 weeks, 10 = 33 weeks, 15 = 37 weeks, and 20 = 40 weeks.

D. Silverman/Anderson[4]
1. This scoring method assesses the severity of lung disease by observing the chest wall retractions as the infant breathes.[5]
2. Chest wall retractions are observed by the drawing in of the chest wall skin between the bony structures.
3. Retractions indicate a decreased work of breathing, usually due to decreased pulmonary compliance.
4. A score (Grade 0, 1, or 2) is determined by observing the severity of the inward movement of the chest wall, which indicates the amount of effort necessary to do ventilatory work.
5. Retractions occur in the intercostal, substernal, and suprasternal areas as the infant with paradoxiacal breathing draws in the chest wall.

IV. Lecithin-sphingomyelin (L/S) ratios are the most frequently used amniotic fluid study for evaluation of fetal maturity.[4]

A. Lecithin and sphingomyelin are phospholipids (90%) and protein (10%) that reflect fetal pulmonary surfactant production. Surfactant is secreted by the Type II cell during inspiration, lining the alveoli to maintain surface tension at the alveolar air interface.

B. Sphingomyelin remains fairly constant during development, while lecithin amounts surge abruptly at about the 34th gestational week.

C. L/S ratios greater than 2.0 indicate minimal evidence of hyaline membrane disease. An L/S ratio of greater than 2.0 correlates with a gestational age of 35–36 weeks, and mature lungs. An L/S ratio of less than 1.0 correlates with immature lungs and is associated with respiratory distress.

V. Insertion of umbilical lines[4]

A. Use of an indwelling arterial catheter is the preferred method for obtaining blood for assessment of oxygen requirements.

B. Its use is generally limited to the first week of life.
C. The catheter, connected to a three-way stopcock and filled with sterile heparin, is inserted into one of two umbilical arteries. It is advanced into the lower thoracic aorta between the ductus arteriosus and the celiac artery.
D. Once in place, the position should be confirmed by X-ray.
E. The most common problems associated with umbilical arterial cannulation include:[4]
   1. Selecting the umbilical vein instead of the artery
   2. Producing a false tract or perforation of the arterial wall
   3. Cannulating a patent urachus (a canal in the fetus that connects the bladder with the allantois, a rudimentary structure that gives rise to the blood vessels of the umbilical cord)
F. Infection can be avoided by maintaining strict attention to sterile technique during catheter insertion and aspiration of blood.
G. Never flush an obstructed arterial line as thromboembolism may occur. Also, if the line is obstructed, you will not be able to aspirate blood through it.

References

1. Lough, M. D., Doershuk, C. F., and Stern, R. C., *Pediatric Respiratory Therapy*, 2nd ed., Yearbook Medical Publishers, 1982.
2. Alone, C. A., and Hill, T. V., *Respiratory Care of the Newborn and Child, 2nd ed.*, Lippincott, 1997.
3. Scanlon, C. L., Wilkins, R. L., and Stoller, J. K., *Egan's Fundamentals of Respiratory Therapy*, 7th ed., Mosby, 1999.
4. Koff, P. B., Eitzman, D. V., and Neu, J., *Neonatal and Pediatric Respiratory Care, 2nd ed.*, Mosby, 1993.

Assessment Questions

1. Which of the following factors are responsible for initiating respiration in the newborn infant?

   I. Hypoxia
   II. Hypercapnia
   III. Acidosis

   A. I and II only
   B. I, II and III
   C. II and III only
   D. III only

2. Infants of diabetic mothers are at increased risk of

   I. Infection
   II. Hypocalcemia
   III. Hypoglycemia

   A. I only
   B. I and II only
   C. I, II and III
   D. II and III only

3. A newborn with active motion of the extremities, irregular respiration, pulse rate of 132 beats/min., and acrocyanosis would have an APGAR score of
   A. 2
   B. 4
   C. 6
   D. 8

4. An amniocentesis shows a lecithin/sphingomyelin (L/S) ratio of 1:1. The newborn infant will probably exhibit which of the following?
   A. Bradycardia
   B. Expiratory grunting
   C. Biots breathing
   D. Very high SaO_2

5. An infant is considered to be full-term after how many weeks of gestation?
   A. 30–34 weeks
   B. 35–37 weeks
   C. 38–42 weeks
   D. 43–45 weeks

6. Which of the following cells is responsible for the production and secretion of surfactant?
   A. Serous cell
   B. Type I cell
   C. Type II cell
   D. Type III cell

7. While assessing a newborn infant, you notice the baby's chest moves inward as the abdomen rises. You would refer to this type of breathing as:
   A. Grunting
   B. Paradoxical
   C. Lordotic
   D. Pectus excavatum

8. Acrocyanosis would be seen:
   A. In the mucus membranes under the tongue
   B. Circling the lips
   C. In the hands and feet
   D. On the anus

9. An infant has the following laboratory data returned.

   Sodium = 142 mEq/L
   Potassium = 3.0 mEq/L
   Calcium = 5.0 mEq/L
   Chloride = 99 mEq/L

   This information would indicate the infant had which of the following?
   A. Hypocalcemia
   B. Hyponatremia
   C. Hypokalemia
   D. Hyperchloremia

Chapter 10

Analyze Data and Determine Plan

Analyze available data to establish therapeutic goals, determine the pathophysiological state, participate in the prescribed respiratory care plan, and recommend modifications where indicated.

I. The RCP should be able to participate in the development of an appropriate respiratory care plan of establishing therapeutic goals.

A. All recommendations must be based on facts from the appropriate accumulation of data.

B. The following information should be considered when developing a respiratory care plan of action.
   1. The previous history of the patient may give a clue to any concurrent or underlying problems.
   2. Subjective information will help identify the current feelings of the patient.
   3. Base-line laboratory data will give a starting point for decision making. The desirable lab tests include ABGs, PFTs, electrolytes, ECG, CBC, chest X-ray, and sputum for gram stain if indicated.
   4. Base-line vital signs will identify the current status of the patient. This information will also be necessary for monitoring any trends of the patient.
   5. A complete awareness of the type of modalities (See Section 2, EQUIPMENT) available for patient care is essential before an effective treatment plan (See Section 3, THERAPY) may be implemented.

C. A plan for the continual monitoring of the patient should also be included once the care plan is established.

D. A legal liability does exist for the RCP in the daily care of patients. Good documentation is the key to good respiratory care and legal protection.[1]

II. Following is a discussion of individual clinical abnormalities that the RCP may encounter. The discussion of each disease process is subdivided into seven categories: Etiology, Physical Exam, Pulmonary Laboratory, Chest X-Ray, ECG, Clinical Laboratory, and Therapeutic Goals.

III. Adult respiratory distress syndrome (ARDS) is a distinct form of respiratory distress resulting from diffuse pulmonary injury of various causes. The pathological changes include alveolar and interstitial edema and hemorrhage, atelectasis, and sometimes, the formation of hyaline membranes.

A. Etiology: ARDS, in reality, is high permeability pulmonary edema (HPPE). Circulating toxins that are generated as a response to any of the following conditions triggers the permeability changes in the capillary endothelium.
   1. Shock from any cause
   2. Infectious diseases (G^- sepsis, viral or bacterial pneumonias)
   3. Aspirated fluids (gastric contents, fresh or salt water, hydrocarbons)
   4. Toxins (heroin, barbiturates, oxygen, smoke, chemicals)
   5. Trauma (lung contusion, fat emboli, brain)
   6. Hematological disorders (massive blood transfusion, disseminated intravascular coagulation, cardiopulmonary bypass)
   7. Miscellaneous (increased intracranial pressure, uremia, eclampsia, radiation pneumonitis, pancreatitis, etc.)

B. Physical Exam: It is often not very revealing. Labored respirations are quite obvious, with or without cyanosis. Intercostal retractions may occur in the late stages. Bronchial breath sounds with occasional rales may be heard. Abnormal breath sounds, if detected, resemble a harsh short inspiratory phase and a rather normal expiratory phase during mechanical ventilation. Cardiac sounds are usually normal.

C. Pulmonary Laboratory: The data may reveal refractory hypoxemia with metabolic acidosis, and a decreased lung compliance.

D. Chest X-Ray: The chest X-ray indicates diffuse, bilateral, alveolar infiltrates in a honeycomb pattern. The radiographic features are not specific for the nature or the degree of pulmonary insult.

E. ECG: The ECG might indicate tachycardia (due to hypoxemia) with possible irregular rhythms (initially from an alkalosis and later in the disease process an acidosis).

F. Clinical Laboratory: The data may indicate (from a lactic acidosis) a rise in the serum miscellaneous anions and H^+ ions, with a corresponding decrease in HCO_3^-.

G. Therapeutic Goals: The therapeutic goals, while somewhat debatable, generally focus on adequate oxygenation (PEEP), ventilatory support, hemodynamic monitoring, and fluid management. Diuretics, corticosteroids, anticoagulants, and appropriate antibiotics constitute the principal pharmacologic support.

IV. **Asthma is defined as airflow obstruction characterized by episodic dyspnea and usually accompanied by wheezing associated with reactive airways. Common are bronchospasm, mucosal edema, and increased sputum production.**[2]

A. Etiology: The two main classifications of asthma are extrinsic and intrinsic. These classifications are based on differing etiologies and clinical variations.
   1. Extrinsic asthma (allergic asthma) usually affects children and young adults. Attacks are related to specific antigens such as pollens, foods, drugs, dusts, and danders. The skin tests are usually positive.
   2. Intrinsic asthma (idiopathic or infective asthma) usually develops in middle age. The attacks are related to infections, exercise, and other stimuli. Skin tests are usually negative.
   3. Status asthmaticus (refractory asthma) is a true medical emergency and occurs when the patient is unresponsive to aggressive medical therapy.

B. Physical Exam: On physical exam, the patient is dyspneic, in respiratory distress, wheezing, flushing, cyanotic, and using their accessory ventilatory muscles. Other features include flaring of the alae, apprehension, diaphoresis, hyperresonance, and distant breath sounds with wheezing.

C. Pulmonary Laboratory: Pulmonary function tests indicate either normal or increased lung volumes, decreased flow rates, and a normal or increased $D_L CO$. Improvement is noted with the use of bronchodilators. Mild hypoxemia and hypocapnia are common between asthmatic episodes and worsen with severity. Hypercapnia occurs with severe attacks.

D. Chest X-Ray: The chest X-ray is normal between attacks, with demonstration of hyperinflation during the obstruction.

E. ECG: The ECG is usually normal between attacks. During an attack, tachycardia is present, along with P pulmonale and low voltage.

F. Clinical Laboratory: The clinical lab reports commonly indicate an increase in sputum eosinophils and blood eosinophilia. There is an elevation in serum IgE levels associated with extrinsic asthma.

G. Therapeutic Goals: The therapeutic goals are aimed at reversal of the bronchospasm, elimination of secretions, and the decreasing of mucosal edema. Long-term management may include avoidance of irritants, adequate nutrition and hydration, bronchodilators and corticosteroids, and hyposensitization for specific allergens.

V. Bronchogenic carcinoma is the most common malignant neoplasm in the lung originating from the bronchial mucosa. It occurs most frequently in men between the ages of 55–60. The five main classifications related to cell types are squamous cell carcinoma, adenocarcinoma, large cell carcinoma, small or oat cell carcinoma, and alveolar cell carcinoma.

A. Etiology: Although the exact etiology is still unknown, there is a high incidence associated with smoking, exposure to asbestos fibers, and toxic industrial substances.

B. Physical Exam: When symptoms are present, they are nonspecific. The most common symptom is a cough. Other findings on physical exam include hemoptysis, a localized wheeze, chest pain, and sputum production. Breath sounds may be decreased or absent. Rales are seldom heard. Recent weight loss is also noticeable.

C. Pulmonary Laboratory: There are no characteristic pulmonary function findings in bronchogenic carcinoma. Concomitant underlying chronic lung disease may reveal an obstructive component. Hypoxia and hypocapnia are common. The extent is dependent on the amount of parenchymal involvement.

D. Chest X-Ray: The chest X-ray findings are variable depending on the site of involvement. Peripheral lesions may manifest as small circular densities, and are generally referred to as a SPN (solitary pulmonary nodule). With central involvement, hilar enlargement is noted. Secondary effects of carcinoma include pleural effusion, elevated diaphragms, and post-obstructive pneumonias.

E. ECG: The ECG is usually normal.

F. Clinical Laboratory: The clinical lab data is important in the diagnostic process. Identification of the carcinogenic cells is made possible from sputum cytology, bronchoscopic washings, and thoracentesis. Anemia is frequently found. Also occurring are hyponatremia (from inappropriate ADH), hypercalcemia (from bone metastases), and hypokalemic alkalosis (from increased secretion of ACTH).

G. Therapeutic Goals: Therapeutic goals focus on ensuring adequate oxygenation, bronchial hygiene, abstinence from further pulmonary insults (i.e., smoking), and pain relief. Surgical intervention is possible in the early stages.

VI. Chronic bronchitis, also a chronic obstructive pulmonary disease, is defined in clinical terms as a cough with sputum production during at least three months of the year for at least two consecutive years.

A. Etiology: Cigarette smoking is the foremost cause of chronic bronchitis. Other causes include particulate and gaseous air pollutants, and pulmonary infections.

B. Physical Exam: The chronic bronchitic is frequently referred to as a "blue bloater," which is more of an end stage condition indicating pulmonary hypertension and cor pulmonale with resultant peripheral edema, hepatomegaly, and cyanosis. Initially, the patient presents with a productive cough, resonance to percussion of the chest wall, course rhonchi, and wheezes and rales that usually clear with coughing. Dyspnea will generally not occur at rest.

C. Pulmonary Laboratory: In the early stages the pulmonary function data may be normal with some identification of small airways disease. Closing volume may be low. In the later stages, the flow rates will be reduced. With increasing severity, the PO_2 decreases and the PCO_2 increases.

D. Chest X-Ray: Radiographic changes are mostly related to concomitant emphysematous changes, except for the increased vascular markings and hilar enlargement of cor pulmonale.

E. ECG: The ECG may show right ventricular hypertrophy; however, it is frequently nonspecific.[3]

F. Clinical Laboratory: Sputum is the most often monitored clinical lab test. This is obtained to determine the most appropriate antibiotic in the case of a pulmonary infection. Sputum and blood eosinophilia occur. Polycythemia is present in patients with chronic hypoxia.

G. Therapeutic Goals: The therapeutic goals are primarily aimed at the outpatient management of the patient—avoidance of inhaled irritants (smoking), adequate exercise, adequate hydration, nutrition and oxygenation, precautions against infection, and patient education.

VII. Cystic fibrosis is the most frequent lethal hereditary disease among Caucasian children in the United States. It is a form of bronchiectasis from repeated pulmonary infection, with a preference of involvement in the upper lobes.

A. Etiology: It is characterized by a dysfunction of the exocrine glands, and presents as a triad of chronic lung disease, pancreatic insufficiency, and an abnormally high sweat chloride level.

B. Physical Exam: On physical exam, the patient appears malnourished with poor body development and foul-smelling stools. Common findings include clubbing, hyperresonance to percussion, cyanosis, productive cough, and use of the accessory muscles for ventilation.

C. Pulmonary Laboratory: Pulmonary function lab data will generally reveal normal to decreased lung volumes, decreased flow rates, normal to slightly decreased D_LCO, and some response to bronchodilators. Blood gases reveal hypoxemia and hypercapnia late in the disease.

D. Chest X-Ray: On chest x-ray, the peribronchial markings and interstitial infiltrates are increased. There may be evidence of diffuse hyperinflation, and mucoid impaction with areas of atelectasis.

E. ECG: The ECG is usually normal, but may show evidence of cor pulmonale.

F. Clinical Laboratory: The diagnosis of CF is based on the clinical lab tests that measure sweat chlorides, which are characteristically high. Anemia of chronic disease is also common. Stool analysis and testing for pancreatic enzymes are also useful.

G. Therapeutic Goals: Because bacterial infection of the airways are the major concern for mortality in CF patients, therapeutic goals should center on an aggressive bronchial hygiene program (hydration, mist therapy, postural drainage, and percussion), proper nutrition, and prevention of lung infection. The progression of infection usually means the patient is initially colonized with *Haemophilus influenzae,* followed by *Staphylococcus aureus,* and later with *Pseudomonas aeruginosa.*

VIII. Emphysema is a chronic obstructive pulmonary disease (COPD), defined in anatomic terms, as a nonreversible enlargement of the airspace's distal to the terminal bronchioles associated with destructive changes in the alveolar walls.

A. Etiology: Emphysema may be divided into two main classifications.
 1. Centrilobular emphysema is a lesion of the center of the lobule. It occurs most frequently in the upper lobes. More common in men than women, it is associated with heavy smoking and chronic bronchitis.
 2. Panlobular emphysema, although less common than centrilobular, effects most of the entire acinus. The lower lung fields are frequently affected. There is a high correlation with alpha-1 antitrypsin deficiency.

B. Physical Exam: On physical exam, the patient is short of breath (dyspneic), which may worsen with exercise. The A-P diameter of the chest is frequently increased, and accessory muscles are in use. The expiratory phase of respiration is prolonged. Breath sounds are reduced with some expiratory wheezing. The chest is tympani to digital percussion. Clubbing of the digital phalanges may be present. Heart sounds are generally distant, but an accentuated second heart sound may be heard in the pulmonic area. The point of maximum impulse (PMI) is drawn downward. Cyanosis and neck vein distension may be present in the later stages. Increased oxygen administration (greater than 2 L/m) may satisfy the hypoxic drive, depress breathing, and lead to patient somnolence.

C. Pulmonary Laboratory: Pulmonary function data would indicate an increased RV, FRC, and TLC, with a decreased FEV_1 and $FEF_{25-75\%}$. Arterial blood gas studies might show normal findings initially with a decreasing PaO_2 and increasing $PaCO_2$ in the later stages. The D_LCO decreases with severity.

D. Chest X-Ray: Radiographically, the diaphragms are frequently depressed with at least 7 anterior ribs showing, and visible are hyperlucent lung fields, decreased vascular markings, an increased retrosternal space, a narrowed mediastinum, and the presence of bullae.[4]

E. ECG: Decreased voltage is seen on ECG, with right axis deviation and a large R wave in lead V_1, indicating cor pulmonale and pulmonary hypertension (late stage).

F. Clinical Laboratory: Clinical lab data is most useful for the monitoring of sputum. COPD patients are susceptible to infection and appropriate identification of bacterial growth is required.

G. Therapeutic Goals: Considerations for therapeutic goals include adequate oxygenation, good bronchial hygiene, bronchodilation, proper nutrition, exercise and breathing retraining (pursed lip breathing), improvement in the activities of daily living (ADL), and patient education.

IX. Inflammation of the upper airway primarily occurs in childhood. Young children are especially predisposed to laryngeal obstruction due to its relatively small size.

A. Etiology: It is determined by the major site of involvement.
1. Croup, also known as laryngotracheobronchitis (LTB), is a subglottic infection caused primarily by the parainfluenza virus (approximately in 85% of the cases), and the bacteria *Hemophilus influenzae* (15%). The bacterial form is more acute and severe. It is a disease occurring generally between the ages of 6 months and 3 years. There is a higher incidence in males.
2. Epiglottitis occurs generally between 4–8 years of age, and is primarily caused by *Hemophilus influenzae*. It is a supraglottic inflammation, and is considered a true pediatric emergency.

B. Physical Exam: The physical exam will be different depending on the site of involvement.
1. The child with croup will present with a barking cough, inspiratory stridor, dyspnea, and restlessness. These symptoms are generally preceded by an upper respiratory tract infection with fever, rhinorrhea, and cough times 2–3 days. The presence of chest retractions reflect respiratory distress.
2. The child with epiglottitis, along with the already mentioned signs and symptoms for croup, may exhibit air hunger, cyanosis, and fatigue, which may lead to coma and death in a very short time (1/2 to 2 hours). The child prefers to sit up with the jaw thrust forward, and drooling due to the pain associated with swallowing.

C. Pulmonary Laboratory: Blood gases initially would reveal a decreasing PO_2 with a normal PCO_2. As the obstruction continues, the patient may go into acute respiratory failure with decreasing PO_2 and increasing PCO_2.

D. Chest X-Ray: The upper airway obstruction of croup will normally not be seen on a lateral roentgenogram of the neck. The supraglottic swelling of epiglottis however will be noted.

E. ECG: The primary ECG abnormality is tachycardia.

F. Clinical Laboratory: Clinical lab data will reveal an increased WBC in bacterial infections, and possible results of lactic acidosis in severe obstruction.

G. Therapeutic Goals: Therapeutic goals should focus on airway support (immediate consideration with epiglottitis), adequate oxygenation, antibiotics for bacterial infection, nebulized racemic epinephrine for viral croup, and cool mist therapy.

X. **Neuromuscular disorders affect respiration in a variety of mechanisms: (1) reduced muscular force for adequate ventilation; (2) alteration of the upper airway protective reflexes; (3) impairment of an effective cough; (4) decreased or absent deep-breathing maneuvers; (5) inability to move and concomitant atelectasis; and (6) dysfunction of the respiratory center.**

A. Etiology: The etiology of the neuromuscular disorders is quite varied.
1. Amyotrophic lateral sclerosis (ALS) is an irreversible muscle disease, usually beginning with weakness of one of the extremities and progressing to the respiratory muscles. The primary abnormality is a loss of motor neurons. The etiology is unknown at the present.
2. Botulism is caused by *Clostridium botulinum*. It is an obligate anaerobic, gram-positive, spore-forming bacilli that produces a neurotoxin, which enters the nerve endings and interferes with the release of acetylcholine, producing a descending muscular weakness. Home canned foods are responsible for the majority of cases.
3. Guillain-Barrè Syndrome (acute polyneuritis) is a symmetrical muscle paralysis that is usually ascending in nature, and is accompanied by a sensory loss. Its etiology is unknown, but has been shown to be associated with the influenza vaccines.
4. Myasthenia gravis usually has an autoimmune basis that is characterized by a reduction in the sensitivity to acetylcholine at the neuromuscular junction. It has also been associated with hyperplasia of the thymus gland. It is primarily a descending paralysis, which may be asymmetrical. Usually the ocular muscles are the first to be affected. The highest incidence occurs in females in their third decade of life.
5. Poliomyelitis is a paralysis of the primary proximal muscle groups of the extremities. It is caused by the enterovirus.
6. Tetanus is caused by *Clostridium tetani*, an anaerobic gram-positive, spore-forming bacillus. It produces a neurotoxin that acts on the spinal cord to inhibit neurons, and on the peripheral motor neurons to inhibit the release of acetylcholine. Wound infections are the most common associated condition.
7. Traumatic injury to the spinal cord below the fourth cervical vertebrae will result in quadriplegia, while still maintaining function of the respiratory muscles. Injury above the fourth cervical vertebrae (C3-5) results in complete paralysis, to include the respiratory muscles.

Chapter 10: Analyze Data and Determine Plan 141

B. Physical Exam: The physical exam will vary depending on the particular neuromuscular disorder.
  1. In botulism, the patient initially appears lethargic, listless, and anorexic, followed by a decreased gag reflex. It may proceed into a rapid ventilatory failure due to muscle paralysis.
  2. The onset of symptoms of the myasthenia gravis patient is usually slow, with weakness of the eye muscles being the first manifestation. This may be followed by abnormal speech, dysphagia, and excessive fatigability of the muscles of the trunk and extremities. A decrease in VC and MIP indicates progressive weakness.
  3. In tetanus, the symptoms may range from an alert but restless patient with trismus (lockjaw), to the more severe form with paroxysmal hypertension and hypotension, high fever, profuse sweating, and severe spasms resulting in respiratory impairment and opisthotonos (a form of spasm with the head and feet bent backward and the body bent forward).
  4. In other neuromuscular disorders, depending on the process, the patient may have decreased breath sounds, ineffective cough, and dullness to percussion of the thorax if resulting atelectasis is present.
C. Pulmonary Laboratory: Pulmonary function data will reveal normal to decreasing lung volumes, decreased flow rates, and a normal to low $D_L CO$. Hypoxemia occurs first in the face of hypo- to normocapnia. Hypercapnia will result from increased severity of the disorder.[5]
D. Chest X-Ray: The chest X-ray is generally clear with elevated hemidiaphragms. As the respiratory muscle involvement increases (and lung volume decreases), there will be a greater opacification of the lung fields.
E. ECG: The ECG is essentially normal with occasional tachycardia.
F. Clinical Laboratory: The clinical lab data may reveal anemia associated with chronic disease. *Clostridium* species will be identified in the blood of the patient with tetanus or botulism.
G. Therapeutic Goals: The therapeutic goals are aimed at airway maintenance and supportive ventilation, prevention of infections, and anticholinesterase drugs if indicated (myasthenia gravis).

XI. Pneumoconiosis is a term given to inhaled or occupational lung diseases.

A. Etiology: This disease refers to any change in the lung as a result of inhaled dusts. Refer to Table 10-1 for a partial listing of occupational toxins known to cause pneumoconiosis. Most of the chronic occupational lung diseases take 20 or more years to become symptomatic.

TABLE 10-1: Inhaled Substances That May Lead to Pneumoconiosis[6]

Category	Occupation Source	Disease Name
acute airway or lung reaction	irritant gases from variable sources	none specific
	nitrogene dioxide in filled silos or welding	Silo filler's
	copper, zinc, iron, welding, mining, electroplating	Metal fume fever Galvanization
acute or subacute allergic reactions	toluene diisocyanate from plastic and foam, proteolytic enzymes	hypersensitivity pneumonitis
	contaminated water in air conditioners	Air conditioner
	droppings, feathers from birds	Ornithosis
	organic dusts from cotton	Byssinosis
	fungal spores, moldy hay	Farmer's Lung
	malt	Malt Worker's
	sugar cane	Bagassosis
	mushrooms	Mushroom Handler
chronic occupational lung diseases	sandblasters, manufacturers of ceramics, miners, diatomaceous earth	Silicosis
	coal	Coal Miner's
	coal with rheumatoid arthritis	Caplan's Syndrome
	asbestos	Asbestosis
	auxite	Shaver's Disease
	tungsten	Siderosis
	talc	Talcosis
	beryllium	Berylliosis
	barium	Baritosis
	paraquat from agriculture	Pulmonary granuloma

1. There are strong geographical relationships to certain fungal diseases.
   a. Coccidioidomycosis is most common in the San Joaquin Valley of California, Arizona, Nevada, Utah, New Mexico, and Texas.
   b. Histoplasmosis is most frequently seen in the Ohio and Mississippi River valleys.
   c. Blastomycosis is most commonly seen in the southeastern United States, as well as South America.

B. Physical Exam: Several factors determine the outcome following exposure (chemical nature, particle size, severity, duration, and individual susceptibility to pulmonary injury). As a result, a complete occupational and environmental history is imperative. Hypersensitivity reactions may be acute or delayed. The patient may appear short of breath, with wheezes or flu-like symptoms, which usually occur in 4–8 hours.
   1. Expectoration of black material is common in Coal Miner's or Black Lung.
   2. The primary symptom with complicated silicosis is dyspnea, with or without a cough.
   3. Dyspnea, with or without a cough, is the most common symptom of asbestosis. In addition, digital clubbing is common, as well as the presence of basilar rales.

C. Pulmonary Laboratory: In simple cases, the pulmonary function values are frequently normal. As the disease progresses, restrictive, obstructive, or mixed patterns of impairment may be demonstrated. Frequently the D_LCO is reduced.

D. Chest X-Ray: The X-ray may appear different depending on the cause of the pneumoconiosis.
   1. Coal worker's pneumoconiosis (CWP) is characterized by reticular and nodular densities throughout the lung fields. Cavitating lesions, if formed, most often are restricted to the upper lung fields.
   2. The characteristic finding in silicosis is the presence of "egg-shell" nodes at the hila. They are enlarged, numerous, and characterized by calcifications at their periphery (pathognomonic).
   3. Bilateral parenchymal fibrosis, with diaphragmatic calcifications are most significant in asbestosis. Pleural changes are very common (pleural thickening, plaques, calcification, and effusion).
   4. The fungal infections will most likely appear as localized parenchymal consolidation with or without hilar or mediastinal lymph node enlargement. Thin-walled cavities may occasionally form.

E. ECG: The ECG is generally nonspecific. Increasing disease and resultant hypoxemia may lead to tachycardia.

F. Clinical Laboratory: Sputum samples and lung biopsies may be useful in identifying the cause of the pneumoconiosis (relate to the patient's history).

G. Therapeutic Goals: The most effective program is based on prophylactic measures. The principles of treatment are similar to those of chronic obstructive pulmonary disease and pulmonary fibrosis. Amphotericin B is of use with fungal infections.

XII. Pneumonia is an inflammation of the lungs with consolidation.

A. Etiology: The etiology of pneumonia may be from a wide assortment of microbial growth.
   1. The gram negative pneumonias (GNP) are the most common cause of nosocomial respiratory infections. This is due to (1) the wide spread use of broad spectrum antibiotics; (2) the potential for respiratory equipment contamination from the common use of assisted ventilation; (3) compromised defenses with endotracheal tube use; and (4) the use of immunosuppressants.
   2. The pneumocystis virus is most well known for its relationship, as an opportunistic infection, in patients with acquired immunodeficiency syndrome (AIDS). The human immunodeficiency virus (HIV), the virus thought to cause AIDS, may enter the body via homosexual activities, infected needles from IV drug abusers, or blood transfusions.
   3. Refer to Table 10-2 for the classifications of microorganisms that cause pneumonia.[3]
B. Physical Exam: The following signs and symptoms indicating the onset of pneumonia may be observed on physical exam: fever, chills, sweats, pleuritic chest pain, cough, dyspnea, hemoptysis, expectoration, headache, and prostration.
   1. Patients with lobar pneumonia will demonstrate signs of consolidation, such as dullness to percussion, increased fremitus, and bronchial breath sounds with rales often present.
   2. Patients with bronchopneumonia will normally only have the listed signs and/or symptoms if the process is extensive.
   3. Patients with AIDS present with a serious systemic illness, manifested by fever, weight loss, lymphadenopathy, and various neoplasms (Kaposi's sarcoma), and opportunistic infections (*Pneumocystis carinii* pneumonia).[7] In addition, the cytomegalovirus (CMV), previously thought of as a virus afflicting premature infants and clinically immunosuppressed patients, is almost always isolated from throat and urine cultures of AIDS patients.[7]
C. Pulmonary Laboratory: Hypoxemia is the most common pulmonary lab occurrence. The pulmonary function tests, although not clinically useful, would reveal a restrictive lung component.
D. Chest X-Ray: Pneumonia as observed on chest X-ray may be manifested in several ways.
   1. Alveolar pneumonia describes the fluffy pattern of an inflammatory response in the peripheral lung fields.

TABLE 10-2: Causative Microorganisms of Pneumonia

Classification	Causative Microorganism	Type of Pneumonia
Bacteria	Streptococcus pneumoniae	Bacterial (Pneumococcal)
	Staphylococcus aureus	(Staphylococcal)
	Klebsiella pneumoniae	(Friedlander's)
	Pseudomonas aeruginosa	
	Haemophilus influenzae	
	Escherichia coli	
	Legionella pneumophila	(Legionnaires Disease)
	Bacteroides sp.	(Aspiration pneumonia)
Fungi	Coccidioides immitis	Coccidioidomycosis
	Histoplasma capsulatum	Histoplasmosis
	Blastomyces dermatidis	Blastomycosis
	Aspergillus fumigatus	Aspergillosis
Rickettsia	Coxiella burnetii	Q fever
Chlamydia	Chlamydia psittaci	Ornithosis
Mycoplasma pneumonia	Mycoplasma pneumoniae	Mycoplasmal
Viruses	Influenza virus, adenovirus, respiratory syncytial virus, chicken-pox, etc.	Viral pneumonia
	Cytomegalovirus	CMV pneumonia
Protozoa	Pneumocystis carinii pneumonia	Pneumocystis (AIDS)

2. Interstitial pneumonia represents an increased inflammatory material within the tissue surrounding the air spaces. It generally represents chronic changes such as fibrosis.
3. Bronchopneumonia describes patchy, fluffy infiltrates that follow the conducting airways. Air bronchograms are rarely seen.
4. Lobar pneumonia describes an opacification, usually of an entire lobe. The air bronchogram is generally seen.
5. Necrotizing pneumonia represents the effect from destruction of the lung parenchyma due to the inflammatory process, and resultant formation of cavities.

E. ECG: The ECG is usually normal. However, pneumonias in anatomic contact with the pericardium, may cause transient atrial fibrillation and flutter.[5]

F. Clinical Laboratory: While usually normal in viral pneumonias, the clinical lab data may be used to differentiate between the different etiologies of the bacterial pneumonias. Sputum Gram stains and cultures are useful in identification. Leukocytosis (immature forms) and hyponatremia are common.

G. Therapeutic Goals: The therapeutic goals should aim at adequate oxygenation, good bronchial hygiene, the use of appropriate antibiotics (i.e., in bacterial pneumonias), proper hydration and nutrition, and pain relief.

XIII. Postoperative pulmonary complications

A. Etiology: The most common postoperative pulmonary complications include arterial hypoxemia, atelectasis, difficulty in weaning from mechanical ventilation, gastric aspiration, thromboembolism, pleural effusion, and bacterial pneumonia.
   1. Preoperative assessment is essential in anticipating the presence of postoperative respiratory complications. Baseline pulmonary functions and ABGs should be obtained.
   2. Increased risk is expected if any of the following values are less than 50% of predicted: FEV_1 (or less than 2.0 L), FVC, FEV_1/FVC, or $FEF_{25-75\%}$.
   3. High risk is anticipated if the FEV_1 is less than 1.0 L, FEV_1/FVC is less than 35%, MVV is less than 50% predicted, and/or the $PaCO_2$ is greater than 45 mmHg when stable.

B. Physical Exam: The clinical presentation varies according to the type and location of surgery, and the primary cause of the pulmonary complication. For example, there is a greater incidence of postoperative pulmonary complications with thoracic and upper abdominal surgery.
   1. In postoperative atelectasis, the patient would appear tachypneic, with an elevated temperature, abnormal auscultatory lung findings, and possible cough.
   2. Aspiration of low pH gastric juice in sufficient volume produces a distinct clinical syndrome manifested by dyspnea, cyanosis, bronchospasm, and shock.
   3. A greater incidence of thromboembolism follows orthopedic surgery. Refer to the physical exam section for pulmonary embolism.
   4. Refer to physical exam section for pneumonia.
   5. A decrease in volume exchange and splinting may be noted following thoracic and abdominal surgery.
   6. A decrease in volume exchange may exist post anesthesia.

C. Pulmonary Laboratory: Postoperatively, pulmonary evaluation would reveal hypoxemia, respiratory alkalemia, and decreased lung volumes and compliance. A metabolic acidemia is the most common ABG abnormality in the ICU.

D. **Chest X-Ray:** Depending on the type of pulmonary complication, the chest film may appear radiopaque bilaterally (atelectasis, gastric aspiration, pneumonia), segmental (thromboembolism), or radiolucent (pneumothorax). Microatelectasis is much more frequent than macroatelectasis.

E. **ECG:** A tachycardia may be present due to postoperative hypoxemia, or PVCs may be noticed due to the presence of irritable foci within the heart.

F. **Clinical Laboratory:** Reduced plasma concentrations of K^+ will result in myocardial irritability and muscle weakness. Sputum culture and sensitivity tests may reveal a bacterial infection.

G. **Therapeutic Goals:** The therapeutic goals should focus on the following: adequate oxygenation and ventilation; good bronchial hygiene; appropriate antibiotics (gastric aspiration, pneumonia); elastic stockings (thromboembolism); proper hydration, nutrition, pain relief; and adequate support during coughing. In addition, the patient should be encouraged to become mobile as soon as possible.

XIV. Pulmonary burns with smoke inhalation

A. **Etiology:** There are two outcomes from exposure to smoke and heat.
   1. Smoke inhalation of the incomplete products of combustion and toxic fumes produces a chemical bronchiolitis of the lower airways with varying degree of alveolitis. Carbon monoxide greater that 20% will exhibit the following symptoms: headache, exertional dyspnea, impaired judgment, lethargy, and mental confusion. If greater than 60–80%, loss of consciousness, convulsions, and coma will occur.
   2. Thermal injuries, usually limited to the upper airway, may lead to mucosal sloughing, bronchorrhea, and edema.

B. **Physical Exam:** On physical exam, the patient with a pulmonary burn will have singed nasal hairs or facial burns, and be tachypneic. Stridor, grunting, and other forms of respiratory distress may not occur for several hours. Sputum is carbon tinted with a productive cough appearing on the second post-burn day. A cherry red color will occur in the more extreme cases of carbon monoxide inhalation.

C. **Pulmonary Laboratory:** Pulmonary lab data would indicate elevated COHb (normal is about 1% or less). Arterial PO_2 is normal, but the O_2 content is decreased. Initially a low PCO_2 would occur. If the patient goes into respiratory failure, a combined respiratory and metabolic acidosis would exist. Vital capacity is decreased.

D. **Chest X-Ray:** Chest X-rays are usually normal for the first 24–48 hours followed by an increase in opacification with the presence of pulmonary edema.

E. **ECG:** Tachycardia is noted on ECG.

F. **Clinical Laboratory:** With severe burns, the clinical lab data would indicate a significant imbalance in the fluid and electrolytes. The reduced plasma volume and insensible water loss would lead to an increase in serum Na^+, K^+, and Cl^-. There would be a corresponding decrease in serum HCO_3^- and serum protein.[8]

G. Therapeutic Goals: Therapeutic goals should focus on adequate oxygenation (increased O_2 delivery in CO poisoning), airway support, fluid and electrolyte balance, corticosteroid therapy, and prevention of bacterial infection.

XV. Pulmonary edema is an excessive movement of fluid from the vascular space into the interstitial and/or air spaces.

A. Etiology: The etiology of pulmonary edema consists primarily of two main categories.
   1. Cardiogenic pulmonary edema is the result of a dysfunction of the cardiovascular system. It may be caused from an acute myocardial infarct, pulmonary embolism, arrhythmias, mitral valve disease, infection, or systemic hypertension.
   2. Noncardiogenic pulmonary edema may be due to altered blood osmolality (overhydration, nephrosis, liver disease), altered capillary permeability (noxious gas inhalation, shock, narcotic overdose), nonuniform arteriolar constriction (high altitude hypoxemia), a shift of blood to the pulmonary circulation from the systemic circulation (brain lesions, trauma), fluid overload (iatrogenic), or an altered lymphatic function.

B. Physical Exam: On physical exam the patient complains of dyspnea, and has rales that may progress to diffuse expiratory wheezing. Initially the patient is tachypneic while still maintaining normal tidal volumes. In the later stages, a cough with frothy blood-tinged secretions will occur.

C. Pulmonary Laboratory: Arterial blood gases most likely will indicate worsening hypoxemia with a normal acid-base to metabolic acidemia. Compliance is markedly reduced, and airway resistance is elevated.

D. Chest X-Ray: Chest X-ray may indicate lymphatic engorgement with the presence of Kerley B lines and the characteristic "butterfly" pattern, or a diffuse haziness with greater involvement in the lower lobes. In cardiogenic pulmonary edema, the heart shadow is also enlarged.

E. ECG: The heart rate is rapid and may be irregular. In AMI, there most likely will be ST depression, inverted T waves, and the presence of Q waves.

F. Clinical Laboratory: Cardiac enzymes (CPK, SGOT, LDH) will be elevated with AMI.

G. Therapeutic Goals: The therapeutic goals should focus on adequate oxygenation, ventilatory assistance (if indicated), improving cardiac function (if cardiogenic in origin), elimination of excess fluid (diuretics, rotating tourniquets), and stabilization of the patient. In the acute phase, the patient should be placed in a semi-Fowler's position.

Chapter 10: Analyze Data and Determine Plan

XVI. Pulmonary embolism, the classic dead space-producing disease, is defined as the occlusion of the pulmonary artery or one or more of its branches by matter carried by the blood.

A. Etiology: The embolus, although most commonly a blood clot, may be a fat particle, air bubble, amniotic fluid, tumor or other tissue, parasite, or any type of foreign body.
  1. The three most important factors facilitating clot formation include:[3]
     a. Damage to the vessel wall, such as found in trauma to the vein, thrombophlebitis, and myocardial infarction
     b. Venous stasis due to prolonged bedrest, general debility, paralysis, pregnancy, heart failure, and immobility from trauma or surgery
     c. Increased clotting tendency from trauma, major surgery, pregnancy, or malignant diseases.
  2. The physiologic hallmark is the development of an increase in dead-space or "wasted ventilation."
  3. Pulmonary hypertension is the most important physiologic alteration.

B. Physical Exam: On physical exam, the symptoms, although rapid in onset, are generally nonspecific.
  1. Breathlessness with tachypnea and shallow exchange occurs in almost all patients following a symptomatic episode.
  2. Chest pain may be initially anginal, and later more pleuritic.
  3. Other findings may include hemoptysis, cough, anxiety, and syncope. A local decrease in breath sounds with wheezing, rales, and a pleural friction rub may be present.

C. Pulmonary Laboratory: Pulmonary functions would reveal decreased lung volumes and compliance, and a mismatching of the $\dot{V}/\dot{Q}$. There would be an increase in the V_D/V_T. Blood gases would reveal arterial hypoxemia with a widened $P_{(A-a)}O_2$, and low PCO_2.

D. Chest X-Ray: The chest radiograph may be normal even with a massive embolus. Findings may include pleural effusion, infiltrates, areas of consolidation, plate-like atelectasis, or elevated hemidiaphragms.

E. ECG: ECG may indicate right axis deviation and p-pulmonale in smaller emboli, and a complete right bundle branch block in massive blockage. Tachycardia is present.

F. Clinical Laboratory: There are no specific diagnostic findings from the standard laboratory tests. Detection of the breakdown products of fibrin may indicate thrombi formation.

G. Therapeutic Goals: The therapeutic goals focus on proper diagnosis (pulmonary angiography), alleviation of hypoxemia, anticoagulation therapy (heparin), thrombolytic therapy (streptokinase), and surgical intervention. The best approach is prophylaxis via proper positioning, mobilization, elastic stockings, and prophylactic anticoagulation for high-risk cases.

XVII. Pulmonary tuberculosis is a chronic infection that, besides the lungs, may infect the bones, meninges, gastrointestinal tract, and genitourinary tract. There are two forms of pulmonary TB: primary infection and reactivation.[5]

A. Etiology: Pulmonary TB is caused by *Mycobacterium tuberculosis,* an acid-fast bacillus. Transmission is primarily via droplet formation. Those at risk include the immunosuppressed, taking high-dose corticosteroids, pregnant, alcoholic, chronic renal failure, or postgastrectomy.

B. Physical Exam: The early symptoms, on physical examination, are rarely diagnostic. The patient may present with easy fatigue, weight loss, low-grade fever, and pleurisy. Later symptoms include chronic cough with purulent secretions, hemoptysis, night sweats, and general ill health with malnutrition.

C. Pulmonary Laboratory: The pulmonary function data is not generally helpful. Hypoxemia is frequently seen by arterial blood analysis.

D. Chest X-Ray: There is a wide variety of chest X-ray patterns that may occur. The most common finding is an upper lobe infiltrate and cavities with or without pleural effusions.

E. ECG: The ECG is usually normal.

F. Clinical Laboratory: Diagnosis of TB is most effectively done by clinical lab analysis. Sputum smears will reveal the acid-fast bacilli. There will be a positive Mantoux test within 48–72 hours. Leukocytes are variable, and the presence of anemia of chronic disease is common.

G. Therapeutic Goals: Therapeutic goals are primarily pharmacologically oriented. The following bacteriocidal agents are generally used (isoniazid (INH), rifampin (RFP), and Pyrazinamide) in short-term regimens. Along with these agents other drugs utilized may include streptomycin (SM), ethambutol (EMB), and para-aminosalicylic acid (PAS). Emphasis is broad until drug susceptibility results are known.

XVIII. Respiratory distress syndrome (RDS) of the neonate (also referred to as hyaline membrane disease or HMD, or surfactant deficiency disease or SDD), is the leading cause of death during the neonatal period. Primarily premature infants in the range of 1.0–1.5 kg birth weight, are affected.[9]

A. Etiology: Although not clearly understood, the primary cause is a decrease or alteration in pulmonary surfactant, leading to inadequate expansion of the lung and diffuse atelectasis. Predisposing factors, besides prematurity and low birth weights include delivery by cesarean section, maternal diabetes, precocious pregnancy, smoking, previous sibling with RDS, vaginal bleeding, and intrauterine distress. The likelihood of moderate to severe RDS increases with lower lecithin-sphingomyelin (L-S) ratios.[3]

B. Physical Exam: The clinical manifestations include expiratory grunting, nasal flaring, retractions of the soft tissues of the chest, tachypnea, cyanosis on room air, and harsh breath sounds with possibly some fine rales present.[3] A "cog-wheeling" type of respirations would reflect CO_2 retention.

C. Pulmonary Laboratory: Wasted ventilation and inefficient perfusion initiate a series of events leading to the clinical and pathological manifestations. There is an increased work of breathing from decreased lung compliance. Hypoxemia and hypercapnia occur late in the disease, along with combined respiratory and metabolic acidosis.

D. Chest X-Ray: On X-ray, the earliest findings are a fine mottling effect with central consolidation. Air bronchograms are frequently present. With disease progression, the chest appears to have a ground glass appearance, or a miliary reticulogranularity of the lung parenchyma. There is also an increase in the cardiothymic thoracic ratio (CTT).

E. ECG: A distressed fetus may demonstrate bradycardia due to cord compression. Postpartum ECG might reflect either tachycardia or a bradycardia. Specific changes are not regularly seen in HMD.

F. Clinical Laboratory: Clinical lab data might reveal a low L-S ratio, low serum protein from malabsorption, anemia from obstetric or iatrogenic loss, and hypocalcemia and hypernatremia from bicarbonate administration. Cellular injury indicator elevation (i.e., SGOT) is dependent on the extent of poor perfusion and anoxia that develops.[10]

G. Therapeutic Goals: The therapeutic goals should address adequate oxygenation, distension of the lung parenchyma (i.e., CPAP), supportive ventilation if indicated (with or without PEEP), and proper hydration and nutrition. There is a notable difference in disease remission between the over-1500-gram newborns and the under-1250-gram newborns.

XIX. Sleep apnea, according to sleep apnea experts, is defined as pauses in breathing that occur for more than 10 seconds and more than 30 times during 7 hours of sleep.[11]

A. Etiology: There are two primary types of sleep apnea:
 1. Obstructive sleep apnea (OSA) refers to significant pauses in breathing during sleep as a result of upper airway obstruction. The drive to breathe is intact, but air flow into the lungs is temporarily blocked because of intermittent upper airway obstruction. Most episodes of apnea are about 20–30 seconds in length.

a. Obesity is thought to play an important role in most cases.
b. Only a minority of patients with OSA will have an anatomical defect such as tonsilar hypertrophy, micrognathia (small lower jaw), or macroglossia (large tongue).
c. The decrease in tonic activity of the upper airway muscles combined with the subatmospheric pressure within the upper airway that occurs with each inspiratory effort may cause an imbalance of the forces holding the upper airway open. This may occur with:
   (1) alternations in the level of consciousness
   (2) alcohol consumption
   (3) sedative-hypnotic consumption
2. Central sleep apnea (CSA) refers to pauses in breathing that occur when the drive to breathe is intermittently absent. CSA is a relatively uncommon disorder that occurs at about 10% the rate of OSA. The exact causes of CSA are not clear.
   a. The central drive to breathe can be temporarily abolished by defects in the respiratory control system or muscles.
   b. Transient instabilities in respiratory drive, such as occur with the onset of sleep, can contribute to CSA.
   c. Reflex inhibition of central respiratory drive may occur with aspiration during sleep or the collapse of the upper airway.
3. Mixed apnea is present when both OSA and CSA occurs during sleep. This is commonly seen in patients with sleep apnea.

B. Physical Exam:
1. The patient with OSA most often complains of excessive daytime sleepiness (EDS). Other symptoms include memory loss, morning headaches, decreased ability to concentrate, and personality changes. Loud snoring, obesity, and a short neck are common findings in OSA.
2. Patients with CSA typically present the clinical picture of chronic hypoventilation syndrome with chronic respiratory failure (e.g., cor pulmonale).

C. Pulmonary Laboratory:
1. Daytime arterial blood gases and routine pulmonary function studies may be normal unless right heart failure or some underlying cardiopulmonary problem exists.
2. The polysomnogram (PSG) is an all-night recording of the patient's sleep. It typically includes recordings of:
   a. Electroencephalogram (EEG) to document stages of sleep
   b. ECG to record changes in heart rhythm
   c. Pulse oximetry to record episodes of desaturation
   d. Air flow at the mouth and nose to document periods of apnea

Chapter 10: Analyze Data and Determine Plan 153

   e. Chest and abdominal movements to identify efforts to breathe
   f. Electrooculogram (EOG) to record eye movements.
D. Chest X-Ray: Daytime studies are normal unless right heart failure or some underlying cardiopulmonary problem exists.
E. ECG: Daytime studies are normal unless right heart failure or some underlying cardiopulmonary problem exists.
F. Clinical Laboratory: Most patients with OSA do not have significant abnormalities in the complete blood count or electrolytes.
G. Therapeutic Goals:
   1. The therapeutic goals of OSA should include elimination, minimization, or stabilization of apneic periods. Once the diagnosis is made, the PSG is useful to assess the patient's response to treatment. Mild to moderate OSA often improve by avoiding alcohol and sedative; sleeping in the lateral position; weight reduction; or administration of protriptyline (a nonsedating tricyclic antidepressant that may be beneficial by increasing upper airway muscle tone). Severe cases will require trials of nasal continuous positive airway pressure; transtracheal oxygen therapy; or tracheostomy.
   2. CSA's therapeutic goals include supplemental nocturnal oxygen; respiratory stimulants (e.g., medroxyprogesterone); and nocturnal use of positive pressure ventilation.

XX. Thoracic trauma

A. Etiology: Serious respiratory and hemodynamic consequences may result from both blunt and penetrating chest trauma.[3]
   1. Pulmonary complications may result from rib fracture, traumatic pneumothorax, hemothorax, sucking chest wounds, flail chest, lung contusion, ruptured diaphragm, ruptured bronchus, or infection.
   2. Hemodynamic complications may result from a rupture of the aorta, cardiac tamponade, or cardiac contusion.
B. Physical Exam: On physical exam the patient is tachypneic, with a shallow ventilatory pattern (due to pain), often is cyanotic, hypotensive, and may have hemoptysis. There may be crepitus and pain on palpation, and altered sounds on percussion (dull over consolidation and hyperresonance over pneumothorax). Chest bruises may be present, and the site of penetration of either ribs or foreign object may be visible. On auscultation, there may be either moist rales or absent breath sounds.
C. Pulmonary Laboratory: Pulmonary evaluation would reveal hypoxemia, an elevated $P(A-a)O_2$, and an initial respiratory alkalemia that may progress into a respiratory and metabolic acidemia with impending respiratory failure. There is a decrease in the lung compliance and a reduction in vital capacity.

D. Chest X-Ray: Chest X-ray is the diagnostic choice for fractured ribs and pneumothorax. Any lung contusion would appear like a patchy, irregular, ill-defined density or homogenous consolidation. Occurring atelectasis is demonstrated by elevation of the diaphragm on the affected side, hilar shift, compensatory hyperinflation, and opacification of the collapsed segment.

E. ECG: Tachycardia will be noted on ECG, as well as assorted arrhythmias caused from concomitant cardiac damage.

F. Clinical Laboratory: Laboratory data is of secondary importance in the initial care of the chest trauma victim. Items to monitor however would include Hb and Hct for fluid management and tissue oxygenation status.

G. Therapeutic Goals: Therapeutic goals would include stabilization of the chest wall (i.e., internal with continuous controlled mechanical ventilation and PEEP), pain relief, prevention of atelectasis, adequate oxygenation, prevention of blood loss, and surgical repair if indicated. In the presence of a tension pneumothorax, the pleural space gas should be immediately evacuated.

References

1. Bunch, D., "Case Studies Examine RT Liability," *AARTimes,* Vol. 7, No. 9, September, 1983.

2. National Institute of Health Publication # 97-4053, *Practical Guide for the Diagnosis and Management of Asthma,* 1997.

3. Netter, F. H., *Respiratory System,* Vol. 7, CIBA Collection of Medical Illustrations, 1979.

4. Burki, N. K., and Krumpelman, J. L., "Correlation of Pulmonary Function with the Chest Roentgenogram in Chronic Airway Obstruction," *American Review of Respiratory Disease,* Vol. 121, 1980.

5. Glauser, F. L., *Signs and Symptoms in Pulmonary Medicine,* Lippincott, 1983.

6. Wilkins, R .L., Sheldon, R. L., and Krider, S. J., *Clinical Assessment in Respiratory Care,* 3rd ed, Mosby, 1995.

7. Hmelo, C. E., "AIDS: Issues for Respiratory Care Practitioners," *Respiratory Management,* November/December, 1987.

8. Collins, R. D., *Illustrated Manual of Fluid and Electrolyte Disorders,* Lippincott, 1976.

9. Koff, P. B., Eitzman, D. V., and Neu, J., *Neonatal and Pediatric Respiratory Care,* 2nd ed., Mosby, 1993.

10. Burton, G. G., Hodgkin, J. E., and Ward, J. J., *Respiratory Care: A Guide to Clinical Practice,* 4th ed., Lippincott, 1997.

11. Wilkins, R., and Parks, T., "Causes and Care of Sleep Apnea," *Master Modules,* Vol. II, No. 3, Education Resource Consortium, Inc., 1994.

Chapter 10: Analyze Data and Determine Plan

Assessment Questions

1. What are the usual pathogens found in the lower airways of patients with CF?

   I. Haemophilus influenzae
   II. Pseudomonas aeruginosa
   III. Staphylococcus aureus
   IV. Aspergillus

   A. I and II only
   B. I, II and III only
   C. II and III only
   D. II, III and IV only

2. A 57-year-old man with a 30-year history of working in a coal mine and a primary diagnosis of pneumoconiosis arrives for a scheduled pulmonary function work-up. You would expect which of the following values to be **ABNORMAL?**

   A. FVC
   B. FRC
   C. ERV
   D. $D_L CO$

3. Bronchopneumonia is best described on the chest X-ray as:

   A. A fluffy pattern seen in the peripheral lung fields
   B. Increased inflammatory tissue surrounding the air spaces
   C. Opacification of an entire lobe
   D. Fluffy infiltrates following the conducting airways

4. A patient with pulmonary edema secondary to pulmonary hypertension is admitted to the ICU with an acute myocardial infarction (AMI). Which of the following enzymes would you expect to be elevated?

   I. CTO
   II. CPK
   III. LDH
   IV. SGOT

   A. I and II only
   B. I, II, III and IV
   C. II, III and IV only
   D. IV only

5. Cytomegalovirus (CMV) is almost always isolated from the throat and urine of:

   A. Premature infants
   B. AIDS patients
   C. COPD patients
   D. TB patients

6. Rifampin and Isoniazid are bacteriocidal agents used to treat patients with:

   A. TB
   B. AIDS
   C. COPD
   D. Asbestosis

7. Most apneic episodes associated with obstructive sleep apnea (OSA) last from:

   A. 5–10 seconds
   B. 10–20 seconds
   C. 20–30 seconds
   D. 45 seconds

8. Which of the following patients are at risk for developing ARDS?

   A. Cancer patients
   B. AIDS patients
   C. Septic patients
   D. COPD patients

9. The ECG of a patient with bronchogenic carcinoma would be expected to exhibit which of the following?

   A. Normal sinus rhythm
   B. Premature ventricular contractions
   C. Right axis deviation
   D. Depressed S-T segment

Section II:

Equipment

Setting

In any patient care setting the respiratory care practitioner is responsible for the proper operation, function, cleaning, and stabilization of respiratory care equipment.

Chapters within this section include:

11. Resuscitation Devices

12. Oxygen Delivery Systems

13. Aerosol Generators and Humidification Equipment

14. Respiratory Support Equipment

15. Ventilator Systems and Support Accessories

16. Monitoring, Analyzing, and Testing Devices

17. Sterilization

Chapter 11

Resuscitation Devices

I. Manual resuscitators

A. Manual resuscitators employ a self-refilling 1.5 liter reservoir bag for adults, a 750 ml bag for pediatrics, or a 250 ml bag for neonates. Inlets for air/oxygen, a non-rebreathing valve, an air intake valve, and the standard 15mm (I.D.) and 22mm (OD) adaptor complete the resuscitation system.
B. As the bag is released, exhaled gas is directed to an exhalation port, while gas (room air/O_2) is being pulled in through a one-way inlet valve opening into the bag. Approximately 700–1100 ml are delivered when the bag is compressed with one hand, provided the patient is intubated. Delivered volumes are much less when using a face mask.
   1. Face masks are constructed of antistatic rubber or plastic. The main body of the mask incorporates a molded frame that provides strength and prevents collapse.
   2. Some manufacturers allow the mask face seal to be inflated with air that helps to prevent gas from escaping between the face and the mask.
   3. All adult and pediatric masks have a thickened connector with an internal diameter of 22 mm.
C. Relief valves may be incorporated within the resuscitator in order to comply with The American Society for Testing and Materials (ASTM) recommendations.
   1. Relief valves limit ventilation pressure. When the preset pressure limit is exceeded, the relief system (spring-tension, restricted orifice, or magnetic valve) allows for venting the excess pressure to the atmosphere.
   2. Not all adult resuscitators contain relief valves. Those that do incorporate some type of override mechanism (e.g., occluding an orifice with a finger) to allow use of pressures up to 70 cmH_2O.
   3. Neonatal and pediatric resuscitators are required to provide a relief system capable of preventing pressures greater than 40 cmH_2O from being exerted. These resuscitators may or may not incorporate an override system. The average pressure relief range is from 35–50 cmH_2O.

D. Successful resuscitation with a bag-type device depends upon obtaining the highest oxygen concentration possible. ASTM standards recommend that each bag be capable of maintaining a FIO_2 of 0.85 (85%) and a minimum minute ventilation of 12 liters.
   1. Use the highest possible liter flow to bring oxygen into the bag. However, excessively high flow rates have been known to jam the breathing valve in some bags. Newer devices are able to prevent valve malfunction at flow rates of 30 L/min or less.
   2. Use the longest refill time possible by manually restricting the expansion of the bag.
   3. Attach a reservoir system to the bag whenever possible.
E. Refer to Trouble Shooting Guide 11-1 regarding manual resuscitators.

II. Pneumatic resuscitator

A. This gas-powered, manually operated device can be used as a pressure-limited resuscitator. It will ventilate the nonbreathing patient or assist the breathing patient, on demand, with 100% oxygen.
B. Inspiration can be initiated by depressing the manual control button (cycling mechanism) or by a subatmospheric pressure generated by the patient's effort.
C. The resuscitator unit includes the standard 15mm (I.D.) and 22mm (OD) adapters. Operating pressure comes from a 50 psig gas source that provides a flow rate of 100 L/min and occurs only if the pipeline pressure remains constant and does not vary under 50 psig. Flow rates of greater than 100 L/min are not obtainable with these resuscitators.

Trouble Shooting Guide 11-1

Manual Resuscitators

Problem	Possible Causes	Corrective Actions
Will not function properly	Not utilizing device correctly Improper assembly Loose connections	Administer correctly Assemble correctly Tighten all connections
Bag is over-inflated	Liter flow is too high for the valving mechanism within bag Restriction to exhalation	Decrease liter flow Eliminate restriction Change resuscitator

Chapter 11: Resuscitation Devices

1. The unit is a pressure-limited device and functions similar to a reducing valve in that a step-down regulator reduces a 50 psig gas source to approximately 50 cmH$_2$O.
2. To deliver an 800 ml tidal volume in the allotted time a flow rate of 96 L/min is required.
3. There is a high risk of gastric insufflation if a mask seal is used instead of a tracheal tube.
4. There is an inability to detect changes in patient compliance and resistance with this device.

D. All resuscitators incorporate a pressure pop-off device (spring-tension, restricted orifice, or magnetic valve) capable of venting pressures greater than 50 cmH$_2$O to the atmosphere. Some units contain a switch that prevents pressure from exceeding 30 cmH$_2$O for infants and children.

E. Refer to Trouble Shooting Guide 11-2 regarding pneumatic resuscitators.

III. Automatic pneumatic chest compressors

A. Compressed gas powers a device that mechanically depresses the sternum, and also automatically ventilates the lungs.
1. An adjustable piston with a fist-sized head directs a 1.5–2 inch stroke to the sternum.
2. A demand valve (pneumatic resuscitator that inflates the lungs with 100% oxygen) incorporating a timer allows the compression to ventilation ratio to be adjustable. The rate is normally set at 5:1.

Trouble Shooting Guide 11-2

Pneumatic Resuscitators

Problem	Possible Causes	Corrective Actions
Will not function properly	Not utilizing device correctly Improper assembly Loose connections	Administer correctly Assemble correctly Tighten all connections
Decreased volume	Line pressure not high enough to produce maximum amount of flow	Make sure line pressure is at 50 psi

B. Their use is limited to adults only, while providing a steady manual compression to the chest that has shown to be very efficient on some patients. There are some strong safety points to consider prior to their use however.
 1. The piston will not adequately compress the chest if the piston head fails to maintain the set position.
 2. Fractured ribs and sternum, punctured lungs, and liver and lung lacerations have occurred due to the piston head shifting position.[1]
C. Vest CPR uses the method of utilizing the entire thorax as a pump to create blood flow.
 1. This is accomplished by simultaneous ventilation and chest compression.
 2. Depending on vest chest design, some models have been shown to increase arterial pressure significantly over standard CPR.[1]

IV. Defibrillators

A. The majority of sudden cardiac arrests are due to ventricular fibrillation (VF), caused by the heart's normally coordinated heartbeat suddenly becoming chaotic and abruptly stopping the pumping action of the heart. The defibrillator delivers an extremely short, high intensity electrical pulse designed to shock the heart, similar to a warm reboot on a locked-up computer system. For a defibrillation pulse to be effective in terminating VF, sufficient energy must reach the heart. Because therapists only perform external defibrillation, the energy burst must first travel through muscle, bone, organs, and other tissues to stop the heart's abnormal electrical activity. Most commercial automatic external defibrillators accomplish this by using a monophasic waveform (delivering an adjustable high voltage direct current (dc) power in one direction from one electrode pad, through the body, to the other electrode pad to the tissues).
 1. Electrode pads are circular in shape and are of three sizes, 13 cm for adults, 8 cm for older children, and 4 cm for infants.
 2. Electrode jelly helps to conduct the electrical impulse from the electrode to the skin.
 3. The delivered voltage is used to stimulate the entire cardiac muscle, with the hope of the SA node regaining control as the pacemaker.
 4. Any amount of energy delivered to the heart is potentially toxic, making first shock efficiency a priority, as continuous high-energy shocks produce negative consequences on the heart muscle.
B. Countershock energy release is expressed in joules or watt seconds. The defibrillator will administer up to 360 joules/W-sec.

$$\text{Energy} = \text{Power} \times \text{Duration}$$
$$\text{(Joules)} \quad \text{(Watts)} \quad \text{(Seconds)}$$

Chapter 11: Resuscitation Devices

1. Initial settings for a normal adult typically start at 200 joules.
2. A very short burst of high voltage energy is released in 0.01 seconds, which is intended to reestablish a normal cardiac rhythm.[1]

C. Automatic external defibrillators (AED) are capable of accurately assessing the cardiac state of the patient by sensing electrical signals from the patient's heart via electrodes. A computerized algorithm then interprets the electrical signals from the electrode and makes a therapy decision.
1. The algorithm is capable of discriminating between normal rhythms and life-threatening arrhythmias. The AED will automatically deliver an electrical pulse to shock the heart if the patient's rhythm requires it.
2. The AED activates the shock button only when a life-threatening arrhythmia is identified. At no other time will the device activate the shock button or permit the operator to deliver a shock.
3. The AED is now being used when transporting patients via air and ambulance, and is available on many commercial air carriers.

V. Laryngoscope

A. This device is used for exposure of the glottis prior to intubation. The laryngoscope consists of a handle containing batteries and is designed to accommodate both pediatric and adult-sized interchangeable blades.
1. The batteries power a replaceable light bulb to provide illumination for direct observation of the trachea, larynx, epiglottis, and vocal cords.
2. The handle has a rough surface to provide traction and has a connection point for the blade at the handle top.
3. The blade is inserted into the patient's oropharynx, and consists of the spatula, flange, tip, and light source.
   a. The straight blade (Miller) is long enough to expose the glottis by allowing the epiglottis to be lifted with an upward motion, thereby allowing the tube to be guided into the trachea. This extra length may allow the practitioner to exert pressure on the upper incisors during intubation. This extra pressure many times results in trauma to the teeth and gums.
   b. The curved blade (Macintosh) fits between the base of the tongue and the epiglottis. The blade conforms to the curve of the tongue and the shorter length prevents dental trauma. The glottis is visualized and then exposed by lifting with an upward and forward motion.[2]
4. Blade sizes range from infants to adults, and are attached to the handle by use of a hook and snap mechanism. Refer to Table 11-1.

B. A fiberoptic laryngoscope is now available as an alternative to the conventional laryngoscope. The tip of the laryngoscope is designed to fit inside the endotracheal tube.

TABLE 11-1: Laryngoscope Blade Dimensions

Age	Size	Length (mm)
Premature Infant	0	75
Infant	1	90–100
Child	2	100–150
Adult	3	150–190

1. A bundle of flexible optical fibers transmits a high-intensity beam of light.
2. The endotracheal tube and the laryngoscope are advanced into position together, with the light allowing excellent visualization of the vocal cords and carina.
3. The laryngoscope uses a self-contained nicad rechargeable battery pack as its power source.

VI. Esophageal obturator airway (EOA)

A. The EOA is a temporary emergency device, designed to be inserted into the esophagus to maintain ventilation in comatose patients during cardiac or respiratory arrest.

B. The device is constructed of a transparent inflatable face mask and a curved hollow plastic tube. The tube tip is closed and has sixteen small vent holes that allow air and oxygen to reach the laryngeal area.

C. Once properly positioned into the patient's esophagus, a balloon cuff is inflated with 30–35 ml of air. This seals the esophagus and prevents possible aspiration of gastric contents.[3]
   1. The balloon is inserted below the level of the carina prior to cuff inflation to prevent tracheal obstruction.
   2. Over-inflation of the cuff (greater than 35 ml) may compress the posterior membranous portion of the trachea causing an obstruction.

D. Complications include esophageal rupture, misplacement of the tube into the trachea, and vomiting and aspiration upon removal.

E. Use is limited to unconscious patients sixteen years of age or older. Pediatric and neonatal sizes are not available.

Chapter 11: Resuscitation Devices

F. The Esophageal Gastric Tube Airway (EGTA) is similar to the EOA except for a central channel that allows passage of a gastric (Levin) tube. This permits suction of stomach contents and relief of gastric distension.
  1. The major advantage of this device is that personnel do not need to be trained in intubation in order to insert the EOA/EGTA.
  2. Placement is relatively simple and the visualization of vocal cords is not required.

VII. Oral pharyngeal airway

A. Oral airways are intended to provide short-term airway management of spontaneously breathing patients. These patients need to be unconscious or heavily sedated as insertion of the airway readily stimulates the gag reflex, thereby greatly increasing the chance of vomiting and aspiration.

B. Oral airways are constructed of plastic, rubber, or metal, and are curved (S-shaped) to fit over the back of the tongue. This holds the tube away from the posterior wall of the pharynx. Inserting the airway through the mouth into the oropharynx allows the flange to lie against the lips and permits the tube body to lie against the roof of the mouth. Refer to Table 11-2.
  1. The Guedel airway has a reinforced bite area and a large central opening for suctioning and exchanging air.
  2. The Berman airway has its reinforced bite area through the center, and is open on each side to allow for the exchange of air and passage of a suction catheter.
  3. The Brook/Safar airway utilizes a flange mouthpiece on one end (rescuer side), and a Berman type airway on the other end (patient side). The bite area is reinforced with metal, and the airway is designed for mouth-to-mouth use only. This permits the rescuer to put their mouth on the airway without coming in contact with the patient.

TABLE 11-2: Oral Airway Dimensions

Age	Size	Length (mm)
Infant	1	40
Child	2	70
Adult	3–5	80–100

C. The airway allows the option of being inserted with the tip pointing toward the hard palate. When the airway is advanced it is turned 180 degrees, sliding into place behind the tongue.

D. To determine the correct size airway size, hold the airway up to the patient's cheek. The airway should reach from the corner of the mouth to the angle of the jaw. If the airway is too small the tongue will obstruct the airway. [4]

VIII. Nasopharyngeal airway

A. The airway is made of soft rubber, latex, or plastic, is uncuffed, and incorporates a beveled tip with a funnel-shaped nasal end. The tube is inserted into one of the nares and lies between the base of the tongue and the posterior wall of the oropharynx.
   1. Normal tube length is approximately 15 cm. Coughing or gagging by the patient indicates that the tube is too long and should be trimmed.
   2. The soft rubber or plastic construction causes the airway to kink and clog easily. Because the airway will normally rest against the skin of the nostril it may cause pressure necrosis. Therefore, the airway needs to be checked periodically for irritation to the nasal mucous membranes.

B. The nasopharyngeal tube maintains a patent airway and allows for repeated suctioning without damaging the nasal turbinates, and is not designed for use with mechanical ventilation.

C. Use of this tube is limited to patients having difficulty maintaining a patent airway (usually facial surgery, burns or injury) but are still breathing spontaneously.
   1. Close inspection is required to see that the tube does not slip out of position. Should the tube slip posteriorly the trumpet-shaped end can become lodged in the nasal passage and be extremely difficult to remove.
   2. Pins, or rings are used to secure the proximal end of the airway, because aspiration of the nasal airway down into the trachea or esophagus can occur.

D. Refer to Trouble Shooting Guide 11-3 for corrective actions taken if problems occur utilizing oral, nasal, or pharyngeal airways.

IX. Laryngeal mask airway (LMA)

A. The LMA is intended as an alternative to using a face mask for ventilation during anesthesia. The mask is made of silicone rubber and consists of an airway tube, mask, and mask inflation line.

B. One end of the airway tube incorporates the standard 15mm adaptor, while the other end is fitted with a specifically shaped mask containing an elliptical cuff. Cuff inflation is accomplished through a valve in the cuff inflation line.

Chapter 11: Resuscitation Devices

Trouble Shooting Guide 11-3

Oral/Nasal Pharyngeal Airways

Problem	Possible Causes	Corrective Actions
Patient gags during insertion	Upon insertion the oropharyngeal A/W touches the pharyngeal wall causing stimulation of the pharyngeal reflex	Use only in unconscious patients whose protective reflexes are obtunded
	The nasal airway length is too long	Trim the distal end of the nasopharyngeal tube
Sizes of the A/Ws are dissimilar with various brands	Sizing is not standardized from one manufacturer to another	Find one brand that meets your needs and stay with it for consistency

C. When properly inserted, the distal end of the LMA cuff lies with the tip of the airway tube resting just above the esophageal sphincter, allowing the upper border of the mask to rest against the base of the tongue. The anterior cuff tip must not enter the glottic opening (valleculae).

D. The device is available in various sizes to accommodate infants through adults. LMA tube lengths are 11.5–23.5 cm long. Internal diameter sizes range 5.25–11.5 mm. Cuff inflation volumes run from 4 ml for the smallest tube, and 40 ml for the largest tube.[5]

E. Steam sterilization is required to sterilize with the LMA.

F. The LMA has been found to provide a clear upper airway that is well tolerated during anesthesia and a low incidence of postoperative effects.

X. Esophageal-tracheal combination tube (ETC)/Pharyngotracheal lumen airway (PTL)

A. The ETC/PTL merge the characteristics of an esophageal airway tube (EOA), with the features of a endotracheal tube, consequently creating a double lumen airway.

B. The twin-lumen tube is inserted into the oropharynx without visualization of the vocal cords. With tubes going to the esophagus and trachea, ventilation is accomplished through the lumen (port) that provides lung inflation.

C. Once the airway is inserted, a large balloon located proximal to the tip is inflated filling the oropharynx and sealing the airway. A small balloon located at the distal end of the tube is also inflated, and the airway is secured by a strap fastened around the neck.

D. The two ports allow whichever one is not used for ventilation to be used to immediately suction gastric contents.

E. Multiple small ports in the unused lumen will allow the patient to breathe spontaneously, similar to the EOA.

F. Incidents involving complications have been minimal, however use has been studied only in-hospital, and has not been widespread to date.[1]

XI. Oral endotracheal tubes

A. The endotracheal tube circumvents the nose, mouth, larynx, and pharynx, thereby reducing the anatomical dead space. The tube creates significant resistance to airflow, and reduces the cough efficacy, which encourages retention of secretions. The oral tube is the tube of choice for short-term airway management in emergency use, because it allows for rapid insertion through the mouth into the trachea.

B. A stylet (malleable metal or plastic) may be inserted into the tube prior to intubation to alter the curve of the endotracheal tube. Care must be taken to prevent the stylet from protruding from the patient end of the endotracheal tube.

C. The oral airway can tolerate a larger size tube than the nasal airway, which may aid in decreasing a patient's work of breathing.
  1. The general rule for tube size is that it should be no larger than 2/3 the size of the patient's trachea.
  2. Conscious patients with a gag reflex may not tolerate an oral tube.
  3. The oral tube uses the simplest and most direct route. The tube should continue to be inserted until the cuff is 3–5 cm past the vocal cords.

D. Oral endotracheal tubes are long, hollow, and slightly curved. The tube is constructed of semi-rigid plastic (polyvinyl chloride, PVC) and contains the standard 15mm removable adapter.
  1. Many oral tubes incorporate a Murphy eye at the distal end that provides an alternative pathway for gas flow if the beveled end of the tube becomes obstructed.
  2. The tube is prone to kinking or becoming obstructed with mucus, making suctioning difficult.

E. Oral tubes (Portex style/Cole) that are used for neonates only do not incorporate a cuff.
  1. These tubes are generally larger at the machine end and taper to a short, small diameter intratracheal section. Usually these tubes measure 2.4–4.5 cm in length.

2. Increased resistance to flow is great due to an extremely small internal diameter.
3. Vocal cord trauma can be a complication due to the use of this type tube.
F. The Carlens tube is a flexible rubber double lumen endobronchial tube with two low-volume, high-pressure cuffs. A disposable brand is now available using low-pressure cuffs.
   1. One cuff is inflated in the trachea, and the other is inflated in the left main stem bronchus.
   2. This allows for separate lung ventilation that permits different expired volumes for each lung.

XII. Nasal endotracheal tubes

A. Nasal tubes are inserted through the nose into the trachea and are better suited for long-term intubation.
   1. A Murphy eye is a lateral eye (opening on the side of the tube), which provides an alternative pathway in the event the distal end of the tube becomes lodged against the tracheal wall or obstructed by mucus.
   2. Nasal tubes are slightly narrower and longer, which makes them less prone to kinking, but increases the resistance to gas flow making the work of breathing harder.
   3. The tube needs to be well anchored and secured to prevent pressure necrosis at the tip of the nares.
B. Tube markings are read from the patient end of the tube to the machine end and incorporate the following:
   1. The words "oral" or "nasal"
   2. The internal diameter in millimeters or French size
   3. The external diameter in millimeters or French size
   4. The length in centimeters, measured from patient end
   5. "IT" (implant tested) or "Z 79" (indicating the tube material is nonreactive when exposed to patient tissue)
C. Tubes with the same internal diameter may not have the same external diameter due to differences in wall thickness. This distinction is important because the tube must pass through the larynx to get into the trachea. Refer to Table 11-3.
D. French(Fr) sizing is determined by the circumference of the outer diameter of the tube, and conversion to Fr is allowed by the following formula. Fr sizes can be converted to millimeters by dividing by three, and vice versa.

$$\text{Maximum diameter (Fr)} = \text{Inside diameter (mm)} \times 3$$

Example: 33 Fr / 3 = 11 mm ID

10 mm ID $\times$ 3 = 30 Fr

TABLE 11-3:	Endotracheal Tube Dimensions		
Age	I.D. mm	O.D. mm	French
Premature	2.5	4.0	12
Newborn	3.0–3.5	4.5–5.0	12–15
1 yr. old	3.5–5.0	5.0–5.5	14–16
3 yr. old	4.5	6.0	18–20
5 yr. old	5.0	6.5	20–22
8 yr. old	5.5–6.0	7.0–8.0	21–24
12 yr. old	6.5	8.5	26
16 yr. old	7.0	9.0	27
Adult Female	7.0–8.0	9.0–10.0	27–30
Adult Male	8.0–9.0	10.0–12.0	30–36

XIII. Tracheostomy buttons

A. "Trach" buttons are used to help maintain the tracheal stoma by preventing it from closing. They also allow the patient to use their upper airway to breathe without tracheal obstruction.
   1. The teflon button consists of a short outer cannula that fits into the stoma and contacts the trachea, and a solid cap that completely plugs the tube when inserted. The cannula is flared on one end to prevent slippage into the trachea
   2. The inner edge is flanged, which keeps it against the tracheal wall. It lies flat so that it does not compromise tracheal air space. When the tube is capped, breathing occurs through the nose and mouth, allowing for coughing, talking, and eating.[6]
B. Various spacers are provided to adjust the distance between the patient's skin and the anterior wall of the trachea assuring the airway remains unobstructed.
C. An inner cannula can be inserted and may be used to ventilate and suction through should the need arise.
D. Refer to Trouble Shooting Guide 11-4 regarding oral/nasal endotracheal tubes.

XIV. Tracheostomy tubes

A. Tracheostomy tubes are inserted through a surgically created stoma into the trachea with the cuff placed between the carina and vocal cords.
   1. They are commonly used when long-term ventilation is required.
   2. They provide an alternate method of weaning a patient from a tracheostomy tube other than plugging the tube.

Trouble Shooting Guide 11-4

Oral/Nasal Endotracheal Tubes

Problem	Possible Causes	Corrective Actions
Abraded or punctured tracheal tissue	Protruding stylet from end of tube	Alter the position of the stylet or remove for patient safety
Obstructed oral tube	Patient biting the tube	Apply bite block or insert nasal tube
Pressure necrosis on the trachea	Tube is too large for size trachea, even with a small amount of air in the cuff	Replace with smaller tube
Pressure necrosis on the external nares	Tube is exerting constant pressure to inflamed area	Relocate tube

B. The tracheostomy tube provides a patent airway that is easy to suction through. A large internal diameter and a shorter length create less airway resistance with this tube.

C. Construction consists of rubber, plastic, or metal, and may or may not incorporate a radiopaque (X-ray) indicator. Many manufacturers include an obturator that has a rounded head, making it less traumatic to insert the outer cannula into the tracheostomy.

1. The obturator is used similar to the stylet during insertion of the tracheostomy tube. It provides rigidity during insertion, and the rounded tip protrudes beyond the end of the tube to assist in passing through the tracheal cartilage.
2. Commonly used tubes contain either single or double cannula. If a single cannula tube becomes plugged with secretions the entire tube must be removed. The double cannula tube contains one cannula inside the other, meaning the inner cannula must be removed to clear the airway, if obstructed.
3. A single lumen tube distends equally in all directions holding the cannula in place. The double lumen tube uses an extra outer wall to hold the cannula in place maintaining better stability.

D. Fenestrated tracheostomy tubes contain a window (fenestration) cut into the posterior wall of the outer cannula, above the inflatable cuff. This window allows air to pass through into the tube and down to the lungs. The tube can be capped with a plug that permits the patient to try breathing without removing the trach tube.
  1. The inner cannula can be inserted to allow for ventilation if desired. The inner cannula will increase resistance due to a smaller internal diameter.
  2. This tube is commonly utilized as an aid to weaning from mechanical ventilation.
E. Refer to Trouble Shooting Guide 11–5 for information regarding tracheostomy tubes.

XV. Tube cuffs

A. Tube cuffs are essential in order to seal the trachea. Plastic tubes have a securely bonded cuff, with the cuff inflation line incorporated into the tube wall. Metal tubes use cuffs that slip on the neck of the tube.

Trouble Shooting Guide 11-5
Tracheostomy Tubes

Problem	Possible Causes	Corrective Actions
Excessive air leak through nose and mouth	Insufficient air in cuff	Deflate and reinflate cuff to check balloon pressure
	Leak in cuff, inflation line, pilot balloon	Change tracheostomy tube
	Trachea too large for sized tube	Insert larger tube
	No cuff on tube	Apply tube with cuff
Trach tube becomes dislodged within trachea	Excessive weight or pulling at neck plate	Reposition ventilator circuit to reduce weight and pull of tubing
	Trach is tied too loose	Reposition tube and secure trach ties
Difficult removal or insertion of inner cannula on fenestrated tube	Tissue growing in through fenestration	Contact physician

Chapter 11: Resuscitation Devices

1. The inflation line continues as a separate line outside the trachea, and connects the cuff, pilot balloon, and Luer valve.
2. The cuff is the balloon-like component that directs airflow through the tube, and acts as a seal to eliminate or decrease airflow through the nose and mouth.
3. Cuff variety is generally limited to cuffs that contain a large volume of gas that seals the trachea using a low pressure, or cuffs that contain a small volume and seal the trachea with high pressure.
   a. High-volume, low-pressure cuffs (less than 25 mmHg) exert their force over a large surface area as they conform to the tracheal wall. Due to the high cuff residual volume the trachea can be sealed with less internal pressure.
   b. Low-volume, high-pressure cuffs exert their force against a very small area on the trachea's surface due to low cuff residual volume, which requires high intracuff pressures (25–200 mmHg) to maintain an effective tracheal seal.

XVI. Cuff inflation devices

A. Equipment necessary for assessment of proper cuff inflation includes a 3-way stopcock, a pressure manometer, and a calibrated syringe.
   1. Newer devices are able to connect to the cuff inflation line and incorporate a pressure manometer displaying cuff pressure in cmH_2O and mmHg.
   2. The idea is to effectively seal the trachea using the lowest possible lateral wall pressure.
   3. Some tubes contain a pressure relief valve (PRV), which automatically limits internal cuff pressure to 25 mmHg.
   4. An adequate seal against liquid aspiration should be attained with an intracuff pressure of 20–25 mmHg provided the tube is a good fit.
B. Trach mate devices monitor lateral wall pressure, use a red light to indicate when pressures are greater than 25 mmHg, and can provide room air to inflate the balloon to the desired pressure.
C. Most facilities monitor cuff pressure at least once each eight hour shift.

XVII. Suction catheters

A. This hollow cylindrical rubber or plastic tube is used for removing secretions from the respiratory tract. The distal end of the catheter may have one or more openings, used for aspiration of secretions.[7]
B. The catheter tip is open and may be straight, angled, beveled, or have a rolled lip. The proximal end is vented (thumb port) in order to apply subatmospheric pressure.
C. The outer diameter (OD) of the catheter should be no larger than 1/2 the inner diameter (ID) of the artificial airway. The most commonly used sizes are #12–#14 French. Refer to Table 11-4.

TABLE 11-4: Suction Catheter Sizes*

Age	Tube Size I.D.	Catheter Size O.D.	Catheter Size French
Newborn	3.0 mm	1.5 mm	4
1 yr. old	4.0 mm	2.0 mm	6
5 yr. old	5.0 mm	2.5 mm	8
12 yr. old	6.0 mm	3.0 mm	8
Adult Female	7.0 mm	3.5 mm	10
Adult Male	8.0 mm	4.0 mm	12
Large Adult	9.0 mm	4.5 mm	14

* This table represents the optimal maximum size usually recommended. It is not meant to indicate the only size catheter to use.

D. The normal standard used to determine catheter tube size is:

$$French = Tube\ ID \times 3\ divided\ by\ 2$$

Example: Trach tube with a size 8mm ID

$$8\ mm \times 3 = 24$$

$$24 / 2 = 12\ Fr\ suction\ catheter$$

E. Disposable specimen collectors (Lukens traps) are intended to be used in-line with suction equipment for the purpose of sputum collection in a sterile container. Collectors are inserted between the suction catheter and the connecting tubing.

F. The oropharyngeal suction device (a Yankauer tonsillectomy suction tip catheter) is used for suctioning large amounts of liquid, food particles, or vomitus from the upper airway or mouth.
   1. The Yankauer is designed for use during surgery or for clearance of the upper airway.
   2. This device is not flexible and suction is applied continuously because it does not incorporate a thumb-vent or vacuum control.

G. Refer to Trouble Shooting Guide 11-6 for information regarding suction catheters.

Chapter 11: Resuscitation Devices

Trouble Shooting Guide 11-6

Suction Catheters

Problem	Possible Causes	Corrective Actions
Unable to pass suction catheter through airway	Secretions blocking tube	Remove and clean/discard inner cannula
		Suction airway to clear secretions
	Suction catheter too large for airway	Change size of suction catheter
	Tube dislodged from trachea	Reposition tube
Unable to get secretions to pass through airway	Suction pressure too low	Readjust suction pressure
	Secretions too thick	Liquify secretions prior to inserting suction tube

References

1. *Advanced Cardiac Life Support,* American Heart Association, 1997.
2. Scanlon, C. L., Wilkins, R. L., and Stoller, J. K., *Egan's Fundamentals of Respiratory Therapy,* 7th ed., Mosby, 1999.
3. Cosgriff, J. H., and Anderson, D. L., *The Practice of Emergency Care,* 2nd ed., Lippincott, 1984.
4. Alone, C. A., and Hill, T. V., *Respiratory Care of the Newborn and Child,* 2nd ed., Lippincott, 1997.
5. Laryngeal Mask Airway Instruction Manual, LMA Co., 1997.
6. McPherson, S., *Respiratory Care Equipment,* 5th ed., Mosby, 1995.
7. Burton, G. G., Hodgkin, J. E., and Ward, J. J., *Respiratory Care: A Guide to Clinical Practice,* 4th ed., Lippincott, 1997.

Assessment Questions

1. Which of the following is correct for a single rescuer using a bag mask resuscitator?
   I. It's easy to deliver the volume using one hand
   II. It's difficult to protect the airway with one hand
   III. It's difficult to maintain a mask seal with one hand

IV. It's easy to deliver the recommended FIO₂ with one hand

A. I, II, III and IV
B. I and IV only
C. II and III only
D. III only

2. While auscultating a patient you just intubated, you hear decreased breath sounds on the left side of the chest. These breath sounds indicate:

    A. The tube is in the left mainstem bronchus
    B. The tube is in the esophagus
    C. The tube is in the right mainstem bronchus
    D. There is a pneumothorax

3. A 30-year-old unresponsive male patient requiring ventilation is airlifted to the emergency room after having been recovered from a car that had a hose from the tailpipe stuck in the back window so he could breathe carbon monoxide. What device would deliver the highest FIO₂ and still provide ventilation?

    A. Manual resuscitator with a reservoir tube
    B. Oxygen-powered demand valve resuscitator
    C. Manual resuscitator without a reservoir tube
    D. Nonrebreathing mask

4. Which of the following is NOT A CONSIDERATION when administering ventilation to an infant with a manual resuscitator?

    A. Choosing the proper-sized bag for the infant
    B. Attaching the resuscitator to an oxygen source
    C. Setting the pressure pop-off to 15 cmH₂O
    D. Choosing the proper-sized mask for the infant

5. The device designed to maintain the patency of a tracheal stoma yet still allow for weaning from the trach tube is a:

    A. Fenestrated tube
    B. Trach button
    C. Tracheal tube with inner cannula
    D. Carlen's tube

6. When inserting an oropharyngeal airway into a child, the correct size airway can be determined by holding the airway up to the corner of the mouth, and having the airway extend to the

    A. Angle of the jaw
    B. Corner of the eye
    C. Tip of the nose
    D. Tragus of the ear

7. Insertion of the LMA requires the anterior cuff tip to

    A. Rest against the base of the tongue
    B. Lie just inside the glottic opening
    C. Lie just inside the valleculae
    D. Lie just above the esophageal sphincter

8. A patient returning from a right lung lobectomy needs to be ventilated using the Independent Lung Ventilation (ILV) mode. You would choose a:

    A. Oral endotracheal tube
    B. Oral double lumen endobronchial tube
    C. Laryngeal mask airway
    D. Pharyngotracheal lumen airway

9. A eight-year-old boy requires intubation with a size 4 mm internal diameter oral tube. What size suction catheter will you obtain for this eight-year-old?

    A. 4 French
    B. 6 French
    C. 8 French
    D. 10 French

Chapter 12

Oxygen Delivery Devices

I. Bulk oxygen systems

A. Bulk liquid oxygen systems range in size from 3000 cubic feet to 300,000 cubic feet. Liquid systems keep the temperature of oxygen below −297°F. The pressure inside the cylinder is maintained at 250 psig.

B. One cubic foot of liquid oxygen at −297°F yields 860 cubic feet of gaseous oxygen at 70°F.[1] This means oxygen expands approximately 860 times to become gaseous. One cubic foot of gaseous oxygen is equal to 28.3 liters.

C. Bulk systems function similar to a thermos bottle. An outer shell is made from carbon steel, the middle space holds powdered insulation material, and the inner shell is composed of stainless steel.
   1. The temperature inside the storage vessel is approximately −300°F.
   2. A pressure relief mechanism is incorporated to allow liquid oxygen to expand and become gaseous oxygen.

D. A seamless copper piping system distributes the gas to suitable station outlets throughout the hospital. All fittings and connections have been brazed or soldered.
   1. An in-line pressure relief valve is set 50% greater than line pressure. This pressure relief valve will allow gas to escape (vent off) should the pressure inside the container rise above 75 psig.
   2. System design includes using smaller diameter pipe in order to keep the system pressure at 50 psig.
   3. The piping system branches to different areas that are controlled by a zone valve. Each zone valve can shut off gas to a specific area for use during system repair, fires, or massive leaks.
   4. The piping system is tested for leaks by being charged 1.5 times its working pressure (250 psig) for a period of 24 hours.

E. Oxygen manifold systems are individual cylinders connected together (called banks) with copper or "Type K" brass pipes. This system, which serves as a backup

for the liquid storage unit, contains a bank of cylinders (one set for use and one set for backup) that supply the hospital pipelines with medical gas during failure of the primary system.[1]
1. These cylinder banks need to be capable of providing at least a one-day (24 hrs.) supply of gas.
2. A check valve must be between each tank to prevent back flow of gas contents and contamination of the other cylinders. This valve also prevents the whole bank from losing pressure should one cylinder develop a leak.
3. Each bank contains a regulator/reducing valve capable of maintaining whatever pressure is needed (usually 50 psig).

II. Gas cylinders

A. Cylinders for medical gas use are manufactured from seamless steel or spun aluminum and are available in sizes ranging from "AA" to "K." Sizes "E" through "K" are common and are somewhat portable.
1. Gas cylinders are governed by the Department of Transportation (DOT), which establishes the regulations for marking, testing, and transport of cylinders.
2. Cylinder markings represent technical information that is stamped into the steel cylinder (e.g., size, weight, pressure).[1]
3. Gas cylinders normally contain 2000 psig. In order to overfill the cylinder by 10% (2200 psig), a "+" mark must be stamped into the cylinder.
4. Hydrostatic testing is done every five–ten years to determine the elastic expansion of the cylinder. The cylinder is immersed inside a container that is filled with water. The cylinder is also filled with water, and that water is then pressurized to 3,000 psig to determine the compliance (elastic expansion) of the cylinder. A decrease in the cylinder's ability to expand indicates the cylinder is aging.
5. A star stamped into the cylinder represents a ten-year hydrostatic recertification as opposed to the normal five years.
6. Each gas cylinder has a specific color indicating the type of gas contained in the cylinder. Refer to Table 12-1.

B. At times it is necessary to calculate how long the gas inside a cylinder will last. Duration of cylinder flow is not applicable for liquid gas in a cylinder. Cylinder factors apply only after the liquid has been converted into the gaseous phase. Refer to Table 12-2.
1. Calculating cylinder factors is based on an assumption of 28.3 L/ft³. Calculation for an "E" cylinder:

$$\frac{22 \text{ ft}^3 \times 28.3 \text{ L/ft}^3}{2200 \text{ psig}} = 0.28 \text{ L/psig}$$

Chapter 12: Oxygen Delivery Devices

TABLE 12-1: Color Codes for Medical Gas Cylinders

Gas	Color
Oxygen (O_2)	Green
Ethylene (C_2H_4)	Red
Nitrous Oxide (N_2O)	Blue
Cyclopropane (C_3H_6)	Orange/Chrome
Carbon Dioxide (CO_2)	Grey
Helium (He)	Brown
Oxygen/Carbon Dioxide >7%	Top Green/Body Grey
Oxygen/Helium >80%	Top Green/Body Brown
Carbon Dioxide/Oxygen <7%	Top Grey/Body Green
Helium/Oxygen <80%	Top Brown/Body Green

2. Calculating remaining gas volume in order to determine time estimates requires that the total gas pressure in the cylinder be multiplied by the factor for that size cylinder. The result is then divided by the total liter flow (L/min) to determine how many minutes the cylinder will last. Divide by 60 to convert minutes into hours. Refer to Equation 12-1.

TABLE 12-2: Calculating Factors for Oxygen Flow

Cylinder Size	Factor
"D" cylinder	0.16 L/psig
"E" cylinder	0.28 L/psig
"M" cylinder	1.36 L/psig
"G" cylinder	2.41 L/psig
"H" cylinder	3.14 L/psig
"K" cylinder	3.14 L/psig

> **EQUATION 12-1:** **Duration of Cylinder Gas Flow**
>
> $$\frac{\text{Gauge pressure} \times \text{Factor}}{\text{Total liter flow}} = \text{Time in min (divide by 60 to calculate hrs)}$$
>
> **Example:** An "H" cylinder with a pressure of 2000 psig is running at a flow rate of 10 L/min. How long will the cylinder run before it is empty?
>
> $$\frac{2000 \times 3.14}{10} = \frac{6280}{10} = 628 \text{ min} \qquad \frac{628}{60} = 10.4 \text{ hours}$$

3. Specific psig safety factors must be subtracted prior to working the equation. A "H" cylinder containing 2000 psig needs to be changed when the pressure reaches 500 psig. Leaving this 500 psig safety factor would leave the equation looking like this: 2000 psig $-$ 500 psig $\times$ 3.14
4. Specific hours of prior use must be subtracted after working the equation. A "H" cylinder has been in use for 5 hours, how many additional hours of gas flow are left in the cylinder? 10.4 hours $-$ 5 = 5.4 hours

C. Refer to Trouble Shooting Guide 12-1 regarding bottled gas systems.

III. Oxygen extraction devices

A. Oxygen concentrators use electrical power to pump room air through a separating device, allowing the device to filter out molecules other than oxygen. Oxygen is sepa-

> **Trouble Shooting Guide 12-1**
>
> **Bottled Gas Systems**
>
> | Problem | Possible Causes | Corrective Actions |
> |---|---|---|
> | Gas fails to flow from cylinder | Decreased pressure in cylinder | Check pressure gauge; Replace cylinder |
> | | Faulty regulator | Repair or replace |
> | | Gas leak | Check connections and secure/tighten |
> | | Obstructed outlet | Remove regulator and go through cylinder "cracking" procedure |

TABLE 12-3: O₂ Percentage at Varying Concentrator Flow Rates

LPM	O₂%
2	94
4	88
6	74
8	60
10	50

rated from the air and concentrated into a reservoir for breathing. The remaining nitrogen is redistributed into the room.
1. A molecular sieve device uses a vacuum to draw room air into cylinders packed with a filtering compound (crystallized zeolite), which absorbs nitrogen from atmospheric air while allowing oxygen to pass through a semipermeable membrane.
2. The sieve is capable of increasing the oxygen concentration of delivered gas to 90% at a flow of 2 L/min. As flow is increased, oxygen percentage is decreased. Refer to Table 12-3.

B. The air inlet filters need to be changed periodically as they become obstructed. Clogged filters mean less oxygen available for the concentrator reservoir. Some concentrators incorporate oxygen alarms that sense pressure decreases inside the oxygen reservoir.

C. Concentrators are designed to deliver a continuous uninterrupted flow of oxygen and are mainly used by the home care patient.

D. Oxygen enrichers provide 40% oxygen and simultaneously function as a humidifier. A compressor maintains a vacuum across a one micron thick (1/25,000th of an inch) plastic membrane that filters out nitrogen while permitting water vapor containing oxygen to pass through.[2]
1. With moisture available in the inspired air the need for a humidifier is eliminated.
2. Because this device provides 40% oxygen concentration at all flow rates, higher gas flow rates may be required to maintain the same blood gas levels for patients that were using other oxygen administering equipment.

E. Refer to Trouble Shooting Guide 12-2 for trouble shooting oxygen extraction systems.

IV. Portable oxygen systems

A. Liquid oxygen placed in portable thermos bottle-type containers are referred to as walkers, companions, strollers, or liberators. The most common type is the Linde

Trouble Shooting Guide 12-2

Oxygen Extraction Systems

Problem	Possible Causes	Corrective Actions
Compressor not turning on	No power to electric outlet	Verify outlet has electrical power
	Fuse is broken	Replace with new fuse
	Compressor malfunction due to parts breakdown	Repair or replace compressor
Inadequate oxygen flow rate	Obstructed air inlet filter	Clean or replace filter
	Leak in tubing	Check and tighten all

Walker System, which consists of a carrier pack and a 40 lb. liquid reservoir from which the walker may be refilled.

1. The full walker (11 lbs.) contains oxygen in the liquid state, which is allowed to expand to 1025 liters of gaseous oxygen.
2. Depressing buttons for 1, 2, or 4 L/min sets flow rates. More than one button may be pressed at one time to provide a total flow capability of 7 L/min maximum.

B. Time estimates for walker systems utilize a formula where the walker gas content is divided by the gas flow to determine how long the oxygen will last. Refer to Equation 12-2.

EQUATION 12-2:   Time Estimates for Portable Oxygen Systems

$$\frac{\text{Content}}{\text{Flow}} = \text{Duration}$$

Example: A patient is going home on a walker system that contains 1000 liters and is running at a flow rate of 4 L/min. How long could the patient be gone and still have fresh oxygen?

$$4 \text{ L/min.} \times 60 = 240 \text{ L/hr.}$$

$$\frac{1000}{240} = 4.1 \text{ hours (4 hr. 6 min.)}$$

Chapter 12: Oxygen Delivery Devices

Trouble Shooting Guide 12-3

Portable Oxygen Systems

Problem	Possible Causes	Corrective Actions
No gas flow	Decreased gas flow from reservoir	Refill system from gas reservoir
	Leaks at connections	Check connections and tighten if loose
	Obstructed/kinked tubing	Check tubing system and repair or replace

C. Refer to Trouble Shooting Guide 12-3 for trouble shooting portable oxygen systems.

V. Cannula

A. The cannula consists of a green plastic supply tube and two prongs (straight or curved) inserted into the nostrils to provide low-flow oxygen administration.
   1. The patient's total minute volume cannot be delivered at cannula flow rates, resulting in a FIO_2 that is variable and unpredictable.[3]
   2. Variable-performance (low-flow) devices are generally used when the patient's respiratory rate is less than 25 BPM, and their tidal volume is constantly between 300–700 ml.
   3. An FIO_2 of up to 0.40 can be achieved with a well-placed cannula at flow rates up to 6 L/min.
   4. Flow rates in excess of 6 L/min will only provide small increases in the delivered FIO_2, and can cause pain due to the high gas flow stream impinging on the frontal sinuses.

VI. Oxygen conservation devices

A. Variations of the cannula design are combined with oxygen storage versions to lower the cost of oxygen for long-term patients.
B. Oxygen conservation devices such as the Oxymizer pendant cannula and the Oxymizer mustache cannula provide slightly higher oxygen concentrations than the typical cannula.
   1. The Oxymizer pendant cannula contains a diaphragm that is shifted as oxygen enters the device.

a. The pendant is capable of holding 40 ml of oxygen and an additional 20 ml of oxygen in the tubing directed to a typical cannula apparatus.
   b. The movement of the diaphragm provides a reservoir of oxygen that is inhaled by the patient on their next breath.
 2. The Oxymizer mustache cannula incorporates a diaphragm at the base of the cannula instead of a pendant. The diaphragm displaces the oxygen, allowing a reservoir of enriched gas for the patient to breathe from on the subsequent breath.[2]
   a. The first part of the patient's breath removes the oxygen from the reservoir and accounts for the slightly higher oxygen concentration than the regular cannula provides at the same liter flow. The reservoir refills with oxygen as the patient is exhaling.
   b. The reservoir is capable of storing 20 ml of oxygen.

VII. Catheter

A. The catheter is a soft, flexible, plastic tube containing several small holes in the terminal end for directing low-flow oxygen to the oropharynx. It is designed to enter either nare and proceed into the oropharynx until the catheter tip lies behind the uvula.
 1. Over-insertion into the esophagus can lead to gastric insufflation that could lead to gastric rupture.
 2. FIO_2s of 0.50 may be achieved with a well-placed catheter at flow rates up to 8 L/min.
 3. The catheter, like the cannula, is considered to be a variable performance device because patient's total minute volume is not being delivered.
 4. A fresh catheter is usually inserted into the opposite nare every 8–16 hours, because nasal secretions may cause the catheter to adhere to the nasal mucosa.[3]

VIII. Transtracheal oxygen catheter

A. This device allows for long-term transtracheal oxygen (TTO) administration. The appliance is an intravenous size catheter made of a high-tech biopolymer tubing, approximately 20 cm in length with a 9-French tract.
 1. The catheter is inserted somewhere between the cricothyroid membrane and the notch of the manubrium, close to the second cartilage ring at the base of the neck.
 2. Oxygen is delivered directly into the trachea without any gas being lost to the atmosphere, bypassing the hypopharynx, a considerable volume of anatomical dead space.
 3. The catheter tip lies against the posterior membrane of the tracheal wall, with the oxygen ports directed away from the respiratory mucosa.

Chapter 12: Oxygen Delivery Devices

Trouble Shooting Guide 12-4

Variable Performance Oxygen Systems

Problem	Possible Causes	Corrective Actions
Absent or inadequate oxygen flow rate	Leaks in the system	Check connections between patient and source (flowmeter)
	Low oxygen pressure	Check source for adequate pressurized supply of gas
	Tubing obstruction	Check tubing for kinks or obstruction
Patient complains of dryness, irritation	Humidifier operation failure	Correct or replace humidifier

    4. Adequate oxygenation can occur at lower flow rates, when the anatomical dead space is decreased as oxygen travels to the lung. Acceptable PO_2 levels may be realized with oxygen flows as low as ½ L/min.

B. The tracheal catheter is comfortable, offers cosmetic improvement over other methods of oxygen administration, and may remain in place for a period of 3–6 months before replacement.[4]

C. Stomal site infection, stoma maintenance, inadvertent catheter displacement, catheter kinking, and mucous plugs adhering to the catheter partially obstructing the trachea are considerations needing attention prior to a long-term commitment.

D. Refer to Trouble Shooting Guide 12-4 for information regarding variable performance oxygen systems.

IX. Simple oxygen mask

A. A simple mask is made of disposable plastic with small holes or ports on each side and does not incorporate any valves. The ports allow exhaled gases to exit the mask, while providing for entrainment of room air during the next inspiration.

    1. Delivered oxygen percentages range from about 35–55% with flow rates of 6–10 L/min.

    2. The simple mask is considered to be a variable performance device in that it does not meet or exceed the patient's peak inspiratory flow rate.

Trouble Shooting Guide 12-5		
Variable Performance Oxygen Masks		
Problem	**Possible Causes**	**Corrective Actions**
Inadequate gas flow rate	Leaks within the system Low pressure other than leaks	Ensure system integrity Ensure proper gas flows

    3. The space under the mask is an extension of anatomical dead space and may lead to an increased $PaCO_2$ with flow rates less than 5 L/min.[3]

B. The mask is designed to fit over the nose and mouth and be secured by a strap that goes around the head. Care must be taken to ensure that the mask does not press too tightly against the patient's face to avoid interference with circulation.

C. Refer to Trouble Shooting Guide 12-5 for information regarding variable performance oxygen masks.

X. Partial rebreathing mask

A. The overall structure is similar to a simple mask with the addition of a 500–1000 ml reservoir bag. The design is to provide for oxygen conservation by permitting the patient to rebreathe a portion of the exhaled gas from their last breath.
    1. With the proper oxygen flow rate being administered, the reservoir bag should be full by the time the first one-third of the patient's tidal volume is exhaled.
    2. A well-fitted mask that has the flow rate adjusted so the bag does not collapse on inspiration will deliver an FIO_2 in the range of 35–60%.

B. The small holes or vents serve as ports for exhaled gas and as an inlet for room air in the event of source gas failure.

XI. Nonrebreathing mask

A. The structure is similar to the partial rebreathing mask, but incorporates a one-way valve that directs gas flow from the bag into the mask. Two one-way valve exhalation side ports serve to prevent exhaled gas from being rebreathed. A flap or spring loaded valve (not available in the disposable mask) allows room air to enter in the event of source gas failure.
    1. A properly positioned disposable mask, with the flow rate adjusted so the bag does not collapse on inspiration, will deliver oxygen concentrations in the range of 55–70%.[3]

Chapter 12: Oxygen Delivery Devices

2. Higher concentrations can be obtained with masks that are not made of disposable plastic and incorporate superior seals.
    a. Leaks around the disposable masks are common, allowing room air to enter on inspiration and thereby decrease the FIO_2.
    b. The one-way valve can become saturated with moisture and stick in the closed position, preventing the reservoir bag from deflating during inspiration. It may also prevent the patient from obtaining a breath.
B. This type of mask is intended for the short-term support of patients who require high FIO_2s, or those who require the administration of mixed gases such as helium/oxygen or oxygen/carbon dioxide therapy.

XII. Tracheostomy mask

A. The tracheostomy mask (collar) is a small shell-shaped aerosol mask made of disposable plastic. It lies loosely over the tracheostomy site and is held in place with an elastic strap. Administration of oxygen, high humidity, or aerosol therapy is its primary function.

B. Oxygen concentration depends upon the limitation of the humidifier or nebulizer being used. Precise FIO_2 control can be achieved provided the flow rates are set to meet or exceed the patient's peak inspiratory flow.

XIII. Briggs "T" adaptor

A. The Briggs adaptor is a manufactured plastic "T," which utilizes a 15mm ID and 22mm OD endotracheal connector at the stem and is usually fitted with wide bore tubing for the administration of oxygen, high humidity, or aerosol therapy.

B. The adaptor allows for the addition of a reservoir tube on the exhalation side of the "T." This helps prevent a large portion of the patient's tidal volume from being drawn from room air, while at the same time, maintains a prescribed FIO_2.
    1. Most reservoir tubes hold from 60–120 ml of volume. 10 ml/inch is the average conversion factor for tubing volume.
    2. The reservoir also helps to counterbalance the weight of the overall circuit at the tracheostomy site.
    3. Flow rate must be adjusted to meet the patient's peak inspiratory flow rate at rest.

XIV. Air entrainment mask

A. Air entrainment masks are fixed-performance devices where oxygen flows through a jet (Bernoulli effect) that can be changed to vary air entrainment and oxygen percentage.[2]

1. Generally fixed-performance devices are desired when the patient's ventilatory pattern is neither consistent nor predictable.
   2. Many times this entrainment device is referred to as a "venturi mask," even though it does not incorporate a venturi. Because the mask is comprised of a jet that entrains air, the name "venturi mask" is misleading.
   3. The entrainment mask contains at least two large holes to permit free expiration and to prevent pressure from building up inside the mask and reducing air entrainment.
   4. The total flow of mixed gases needs to be 40–60 L/min regardless of the prescribed oxygen concentration. The total gas flow must exceed the patient's peak inspiratory flow (normally $4 \times$ patient minute volume).
B. Air-entrainment masks are called fixed-performance devices because they maintain a precise oxygen percentage. The mask fits over the mouth and nose and is secured by tightening an elastic strap.
   1. Controlling the jet size and entrainment port size delivers all of the inspired gas at a preset FIO_2. In other words, the ratio of source gas to gas entrained can be controlled. Refer to Table 12-4.
   2. As long as the patient's peak inspiratory flow is being met, the entrainment mask will not be affected by changes in the patient's ventilatory pattern.
   3. Increasing the oxygen liter flow will increase the total flow, but will not effect the entrainment ratio or the O_2 percent.
C. The air to pure oxygen ratio can be manipulated to calculate total flow. Refer to Equation 12-3.
D. Refer to Trouble Shooting Guide 12-6 for information regarding fixed performance oxygen systems.

TABLE 12-4: Air/Oxygen Entrainment Ratios

FIO_2	Ratio	Flow Rate	Total Flow
0.24*	25:1	4 L/M	104 L/M
0.28*	10:1	4 L/M	44 L/M
0.35	4:1	7 L/M	35 L/M
0.40	3:1	8 L/M	32 L/M
0.60	1:1	15 L/M	30 L/M

*21 is substituted for 20 whenever the FIO_2 calls for less than 0.35.

Chapter 12: Oxygen Delivery Devices

EQUATION 12-3: Air/Oxygen Ratio

$$\frac{(\text{source}) \ 100 - O_2\% \ (\text{desired})}{O_2\% \ (\text{desired}) - 20 \ (\text{room air})} \quad \text{OR} \quad \frac{1 - FIO_2}{FIO_2 - 0.2}$$

Example: $\dfrac{100 - 40}{40 - 20} = \dfrac{60}{20} = \dfrac{3 \text{ liters of air @ } 20\%}{1 \text{ liter of oxygen @ } 100\%}$

$+ \dfrac{\dfrac{3 \times 0.2}{1 \times 1.0}}{4} = \dfrac{\dfrac{0.6}{1.0}}{1.6} \div 4 = 0.4 \times 100 = 40\%$

3 liters of room air (20%) are entrained for every 1 liter of oxygen (100%) providing an FIO_2 of 40%

Note: Once the air/oxygen ratio is obtained, total flow can be established by taking the total number of parts (air + oxygen) times the flowmeter setting. In this example if the flowmeter were set to 8 L/min the total flow would equal 32 L/min.

4 total parts $\times$ 8 (flowmeter setting) = 32 L/min.

Trouble Shooting Guide 12-6

Fixed Performance Oxygen Systems

Problem	Possible Causes	Corrective Actions
Inadequate gas flow rate	Leaks within the system	Check connections from gas source, flowmeter, and humidifying equipment
	Low pressure other than leaks	Change or replace gas supply
	Inadequate flow rate to meet patient demands	Increase oxygen flow rate
Incorrect FIO_2	Inadequate flow rate to meet patient demands	Increase flow rate
	Use of improper jet orifice	Replace with proper orifice size

XV. CPAP (PEP) mask

A. A soft plastic mask is used for short-term application of continuous positive airway pressure (CPAP) in the alert, cooperative, spontaneously breathing patient, averting the need for intubation.

B. When the CPAP mask is snugly fit, positive pressure remains in the airway throughout the entire respiratory cycle.
  1. A flowmeter regulates a continuous flow of gas through oxygen tubing to the mask's inlet valve.
  2. Two straps help position the mask. One strap is secured behind the patient's neck, with the other strap going over the head and above the ears to hold the mask securely over the nose and mouth.
  3. A fixed-orifice resistor provides the positive expiratory pressure (PEP) during exhalation. The resistor normally has four positions that limit the size of the orifice through which the patient exhales.
     a. The standard method is to pick the resistor setting that provides a PEP of 10–20 cmH$_2$O, and an I:E ratio of 1:3.
     b. A spring tension dial-in PEEP valve that maintains expiratory pressure above ambient can also be used. The expiratory resistance can usually be adjusted up to 15 cmH$_2$O.[5]
  4. Aspiration, pressure necrosis to the face, leaks around the mask, and increased dead space are complications of using this device.
  5. Blended gas flow from a metering device to the reservoir bag needs to be sufficient to keep it fully distended during tidal breathing.

C. Inadequate flow rates that do not meet a patient's peak inspiratory flow demands will lead to decreased CPAP levels.

XVI. Nasal CPAP

A. Administration of nasal CPAP requires short plastic nasal prongs to be fitted into an infant's nares similar to a nasal cannula.

B. A flowmeter regulates a continuous flow of gas and a fixed-resistor or PEEP device maintains expiratory pressure above ambient. They can usually be adjusted up to 15 cmH$_2$O.

C. The infant still maintains glottic control as opposed to use of an endotracheal tube. A mouth leak provides an adequate pressure pop-off.[3]

D. Refer to Trouble Shooting Guide 12-7 for information regarding CPAP devices.

XVII. Oxygen hoods

A. Oxygen hoods are small transparent plexiglass enclosures that are designed to fit over the head of an infant weighing up to 18 lbs. The hood provides an environment for delivering preblended concentrations of oxygen and aerosol.

Chapter 12: Oxygen Delivery Devices

Trouble Shooting Guide 12-7
CPAP Devices

Problem	Possible Causes	Corrective Actions
Low expiratory pressure	Leaks in the system	Check all connections, problem usually relates to the mask seal around the patient's nose and mouth
Gastric distension	Air is being pushed into the stomach by positive pressure, distending the abdomen	Notify physician, gastric decompression may be required. Repositioning of the mask may help
Expiratory time too short	Expiratory resistor setting selected is too large, the desired PEP will not be realized	Select a smaller setting on the expiratory resistor
Expiratory time too long	Expiratory resistor setting selected is too small, the desired PEP will not be realized	Select a larger setting on the expiratory resistor
Increased work of breathing	Prolonged expiratory time leads to air-trapping and difficulty breathing	Select a larger setting on the expiratory resistor

1. Gases need to be warmed as well as humidified, and care must be taken so that the gas flow does not blow directly onto the infant's face. Cold air can cause an increase in the baby's oxygen consumption.
2. A blending device prior to the gas being warmed usually administers oxygen and air.
   a. When oxygen is administered, layering occurs due to oxygen being heavier than air, resulting in higher oxygen percentages at the bottom of the hood.
   b. An oxygen analyzer probe should be placed near the infant's face to determine the actual FIO_2 delivered.
B. High gas flow rates can cause increased noise levels that may affect the infant's psychological well-being and hearing. The danger limit for noise levels is anything greater than 65 dB.[6]

XVIII. Incubators/warmers

A. An incubator is a transparent enclosure that accommodates the infant while maintaining a controlled environment (temperature, FIO_2, and humidity).
   1. Heating coils maintain temperature using a thermostat (infant servo control, ISC). Temperature monitoring is available on some models.
   2. A jet-entrainment device controls the FIO_2 by opening or closing the entrainment port. On some brands moving a red flag closes the entrainment port, which exposes the interior to 100% source gas.[2]
   3. A blower moves filtered room air over a water chamber (blow-by humidification), providing moisture to the interior. External cascade-type humidifiers are used to obtain higher humidity levels.
   4. Entry ports (portholes), which allow access to the infant, are positioned on both sides of the unit.
   5. Newer models have alarms that indicate excessive FIO_2, acute temperature changes, or power failure.
B. Radiant warmers use a servo-controlled radiant heat source to help the infant maintain temperature. An adjustable table with a mattress provides easy access and space for equipment.

XIX. Oxygen tents

A. Oxygen tents incorporate a transparent plastic canopy that encloses a patient, which allows for environmental control of oxygen concentration, temperature, humidity, and aerosol.
   1. Oxygen concentration is difficult to maintain and is usually limited to 0.5 FIO_2 at 12–15 L/min for large tents, and 8–10 L/min for smaller pediatric-size tents. This liter flow also ensures the percentage of CO_2 remains less than 1%.
      a. Any time the canopy is opened the oxygen percentage will drop drastically.
      b. High flows (flush setting on the flowmeter) will help build up the oxygen concentration quickly in the event the canopy is opened.
   2. Cooling the gas controls temperature.
      a. Several tents cool the gas electrically, similar to the air conditioner in a car. The refrigeration cycle is capable of cooling the gas to 12–21°F below room temperature.[2]
      b. Smaller tents allow oxygen to enter through a jet, entraining air and exposing the gas mixture to a chamber of melting ice, which dries and cools the gas resulting in a 6–8°F drop below room temperature.
   3. Aerosol can be provided by any of the various aerosol generators. Increased humidity levels are provided by aerosol evaporation within the tent.

Chapter 12:   Oxygen Delivery Devices

Trouble Shooting Guide 12-8

Oxygen Enclosures

Problem	Possible Causes	Corrective Actions
Inadequate gas flow	Leaks within the system	Check all components for tightness
	Leaking seals within the enclosure	Check all seals, tuck in any canopies
Decreased oxygen percent	Leaks in seals, canopies, or space between canopy and mattress	Check system for leaks
	Oxygen sensor not reading accurately	Position oxygen sensor near patient's mouth
	Possible contamination or decreased source at outlet	Replace or correct
Decreased mist or humidity	Circulation outlets obstructed	Check outlets and correct
	Improper nebulizer/humidifier function	Check for obstruction and function

B. Open top tents allow the heat to rise and escape out the top. Cooling takes place by evaporation or aerosol mist within the tent.

C. There is an increased risk of fire in the enclosed oxygen-enriched environment. Maintaining 60% relative humidity within the canopy helps to decrease this hazard.

D. Refer to Trouble Shooting Guide 12-8 for a trouble shooting oxygen enclosures.

XX. Environmental scavenging systems (ESVS)[7]

A. The advent of aerosolizing anti-infective/antiviral agents (pentamidine & ribavirin) has put the healthcare worker at risk. Exhaust from the nebulizer exposes the worker to the drug itself, along with the possibility of infection from tuberculosis.

B. Double enclosure and double vacuum scavenging systems help protect the therapist from the effects of aerosol administration.
  1. An oxygen hood containing aerosol is administered inside an oxygen tent while two high-flow vacuum units scavenge the aerosol through HEPA filters.
  2. Nebulizers with one-way valves that exit into an expiratory filter is one method of dealing with pentamidine administration.

3. Isolation booths are employed with similar results provided an exhaust fan removes aerosol through a HEPA filter.
4. Negative pressure rooms where the air is exchanged many times per hour are efficient but very expensive options.

XXI. Hyperbaric oxygen (HBO)

A. HBO therapy is a medical treatment by which oxygen is administered at greater than atmospheric pressure. Because the chamber pressure increases the volume inside the chamber decreases (Boyles Law), this increases the gas density since the number of molecules stay the same, and allows large amounts of oxygen to be administered at a lower FIO_2.

B. A hyperbaric chamber is an airtight vessel, usually made of metal, in which a patient is entirely enclosed. Oxygen or air is available at pressures from one to three atmospheres. A compressor increases the chamber pressure through a series of reducing valves.[1]
   1. Monoplace describes a chamber that encloses one person.
   2. Multiplace describes a chamber that has more space and can contain several persons.

C. The entire chamber is filled with gas.
   1. Many chambers recycle the gas by absorbing the CO_2 and removing the water vapor.
   2. Some chambers periodically purge themselves as fresh oxygen enters the system.

D. Policy for disease problems and treatment are controlled by the Underwater Medical Society (UMS).

E. HBO is a treatment mode for patients with deficient tissue oxygenation, carbon monoxide poisoning, anaerobic bacterial infections, crush injuries, radionecrosis, compromised skin grafts, cyanide poisoning, and thermal burns.
   1. During treatment 100% oxygen is administered while the pressure inside the chamber is slowly increased.
   2. The amount of pressure increase and the length of time under pressure is determined by the condition being treated.
   3. Treatment usually lasts from 1–2 hours at full pressure.

F. By breathing pure oxygen at 3 times the normal pressure (3 ATA or 29.4 psig or 44.1 psia), fifteen times as much oxygen is physically dissolved into the blood plasma. During HBO therapy the PaO_2 ranges from 800 to 2000 torr, depending on the degree of pressurization and the FIO_2.

G. Refer to Trouble Shooting Guide 12-8 for information regarding oxygen enclosures.

Chapter 12: Oxygen Delivery Devices

References

1. Burton, G. G., Hodgkin, J. E., and Ward, J. J., *Respiratory Care: A Guide to Clinical Practice,* 4th ed., Lippincott, 1997.
2. McPherson, S., *Respiratory Care Equipment,* 5th ed., Mosby, 1995.
3. Scanlon, C. L., Wilkins, R. L., and Stoller, J. K., *Egan's Fundamentals of Respiratory Therapy,* 7th ed., Mosby, 1999.
4. Spofford, B, et al., "Transtracheal Oxygen Therapy, A Guide for the Respiratory Therapist," *Respiratory Care,* Vol. 32, no. 5, 1987.
5. Mahlmeister, M. J., et al., "Positive-Expiratory-Pressure Mask Therapy: Theoretical and Practical Considerations and a Review of the Literature," *Respiratory Care,* 36, no. 11, 1991.
6. Barnes, T. A., *Respiratory Care Practice,* Year Book Medical Publishers, 1988.
7. Rau, J. L., *Respiratory Care Pharmacology,* 5th ed., Mosby, 1998.

Assessment Questions

1. Which device would you choose to administer 45% oxygen to a two-year-old?
   A. Oxygen hood
   B. Oxygen tent
   C. Incubator
   D. Nasal cannula at 6 l/min

2. What is the minimum flowrate required to flush the accumulated CO_2 out of an oxygen mask?
   A. 4 l/min
   B. 6 l/min
   C. 8 l/min
   D. 10 l/min

3. The psig associated with 3_{atm} is
   A. 0 psig
   B. 14.7 psig
   C. 29.4 psig
   D. 44.1 psig

4. The psia associated with the preceding question at 3_{atm} would be?
   A. 0 psia
   B. 14.7 psia
   C. 29.4 psia
   D. 44.1 psia

5. A COPD patient is going to be exercising on a treadmill at home. On occasion he feels dyspneic and needs oxygen. Which type of delivery system would you recommend?
   A. Liquid oxygen system (walker)
   B. Oxygen pulse dose system
   C. Oxygen concentrator
   D. Oxygen enricher

6. An asthmatic patient has an increased inspiratory flowrate of 50 L/min, and requires 28% oxygen by entrainment mask. What flowrate would you set on the flowmeter?
   A. 5
   B. 8
   C. 10
   D. 12

7. A home care patient complains that his oxygen concentrator is unable to maintain the desired flow of oxygen even though the device seems to be running fine. You would look for which of the following problems?
   I. Faulty gas outlet pressure
   II. Obstructed delivery tubing

III. Obstructed humidifier
IV. Obstructed filter

A. I only
B. I, II, III and IV
C. I and IV only
D. II and III only

8. A patient receiving 35% oxygen via entrainment mask is receiving a bed bath, and the bath blanket completely blocks the entrainment ports on the oxygen mask. Which of the following statements are true?

I. The FIO_2 will increase
II. The FIO_2 will decrease
III. The FIO_2 will remain the same
IV. Total flow will increase
V. Total flow will decrease

A. I and V only
B. I and IV only
C. II and IV only
D. III only

9. A patient that has a continuing decreased tidal volume would obtain an FIO_2 that is higher than expected if she were on which of the following oxygen delivery devices?

I. Simple oxygen mask
II. Oxygen cannula
III. Entrainment mask
IV. Partial rebreathing mask

A. I and III only
B. I, II, III and IV
C. I, II and IV only
D. III only

Chapter 13

Aerosol Generators and Humidification Equipment

I. Relative humidity

A. The ratio between water vapor actually present in a volume of gas at a given temperature (absolute humidity) compared to the water vapor that the gas would be capable of holding at a given temperature (relative humidity) is usually expressed as a percentage. Refer to Equation 13-1.

B. At normal body temperature (98.6°F, 37°C), gas that is fully saturated with water vapor will contain 44 mg/L and exert a pressure of 47 mmHg. This means that at 37°C, 100% RH = 44 mg/L or 47 mmHg.

C. It is important to note that if the humidity is expressed in mg/L, the equation is divided by 44. If the humidity is expressed in mmHg, the equation is divided by 47.

D. A humidity deficit is the difference between inspired absolute humidity and the content of water vapor in alveolar air. Humidity deficits are found by subtracting actual water vapor content from 44 mg/L (the maximum amount of water vapor held in a gas at body temperature, i.e., Body Humidity). Refer to Equation 13-2.

II. Aerosol generators

A. Nebulizers produce particulate water that becomes suspended in the air and appears as a fog or light mist.
  1. The size of the particles (in microns) that exit the nebulizer is mainly determined by the amount of baffling that occurs within the system.
  2. A baffle (sides of the container, a sphere, anything the particle comes in contact with) reduces the size of the particles that the nebulizer produces.
  3. The range of particles produced is normally between one and ten $(1-10\mu)$ microns.

B. Nebulizers are connected to a gas source and then placed in either the main stream or side stream positions in order to pick up the particles produced and deliver them to the patient.[1]

EQUATION 13-1: Calculating % Relative Humidity

$$\text{Relative humidity } (\%) = \frac{\text{Absolute humidity}}{\text{Capacity}} \times 100$$

Example 1: If the gas is holding 22 mg of water at body temperature, what is the percent R.H.?

$$\frac{22 \text{ mg/L}}{44 \text{ mg/L}} = 0.5 \times 100 = 50\% \text{ RH}$$

Example 2: If the gas is holding water vapor that exerts a pressure of 22 mmHg at body temperature, what is the percent R.H.?

$$\frac{22 \text{ mmHg}}{47 \text{ mmHg}} = 0.468 \times 100 = 47\% \text{ RH}$$

EQUATION 13-2: Calculation of Humidity Deficit

$$\text{Humidity deficit} = 44 \text{ mg/L} - \text{Actual water content}$$

Example: If the water content of the inspired gas is measured to be 22 mg/L of water, the humidity deficit that the airway needs to make up for is calculated as:

$$44 - 22 = 22 \text{ mg/L deficit}$$

1. In the main stream position the entire stream of gas (main flow and jet) enters the nebulizer. This results in a larger particle size and a greater amount of aerosol being carried out of the nebulizer.
2. In the side stream position the aerosol is carried by the jet into the main flow of gas. This results in a smaller particle size and a smaller amount of aerosol being carried out of the nebulizer.

C. Some nebulizers have provisions for heating the gas with immersion heaters as a means of increasing the moisture-carrying capabilities of the aerosol. The immersion heater thermostat can be adjustable or factory preset to maintain the temperature of the water at 55–60°C (135–145°F).

Chapter 13: Aerosol Generators and Humidification Equipment

D. Medication nebulizers contain a reservoir (medication cup) with a capacity of 5–30 ml. These devices are mostly of the disposable variety and are used for aerosolized medication treatments.
  1. Earlier models were powered by having the patient squeeze a rubber bulb creating an aerosol for inhalation.
  2. Pneumatic nebulizers use source gas to power a jet creating an aerosol, which is carried to the patient for inhalation. They are capable of nebulizing 3–5 ml of medication in 5–10 minutes using a flow of 5–10 L/min.

E. Entrainment nebulizers (large volume jet nebulizers) accommodate reservoirs ranging from 250–2500 ml. They contain provisions for heating the liquid and varying the oxygen concentration.
  1. This type of nebulizer uses a 50 psig gas source, which enters the nebulizer through a jet, resulting in a high speed stream of gas being directed to the end of a capillary tube that produces an aerosol mist.
     a. Clogged capillary tubes are a primary cause of inadequate mist being created by the nebulizer.
     b. Aerosol being produced in short rapid puffs is normally caused by liquid water pooling in the delivery tube.
  2. The nebulizer depends upon the Bernoulli effect to provide air entrainment to increase the total flow and decrease the FIO_2.
  3. Subatmospheric pressure generated by the jet causes liquid to be entrained from the reservoir and added to the gas stream. This liquid is broken up into small droplets by the high velocity gas and is carried in the gas stream as a mist.

F. The Babington hydronamic nebulizers (Hydrosphere/Solo-sphere) use pneumatic source gas and a glass sphere to generate particles in the 3–5 micron range.
  1. A siphoning system directs a thin liquid film over the surface of the glass sphere where the liquid is exposed to gas pressure.
  2. Source gas exits at supersonic speed through a small pinhead-sized orifice in the glass sphere. This high speed gas flow ruptures the liquid film at the point of contact creating aerosol particles that impact on a baffle (bead).
  3. Air entrainment occurs through ports, which can be adjusted to provide variable oxygen concentrations.

G. The small particle aerosol generator (SPAG-2) is used for administration of Virazole (Ribavirin) aerosol only, and is limited to infants with respiratory tract infections caused by the respiratory syncytial virus (RSV).
  1. The SPAG-2 is driven by compressed or blended gas, which is reduced from source pressure (50 psig) to 26 psig and then directed to two pressure-compensated flowmeters.
     a. One flowmeter directs gas to the nebulizer that generates the Virazole aerosol mist. The recommended setting is 6–10 L/min.

Trouble Shooting Guide 13-1

Aerosol Generators

Problem	Possible Causes	Corrective Actions
Absent or inadequate gas flow rate	Gas source is not suitable for flow demands of the system	Change or increase gas source flow
	Check flowmeter range setting is correct	Set flowmeter for correct range
	Nebulizer jet is clogged or obstructed	Clear jet of debris
	Leaks within the system	Ensure fittings and connections are tight
Decreased aerosol mist	Decreased water level	Fill to appropriate level with water
	Kinks/obstruction in water feed tube	Repair/replace feed tube
	Gas flow rate set too low	Increase liter flow accordingly

  b. A second flowmeter powers a drying chamber that dehumidifies the aerosol, resulting in a decrease in the particle size of the delivered mist. The recommended setting is 3–8 L/min.

 2. The mass median diameter of the aerosol particles is approximately 1.3 microns.[2]

H. Refer to Trouble Shooting Guide 13-1 for information regarding aerosol generators.

III. Metered-dose inhalers (MDI)

A. Metered cartridges provide unit doses of medication from fluorocarbon-pressurized canisters. The cartridge is powered by freon (chlorofluorocarbons CFCs) an inert gas, and contains an active bronchodilator as a suspended powder or solution. The freon propellant is in a liquid state within the canister, and is pressurized to approximately 58 psi. A full MDI contains approximately 200 puffs.

B. The standard for most MDIs is that they utilize a (Riker) valve that administers a single unit dose from the fluorocarbon-pressurized canister as the valve is depressed. Cardio-toxicity from high concentrations of inert fluorocarbons have been known to cause arrhythmias.[3]

Chapter 13: Aerosol Generators and Humidification Equipment

1. These gaseous agents are liquefied by pressure. When the product is released from the cartridge, the freon becomes gaseous, and a cloud of droplets is created.
2. The MDI must be inverted (held upside down) prior to depressing the valve, or only the freon propellant will be expelled from the cartridge instead of the medication.

C. Aerochambers, spacers, or extension/reservoir tubes may be used in combination with the inhaler.
1. As the patient actuates the MDI, the aerosolized solution enters the spacer, and is inspired by the patient using a mouthpiece.
   a. As the aerosol is delivered into the extension device, the speed of the particles slows down and a reduction of particle size occurs due to propellant evaporation.
   b. This process allows for impaction and fall out of large aerosol particles that would otherwise deposit in the mouth and pharynx and cause adverse effects. This also allows for greater penetration of particles to the smaller airways.

D. Dry powder inhalers (DPI) use single unit dose capsules mixed with a carrier substance to aid drug delivery. By placing the capsule inside the DPI, the patient initiates a breath. Inspiration activates a rotohaler (spinhaler), puncturing the capsule and sending the dry powder medication into the airways with the patient's inspiratory flowrate.

IV. Ultrasonic nebulizers

A. This is an electronic aerosol generating device where high frequency sound waves are applied to a ceramic disk (piezoelectric transducer), which vibrates at a rate that exceeds 1.35 million cycles/sec (1.3–1.4 MHz).
1. A couplant chamber is filled with liquid and has the transducer at its base. This chamber helps transfer the ultrasonic sound waves from the transducer to the liquid thereby creating an aerosol.
2. The particle size of the aerosol is determined by the frequency and has a normal size distribution of 1–10 microns with the average range being 3–5 microns.[1] The frequency, and thus the particle size, is not adjustable.

B. Due to the use of high frequency sound waves, the vibration produced may interfere with the frequency of cardiac pacemakers. These devices may be contraindicated in patients with artificial pacemakers.

C. Large volume output nebulizers used for bland mist therapy can generate volume output ranges up to 6ml/min. The volume of aerosol (density) generated is determined by the amplitude control. Small handheld output nebulizers (<10ml) for administration of medications generally generate 0.5 ml/min., with a mass median diameter ranging from 1.6 μm to 5.4 μm.

Trouble Shooting Guide 13-2

Ultrasonic Nebulizers

Problem	Possible Causes	Corrective Actions
Decreased or absent aerosol output	Low water volume in couplant chamber	Return proper fluid amount to cup
	Tubing is kinked/obstructed	Repair/replace tubing
	Float is not working on continuous feed system	Repair float or replace unit
	Power setting too low	Increase power setting on unit
Nebulizer fails to operate	Unit not plugged into power	Ensure power gets to the unit
	Fuse not operating properly	Replace with proper size fuse

D. Transportation of particles to the patient is provided by a small blower through large bore tubing at a flow rate of 30 L/min. for the large volume units.

E. Refer to Trouble Shooting Guide 13-2 for trouble shooting ultrasonic nebulizers.

V. Bubble humidifier

A. This device is designed to increase the water vapor content of a gas by allowing the gas to enter below the water surface and bubble to the top. A diffuser at the end of the tube below the water breaks the gas up into very small bubbles, increasing the relative humidity.

B. Increasing the flow rate can decrease the humidifier's efficiency in terms of output. This is due to the cooling effect of the increasing flow rate, thereby decreasing the capacity of the gas to carry water.[3]

C. Pressure relief is accomplished by either spring-tension or magnetic force that permit venting of any pressure over 2 psig. Some manufactures incorporate a pop-off device which releases pressure over 40 mmHg.

VI. Passover humidifiers

A. The passover or blow-by humidifier requires the gas to pass over the surface of the water, adding moisture to the gas by evaporation. Currently this humidifier design is used to provide humidification in isolettes.[1]

B. Efficiency is low due to the short exposure time that the gas is in contact with the water. Heating the water increases the efficiency of the unit as the capacity of the gas to carry water is greater.

VII. Cascade-type humidifiers

A. This advanced bubble humidifier combines the diffuser head and passover principles. Gas is directed through a tower into heated water and up through a grid, creating an excellent gas-water interface.[2]
B. The unit is heated and is designed to provide 100% relative humidity at body temperature, which indicates its use in patients whose upper airways are bypassed by artificial airways.
   1. Due to the cooling of hot saturated air as it moves from the humidifier to the patient, the relative humidity remains at 100%, while absolute humidity decreases due to condensation of water within the tubing.
   2. Temperatures as high as 48–50 degrees C at the humidifier outlet may need to be set in order to provide the patient with saturated gas at body temperature. Temperature normally decreases by six degrees for every foot of tubing (6°/ft).
   3. When the water level falls below the fill mark, the absolute humidity delivered to the patient falls below body humidity requirements. A metal shunt permits heat transfer from the heating element to the thermistor switch shutting the heater off when water levels are decreased.
   4. Some unit's operating temperatures are servo-controlled by means of a thermistor bead placed in the patient circuit at the proximal airway.
C. A sensing port is incorporated in the tower assembly that allows the ventilator to sense the patient's inspiratory effort when an assisted breath is needed. This tower is usually removed when weaning patients from the ventilator so as not to increase the patient's work of breathing.

VIII. Wick-type humidifiers

A. This device uses a water-absorbing substance (sponge) referred to as a wick, which is partially submerged in a liquid reservoir. This wick provides a source of water for gases to contact as they move through the humidifier.
B. The wick absorbs the water and functions similar to a passover humidifier. The gas passes over the water and next to the saturated wick, increasing the moisture content of the gas.
C. Because the wick is surrounded by a heating element or plate, the humidity of the gas is increased. Body humidity levels greater than 90% can be achieved as long as the humidifier water level is high enough to keep the wick saturated.[4]

IX. Vapor-phase humidifier

A. The vapor-phase type of humidifier incorporates a hydrophobic filter, which repels water but allows water vapor to pass through.
   1. The humidifier sits on top of the heater.
   2. A water reservoir supplies a constant 10 ml of water to the surface of the heater.
   3. Water lies below the filter and is warmed by a heating element creating water vapor.
B. Because the water is vaporized, only the water vapor diffuses through the filter free of pathogens en route to the patient.
C. Refer to Trouble Shooting Guide 13-3 for information regarding humidifiers.

Trouble Shooting Guide 13-3

Humidifiers

Problem	Possible Causes	Corrective Actions
Inadequate gas flow rate	Gas source is not suitable for flow demands of the system	Change or increase gas source flow
	Flowmeter range setting is incorrect	Set flowmeter for correct range
	Humidifier capillary tube clogged or obstructed	Clear capillary tube of debris
	Leaks within the system	Ensure fittings and connections are tight
Humidity output inadequate	This type of problem is generally related to a restricted water feed system	Check installation of the upper and lower feed lines going to humidifier
	Humidifier not designed for the job required	Pick humidifier with higher output
	Humidifier malfunctioning	Replace unit
Temperature too high or too low	Heater or servo mechanism monitoring heater is malfunctioning	Replace with other unit, these problems generally need to be corrected by the manufacturer

Chapter 13: Aerosol Generators and Humidification Equipment

X. Heat-moisture exchangers (HME)

A. Heat-moisture exchangers are occasionally connected in the ventilator circuit in place of a humidifier to provide moisture to the inspired gas. These exchangers contain a hygroscopic plastic foam material that is porous and absorbs water.
  1. The HME is installed between the endotracheal or tracheostomy tube and the patient-Y of the ventilator circuit, thus becoming part of the rebreathed volume.
  2. During exhalation, the moisture and heat from the patient's respiratory tract condenses on the HME's sponge-like (hygroscopic) material.
     a. This sponge-like material causes cooling of the exhaled gas, which causes condensation of the water molecules.
     b. Hygroscopic fibers absorb the water molecules from the exhaled gas.
     c. On inspiration, warm, dry gas enters the sponge-like material, causing the hygroscopically bound water molecules to be released into the inspired air.
  3. Many of the HMEs provide a relative humidity of 50–80% at body temperature, although problems have occurred with their use in patients having excessive secretions.[5]
  4. They are not designed to be used in combination with humidifiers or nebulizers.
     a. If the moisture provided by the HME is inadequate, then the device needs to be replaced by a conventional heated humidifier.
     b. The HME is designed for single patient use, and needs to be changed every 24 hours.
B. HMEs mimic the heating and humidifying actions of the upper airway. They are referred to as artificial noses or hygroscopic condenser humidifiers (HCH).
C. Should the filter material become less patent, it will cause the ventilator to increase its delivery pressure in order to compensate for the greater resistance.
D. Refer to Trouble Shooting Guide 13-4 for trouble shooting heat moisture exchangers.

XI. Heated tubes

A. The inspiratory breathing tube of a ventilator circuit is heated and contains a thermistor bead that is located at the proximal airway. Gas leaves the humidifier at near body temperature and that temperature is maintained throughout the circuit en route to the patient.
  1. The temperature sensed at the thermistor bead is servo-controlled to the wire-heating elements so the delivered gas for the patient maintains its preset temperature.
  2. The key to heated tubes is that they allow only a 1–2°C decrease in temperature from the humidifier to the patient.
B. Because the gas temperature remains the same, condensate is appreciably eliminated within the ventilator circuit.

Trouble Shooting Guide 13-4

Heat Moisture Exchangers

Problem	Possible Causes	Corrective Actions
Increased peak airway pressure	Obstruction to airflow	Replace moisture exchanger
Increased work of breathing	Obstruction to airflow	Replace moisture exchanger
Thickening secretions	Moisture exchanger not providing enough humidification to manage patient secretions	Replace moisture exchanger with heated humidifier

References

1. McPherson, S., *Respiratory Care Equipment*, 5th ed., Mosby, 1995.
2. SPAG-2 Instruction Manual, ICN Pharmaceuticals, Inc., 1986.
3. Burton, G. G., Hodgkin, J. E., and Ward, J. J., *Respiratory Care: A Guide to Clinical Practice*, 4th ed., Lippincott, 1997.
4. Cairo, J. M., and Pilbeam, S. P., *Mosby's Respiratory Care Equipment*, 7th ed., Mosby, 1999.
5. Branson, R. D., and Hurst, J. M., "Laboratory Evaluation of Moisture Output of Seven Airway Heat and Moisture Exchangers," *Respiratory Care*, 1987.

Assessment Questions

1. The amount of water existing in normal alveolar gas is:

    A. 47 mg/L
    B. 44 mg/L
    C. 37 mg/L
    D. 0.8 mg/L

2. The humidification device that collects exhaled heat and moisture and reuses it to warm and humidify the inspired air is referred to as a:

    A. Bubble humidifier
    B. Wick humidifier
    C. Hygroscopic humidifier
    D. Ultrasonic humidifier

3. Heat moisture exchangers are contraindicated on infants where humidification is going to be required for:

    A. 8 hours
    B. Less than 24 hours
    C. Less than three days
    D. More than five days

Chapter 13: Aerosol Generators and Humidification Equipment 207

4. The type of breath-triggered device utilizing single-unit-dose capsules to deliver medication to the airways is a:
   A. SPAG
   B. MDI
   C. Small-volume USN
   D. Dry powder inhaler

5. In preparation for a bronchoscopy procedure, you receive an order to nebulize lidocaine. You would choose a nebulizer that is capable of generating particles in the range of:
   A. > than 10 μ
   B. 8 to 10μ
   C. 5 to 8 μ
   D. < than 3μ

6. In preparing to administer an albuterol treatment to a severely asthmatic patient, you would chose a nebulizer that is capable of generating particles in the range of:
   A. > that 10μ
   B. 8 to 10μ
   C. 5 to 8μ
   D. < than 3μ

7. The calculated humidity deficit while breathing room air with a RH of 22 mg/L would be:
   A. 40%
   B. 50%
   C. 60%
   D. 70%

8. Humidifiers operate on the basis of:
   A. Venturi's principle
   B. Bernoulli's principle
   C. Pitot's principle
   D. Evaporation

9. The number one priority when administering aerosol with an MDI is:
   A. Patient instruction
   B. Care and cleaning of the MDI
   C. Using a spacer
   D. Breathing pattern

Chapter 14

Respiratory Support Equipment

I. Safety systems

A. Safety systems are really connectors designed to prevent misconnection between gases and the different delivery systems.

B. The American Standard Safety System prevents accidental connection of a reducing valve or regulator to the incorrect cylinder.
   1. This standard is used for indexing all large cylinder outlet valves.
   2. Individual gas lines and medical gas administering equipment use this standard when the gas pressures are 200 psig or greater.

C. The Diameter Index Safety System (DISS) is used in indexing medical gas piping systems (including quick-disconnects) and medical gas administering equipment, using pressures of 200 psig or less.

D. Pin Index Safety System (PISS) is for use on small cylinders (up to size "E") with post-type valve or flush valve stems.[1] The system incorporates a yoke connection with protruding pins that matches to holes located in the post-type cylinder valve stem. Refer to Table 14-1.

E. All main cylinder valve stems on cylinders above size "E" contain a fusible plug constructed of a low-melting-point material (Woods metal). Should the temperature reach 170.6°F (77°C) the plug will melt, allowing the cylinder gas to vent off to the atmosphere. The stem also employs a copper frangible disk that bursts if gas pressure reaches 3360 psig, and allows gas to escape to the atmosphere.

II. Regulator/reducing valve

A. A regulator controls both pressure and flow. Operating on the principle of spring tension versus gas pressure, it reduces cylinder pressure to workable levels and maintains a constant flow rate regardless of changes in cylinder pressure.[2]

Chapter 14: Respiratory Support Equipment

TABLE 14-1 Pin Index Connections

Gas	Pin Connections
Ethylene	1–3
Medical Air	1–5
Oxygen/Carbon Dioxide >7%	1–6
Oxygen/Helium <80%	2–4
Oxygen	2–5
Carbon Dioxide/Oxygen <7%	2–6
Nitrous Oxide	3–5
Cyclopropane	3–6
Helium/Oxygen >80%	4–6

1. A multiple stage pressure regulator reduces pressure in two or three steps instead of one. The number of stages can be determined by the number of spring tension pop-offs (pressure-relief valves). The multiple stage regulator is used when greater accuracy is required than can be obtained with a single stage regulator.
2. Preset-regulators have their spring tension set at the factory. The pressure chamber is supplied with a spring tension pressure pop-off that is usually set 50% higher than the regulator's output (working pressure).

B. Adjustable pressure regulators allow for adjustment of the spring tension, which varies the pressure within the regulator.
   1. The Bourdon gauge operates by having a fixed orifice and being able to vary the pressure gradient across that orifice, which determines the flow rate of the gas.
   2. The face-plate has a scale that indicates flow in L/min even though the regulator is measuring pressure in the reducing chamber.

C. Refer to Trouble Shooting Guide 14-1 regarding regulators.

III. Flowmeters

A. Flowmeters measure the flow rate of gas. They attach to a gas outlet and allow the adjustment and regulation of gas flow. Some flowmeters will read accurately in the presence of back pressure (pressure compensated) and some will not (uncompensated).

Trouble Shooting Guide 14-1

Regulators

Problem	Possible Causes	Corrective Actions
Regulator does not fit on the O_2 cylinder	Safety system prevents regulators from attaching to gas cylinders they are not calibrated for	Switch to a DISS connection for that regulator/cylinder system
Leaks	Diaphragm-sealing gaskets, "O" rings, washers, springs wear out	Replace worn-out components
	Leaky high pressure threaded connections	Use teflon-type tape at all connections

1. The Bourdon flowmeter is actually a pressure gauge but employs a face-plate that is calibrated to read flow rate.
   a. When the Bourdon device is subjected to back pressure due to restricted gas flow, the gauge will always read greater than the actual flow delivered (uncompensated).
   b. The unit is not influenced by gravity so its major advantage is that it is capable of working in any position.
2. Thorpe tubes consist of a transparent tapered tube containing a spherical float (metal ball-bearing) that moves up and down inside the tube in response to gas flow; thus indicating flow rate.
   a. Kinetic flowmeters are shaped and function the same as Thorpe tubes, except they contain a plunger instead of a spherical float.
   b. Gas flow is read on a calibrated scale from 0–15 L/min plus flush. The "flush" setting can provide flow rates in the range of 60–120 L/min.
   c. Recently flowmeters have been introduced that are capable of providing flows in the 0.2–2 L/min range, and the 0–70 L/min range.
   d. Uncompensated Thorpe tubes are calibrated at atmospheric pressure without restriction or back pressure. In the presence of a restriction or back pressure, flow will read lower than the actual flow rate delivered to the patient.
   e. Compensated Thorpe tubes place the needle valve downstream of the flow meter. The flow tube is always exposed to pipeline pressure so it is calibrated against a 50 psig source gas to ensure that the proper flow rate will be accurately displayed in the face of a restriction or back pressure.

Chapter 14: Respiratory Support Equipment

      f. Thorpe tubes are influenced by gravity and only display flow rate accurately when placed in the upright position.

B. The following air-entrainment equations are determined by knowing the numerical values of two of the three components: oxygen flow rate, air flow rate, and FIO_2.
  1. When the oxygen and air flow rates are known, the FIO_2 can be computed. Refer to Equation 14-1.
  2. When the FIO_2 and oxygen flow rate is known, the total flow can be calculated. Refer to Equation 14-2.

EQUATION 14-1: **Calculating FIO_2**

$$FIO_2 = \frac{O_2 \text{ flow} + (0.2 \times \text{air flow})}{\text{Total flow rate}}$$

Example: An oxygen flowmeter is running at 3 L/min and an air flowmeter is running at 7 L/min. What is the FIO_2? (7 L air + 3 L oxygen = 10 L/min Total Flow)

Step 1: $FIO_2 = \dfrac{3 + (0.2 \times 7)}{10}$

Step 2: $FIO_2 = \dfrac{3 + 1.4}{10} = \dfrac{4.4}{10} = 0.44$

Note: Liters of 100% O_2 + Liters of 21% O_2 = Total flow at some FIO_2 between 0.21 and 1.0.

EQUATION 14-2: **Calculating Total Flow**

$$\text{Total Flow} = \frac{O_2 \text{ flow} \times 0.8}{FIO_2 - 0.2}$$

Example: What is the total flow rate available when oxygen flow is 2.5 L/min. and the FIO_2 is 0.4?

$$\text{Total Flow} = \frac{2.5 \times 0.8}{0.4 - 0.2} = \frac{2}{0.2} = 10 \text{ L/min}$$

3. When the total flow and FIO_2 are known, the oxygen flow rate can be determined. Refer to Equation 14-3.
C. Computation of gas flow rates using more than one flowmeter with more than one oxygen percentage requires computing total flow for each oxygen percentage. Refer to Equation 12-3 for computing total flow rate. Refer to Equation 14-4 and 14-5 for examples.
D. When computing flow rates using an oxygen flowmeter with oxygen and helium gas mixtures, a correction factor must be applied, because the flowmeters are calibrated for oxygen rather than oxygen and helium, which is less dense. Refer to Equation 14-6.
   1. When using a 80%–20% mixture of helium and oxygen the computing factor is 1.8. Take this factor times the flowmeter reading to determine the actual flow rate.
   2. When using a 70%–30% mixture of helium and oxygen the computing factor is 1.6. Take this factor times the flowmeter reading to determine the actual flow rate.
E. Refer to Trouble Shooting Guide 14-2 for information regarding flowmeters.

EQUATION 14-3: Calculating Oxygen Flow Rate

$$O_2 \text{ flow} = \frac{\text{Total Flow} \times (FIO_2 - 0.2)}{0.8}$$

Example: What flow rates must be set on oxygen and air flowmeters in order to deliver 0.6 FIO_2 with a total flow of 10 L/min?

Step 1: To determine flow for O_2 flowmeter

$$O_2 \text{ Flow} = \frac{10 \times (0.6 - 0.2)}{0.8}$$

$$= \frac{10 \times 0.4}{0.8} = \frac{4.0}{0.8} = 5 \text{ L of } O_2$$

Step 2: To determine flow for air flowmeter

Total Flow − O_2 Flow = Air Flow

10 L/min − 5 L/min = 5 L/min

Note: Table 12-4 identifies a 1:1 ratio of oxygen to air for a 0.6 FIO_2.

Chapter 14: Respiratory Support Equipment

EQUATION 14-4: Calculating Gas Flow Rates with Two Flowmeters

$$FIO_2 = \frac{(FIO_2 \, A)(Flow \, A) + (FIO_2 \, B)(Flow \, B)}{Flow \, A + Flow \, B}$$

Example: In order to maintain a fairly precise O_2 percentage in a console tent, two flowmeters are used together. One flowmeter is set at 12 L/min through a nebulizer on the 60% setting. The second flowmeter is set at 10 L/min through a nebulizer entraining air at the 40% setting. What is the FIO_2 delivered inside the tent?

Step 1: Compute total flow for each nebulizer
(Refer to Equation 12-3: Air/Oxygen Ratio)

Flowmeter A: 60% at 12 L/min = 24 L/min Total flow

Flowmeter B: 40% at 10 L/min = 40 L/min Total flow

Total flow of both flowmeters (24 + 40) = 64 L/min

Step 2: Compute combined FIO_2

$$FIO_2 = \frac{(0.6)(24) + (0.4)(40)}{64}$$

$$FIO_2 = \frac{14.4 + 16}{64}$$

$$FIO_2 = \frac{30.4}{64} = 48\%$$

IV. Flow restrictors

A. The commercial name for the most basic flowmeter is the flow restrictor. Flow restrictors provide a set flow of oxygen, eliminating the need for a flowmeter. They are normally used in a patient's home as an alternative to Thorpe tubes and Bourdon gauges. The two types are the fixed restrictor, and the adjustable restrictor.
  1. The fixed restrictor contains a fixed orifice insert that determines the resistance and thus the oxygen flow rate that is delivered to the patient.
     a. Set-sized restrictors are available ranging from 1/4 L/min to 6 L/min. In order to change the oxygen flow rate the restrictor must be changed.[3]
     b. Once a size is selected, no change occurs in flow because no moving parts or adjustments are involved.

EQUATION 14-5: Shortcut Equation to Determine FIO_2 from Two Flowmeters

$$FIO_2 \text{ Combined} = \frac{(FIO_2 \text{ A} + FIO_2 \text{ B})}{2} - (\text{high flow} - \text{low flow})$$

Example: Utilizing the same data given in Equation 14-4, calculate the new FIO_2.

$$\frac{0.6 + 0.4}{2} - (12 - 10) \quad 50 - 2 = 48\%$$

EQUATION 14-6: Calculating Flow Rate of Helium/Oxygen Mixtures[2]

For 80% Helium, 20% Oxygen Mixture

Example: If the flowmeter is reading 10 L/min, the actual flow rate would be:

$$10 \times 1.8 \text{ or } 18 \text{ L/min}$$

For 70% Helium, 30% Oxygen Mixture

Example: If the flowmeter is reading 10 L/min, the actual flow rate would be:

$$10 \times 1.6 \text{ or } 16 \text{ L/min}$$

---

      c. The flow restrictor needs to be checked periodically by a calibration flowmeter because there is no way to obtain a reading of the flow rate.

  2. The variable or adjustable restrictor employs several orifices and restrictions. The restrictor rotates to different orifice sizes thereby providing variable oxygen flow rates.

B. Some restrictors are limited to 50 psig source pressure. Other rotary restrictors are manufactured to operate at 20 psig in order to accommodate the liquid reservoir systems in the home. The most common usage of rotary restrictors are the various oxygen concentrators.

Chapter 14: Respiratory Support Equipment

Trouble Shooting Guide 14-2

Flowmeters

Problem	Possible Causes	Corrective Actions
Pressure compensated flowmeter will not indicate actual flow	Source gas pressure is not being maintained at 50 PSI Flowmeter is adjusted to deliver a higher flow than available from current gas source	Reestablish source gas pressure Change flowmeter or reestablish source gas pressure
Leaks	Diaphragm-sealing gaskets, "O" rings, washers, springs wear out Leaky high pressure threaded connections	Replace worn components Use teflon-type tape at all connections
Erratic flow rate	Flowmeter out of calibration Diaphragm-sealing gaskets, "O" rings, washers, springs wear out	Check actual flow with calibration flowmeter Replace worn components

V. Blenders/Controllers

A. Air-oxygen blenders permit the air/oxygen gas mixture to be directly selected by a control knob (proportioning valve). As one side is proportionately opened, the other side is proportionately closed. By changing the openings through which each gas has to pass, variable oxygen concentrations can be delivered.
   1. Step-down regulators are incorporated within the blender to regulate the output pressure for both air and oxygen. By the time the gases reach the proportioning valve, the pressures of the two incoming gases need to be equal.
   2. Most controllers have a means of providing gas flow to the patient in spite of a loss of source pressure in one of the lines.
      a. The total flow rate may be reduced when one source line is not operational, although flow will continue through the remaining functioning line.
      b. Many controllers contain audible alarm systems that warn of pressure fluctuations in a line, or are activated by low pressure in either the O_2 or compressed air lines.

3. Most blenders need substantial pressure differences between oxygen and air before changing the gas concentration. The fractional concentration of delivered oxygen (FDO_2) may fluctuate in some units when line pressure drops below 50 psig.
B. As long as pipeline pressures remain constant, the typical maximum flow rate is about 120 L/min on the 60% setting. Inadequate maximum flow output can occur when the blender is powering a ventilator and the FIO_2 is approaching either 0.21 or 1.0. Generally speaking, high-flow blenders become more inaccurate at low flows and low-flow blenders become more inaccurate at high flows.
C. At times it is essential to be able to measure the individual flow rates of the components of a gas mixture. Total gas flow and the individual component concentrations can be calculated whenever blenders or entrainment systems are employed.[2] Refer to Equations 12-3, 14-1, 14-2, and 14-3.
D. Pulse dose/demand oxygen controllers are electronically controlled devices that conserve oxygen by delivering it only during inspiration. They are designed to work with the nasal cannula, and sense the subambient pressure created when the patient inhales.
 1. Some units are designed to work with yoke systems (E cylinder), some with large tanks, and some work with liquid systems. All of them can be operated by battery for portability.
 2. As the patient inspires, a sensitive pressure transducer inside the device recognizes subambient pressure. This subambient pressure generates an electrical signal that is sent from the pressure transducer, which sends it on to a solenoid valve. The valve opens and oxygen is dosed to the patient at the predetermined liter flow. When the patient exhales the sensor no longer detects subambient pressure, eliminating the electrical signal, and the solenoid valve closes, stopping the flow of oxygen to the patient.
 3. Oxygen flow is determined by operator setting on the device. Because it is designed for a cannula, flow usually limits at 6 L/min. By increasing or decreasing the flow, the operator is actually determining how long the solenoid valve remains open. Therefore, the volume of oxygen delivered to the patient is determined only by the amount of time the solenoid valve stays open (flow per time).
 4. If the patient's respiratory rate increases, the patient receives more oxygen. When this occurs it is referred to as a "rate response" type of oxygen delivery [4]
E. Refer to Trouble Shooting Guide 14-3 for information regarding blending and controlling devices.

VI. Manometers and gauges

A. Aneroid-type or mercurial-type pressure gauges display generated positive (+) and negative (−) pressures. The pressure recorded by a manometer or gauge is a reflection of gas pressure in the system (system pressure).

Chapter 14: Respiratory Support Equipment

Trouble Shooting Guide 14-3

Blending and Controlling Devices

Problem	Possible Causes	Corrective Actions
Regulator does not fit on the O_2 cylinder	Safety system prevents attaching to source gas	Switch to a DISS connection or quick-disconnect for proper attachment
Leaks	Diaphragm-sealing gaskets, "O" rings, washers, springs wear out	Replace worn components
	Leaky high pressure threaded connections	Use teflon-type tape at all connections
	High pressure hoses and their fittings on the blender outlet or source outlet	Check hoses and fittings
Inaccurate oxygen percentage	Proportioning valve out of alignment	Replace blender/controller
	Oxygen analyzer not analyzing correctly	Repeat procedure with different unit

1. Gauge pressure (psig) is 14.7 lb. and is referenced to atmospheric pressure (pisa) and is not displayed on the gauge (1 psig = psi recorded + 14.7).
2. The face-plate on the manometer can be incremented in psig, cmH_2O, or mmHg. Refer to Table 14-2.
3. The manometer is calibrated so atmospheric pressure displays as zero on the scale face.

B. The sphygmomanometer consists of a rubber bag inside a cloth cuff that is inflated with air by squeezing a rubber bulb. As the bag is inflated, the force that blood exerts on the arterial wall is measured on the pressure gauge.
   1. The cuff is wrapped around the upper arm, compressing the vessels by the air pressure in the bag. The manometer displays the changes in pressure that are directly proportional to the expansion and contraction of the rubber diaphragm located inside the cuff.
   2. As the cuff is deflated, arterial blood flows past the cuff, arterial pressure exceeds cuff pressure, and results in visual display on the manometer.

TABLE 14-2: Pressure Conversion Factors

psia = 14.7 lb.
1 psi = 70 cmH$_2$O
1 mmHg = 1.36 cmH$_2$O
1 inHg = 25.4 mmHg
1 cmH$_2$O pressure = 0.74 mmHg
1 cmH$_2$O pressure = 0.1 kPa

3. The manometer displays the pressure (mmHg) within the inflated cuff in proportion to the contraction and expansion of a simple diaphragm within the pressure gauge.

VII. Vacuum systems

A. A centrally located rotary vane pump provides a wall vacuum source and is monitored by a vacuum gauge calibrated in mmHg. Each wall outlet is connected to this electrically powered pump. The pump provides a continuous even flow of negative pressure without pulsation in the line. The operating range of negative pressure generated is approximately 600 mmHg.

B. Hospital compressors create up to −600 mmHg. of subambient pressure, which is reduced to clinically acceptable levels (−20 to −120 mmHg.) by in-line single-stage reducing valves.

   1. A suction regulator with the vacuum gauge is attached to the wall outlet using DISS connections.
   2. A 2-liter reservoir container is part of the regulating system that allows for a rapid buildup of negative pressure and collects the material suctioned by the catheter.
   3. Negative pressure is exerted through a suction catheter to assist in removal of secretions. The maximum pressure that can be exerted through the system is typically −200 mmHg. Refer to Table 14-3.
   4. Insert the catheter tip under water and occlude the thumb port to determine maximum pressure.
   5. Damage to the tracheal mucosa has been reported using negative pressures in excess of −120 mmHg.[5]

Chapter 14: Respiratory Support Equipment

TABLE 14-3: Optimal Pressure Range for Suction Catheters

Patient	Pressure Range
Adults	−100 to −120 mmHg
Pediatrics	−50 to −80 mmHg
Neonates	−40 to −50 mmHg

C. Portable compressor pumps generate negative pressure and contain a collection bottle for secretions.
   1. Negative pressure is generated by a diaphragm-type compressor calibrated in mmHg.
   2. Pressure buildup within the collection jar and generated pressures are not as high as with wall systems.
D. Refer to Trouble Shooting Guide 14-4 for information regarding vacuum systems.

Trouble Shooting Guide 14-4

Vacuum Systems

Problem	Possible Causes	Corrective Actions
Inability to suction secretions from the airway	Collection reservoir is full	Empty reservoir
	Suction tubing is kinked or disconnected	Reconnect or repair tubing system
	Secretions are plugged in suction catheter	Remove obstruction
Decreased pressure	Leaks in vacuum line or suction trap	Check connections
	Leaks in tubing system	Check tubing system
	Faulty suction regulator	Replace regulator
Fails to operate	Faulty suction motor	Check regulator motor Repair/replace

VIII. Compressors

A. A compressor is used to power other respiratory care devices by providing a source of air. The compressor is motor driven and moves a piston, rotary fan, or diaphragm that takes in ambient air. The air is filtered, the gas molecules are compressed to a preset pressure level, and the gas is stored in an accumulator for use.

B. A piston moves up and down within a cylinder drawing in room air. The piston compressor is able to generate high flows and high pressures (for driving ventilators and respirators).
  1. The piston-type compressor is the main source of air for hospital piping systems and oxygen concentrators.
  2. These compressors incorporate outflow filters to trap any debris that is created as the piston rings wear to prevent foreign material getting into the main piping lines.
     a. Inflow and outflow filters need to be changed periodically as recommended by the manufacturer.
     b. Lubrication of the compressor with oil is to be avoided because it may enter the piping system.[3]
  3. As ambient air is compressed, the gas molecules move closer together, generating heat. The high pressure gas passes through the regulator and into the hospital piping system. The gas cools and the moisture in the air condenses, leaving water in the system.
     a. Refrigerated dryers remove heat and extract excess water from the compressed gas as it leaves the compressor.
     b. A regulator maintains pipeline pressure at a range of 50–55 psig.

C. The diaphragm compressor functions similar to the piston compressor (diaphragm moves up and down within a cylinder) but is not able to generate the same high pressure and flow capabilities.
  1. The diaphragm movement is quieter and produces less vibration than the piston type.
  2. They are the primary source of air for powering large volume pneumatic nebulizers, medication nebulizers, and some portable IPPB units.
  3. Some small oil-free compressors with outputs of 7–10 L/min are used to power handheld nebulizer units within the home.
     a. Some have internal batteries allowing approximately 60 total minutes of treatment time.
     b. There are units that contain DC adaptors to allow for treatments to be taken while in a vehicle. The unit plugs into a cigarette lighter for its DC power.

D. The rotary compressor uses a fan to draw gas into the system. The air then exits out the exhaust port like a fan blows air.

Trouble Shooting Guide 14-5

Compressors

Problem	Possible Causes	Corrective Actions
Low power output	Inlet filter dirty and obstructing flow	Clean/replace filter
	Obstruction within tubing system	Clear/replace tubing
Fails to operate	Malfunction in power cord/electric outlet	Repair/replace
	Broken fuse	Replace fuse
	Ruptured diaphragm	Send for repair/replace unit
Leaks	Tubing system and high pressure connections	Check tubing system and connections

1. Small rotary compressors power portable IPPB units and some medication nebulizers in the home.
2. Large rotary compressors are the primary source of power for many volume ventilators.

E. Refer to Trouble Shooting Guide 14-5 for information regarding compressors.

IX. Pleural drainage devices

A. Chest tubes evacuate air or fluid from the pleural cavity to reexpand the lung. Chest tube sizes range from 12–42 French.
  1. A small size chest tube (28–32) that is removing air from the pleural space is normally inserted into the second interspace in the midclavicular line of the anterior chest.
  2. A large size chest tube (34–40) that is draining fluid from the pleural space is typically placed between the fifth and sixth interspace in the midaxillary line.[6]
  3. Should the pleural space contain both air and fluid you may expect to see tubes placed at both sites.

B. The viscosity of the material being evacuated determines the size of the chest tubes. Thin liquid or air is easily drained through a 28–32 French tube, while thick pus or clotted blood needs a 34–40 French tube.

C. The tubes are not to be clamped except in emergency situations, and then only for brief periods of time. The tubes are never clamped if the patient is suspected of having an air leak within the lung.
D. Chest drainage involves the use of a vacuum system that provides for the removal of air or fluid from the chest. Wall suction incorporates an electrically driven vacuum pump that is capable of bringing the suction levels down to -40 cmH$_2$O or less in order to overcome resistance and allow for proper drainage.
   1. Common suctioning pressures in the chest are generally in the 15–20 cmH$_2$O range. The idea is to remove air/fluid swiftly enough to maintain normal pleural pressures and reexpand the lung.
   2. The collection unit must always be placed below the patient's chest.
   3. The one-bottle system consists of an underwater seal with the stem submerged to allow air to leave but not to enter (unidirectional system).
      a. A vented stopper prevents pressure buildup in the bottle. This system allows pressure to equalize between the air space of the bottle and the atmosphere.
      b. The one-bottle system is appropriate for the removal of air but not fluid. As the fluid level rises within the system resistance is created, impeding further drainage.
   4. The two-bottle system permits collection of fluid in the first bottle while the second bottle contains the water seal.
      a. A one-way valve prevents air from entering the pleural cavity.
      b. Fluids can be accurately measured in an evacuation reservoir designed for collection.
   5. The three-bottle system requires adding a vacuum control bottle to regulate the amount of suction applied to the system.
      a. If large amounts of air are exiting the patient's lung into the pleural space, then the amount of air removed from the lung is not sufficient to establish normal pleural pressure, which is needed to reexpand the lung.
      b. Suction control quickens the time needed to reexpand the lung and aids in the evacuation of air and fluid.
   6. One-piece plastic-molded evacuation systems like the Pleur-Evac units contain intercompartmental reservoirs and valves that function exactly like the three-bottle system.
      a. They employ a collecting chamber that provides an accurate means of measuring the rate of fluid drainage from the chest.
      b. A suction regulator maintains a negative intrapleural pressure and is adjusted so it just bubbles slightly.
      c. Bubbling during exhalation indicates the patient has an air leak from the lung into the intrapleural space.
E. The tubing system transports fluid or air to the evacuation chamber.

Chapter 14: Respiratory Support Equipment

1. If there is no fluid level movement within the tube, the indications are generally a plugged or kinked chest tube, a leak somewhere, or an apneic patient. Fluid movement in the tube is normal and expected.
2. Mediastinal tubes may be placed in addition to or instead of chest tubes following mediastinal injuries or surgery.
3. It is common to have more than one tube inserted.
   a. One tube for air and one for fluid.
   b. Two or more fluid tubes for an active bleed.

F. Chest tubes can be considered for removal once drainage from the tube is less than 150ml/24 hours. If the tube was used for pneumothorax, the lung should be fully expanded, and free of any air leak for the previous 24 hours. In some cases the tube is clamped for several hours to ensure patient stability prior to removal.[7]

X. Bronchoscope

A. The bronchoscope allows the trachea and major bronchi to be visualized directly, usually to investigate an abnormality observed on X-ray. The flexible fiberoptic bronchoscope (FFB) is the standard when it comes to bronchoscopes. It will usually enter most third and fourth level bronchi.
   1. The FFB is able to bend from 96–160 degrees from the axial plane, providing excellent visualization. A high-powered light source provides illumination for inspection.
      a. Adult scope (5.0 mm OD)/6.0 mm OD for lavage.
      b. Pediatric scope (3.5 mm OD).
   2. The FFB contains four ports: two light channels to provide illumination, a viewing channel to look through, and an open channel that accommodates a biopsy forceps, cytology brush, or suction for aspiration of secretions.
      a. The grasping forceps employs various bite sizes to obtain tissue for culture or foreign body removal.
      b. The viewing channel allows for a separate head to be inserted so others may observe the procedure.
      c. Bronchoalveolar lavage (BAL) may be performed during the bronchoscopy procedure by the injection of sterile fluid into the lung.

B. The rigid bronchoscope is preferable for large foreign body aspiration and for YAG (yttrium, aluminum, garnet) laser (light amplification by stimulated emission of radiation) therapy.
   1. The YAG laser incorporates quartz monofilaments (lenses and mirrors) that permit a laser beam to emit energy for debulking large airway tumors. These tumors infringe on the airway wall causing obstruction.

2. The laser light has a wide range of intensities and does not diffuse as ordinary light sources do. Small blood vessels can be coagulated at low-power settings, while tissue can be cut or vaporized on high-power settings.

XI. Stethoscope

A. The acoustic stethoscope emphasizes the frequency of sounds heard during auscultation. It allows the sounds produced by the body to be clearly heard by filtering out extraneous noise.

B. The stethoscope components consist of short (10–12 inches long) thick rubber tubes, ear pieces, and a reversible end-piece for listening to different frequencies of sound.

C. The diaphragm is best used for the high frequencies associated with breath sounds. The bell detects a broad spectrum of sounds and is typically used to evaluate the lower sound frequencies produced by the heart.[8]

XII. Chest physical therapy devices

A. Percussors are mechanical devices used to loosen tracheobronchial secretions. The mechanical percussor incorporates a flexible drive cable with a variable speed control (rheostat or belt placement) and a padded cup-shaped head. An electric motor drives the shaft up and down against the chest, creating percussion.
   1. The shaft speed is variable with an output range of 20–60 cps (cycles per second), which creates the rhythmic force on the chest. The speed control is typically set at 20–30 cps for normal-sized patients.
   2. The cuff is adequately padded to eliminate irritation and discomfort.
      a. Extra padding, like thick towels and blankets, needs to be used with caution, as they absorb the energy rather than transmit it to the lung field.
      b. Mechanical percussors are normally contraindicated in fragile or brittle-boned patients in order to avoid trauma to soft tissues and chest wall.
   3. Recently pneumatic percussors have become available for use in neonates, infants, and children.
      a. These devices require a 45–55 psig wall source for power, and consist of a high-pressure hose, a power unit, and a percussor head.
      b. Controls are available on the power unit to adjust the frequency and force of percussion.

B. Mechanical vibrators incorporate an electric motor to provide uniform vibration at various speeds (frequency in excess of 200 vibrations per second) via a rheostat control.
   1. The practitioner provides perpendicular and horizontal force to the chest wall during exhalation with the applicator head (cupped pad).

Chapter 14: Respiratory Support Equipment 225

2. Controls are available for adjusting the frequency and intensity of the vibration.
3. High frequency vibration is most efficient for the peripheral areas of the lung, while low frequency vibration is most effective for the larger upper airways of the lung.

C. Flutter valve therapy applies a rapidly oscillating positive expiratory pressure that acts as a mechanical split to keep the airway open. The patient inspires to maximum volume and exhales against a weighted ball valve creating the positive pressure. The rapid oscillating pressure from the vibrating ball encourages coughing that facilitates secretion removal.[9]

XIII. Incentive breathing exercisers

A. These exercisers require a patient to perform a SMI (sustained maximal inspiration) maneuver, thereby increasing their inspired volume of air. Indicators provide immediate feedback to the patient on how much air is being inspired with each breath. This feedback rewards the patient for their achievement and provides motivation for continued performance.

B. Flow incentive spirometers direct a float (usually a ball) to rise and remain suspended in the spirometer housing for a sustained time period.
 1. Flow spirometers require a minimum inspiratory flow rate to keep the indicator elevated.
    a. The patient is encouraged to keep the balls suspended as long as possible.
    b. Slow inspirations do not generate sufficient flow to raise the float.
    c. Patients with low peak inspiratory flow rates may achieve a maximum inspiration without ever elevating the indicator.
    d. Some spirometers incorporate a controlled leak in order to require that the patient maintain the indicator in the elevated position for as long as possible.
 2. Normal operating range is 600–900 ml/sec of inspiratory flow to suspend the float.
    a. To calculate inspiratory capacity ml/sec must be converted to ml.
    b. The number of seconds the balls are suspended times the flow per second calculates inspired volume.
    c. If the balls are suspended for 3 sec. at 500 ml/sec.

    $$500 \text{ ml/sec} \times 3 \text{ sec.} = 1{,}500 \text{ ml inspiratory capacity}$$

 3. In order to accurately indicate the patient's effort, most flow incentive spirometers need to remain in the upright position.
 4. Some manufacturers provide a nebulizer for adding medicated aerosol to the patient's inspired flow.

C. Volume incentive spirometers allow the patient to inhale until a preset volume of gas is inspired. Some exercisers measure the intake of air electronically and record the result visually.
   1. The normal operating range is 200–4000 ml in 200 ml increments.
   2. Accuracy of these spirometers is not influenced by the patient's peak inspiratory flow. They allow for volume measurement and adjustment and will register a reading regardless of the patient's peak inspiratory flow rate.[1]

References

1. Eubanks, D. H., and Bone, R. C., *Comprehensive Respiratory Care, 2nd ed.*, Mosby, 1990.
2. McPherson, S., *Respiratory Care Equipment, 5th ed.*, Mosby, 1995.
3. Mcpherson, S. P., *Respiratory Home Care Equipment*, Kendal/Hunt Co., 1988.
4. White, G. C., *Equipment Theory for Respiratory Care, 3rd ed.*, Delmar Publishers, 1999.
5. Shapiro, B. A., *Clinical Application of Respiratory Care, 4th ed.*, Yearbook Medical Publishers, 1991.
6. Burton, G. G., Hodgkin, J. E., and Ward, J. J., *Respiratory Care: A Guide to Clinical Practice, 4th ed.*, Lippincott, 1997.
7. Parsons, P. E., and Heffner, J. E., *Pulmonary/Respiratory Therapy Secrets*, Hanley and Belfus Inc.,1997.
8. Wilkins, R. L., Hodgkin J. E., Lopez, B. L., *Lung Sounds: A Practical Guide, 2nd ed.*, Mosby, 1995.
9. Alone, C. A., and Hill, T. V., *Respiratory Care of the Newborn and Child, 2nd ed.*, Lippincott, 1997.

Assessment Questions

1. The proper-sized chest tube used for treatment of a spontaneous pneumothorax would normally be in the range of:
   A. 12–22 French
   B. 22–28 French
   C. 28–36 French
   D. 35–42 French

2. Quick-disconnect station outlets:
   I. Are indexed by the American Standard Safety System
   II. Prevent incorrect gas delivery to the patient
   III. Are indexed by the Diameter Index Safety System
   IV. Are indexed by the Pin Index Safety System

   A. I and II only
   B. II only
   C. II and III only
   D. II and IV only

3. A post-surgical patient reaches the goal of 700 ml/sec using a flow-dependent incentive spirometer. The patient is able to keep the float suspended for three seconds.

Chapter 14: Respiratory Support Equipment

What inspired volume would you document on the patient's chart?

A. 0.7 Liters
B. 1.4 Liters
C. 2.1 Liters
D. 2.8 Liters

4. The procedure of cracking an oxygen cylinder prior to use is performed:

   A. To expel debris from the cylinder valve outlet
   B. After the regulator is attached to the cylinder
   C. To establish there is gas pressure in the cylinder
   D. To make it easier to attach the regulator the cylinder valve

5. Bourdon gauge flowmeters have their accuracy affected by which of the following?

   A. Downstream resistance
   B. Flow rate
   C. Position
   D. Wall/cylinder pressure

6. A device that measures pressure would be referred to as a:

   A. Barometer
   B. Parameter
   C. Hygrometer
   D. Manometer

7. Oxygen and air are mixed simultaneously by a:

   A. Oxygen compressor
   B. Oxygen concentrator
   C. Oxygen enricher
   D. Oxygen proportioner

8. While suctioning a patient, all vacuum is lost, causing you to do which of the following?

   I. Empty the collection bottle if full
   II. Make sure the catheter isn't obstructed
   III. Establish that the connection between the suction tubing and the catheter is secure

   A. I only
   B. I, II and III
   C. II only
   D. III only

9. Where should a chest tube be placed for treatment of a pneumothorax?

   A. 2nd intercostal interspace in the midclavicular line
   B. 3rd intercostal interspace in the midclavicular line
   C. 4th intercostal interspace in the midclavicular line
   D. 5th intercostal interspace in the midclavicular line

Chapter 15

Ventilator Systems and Support Accessories

I. Pneumatic ventilators

A. Pneumatic ventilators require a 50 psig compressed gas source to provide a positive-pressure breath. When all ventilator controls are influenced by gas pressure, the ventilator is considered to be pneumatic in nature.
   1. Because the controls require pressurized gas as the power source for operation, a venturi mechanism (injector) is utilized to deliver a volume of gas to the patient system. Line pressure of 50 psig is reduced down to approximately 40–60 cmH$_2$O for mechanically inflating the lungs.
   2. The venturi drive is responsible for boosting the flow capabilities through air-entrainment. The venturi is a low pressure drive system and is susceptible to a decrease in total flow when exposed to back pressure (resistance and compliance changes in the patient's lungs).[1]
      a. Flow starts out at maximum and continues to decrease throughout the inspiratory phase (high initial and low terminal flow pattern).
      b. Pressure starts out by building up in a linear fashion (increasing rapidly from baseline) and displays a plateau effect as it slowly accelerates up to peak pressure (shark fin look).
B. The air-mixture control determines whether source gas bypasses the venturi or not. If oxygen is used as the source gas in the air-mix mode, FIO$_2$ is virtually uncontrollable as percentages may range from 60–90%.
   1. A venturi responds to backpressure by entraining less air, resulting in higher oxygen percentages.
   2. When moving to the 100% mode, peak flow can decrease due to elimination of air entrainment at the venturi.
   3. Oxygen blending devices or accumulator bags may need to be used to provide more precise control of FIO$_2$.

Chapter 15: Ventilator Systems and Support Accessories

C. The pressure control determines the pressure limit. Delivered gas volume and duration of delivery at a given pressure will be the result of the compliance of the patient's lung and chest wall and the resistance encountered as gas flows from the machine to the patient.
   1. Because resistance is encountered as gas flows from the machine to the patient, the pressure will remain constant and the volume will vary.
   2. Use of these devices for continuous ventilation is not usually indicated in patients with abnormal lungs.
D. Pressure limited (cycled off) refers to termination of the inspiratory phase when a preselected airway pressure is reached. Expiration then begins and the patient exhales passively.
E. Peak flow is determined by a needle valve sitting inside a variable orifice. At its maximum setting, most pressure preset ventilators will provide approximately 60–80 L/min. The inspiratory wave form then will decline throughout inspiration as the venturi responds to the pressure building up in the patient system.
   1. Flow rate is equal to the volume of gas delivered per unit of time.
   2. Variation of the flow rate will result in changing the speed at which the gas flows from the ventilator to the patient.
F. The rate control (expiratory timers on pressure preset ventilators) establish how much time the ventilator will spend in the expiratory phase. Inspiration is a function of the set flow rate, pressure setting, and patient resistance and compliance.
   1. Once the expiratory time is set, it is the only period of the ventilatory cycle (inspiration plus expiration) that is not subject to change (unit must be in the control mode).
   2. The respiratory rate, minute volume, and inspiratory time can change from one minute to the next because only expiratory time is controlled.
   3. The rate will change each time the patient initiates an assisted breath, which changes the time allowed for expiration.
G. Patient sensitivity can be adjusted to range from self-cycling to locking out all response to patient effort (controlled ventilation).
   1. Adjusting the sensitivity control alters the effort the patient is required to create in order to cycle the ventilator on.
      a. Less sensitive means the patient needs to exert a greater effort to cycle the machine on.
      b. More sensitive means that it is easier (less effort) for the patient to cycle the machine on.
   2. All sensitivity controls function only during the expiratory phase of the ventilatory cycle. Once the machine cycles on, the control no longer operates.

H. Pneumatic volume cycling applies to a ventilator that allows minute volume to be set on a controlling device (blender).
 1. Volume is calculated by dividing the blender flow rate by the set ventilation rate per minute; for example, 10 liters set on a blender, divided by a respiratory rate of 10 BPM, would equal a tidal volume of 1000 ml.
 2. Patients assisting at a faster rate than the backup rate set will receive a smaller tidal volume each time the machine cycles on.
I. Pneumatic time cycling terminates the inspiratory phase after a preset time is reached, which allows the volume to change as dictated by the compliance and resistance of the patient's lungs.
 1. By setting an inspiratory and expiratory time, these two controls together provide a rate per minute.
 2. The inspiratory timer determines how long source gas will flow to the patient.
 3. The expiratory timer determines how long the machine will wait before initiating the next inspiratory phase.
J. Some pneumatically powered ventilators incorporate the use of fluidic components that have no moving parts and depend solely on gas flow and pressure to function.
 1. These ventilators utilize fluid logic in order to determine the sensing, information processing, analyzing, and decision-making control functions.
 2. Operational principles consist of the Coanda effect and beam deflection.
  a. When a high stream of gas emerges from a jet orifice and passes by a wall, the gas stream is attracted to and attaches itself to the wall (Coanda effect).
  b. A high-speed stream of gas, if directed at a ninety degree right angle, will cause the stream of gas to separate from the wall it is attached to. This separation then changes the direction of the gas flow (beam deflection principle).
 3. Fluidic elements (switches and gates) are blocks of inert material (Corning glass) that contain a network of internal channels.
 4. The common fluidic elements used in ventilator systems include:
  a. And/nand gate
  b. Back-pressure switch
  c. Flip-flop
  d. Or/nor gate
  e. Schmitt trigger
 5. Fluidic components are not affected by any atmospheric conditions such as temperature, humidity, or radiation. Liquid water or dirt accumulating in the tubing that connects each component affects their output.
K. Refer to Trouble Shooting Guide 15-1 for corrective actions of pressure ventilator problems.

Chapter 15: Ventilator Systems and Support Accessories

Trouble Shooting Guide 15-1

Pressure Ventilators

Problem	Possible Causes	Corrective Actions
Fail to cycle	System leaks	Perform leak test
Loss of pressure	Exhalation valve diaphragm	Check
	Holes in circuit tubing	Check
	All circuit connections	Check
	Internal ventilator leak	Check
Deficient flow rate	Venturi gate chatter	Check machine against manufacturer list of tolerance ranges. If ventilator unable to meet calibration ranges remove from service.
	Ventilator out of calibration	

II. Electric ventilators

A. Electric current is required to provide the power necessary for operation and control of the ventilator. Electronic components power all ventilator logic systems for controlling inspiration and expiration.

B. Circuitry is the path gas takes inside a ventilator and determines the driving mechanism.
   1. A single-circuit ventilator sends the gas that is inside the ventilator directly to the patient.
   2. A double-circuit ventilator uses two separate pressurized gas volumes. One ventilator gas volume is used to compress another gas volume in the system, which is delivered to the patient.

C. Cycling modes are incorporated within the ventilator system, which control inspiration and expiration.
   1. Volume limiting (cycling off) refers to inspiration ending after a preset volume is delivered from the ventilator.
   2. Time cycling/limiting refers to a certain period of time elapsing before the mode function will change.
   3. Controlled ventilation is where the ventilator delivers positive-pressure breaths automatically during inspiration and allows pressure to return to atmospheric during expiration.

a. The initiation of inspiration and the volume of the breath are completely independent of patient control.
  b. A timing mechanism determines when the ventilator will deliver the number of preset breaths.
D. An automatic cycling mechanism combined with an assist mechanism provides an assist-control mode. The ventilator assists the patients in response to their inspiratory effort. In this case, the control rate can assist a weakened ventilatory effort and provide backup support should it be required by the patient.
  1. Assist-cycling occurs as the ventilator senses a slight subatmospheric pressure generated by the patient and delivers a pressurized breath.
  2. If the amount of effort required to trigger inspiration is adjustable, the ventilator is said to have sensitivity.
      a. Patient sensitivity can be adjusted to range from self-cycling to locking out any response to patient effort.
      b. The inspiratory cycle usually begins when the sensitivity is set approximately $-1 \text{ cmH}_2\text{O}$.
      c. The sensitivity may compensate and allow for the assist cycle to occur at elevated baseline pressures (PEEP/CPAP).
E. Establishing the ventilator rate means the ventilator must incorporate some mechanism of dividing a minute into so many ventilatory cycles (set number of breaths).
  1. Many ventilators incorporate a rate control. Inspiratory time is determined by the volume set, inspiratory flow rate, and the patient's resistance and compliance. Expiration is whatever is left over prior to the machine cycling into the next inspiration.
      a. A rate of 15 indicates 15 breaths per minute. Because flow rate is measured in L/min, this rate would mean the unit must get inspiration and expiration over in a four-second time period prior to the next breath being delivered.
      b. Inspiratory time in most adults is maintained between 0.5 and 2.0 seconds.
  2. Some ventilators incorporate two separate timers. One timer starts inspiration and another timer starts expiration. Any change in either of the timers will change the ventilator mechanical rate.
  3. The inspiratory/expiratory ratio (I:E) is normally averaged over a certain period of time and is displayed on the ventilator panel.
      a. Unless specific situations occur requiring inverse I:E ratios, inspiration is normally shorter than expiration (1:1.5–1:4.0).
      b. When calculating the I:E ratio, both the numerator and denominator are divided by inspiratory time to reduce the value to its simplest form. Refer to Equation 15-1.
F. Ventilator volume is produced and regulated inside the machine. An adjustable control knob on the ventilator's front panel allows control of the volume setting

Chapter 15: Ventilator Systems and Support Accessories

> **EQUATION 15-1:   Calculating I:E Ratio**
>
> $$I/E = (I/I):(E/I)$$
>
> **Example:** Given an inspiration that lasts 2 sec and an expiration that lasts 3 sec, determine the I:E ratio?
>
> $$I/E = \frac{2}{2}:\frac{3}{2}$$
>
> $$I/E = 1:1.5$$

(minute volume or tidal volume). It provides for adjustment of a preset volume limit that terminates the inspiratory phase.

1. Not all of the preset volume reaches the patient's lungs. Discrepancies exist between the volume delivered to the patient and the actual amount set on the volume control. This difference is a result of the compliance and distensibility of the circuitry, and the compressibility of the gas molecules within the system.
2. Because the tubing system will hold a certain amount of volume for each cmH_2O developed within the system, the volume compressed in the circuitry is directly related to the generated system pressure. This volume must be subtracted from the volume recorded by the spirometer. It is known as correcting for tubing compliance. Refer to Equation 15-2.
3. Depending upon the various components incorporated within the ventilator and tubing system, 3–6 ml/cmH_2O is the general amount of volume compressed.
4. The normal approach for determining the compressed volume factor is to put 100 ml of gas into the ventilatory circuit and plug it off. Then turn the ventilator on and see how much pressure it takes to compress the gas. If it takes 25 cmH_2O to move 100 ml of gas into the circuit, then the factor you use to determine compressed volume is 4 ml/cmH_2O (100/25).
5. A sigh breath is a deeper ventilator-delivered breath than an ordinary ventilator delivered breath. A timing mechanism determines periodic delivery of a ventilator generated breath that is generally 50% greater than the patient's set mechanical tidal volume.
    a. Sigh rate limits are preset by the therapist on the sigh rate control. Single or multiple sighs are set per hour.
    b. The general recommendation is when less than 10 ml/kg is used for delivered tidal volume, a sigh of 1–1.5 times patient's tidal volume is given 6 times hr (q 10 min).

> **EQUATION 15-2: Correcting for Tubing Compliance**
>
> Volume delivered = Spirometer reading minus compressed volume
>
> **Example:** A spirometer is reading 500 ml delivered volume from a patient with the peak inflation pressure at 25 cmH$_2$O. In this example, 4 ml of volume is captured and compressed in the system for every 1 cmH$_2$O pressure developed (tubing compliance).
>
> The corrected volume can be calculated as follows:
>
> | | |
> |---|---|
> | 500 ml | spirometer reading |
> | −100 ml | compressed volume (25 cmH$_2$O × 4 ml/cmH$_2$O) |
> | 400 ml | delivered volume |
>
> **Note:** This calculation does not apply when taking the volume reading from the ventilator setting. It only applies when the volume reading is taken from the spirometer.

G. Gas flow for a given period of time establishes volume. The ventilator flow rate control determines the speed at which the gas flow moves from the ventilator system to the patient. This influences (along with volume and patient resistance and compliance) the time that the ventilator spends in inspiration.

1. Decreasing the flow rate will increase the inspiratory time, and increasing the flow rate will decrease the inspiratory time.
2. For most adult patients, normal flow rate settings are between 30 and 70 L/min and are dependent on the desired inspiratory time, set tidal volume, and patient effort.
3. Most ventilators are capable of delivering flows in the range of 100–150 L/min, although some ventilators are capable of producing flow rates greater than 200 L/min.

H. Ventilator flow wave form controls directly encroach upon the inspiratory phase of the ventilatory cycle, and provide adjustment for obtaining various wave forms.

1. Square wave flow patterns are the result of a ventilator generating and maintaining a constant flow throughout the inspiratory phase. Flow at the end of inspiration is the same as at the beginning of inspiration.
   a. Changes in airway resistance and compliance will not influence the flow pattern.
   b. This type of flow pattern is advantageous to the patient with an increased respiratory rate.

Chapter 15: Ventilator Systems and Support Accessories

2. Accelerating flow (an electronically generated sine wave) results when the wave form controls influence the ventilator to generate a nonconstant flow throughout the inspiratory phase. Flow accelerates from baseline and decelerates back to baseline in the same manner for each breath.
    a. Rotary piston ventilators (Emerson/Engström) can produce mechanically generated sine waves.
    b. The accelerating flow pattern succeeds in reducing airway turbulence for the patient with problems of increased resistance.
3. Decelerating flow (ramp-shaped) patterns are the result of a ventilator that generates a high initial flow at the beginning of inspiration, and permits flow to taper to a terminal point (above zero) at the end of inspiration.
    a. Decelerating flow is advantageous to the patient with poor compliance since it allows ventilation to occur at a decreased intrathoracic pressure.
    b. Decelerating flow will cause an increase in the inspiratory time since the same volume is delivered at a lower pressure. Refer to Figure 15-1.
I. Some flow rate controls establish the available flow for spontaneous breathing. This flow can be used for IMV or CPAP continuous flow, or IMV/CPAP demand flow.
    1. In the continuous flow mode the flow rate control sets the flow rate available for spontaneous breathing as well as the flow for mandatory breaths.
    2. With the fast-reaction demand systems (proportional solenoids), there is a response to patient effort. A pressure gradient is produced between the airway and the ventilator, resulting in a flow that varies since it is based on the size of the gradient. The demand valve also responds when the proximal airway pressure drops below the ambient or above the baseline (PEEP/CPAP) pressure.
J. The flow rate formula is a calculation utilized during ventilatory support. The following equation, algebraically manipulated, may be used to solve for tidal volume, average flow rate, or inspiratory time. Refer to Equations 15-3, 15-4, and 15-5.

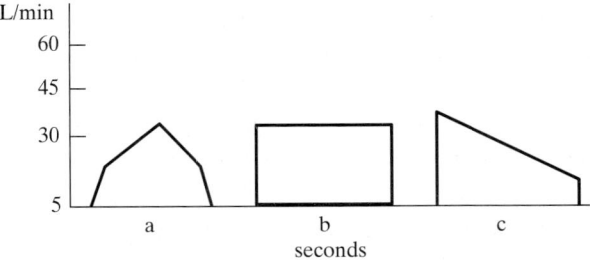

FIGURE 15-1: Sample of electronically generated flow waveforms, a = accelerating, b = square, and c = decelerating (rampshaped/tapered).

> **EQUATION 15-3: Solving for Ventilator Tidal Volume**
>
> $$\text{Tidal volume} = (\text{Flow rate})(\text{Inspiratory time})$$
>
> **Example:** Given a mean flow rate of 56 L/min, and an inspiratory time of 0.8 seconds, what is the approximate tidal volume?
>
> **Step 1:** Convert L/min to L/sec*
>
> $$\frac{56 \text{ L/min}}{60 \text{ sec}} = 0.933 \text{ L/sec}$$
>
> **Step 2:** Tidal Volume = 0.933 × 0.8 = 747 ml
>
> * Because the flow rate stated is in L/min and inspiratory time is in seconds, the flow rate must be divided by 60 to convert into seconds.

K. The oxygen percentage control adjusts the FIO_2 delivered. The method used to deliver oxygen percentage varies. Accumulators, blenders, controllers, mix-boxes, reservoir bags, and the venturi are among the different systems. FIO_2 values can be controlled by the user and vary from 0.21 to 1.0.

> **EQUATION 15-4: Solving for Average Ventilator Flow Rate**
>
> $$\text{Average flow rate (L/sec)} = \frac{\text{Tidal volume (L)}}{\text{Inspiratory time (sec)}}$$
>
> **Example:** A ventilator is delivering 750 ml in 0.8 seconds. What is the average inspiratory flow rate in L/min?
>
> **Step 1:** $\text{Flow rate} = \dfrac{0.750}{0.8} = 0.9375 \text{ L/sec}$
>
> **Step 2:** Convert to liters per minute (L/min)
>
> 0.9375 × 60 = 56 L/min

...ms and Support Accessories

...for Inspiratory Time

...y time = $\dfrac{\text{Tidal volume}}{\text{Flow rate}}$

...of 750 ml and a mean flow rate of 56 L/min, ...iratory time.

...t L/min to L/sec

$\dfrac{\text{in}}{} = 0.933$ L/sec

...ory Time = $\dfrac{0.750}{0.933} = 0.8$ sec

...button) delivers one mandatory breath in all ...han one breath be desired, the button is pushed

...ors

...sors, microprocessor electronics, and engineer... ...ch more versatility and control than the knob-turning gas delivery systems of years past.

1. Microprocessor technology (through use of a keypad or mouse) allows the RCP to capture, process, transmit, and display information concerning the patient-ventilator system immediately in real time.
   a. Data can be manipulated to display graphical plots or numerical results.
   b. Data can be distributed to storage areas, and transmitted to remote locations.
   c. The microprocessor is able to digitally execute software coded instructions to run almost any new mode of ventilation, and to collect information from a vast array of sensors (pressure/flow transducers).
2. Gas delivery is a function of electronic microprocessor control.
   a. Present-day ventilators use the microprocessor to regulate and oversee flow control valves that open and close proportionally.
   b. Some ventilator systems incorporate digital flow valves, where one valve is either open or closed, but under direct microprocessor control.

c. The microprocessor also has sensors that monitor the patient-ventilator system, and provides feedback capability, allowing the system to readjust and self-correct its own performance.

IV. Ventilator modifications

A. Airway pressure release ventilation (APRV)
 1. The mode APRV is a method that provides for spontaneous ventilation, while allowing intermittent levels of CPAP. It allows two levels of CPAP, and the patient is able to breathe spontaneously in both modes.
 2. APRV is designed to help maintain oxygenation, decrease physiologic deadspace ventilation, decrease peak airway pressure, and increase alveolar ventilation compared to CPAP alone.[2]
 3. The patient is placed on a elevated baseline pressure (CPAP) and allowed to breathe spontaneously.
    a. The elevated baseline pressure is then released intermittently to lower CPAP pressure and may on occasion be allowed to return to atmospheric pressure.
       (1) This drop in baseline pressure, is performed by briefly (approximately 1 second) opening a solenoid valve that opens the CPAP circuit to atmosphere.
       (2) Once the baseline pressure has been released, the patient will exhale more gas.
       (3) The solenoid valve is then closed, restoring the baseline pressure.
       (4) As the baseline is restored, additional gas ventilates the patient's lungs.
    b. The patient's volume exchange then depends upon their lung compliance and the level of elevated baseline pressure (CPAP).
B. Bilevel positive airway pressure (BiPAP)
 1. The BiPAP system incorporates a standard nasal CPAP blower modified with a solenoid valve making it act as a ventilatory assist device that's totally noninvasive.
    a. A various array of ventilation masks similar to a standard nasal CPAP mask is connected to the BiPAP device and held in place by head straps.
    b. An electric solenoid valve produces a timed positive airway pressure boost (PB) (difference between IPAP and EPAP) that permits the unit to provide the patient with ventilatory assistance.
    c. Self-adjusting/auto-CPAP units allow for variance of the pressure needed to treat upper airway collapse. Should a patient start to snore during a sleep period, the baseline pressure will automatically increase to clear the obstruction. This adjustment is accomplished by a sensor that sends information to a computer algorithm resulting in changes in the CPAP level (lower/baseline pressure) as upper airway physiology changes in the patient's sleep.[3]

Chapter 15: Ventilator Systems and Support Accessories 239

2. BiPAP is a device that provides a fixed amount of pressure during the night, responds to the patient's inspiratory flow rate, or cycles at timed intervals of preset IPAP and EPAP.
    a. Inspiratory positive airway pressure (IPAP), with a selective range of 2–25 cmH$_2$O, is available to set the preselected pressure support level.[2]
    b. A pressure transducer senses the patient starting to take a breath due to a decrease in the level of circuit flow.
    c. The unit switches to IPAP mode and increases the amount of airflow in the circuit, supporting the patient's effort, and increasing the tidal volume.
    d. Expiratory positive airway pressure (EPAP), with a selective range of 2–20 cmH$_2$O, which sets the CPAP level (pressure patient has to breathe against during expiration). This baseline level must be high enough to prevent upper airway obstruction of the soft tissues.
    e. Spontaneous mode (really a pressure cycled assist) with a selective range of 6–30 cycles per minute between IPAP and EPAP.
    f. CPAP mode is where the system is used to provide continuous positive pressure in response to patient effort.[4]

C. Expiratory retard/resistance occurs during exhalation; where the patient's expiratory gas flow is delayed as it returns to baseline pressure.
    1. The maneuver functions much like pursed-lip breathing in that it takes a longer time for the gas to decrease from peak pressure to baseline.
    2. Expiratory time will need to be increased if this modality is used during controlled ventilation.

D. High-frequency ventilation (HFV) incorporates four different types of ventilating devices that meet the patient's gas exchange needs by employing higher than normal frequencies (breathing rates greater than 150 BPM), with a noncompliant ventilator circuit.[5]
    1. High-frequency positive-pressure ventilation (HFPPV) incorporates a conventional volume or pressure-limited ventilator that has been modified with special pneumatic valves (solenoid valves) to produce very high breathing rates and small tidal volumes.
        a. The estimated tidal volume with each breath is slightly larger than dead space ventilation (1–3 ml/kg), but overall total minute ventilation will be substantially greater than normal.
        b. The small tidal volumes are delivered at a significantly reduced peak pressure.
        c. The fast breath rate is due to a short inspiratory time and passive inspiration. I:E ratio is usually maintained at 1:1 to prevent auto-PEEP effects.
    2. High-frequency jet ventilation (HFJV) uses small puffs of air (there is no deep in-and-out breathing) that exit a side port in the endotracheal tube at a high frequency to ventilate the lungs. Breathing frequency ranges from 100–600 cycles/minute.

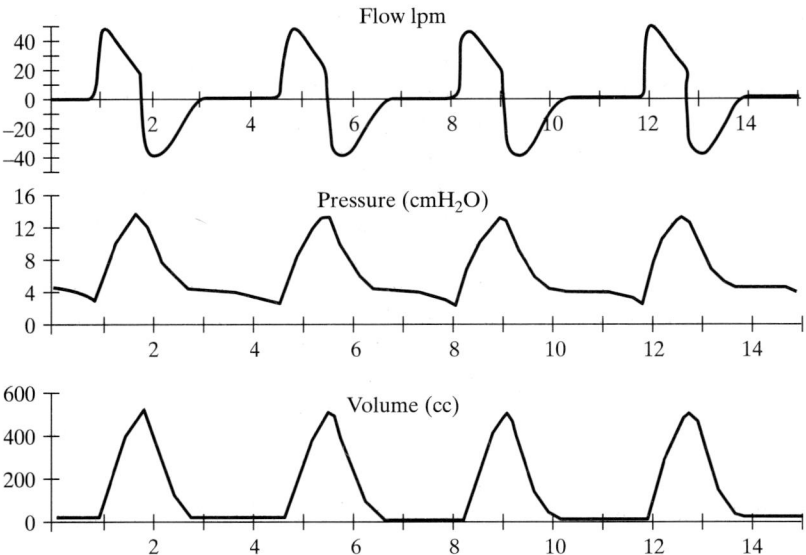

FIGURE 15-2: BiPap. Flow/time waveform shows descending flow abruptly drops to baseline at a system-specific terminal flow. Pressure/time tracing reveals a preselected inspiratory pressure, and indicates a patient-triggered breath. Volume/time waveform shows consistent volume but will vary with patient effort. This waveform has many similarities: when used with an endotracheal tube, the tracing reflects PSV with CPAP; when used without an endotracheal tube, it may also be termed noninvasive positive pressure support (NPPV). Modified from Waugh, J., Deshpande, V., and Harwood, R., Rapid interpretation of Ventilator Waveforms, Prentice-Hall, Inc., 1999, with permission.

    a. The small tidal breaths are pulsed down the airway through a jet with extremely short inspiratory times (20–40 milliseconds), allowing for passive exhalation.

    b. The high pressure is delivered through a small 5 cm long cannula (injector) 1.06–1.62 mm in diameter (14–18 gauge for adults and 22–25 gauge for children).[6]

    c. Current terminology expresses the frequency of breaths in Hertz (Hz), 1 Hz = 1 cycle/second = 60 BPM.

3. High-frequency flow interrupter ventilation (HFFIV) delivers short bursts of inspiratory flow via microprocessor-controlled solenoid valves.

    a. Breathing rates can be as high as 22Hz, or 1300 cycles per min.

    b. Expiration is active as opposed to passive in that a mechanical airway pressure drop occurs during exhalation to facilitate the removal of exhaled gas.

Chapter 15: Ventilator Systems and Support Accessories 241

   4. High-frequency oscillation ventilation (HFOV), also known as high-frequency chest-wall compression (HFCWC), generates breathing rates in excess of 3000 cycles/minute by use of a diaphragm oscillator or low-frequency speaker.
      a. Inspired tidal volumes are less than physiologic dead space.
      b. A diaphragm vibrates a volume of gas causing that gas to oscillate throughout the conducting airways. A low frequency woofer-type speaker that vibrates the chest wall externally causes gas to oscillate and mix in the airways in the same fashion.

E. Intermittent mandatory ventilation (IMV) combines spontaneous patient breathing with a predetermined automatic-controlled ventilator rate.
   1. The patient inhales spontaneously from a fresh gas source at their own desired rate and tidal volume. The volume of the breath and the initiation of the breath are under patient control. A spontaneous breath is a breath without machine intervention.
   2. The controlled (mandatory) breaths receive the full predetermined volume. The control rate is preset and not synchronized with the patient's inspiratory efforts.

F. Inspiratory plateau (inspiratory hold, inflation hold, post-inspiratory hold, end-inspiratory pause) is a maneuver that lengthens the interval between active inspiration and active expiration.
   1. The delivered volume is held in the system providing extra time for gas within the lung to distribute more equally to less ventilated areas.
   2. The opening of the exhalation valve is delayed for a preset period of time (generally from 0–2 sec.) prior to the beginning of the expiratory phase.

G. Inverse ratio ventilation (IRV)
   1. IRV is a method of ventilation where the inspiratory phase lasts longer than the expiratory phase.
   2. The I:E ratio is prolonged by increasing the inspiratory time. The options are:
      a. Slowing down the inspiratory flow rate, and allowing the inspiratory phase to encroach upon the expiratory time.
      b. Use of an end-expiratory pause maneuver (up to 2 sec.) after a preset volume delivery, which increases inspiratory time and encroaches upon expiratory time.
      c. Increasing the inspiratory time percent, provided the ventilator has an "insp. time %" control, which essentially slows down the inspiratory flow rate, resulting in inspiration lasting longer than expiration.
      d. PC-IRV uses a rapid insufflation combined with a rapidly decelerating flow rate.
      e. Rapid insufflation achieves the preset pressure early in the inspiratory phase, and maintains that pressure throughout the remainder of the inspiratory period.
      f. The rapidly decelerating flow rate produces a even distribution of ventilation resulting in improved oxygenation.[7]

3. Appropriate selection of the I:E ratio and respiratory rate results in a PEEP-like effect, where the ventilator begins a new breath just prior to terminal flow being concluded from the previous breath.
   a. Because the expiratory flow does not reach zero, and the expiratory pressure does not reach baseline, PCV ventilation is selected as the mode so that when air trapping takes place, breath stacking does not occur.
   b. With PC-IRV, the lungs are kept in a splinted position prior to the next breath, preventing the small lung units from collapsing. This PEEP-like effect helps to avoid a high positive inspiratory pressure (PIP).

H. Mandatory minute ventilation (MMV)
   1. MMV is a ventilatory technique where the ventilator is adjusted to administer a preset mandatory minute volume. This method prevents the patient's minute volume from falling below a preset rate, regardless of their spontaneous minute volume.
      a. A guaranteed minute volume is preset on the ventilator, and the patient is allowed to breathe spontaneously.
      b. Whatever portion of the preset minute volume the patient is unable to spontaneously attain, the ventilator provides in terms of positive pressure mechanical breaths.
      c. The ventilator can provide ventilation as a pressure supported breath, or a breath with a preset volume.
      d. Once the patient's spontaneous breathing meets the required MMV setting, no mandatory assistance by the ventilator will be provided.
   2. Because the ventilator monitors minute volume, alveolar ventilation is not reflected.
      a. The ventilator only knows that the preset minute volume values have been met.
      b. A patient could increase their spontaneous breathing rate to 60 BPM in order to meet the preset minute volume value, although inadequate alveolar ventilation is likely to occur.[8]

I. Pressure-control ventilation (PCV)
   1. PCV produces a rapid ascent to peak pressure and maintains it while inspiratory flow decelerates throughout the inspiratory phase until the exhalation valve opens.
      a. Because the pressure remains constant throughout inspiration, and respiratory rate and inspiratory time are controlled, a consistant tidal volume is delivered with each breath. Volume delivery is dependent upon lung characteristics.
      b. Again, because pressure is constant, flow is greatest at the start of inspiration and decelerates throughout the inspiratory phase.

Chapter 15: Ventilator Systems and Support Accessories **243**

2. The higher the preset inspiratory pressure level (actually a pressure hold or plateau maneuver), the larger the patient's tidal volume, since more gas will flow into the lungs.
3. PCV can be employed in combination with PSV, and is commonly used in the CMV mode with inverse ratio ventilation (PC-IRV) when treating some ARDS patients.
    a. In CMV, any spontaneous effort results in a patient-initiated mandatory breath.[8]
    b. In SIMV, any spontaneous effort results in either a patient-initiated mandatory or spontaneous breath. See Figure 15-3.

J. Pressure support ventilation (PSV) is a form of mechanical ventilatory support that augments the patient's spontaneous inspiratory efforts with a preselected level of positive airway pressure (pressure assist).[9]
    1. The patient controls the ventilatory rate and inspires a tidal volume with which they feel comfortable. As the patient creates a spontaneous inspiratory effort, a predetermined pressure is rapidly established in the ventilator system.
    2. As the patient's spontaneous inspiratory flow rate decreases (usually 25% of peak inspiratory flow or some preset value), the level of positive pressure returns to baseline. It allows the patient to exhale passively, without pressure support.
    3. Pressure support ventilation can be used independently, with elevated baseline pressures (CPAP), or in combination with CPAP/SIMV.

K. Synchronized intermittent mandatory ventilation (SIMV) allows the patient to breathe spontaneously between positive pressure breaths, and those breaths are synchronized to patient inspiratory effort.
    1. This mode requires that the ventilator incorporate a mechanism that senses patient effort consistent with the times set on the rate (SIMV) control. A sensor ignores the patient inspiratory effort during the time the patient is spontaneously breathing, which prevents the ventilator from cycling on.
    2. The assist sensor (usually a electronic window) within the ventilator responds to the time frame set on the SIMV rate control. Once the window is open the ventilator assist mechanism reacts to the patient's initial inspiratory effort, which synchronizes and triggers the mandatory breath.

L. Proportional assist ventilation (PAV) is where pressure, flow, and volume delivery are proportional to the patient's spontaneous effort. The clinician preselects and adjusts the ventilatory response to patient effort, while the ventilator produces pressure appropriate to the amount of inspiratory flow and volume demanded by the patient's effort.
    1. The system currently cannot compensate for system leaks.
    2. Assisted ventilation is the only available mode.
    3. The patient has difficulty triggering the ventilator in the presence of auto-PEEP.[9]

M. Refer to Trouble Shooting Guide 15-2 for information regarding electric ventilators.

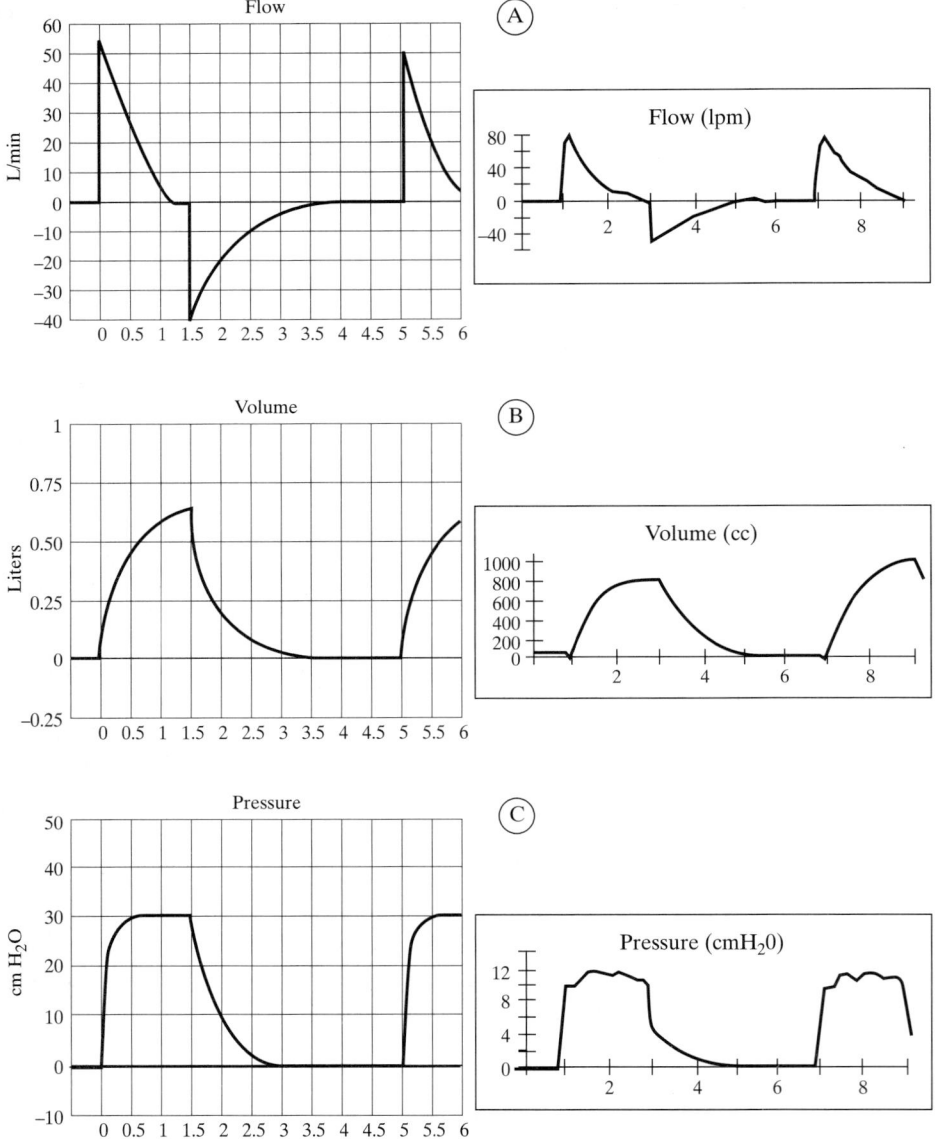

FIGURE 15-3: Pressure controlled ventilation (PCV). A. Flow/time waveform shows flow continues to taper down throughout the inspiratory phase, and may reach zero flow at or before the inspiratory time (1.5 seconds) elapses. This occurs because PCV is a time-cycled mode of ventilation. B. Volume/time tracing shows volume delivery is terminated at the end of the inspiratory phase, and the delivered volume is dependent upon lung characteristics. C. Pressure/time waveform reveals pressure maintained at 30 cm H_2O throughout inspiration (1.5 seconds), and a baseline that returns to zero. Modified from Waugh, J., Deshpande, V., and Harwood, R., Rapid interpretations of Ventilator Waveforms, Prentice-Hall, Inc., 1999, with permission.

Chapter 15: Ventilator Systems and Support Accessories 245

Trouble Shooting Guide 15-2

Electric Ventilators

Problem	Possible Causes	Corrective Actions
Loss of pressure	System leaks	Perform leak test
Loss of volume	Humidifier	Check
	Exhalation valve diaphragm	Check for rupture
	Holes in circuit tubing	Check
	All circuit connections	Check
	Internal ventilator leak	Check
Erroneous tidal volume, flow rate, or breathing rate	Ventilator out of calibration	Check machine against manufacturer's tolerance ranges; if ventilator unable to meet calibration ranges remove from service
Unwanted high or low pressure; inaccurate FIO_2; inadvertent PEEP	Failure of alarm system to properly identify malfunction or changes in patient status	Set alarm systems to identify the slightest of system changes
		Evaluate each alarm system with initial ventilator check

V. Ventilator alarm systems

A. Ventilator alarm systems are intended to detect and draw attention to undesirable changes or failure in performance of the ventilator.

B. Audible and visual alerts will be activated should violation of preset values occur concerning the patient's status.

C. Most alarms are incorporated into the ventilator and are of three types: high pressure, low pressure, and loss of PEEP. Supplemental alarms are free-standing and not incorporated into the ventilator system. Refer to Table 15-1.
   1. Free-standing alarms are usually pressure sensitive (alarms that respond to changes in pressure). They are normally battery powered and are connected to the ventilator circuit by narrow-bore tubing at a point near the patient's airway.

TABLE 15-1: Ventilator Alarms

Event	Alarm
Apnea	Low pressure
No gas delivery	Low pressure
Excessive gas delivery	High pressure
Timing failure	Ventilator inoperative
Electric power failure	Ventilator inoperative
Gas power failure	FIO_2 or blender alarm
Loss of PEEP	Low pressure
Excessive PEEP	High pressure
Circuit Leaks	Low pressure
Inappropriate I:E ratio	I:E ratio alarm
Circuit partly occluded	High pressure

2. The apnea alarm is activated after a preset time interval has passed without the patient initiating a inspiratory effort. Default is usually somewhere between 10 and 30 seconds.
3. Low inspiratory pressure alarms indicate pressure has fallen below ventilating pressure. Activation of this alarm usually indicates a leak somewhere in the system, inappropriate control settings, or that the PEEP/CPAP levels are not remaining constant. Most PEEP/CPAP alarms are really low pressure alarms. This alarm is typically set 5–10 cmH$_2$O below normal ventilating pressure.
4. Setting the pressure limit control (usually 5–10 cmH$_2$O above peak pressure) directs the ventilator to end inspiration immediately upon reaching the preset pressure. Common causes include acute increases in system pressure (i.e., kinked ventilator tubing, the patient being out of phase with the ventilator, water pooling in the ventilator tubing, the patient coughing, or the patient needing to be suctioned).
   a. Pressures at the patient airway will differ (as much as 5–15 cmH$_2$O depending upon the flow rate) from machine pressure. If the manometer measures pressure inside the ventilator prior to the humidifier rather than at the patient's airway, the pressure displayed will be greater than the actual patient pressure measured at the proximal airway during a positive pressure inspiration.
   b. Excess pressures may also be vented by a pressure pop-off (pressure relief valve), which results in a continuation of the inspiratory phase until a volume or time limit occurs. The high pressure alarm still becomes activated.

Chapter 15: Ventilator Systems and Support Accessories

5. The inspiration/expiration (I:E) alarm normally limits (ends inspiration) when the ratio reaches 1:1.
   a. This alarm can be overridden on some ventilators so as to provide inverse I:E ratios.
   b. The I:E ratio display is a calculated relationship of the duration of inspiration compared with the duration of expiration.
   c. Inspiration is always expressed as 1 while expiration is shown with a decimal or as a whole number followed by tenths (1:2.6).
6. The oxygen low pressure alarm is activated when line pressure from the source has decreased below a certain value.
   a. The alarm does not measure the concentration of oxygen unless it is an oxygen analyzer alarm. The alarm can only sense the pressure in the system (supply line). It does not prevent inadvertent connection to an incorrect gas source, because the incorrect gas could exert the proper amount of pressure.
   b. High and low oxygen percentage alarms may be activated when the set values are not realized, provided the alarm is an oxygen analyzer that is measuring oxygen percentage.
7. A low exhaled volume alarm signifies that the expired volume has not exceeded the control setting for a certain number of breaths (usually a minimum of three). This alarm is usually activated by a leak within the circuit system.
8. The high rate (BPM) alarm is typically calibrated somewhere between 10 and 80 breaths/min. The high rate alert is normally activated once the total rate exceeds the alarm setting.
9. Alarm silence/alarm delay is used when it becomes desirable to disable the audio portion of a alarm system for a certain period of time (usually 60 sec). When the alarm silence is activated a visual light is illuminated signaling that the audible portion of the alarm system has been silenced.
10. The ventilator inoperative alarm signifies either total gas failure, AC power failure, or an electronic malfunction in the volume measuring circuitry.
    a. The operator is notified that the electronics have detected a problem that renders the ventilator unsafe and has shut the ventilator down.
    b. When this alarm activates, gas flow ceases and the ventilator valve opens, venting the patient circuit to ambient pressure.

VI. Noninvasive ventilatory support systems

A. The iron lung is constructed from a cylinder that encloses the entire body of the patient except for the head. It allows negative pressure to be applied to the patient's entire body from the neck down. The bottom of the cylinder is enclosed by a diaphragm connected to an electric motor.

1. Inspiration occurs when the motor moves the diaphragm outward thereby causing pressure to drop inside the cylinder. This negative force creates a pressure gradient causing the patient's chest wall to move outward. The pressure gradient allows atmospheric pressure to enter the patient's upper airway and inflate the lungs.
2. As the motor displaces the diaphragm back to the starting position, expiration occurs passively due to lung recoil as the negative pressure around the chest returns to atmospheric levels.
3. The generated pressure can reach 60 cmH$_2$O, but is normally set for 15 cmH$_2$O. A rheostat connected to the variable speed motor permits the rate to be adjusted in the range of 10–40 BPM.
4. The timing mechanism functions in the control mode only, and the I:E ratio is fixed at 1:1.
5. Tank shock (abdominal pooling of blood) is a precaution that always needs to be considered when placing a patient inside an iron lung.

B. The chest cuirass is generally constructed of a dome-shaped fiberglass shell that covers the anterior thorax and abdomen. Use of this device is usually limited to assisting patients with impaired ventilatory function, and can be electrically or battery powered.
1. Large diameter (2 inch) tubing is inserted into the center of the cuirass and connects the patient to an vacuum-type blower that generates pressure.
2. Negative pressure is transmitted under the shell to the chest causing the thorax to expand and atmospheric air to enter the upper airway and ventilate the lungs.
3. Both the negative pressure control and the ventilatory rate control can be managed by dial adjustment, which provides for control of tidal volume and minute ventilation.
4. Some manufacturers have incorporated flow-sensors that are inserted into the nose allowing the cuirass to sense patient effort and provide a synchronized assist breath.
5. The cuirass produces a negative inspiratory pressure and does not impede cardiac filling during pressurization.

C. The rocking bed is designed for patients with impaired ventilatory effort. The rocking rate and pitch of the bed can be adjusted, however it normally swings the patient +/−20 degrees from horizontal.
1. As the foot of the bed rocks down, the abdominal contents are shifted, and the weight forces the diaphragm to move downward generating inspiration.
2. As the foot of the bed rocks up, the abdominal contents push the diaphragm back up, resulting in expiration.
3. Tidal volumes produced are below the patient's resting level.

Chapter 15: Ventilator Systems and Support Accessories 249

VII. External circuitry for ventilators

A. The external continuous mechanical ventilation (CMV) patient-ventilator circuit contains a main inspiratory drive line that connects the ventilator to the patient airway, and an expiratory line carries exhaled gas away from the patient. These breathing lines are usually constructed of corrugated silicone, latex, or disposable polyethylene.
  1. In addition to the connecting tubing, the inspiratory side of the circuit contains a support manifold, a humidification system, a temperature probe, proximal airway pressure and oxygen monitoring ports, a nebulizer, and water trap connections.
     a. CMV circuits contain some mechanical dead space that is dependent upon circuitry designs, with 25–100 ml being common to most circuits. This rebreathed volume includes the tubing between the patient wye and the connector.
     b. Bacteria filters contribute to the rebreathed volume when placed between the patient and the wye, and add to the compressed volume on the inspiratory and expiratory sides of the circuit. Most filters have a 99.99% efficiency for trapping bacteria averaging 1–5 micrometers in size.[10]
  2. The expiratory limb is usually comprised of connecting tubing, a volume measuring device (spirometer), and an exhalation valve that is pressurized during inspiration. Some ventilators incorporate the exhalation valve inside the ventilator as opposed to an external circuit.
     a. The area under the exhalation valve is smaller than the surface area of the rubber valve itself. When the exhalation valve is pressurized during inspiration, the valve will remain closed.
     b. Extra-large exhalation valves contribute to the surface area ratio at the valve seat, resulting in greater pressures being required within the tubing system to overcome the extra surface area ratio and open the exhalation valve.
  3. "H"-valve circuits are designed for patients on the SIMV mode.
     a. The "H" configuration allows for spontaneous breaths to be separated from ventilator breaths.
     b. The exhaled spirometer counts and displays the exhaled value for spontaneous breaths and ventilator breaths independently.
  4. Tight seals are required to provide a leak-free system to connect the circuit components together. Because the circuit is a positive pressure system, the circuit is capable of maintaining 80 cmH_2O for a period of 2–4 seconds without leaking.
  5. Various products are utilized to merge the different components of a ventilator circuit together.
     a. A connector is a fitting that joins like components together.
     b. An adaptor is a specialized connector that allows unlike components to be connected together.

c. The so-called "universal adaptor" that fits on many different pieces of respiratory equipment incorporates a 15 mm internal diameter and a 22 mm external diameter.
d. A wye connector/adaptor attaches the inspiratory and expiratory breathing lines to the patient.
e. A bushing is a connector that alters the internal diameter of a component.
f. A sleeve is a connector that alters the external diameter of a component.
g. Elbow connectors incorporate occlusive (plug-up/close-off) sealing ports, allowing for suctioning of the patient without disconnecting them from the circuit. They prevent pressure losses from occurring within the circuit.

B. CPAP circuits are similar to CMV circuits except that they are designed to deliver a high gas flow to the patient while keeping a constant level of positive pressure within the system.
 1. The delivered gas must meet the patient's peak inspiratory demands as the patient is entirely dependent upon the system for their total gas volume.
 2. For continuous flow CPAP systems, 3–5 liter reservoir bags permit gas to accumulate and be available for the next inspiration. This gas is also available to maintain flow to the patient should their peak inspiratory flow demands increase.

C. IMV circuits are CMV circuits with the addition of a controlled FIO_2 source and one-way valves. The combination of these components results in a circuit that can be utilized for continuous ventilation and spontaneous patient breathing.
 1. Blended source gas needs to be at least sufficient to keep the 3–5 liter reservoir expanded during inspiration. Adjustment of the flow to exceed the patient's peak inspiratory flow reduces their inspiratory work.
 2. As the ventilator cycles, a one-way valve between the circuit and the bag is closed, preventing the continuous flow from entering the circuit.
    a. The valve prevents the ventilator from ventilating the bag instead of the patient.
    b. The bag should contain a pressure relief valve that can be used to vent excess pressure accumulating in the bag during a mechanical breath.

VIII. PEEP administering devices

A. Threshold resistors are devices or systems that oppose expiratory flow by applying constant pressure at the airway throughout the expiratory phase. This pressure may be applied during mechanical or spontaneous ventilation.
 1. Underwater seal devices require submerging a portion of the expiratory limb under water. Patient-exhaled gas bubbles up through the water and vents to the atmosphere. Pressure is directly proportional to the distance the expiratory limb is submerged under the water. If the tube is submerged 5 cm under the water the expiratory pressure exerted at the patient airway will be 5 cmH_2O.

Chapter 15: Ventilator Systems and Support Accessories 251

2. A water column device applies water to the top of a diaphragm with the patient circuit connected to the bottom of the diaphragm (exhalation valve). The weight of the water on top of the diaphragm is the amount of force (PEEP pressure) the patient has to exert in order to open the valve to atmosphere.
3. Gravity-dependent steel balls of specific weight rest on an orifice that permits the exhaled gas to vent to atmosphere.[11]
   a. The threshold pressure varies directly with the weight of the ball over the expiratory orifice. The valve must be kept in a vertical position to function properly.
   b. The patient must generate a greater gas pressure than the ball's weight in order to open the orifice and vent the exhaled gases to the atmosphere.
4. Exhalation balloons can trap a specific amount of gas in the balloon. This balloon pressure then opposes the pressure in the expiratory line of the patient circuit. The patient must exert a pressure greater than the pressure inside the balloon to move the valve off its seat and vent the exhaled gases to atmosphere.
5. Magnets incorporate the opposing force of gas pressure and magnetic attraction to create a positive-end expiratory pressure.
   a. A disk of ferromagnetic metal is positioned against the exhalation valve seat by a magnet. The position of the magnet can be located closer to or further away from the exhalation valve.
   b. This changes the pressure the patient must generate to overcome the magnet's attraction and open the exhalation port thereby venting the exhaled gases to the atmosphere.
6. A spring-loaded valve can be adjusted to provide tension (force) against a disk that rests on the exhalation port, sealing it from the atmosphere. The patient must overcome the tension of the adjustable spring to open the exhalation valve.

B. Flow resistor systems provide positive-end expiratory pressure by establishing resistance to gas flow through an orifice. Flow must be continuous through the system in order to maintain pressure. If flow stops the pressure will immediately drop to atmospheric.
  1. Orifice resistors establish resistance at the exhalation valve of a continuous flow circuit. These devices are flow dependent, which means the PEEP levels will change if the flow changes.
     a. If the orifice diameter is decreased in size, the pressure the patient must exert in order to exhale increases.
     b. If the orifice diameter is increased in size, the pressure the patient must exert to exhale decreases.
     c. There is no exhalation valve, just an orifice that is always open, with the resistance being varied across it.
  2. The use of flow resistors is mostly limited to neonatal and pediatric ventilators.

C. Opposing-flow devices incorporate a venturi that opposes the patient's exhaled gas flow causing resistance at the exhalation valve. A needle valve is responsible for regulating the flow rate, which in turn increases or decreases the pressure the patient must exert to open the exhalation valve.

D. Regardless of the type of PEEP-generating system, the intent is to initiate the proper level of PEEP and maintain that PEEP level throughout the ventilatory cycle.

References

1. Mushin, W. W., et al., *Automatic Ventilation of the Lungs, 3rd ed.*, Blackwell Scientific Publications, 1980.
2. Strumpf, D. A., et al., "An Evaluation of the Respironics BiPAP Bi-Level CPAP Device for Delivery of Assisted Ventilation," *Respiratory Care* 35, no. 90, 1990.
3. Atwood, C. W., "Positive Pressure Therapy: Theory and Application," *Respir Care* 43, no. 4, 1998.
4. Waugh, J., Deshpande, V., and Harwood, R., *Rapid interpretation of Ventilator Waveforms,* Prentice-Hall, Inc., 1999.
5. Alone, C. A., and Hill, T. V., *Respiratory Care of the Newborn and Child, 2nd ed.,* Lippincott, 1997.
6. Sjostrand, U. H., "High-Frequency Positive-Pressure Ventilation (HFPPV): A Review," *Critical Care Medicine* 8, no. 3, 1980.
7. Chan, K., and Abraham, E., "Effects of Inverse Ratio Ventilation on Cardiorespiratory Parameters in Severe Respiratory Failure," *Chest* 102, no. 5, 1992.
8. Quan, S. F., et al., "Mandatory Minute Volume (MMV) Ventilation: An Overview," *Respiratory Care* 35, no. 9, 1990.
9. Pilbeam, S. P., *Mechanical Ventilation Physiological and Clinical Applications, 3rd ed.,* Mosby, 1998.
10. Griggs, B. L., and Reinhardt, D. J., "Fundamentals of Nosocomial Infections Associated with Respiratory Therapy," *Projects in Health Inc.*, 1975.
11. Dupuis, Y. G., *Ventilators Theory and Clinical Application,* Mosby, 1986.

Assessment Questions

1. While working in the sleep lab monitoring a patient on BiPAP, you notice loud snoring during a sleep period. You would adjust the BiPAP by:
   A. Increasing the IPAP
   B. Increasing the EPAP
   C. Increasing the flow rate
   D. Increasing the respiratory rate

2. A constant flow ventilator would exhibit which of the following characteristics?
   I. The inspired flow remains the same throughout inspiration
   II. The ventilator is not influenced by the patient's lung characteristics
   III. Pressure would increase in a linear fashion throughout inspiration

A. I and II only
B. I, II and III
C. I and III only
D. II and III only

3. A volume ventilator that you are monitoring experiences a low exhaled volume alarm situation. Which of the following could cause this occurrence?

   I. Change in inspired tidal volume
   II. Change in the set frequency
   III. A decrease in the patient's spontaneous ventilation
   IV. A leak somewhere in the inspiratory side of the system

   A. I and II only
   B. I, II and III only
   C. I, II, III and IV
   D. II, III and IV only

4. When using the expiratory retard option during mechanical ventilation you would expect:

   A. The inspiratory flow to increase
   B. The expiratory time to increase
   C. Patient-ventilator asynchrony
   D. Auto-PEEP

5. High frequency jet ventilators (HFJV) exhibit which of the following characteristics?

   I. Requires a special endotracheal tube to support high ventilator rates
   II. Allows for passive exhalation
   III. Permits breathing rates up to 600 breaths per minute
   IV. Requires active exhalation

   A. I, II and III only
   B. I, III and IV only
   C. II and III only
   D. III and IV only

6. The most popular method of adjusting the low inspired pressure alarm is to:

   A. Set the alarm 10 cmH_2O above the peak inspiratory pressure
   B. Set the alarm 10 cmH_2O below the peak inspiratory pressure
   C. Set the alarm 15 cmH_2O below the peak inspiratory pressure
   D. Set the alarm 1 cmH_2O below the peak inspiratory pressure

7. Activation of the low-pressure alarm would require the therapist to first:

   A. Run the ventilator self-test
   B. Determine patient's level of dyspnea
   C. Immediately check source (wall) pressure
   D. Immediately check for patient disconnection

8. The patient's inspired gas volume is indicated on the expiratory spirometer. The reason for it is that:

   A. Not all ventilator gas gets through the inspiratory HEPA filter
   B. There are built-in leaks in every ventilator
   C. Positive pressure is compressing volume in the ventilator circuitry
   D. Some gas diverts to the exhalation side of the tubing at the patient wye

9. The physician asks you to remove 12 inches of tubing that lie between the wye connector of the ventilator circuit and the patient's airway. Removal of this tube will have which of the following effects?

   I. Remove some compressible volume due to positive pressure
   II. Decrease the patient's mechanical deadspace
   III. Increase the patient's FRC
   IV. Allow the exhaled gas to flow out the expiratory port

   A. I and II only
   B. I, II and III only
   C. I, II, III and IV
   D. II, III and IV only

Chapter 16

Monitoring, Analyzing, and Testing Devices

I. Electrocardiography

A. The electrocardiometer is a voltmeter that records the electrical charges occurring in the heart. Electrodes (sensors) are placed in direct contact with the skin and transmit the electrical signals to the ECG machine. The use of a digital computer for ECG measurement provides analysis and diagnosis with waveform comparison against a large database of prerecorded waveforms. Large numbers of records are allowed to be processed and transmitted anywhere online.

B. Cardiac leads consist of positive and negative electrodes that sense the magnitude and direction of the heart's electrical forces. Leads are used to record electrical activity on graph paper, on a oscilloscope, or on a computer, thus displaying the P, QRS, and T waveforms.

C. For dynamic information like ECG waveforms, the most effective display is oscilloscopic. New technology computer monitors continuously trace the incoming signals on the tube face. A memoscope is used to retain a trace as a fixed image with uniform undiminished brightness until an erase signal is given. It provides an appropriate means for displaying the trends of slowly changing data.

D. A plotting recorder permits immediate observation of trends and cross-correlations of different recorded data.

    1. The ECG plotting recorder makes an upward deflection on the graph paper when the electrical impulse of the heart moves towards the positive lead.

    2. The ECG recorder makes a downward deflection on the graph paper when the electrical impulse moves away from the positive lead.

    3. Six limb leads are placed on the arms and legs, and six standard precordial leads for the chest. Refer to Table 16-1.

Chapter 16: Monitoring, Analyzing, and Testing Devices

TABLE 16-1: EKG Leads[3]

The right leg lead is always considered the ground lead.
All chest leads are positive.

Standard leads:

Lead I	Left arm	(+)	Right arm	(−)
Lead II	Left leg	(+)	Right arm	(−)
Lead III	Left leg	(+)	Right arm	(−)

Unipolar leads:

AVR*	Right arm	(+)	All other leads	(−)
AVL	Left arm	(+)	All other leads	(−)
AVF	Left foot	(+)	All other leads	(−)

Precordial (chest) leads:

V_1	Fourth intercostal space, right sternal border
V_2	Fourth intercostal space, left sternal border
V_3	In-between V_2 and V_4
V_4	Fifth intercostal space, midclavicular line
V_5	Fifth intercostal space, anterior axillary line
V_6	Fifth intercostal space, midaxillary line
V_7	Fifth intercostal space, posterior axillary line
V_8	Fifth intercostal space midscapular line

*It is the only limb lead that produces an upside-down or negative electrical pattern; augmented voltage (Foot)(Lead).

II. Arterial catheter

A. Arterial catheters are used to continuously monitor moment to moment arterial pressure as part of a catheter-transducer monitoring system.
  1. They are designed to provide access to arterial blood for acid-base and oxygenation measurements, and supply a site for rapid removal of blood in the event of fluid overload.

2. The catheter also provides reproducible measurements of mean, systolic, and diastolic blood pressure, and derives mean arterial pressure (MAP) by computer calculation.
3. When the catheter is used to monitor right ventricular function it will provide precise measurement of right ventricular filling pressure or central venous pressure (CVP).

B. Sites for placement of a 18–20-gauge catheter include the femoral, radial, brachial, and dorsalis pedis, with the radial artery the most commonly used due to its superficial location and collateral anastomoses with the ulnar artery.
  1. The 20-gauge teflon catheters have shown to have the least amount of thrombosis, as high as 8%.[1]
  2. The 18-gauge polypropylene catheter was most likely to thrombose.[1]

C. Refer to Trouble Shooting Guide 16-1 for information regarding arterial catheters.

III. Swan-Ganz catheter

A. A soft flow-directed catheter is inserted into a femoral, subclavian, jugular, or brachial vein, and threaded through the right heart into the pulmonary artery. The

Trouble Shooting Guide 16-1

Arterial Catheters

Problem	Possible Causes	Corrective Actions
Bleedback into tubing or transducer dome	Insufficient pressure on IV bag	Maintain 300 mm Hg pressure on IV bag
	Loose connections	Tighten all connections Use luer-lock
Sepsis	Break in sterile technique	Antibiotic Rx, use aseptic technique
	Prolonged catheter use	Remove catheter after 72–96 hours
	Bacterial growth in IV fluid	Proper flushing of stopcocks after blood sampling
Emboli	Clot from catheter tip into bloodstream	Heparin

catheter is constructed of polyvinyl chloride and measures 110 centimeters in length. Available sizes are 4 Fr for pediatric patients and 5–7 Fr for adults.[2]

B. The catheter is a multipurpose device that is used to monitor cardiac output, central venous pressure (CVP), right/left heart pressures, pulmonary artery pressure (PAP), and permit blood sampling and drug administration. Some catheters are equipped with a pacer wire for adjusting heart rate.
1. A proximal port opens into the right atrium that allows administration of medication, delivery of cardiac output injectate, and measurement of CVP.
2. 10 ml of cooled 5% dextrose in water or normal saline is infused into the right atrium. A thermistor bead located just behind the balloon on the tip of the catheter measures the temperature of the blood in the pulmonary artery, thereby determining cardiac output.
3. A distal lumen port (catheter tip) opens into the pulmonary artery to monitor PAP. Blood samples are withdrawn here to determine mixed venous oxygen content.
4. A balloon inflation valve connects to a syringe for insertion of 1.25–1.50 ml of air to measure pulmonary capillary wedge pressure (PCWP). Balloon bursting volume occurs with 3 ml of air.
5. The catheter connects directly to a cardiac output computer and to a pressure transducer. Fluid motion in the vascular system is transformed into an electrical signal that is amplified and displayed as a pressure tracing.

IV. Metering devices

A. Respirometers (like the Wright) operate by directing a flow of gas against a vane. The gas flow manipulates a watch-like set of gears in order to display the recorded gas volume on a dial face calibrated in liters.
1. These devices are handheld and have a stopwatch-like push-button control for stop, start, and reset.
    a. Timed flows are not possible with this device.
    b. Measures flow in one direction only.
    c. There is no printout or recording of the patient's effort other than the volume indicators on the dial face.
2. The respirometer is also referred to as a turbinometer, because it records gas volume through the measurement of gas flow.
3. The normal flows this device will measure are between 3 and 300 L/min.
    a. The primary uses are to measure tidal and minute volumes.
    b. The device is easily adapted to fit on the expiratory side of most ventilator circuits.
4. Low flow rates (less than 3 L/min) are not high enough to overcome inertia of the vane/gear drive mechanism, thereby causing erroneous readings to occur.

5. Flow rates above 300 L/min can damage the turbinometer causing the rotor mechanisms to lock (jam) up.[4]

B. Inspiratory/expiratory force meters are normally Bourdon-type pressures gauges.
   1. A pressure manometer indicates both positive and negative changes from ambient air. The pressure gauge attaches to the patient's endotracheal tube and measures the subambient or peak pressure generated.
   2. A red pointer indicates the highest inspiratory pressure, and a black pointer indicates breath to breath measurements. Most gauges indicate a pressure range of −60 to +60 cmH$_2$O even though most patients are capable of generating much greater pressures during both inspiratory and expiratory maneuvers.

C. Refer to Trouble Shooting Guide 16-2 for information regarding a gas driven turbinometer.

V. Pressure transducers

A. The transducer is an electronic device that receives data in one form and transduces (transforms) it into another form. In this case, energy is converted into an electrical signal, which is amplified and displayed on a monitor screen.

Trouble Shooting Guide 16-2

Gas Driven Turbinometer

Problem	Possible Causes	Corrective Actions
Volumes being displayed are not accurate	Exposure to flows, temperatures, or pressures beyond design limits	Design accuracy is +/− 6%
	Dial has been reset with the unit switched on	Vanes warped, repair
	Unit has been dropped or struck a hard surface	Repair
	Humidity damage from continuous in-line use	Vanes warped, repair
Not recording exhaled volume	Wright respirometer is turned off	Flip the switch to the on position
Dial indicators aren't moving	Expiratory hose attached to outlet	Attach hose to inlet

Chapter 16: Monitoring, Analyzing, and Testing Devices

1. The transducer has a pressure-sensing device (diaphragm) enclosed in a sealed chamber. This diaphragm distorts or deforms away from the greatest pressure change.
    a. The diaphragm of a pressure transducer has one side exposed to source pressure and one side exposed to barometric pressure.
    b. The diaphragm of a differential-pressure transducer (difference in pressure between two points) has one side exposed to pressure sources. The diaphragm then responds only to the difference between those two pressures, by bending away from the greatest pressure change.
2. The diaphragm responds to pressure by bending out of proportion. A strain gauge (pressure-sensitive semiconductor) is bonded to the diaphragm. This gauge senses the bending and converts it into an electrical signal.
    a. Electronic circuits encased in the transducer convert the movement of the strain gauge into a representative voltage that is transmitted to the pressure monitor.
    b. Gas bubbles that become trapped in the transducer dome reduce the frequency response of the system resulting in a pressure waveform that appears dampened (reduced in size for maximum inflections and deflections). This result applies only to blood or liquid manometer systems.

VI. Pneumotachometers

A. A pneumotach is an electronic monitoring device that measures continuous or intermittent flow. Advanced electronics change (integrate) the flow into a signal that is proportional to volume.
   1. A fine mesh screen of small capillary tubes makes up the flow-resistive element that creates a fixed resistance (obstruction) to airflow. As gas flow meets the obstruction, a pressure difference is created, which is proportional to flow. By electronically integrating a pressure-differential signal (flow) with time, a volume signal is created and measured.
   2. Laminar flow provides the most accurate measurements. The more turbulent the gas flow, the more increasingly inaccurate the flow rate measurement.
   3. Condensed water droplets increase the pressure difference at any given flow rate. Heated thermistor beads (hot wires) are used on some units to raise the temperature of the gas, thereby preventing condensation from changing the resistance.[1]
B. Anemometry (heated-wire thermistor bead pneumotachs) detect flow by measuring the resistance to electric current according to temperature change. A sensor contains two heated thermistor beads (elements) suspended in the main flow channel so incoming gas passes over them. The gas flow cools the wire elements. Electronic chips regulate the current needed to keep the wire elements (heat-transfer) at a stable temperature. In theory, temperature is proportional to flow rate.

1. The wire mesh is designed to trap foreign material and evenly distribute the incoming gas.
2. Sensing elements must be cleaned and reused.
3. Calibration is normally required and the technology is primarily reserved for neonatal application.

C. Vortex shedding pneumotachs incorporate a calibrated flow tube with a strut placed in the airstream to create turbulence. As gas flows over the strut, the turbulent sheet of air tumbles, thus creating a vortex.
  1. Normally each vortex produced represents 1 ml of gas.
  2. An ultrasonic transmitter sends sound waves through the vortices to an ultrasonic receiver, producing an electric signal (pulse) that is calculated and displayed as a measurement of volume or flow. The number of pulses produced is proportional to gas flow.
  3. The electric circuitry does contain a dead-band zone where the electronic signal cannot be accurately produced if the gas flow is less than 10 L/min or greater than 250 L/min. Moisture condensation on the receiver will also cause inaccurate electronic signals to be produced.

D. Photoelectric pneumotachs contain a rotating vane and photoelectric cell mechanism to provide volume measurement and display.
  1. As gas passes through the device a vane rotates, interrupting an infrared light beam emitting from a photoelectric cell. The breaks in the light are counted electrically and are proportional to volume.
  2. Flow rates of 12–150 L/min produce the most accurate results. Exhaled gas moisture that contacts the rotating vane will produce inaccurate volumes.[1]

VII. Blood gas analysis systems

A. Invasive analysis of blood gases requires equipment that obtains and collects the blood sample, equipment for acquiring accurate analysis of the sample, and calibration and control of that equipment.

B. In order to obtain the blood sample a syringe with an accompanying needle (unless sample is extracted from an arterial line) is required.
  1. Syringes are composed of glass or plastic and can be reused or disposable.
     a. Glass syringes generally fill more smoothly than the plastic syringes. A small amount of aspirator force may be required with some brands of plastic syringes.
     b. Some syringes come with the hub and barrel precoated (liquid sodium heparin, 1000 IU/mm) to prevent clotting of the sample.
     c. Syringes (evacuation/collection tubes) containing a partial vacuum are contraindicated when obtaining arterial samples.

Chapter 16: Monitoring, Analyzing, and Testing Devices

2. Hypodermic needles are designed of different lengths, gauges, and hubs.
    a. The shorter 5/8 in. needles are used to administer a local anesthetic solution (0.5%–2% lidocaine), or for puncture of the radial artery. The longer 1½ in. needles are more generally used for brachial and femoral artery puncture.
    b. Smaller-gauge (23–25 gauge) needles are normally used for radial artery punctures, while larger-gauge needles (18–20) are used for brachial and femoral puncture.
    c. Needles with translucent hubs are preferred as they make it more obvious when the artery is punctured.

C. Analyzing gas tension and blood pH require electrodes that are connected to an amplifier system so results can be displayed on a voltmeter calibrated in pH units. Newer automated systems with computer interface allow for interpretation and statistical analysis of the analyzed sample.
    1. The Sanz (pH electrode) is used to measure the hydrogen ion activity in a sample of blood. The measurement is obtained by a comparison of a known hydrogen ion concentration (6.840 at 37°) to an unknown hydrogen ion concentration in the blood sample.
        a. A silver chloride anode (negative pole) contained in a separate inner chamber within the electrode measures the known hydrogen ion concentration.
        b. The anode makes its connection between the outside of the electrode and the inner chamber.
        c. Once contact is made, an electrical gradient is established, which represents the hydrogen ion concentration. This difference is read by the blood gas machine as pH, and indicated by a numerical value display.
        d. Temperature, protein buildup, bacteria metabolism, and disruption of the electrode-membrane integrity will cause erroneous test results.[1]
    2. The Stowe-Severinghaus (PCO_2) electrode is essentially a glass pH electrode with a membrane permeable to CO_2 molecules.
        a. As CO_2 diffuses across a teflon semipermeable membrane, it dissolves into an electrolyte solution. Upon dissolving, an acid is formed creating an electrical reaction within the electrolyte solution. This reaction changes the pH of the electrolyte solution, which is measured by the electrode.
        b. The hydrogen ion change in the electrolyte is what is measured by the electrode, then amplified and displayed as PCO_2.
        c. Temperature, protein buildup, bacteria metabolism, and membrane integrity will affect the test results.[1]
    3. The polarographic Clark electrode (PO_2) polarizes two electrodes that provide the analysis of oxygen in the blood.
        a. Oxygen molecules diffuse through a teflon or polypropylene membrane into an electrolyte bath that is connected to a platinum wire.

b. Oxygen molecules are broken down in an oxidation reaction that changes the amount of current flowing through the electrolytic bath. The blood gas machine converts this current flow into a corresponding PO_2 value that is displayed in mmHg.
c. Excess heparin, anesthetic agents, or protein buildup on the membrane will affect the integrity of the displayed results.[1]
4. In-dwelling arterial optical biosensors (optodes) are in use for ECMO and cardiopulmonary bypass.[5]
a. Miniature optodes are fitted into a 20-gauge arterial catheter and reside inside the artery. Optodes work on the principle of fluorescence.
b. Each optode incorporates a fluorescent indicator dye that is capable of absorbing wavelengths of light specific to O_2, CO_2, and H^+ molecules and ions.
(1) Photosensors measure the amount of light absorbed and transmit an electrical signal in proportion to the absorbed light to a display that shows numerical values.
(2) Optodes are presently available to measure O_2, CO_2, and pH.
(3) System failure of optode sensors has been shown to be faulty in monitoring patients over the long term.[1] Refer to Trouble Shooting Guide 16-3 on blood gas electrodes.

Trouble Shooting Guide 16-3

Blood Gas Electrodes

Problem	Possible Causes	Corrective Actions
Contamination of electrode membrane	Blood products (protein) buildup on the membrane surface	Replace
	Erosion of membrane surface allowing electrolyte solution to leak	Replace
Preanalytic errors	Incorrect calibration	Requires recalibration
	Incorrect temperature in electrode chamber	Maintain temperature in chamber
	Air bubbles in blood sample	Remove air bubble or resample
	Excessive amount of heparin coating syringe	Obtain alternate syringe
	Clotting in the sample	Resample

Chapter 16: Monitoring, Analyzing, and Testing Devices

D. Calibration and quality control of the equipment is essential for accurate assessment of the obtained blood sample.
   1. The quality control program needs to be established according to the following:
      a. Allowable limits need to be set for variation of test results.
      b. All control data must be evaluated according to those established limits.
      c. Documentation in the logbook showing action taken to correct excessive limits.
   2. Because electrode stability is subject to sudden malfunction and the inherent temperature/pressure drift characteristics within the amplifier system, the electrodes need to be calibrated over the span of physiologic range that is measured clinically. They require a two-point calibration of the baseline-reference (zero) and high-reference (gain) points of each electrode. This calibration can be accomplished either manually or automatically.
      a. In manual calibration, the pH electrode is exposed to two buffer solutions that establish the electrode range. Zero reference is verified by a buffer with a pH value of 6.840. High reference is verified by a buffer with a pH value of 7.384.
      b. Manual calibration of the gas electrodes establishes the zero-range by exposing them to FO_2 of 0.2 and a FCO_2 of 0.05. The gain is set by exposing them to a FO_2 of 0 and a FCO_2 of 0.1. This procedure sets the oxygen electrode range at 0–150 mmHg, and the carbon dioxide electrode range 30–80 mmHg.
      c. Automatic analyzers perform this same calibration process at preselected intervals. Instead of reference adjustment by the practitioner, a microprocessor adjusts each electrode output to match the known values.
   3. Equipment quality control is typically determined by tonometry or commercially available controls that are pretonometered.
      a. Tonometry is the rapid equilibration of gas mixtures with known partial pressures for CO_2 and PO_2 with a liquid (blood samples or buffer solution).
         (1) This mixing occurs when the gas and liquid are exposed to each other in a tonometer.
         (2) Tonometered sample results are then compared to predicted values, thereby checking the accuracy of the blood gas analyzer.
      b. Commercially prepared controls consist of buffered fixed human red cells or aqueous/perfluorinated compounds that are designed to simulate the characteristics of blood.
         (1) They come prepackaged in 2–3 ml sealed glass ampoules.
         (2) Barometric pressure, instrument temperature, and observed pH are recorded into the daily log. Electrode pH values are compared to the buffer values.
   4. Should a series of calibration parameters be outside the standardized limits, an out-of-control situation has occurred and reporting accuracy has become compromised.

a. An out-of-control situation exists when a set of calibration values are outside the established limits. Either random error or systemic error is responsible for the analyzed values.
b. An in-control situation exists when a set of calibration values are within two standard deviations of the established limits (mean).

VIII. Oxygen analyzers

A. The paramagnetic oxygen analyzer (Beckman) actually measures the partial pressure of oxygen molecules present in a sample of gas by applying Pauling's principle of paramagnetism. When a gas containing oxygen is exposed to a magnetic field, the oxygen molecules are attracted to that field.[7]
 1. Two hollow glass spheres filled with nitrogen are suspended on a platinum-iridium wire between the poles of a magnet. When oxygen is exposed to the magnetic field, the field acts upon the nitrogen filled glass spheres making the dumbbell rotate.
    a. A mirror attached to the dumbbell reflects light onto a scale calibrated in mmHg and oxygen percent.
    b. Because only factory calibration is possible, a nomogram is supplied with the analyzer in order to compensate for changes on the oxygen percent scale due to altitude.
 2. This analyzer provides for the intermittent analysis of oxygen, by aspirating the sample gas via a squeeze bulb.
B. The thermal conductivity oxygen analyzer measures the partial pressure of oxygen molecules present in a sample of gas by applying the principle of thermal conductivity (where oxygen has the ability to remove heat faster than nitrogen).
 1. Two thermistor beads (temperature-sensitive electrical resistors) are connected in a wheatstone bridge circuit. One bead serves as a reference and one bead is exposed to the sample gas.
    a. Constant electrical current heats the sensor. As the sample gas is passed over the sensor, heat is conducted away from the sensor at a rate dependent upon the thermal conductivity of oxygen.
    b. The sample gas is directed over a heated thermistor bead, so these analyzers are not recommended for use in an environment where explosive anesthetic gases are present.
 2. Because carbon dioxide molecules are heavier than oxygen molecules, this device is designed to sample oxygen on the inspiratory side of the ventilator circuit.
 3. This analyzer also analyzes gas intermittently via a squeeze bulb.
C. The electrochemical oxygen analyzer provides for intermittent or continuous measurement of oxygen concentration by employing a galvanic fuel cell.

Chapter 16: Monitoring, Analyzing, and Testing Devices   265

1. The fuel cell uses the current generated from oxygen reduction to analyze the oxygen concentration.[7]
   a. Two electrodes, a lead cathode and a gold anode, are immersed in an electrolyte solution separated by a semi-permeable membrane.
   b. Oxygen molecules diffuse across the membrane producing an electronic current between the two electrodes. This current flow is measured and displayed as oxygen percentage.
2. Proper calibration technique requires that the unit be calibrated at 0.21 when the FIO_2 is less than 0.60. When the FIO_2 is greater than 0.60 the unit is calibrated at 1.00.

D. The polarographic (Clark electrode) uses an external power source (battery) to polarize two electrodes, a silver cathode and a platinum or gold anode that provides intermittent or continuous breath-to-breath oxygen analysis.
   1. Oxygen molecules diffuse through a teflon or polypropylene membrane into an electrolyte bath. The electrolyte uses the oxygen molecule to establish current flow that is converted to oxygen percentage.
   2. The percentage reading is proportional to the partial pressure. The oxygen percentage will fluctuate slightly when used in-line with a ventilator due to the positive pressure occurring on inspiration.
   3. The polarographic electrode may require frequent calibration due to drift problems.
   4. Proper calibration technique requires that the unit be calibrated at 0.21 when the FIO_2 is less than 0.60. When the FIO_2 is greater than 0.60 the unit is calibrated at 1.00.

E. Refer to Trouble Shooting Guide 16-4 for information regarding oxygen analyzers.

IX. Oximetry[1]

A. The co-oximeter (IL282) measures the absorption of light. A hollow cathode lamp is used to measure optical density at four well-defined wavelengths. This determines the oxygen saturation of the blood by measuring the amount of light reflected through a layer of blood.
   1. As light passes through a transparent container holding a sample of blood, some of the light is absorbed. Electronic circuitry converts it into an electrical signal.
   2. The oximeter then computes the total hemoglobin, oxyhemoglobin, methemoglobin, and carboxyhemoglobin saturation, and derives the oxygen content value.

B. The pulse oximeter is noninvasive and monitors hemoglobin arterial oxygen saturation. Two different wavelengths of light are used to measure the optical density of hemoglobin, allowing the adequacy of perfusion to be identified.

Trouble Shooting Guide 16-4

Oxygen Analyzers

Problem	Possible Causes	Corrective Actions
Analyzer does not function correctly	Power supply, fuel cell, or battery may be exhausted	Fix or replace
Decreased response time	Sensor probe faulty	Fix or replace
	Exhausted fuel cell or battery	Replace
Drifty O$_2$ reading	Analyzer out of calibration	Recalibrate/recheck oxygen concentration
	Moisture or debris resides on sensor probe	Remove moisture/debris or replace sensor probe
Erratic reading with new sensor	Installation of new probe requires stabilization time prior to first sample being run	Turn unit off, wait for unit to stabilize on room air, calibrate, and then sample

1. This measurement is accomplished by measuring pulsed red (660 NM) and infrared (940 NM) light absorption through the skin. These two wavelengths are used to gauge the presence of oxygenated and reduced hemoglobin.
2. Because oxygenated hemoglobin (HbO$_2$) and reduced hemoglobin (Hb) absorb light differently, this difference of HbO2 and Hb can be calculated. Oxygen-depleted blood absorbs more red light than oxygen-saturated blood.
3. The oximeter oxisensor (probe/transducer) transmits the two wavelengths of light (red and infrared) from a LED (light-emitting diode) through a finger or toe.
   a. A photodetector picks up the transmitted light and converts the light into an electronic signal.
   b. The oximeter amplifies the electronic signals it receives and converts this information into the SaO$_2$ and pulse rate values that are displayed on the front panel.
   c. Due to the pulsing of the vascular bed between the light source and the detector, a familiar waveform (optical plethysmograph) results.
4. The presence of a strong arterial pulse (pulse amplitude) is important. The red light passing through oxyhemoglobin generates a small pulse amplitude, while

Chapter 16: Monitoring, Analyzing, and Testing Devices

a red light passing through deoxyhemoglobin generates a large pulse amplitude. It allows the oximeter to measure the rate and strength of the pulse, due to the amount of light transmitted through a finger or toe varying with the pulse.

5. Pulse oximeters cannot recognize the different forms of hemoglobin such as oxyhemoglobin (HbO_2), carboxyhemoglobin (HbCO), and methemoglobin (Hbmet).
   a. As a result, the oximeter reading may be affected by the amount of HbCO and Hbmet present in the blood sample.
   b. The oximeter can detect the differences of arterial blood, venous blood, and tissue. Venous blood does not pulse because the arterial bed expands and relaxes, which modifies the amount of light detected.
6. Acceptable values for percent saturation and heartbeat are based on the following:
   a. Accuracy would be expected to fall between 3%–5%, meaning a SaO_2 of 94% would fall somewhere between 89% and 99%.
   b. Heart rate results should fall between 5 beats per minute of a manually taken pulse.
   c. Sensor probe type has been shown to affect response time significantly during a desaturation event. This time frame elapses from the beginning of the event until the unit alarms, warning the event occurred. Refer to Table 16-2, and to Trouble Shooting Guide 16-5 for information regarding oximetry.

X. Transcutaneous oxygen and carbon dioxide monitors

A. These monitors are really blood gas electrodes that contain built-in heaters to warm the body surface beneath the electrode to approximately 42–45°C.
   1. Heating the skin (hyperemia) causes dilation of the underlying capillary bed and an increase in local blood perfusion, which makes it possible to estimate the partial pressures of oxygen and carbon dioxide.

TABLE 16-2: Desaturation Event Response Time[8]

Sensor Type	Response Time
Ear sensors	10–20 sec
Finger sensors	24–35 sec
Toe sensors	56.8 sec

Trouble Shooting Guide 16-5

Oximetry

Problem	Possible Causes	Corrective Actions
Inaccurate results	Patient motion	Correct
	Strong light source	Shield probe from strong light source
	Dirty sensor	Clean/replace
	Oxisensor misaligned	Realign
	Fingernail polish	Select alternate site/remove
Reading varies with site location	Oxisensor malfunction	Replace
	Site location not well perfused	Realign same site, or try alternate site

    2. The increase in skin temperature increases cutaneous blood flow, allowing for diffusion from the arterialized capillaries through the skin to the sensor on the surface.

    3. The measured transcutaneous gas tensions ($tcpO_2$ and $tcpCO_2$) are indicative only of local tissue perfusion and not necessarily indicative of the arterial tension.

B. The measuring component consists of a base monitor, cable, and electrode that attaches to the skin in such a manner as not to allow room air to be present between the membrane and skin surface.

    1. Membranes are constructed of a teflon material that allows gases to pass through it while preventing the electrolyte solution from passing through.

    2. A contact gel is placed on an adhesive disk and attaches to the electrode on the patient's chest.

    3. Gas diffuses in the following manner:

        a. Across the skin surface

        b. Through contact gel

        c. Through the teflon membrane

        d. Through the chemical reaction within the electrolyte

        e. Into the electrode to be measured

C. The ideal skin temp is 43°C. At this point, the $tcpO_2$ and $tcpCO_2$ correlate well with each other and the skin is not seriously burned.

Chapter 16: Monitoring, Analyzing, and Testing Devices 269

1. The skin sites should be changed every two to four hours (recalibration recommended). Hyperemia causes vasodilatation of the capillaries and may allow tissue edema and burning to develop.
2. Too much pressure from the sensor on the skin may reduce perfusion.
3. Erroneous readings will be introduced if blood flow is insufficient to the region due to impaired diffusion. Refer to Trouble Shooting Guide 16-6.
4. The electrodes need to be calibrated prior to use.
    a. The miniaturized Clark oxygen electrode may use solutions with known values, or gases, for calibration. Two-point calibration is used, with a low value of zero, and a high value, which is room air or an arterial sample.
    b. The Stowe-Severinghaus carbon dioxide electrode must be calibrated with gases of known values. Two-point calibration requires the low level to be 4–5% CO_2, and 10% CO_2 for the high level.

XI. Mass spectrometer

A. The mass spectrometer is designed to separate charged gas molecules according to their specific mass, making it possible to quickly measure the true concentration of respiratory gases. An electron beam ionizes the sample gases in a magnetic field,

Trouble Shooting Guide 16-6

Transcutaneous Electrodes

Problem	Possible Causes	Corrective Actions
Reading varies up and down, or varies with ABG results	Air is present between the skin and the electrode	Clean and apply contact gel
	Membrane is no longer permeable and leaking electrolyte	Replace membrane
	Skin is blistered and burned	Relocate sensor site
Low results	Temperature is less than required 42–45°C	Repair or replace
	Site location not well perfused	Relocate sensor site
Erratic reading with new membrane	New membrane installation requires stabilization time prior to first sample being run through	Turn unit off, wait for unit to stabilize on room air, then calibrate, then sample

counts the number of ionized molecules present in the sample, and separates the gases according to their specific mass.
1. A sample of patient's exhaled gas is drawn into a capillary tube using a vacuum pump. A "T"-piece at the end of the endotracheal tube allows the gas to be removed from the patient.
2. An extremely hot filament provides a current to knock electrons from the gas molecules thereby ionizing them. A magnetic analyzer then separates the gases according to their charge and mass.
3. As the gases separate they impinge on collecting plates where electrometers count the number of molecules to determine the concentration of each gas. This information is then converted into a signal that is amplified and displayed.
4. Both inspired and end-tidal respiratory gases can be measured and displayed.
5. Multiple patients can be monitored in the ICU or surgical setting for concentrations of oxygen, nitrogen, carbon dioxide, and anesthetic gases.

XII. Capnometer/capnography

A. Carbon dioxide monitors measure the percentage of CO_2 in a given sample of gas. Capnometry is the measurement and numerical display of airway CO_2. The capnometer is the device that provides the numeric display. Capnography is the measurement and graphic display of CO_2, while the CO_2 waveform display is called a capnogram.
1. Exhaled gas enters a sample chamber and is exposed to a high-intensity infrared light beam.
   a. The CO_2 absorbs the infrared light in proportion to the number of CO_2 molecules present in the sample chamber.
   b. Capnometers are constructed of an incandescent filament to generate the infrared light, and a detector to measure the radiation. The radiation is converted into an electrical signal, which is amplified and sent to a display.
2. Monitors continue to display the measured value (as a percent or in mmHg) and graph the exhaled CO_2 waveform (capnogram).
B. The expired gas sample is obtained through tubing placed at the airway and transported to the sample chamber. This technique allows for microsampling volumes of exhaled gas. There are two types of sampling techniques used by infrared technology.
1. The sidestream (aspirating) capnograph draws gas from the patient's airway via a sampling adapter.
   a. The sample gas is transported through fine-bore tubing to the capnograph that houses the measurement chamber. The infrared light source and photodetector lie inside the measurement chamber.

Chapter 16: Monitoring, Analyzing, and Testing Devices

      b. Transportation of the sample gas to the remote site delays the response time of the unit.

      c. Moisture easily obstructs tubing causing inaccuracies.

      d. Most capnographs sample exhaled gas at a flowrate of 150 ml/min.

  2. The mainstream (in-line) capnograph has the measurement chamber placed in-line with the patient's airway.

      a. The infrared light source and photodetector are inside the measurement chamber.

      b. This system results in a crisp capnogram display almost instantly without a delay in response time.

      c. The mainstream sensor is fragile and subject to damage.

      d. The mainstream sensor has added weight and may threaten tubing disconnect.

  3. A monitoring lumen is used with the sampling adaptor. There is a separate tube within the wall of the endotracheal tube incorporating a port located at the tip for sampling end-tidal concentrations of gas.

  4. Waveforms are produced by changes in the level of expired CO_2. The highest point of the waveform is referred to as end-tidal CO_2 ($EtCO_2$).

  5. Calibration is done on room air, and the unit is set at "zero mm Hg.", because atmospheric air only contains a trace amount of carbon dioxide.

C. Refer to Trouble Shooting Guide 16-7 for information regarding capnographs.

XIII. Exhaled carbon dioxide detection device[5]

A. The Easy Cap end-tidal carbon dioxide detector is a disposable device using a chemical reaction to produce a color change (colorimetric end-tidal CO_2 detection) from purple to yellow in the presence of carbon dioxide.

B. The device is inserted between the manual resuscitator bag and the endotracheal tube to determine tube position within the trachea.

  1. When exposed to alveolar gas the device reads yellow indicating endotracheal intubation has occurred. If the color remains purple the tube has been inserted into the esophagus. Breath-to-breath visualization is assured as the color changes with each inspiration and expiration.

  2. The detector contains 38 ml of dead space, which could put small children at risk of rebreathing CO_2 should the device be used on them.

  3. The detector should only be used for short-term determination, as humidity in the exhaled gas makes the device ineffective.[1]

C. The Easy Cap functions well (100% accuracy) in emergency situations as long as the patient is in respiratory failure.[1]

Trouble Shooting Guide 16-7

Mainstream and Sidestream Capnographs

Problem	Possible Causes	Corrective Actions
Drifty/erratic CO_2 reading	Secretions block sensor window or sample tubing	Use line from suction machine to remove blockage/replace tubing
	Humidity interferes with sensor window or obstructs sample tubing	Suction sensor line or replace tubing
	Obstruction of inlet filter	Replace filter
Delayed response to CO_2 changes	Out of calibration	Recalibrate at regular intervals
	Tubing too long, dampens reading	Shorten tubing
	Tubing disconnected from ventilator circuit	Reconnect
Low CO_2 reading	Leak in ventilator citcuit	Correct leak
	Tubing too long, dampens reading	Shorten/replace tubing

1. Results are much less reliable for detection of esophageal intubation during cardiac arrest due to inadequate pulmonary blood flow.
2. Pulmonary edema fluid contaminates the device and makes the detector ineffective.

XIV. Helium analyzer[6]

A. The helium analyzer (Cartharometer) works on the principal of thermal conductivity. The device is normally used for measuring small fractional concentrations of helium (up to 10%).
   1. An electrical current constantly heats two thermistor beads (sensors). As the analyzed gas passes over the sensor, heat is removed in proportion to the molecular weight of the gas.
   2. The thermistor beads (temperature-sensitive electrical resistors) are connected in an electrical circuit (wheatstone bridge). One bead (sensor) is subjected to a reference gas whose concentration is known, while the other sensor is subjected to the sample gas whose concentration is unknown.
   3. A difference that is measurable then exists between the reference sensor and the sample sensor. The concentration change of helium is actually measured by

Chapter 16: Monitoring, Analyzing, and Testing Devices

the resistance changes of the sensor. This difference is expressed as a percentage of helium.

XV. Spirometers[6]

A. Spirometers are used for clinical and diagnostic testing and should meet the standards for pulmonary function analysis as established by the American Thoracic Society (ATS).

B. Calibration of pulmonary function spirometers require a Super-Syringe capable of delivering a known 3-liter volume.
   1. The syringe can provide test signals for both volume-type and flow-type spirometer systems to indicate any leaks.
      a. The entire syringe volume is displaced and the spirometer reading is observed.
         (1) If no leak is found, the volume shown on the computer screen or on printout will be within $+/-3\%$ of the syringe volume.
         (2) The results are then documented in the equipment logbook.
      b. Some spirometers require the entire syringe volume to be injected at different speeds. ATS suggests emptying the syringe in 0.5-sec increments, up to 5 seconds.
   2. Should the spirometer be unable to meet the standards within the $+/-3\%$ limit, it needs to be pulled from service until repaired, then recalibrated.

C. Rolling-seal spirometers use a rolling diaphragm and a lightweight aluminum piston that is displaced as exhaled gas enters the cylinder.
   1. As gas enters the system, a piston moves a U-shaped seal that rides on low friction bearings back and forth on a horizontal plane.
   2. A potentiometer (changes the pistons movement into an electrical signal) is attached to the piston to provide a digital readout or a waveform tracing of flow and volume.
      a. The voltage output produced is proportional to the volume change in the cylinder.
      b. Cylinder volume is normally 10–12 liters.

D. Water seal (direct volume displacement) spirometers incorporate a bell that is inverted into water to prevent atmospheric air from entering the system. The water seal helps to contain the patient's exhaled air and is used for pulmonary function screening of basic laboratory tests.
   1. A patient normally exhales into the bell causing the bell to rise. This permits a rotating drum (paper drive mechanism) to display volume per time on graph paper.
   2. A pen connected to the chain and pulley assembly traces the movement of the bell (a spirogram representing the exhaled volume) on graph paper attached to the rotating drum (kymograph).

3. The kymograph rotates at speeds of 32 mm/min for the He dilution test, 160 mm/min for a MVV maneuver, and 1,920 mm/min for the purpose of recording a forced vital capacity.
E. Wedge spirometers incorporate an accordion-type bellows that folds and unfolds in response to breathing excursions.
   1. The fan-like movements of the wedge bellows produce the mechanical movement that is transmitted to a mechanical recording device (pen).
   2. A transducer converts the fan-like motion into an output voltage that is proportional to volume.
F. Plethysmography (body box)
   1. The body plethysmograph is used to measure thoracic gas volume (TGV) based on Boyle's law (a volume of gas at constant temperature varies inversely to the pressure applied to it).
      a. The plethysmograph is constructed of plexiglass and has the appearance of a telephone booth. This booth has an approximate capacity of 600 liters, and provides an air tight seal.
      b. When a patient is placed inside the box, the pressure change produced by the patient's ventilatory movements inside the box can be measured.
   2. Pressure transducers are used to measure the pressure inside the box that is converted electronically by computer to a volume measurement. This signal is then sent to a printer or oscilloscope for visualization.
   3. A pneumotachometer is used to measure flow rates, utilizing an electronic shutter apparatus to measure mouth pressure.

XVI. Holter monitors[9]

A. A portable ECG that can be worn for long periods of time for the purpose of monitoring abnormal cardiac activities.
B. The device is noninvasive and is capable of generating a hard copy (graph) of abnormalities.
C. The main intent of the unit is detecting arrhythmias, observing the effects of a medication to determine its effectiveness, and to detect episodes of silent ischemia.
   1. The monitor is worn underneath the clothing with the cardiac leads attached to the chest.
   2. The Holter is available as a tape system, a digital flash card, or a combination of both. Each system will operate with modern computer components to maximize accuracy reporting speed.
   3. Transfer and analysis of 24-hour Holter data can be archived in less than five minutes.

Chapter 16: Monitoring, Analyzing, and Testing Devices

References

1. Kacmarek, R. M., et al., *Monitoring in Respiratory Care,* Mosby, 1993.
2. *Advanced Cardiac Life Support,* American Heart Association, 1997.
3. Shoemaker, W. C., et. al., *The Society of Critical Care Medicine Textbook of Critical Care, 3rd ed.,* W. B. Saunders Co., 1999.
4. Wernerus, H., et al., "Accuracy of Drager and Wright Ventilation Meters," *Respiratory Care* 23, no.9, 1978.
5. Scanlon, C. L., Wilkins, R. L., and Stoller, J. K., *Egan's Fundamentals of Respiratory Therapy, 7th ed.,* Mosby, 1999.
6. Ruppel, G., *Manual of Pulmonary Function Testing, 7th ed.,* Mosby, 1998.
7. McPherson, S., *Respiratory Care Equipment, 5th ed.,* Mosby, 1995.
8. Quan, S. F., et al., "Mandatory Minute Volume (MMV) Ventilation: An Overview," *Respiratory Care* 35, no. 9, 1990.
9. http://software.bu.edu/COHIS/cardvasckvd.htm

Assessment Questions

1. Placement of the arterial catheter include which of the following?

    I. Brachial artery
    II. Dorsalis pedis
    III. Femoral artery
    IV. Radial artery

    A. I and II only
    B. I, II, III and IV
    C. I and III only
    D. I and IV only

2. The type of device that senses flow by measuring a change in electric current created by a change in temperature describes a:

    A. Capnometer
    B. Pressure differential pneumotach
    C. Turbinometer
    D. Cathrotach

3. Which of the following types of hemoglobin can be analyzed by the co-oximeter?

    I. Carboxyhemoglobin
    II. Methemoglobin
    III. Oxyhemoglobin

    A. I only
    B. I and II only
    C. I, II and III
    D. III only

4. Which of the following values can be measured with a pulmonary artery catheter?

    I. Pulmonary artery pressure
    II. Pulmonary wedge pressure
    III. Mixed venous blood parameters
    IV. Cardiac output

    A. I and II only
    B. I, II and III only
    C. I, II, III and IV
    D. II, III and IV only

5. When calibrating an ABG machine, the values derived are considered in control when the calibration values are:

    A. Within two standard deviations from the mean
    B. Within three standard deviations from the mean

C. Within four standard deviations from the mean
D. Within five standard deviations from the mean

6. A patient undergoing a stress test is connected to an ECG monitor and a pulse oximeter. The ECG monitor displays a heart rate of 92, while the pulse oximeter exhibits a heart rate of 122, and a SaO_2 of 85%. Which of the following actions are most appropriate?
   A. Obtain an arterial blood sample and run it through a co-oximeter
   B. Inspect and secure all the ECG leads
   C. Move the pulse ox sensor to an alternative site
   D. Obtain an arterial blood sample and run it through the ABG analyzer

7. Sources of blood gas analyzer calibration errors include which of the following?
   I. Imprecise barometer readings
   II. Contaminated buffers
   III. Air bubble injected into the analyzer
   IV. Deteriorated blood sample

   A. I and II only
   B. I, II, III and IV
   C. II, III and IV only
   D. III and IV only

8. The low and high values used in the two-point calibration method with transcutaneous CO_2 monitors are:
   A. 1% and 4% CO_2
   B. 5% and 10% CO_2
   C. 8% and 12% CO_2
   D. 12% and 15% CO_2

9. The type of glass used in the pH electrode:
   I. Is permeable to bicarbonate ions
   II. Is permeable to hydrogen ions
   III. Is the reason a potential voltage difference is created between two solutions

   A. I only
   B. I and II only
   C. I, II and III
   D. III only

Chapter 17

Sterilization

I. Categories and techniques of isolation

A. Care of the hospitalized patient with a contagious disease requires an aseptic barrier to be created, which will prevent the spread of infection. The various categories of isolation are designed to prevent the spread of pathogenic microbes that are transmitted in the air (airborne), and by direct or indirect contact. Protective clothing is required in various types of isolation.
   1. Hand-washing is the most important method of preventing cross-contamination between patients.
      a. Hexachlorophene and Betadine solutions are common agents utilized for scrubbing the hands between patients.
      b. Hand-washing should be done before and after contact with each patient.
   2. Masks are required when contact is made with diseases that are transmitted by air, as they are designed to filter most airborne species of bacteria.
      a. The mask should fit snugly around the nose and mouth in order to prevent any pathogen from invading the body.
      b. The mask needs to be changed frequently as exhaled air contains moisture, which makes the masks filtering abilities inefficient.
   3. Gloves are used to protect the patient and the attending from direct or indirect transmission of pathogens.
      a. They may be either sterile or nonsterile disposable type gloves.
      b. The use of gloves does not eliminate or replace the procedure of washing the hands.
   4. Gowns are worn to protect the attendant's clothing from being soiled.
      a. Gowns may be disposable (paper) or reusable (cloth).
      b. Gowns are generally used once and then placed in isolation laundry bags or isolation trash bags if disposable.

B. Strict isolation is required for the diseases which are highly contagious (AIDS, diphtheria, smallpox, rabies). These diseases may be spread by either direct contact or by air.
   1. All personnel entering the room require gloves, gowns, and masks.
   2. All articles need to discarded or bagged prior to removal from the room.
C. Respiratory isolation is required for pathogens that are spread in the air (pertussis, *Staphylococcus aureus* pneumonia, tuberculosis).
   1. All personnel entering the room require masks and gloves. New OSHA regulations require the use of high efficiency particulate aerosol (HEPA) filters for personal protection against tuberculosis. The HEPA 100 mask carries a 99.97% efficiency rate.[1]
   2. All articles contaminated by the patient's secretions need to be discarded or sent for sterilization.
D. Reverse isolation is designed to protect the patient that is immunosuppressed or burned. It is not possible however to create a bacterial-free environment.
   1. Gloves and gowns are required only if the attending is going to be in direct contact with the patient.
   2. All personnel entering the room wear masks.
E. Skin, blood, and secretion precautions require that the attending be protected from pathogens found in wounds, dressings, and linens.
   1. All body fluids need to be considered contaminated and handled accordingly. Refer to Table 17-1 for a listing of human body fluids.
   2. Gowns, gloves, and masks are required to prevent cross-contamination.
   3. The Centers for Disease Control recommends isolation precautions for all patients. Refer to Table 17-2 universal precautions.

II. Handling contaminated equipment

A. Disposable equipment that has come in contact with a patient's exhaled gas, body fluids, or aerosols needs to be disposed of in the patient's room.
B. Small equipment to be sterilized needs to be placed in a water-soluble red plastic bag, tied, placed in another red bag (double-bag procedure), and taken to the decontamination area for disassembly and cleaning. Refer to Table 17-3 for a listing of definitions related to sterilization.
C. Because it is difficult to sterilize large equipment, it needs to be disinfected prior to removal from an isolation room.
   1. Remove all visible secretions using soap and water.
   2. Remove all surface pathogens by wiping the surface down with alcohol on a disposable cloth.

TABLE 17-1: Human Body Fluids
Amniotic fluid
Blood
Cerebrospinal fluid
Pericardial fluid
Peritoneal fluid
Pleural fluid
Semen
Saliva
Synovial fluid
Vaginal secretions
Vitreous humor

D. All equipment that has come into direct contact with the patient needs to be collected from patient areas in a plastic bag, taken to the dirty area, and disassembled into the smallest parts possible prior to washing.
   1. Equipment needing to be washed should be immersed in water, washed with alkaline soap, and scrubbed with a brush if required.
   2. Rinsing provides for the removal of contaminates and soap residues.
   3. Warm, filtered air should be utilized for drying equipment prior to packaging.
   4. Equipment must remain sealed prior to assembly at the treatment site.
E. Documentation of the sterilization process is required and is achieved through the use of indicators.
   1. Heat-sensitive tape indicators are used for items to be autoclaved. They indicate that the desired temperature is achieved during the sterilization process. The indicator tape does not signify the equipment has been sterilized.
   2. Chemical indicator tape is used for items to be gas (ETO) sterilized, and indicates only that the specific conditions for sterilization have been met.
   3. Biological indicators (spore strips) are actual microorganisms (*Bacillus stearothermophilus*) that provide factual information that the actual conditions for sterilization have been met. The death of these organisms shows that sterilization did indeed occur.
F. Filters are utilized in mainflow and nebulizer circuits to remove microbes from gas that is being delivered to the patient.

TABLE 17-2: Isolation Precautions

1. All health-care workers should routinely use appropriate barrier precautions to prevent skin and mucous-membrane exposure when contact with blood or other body fluids of any patient is anticipated. Gloves should be worn for touching blood and body fluids, mucous membranes, or non-intact skin of all patients, for handling items or surfaces soiled with blood or body fluids, and for performing vascular access procedures (including arterial blood gas punctures). Gloves should be changed after contact with each patient. Mask and protective eyewear or face shields should be worn during procedures that are likely to generate droplets of blood or other body fluids to prevent exposure of mucous membranes of the mouth, nose, and eyes. Gowns or aprons should be worn during procedures that are likely to generate splashes of blood or other body fluids.

2. Hands and other skin surfaces should be washed immediately and thoroughly if contaminated with blood or other body fluids. Hands should be washed immediately after gloves are removed, and after handling contaminated equipment.

3. All health-care workers should take precautions to prevent injuries caused by needles, scalpels, and other sharp instruments or devices during procedures; when cleaning used instruments; during disposal of used needles; and when handling sharp instruments after procedures. To prevent needle stick injuries, needles should not be recapped, purposely bent or broken by hand, removed from disposable syringes, or otherwise manipulated by hand. After they are used, disposable syringes and needles, and other sharp items should be placed in puncture-resistant containers for disposal; the puncture-resistant containers should be located as close as practical to the use area.

4. Although saliva has not been implicated in HIV transmission, to minimize the need for emergency mouth-to-mouth resuscitation, mouthpieces, resuscitation bags, or other ventilation devices should be available for use in areas in which the need for resuscitation is predictable.

5. Health-care workers who have exudative lesions or weeping dermatitis should refrain from all direct patient care and from handling patient-care equipment until the condition resolves.

6. Pregnant health-care workers are not known to be at greater risk of contracting HIV infection than health-care workers who are not pregnant; however, if a health-care worker develops HIV infection during pregnancy, the infant is at risk of infection resulting from perinatal transmission. Because of this risk, pregnant health-care workers should be especially familiar with and strictly adhere to precautions to minimize the risk of HIV transmission.

Source: J. Henry, *Contagious Diseases and Universal Precautions,* ERC Inc., 1991.

TABLE 17-3: Definitions of Sterilization

Antiseptic:	An agent or substance capable of destroying or inhibiting the growth of microorganisms
Asepsis:	The complete absence of microbial contamination or infection
Bactericide:	A chemical or physical agent that is used to destroy bacteria
Bacteriostatic:	A chemical or physical agent used to inhibit or retard the growth of bacteria
Colonization:	Presence of potentially pathogenic microorganisms without tissue invasion or infection
Contamination:	The process of soiling with infectious material
Decontamination:	Removal or neutralization of a contaminant by a chemical or physical agent
Denature:	To alter or change from normal any of a subject's characteristics, usually proteins
Disinfectant:	A chemical or physical agent that possesses the ability to destroy or inhibit microorganisms; does not apply to bacterial spores
Fungicide:	Any chemical or physical agent that is capable of destroying fungi
Germicide:	A chemical or physical agent capable of destroying all types of microorganisms
Infection:	Presence of pathogenic microorganisms with evidence of disease
Pathogen:	Any microorganism capable of producing disease
Resident flora:	Those microorganisms that normally inhabit various anatomical sites and can be repeatedly cultured and cannot be eliminated by washing
Sanitizer:	A chemical or physical agent that will reduce the total bacterial contamination to a safe level as established by the Public Health Department
Sporicide:	Any chemical or physical agent capable of destroying vegetative spores
Sterile:	Free of all microorganisms
Sterilization:	The act or process of destroying all microorganisms including spores
Transient flora:	Microbes that normally inhabit various anatomical sites and can be removed by washing
Viricide:	A chemical or physical agent capable of destroying all types of viruses

1. Most filters have a 99.99% efficiency against organisms 1–5 microns in size.
2. Some filters are disposed of when the circuit is changed, and some are designed to withstand repeated sterilization.

III. Methods of sterilization

A. Refer to Table 17-4 for a comparison of the different methods of sterilization.
B. Acetic acid will effectively decontaminate respiratory therapy equipment against gram-negative bacteria. A 2–2.5% solution of white vinegar and distilled water (1 part vinegar and 3 parts water) is mainly used for soaking humidifiers and nebulizers (30–60 min.) in the home.
C. Sodium hypochloride (5.25% chlorine, pH = 11.4) is readily available from the Clorox Co. (liquid chlorine bleach, Clorox liquid bleach, Clorox germicidal bleach), and can be an effective disinfectant for humidifiers and nebulizers in the

TABLE 17-4: Methods of Sterilization

Method	Action	Effective against			Temp.	Time
		G+	G−	Spores		
Aldehydes	destroy cell walls	X	X	X		10 hrs.
Dry heat	dehydrates intracellular substances	X	X	X	160°C	2 hrs.
ETO	alters cell metabolism	X	X	X	50°C	4 hrs.
Cobalt 60	prevents reproduction	X	X	X		
Moist heat (autoclave)	coagulate cell proteins	X	X	X	121°C	15 min.
Pasteurization	denatures cell proteins	X	X		63°C	30 min.
Quats	destroy cell enzymes	X				

home. A one-eighth cup of chlorine bleach in one gallon of water is normally used to soak the equipment for 10–15 minutes.

D. Alcohols (ethyl and isopropyl) are effective against bacteria and fungi but not effective against spores and hepatitis. Alcohol has the ability to change the nature of (denature) proteins causing the cell membrane to shrink.
  1. Ethyl alcohol (ETOH), in order to achieve maximum germicidal action, needs to be mixed with water. The optimal concentration is 70% ETOH and 30% H_2O.
  2. Isopropyl alcohol is more rapidly germicidal when it is at 90% strength and 10% water.

E. Chemicals are effective against vegetative forms, fungi, and tuberculosis organisms. With the exception of glutaraldehyde and ethylene oxide, chemicals cannot guarantee sterility.
  1. Ethylene oxide (C_2H_4O) has remarkable penetrating power and kills all microbes and endospores. The mechanism of action is to alter the nucleic acids that interfere with normal metabolism and reproduction.
     a. Ethylene oxide is an alkaline oxide that is administered in a special airtight chamber. The concentration is normally 12% or 800–1000 mg/L. Ethylene oxide is most effective when chamber temperature is 50°C and the relative humidity is approximately 50%.
     b. The materials need to be completely dry prior to exposure or the ethylene oxide will mix with the water and form ethylene glycol (antifreeze), which is toxic to human tissue.
     c. Aeration time following sterilization is usually a minimum of 24 hours. This time may be shortened by using an aeration chamber connected to a vacuum source.
  2. Acid (Sonacide) or alkaline (Cidex) aqueous solutions of glutaraldehyde are broad spectrum bacteriocides. Their mechanism of action is to disrupt the proteins in the cell membrane permitting the contents inside to leak out.
     a. Sonacide's pH range is 2.70–3.50. This solution effectively kills bacteria and viruses in 20 minutes at room temperature. It becomes sporicidal in one hour at room temperature.
     b. Cidex has a pH range of 7.50–8.50 and kills viruses and bacteria in 10 minutes, but takes 10 hours to be sporicidal.
  3. Quaternary ammonium compounds (Quats) have high bactericidal action against gram positive organisms. Their mechanism of action is to destroy the enzymes, which results in leakage of the cell walls. Quats have no effect on *Pseudomonas* and most other gram negative bacteria.

F. Dry heat can be effective against all organisms provided the exposure time is 2 hours and the temperature is 160°C. The mode of action is by coagulating the plasma proteins into a solid gelatin mass.

G. Ionizing radiation (gamma rays) is where radioactive isotopes of Cobalt 60 emit radiation toxic to all organisms. Gamma irradiation is the result of very short wavelengths of light comprised of extreme high energy that will ionize an organism.
   1. The high-energy short wavelengths of light form hydroxyl radicals within the cell. This process prevents reproduction by interfering with the cells normal metabolic pathways.
   2. Ethylene chlorohydrin is toxic to human tissue and is formed when using ethylene oxide to resterilize previously gamma irradiated material.

H. Moist heat (autoclave) is high pressure steam at two atmospheres of pressure with a temperature of 121°C. It will kill all organisms exposed over a period of 15 minutes. Once exposed to this temperature and pressure the plasma proteins of the organism coagulate into a solid gelatin mass.

I. Pasteurization involves the immersion of equipment for 30 minutes at a temperature of 62°C/172°F. This mild application of heat will kill vegetative bacteria including tuberculosis.

IV. Multiple-drug resistant bacteria

A. Modes of transmission of multiple-drug resistant bacteria include unwashed hands, gloves worn from patient to patient, contaminated environmental surfaces, inadequately cleaned equipment, and inappropriate use of antibiotic agents.

B. Methicillin resistant staphylococcus aureus (MRSA), Vancomycin resistant enterococci (VRE), Multiple-drug resistant mycobacterium tuberculosis (MDR-TB), and Penicillinase producing Neisseria gonorrhoeae (PPNG) are examples of drug resistant bacteria.

C. Using contaminated medical devices is one of the principal reasons for infections in patients, and these devices fall into three classifications:
   1. Critical devices that enter sterile tissue or the vascular system (implants/needles) require sterilization.
   2. Semicritical devices that touch mucous membranes or broken skin (bonchoscope) require high-level disinfection ($>$ than 20 minutes).
   3. Noncritical devices that touch intact skin (stethoscope) require low-level disinfection ($<$ than 10 minutes).

Reference

1. Butler, T. J., Close, J. R., and Close, R. J., *Laboratory Exercises for Competency in Respiratory Care*, F. A. Davis Co., 1998.

Chapter 17: Sterilization

Assessment Questions

1. When instructing a patient in the home care setting on how to decontaminate their respiratory therapy equipment, you would recommend:

    A. Sodium chloride
    B. Sodium bicarbonate
    C. Clorox
    D. Baking soda

2. When decontaminating a reusable ventilator bacterial filter, you would use which of the following methods:

    A. Alcohol
    B. Steam autoclave
    C. Acid glutaraldehyde
    D. Pasteurization

3. Which of the following methods are capable of destroying all microbial life?

    A. Quaternary solutions
    B. Alcohol solutions
    C. Acetic acid solutions
    D. Ethylene oxide

4. The widest variety of respiratory therapy equipment can be sterilized by using:

    A. Gas sterilization
    B. Steam sterilization
    C. Glutaraldehyde
    D. Pasteurization

5. When cleaning and disinfecting a fiberoptic bronchoscope you would:

    A. Soak the bronchoscope in Betadine
    B. Soak the bronchoscope in sterile water
    C. Soak the bronchoscope in glutaraldehyde
    D. Wipe the bronchoscope with Betadine and steam autoclave it

6. Which of the following is NOT capable of complete sterilization?

    I. Quaternary compounds
    II. Alcohol
    III. Pasteurization
    IV. Gluteraldehyde

    A. I, II, and III only
    B. I, II, III and IV
    C. II and III only
    D. IV only

7. Mask and gloves should be worn when suctioning a patient with:

    I. Bacterial pneumonia
    II. Influenza pneumonia
    III. Hepatitis B
    IV. Tuberculosis

    A. I only
    B. I and II only
    C. I, II and III only
    D. I, II, III and IV

8. In order for sterilization to occur the sterilizing agent must be:

    I. Bacteriocidal
    II. Fungicidal
    III. Sporicidal
    IV. Viricidal

    A. I only
    B. I and II only
    C. I, II and III only
    D. I, II, III and IV

9. Additional aeration time would be required prior to patient use if the equipment was sterilized by:

    A. Dry heat
    B. Moist heat
    C. Gluteraldehyde
    D. Ethylene oxide

Section III:

Therapy

Setting

In any patient care setting the respiratory therapist initiates, conducts, and modifies prescribed therapeutic procedures to achieve one or more specific objectives, maintains patient records, and communicates relevant information to members of the health care team. In addition to these duties, the advanced respiratory therapist will assist the physician in performing special procedures and conduct pulmonary rehabilitation and home care.

Chapters within this section include:

18. Removal of Bronchopulmonary Secretions
19. Respiratory Pharmacologic Agents
20. Ensuring Adequate Ventilation
21. Mechanical Ventilation of Adults
22. Mechanical Ventilation of Neonates
23. Monitoring of Blood Gases
24. Achieving Adequate Oxygenation
25. Cardiovascular Monitoring
26. Cardiopulmonary Resuscitation
27. Pulmonary Rehabilitation and Home Care
28. Assistance with Special Procedures
29. Record Maintenance and Documentation

Chapter 18

Removal of Bronchopulmonary Secretions

I. Coughing techniques[1]

A. The patient must have the ability and general awareness to receive adequate instruction to perform the maneuver.

B. The appropriate administration of pain medication prior to attempting the procedure may determine its success. It may be necessary to wait several minutes for the medication to take effect.

C. Position the patient for effective coughing.
  1. Patients with a strong cough usually benefit most from a semi-Fowlers or sitting position.
     a. This position allows initial relaxation of the abdominal muscles.
     b. It facilitates effective contraction of the abdominal muscles during the cough maneuver.
  2. A different position is required in patients having weak, nonproductive coughs.
     a. Some patients with inadequate cough strength to clear tracheal secretions, supine or sitting, may be able to do so in the semi-prone position.
     b. The semi-prone position allows gravity to help with the movement of mucous to the larynx, making a weak cough effort far more effective.
     c. A weak cough effort will move mucous in a horizontal direction more easily than in a vertical direction.

D. Coughing is usually performed by taking a relatively deep breath, closing the glottis, and forcefully contracting the abdominal muscles, and then expelling the air trapped in the lungs.

E. A *deep breath* is a relative term and is not a maximum inhalation or inspiratory capacity maneuver.
  1. Even a normal tidal volume may feel excessive to a patient who has had thoracic or abdominal surgery.

2. Coughing against an open glottis ("huff coughing") has been shown to be more effective in patients with COPD.
   a. Also known as forced expiratory technique (FET), it is performed as one or two forced expirations ("huffs") at mid to low lung volumes with the glottis open.
   b. This technique can be enhanced by self-compression of the chest wall, briskly compressing the upper arms against the sides of the chest wall.
3. After one inspiration, two hollow sounding coughs should be given, one to "shift" and the other to "lift" secretions.

F. Splinting of the chest wall during a cough is necessary when the patient has had recent chest or abdominal surgery.
   1. The effectiveness of the cough procedure is increased by having patients hug a pillow against their chest and/or abdomen while in the sitting position.
   2. Patients squeezing the pillow tightly against their abdomen may assist in creating the increased intrapulmonary pressure necessary to help move secretions up the airway.
   3. Patients having had lateral thoracotomies may need towel splinting to support the area of incision.

II. Chest physical therapy: postural drainage, percussion, and vibration

A. Indications (adults and older children)[2]
   1. Patients who have copious secretions (25–30 ml/day) or have difficulty raising secretions will benefit.
   2. Chest physical therapy techniques are particularly effective in cystic fibrosis, bronchiectasis, and stable chronic airflow limitation.
   3. Positioning the patient may drain lung abscess. Care must be taken because, in some instances, large volumes (200 ml or more) may be drained spontaneously from the abscess and a "drowning" effect may occur.
   4. Other indications include evidence of retained secretions in patients with artificial airways, atelectasis suspected to be caused by mucus plugging, or the presence of a foreign body in the airway.
   5. It is important to note possible exceptions to what are thought to be standard indications for chest physical therapy.
      a. When there is no improvement in elimination of sputum, arterial blood oxygen tension, or the clinical course of uncomplicated pneumonia when these techniques are applied.
      b. In patients with chronic bronchitis or emphysema who develop acute exacerbations, no effect has been demonstrated on duration of fever, radiographic clearing, volume of secretions expectorated, arterial blood gases, duration of hospital stay, or mortality.

Chapter 18: Removal of Bronchopulmonary Secretions

B. Contraindications[3]
 1. Absolute—unstabilized head or neck injury and/or active hemorrhage with hemodynamic instability.
 2. Relative—intracranial pressure over 20 mmHg, recent spinal surgery, acute spinal injury, acute hemoptysis, bronchopleural fistula, congestive heart failure with pulmonary edema, large pleural effusions, pulmonary embolism, rib fractures, or fresh surgical wounds.
 3. The Trendelenburg position is contraindicated for intracranial pressure over 20 mmHg, recent neurosurgery, cerebral aneurysms, recent eye surgery, uncontrolled hypertension, distended abdomen, esophageal surgery, recent gross hemoptysis, tube feedings, or a recent meal.
 4. Reverse Trendelenburg is contraindicated with hypotension or vasoactive medication.
C. Indications (infants and young children)[3]
 1. Respiratory distress syndrome, intubation, meconium or other aspiration syndromes, chronic pulmonary disease, pneumonia, transient tachypnea of the newborn, congenital lobar emphysema, intrapulmonary malformations, atelectasis, or neurologic damage, and as postoperative care following abdominal or thoracic surgery.
D. Contraindications (infants and young children)[4]
 1. Whenever the FIO2 must be increased by greater than 0.25 during the procedure because of patient agitation.
 2. Feedings within the previous hour.
 3. History of gastroesophageal reflux.
 4. Neonates less than 1000 grams birth weight or less than 32 weeks gestation.
 5. Histories of intraventricular hemorrhage of greater than Grade I, or less than seven days post-bleed.
 6. Children in status asthmaticus.
 7. Severe, acute congestive heart failure.
 8. Increased intracranial pressure.
E. Postural drainage
 1. Relaxation is very important during postural drainage and no effort should be spared in gaining the patient's cooperation.
    a. Physical discomfort leads to restlessness and anxiety, especially when a position must be maintained over a prolonged period of time.
    b. Hips and knees should be flexed and pillows used for support.
 2. Postural drainage should begin with positioning for the uppermost involved pulmonary segment.
    a. This segment should be determined by auscultation and/or review of chest X-rays. (Refer to Table 7-1 for relative anatomic positions of lung segments).

      b. In the case of a chest that is "quiet" to auscultation, it may be necessary to perform a complete segment-by-segment procedure in order to identify the major sites of obstruction.

      c. In general, if no increase in cough or expectoration occurs after 5–10 minutes of therapy, the therapist should move on to another lobe or segment.

3. The time and duration of postural drainage depends on the patient's needs.
    a. In patients with large amounts of sputum, postural drainage should usually be performed four times a day for at least half an hour each session.
    b. If two or more areas are to be drained, an hour per session may be necessary.
    c. The most essential times for postural drainage are immediately on waking and just before bedtime at night.
        (1) The early session clears the secretions accumulated during the night.
        (2) The late session helps to provide a more peaceful night's rest.
4. Precautions and complications
    a. In some bronchitic patients with very large amounts of secretions, the prolongation of drainage and the movement of the secretions may promote paroxysmal coughing and bronchospasm.
    b. Position changes can cause significant physiologic stress, especially in critically ill patients.
    c. Positioning should not place stress on "healing" tissue such as recent spinal fusions and skin grafts.
    d. Positioning should not cause compression of sites of recent surgical or nonsurgical trauma.
    e. When drainage is performed for a disease present in only one lung, secretions may drain into the opposite "clean" lung. Therefore, after the affected lung is drained, the "clean" lung should be prophylactically drained as well.
    f. Empyema should be surgically drained before chest physical therapy is applied, because as much as four to five liters of pus may be present in the pleural space. Any release of the empyema to the intrapulmonary space would cause gross contamination of lung fields.
    g. Pulmonary rupture and hemorrhage may occur.
    h. Dislodgment of pulmonary emboli is a theoretical consideration.
    i. Worsening hypoxemia may occur from increased exertion and oxygen demand as well as the positioning of poorly ventilated areas of lung in the down position.
        (1) Placing of a poorly ventilated area of lung in the down position will worsen the matching of blood and ventilation.
        (2) The weight of the body may cause "splinting" of the dependent lung and cause ventilation of that area to worsen further.

Chapter 18: Removal of Bronchopulmonary Secretions

      j. Cardiovascular collapse can occur from a combination of head-down positioning, increased hypoxemia, compromise of diaphragm action, and/or exertion.

      k. Nonspecific cardiac arrhythmias may occur.

  5. Positioning—the involved segmental bronchus should be placed in a vertical position so drainage is effected as much as possible by gravity. Positions are normally held for a minimum of five minutes and a maximum of ten minutes

      a. The upper lobes are best drained during upright positioning.

      b. The right middle lobe and lingula of the left upper lobe are best drained with the patient in a supine position, with the head lowered, and body turned at a 45 degree angle.

      c. The superior segments of the lower lobes are drained while in the prone position.

      d. The remainder of the lower lobes should be drained with the patient supine and tilted head down so the legs are 6–9 inches above the level of the heart (Trendelenburg position).

      e. Due to positioning associated with the bedridden patient, the superior and posterior basal segments are the greatest potential sites for secretions to accumulate.

F. Percussion—should be done with the cupped hand applied to the rib cage immediately over the pulmonary segment being drained. The hand should make a hollow "popping" sound as it strikes the chest wall.[5]

  1. Percussion is performed continuously throughout inspiration and expiration.

  2. Care should be taken to avoid percussing the sternum, scapula, spine, kidney area, abdomen, and the female breast.

  3. It is a matter of opinion whether to percuss directly against bare skin when using the hands.

      a. A towel or gown covering the area to be percussed may decrease the vibratory effect on the tracheobronchial tree.

      b. To tolerate the procedure in some patients it may be necessary for some type of covering to be placed over the percussed area.

  4. In some patients, manually compressing the lower thorax and upper abdomen during a slow and complete exhalation may improve the ability to expectorate.

  5. Percussion should not be applied to patients who fall into the following categories:

      a. Those prone to hemorrhage, such as patients with tuberculosis or bronchiectasis.

      b. Those with acute inflammatory conditions where inflammation might spread to other areas of the lung.

      c. Aged and very nervous patients.

      d. Recent postoperative cases where pain is increased.

G. Vibration
   1. The technique is usually performed over the effected area of the thorax during the expiratory phase. The practitioner should be aware of stimulation of intercostal muscle spindle endings in regard to breathing sensation.[6]
      a. Vibration of the upper rib cage during inspiration results in an illusion of chest expansion.
      b. Vibration of the lower rib cage during expiration causes an illusion of chest deflation.
      c. Out-of-phase vibration of the upper chest during deflation or the lower chest during inflation results in a sensation of dyspnea.
   2. Manual vibrations are done at a frequency of 30–50 per minute with the elbows locked and rigidly vibrating the hands.
   3. Hand placement
      a. Vibration can be done with the hands placed anteriorly and posteriorly at the same time, as well as placing the hands side by side on the same chest wall surface.
      b. It can be done with one hand placed on top of the other.
   4. As the vibrations are applied, a gentle squeeze is provided throughout expiration.
   5. It has been observed during bronchoscopy under general anesthesia that vibrations given on expiration squeeze the secretions from the bronchioles into the larger bronchi.
   6. Electrical percussors/vibrators exist in many forms and can be effective and much less tiring for the therapist.
      a. Such equipment must be appropriately adjusted and adequately padded to avoid injury to the patient.
      b. Use of such equipment depends on the user's knowledge and the psychological acceptance by the patient.
      c. An added advantage of mechanical devices appears to be the frequency attainable.
         (1) The optimal percussion energy frequency range for the transport of mucus has been shown in one study to be 25–35 Hz (vibrations per second).[7]
         (2) This frequency range is usually beyond manual capability.

H. Positive airway pressure adjuncts (PEP and EPAP)[8]
   1. Indications
      a. Airtrapping disease such as COPD or asthma
      b. Retained secretions
      c. Prevention or reversal of atelectasis
      d. For optimal delivery of bronchodilators

Chapter 18: Removal of Bronchopulmonary Secretions 295

2. Contraindications
   a. Patients who may not tolerate the increased work of breathing
   b. Intracranial hypertension (ICP greater than 20 mmHg)
   c. Hemodynamic instability
   d. Any medical or surgical condition that will not allow the patient to tolerate a snugly fitting face mask
   e. Acute sinusitis
   f. Nose bleeds and/or active hemoptysis
   g. Esophageal surgery and/or nausea
   h. Untreated pneumothorax
   i. Any type of known or suspected middle ear pathology
3. Positive expiratory pressure (PEP)
   a. The patient is seated comfortably and holds a mask over the mouth and nose, to which is attached a flow resistance device.
   b. A fixed-resistance cap is used that results in a measured expiratory pressure of 10–20 cmH_2O during the mid-part of expiration. This requires only minimal active expiratory effort by the patient.
   c. Tidal volumes slightly above normal can be used, and forced and complete exhalation should be avoided to prevent lung collapse.
   d. After about 10 PEP breaths, "huff" coughing and then spontaneous coughing can be used bring up secretions mobilized by PEP therapy.
   e. The maneuver should be repeated several times.
      (1) Fifteen minutes BID is appropriate for prophylaxis during stable chronic pulmonary disease.
      (2) Thirty breaths per hour during waking hours and less frequently during the night may be useful in postoperative patients.
4. Expiratory positive airway pressure (EPAP)
   a. This technique differs from PEP therapy in that a threshold rather than a fixed orifice resistor is used.

I. Autogenic Drainage[8]
   1. This technique involves breathing control in addition to "huff" and spontaneous coughing for secretion removal.
   2. Advantages
      a. It can be done anywhere (home, school, car, etc.) and can be done in as little as five minutes, or as full treatment for 20–30 minutes.
      b. There is no positional dyspnea, desaturation, thoracic cage pain, of "assault" perception by the patient.

c. It can be self-administered and does not require any equipment.
d. The patient may stop and rest anytime during the procedure and then begin again, having retained the progress made prior to the rest.
3. Disadvantages
   a. It is notably time intensive to teach, requiring 12–20 hours for younger patients (is difficult to teach to children under 12 years) and an average of five hours for adults.
   b. Patients may complain of headaches when learning this therapy due to intense concentration or hyperventilation.
4. Goals
   a. To drain whole areas of lung simultaneously, from peripheral areas into large areas, large areas into central airways, central airways into large airways, and then through "huff" coughing, to eliminate secretions.
   b. To achieve the highest possible airflow in as many generations of bronchi as possible.
5. Procedure
   a. The patient should be relaxed in the upright position, using diaphragmatic breathing, and breathing in through the nose and out through the mouth with the neck slightly extended.
   b. Inspiratory flow rate should be limited so as to enhance gas distribution, and the breath should be held 1–3 seconds.
   c. When exhaling, the expiratory flow should be controlled so as to avoid wheezing.
   d. Three volumes of breathing are used.
      (1) At the first volume, the patient exhales down to residual volume, inhales to functional residual capacity (FRC), holds the breath for 1–3 seconds, and then exhales down to residual volume (RV).
         (a) Crackles will be present and will move from end-expiratory to mid-expiratory to beginning expiratory during this phase.
         (b) Once the crackles have moved to beginning expiratory (usually 1–3 minutes), the patient moves on to the next volume.
      (2) At the second volume the patient is breathing out to between FRC and RV and then inspires a normal tidal volume and holds their breath for 1–3 seconds.
         (a) The effect of this phase is to move the secretions through the larger airways and another 1–3 minutes may be spent here.
         (b) This level of breathing seems most comfortable for patients because they are not forcing inspiration or expiration.
         (c) When starting to teach autogenic drainage to a new patient, this volume level is often where you would start.

Chapter 18: Removal of Bronchopulmonary Secretions

(3) The third volume phase using normal to high lung volumes starting at FRC with attempt to control spontaneous coughing.
   (a) The goal is to move secretions from central to large airways where they can be removed by "huff" coughing and minimal effort.
   (b) A hazard of this phase can be hyperventilation.
(4) The last step is for the patient to take a deep breath, hold for 1–3 seconds, and exhale rapidly to mid-lung volumes, saying the word "huff" as they exhale. This procedure is repeated 2–3 times.
(5) If secretions have not been expelled after three "huff" coughs, the patient resumes level three breathing until secretions seem on the verge of being expelled.

III. Suctioning[9]

A. The purpose of suctioning is twofold. When secretions accumulate in the airways of patients who are unable to clear them adequately, the work of breathing increases significantly and blood gas alteration occurs. The continued accumulation of secretions may become life threatening. It is the purpose of suctioning to reverse this situation and produce decreased work of breathing with improved ventilation.
   1. Decreasing the work of breathing relates directly to improving airway resistance through the removal of collected secretions.
      a. Under conditions of laminar or streamlined flow, airway resistance varies directly with the viscosity of the gas and the length of the tube and inversely with the fourth power of the radius of the airway lumen.
      b. Equation 18-1 demonstrates the application of Poiseuille's law and its impact on airway resistance.
   2. Gas flow follows the path of least resistance and when secretions are present in the airway, gas flow through that airway will decrease.
      a. Reduced ventilation to any area of lung that still has good blood flow will result in an increase in the number of low ventilation/perfusion lung units.
      b. As ventilation decreases to specific areas of lung, the alveolar PO_2 will fall, and the blood leaving those areas will be low in oxygen.
B. Tracheostomy suction procedure in adults and children
   1. Preparation
      a. Auscultate the patient's chest to determine the degree of congestion; suction should be performed only as needed. Other indications may include:
         (1) Increased peak inspiratory pressure during volume ventilation or decreased tidal volume during pressure ventilation.
         (2) A patient who is unable to cough effectively.
         (3) Secretions that are seen in the airway.

> **EQUATION 18-1: Application of Poiseuille's Law and Airways Resistance**
>
> $$\text{Resistance of flow through an airway} = \frac{\text{viscosity} \times \text{length}}{(\text{radius})^4} \times \frac{8}{\pi}$$
>
> **Example:** If the radius of an airway is decreased by one-half, there is a tremendous increase in airway resistance. Given an airway with a radius of 6 relative units (RU), determine the impact on the airway resistance (R_{air}) if the radius is reduced to 3 relative units.
>
> Radius of 6 RU
> R^2 $6 \times 6 = 36$
> R^3 $36 \times 6 = 216$
> R^4 $216 \times 6 = 1296$
>
> Radius of 3 RU
> R^2 $3 \times 3 = 9$
> R^3 $9 \times 3 = 27$
> R^4 $27 \times 3 = 81$
>
> $$\text{Impact on } R_{air} = \frac{R^4 \text{ at 3 RU}}{R^4 \text{ at 6 RU}} = \frac{81}{1296} = 1/16^{th}$$
>
> **NOTE:** If the patient does not increase their effort to breathe, flow through the airway will drop to $1/16^{th}$ of its original value.

      (4) Changes in monitored flow and pressure graphics.
      (5) Suspected aspiration.
      (6) Increased work of breathing (higher respiratory rate, accessory muscle use, anxious retractions, etc.).
      (7) Deterioration of arterial blood gases.
      (8) X-ray changes consistent with major airway plugging (unilateral whiteout).
  2. Procedure
    a. Before suctioning the tracheostomy, pre-oxygenate the patient.
      (1) Inflating the lungs with a manual ventilation bag with 100% oxygen running to the bag (it may be difficult to obtain 100% O_2).
      (2) If the patient is on a mechanical ventilator, the FIO_2 control may be turned to 1.0, but caution must be taken to remember to return the FIO_2 control to its original setting following suctioning.

Chapter 18: Removal of Bronchopulmonary Secretions

(3) A single lumen oxygen insufflation catheter may be used where oxygen is delivered at 15 L/M through the catheter for 15 seconds prior to suctioning.

b. If the patient is on distending pressure (CPAP, PEEP) and a manual ventilation bag is used for pre- and post-oxygenation, a PEEP attachment should be used if the patient requires more than 5 cmH$_2$0 distending pressure.

c. A closed circuit suction catheter (Ballard) may be used to avoid removing the patient from their current level of distending pressure and ventilatory support. These devices appear to work as effectively for secretion removal as conventional catheter use.[10]

d. Directed suctioning of the left mainstem bronchus, as opposed to the right mainstem bronchus, is difficult to accomplish with a standard catheter, but is greatly enhanced with the use of a closed-system directional-tip catheter.

e. Prior to suctioning, instillation of a 5 ml bolus of normal saline has been shown to stimulate coughing and result in removal of a greater amount of secretions. The effects on hemodynamics, lung mechanics, gas exchange, and patient comfort were not significantly different from suctioning without saline instillation.[11]

f. Direct the catheter tip through the tracheostomy tube and insert the catheter gently until resistance is met.

g. Apply suction only as you withdraw the catheter.

h. Roll the catheter between your thumb and finger during withdrawal.

i. DO NOT maintain the catheter in the airway for more than 15 seconds as you may evacuate too much air from the lungs, and the patient may suffer a cardiopulmonary arrest. A practical guide for how long you are staying down is to hold your own breath as you begin to suction. When you need to draw a breath, so will the patient.

j. Reinflate and reoxygenate the patient's lungs.

k. Repeat the suction as necessary and while the suctioning is being productive. Do not suction when there is nothing to suction out, regardless of whether the orders say to suction every hour on the hour.

C. Nasotracheal suctioning[12]
 1. Indications
    a. Inability to clear secretions.
    b. Secretions heard in the larger central airways that the patient is unable to cough up in spite of their best effort.
 2. Relative contraindications
    a. Occluded nasal passages
    b. Nasal bleeding
    c. Acute injury to the head, neck, or face

d. Low platelet count, prolonged bleeding time, prolonged partial thromboplastin time (PTT), prolonged prothrombin time (PT)
   e. Laryngospasm
   f. Spastic airways
   g. Upper respiratory tract infection
3. This form of suctioning is absolutely contraindicated in acute upper airway inflammation in children (croup, epiglottis).
4. This is considered to be the most dangerous form of suctioning.
   a. It offers greater occasion for stimulation of the vagus nerve and resultant bradycardia.
   b. The trauma of the nasal introduction of the catheter may result in catecholamine release. This, with attendant hypoxia, increased work of breathing, and vagal stimulation may result in serious arrhythmias.
   c. Oxygen should be administered during nasotracheal suctioning even more often and more vigorously than with other forms of suctioning. It can be done with an oxygen mask or IPPB machine with mask or mouthpiece.
   d. The patient should be in the sitting position and breathing through their mouth.
   e. The equipment is the same as for tracheal suction, although lubrication of the catheter with 1% xylocaine jelly may help to alleviate discomfort from the introduction of the catheter.
   f. The catheter, while disconnected from the vacuum line, is slowly advanced through the selected nare to a point just above the larynx.
      (1) Sounds of airflow are listened for at the proximal end of the catheter.
      (2) When airflow is felt to be the strongest and the respiratory sounds are the loudest, the tip of the catheter is just above the epiglottis.
      (3) If the catheter is advanced too far, it will usually have entered the esophagus and sounds of respiration will cease to be heard at the proximal end of the catheter.
   g. The catheter is advanced into the trachea through the larynx while the patient is instructed to breathe in deeply. This will open the epiglottis and facilitate entry of the catheter.
   h. If a successful tracheal intubation with the catheter has been achieved, the cough will become hoarse and the patient will be unable to talk in a normal tone.
   i. After the vocal cords are passed, a few deep inspirations are allowed while the patient is reoxygenated.
   j. Suctioning is then begun in the standard way, following reconnection of the catheter to the vacuum line.
      (1) Violent coughing may begin once the catheter enters the trachea, and the patient should be warned of this prior to initiating the procedure.
      (2) If the procedure is to be performed often, a nasal trumpet (airway) should be inserted, using Xylocaine jelly.

Chapter 18: Removal of Bronchopulmonary Secretions

(3) If suctioning of the left mainstem bronchus is desired, it takes a curved tipped catheter (Code'). It is not effective if suctioning through an endotracheal tube.

D. Suctioning in infants[4]
1. Hazards include:
   a. Anoxia as a result of discontinuation of mechanical ventilation.
   b. Extraction of gas from small airways, leading to severe hypoxemia.
   c. Atelectasis.
   d. Lesions in the trachea at the site of the suction catheter tip.
2. Procedure
   a. It is recommended that suctioning be done with two people; one to suction and the other to monitor the patient and provide support as needed.
   b. A strict sterile technique should be used with gloves and catheter.
   c. The FIO2 should be increased 10–20% above presuctioning levels for recovery between each suctioning episode.
   d. The use of a closed suction device (Ballard Medical Products) or of a suction adaptor (Novametrix Medical Systems) or of a self-sealing one-way valve in the patient wye (Neo$_2$Safe Valve) may reduce the hazard of extreme hypoxemia and instability while suctioning.
   e. If using a manual ventilation bag before, during and after the procedure, a pressure manometer should be inline and a pressure 20% higher than on the ventilator may be used to reexpand the lungs.
   f. The suction catheter should only be inserted to the tip of the endotracheal tube to avoid tracheal damage.
      (1) The proper distance is determined by noting the centimeter marking on the endotracheal tube at the level of the ET tube adaptor.
      (2) This ET adaptor is about 4 cm in length and it is added to the cm length marked on the ET tube at the level of the ET tube adaptor to determine the length the suction catheter should be inserted.
   g. A few drops to 0.3 ml of normal saline may be instilled through the ET tube to facilitate removal of secretions.
   h. When suctioning, the maximum amount of time spent in the airway should be 10 seconds, with no more than 5 seconds spent actually applying negative pressure to the airway.

IV. Aerosol/humidity therapy[6]

A. Penetration and deposition of aerosols are dependent upon several factors.
1. Gravity—the settling rate of a particle is proportional to its density times the square of its diameter.

2. Kinetic activity of gas molecules—particles of 0.1 micron and less are effected by bombardment from the gas molecules in their carrier stream.
   a. These minute aerosol particles can be "driven" towards the bronchial wall and settle out.
   b. This process is referred to as diffusion deposition.
3. Inertial impaction—the deposition of an aerosol particle when it is carried in a gas stream and the gas stream is diverted suddenly.
   a. Sudden diversions occur when gas flows through the tracheobronchial tree.
   b. Two conditions determine the extent to which the particle will impact against the bronchial wall as opposed to continuing to be carried with the gas stream.
      (1) The larger the particle, the greater the chance it will impact because its mass will keep it moving in a relatively straight line instead of making the turn at the bifurcations of the airway.
      (2) The faster the particle is moving, the greater the chance it will impact because it will fail to make the turns at the bifurcations of the airway.
4. Ventilatory pattern—the deposition of an aerosol is directly related to inhaled volume and inversely related to respiratory rate.
   a. Deposition is increased with increased tidal volume and decreased respiratory rate.
   b. If tidal volume and rate change at the same time, the effects on increased deposition are additive.
      (1) Shallow breathing carries a decreased volume of aerosol per tidal volume.
      (2) Rapid breathing reduces the time available for the particle to settle.
5. Devices selected for aerosol medication delivery should be capable of producing particles of a mass median aerodynamic diameter (MMAD) of 2–5 microns. The devices capable of this goal are metered dose inhalers with or without spacers (MDI), dry powder inhalers, as with cromolyn sodium (DPI), small volume nebulizers (SVN), large volume nebulizers (LVN), and ultrasonic nebulizers (USN).[13]
6. Optimal procedure for the use of therapeutic aerosols
   a. Technique for use of small volume nebulizer (SVN)
      (1) Place the drug in the nebulizer and dilute with 0.9% saline to a total volume of 4 ml.
      (2) Install a finger port in the driving gas system so that the patient or therapist can cause nebulization to occur only during inspiration.
      (3) Set the driving gas flow at 6–8 L/M.
      (4) If using a mouthpiece, instruct the patient to seal their lips around the mouthpiece. With a mask, the patient should be instructed to breathe with their mouth open.
      (5) Grasp the nebulizer firmly in the hand to warm the nebulizer solution and result in smaller particle delivery to the patient.

Chapter 18: Removal of Bronchopulmonary Secretions

(6) The patient should inhale slowly (0.5 L/s) to normal tidal volume with occasional inspiration to total lung capacity with a 4–10 second breath hold.

(7) As nebulization progresses, tap the sides of the nebulizer to minimize the amount of drug left there.

(8) Continue until no aerosol is being produced from the nebulizer.

b. Use of a metered dose inhaler (MDI)
  (1) Hold the inhaler with the mouthpiece down.
  (2) Shake the container vigorously several times.
  (3) Breathe out in the normal passive fashion.
  (4) Open the mouth widely and let the mouthpiece touch the lips.
  (5) Start to inhale slowly, then squeeze the cartridge to release the spray.
  (6) Continue to inhale slowly and as deeply as possible, then hold the breath for about ten seconds if possible.
  (7) The time for breath holding is especially important to allow the large particles that are coated with propellant to "flash" or evaporate into smaller particles. These will then impact in larger airways and reach the smaller airways through the effect of gravitational sedimentation.
  (8) Exhale slowly and passively.
  (9) Wait 3–10 minutes before the next puff.
  (10) Patients who have difficulty coordinating their breathing when using an MDI may benefit from the addition of a spacer device (large volume reservoir) between the MDI and the mouth.
  (11) The addition of a reservoir to the MDI can improve aerosol delivery to the lower lung and cause less drug to be deposited in the oropharynx. Reducing the drug that is deposited in the oropharynx will reduce absorption into the systemic circulation.
     (a) For the use of MDI in mechanically ventilated adults or older children, a chamber-style device results in greater respirable volume of medication than in-line or elbow style devices, and a cone-shaped chamber is demonstrated to work most effectively.
     (b) It is probable that MDI use is more appropriate and effective than in-line small volume nebulizers for the administration of aerosolized medication to mechanically ventilated patient. Potential benefits may include:
        i) Less delivery time, reducing cost of therapy and freeing the therapist to attend to other duties.
        ii) Avoiding damage or contamination to expiratory flow transducers.
        iii) Avoiding triggering problems during pressure support ventilation by eliminating the flow from the small volume nebulizer.

iv) Avoiding any contamination caused by the small volume nebulizer.
v) Avoiding opening the patient ventilator circuit with subsequent aerosolization of contaminated matter into the environment.
  c. Inpatients and certain selected outpatients may benefit from an inhalant being given by a handheld nebulizer or by IPPB.
    (1) Improved coordination of inhalation may result.
    (2) A larger aerosol dose can be given via this method.
    (3) A slow deep breath with breath holding is important, regardless of the method used.
  d. A bench study suggests that the most effective method for delivery of aerosol from a small volume nebulizer through a neonatal endotracheal tube is with the nebulizer placed in-line on the inspiratory limb of the ventilator circuit, with a 5-inch reservoir tube between the nebulizer and the patient wye.
7. Particle sizes and sites of deposition
  a. 100 microns—too large to enter the respiratory tract.
  b. 100 microns down to 5 microns—trapped in the nose in normal breathing.
  c. 5–2 microns—deposited somewhere before, but up to the alveoli.
  d. 2–1 microns—enter the alveoli and 95–100% of those particles down to 1.0 micron can remain.
  e. 1.0–0.25 microns—stable with minimal settling.
  f. 0.25 microns and less—increased alveolar deposition in this range due to diffusion settling.
  g. As a general statement, a desirable size distribution for an effective therapeutic aerosol, where peripheral airway deposition is desired, would be 2–3 microns.

B. "Bland" aerosol therapy
1. Solutions used for this type of therapy vary from sterile water, 0.45% NaCl, and 0.9% NaCl to 5% NaCl for sputum induction.
2. Accepted uses for bland aerosol therapy include the following:
  a. Upper airway lesions such as laryngotracheobronchitis (croup), and post-extubation laryngeal irritation.
  b. Sputum induction in patients who may not have a sufficient volume of secretions for a laboratory sample, or in patients who have retained secretions.
3. This type of therapy involves the use of a variety of aerosol generators that are designed to add significant quantities of water or saline to the inspired gas.
4. While subjective evidence convinces many therapists to continue to promote bland aerosol therapy to liquify secretions and improve mucociliary transport, objective documentation of therapeutic effectiveness is lacking.
5. In sensitive patients, significant airway constriction may occur following bland aerosol inhalation due to stimulation of vagal mediated pulmonary irritant reflexes.

Chapter 18: Removal of Bronchopulmonary Secretions 305

C. Humidity therapy
  1. Mechanical ventilation[14]
     a. Humidification of inspired gas is mandatory when the upper airways are bypassed with the use of an artificial airway, including tracheostomy or endotracheal tubes. Failure to humidify the inspired gas can result in:
        (1) Patient hypothermia
        (2) Thickened, hardened secretions
        (3) Destruction of airway epithelium
        (4) Atelectasis
     b. Airway humidification can be accomplished with a device that provides 30 mg of H_2O/L of delivered gas at 30 degrees C.
        (1) Heated humidifiers are effective because they heat the inspired gas and increase the water vapor content and are best used in all patients being mechanically ventilated longer than 96 hours.
        (2) Heat/moisture exchangers (HMEs) passively store heat and water from the patient's exhaled gas and release it to the inhaled gas. They can be used effectively for up to 96 hours except where contraindicated in the following circumstances:
           (a) Patients with secretions that would result in the plugging of the device (large volume of secretions, thick or bloody secretions)
           (b) Patients who do not exhale sufficient volume to make the HME a competent humidifier (leaks around the artificial airway cuff, bronchopleural fistulas)
           (c) Patients who are hypothermic (body core temp less than 32°C)
           (d) Patients with high minute ventilation (at greater than 10 L/min. ventilation, the HME may not meet the required humidity content)
     c. For infants and small children whose upper airways are bypassed, gas should be delivered via heated humidifier at 34° ± 1°C.
  2. Oxygen administering devices
     a. In low flow (≤2 L/M) nasal oxygen in adults and older children, unless the patient complains of dry or sore nasal membranes, it is appropriate to eliminate any accessory humidifier.
     b. For all oxygen administering devices in adults and older children, cool bubble humidifiers should be used when using flow greater than 2 L/M.
     c. In small infants and children, cool bubble humidifiers should be used for oxygen cannulas or masks.
     d. Infant hoods.
        (1) Inspired gas should be both heated to neutral thermal environment (NTE), which is the temperature in the environment required to maintain the infant's temperature at normal (37 C), and fully humidified at that temperature.

References

1. "AARC Clinical Practice Guidelines: Directed Cough," *Respiratory Care* 38, no. 5, May 1993.
2. Eid, N., et al., "Chest Physiotherapy in Review," *Respiratory Care* 36, no. 4, April 1991.
3. "AARC Clinical Practice Guidelines: Postural Drainage Therapy," *Respiratory Care* 36, no. 12, December 1991.
4. Koff, P. B., Eitzman, D. V., and Neu, J., *Neonatal and Pediatric Respiratory Care, 2nd ed.*, Mosby, 1993.
5. Burton, G. G., Hodgkin, J. E., and Ward, J. J., *Respiratory Care: A Guide to Clinical Practice, 4th ed.*, Lippincott, 1997.
6. Scanlon, C. L., Wilkins, R. L., and Stoller, J. K., *Egan's Fundamentals of Respiratory Therapy, 7th ed.*, Mosby, 1999.
7. Fishman, A. P., *Pulmonary Diseases and Disorders,* Vol. II, McGraw-Hill, 1980.
8. "AARC Clinical Practice Guidelines: Use of Positive Airway Pressure Adjuncts to Bronchial Hygiene Therapy," *Respiratory Care* 38, no. 5, May 1993.
9. "AARC Clinical Practice Guidelines: Endotracheal Suctioning of Mechanically Ventilated Adults and Children with Artificial Airways," *Respiratory Care* 38, no. 5, May 1993.
10. Witner, M., et al., "An Evaluation of the Effectiveness of Secretion Removal with the Ballard Closed-Circuit Suction Catheter," *Respiratory Care* 36, no. 8, August 1991.
11. Gray, J., et al., "The Effects of Bolus Normal Saline Instillation in Conjunction with Endotracheal Suctioning," *Respiratory Care* 35, no. 8, August 1990.
12. "AARC Clinical Practice Guidelines: Nasotracheal Suctioning," *Respiratory Care* 37, no. 8, August 1992.
13. "AARC Clinical Practice Guidelines: Selection of Aerosol Delivery Device," *Respiratory Care* 37, no. 8, August 1992.
14. "AARC Clinical Practice Guidelines: Humidification During Mechanical Ventilation," *Respiratory Care* 37, no. 8, August 1992.

Assessment Questions

1. Absolute contraindications to chest physical therapy include:
   - I. Unstablized head injury
   - II. Congestive heart failure
   - III. Active hemorrhage

   A. I only
   B. I and II only
   C. I, II and III
   D. I and III only

2. A patient lying on a flat bed in the prone position with a pillow under the abdomen would drain the basal lobes and which of the following segments?

   A. Apical segments
   B. Anterior segments
   C. Lingular segments
   D. Posterior segments

Chapter 18: Removal of Bronchopulmonary Secretions

3. Positive expiratory pressure (PEP) would be indicated in which of the following?

    I. Retained secretions
    II. Prevention of atelectasis
    III. Airtrapping

    A. I only
    B. I and II only
    C. I, II and III
    D. III only

4. Advancing a suction catheter into the airway of an adult patient will result in which of the following?

    I. Removal of existing secretions
    II. Transitory hypoxemia
    III. Removal of air from the stomach
    IV. Removal of air from the lungs

    A. I and II only
    B. I, II and III only
    C. I, II, III and IV
    D. I, II and IV only

5. Which of the following is the most important element in preventing the retention of secretions?

    A. Cough
    B. Ciliary movement
    C. Pursed-lip breathing
    D. Positive expiratory pressure (PEP)

6. In demonstrating how a patient should take an optimal aerosol treatment, you would advise them to:

    A. Breath very deep and normal
    B. Breathe in as deeply and as fast as possible and then hold breath
    C. Breathe in slow and deep with a breath hold prior to expiration
    D. Inspire slowly through the nose and exhale slowly through the mouth

7. Heat moisture exchangers that store heat and moisture from the patient's exhaled gases can be effectively used for:

    A. 96 hours
    B. 72 hours
    C. 48 hours
    D. 24 hours

8. The goal of cool bland aerosol mist when treating inflammatory obstruction like croup is to:

    A. Cause increased coughing and expectoration
    B. Relieve inflamed tissue and reduce edema
    C. Replace the humidity deficit
    D. Maintain the FIO_2

9. Complications of aerosol therapy include which of the following?

    I. Bronchospasm
    II. Overhydration
    III. Infection

    A. I only
    B. I and II only
    C. I, II and III
    D. II and III only

Chapter 19

Respiratory Pharmacologic Agents

I. **Solutions and dosages**

A. A solution consists of a solute (a substance dissolved in a solution) and a solvent (the liquid the solute is dissolved in) or a diluent (an agent that renders a substance less potent or irritating).
B. Drugs may be prepared in three ways:
   1. Weight-volume relationship (1 gm/100 ml).
   2. Volume-volume relationship (1 ml/99 ml).
   3. Weight-weight relationship (1 gm/99 gm).
C. 100 ml of distilled water at 4°C weighs 100 grams.
   1. If one gram of a drug is added to 100 ml of solution, it is 1/100th of the weight or 1%.
   2. When 100 ml of solution contains 1 gram of solute or drug dissolved in it, it is said to be a 1% solution.
   3. 1 kilogram (Kg) = 1000 grams (g).
   4. 1 gram (g) = 1000 milligrams (mg).
D. The strengths of solutions are often expressed clinically in percentage, ratio, or weight per volume (mg/ml). Refer to Table 19-1 for the interrelationship between these expressions.
E. Ratios are also common forms of drug expressions.
   1. 1:100 = 1% = 1 gm/100 ml
   2. 1:200 = 0.5% = 0.5 mg/100 ml
   3. 25:100 = 25% = 25 gm/100 ml
F. Through the use of reasoning power and two basic formulas, correct amounts of ordered drugs may be given. Refer to Equations 19-1 and 19-2.
   1. Dilution—The formula dilution is used whenever a lesser concentration or amount is requested and consequently whenever the concentration or amount on hand must be diluted.

Chapter 19: Respiratory Pharmacologic Agents

TABLE 19-1: Drug Expressions

1 gm/100 ml = 10 mg/ml = 1% = 1:100

In order to calculate the number of mg/ml, simply take the number followed by a percent sign and move the decimal one place to the right. This is shown in the following manner:

$$1\% = 1 \text{ gm/100 ml}$$
$$= 1000 \text{ mg/100 ml}$$
$$= 10 \text{ mg/ml}$$
$$1.0\% = 10 \text{ mg/ml}$$

EQUATION 19-1: Dilution Equation

$$V_1 \times C_1 = V_2 \times C_2$$

where V_1 = desired volume or weight
C_1 = desired concentration or amount
V_2 = volume or weight on hand
C_2 = concentration or amount on hand

Example: Orders have been written to deliver 2.5 ml of 10% Mucomyst, but there is only a 20% bottle on hand. How much of the 20% solution will be used?

$$2.5 \times 10 = V_2 \times 20$$

$$V_2 = \frac{2.5 \times 10}{20} = 1.25$$

Therefore, take 1.25 ml of the 20% solution and add 1.25 ml of the diluent (2.5 − 1.25) to obtain 2.5 ml of 10% solution.

Note: Most often it will be necessary to solve for V_2, which is the amount that must be added to the diluent to obtain the desired amount.

> **EQUATION 19-2:   Concentration Equation**
>
> $$V_1 \times C_2 = V_2 \times C_1$$
>
> **Example:** Orders have been written to deliver 2.5 mg of Isuprel. On hand is a 50 ml bottle of a 1:200 solution. Calculate the number of mls of Isuprel that should be given.
>
> **Note:** A 1:200 solution has 1 gm/200 ml or 0.5 mg/ml (refer to Table 19-1). The volume of the bottle on hand (50 ml) is of no significance in this calculation.
>
> $$V_1 \times 5 = 1 \times 2.5$$
>
> $$V_1 = \frac{1 \times 2.5}{5} = 0.5$$
>
> Therefore, administering 0.5 ml of a 1:200 solution will provide the required 2.5 mg.

2. Concentration—The concentration formula is used whenever a portion of the stock solution or weight is desired without adding a diluent.
3. If you were given a 1:2000 solution and required to reason out the number of mg/ml, you would begin with the statement that a 1:100 solution contains 10 mg/ml.
    a. A 1:1000 solution is ten times more dilute and should contain only 1/10 the amount of drug that a 1:100 solution contains.
    b. A 1:1000 solution therefore contains 1 mg/ml.
    c. A 1:2000 solution is twice as dilute as a 1:1000 solution and therefore contains only 1/2 the amount of drug in an equal volume.
    d. If a 1:1000 solution contains 1 mg/ml then a 1:2000 solution can only contain 0.5 mg/ml.
4. The standard dose of isoetharine is 0.5 ml of a 1% solution. To determine how many mg of drug are being administered, you begin by knowing that a 1% solution equals 10 mg/ml. If you are administering 0.5 ml, then you are giving 0.5×10 mg or 5 mg of drug.

II. Bronchodilators

A. The use of bronchodilator drugs is indicated when it is desirable to relax smooth muscle of the airway. This smooth muscle relaxation and vasoconstriction are ac-

Chapter 19: Respiratory Pharmacologic Agents

complished by stimulation of alpha and beta receptors. (Refer to Tables 19-2, 19-3, and 19-4).

B. Some bronchodilators are available only in metered-dose inhalers (MDI).
   1. Bitolterol—a longer-acting β_2 stimulant that is taken 2–3 puffs every 6–8 hours.
   2. Pirbuterol—usual dose in patients over 12 years of age is 2 puffs every 4–6 hours (comparable in clinical effects to albuterol).
   3. Fenoterol—a very long-acting β_2 stimulant that is taken in 1–3 puffs every 8–12 hours.
   4. Ipratropium bromide (Atrovent)—a longer acting (6 hours) anticholinergic bronchodilator that is taken 2–4 puffs every 4–6 hours and is considered to be more effective than atropine.
      a. Both ipratropium and atropine are beneficial when given with β_2 drugs due to a synergistic effect.

TABLE 19-2: Bronchodilator Drugs for Use in Nebulizers (Adults)

Drug	Dose/Tx	Alpha	Beta 1	Beta 2	Maximum Effect	Duration Action
Epinephrine	2–3 inhal	+++	++++	+++	20–30 min.	1–2 hrs.
R-epinephrine	0.25–0.5 ml of 2.2%	++(+)	+++(+)	++(+)	20–30 min.	1–2 hrs.
Isoproterenol	0.5 ml 1:200	(+)	++++	++++	6 min.	1 hr.
Isoetharine	0.25–1.0 ml of 1:100		+(+)	+++	60 min.	3 hrs.
Metaproterenol	0.5–1.0 ml of 5%	++(+)	++(+)		6–15 min.	1–5 hrs.
Terbutaline	1 ml of 0.1%		+(+)	+++(+)	30–60 min.	4–6 hrs.
Albuterol	0.5 ml of 0.5%		+	++++	15 min.	3–4 hrs.
Atropine	1 mg in 2 ml				30–170 min.	4–6 hrs.
Glycopyrrolate	1.0 mg				120–180 min.	≥6 hrs.

Note: + indicates relative strength, (+) indicates variable response

TABLE 19-3: Bronchodilator Drugs for Use in Nebulizers (Neonates)

Drug	Dosage
Albuterol	0.04 ml/Kg in 1.5 ml NaCl 0.9%
Isoproterenol	0.2 ml of 1:200 in 2 ml of NaCl 0.45%
Metaproterenol	2.0 ml of 0.3% solution; mix 0.12 ml of 0.5% metaproterenol with 1.88 ml of diluent
Atropine	0.05 mg/kg in 2 ml NaCl 0.45%

    b. Ipratropium bromide has been shown to produce no bronchodilator effect following bronchial provocation testing, whereas albuterol still produced good effect. Anticholinergic bronchodilators are effective prior to mast cell degranulation in allergic asthma, but not afterwards.

C. Dosing strategies for β_2 agonists[2]
  1. Stable chronic asthma—standard dosing of β_2 agonists is QID to Q4H.
  2. Moderate-to-severe chronic asthma—some studies suggest that patients in this category may benefit from 2.5–8 times the normal dosage.[2]
  3. Acute severe asthma—continuous nebulization therapy (CNT) is in use in emergency rooms throughout the country and is seen to be effective in this group of patients.
    a. Continuous nebulization is shown to be safer in status asthmaticus than continuous IV therapy of β_2 agonists.
    b. Routine practice is to administer the β_2 agonist continuously until adequate clinical response is seen.
  4. Stable severe COPD—the following method is suggested to find the proper dose for any given patient. This particular method uses the drug albuterol.
    a. Administer albuterol MDI 2 puffs or handheld nebulizer 2.5mg/4ml.
    b. Monitor bronchodilator response by measuring peak expiratory flowrate (PEFR), forced expiratory volume for 1 second (FEV_1), vital capacity (VC), and heart rate (HR) at 15 and 30 minutes and then every 10 minutes until no further improvement is seen in these parameters.
    c. Repeat the initial dose.
    d. Repeat the same measurements used following the initial dose.
    e. Continue the cycle of administration and measurement until no further improvement occurs in any of the measured parameters.

TABLE 19-4: Response to Stimulation of Autonomic Drug Receptors

	Alpha	Beta 1	Beta 2	Cholinergic
Heart		increased rate, contraction, conduction		decreased rate, contraction
Arterioles				
coronary	constrict		dilate	dilate
skeletal	constrict		dilate	dilate
pulmonary	constrict		dilate	dilate
Veins	constrict		dilate	
Lung				
bronchial muscle			relax	contract
bronchial glands				stimulation
Stomach			decreased motility and tone	increased motility and tone
Intestine			decreased motility and tone	increased motility and tone
Kidney			increased renin secretion	
Liver			increased blood sugar	increased glycogen synthesis
Spleen			relax	
Pancreas			increased insulin secretion	

    f. Give QID the dose (or cumulative dose) that produced the greatest bronchodilation.

    g. Monitor daily peak flow, symptoms, and extra bronchodilator use.

D. Oral bronchodilators

  1. Sympathomimetics

    a. They may be used alone or in addition to an aerosolized bronchodilator.

    b. The appropriate dose for each drug is 1–2 low-dose or 1 high-dose tablet(s), three or four times a day, based on individual need and tolerance.

c. The following drugs are the oral sympathomimetic bronchodilators most commonly in use. They are isoproterenol (5–20 mg), metaproterenol (10–20 mg), terbutaline (2.5–5.0 mg), and albuterol (2–4 mg).
d. Tremors and other side effects are usually more severe with oral therapy and caution must be used when combining aerosol and oral therapy in order to avoid overdosing.

2. Theophylline
   a. Mode of action includes antagonism of natural bronchoconstrictors, such as adenosine and prostaglandins, and a possible effect on intracellular calcium movement.
   b. Side effects include nervousness, insomnia, palpitations, tachycardia, nausea, and vomiting. Arrhythmias and seizures can occur at excessively high doses.
   c. The average nonsmoking, nonobese, relatively healthy adult will do well on 10–12 mg/Kg/day.
   d. For a 70 Kg patient, a total of 800 mg/day can be given in two doses of a slow release product, equaling 400 mg every 12 hours.
   e. After three days of therapy, adjustment can be made based on clinical response and/or serum levels (therapeutic levels range from 5–20/μg/ml or mg/L).
   f. Many factors will modify theophylline metabolism, and so in the presence of these factors, dosage adjustments must be made. Refer to Table 19-5.

TABLE 19-5: Dosages for Altered Metabolism of Theophylline

Factor	Dosage Adjustment
Hepatic insufficiency	Less than 5 mg/Kg/day
Heart failure, cor pulmonale	5–8 mg/Kg/day
Therapy with Cimetidine or Troleandomycin	5 mg/Kg/day
Therapy with Estrogen, Erythromycin, Allopurinol	7.5 mg/Kg/day
Dietary factors that include high protein, low carbohydrates, barbecued food, barbiturate therapy, and those age 16–20	12 mg/Kg/day
Therapy with Phenytoin or Rifampin	10–15 mg/Kg/day
Marijuana user	12–15 mg/Kg/day
Smoker	12–18 mg/Kg/day
Age 10–15 years	14–18 mg/Kg/day

Chapter 19: Respiratory Pharmacologic Agents 315

E. Parenteral sympathomimetic bronchodilators used in the management of severe asthma attacks
   1. Subcutaneous injection of epinephrine (0.1 ml of 1:1000 solution) can be given every 20 minutes for 3 or 4 doses.
   2. Subcutaneous injection of terbutaline (0.25 ml of 1:1000) can be given and repeated in 30 minutes.
   3. When patients in severe attack fail to respond to sympathomimetics, intravenous aminophylline is indicated.
      a. A loading dose of aminophylline in the range of 5–7 mg/Kg is recommended for a patient who has not been taking oral theophylline in the previous 24 hours.
      b. In those patients who have taken theophylline in the previous 24 hours, serum level should be obtained.
      c. For a serum level just above $10/\mu g/ml$, give 30% of the usual loading dose.
      d. For a serum level of $5-10/\mu g/ml$, give 50% of the usual loading dose.
      e. For a serum level of less than $5/\mu g/ml$, give the entire loading dose.
      f. A continuous IV drip should be started rate of 0.5 to 0.6 mg/Kg/hour, which should result in a serum level of about $10-15/\mu g/ml$ in most patients. The therapeutic range is $5-25/\mu g/ml$.

III. Mucolytics[3]

A. The movement of retained secretions is the result of combined therapy including IPPB, bronchodilators, postural drainage, percussion, vibration, and chemical alteration of the mucous.
B. Direct chemical alteration of the mucous is largely confined to the use of one drug, acetylcysteine (Mucomyst).
   1. It is intended to be prescribed 3–4 times per day with a dose of 3–5 ml of 20% solution or 6–10 ml of 10% solution.
   2. The action of Mucomyst is to directly disrupt the chemical bonds holding together the long-chain mucoproteins.
   3. The viscosity of the mucous is reduced in direct proportion to the concentration of the drug.
   4. Because of the high solute concentration of Mucomyst, it may cause irritation of the airway and bronchospasm. Therefore, it should only be given accompanied by a bronchodilator drug.

IV. Cromolyn sodium[3]

A. It comes packaged as a powder in 20 mg doses in capsule form, which then requires the use of a special inhaling device that punctures the capsule, thus releasing the powder. It is also available in liquid form (1%) for regular aerosolization.

B. Cromolyn apparently interferes with the release of mediators from mast cells in the airways. These mediators promote allergic reactions in those who come in contact with allergens to which they are sensitive.

C. Cromolyn is intended to be used prophylactically, and if given to patients in distress, can cause deterioration, usually because patients in acute distress are more reactive to inhaled irritants. While this problem is documented with the powder form, it can be expected to occur with the liquid form as well because the drug contains no bronchodilator properties.

D. One study showed effective use of nebulized cromolyn sodium in a population 16 months to five years of age. Method of delivery was with DeVilbiss Pulmo-Sonic nebulizer with mouthpiece or pediatric aerosol mask. Dosages are recommended at 80 mg/day in four divided doses.[4]

V. Steroids[3]

A. These drugs may be used either following severe asthma attacks when the patient has been on IV steroids or for chronic therapy in the severe asthmatic.
   1. When weaning from IV therapy, 40–80 mg/day of prednisone can be used and gradually reduced by 25% every other day or by 5–10 mg/day.
   2. A chronic maintenance dose of 7.5–10 mg/day can be used or an alternate day approach of 5 mg/day on odd days and 15–20 mg/day on even days.

B. Patients with severe asthma who do not respond promptly to bronchodilator therapy will require IV methylprednisolone or hydrocortisone (in doses five times higher).
   1. A loading dose of methylprednisolone of 0.8–1.6 mg/Kg can be followed by 0.2 mg/Kg/hour for 1–3 days.
   2. Peak effect of the drug occurs after 4–6 hours, so it should be given as soon as it is apparent that the patient is not responding to bronchodilator therapy.
   3. If the patient has been on prednisone prior to admission, a loading dose of 1.6–3.2 mg/Kg should be followed by a maintenance dose of 0.2–0.4 mg/Kg/hour.

C. Inhaled anti-inflammatory steroids
   1. Triamcinolone acetonide (Kenalog)
      a. Used primarily to decrease local vascular congestion and cellular infiltration in the lung in response to injury or infection.
      b. An aerosolized dose begins with 10 mg of drug in solution and is adjusted according to patient response.
      c. This drug is poorly absorbed through the lung and therefore shows a sharp reduction in the side effects seen with systemic administration of steroids.

Chapter 19: Respiratory Pharmacologic Agents

2. Beclomethasone dipropionate (Vanceril)
   a. The effects are the same as for Kenalog, with a similar reduction in side effects.
   b. It is administered from a propellant-powered inhaler.
3. Flunisolide (Aerobid)
   a. This drug is given by metered dose inhaler and each activation will result in a greater dose than with beclomethasone.
   b. Because there appears to be higher levels of systemic absorption with flunisolide than with triamcinelone or beclomethasone, patients receiving this steroid should be monitored for systemic signs of reduced adrenal function, and in children, reduced bone growth.

VI. Guidelines for the management of asthma in the adult[5]

A. Chronic mild asthma (intermittent wheeze/cough/dyspnea up to 2 times/week, lasting less than one hour, asymptomatic between exacerbations, less than 30 minutes wheeze/cough/dyspnea with activity, nocturnal cough/wheeze less than twice/month)
   1. Asymptomatic—forced expiratory volume for 1 second (FEV_1) or peak expiratory flowrate (PEFR) are at or greater than 80% of baseline.
      a. Pretreat as needed with 1–2 puffs of a β_2 agonist and/or cromolyn sodium for exercise, allergens, or other exposure.
   2. Symptomatic—the FEV_1 or PEFR vary more than 20% from baseline.
      a. β_2 agonist, 2 puffs every 3–4 hours as needed during the episode.
      b. If there is no response or the response is incomplete, then move to home management of acute exacerbations.
   3. Acute exacerbations—home management consists of using a β_2 agonist, 2–4 puffs every 20 minutes up to one hour if needed.
      a. Good response to therapy occurs when the patient has only mild wheeze/cough/dyspnea/chest tightness; symptoms occur with activity but not at rest; patient can climb one flight of stairs without stopping to rest; and PEFR is ≥70–90% of baseline and can be sustained for over 4 hours.
         (1) Continue treatment every 3–4 hours for 24–48 hours as needed.
         (2) Continue routine medications.
         (3) Contact physician if symptoms recur.
      b. Incomplete response occurs when patient has marked wheeze/dyspnea/repetitive cough/chest tightness occurring at rest; symptoms may interfere with daily activity; patient cannot climb one flight of stairs without resting; and PEFR is 50–70% of baseline.
         (1) MDI or nebulized β_2 agonist every hour.
         (2) Start or increase dose of oral steroids.

(3) If symptoms do not improve to good response within 2–6 hours, PEFR remains 50–70% of baseline or symptoms, or PEFR deteriorates, contact physician or go to the emergency department.

c. Poor response (severe wheezing/dyspnea, speech fragmented, severe symptoms at rest, unable to walk 100 feet without rest, PEFR $\leq$ 50% of baseline.

(1) Contact health provider.
(2) If no response to inhaled β_2 agonists, increase to 4–6 puffs 1–2 times or one nebulized dose every 10 minutes.
(3) Begin or increase dose of steroids.
(4) Go to emergency department if:
   (a) No real improvement after 30 minutes.
   (b) Severity persists and PEFR is $\leq$ 50% of baseline.
   (c) Symptoms persist when using $\beta 2$ agonist every 1–3 hours for more than 6–12 hours with PEFR $\leq$ 70% of baseline or deteriorating.

B. Chronic moderate asthma (symptoms $\geq$ 1–2 times/week, exacerbations may last several days and affect sleep and activity, occasional visits to the ER, PEFR is 60–80% of baseline and varies 20–30% when symptomatic)

1. Inhaled β_2 agonist PRN to TID or QID frequency. If required more often, add one of the following:
   a. Inhaled steroids, 2–4 puffs BID.
   b. Cromolyn, 2 puffs QID.
   c. Sustained release theophylline.
2. If symptoms persist, move to additional therapy.
   a. Increase dose of inhaled steroids, and/or
   b. Increase dose of sustained theophylline, and/or
   c. Add oral β_2 agonist.
3. If PEFR varies more than 30% during worst exacerbations, add a short course of oral prednisone or equivalent followed by inhaled steroids.
4. If symptoms are increasingly frequent, or there is no or only intermittent response to the above therapy, get assessment by a specialist.

C. Chronic severe asthma (continuous symptoms are frequently nocturnal as well, causing limited activity levels. Frequent exacerbations require occasional ER treatment and hospitalization, PEFR $\leq$ 60% baseline and varies 20–30% with routine medication. During acute exacerbations PEFR may vary 50%)

1. Inhaled β_2 agonist PRN-QID and
2. Inhaled steroids 2–6 puffs BID-QID with or without
3. Oral sustained release theophylline (especially for nocturnal symptoms) and/or
4. Oral β_2 agonist

Chapter 19: Respiratory Pharmacologic Agents

5. When PEFR varies more than 50% of baseline add to the preceding regimen:
   a. Extra β_2 agonist 2–4 puffs MDI or nebulizer treatment and
   b. Oral steroids (40mg/day single or divided dose for 1 week, then tapered for 1 week)
D. Emergency department management and initial treatment
   1. Inhaled β_2 agonists times 3 doses over 60–90 minutes. If PEFR ≥ 90% baseline after first dose, additional doses unnecessary.
   2. Subcutaneous β_2 agonist times 3 doses over 60–90 minutes.
   3. Supplemental O_2 to bring SaO_{22} ≥ 90%.
   4. Consider systemic steroids for those already taking oral steroids, or who are not responding to β_2 agonist therapy.
      a. Good response (no wheezing or dyspnea, PEFR ≥ 70% of baseline)
         (1) Discharge and continue medication.
         (2) Consider steroids.
         (3) Close medical follow-up.
         (4) Patient education.
      b. Incomplete response (mild wheezing or dyspnea, PEFR 40–70% of baseline)
         (1) Continue Q1H inhaled β_2 agonist.
         (2) Begin systemic steroids.
         (3) Consider subcutaneous epinephrine.
      c. Poor response (marked of diffuse wheezes or dyspnea, PEFR ≤ 40% of baseline)
         (1) Continue Q1H inhaled β_2 agonist.
         (2) Begin systemic steroids.
         (3) Consider subcutaneous epinephrine.
         (4) Evaluate for admission.
      d. Respiratory failure (extreme distress, impaired consciousness, severe wheezes or "silent" chest, PEFR ≤ 25% baseline, $PaCO_2$ ≥ 40 torr)
         (1) Admit to ICU.
         (2) Begin systemic steroids.
         (3) Give frequent inhaled β_2 agonists.
         (4) Consider intubation and mechanical ventilation.
E. Hospital management
   1. General treatment includes:
      a. Inhaled β_2 agonists Q1-2H
      b. Systemic steroids Q6-8H (IV methylprednisolone 60–80mg)
      c. IV aminophylline or oral theophylline
      d. Supplemental O_2

2. Improved patient breathing
   a. Suggested goals prior to discharge include:
      (1) Minimal or no wheezing
      (2) ≤ one awakening at night with symptoms
      (3) Good activity tolerance
      (4) PEFR ≥ 70% baseline
   b. Preparation for discharge
      (1) Inhaled β_2 agonist no more often then Q3-4H
      (2) Oral steroids
      (3) Oral theophylline
      (4) SaO_2 ≥ 90% on room air
      (5) Patient education provided in areas of:
         (a) Medication use
         (b) PEFR measurement at home
         (c) Contact physician within 7–10 days of discharge
3. Not improved despite maximal therapy
   a. Transfer to ICU.
   b. Nebulized β_2 agonist Q30–60 minutes, may supplement with subcutaneous epinephrine.
   c. IV steroids.
   d. IV aminophylline.
   e. Supplemental O_2.
   f. Intubation and mechanical ventilation for hypercapnic respiratory failure.

VII. Guidelines for the management of asthma in children[5]

A. Chronic mild asthma (wheeze/cough/dyspnea/chest tightness lasting less than 1 hour up to twice a week, asymptomatic between exacerbations, less than 1/2 hour wheeze/cough/ dyspnea/chest tightness with activity, less than twice a month nocturnal cough/wheeze, PEFR ≥ 80% of baseline when asymptomatic, PEFR varies more than 20% when symptomatic)
   1. Pretreat PRN 1–2 puffs β_2 agonist and/or cromolyn for exposure to exercise, allergens, or other stimuli when asymptomatic.
   2. If symptomatic (PEFR varies more than 20% from baseline) then:
      a. If ≤ 5 years of age:
         (1) β_2 agonist MDI 2 puffs Q4–6H (use with spacer device)
         (2) Nebulizer with albuterol 0.1–0.15 mg/Kg in 2ml saline Q4–6H (maximum dose 5.0mg) or metaproterenol 0.25–0.5 mg/Kg in 2ml saline Q4–6H (maximum dose 15mg)
         (3) Nebulizer with cromolyn sodium 20mg BID-QID

Chapter 19: Respiratory Pharmacologic Agents 321

      b. If ≥ 5 years of age:
        (1) β_2 agonist via MDI 2 puffs Q4–6H
        (2) Cromolyn sodium (1 dry powder capsule) Q4–6H for the duration of the episode
   3. Acute exacerbations—home management
      a. Albuterol by nebulizer 0.1mg/kg/dose every 20 minutes up to one hour if needed
      b. MDI/spacer 2–4 puffs every 20 minutes up to one hour if needed
      c. Good response (respiratory rate normal, no dyspnea, no retractions or accessory muscle use, alert, no color change, PEFR is 70–90% of baseline)
        (1) Continue albuterol 0.1mg/kg Q3–4H.
        (2) Continue routine medications.
        (3) Contact physician if symptoms recur.
      d. Incomplete response (respiratory rate normal or increasing, moderate dyspnea, minimal accessory muscle use, mild-moderate intercostal retractions, alert, no color change, PEFR 50–70% of baseline)
        (1) Contact health care provider.
        (2) Continue albuterol 0.1mg/kg/dose Q2H times 3 doses with continued observation.
        (3) Begin oral prednisone 1–2 mg/kg/dose.
        (4) If PEFR or symptoms deteriorate, contact physician or go to ER.
      e. Poor response (respiratory rate increasing, severe dyspnea, severe retractions and nasal flaring with accessory use, decreasing alertness, color change, PEFR ≤ 50 baseline)
        (1) Contact physician.
        (2) Go to ER.

B. Chronic moderate asthma (symptoms ≥ 1–2 times/week, exacerbations may last several days, occasional ER visit, PEFR 60–80% baseline and varies 20–30% when symptomatic)
   1. Inhaled β_2 agonist TID-QID and cromolyn 2 puffs BID-QID or 1 20mg BID-QID.
   2. Inhaled β_2 agonist TID-QID and sustained release theophylline to achieve serum level of 5–15 µg/ml or oral β_2 agonist.
   3. If symptoms persist with above regimen, add inhaled steroids and may drop cromolyn or theophylline.
   4. If there is no response or only an intermittent response, get assessment by a specialist.

C. Chronic severe asthma (continuous symptoms, limited activity, frequent exacerbations, frequent nocturnal symptoms, occasional ER treatment and hospitalization, PEFR ≤ 60% of baseline and varies 20–30% with routine medication)

1. Inhaled β_2 agonist PRN-TID-QID
   a. If ≤ 5 years, use nebulizer.
   b. If ≥ 5 years, 2 puffs QID-Q4H.
2. Inhaled steroid 2–4 puffs BID-QID after β_2 agonist with or without.
3. Cromolyn, 2 puffs BID-QID with or without
4. Oral sustained released theophylline to achieve serum concentration of 5–15/µg/ml, and/or
5. Oral beta agonist.
6. For acute exacerbations, when PEFR varies ≥ 50% of baseline:
   a. Add extra β_2 agonist treatment 2–4 puffs MDI or nebulizer treatment as needed.
   b. Consider oral steroids.
      (1) ≤ 5 years 5–10 mg alternate days, decrease to lowest dose that stabilizes symptoms and PEFR.
      (2) ≥ 5 years use lowest alternate A.M. dose that stabilizes symptoms and PEFR.

D. Emergency department management
   1. Initial care includes:
      a. Supplemental O_2 to keep SaO_2 ≥ 95%.
      b. Nebulized albuterol with 6 L/M O2 at 0.15 mg/kg/dose (maximum dose = 5mg) Q20 minutes up to 1 hour (if PEFR ≥ 90% baseline after first dose, additional doses are unnecessary).
      c. Start steroids if no response after one nebulized treatment or if patient is steroid dependent.
      d. If patient is unable to perform PEFR or has diminished consciousness, give 0.01mg/kg subcutaneous epinephrine immediately.
   2. Good response (PEFR ≥ 70% baseline, heart rate and respiratory rate are decreasing, no wheezing on auscultation, no accessory muscle usage, minimal to no dyspnea, pulsus paradoxus less than 10 torr, SaO_2 ≥ 95%)
      a. Decrease albuterol to Q2H.
      b. Observe for at least 1 hour.
         (1) If stable (PEFR ≥ 70% baseline, SaO_2 ≥ 95%, other parameters improved)
            (a) Discharge with patient education.
            (b) Continue medications (consider steroids).
            (c) Order follow-up.
         (2) Not stable (PEFR ≤ 70% baseline, other parameters not improved)
            (a) Treat as incomplete response.

Chapter 19: Respiratory Pharmacologic Agents

3. Incomplete response (PEFR 40–70% baseline, heart rate and respiratory rate have increased further, mild wheezing, moderate accessory muscle use, moderate dyspnea, pulsus paradoxus ≥ 10–15 torr, SaO_2 91–95%)
   a. Add oral prednisone 1–2 mg/kg/dose.
   b. Continue inhaled albuterol at 0.15 mg/kg/dose every 20 minutes.
   c. Assess severity at 1 hour.
      (1) Good response (PEFR ≥ 70% baseline, SaO_2 ≥ 95%, other parameters improved)
         (a) Discharge with patient education.
         (b) Continue medications.
         (c) Order follow-up.
      (2) Incomplete response (PEFR 40–70% baseline, SaO_2 91–95%, other parameters improving)
         (a) Continue treatment.
         (b) Consider admission if no improvement.
      (3) Poor response (PEFR ≤ 40% baseline, SaO_2 ≤ 91%, other parameters not improved)
         (a) Consider hospitalization.
4. Poor response (PEFR ≤ 40% baseline, heart rate and respiratory rate increasing, decreased air movement, severe dyspnea and accessory muscle use, pulsus paradoxus ≥ 15 torr, SaO_2 ≤ 91%)
   a. Admit.

E. Hospital management
   1. If PEFR ≥ 30% baseline and/or $PaCO_2$ ≤ 40 torr, SaO_2 ≥ 90%, moderate wheezing, moderate dyspnea and accessory muscle use, pulsus paradoxus ≤ 15 torr, admit to monitored unit.
      a. Supplemental O_2 to keep SaO_2 ≥ 90%.
      b. Nebulized albuterol 0.15ml/kg/dose Q1–2H.
      c. Oral or IV methylprednisolone 1–2mg/kg/dose Q6H.
      d. Oral theophylline Q12H or IV aminophylline
         (1) Improved (PEFR ≥ 70% baseline, heart rate and respiratory rate returned to normal, minimal to no wheezing, no dyspnea, moderate to no use of accessory muscles, no pulsus paradoxus)
            (a) Discharge home with patient education.
            (b) Continue medications.
            (c) Order follow-up.
         (2) Not improved (PEFR ≤ 30% of baseline, $PaCO_2$ ≥ 40 torr, and other parameters worsening)
            (a) Admit to ICU.

2. If PEFR ≤ 30% baseline and/or $PaCO_2$ ≥ 40 torr, SaO_2 ≤ 90%, severe wheezing, decreased air movement, severe accessory muscle use, severe dyspnea, pulsus paradoxus ≥ 15 torr, admit to ICU.
    a. Oxygen to keep SaO_2 ≥ 95%.
    b. Continuous nebulized albuterol 0.5ml/kg/hour (maximum dosage 15mg/hour).
    c. IV methylprednisolone 1–2mg/kg/dose Q6H.
    d. IV aminophylline
        (1) If theophylline concentration known, every 1mg/kg will give 2μg/ml increase in serum concentration.
        (2) If theophylline concentration unknown:
            (a) If no previous theophylline, give loading dose of 6mg/kg.
            (b) If previous theophylline administered, give loading dose of 3mg/kg.
        (3) Constant infusion rates to give serum concentration of 15μg/ml
            (a) 1–6 months age: 0.5mg/kg/hr
            (b) 6 months–1 year age: 1.0mg/kg/hr
            (c) 1–9 years age: 1.5mg/kg/hr
            (d) 10–16 years age: 1.2mg/kg/hr
    e. If PEFR ≤ 25% baseline and $PaCO_2$ ≥ 45 torr, and other parameters worsening, consider IV terbutaline with 10μg/kg over 10 minutes as loading dose, then a maintenance dose of 0.4μg/kg/min. Increase as necessary by 0.2μg/kg/min. up to 3–6μg/kg/min.
    f. If $PaCO_2$ ≥ 55 torr or rising ≥ 5–10 torr/hr, increasing dyspnea and fatigue of respiratory muscles, decreased alertness, pulsus paradoxus ≥ 30 torr, with acidosis and desaturation, continue medications and consider adding mechanical ventilation.

VIII. Smoking cessation and nicotine therapy[6]

A. Discuss stopping smoking with all respiratory care patients who smoke.
   1. Spend 2–5 minutes advising patients who smoke to stop.
   2. Personalize the risks of smoking.
       a. Pulmonary disease
           (1) Smoking is the major cause of chronic bronchitis and 80–90% of COPD.
           (2) Smoking is associated with more frequent and severe asthma.
           (3) Smoking is associated with recurrent respiratory infections.
           (4) Smoking is associated with increased respiratory tract infections in infants whose mothers smoke.

Chapter 19: Respiratory Pharmacologic Agents

      b. Cardiovascular disease
         (1) Smoking is a major cause of heart disease in men and women.
         (2) Smoking is associated with up to 30% of cardiac deaths.
         (3) Smoking is associated with increased risk of stroke and is compounded by the use of oral contraceptives.
         (4) Smoking is cited as cause and the most important risk factor of peripheral vascular disease.
         (5) Diabetic men and women who smoke greatly increase their risk of cardiovascular and peripheral vascular disease.
      c. Cancer
         (1) Smoking is associated with about 30% of all cancer deaths each year.
         (2) Smoking is a major cause of lung, laryngeal, oral, and esophageal cancer.
         (3) Smoking is a contributing factor in bladder, pancreatic, and renal cancer.
         (4) Smoking is associated with gastric and cervical cancer.
      d. Pregnancy-related complications
         (1) Smoking is associated with increased risk of miscarriage, stillbirth, and low birthweight infants.
         (2) Smoking is associated with retarded physical and mental development of offspring.
   3. Benefits of quitting
      a. Reduced expenditure.
      b. Improved health.
      c. Impact of smoking in their environment on their children and others.
      d. Reducing the risk of cancer.
      e. Reducing the risk of cardiovascular and peripheral vascular disease.
B. Give each patient literature.
C. Ask the patient if he or she is ready to quit smoking and help them set goals for doing so.
D. Refer the patient to a local smoking cessation program.
E. Follow-up the advice and literature during routine respiratory care visits.
   1. Continue talking to the patient at every opportunity during routine visits.
   2. Ask the patient to describe how he or she thought or felt after your last conversation about smoking.
   3. Repeat your smoking message.
   4. Reiterate your information about a local smoking cessation program.
   5. Provide encouragement and positive reinforcement if the patient starts to consider quitting or makes any attempt to stop smoking.
   6. Use home care visits if possible to reinforce no-smoking messages.

F. Give individualized guidance to smokers receiving respiratory care who want to quit.
   1. Obtain the patient's smoking history.
      a. When and how did they start smoking?
      b. How much do they or have they been smoking?
      c. At what times of the day do they smoke the most?
      d. What other activities do they do while they smoke?
      e. Where do they smoke?
      f. With whom do they smoke?
      g. What feelings make them want to smoke?
      h. If they have tried to quit before, what problems did they have with quitting?
   2. Prepare the patient to quit.
      a. Set a quitting date.
         (1) This date should be set by the patient and should not coincide with especially stressful events.
         (2) Quitting suddenly ("cold turkey") reduces the number of days of withdrawal from nicotine addiction, and most individuals who quit successfully quit in this manner.
         (3) If the patient is unable to quit suddenly, help them set goals to taper to one-half their normal use, prior to quitting altogether.
      b. Teach your patient the Stop-Think-Act technique for coping with quitting.
         (1) **Stop**—Say "STOP!" to yourself when you feel the urge to smoke.
         (2) **Think**—of why you quit and that you can wait out the urge.
         (3) **Act**—
            (a) Get up and move around. Start an exercise program.
            (b) Keep your hands busy.
            (c) Talk to a friend.
            (d) Breathe deeply, sigh, or yawn.
            (e) Chew sugarless gum, eat low calorie foods, or drink water and juice.
G. Discuss weight gain and diet with the patient. Share tips on how to help control weight gain.
   1. Stick to a low-fat diet including foods such as fruits and vegetables, lean meats, poultry, fish, and low-fat dairy products.
   2. Eat three balanced meals per day with moderate portions of food, or eat five or six smaller meals per day.
   3. Broil, bake, or boil foods instead of frying them.
   4. Drink water before meals and throughout the day (six to eight 8 oz. glasses).

Chapter 19: Respiratory Pharmacologic Agents

H. Help the patient obtain a prescription for nicotine polacrilex medication, if needed.
   1. Using nicotine polacrilex. Guidelines include:
      a. One piece of nicotine gum every waking hour as a starting routine.
      b. One piece of nicotine gum per cigarette for the first two weeks, not to exceed thirty pieces per day.
      c. One piece of nicotine gum for every two cigarettes for the next three months.
      d. Gradual tapering off over the next 2–3 months.
   2. Transdermal nicotine patches
      a. Don't use the patch until quit day.
      b. Rotate the patch to a new site each day and don't reuse the same site for 7 days.
      c. Don't apply the patch before bedtime.
      d. Do not attempt to taper off the patch prematurely. Most smokers require 6–10 weeks of patch therapy.
      e. Don't use the patches if still smoking, pregnant, or if suffering adverse physical or skin reactions.
I. Encourage the patient to tell family and friends of the decision to quit.
J. Ask the patient to identify a friend or family member who can be a steady source of support.
K. Tell the patient to get rid of cigarettes, ash trays, and lighters in order to start acting as a nonsmoker.
L. Ensure that some form of follow-up is used.

IX. Antiviral agents[7]

A. Amantadine—aerosol dose is approximately 20 mg/day; effective against Influenza A. Side effects include insomnia, nervousness, slurred speech, dizziness, and ataxia in over 10% of the reported cases.
B. Ribavirin—aerosol dose is 55 mg/hour or 0.82 mg/Kg/hour, given continuously (20 out of 24 hours per day); effective against Influenza A and B, parainfluenza, and respiratory syncytial virus (RSV). Low toxicity has been reported, and there appears to be some response against RSV in infants and small children. Ribavirin must be administered with the SPAG-2 aerosol generator only.
   1. This drug is contraindicated in women or girls who are or who may become pregnant during exposure to the drug.
   2. Specific precautions should be taken by the caregiver when administering ribavirin therapy.
      a. Pregnant practitioners and both male and female workers who are trying to conceive should avoid exposure to this drug, since animal studies have shown teratogenic effects even at low doses.

b. The drug should be administered only in an isolation room with a separate air circulating system equipped with an HEPA filter.
   c. The pressure in the room should be negative with respect to the outside environment to prevent droplet nuclei from leaving the room.
   d. An OSHA approved respirator with a protection factor of at least 10 should be worn.
3. Because ribavirin is specifically administered for RSV, the following precautions should be observed when dealing with these patients, to prevent the spread of this potentially lethal infection.
   a. If the patient is suspected or diagnosed as having RSV, he/she must be placed in a private room, and caregivers should gown, mask, and glove. Gloving is imperative as long as the organism is transferred by direct contact with secretions.
   b. Strict adherence to handwashing procedures (scrub after contact with an infected patient or his/her environment.)
   c. Avoid touching your face and/or mucous membranes.
   d. Use eye protection
   e. In adults, RSV most often causes a common cold. If you have an upper respiratory tract infection, avoid direct contact with infants and young children.

X. Pentamidine isethionate (NebuPent)[8]

A. Pentamidine is indicated for the prevention of *Pneumocystis carinii* pneumonia (PCP) in high-risk, HIV-infected patients.
B. The standard dose is 300mg once every 4 weeks.
C. Preparation and administration
   1. The contents of one vial (300mg) in 6 ml of sterile water for injection USP (the use of saline will cause precipitation of the drug).
   2. The entire reconstituted contents of the vial should be placed in the nebulizer reservoir of the Respirgard II nebulizer.
   3. The dose should be delivered until the nebulizer reservoir is empty (about 30–45 minutes).
   4. The nebulizer flowrate should be 5–7 L/M from a 40–50 PSI air or oxygen source. Less than 20 PSI should not be used.
D. Precautions
   1. The caregiver should take precautions to isolate themselves from the aerosol because asthmatic reactions have been reported.[9]

Chapter 19: Respiratory Pharmacologic Agents

2. These guidelines should be followed when administering pentamidine:
   a. Use single patient rooms or booths.
   b. Six or more room air exchanges per hour should occur.
   c. There should be nonrecirculation of treatment room air.
   d. Negative air pressure should be maintained in the treatment room area with respect to adjacent areas.

XI. Cardiovascular agents (Refer to Table 19-6.)

A. Inotropic agents influence the force of contraction.

B. Chronotropic agents influence the rate of contraction.

C. Vasodilator agents are useful in rapidly decreasing the blood pressure in critical hypertensive conditions by expanding the systemic vascular bed.

D. Vasoconstrictor agents are useful for increasing the blood pressure in hypotensive conditions by constricting the systemic vascular bed.

E. Diuretic agents alter the rate of urine output by increasing or decreasing the glomerular filtration rate. Refer to Table 19-7.

TABLE 19-6: Drugs for Altering Pump Function, Preload, and Afterload

Inotropes	Vasodilators	Vasoconstrictors
Dopamine	Nitroprusside	Methoramine
Dobutamine	Nitroglycerine	Norepinephrine
Isoproterenol	Phentolamine	Metaraminol
Epinephrine	Chlorpromazine	Mephentermine
Norepinephrine	Hydralazine	Phenylephrine
Digitalis	Diazoxide	Epinephrine (high doses)
Calcium	Prazosin	Dopamine (high doses)
	Isoproterenol	
	Dopamine (low doses)	
	Epinephrine (low doses)	

TABLE 19-7: Diuretics

Drug	Mechanisms of Action
Acetazolamide	Interferes with reabsorption of $NaHCO_3$
Amiloride	Interferes with passive $Na+$ entry from lumen to cell and with potassium secretion.
Aminophylline	Increases glomerular filtration
Ethacrynic acid	Interferes with chloride reabsorption
Furosemide	Interferes with chloride reabsorption
Glucocorticoids	Increases glomerular filtration
Mannitol	Interferes with reabsorption of NaCl, $NaHCO_3$, and H_2O
Mercurials	Interferes with chloride reabsorption
Spironolactone	Competitively inhibits mineralocorticoid action
Thiazides	Interferes with NaCl reabsorption

XII. Resuscitation drugs[10]

A. Sodium bicarbonate
1. This drug is given to counteract hypoxia-induced anaerobic metabolism by combining with H+ and elevating pH.
2. The indications for bicarbonate therapy are few, and it should only be considered when there is documented preexisting metabolic acidosis with or without hyperkalemia.
   a. Though sodium bicarbonate buffers free H+, it is then converted to carbonic acid and then dissociates to water and carbon dioxide.
   b. Each 50 mEq dose of sodium bicarbonate contains a high carbon dioxide content. This content exerts a partial pressure of 260–280 mmHg, and the carbon dioxide that is generated crosses rapidly into cells and causes a paradoxical worsening of intracellular acidosis.
   c. Administration of bicarbonate does not facilitate ventricular defibrillation or survival in cardiac arrest.
3. If used, sodium bicarbonate should be given in a dose of 1 mEq/Kg only after interventions such as prompt defibrillation, effective chest compression, endotracheal intubation, and hyperventilation with 100% oxygen, and the use of drugs

such as epinephrine and lidocaine. A maximum of 0.5 mEq/Kg may be given for subsequent doses, but not more frequently than every 10 minutes.
B. Epinephrine—the recommended dose is 0.5–1.0 mg given IV and repeated at least every 5 minutes. Through its adrenergic action and stimulation of alpha and beta 1 receptors, it has the following effects in resuscitation:
  1. Increased systemic vascular resistance
  2. Increased arterial blood pressure
  3. Increased heart rate
  4. Increased coronary and cerebral blood flow
  5. Increased myocardial contraction
  6. Increased myocardial oxygen requirements
  7. Increased automaticity
C. Atropine
  1. Atropine is indicated as initial therapy in patients with symptomatic bradycardia.
  2. It may restore normal AV nodal conduction and stimulate electrical activity during asystolic cardiac arrest.
  3. For patients without cardiac arrest, a dose of 0.5 mg IV, repeated at 5 minute intervals is recommended. This dose is repeated until the desired clinical effect is achieved. For patients in asystolic arrest, a dose of 1 mg, repeated once if necessary, is recommended.
D. Lidocaine
  1. Lidocaine suppresses ventricular arrhythmias by decreasing the automaticity.
  2. Dosage recommendation is a bolus injection of 1 mg/Kg with additional bolus injections of 0.5 mg/Kg every 8–10 minutes if needed to a total dose of 3 mg/Kg. Following resuscitation, the restoration of a continuous IV drip should be started at a dose of 30–50 μg/Kg/min.
E. Procainamide
  1. This drug suppresses ventricular arrhythmias and may be useful when lidocaine has not been effective in life-threatening arrhythmias.
  2. The IV dose for management of premature ventricular contractions or ventricular tachycardia is 50 mg every 5 minutes until one of the following is seen:
     a. The arrhythmia is effectively treated.
     b. Hypotension occurs.
     c. The QRS complex of the ECG is widened by 50% of its original width.
     d. A total of 1 gram of drug has been injected.
F. Bretylium tosylate
  1. The use of this drug is indicated for treating ventricular fibrillation and ventricular tachycardia that does not respond to therapy with lidocaine, procainamide, and/or repeated shocks.

    a. Dosage for ventricular fibrillation is 5 mg/Kg undiluted bretylium IV, followed by attempted defibrillation. If attempts at defibrillation fail, the dose can be increased to 10 mg/Kg and repeated at 15–30 minute intervals to a maximum dose of 30 mg/Kg.
    b. In refractory or recurrent ventricular tachycardia, 500 mg of bretylium can be diluted to 50 ml, and 5–10 mg/Kg can be injected IV over a period of 8–10 minutes.
G. Verapamil
  1. This drug is used primarily for treatment of paroxysmal supraventricular tachycardia (PSVT) where this arrhythmia does not require electrical shock.
  2. A single dose is 0.075–0.15 mg/Kg to a maximum of 10 mg, given as an IV bolus over a 1 minute period.
  3. Repeat doses are 0.15 mg/Kg to a maximum of 10 mg, given 30 minutes after the initial dose.
H. Morphine
  1. It is the drug of choice for the treatment of pain and anxiety associated with acute myocardial infarction. It is also useful for treatment of acute pulmonary edema.
  2. Dosage is 5–10 mg IV every 5–30 minutes until desired clinical effect is achieved.[12]

XIII. Endotracheal drugs[10]

A. Epinephrine
  1. Endotracheal injection produces lower and slightly delayed peak plasma concentrations, but a more sustained physiological effect, probably due to delayed absorption secondary to localized pulmonary vasoconstriction.
  2. Chest compression must be halted momentarily while the drug is instilled through the ET tube.
  3. Positive pressure is then reapplied and compression resumed.
  4. The standard dose should be diluted in either 10ml of normal saline or sterile water prior to administration.
  5. In pediatric patients, good results have been seen with use of the undiluted dose.
    a. Peak blood levels are less than 1/10 of those seen with IV administration of an equal dose.
    b. The minimal recommended dose is 0.5ml of the 1:10,000 solution. Smaller volumes of the 1:1,000 solution are not recommended because they may fail to reach the bronchial mucosa.
    c. CPR should be interrupted briefly while the drug is injected as deeply as possible into the ET tube, followed by several rapid positive-pressure breaths.

Chapter 19: Respiratory Pharmacologic Agents

B. Atropine
1. When given via ET tube, the onset of action is similar to that seen with IV administration.
2. The adult dose is 1.0–2.0mg diluted in 10ml of normal saline or sterile water.
3. The pediatric dose would be 0.02 mg/kg with a minimum dose of 0.1mg and a maximum dose of 1.0mg.
   a. This can be repeated every five minutes up to a total of 1.0mg in the child.
   b. Administration can be repeated every five minutes up to a total dose of 2.0mg in the adolescent.

XIV. Respiratory stimulation

A. When Doxapram is administered IV in low doses, it selectively stimulates respiration and increases the tidal volume by activating carotid chemoreceptors and central respiratory neurons.
B. The duration of respiratory stimulation seldom lasts longer than 5–10 minutes after a single dose.
1. Single or divided IV doses of 0.5–1.5 mg/Kg are used to produce desired stimulation. An IV drip may be used at 5 mg/min and reduced by 50% following response. Recommended maximal dose is 4 mg/Kg or 3 grams.
2. Excessive doses may result in hypertension, tachycardia, arrhythmias, coughing, sneezing, vomiting, itching, tremors, muscle rigidity, sweating, flushing, and hyperpyrexia. Side effects are common.
3. Treatment of acute sedative-hypnotic intoxication, in addition to correction of acute respiratory insufficiency, have been considered indications for this therapy.

XV. Sedatives[11]

A. A sedative drug produces a feeling of relaxation and rest, not necessarily accompanied by sleep. Refer to Table 19-8.
1. Sedative doses of secobarbital (Seconal), or pentobarbital (Nembutal) produce no significant respiratory depression.
   a. Seconal is given in doses of 30–50 mg, 3–4 times per day.
   b. Nembutal is given in a 20mg dose, 3–4 times per day.
   c. Half-life for both Seconal and Nembutal is between 15–48 hours.
2. Chloral hydrate (Note) has been reported to be useful and safe as a sedative in asthmatics and as a hypnotic (a drug that produces sleep) in patients with respiratory insufficiency. A standard dose would be 250 mg, 3 times per day, with a half-life of 4–9.5 hours.

TABLE 19-8: Sedative Drugs

Benzodiazepines

Diazepam
Lorazepam
Midazolam
Clonazepam
Chlordiazepoxide
Temazepam
Triazolam
Alprazolam
Flurazepam
Butyrophenones
Haloperidol
Droperidol

Tricyclic antidepressants

Amitryptaline
Nortryptaline
Imipramine
Desipramine
Doxepin
Maprotiline

Hydrocarbons

Chloral hydrate
Trichlorethanol

Phenothiazines

Chlorpromazine
Promethazine
Thioridazine
Trifluoperazine
Perphenazine
Prochlorperazine
Fluphenazine

Barbiturates

Pentobarbital
Thiopental
Methohexital
Thiamylal
Secobarbital
Amobarbital

Antihistaminics

Hydroxyzine
Diphenhydramine

Other drugs

Clonidine
Propofol
Etomidate

Modified from K. J. S. Anand, "Analgesia and Sedation for Ventilated Children and Infants," *Respiratory Care* 43, no. 11 (1998): 942–951, with permission.

3. Flurazepam (Dalmane), a benzodiazepine, can be used as a hypnotic and produces less respiratory depression than barbiturates. The hypnotic dose is 15–30 mg, with a half-life of 50–100 hours.
4. Diazepam (Valium) can be used as a minor tranquilizer for relief of anxiety and is less likely to cause respiratory depression than the barbiturates. Standard sedative dose is 5–10 mg, 3–4 times per day, with a half-life of 30–60 hours.
5. Hydroxyzine (Atarax, Vistaril) is a tranquilizer that also has antihistaminic and bronchodilator properties (it exerts its bronchodilator effect through its anti-

Chapter 19: Respiratory Pharmacologic Agents

cholinergic properties). It is therefore useful for anxious patients with bronchospastic disease, and is the drug of choice for preoperative preparation of patients with respiratory insufficiency. Duration of action is 6–24 hours, with a single dose being 2.5 mg.

XVI. Respiratory suppressants

A. Morphine has a direct dose-related depressant effect on the brainstem causing respiratory suppressions. The result is a decrease in respiratory rate, leading to a reduction in minute ventilation.
   1. Effective suppression of ventilation can occur within 10 minutes of a 5 mg IV dose. Repeated doses every 10 minutes up to 20 mg may sometimes be necessary.
   2. Potential side effects include nausea, vomiting, hypotension, and gaseous bowel distention.
   3. Because morphine can cause tissues to release histamine, use of this narcotic should be avoided in most asthmatics.

XVII. Muscle relaxants

A. Muscle relaxants (paralysis) are indicated for prevention of spontaneous breathing for a patient on a mechanical ventilator and for endotracheal intubation in the awake patient. In both cases, sedatives or tranquilizers should also be used.
   1. d-tubocurarine (Curare) is normally given in a dose of 6–9 mg, while one-half the dose may be given 3–5 minutes later, if necessary.
   2. Small, rapidly moving muscles are affected first, followed by limb, neck, trunk, intercostal, and finally, diaphragm muscles.
   3. The standard duration of action is about 30–60 minutes.
   4. Major side effects include histamine release followed by severe hypotension, bronchospasm, and excessive bronchial and salivary secretions.
B. Pancuronium (Pavulon) is normally administered in a IV dose of 0.04–0.10 mg/Kg. Relaxation will be produced in 2–3 minutes and last up to 90 minutes with a standard dose.
   1. It is about five times more potent than curare as a competitive neuromuscular blocking agent.
   2. It has minimal cardiovascular side effects and little histamine releasing effects.
C. Succinylcholine (Anectine) is administered IV and has rapid onset, within one minute. Duration of action is short, lasting only about five minutes. The usual dose is 20 mg.
   1. Succinylcholine works by causing depolarization of the motor end-plate, and transient muscle tremors may occur prior to paralysis. Muscle soreness may follow its use.

a. Acute cardiovascular collapse may occur following administration, usually due to potassium loss from skeletal muscle secondary to persistent depolarization.

b. The resulting hyperkalemia may produce myocardial depression and ventricular arrhythmias.

XVIII. Antibiotics[1]

A. Patients with chronic pulmonary disease will often experience increased dyspnea, cough, and an inability to expectorate secretions, which may have turned green or yellow in color.

B. Empirical antibiotic therapy is felt to be indicated, with all common agents effective against *Diplococcus pneumoniae* or *Haemophilus influenzae* being acceptable.

C. A standard course of 7–14 days treatment is given for each exacerbation.

D. Commonly used antibiotics include tetracycline, ampicillin, amoxicillin, erythromycin, and trimethoprim-sulfamethoxazole.

XIX. Artificial surfactants

A. Exosurf Neonatal (a protein-free synthetic lung surfactant)[8]
  1. Indications
     a. Prophylactic treatment of infants with birthweights of less than 1350 grams who are at risk of developing RDS.
     b. Prophylactic treatment of infants with birthweights of over 1350 grams who have evidence of pulmonary immaturity.
     c. Rescue treatment of infants who have developed RDS.
  2. Preparation and administration
     a. Exosurf is stored under vacuum as a sterile lyophilized powder that is then reconstituted with preservative-free sterile water for injection prior to administration.
     b. Reconstitution
        (1) This should be done immediately prior to use because Exosurf contains no preservatives.
        (2) Fill a 10–12 ml syringe with 8 ml of preservative-free sterile water for injection using an 18 or 19 gauge needle.
        (3) Allow the vacuum in the vial to draw the water from the syringe into the vial.

(4) Draw the 8 ml of solution out of the vial and into the syringe while maintaining the vacuum, then release the plunger of the syringe, allowing the solution to move back into the vial.

(5) Repeat the drawing and plunger release step 3–4 times to ensure adequate mixing of the powder and water.

(6) If the vial does not have vacuum when first opened, do not use.

3. Administration
   a. The dose for Exosurf is 5ml/kg of the reconstituted solution.
   b. The appropriate dose should be drawn from the vial from **below** the frothy surface of the solution.
   c. If the solution appears to have separated prior to administration, gently shake or swirl the vial to resuspend the preparation.
   d. Prophylactic treatment
      (1) The first dose should be administered as soon as possible after birth.
      (2) Second and third doses should be administered at 12 and 24 hours for infants who remain on mechanical ventilation.
   e. Rescue
      (1) The first 5ml/Kg dose should be administered as possible after the diagnosis of RDS.
      (2) The second dose should be given at 12 hours following the first dose.

4. Technique
   a. Connect the appropriate size of endotracheal tube adaptor with luer-lock side port that is provided with the solution.
   b. Attach the syringe containing the surfactant solution to the side port of the adaptor.
   c. One-half of the total solution is instilled slowly through the side port over 1–2 minutes (30–50 breaths) in timing with each ventilator breath with the infant supine and the head in the neutral position.
   d. The infant is then turned with the torso and head at a 45 degree angle to the right and held there for 30 seconds while mechanical ventilation continues.
   e. The infant's head and torso are then returned to the midline and the remaining half dose is given in the same fashion.
   f. Following administration of the second half of the dose, the head and torso are turned 45 degrees to the left and held there while mechanical ventilation continues.
   g. The infant is then returned to the midline.

5. Precautions
   a. Rapid improvements in lung function may require immediate reductions in ventilator rate, pressure, and/or FIO_2.
   b. Constant bedside attendance for at least 30 minutes is essential because rapid improvement may require immediate change.
   c. If during administration of the surfactant solution, deterioration of the infant occurs, the procedure should be stopped and necessary adjustment in ventilator parameters and oxygen should be performed.
   d. Suctioning should not be performed for two hours after the Exosurf is given, except when dictated by clinical necessity.

B. Survanta (a natural bovine extract)[8]
   1. Indications
      a. For prevention of RDS in premature infants of 1250 grams or less or with evidence of surfactant deficiency.
      b. For rescue of infants with RDS confirmed by X-ray and requiring mechanical ventilation.
   2. Preparation and administration
      a. Survanta is stored refrigerated at 2–8°C and should be warmed by standing at room temperature for at least 20 minutes or warmed in the hand for at least 8 minutes.
      b. The vial should be visually inspected for discoloration to note that the solution is the proper off-white to light brown color.
      c. Each dose of Survanta is 4ml/Kg of the solution (100mg of phospholipids/Kg).
      d. Any unopened vial of Survanta that has been warmed to room temperature and not used may be returned to refrigeration within 8 hours and stored for future use.
      e. Four doses of Survanta can be given as indicated in the first 48 hours, and should not be given more often than every 6 hours.
   3. Technique
      a. For prevention, the first dose should be administered within 15 minutes of delivery.
      b. The drug is given through a 5 Fr end-hole catheter that is inserted through the endotracheal tube to be positioned just above the carina.
      c. The full dose is given in 1/4 increments, with each 1/4 dose being instilled through the catheter over 2–3 seconds. Each 1/4 dose is given in a different position to aid in as much even distribution of the drug as possible.
         (1) The head and body are inclined slightly down with the head turned to the right.
         (2) The head and body are inclined slightly down with the head turned to the left.

Chapter 19: Respiratory Pharmacologic Agents

- (3) The head and body are inclined slightly up with the head turned to the right.
- (4) The head and body are inclined slightly up with the head turned to the left.
- d. Following each position change and administration of 1/4 dose, the infant should be manually ventilated with a sufficient oxygen concentration to prevent cyanosis, at a rate of 60 breaths/minute, with sufficient pressure to ensure adequate ventilation and chest excursion.
- e. When Survanta is given for rescue, the first dose should be given as soon as possible after the infant is placed on mechanical ventilation. The drug is given in the same fashion as for prophylaxis, while using the ventilator after each 1/4 dose instead of manual ventilation.

4. Precautions
   a. During the dosing procedure, ventilator adjustments should be made to maintain clinical stability of the infant.
   b. Crackles and moist breath sounds can occur after administration of Survanta, but no intervention is required unless there are clear-cut signs of airway obstruction.

C. Surfactant in adult respiratory distress syndrome (ARDS)[3]
   1. A prospective study with placebo control and aerosolized Exosurf revealed the following:
      a. Fifty-two patients with sepsis-induced ARDS showed trend improvement in pulmonary function with aerosolized Exosurf with decreased shunt fractions, improved static respiratory compliance, and decreased mortality.
      b. A protocol was followed where Exosurf was nebulized either 12 or 24 hours a day for up to 5 days using an in-line nebulizer that nebulized only during inspiration, using a dose of 13.5mg/ml.
   2. A follow-up study was performed in 49 patients with sepsis-induced ARDS.
      a. Exosurf was nebulized for 24 hours/day at concentrations of 40.5mg/ml or 81mg/ml.
      b. There was significant improvement in alveolar-arterial oxygen gradient (A-aDO_2) and a reduction in FIO_2.
   3. There is no optimal dose yet determined for this application and it is not clear whether nebulization or instillation would be more effective.
      a. Large quantities of nebulized surfactant may cause problems with some ventilator circuits due to plugging of expiratory filters.
      b. Large quantities of instilled surfactant (estimated at 150–300ml/dose) may causes temporary increases in shunt fraction, airway pressures, bronchial obstruction, and desaturation.

XX. Analgesic/Anesthetic Agents[11]

A. Medications capable of removing pain (analgesics, aspirin/morphine) and removing sensation (anesthesia, pentothal/halothane) function by depressing the central nervous system (CNS). These groups of drugs run the full spectrum of neuromuscular blockade, from mild sedation on one end to complete unconsciousness on the other. Refer to Table 19-9.

B. Local anesthetics, usually amines (lidocaine) do not affect the CNS by creating various degrees of depression, but depress sodium flow to the myocardial cells, thereby increasing their resting potential.[1] The effect is that the nerve is not capable of generating an action potential in response to a pain stimulus. Refer to Table 19-10.

TABLE 19-9: Local/Regional Analgesic Agents and Techniques

Amide Local Anesthetics

Lidocaine
Bupivaciane
Etidocaine
Mepivacaine
Prilocaine
Ropivacaine

Topical Applications

EMLA cream (lidocaine/prilocaine)
TAC (tetracaine/adrenaline/cocaine)
LET (lidocaine/epinephrine/tetracaine)
Lidocaine gel (30%)
Iontophoresis (lidocaine/epinephrine)
Ethylene chloride spray

Peripheral Techniques

Local infiltration
Ring.- block
Nerve blocks
Plexus blocks
Ganglion blocks

Ester Local Anesthetics

Chloroprocaine
Procaine
Tetracaine
Cocaine

Neuraxial Techniques

Epidural anesthesia
Spinal anesthesia
Patient-controlled epidural analgesia

Sympathetic Chain Blocks

Morphine
Fentanyl
Clonidine
Butorphanol
Buprenorphine
Somatostatin
Ketorolac tromethamine

Modified from K. J. S. Anand, "Analgesia and Sedation for Ventilated Children and Infants," *Respiratory Care* 43, no. 11 (1998): 942–951, with permission.

TABLE 19–10: Classification of Analgesic Agents

Pure Opioid Agonists

Morphine
Fentanyl
Alfentanil
Sufentanil
Codiene
Methadone
Hydroxymorphone

Partial Opioid Agonists

Pentazocine
Nalbuphine
Buprenorphine

Nonsteroidal Anti-Inflammatory Agents

Acetaminophen
Acetylsalicylic acid
Ibuprofen
Ketorolac tromethamine
Flurbiprofen

Anesthetic Agents

Ketamine
Nitrous oxide
Propofol
Isoflurane

Miscellaneous Agents

α_2-adrenergic agonists (e.g., clonidine)
Stimulants (e.g., dextroamphetamine, methylphenidate)
Tricyclic antidepressants (e.g., amitryptaline, imipramine)
Anticonvulsants (e.g., phenytoin, carbamazepine)
Corticosteroids (e.g., decadron)
Enkephalinase inhibitors
NMDA antagonists

Modified from K. J. S. Anand, "Analgesia and Sedation for Ventilated Children and Infants," *Respiratory Care* 43, no. 11 (1998): 942–951, with permission.

References

1. Rau, J. L., *Respiratory Care Pharmacology*, 5th ed., Mosby—Yearbook Inc., 1998.
2. Tashkin, D., "Dosing Strategies for Bronchodilator Aerosol Delivery," *Respiratory Care* 36, no. 9, September 1991.
3. Scanlon, C. L., Wilkins, R. L., and Stoller, J. K., *Egan's Fundamentals of Respiratory Therapy*, 7th ed., Mosby, 1999.
4. Marks, M. B., "Nebulization of Cromolyn Sodium in the Treatment of Childhood Asthma," *Respiratory Care* 28, no. 10, October 1983.
5. National Institute of Health Publication # 97-4053, *Practical Guide for the Diagnosis and Management of Asthma*, 1997.
6. Rennard, S., and Koughton, D., "Transdermal Nicotine for Smoking Cessation," *Respiratory Care* 38, no. 3, March 1993.
7. Mathewson, H. S., "Antiviral Drugs for Acute Respiratory Infections," *Respiratory Care* 31, no. 1, January 1986.
8. *Physician's Desk Reference, 52nd ed.*, Medical Economics Data, 1998.
9. Burton, G. G., Hodgkin, J. E., and Ward, J. J., *Respiratory Care: A Guide to Clinical Practice*, 4th ed., Lippincott, 1997.
10. *Advanced Cardiac Life Support,* American Heart Association, 1997.
11. Anand, K. J. S., "Analgesia and Sedation for Ventilated Children and Infants," *Respiratory Care* 43, no. 11 (1998): 942–951.
12. Prudy, R. E., Boucek, M. M., and Boucek, R. J. Jr., *Handbook of Cardiac Drugs*, 2nd ed., Little Brown and Co., 1995.

Assessment Questions

1. The popular drug of choice for treating patients with acute pulmonary edema is:

   A. Nitroprusside
   B. Lasix
   C. Diamox
   D. Furosemide

2. Bronchodilators work by stimulating which of the following receptor(s)?

   A. α and β_1
   B. α and β_2
   C. β_1 and β_2
   D. β_2

3. Bronchial asthma can be treated by MDI containing which of the following steroid inhalants?

   I. Cromolyn
   II. Triamcinolone
   III. Beclomethasone
   IV. Dexamethasone

   A. I only
   B. I, II and III only
   C. II, III and IV only
   D. III and IV only

4. A 1:200 drug solution is the same as:

   A. 0.5%
   B. 1.0%
   C. 10%
   D. 0.1%

5. Your newly extubated patient is complaining of a sore throat and hoarseness. You would recommend:

Chapter 19: Respiratory Pharmacologic Agents 343

    A. Hydralazine
    B. Racemic epinephrine
    C. Acetylcysteine
    D. Cromolyn sodium

6. Albuterol is classed as a:

    A. Parasympathomimetic
    B. Sympathomimetic
    C. Vasodilator
    D. Mucolytic

7. Acute hypertension is best treated with:

    A. Versed
    B. Nitroprusside
    C. Digoxin
    D. Phenylephrine

8. How many milliliters of water need to be added to 10 ml of a 20% solution of sodium bicarbonate in order to make it a 5% solution?

    A. 10
    B. 20
    C. 30
    D. 40

9. The generic name for Alupent is:

    A. Isoproterenol
    B. Terbutaline
    C. Metaproterenol
    D. Salbutamol

Chapter 20

Ensuring Adequate Ventilation

I. Breathing technique

A. Goals for breathing retraining
   1. Promote greater use of the diaphragm as opposed to the accessory inspiratory muscles.
   2. Increase sensory awareness of the muscles of respiration and to decrease hurried and gasping respiration.
   3. Allow the patient to better handle the feeling of dyspnea.
   4. Promote improvement of general tolerance to activity.

B. Pursed-lip breathing
   1. It is a technique often used by COPD patients where the patient is taught to inhale slowly through the nose and then blow out slowly through pursed lips in a prolonged but relaxed manner. Expiration should be at least twice as long as inspiration.
   2. The apparent effectiveness of the technique appears to be related to a decreased rate and an increased depth of breathing that may, by altering the inappropriate length and tension relationships of respiratory muscles, relieve the sensation of dyspnea.

C. Diaphragmatic breathing
   1. This technique can be taught by use of either the patient's or therapist's hand over the abdominal wall with inspiratory effort directed towards outward movement of the abdomen instead of the upper chest wall.
   2. The patient is usually in the recumbent position to practice this form of breathing training.
   3. Weights of up to 10–12 lbs. placed on the abdomen can serve as good sensory cues, which is useful in diaphragmatic breathers.

Chapter 20: Ensuring Adequate Ventilation

II. Incentive spirometry[1]

A. Incentive spirometry (IS) or sustained maximal inspiration (SMI) therapy is designed to have the patient take long, slow, deep breaths. Goals include
   1. Increasing transpulmonary pressure so to encourage expansion of all lung areas, prevent atelectasis, and reexpand the collapsed lung.
   2. Improving inspiratory muscle performance.
   3. Simulating the normal pattern of pulmonary hyperinflation (sighing or yawning).
B. Indications
   1. Patients who have had upper abdominal or thoracic surgery, where the diaphragm is frequently impaired postoperatively and pain inhibits adequate spontaneous sighing.
   2. Patients with COPD who have had surgery.
   3. Presence of atelectasis.
   4. Those with restrictive lung disorders with quadriplegia and/or diaphragm dysfunction.
C. Generally is contraindicated in patients who cannot be taught (developmentally disabled), or who are too weak or debilitated to perform the maneuver.
D. Hazards
   1. Hyperventilation is the main concern due to the patient attempting to inspire to total lung capacity. It can be of particular concern in those patients with existing electrolyte deficits that encourage arrhythmias.
   2. Barotrauma in the emphysematous lung.
E. Several advantages encourage use of an "incentive" device compared to simple encouragement of deep breathing.
   1. The patient can visualize the inspired volume with each breath, and the total number of breaths can be recorded on a counter.
   2. The physician, therapist, and patient can be assured that the proper maneuver is being done frequently enough to maintain alveolar inflation.
   3. The regular use of deep breathing exercises using an incentive spirometer has been shown to decrease the incidence of postoperative pulmonary complications from 30% to 10%.
F. Instruction
   1. For postop patients, the procedure must be taught prior to surgery. Most patients cannot learn breathing exercises in a painful, narcotized, postop state.
   2. The patient is instructed to close his lips around the mouthpiece and exhale slowly and completely, followed by a slow, deep, maximum inhalation.

3. Following a maximum inhalation, the patient is instructed to continue that effort for at least another three seconds.
4. A normal exhalation should follow the inspiratory hold.
5. The patient should relax and breathe normally for 5–6 breaths and then perform the maneuver again. It is essential to have the patient breathe normally in between exercise breaths in order to avoid the dangers of hyperventilation.

III. Respiratory muscle training[2]

A. In a variety of diseases, severe weakness of the respiratory muscles exists.
   1. Weakness of inspiratory muscles may lead to respiratory failure when these muscles are put under additional load with conditions such as respiratory tract infection and/or heart failure.
   2. Expiratory muscle weakness may cause failure by the patient to be able to clear secretions, leading to hypostatic pneumonia.
B. Diseases that may be associated with respiratory muscle weakness include
   1. Neurological: quadriplegia, such as Myasthenia gravis, botulism, poliomyelitis, Guillain-Barre' syndrome.
   2. Muscle disease: such as steroid myopathy, muscle enzyme deficiency.
   3. Connective tissue disease: such as polymyositis, systemic lupus erythematosus (SLE).
   4. Endocrine disorders: such as thyroid disease, Cushing's syndrome.
   5. Electrolyte disorders: such as hypophosphatemia, hypocalcemia, hypomagnesemia, metabolic alkalosis.
C. Three primary principles apply to muscle training.
   1. Overload: in order for muscle fibers to change their structure and improve their function, they must perform work beyond some critical level.
   2. Specificity: the best results are achieved when the muscles are trained using the type of exercise in which the improved performance is desired.
   3. Reversibility: once the training stops, conditioning declines.
D. Respiratory muscle training
   1. Respiratory muscle strength training may be appropriate to patients with primary muscle weakness such as the patient with quadriplegia. It is important to distinguish between respiratory muscle weakness that requires training, and fatigued respiratory muscles that require rest.
      a. Weakness is suggested by a chronic reduction in strength and a chronic elevation of $PaCO_2$.
      b. Sudden onset of weakness, elevated $PaCO_2$, and paradoxical movement of the abdomen (diaphragm fatigue) or chest wall (external intercostals) during inspiration suggests fatigue.

c. Strength training has shown improvement in patients with COPD, cystic fibrosis, and quadriplegia.
    (1) Maximal forced inspiration clearly improved strength.
    (2) Inspiratory resistive loading shows variable results for strength improvement, possible because not enough resistance was used in some groups.
2. Respiratory muscle endurance training has a broader clinical application because the respiratory muscles must remain continuously active even under increased workload.
    a. Nonspecific training includes total body exercise with a significant increase in minute ventilation for a significant time period that will result in improved endurance of the respiratory muscles.
        (1) Positive results are shown in normal individuals and those with cystic fibrosis, but not COPD.
        (2) Because the intensity and duration in COPD patients is often insufficient for training to occur, due to the limitations of their lung function, specific training is needed for this group.
    b. Specific training
        (1) Voluntary isocapnic hyperpnea
            (a) The patient maintains high target levels of minute ventilation for up to 15 minutes.
            (b) The yardstick of improvement is the maximal sustained ventilatory capacity (MSVC), which is the highest minute ventilation the patient can sustain under isocapnic conditions for 15 minutes.
            (c) Normal individuals and COPD patients have shown muscle endurance improvement with this approach.
        (2) Inspiratory resistive loading
            (a) The patient inspires through a simple resistance device for 5–15 minutes.
            (b) Improvement is measured by how much increased resistance can be tolerated or by an increased amount of time at the same resistance.
            (c) Studies have shown improved endurance in patients with COPD and cystic fibrosis.
            (d) It is important to note that, with this form of training, care must be taken to have the patient avoid simply changing their breathing pattern to long, slow, deep inspirations.
                i) Breathing pattern adaptation may cause the appearance of improved endurance when, in fact, it does not exist.
                ii) Such alteration of the breathing pattern may reduce the effort to the point where no muscle training effect occurs.

(3) Inspiratory threshold loading
 (a) The inspiratory pressure load is adjusted by the amount of weight applied to the inspiratory port of a one-way valve. (The Emerson PEEP valve is an upside-down baby bottle filled with a varying amount of water that creates force against the exhalation valve diaphragm.)
 (b) Improvement is measured by the change in time that a subject can breathe against a given load.
 (c) Improved respiratory muscle endurance has been shown with this method for COPD patients.
 (d) The breathing pattern is less critical with this form of training because the patient must exert the required effort for each breath in order initiate inspiration.

E. Weight training in COPD, using dumbbells and backpacking, have the following benefits:
  1. Improved exercise response and maximal exercise capacity.
  2. Reduction in functional residual capacity (FRC) and total lung capacity (TLC), which has been found to improve the strength and endurance properties of the respiratory muscles by enhancing their length-tension characteristics.

F. Inspiratory and expiratory muscle training has been shown to improve respiratory muscle strength and endurance in different groups.
  1. Healthy individuals
  2. Patients with cystic fibrosis and COPD
  3. Patients with quadriplegia
  4. Patients being weaned from mechanical ventilators

G. At present, no clear guidelines exist for respiratory muscle training prescription. Any prescription should include at least the following parameters:
  1. Frequency of training (times per day, days per week, etc.)
  2. Intensity (which resistance, when to change resistances)
  3. Duration (how many times)

IV. IPPB therapy[3]

A. Indications
  1. To provide large inspired volumes for treating atelectasis
  2. To improve delivery of medications
   a. For patients who cannot coordinate their own efforts with a propellant-powered nebulizer.
   b. For patients who are unable to inhale adequately for effective deposition of the medication.

Chapter 20: Ensuring Adequate Ventilation

        (1) Very weak patients

        (2) Patients who are in bronchospasm

3. To improve coughing and expectoration.
    a. Inhaling an aerosol via IPPB may stimulate coughing.
    b. Theoretically, IPPB may cause sufficient mechanical bronchodilation to loosen or move secretions and may promote their movement through increased bronchial gland secretion mediated via the vagal pulmonary irritant reflex.
    c. IPPB is most effective in this category when combined with other modalities such as increased fluid intake, percussion, vibration, postural drainage, and active breathing and coughing exercises.
4. To decrease a rising $PaCO_2$ in the acute treatment of a hospitalized patient, utilization of IPPB for 5–10 minutes every 1/2–1 hour may alleviate the need for endotracheal intubation. This is providing that the IPPB results in bronchodilation and improved mucociliary clearance, as well as augmented breathing.
5. Domiciliary use
    a. Patients with COPD may derive significant benefit from medication delivery and mobilization of secretions via IPPB.
    b. Additional benefits may be realized from the relief of anxiety and the decrease in panic reactions that treatment offers.
    c. Some research, in addition to subjective testimony from patients, suggests that overall improvement in tolerance to the increased work of breathing that accompanies COPD can be seen with periodic (3–4 times per day) rest of accessory inspiratory muscle groups via properly performed IPPB.
    d. Cost of home devices is high and the purchase or rental of such a device is not warranted for such patients unless physiologic benefit can be demonstrated.
6. Special situations
    a. In acute pulmonary edema, IPPB is useful to provide transient relief while standard drugs and procedures are used to bring the problem under control.
    b. Weak patients
        (1) Those who have been weaned from mechanical support
        (2) Those who have neurologic or musculoskeletal disease
        (3) Those who are elderly or chronically debilitated
    c. For kyphoscoliosis, the use of IPPB for 5–10 minutes has been shown to improve pulmonary mechanics in these patients for several hours.
    d. Sputum induction is useful in patients who do not respond to other modalities.
    e. To deliver drugs, IPPB therapy is useful for special applications such as the administration of topical anesthetics for bronchoscopy.

B. Administration of IPPB
   1. The patient's spontaneous tidal volume and vital capacity should be measured so that they can be compared with those achieved during IPPB.
   2. The delivered volumes must be monitored to ensure that they exceed the patient's own spontaneous volume.
      a. The initial tidal volume should exceed the patient's spontaneous volume by more than 25%.
      b. A therapeutic target volume should be 15–20 ml/Kg of ideal body weight.
   3. Explaining the therapy
      a. The patient should be instructed in both the use of the pressure breathing device and the most appropriate pattern of breathing.
      b. The patient must learn how to initiate the breath and then allow passive augmented inspiration without premature exhalation or excessive work during the inspiratory cycle.
      c. For effective therapy, the patient must be encouraged to relax by the therapist who administers the IPPB.
   4. The breathing rate achieved during the IPPB treatment should be as low as possible and certainly less than the patient's own spontaneous rate to avoid hyperventilation. The exception would be the goal of decreasing a rising $PaCO_2$.
   5. Clear objectives for the therapy must be defined prior to starting, as they will dictate the way in which the therapy is administered to the greatest benefit for that patient.

V. Oro-nasal airway insertion[4]

A. Indications
   1. For relief of present or potential airway obstruction from the tongue.
   2. For airway maintenance.
   3. The presence of secretions in the airway that require assisted clearance.
   4. The need for artificial ventilation.
   5. Repeated naso-pharyngeal or naso-tracheal suctioning.
B. Insertion of an oral airway
   1. It should only be placed in an unconscious patient because stimulation of the gag reflex in a conscious patient may cause vomiting and aspiration.
   2. An airway of the proper size should be selected based on the size of the patient's oropharynx.
   3. The oropharynx should be cleared of any foreign material, and then the patient placed in the supine position.
   4. The neck should be hyperextended if possible and/or the mouth opened by prying with your fingers.

Chapter 20: Ensuring Adequate Ventilation

5. The artificial airway should then be inserted over the tongue with the tip pointed at the roof of the mouth, until the tip is past the uvula.
6. Once the tip is past the uvula, the airway should be rotated 180 degrees so the tip is then pointed down towards the trachea and the airway curves properly over the tongue.
7. The airway should then be taped in place.

C. Insertion of a nasal airway
1. Measuring from the tip of the nose to the ear lobe should choose a proper length of airway.
2. The airway should be finely coated with a lubricant.
   a. Water-soluble jelly may be used, but not a petroleum-based jelly, because the petroleum base could cause pneumonitis if aspirated.
   b. 2% xylocaine jelly will significantly ease the pain and discomfort of insertion.
3. The airway should be inserted through the most patent nostril by pushing up on the tip of the nose and inserting it straight back through the inferior passage.
4. The tip of the airway should be seen posterior to the base of the tongue.
5. Fix the airway in place by inserting a safety pin through the flange and taping the safety pin to the cheek or lip.
6. Tracheal, carinal, and gag reflexes will respond to the passage of the tube through the airway.

References

1. Scanlon, C. L., Wilkins, R. L., and Stoller, J. K., *Egan's Fundamentals of Respiratory Therapy*, 7th ed., Mosby, 1999.
2. Pardy, R., et al., "Respiratory Muscle Training," *Problems in Respiratory Care*, 3, no. 3, September 1990.
3. "AARC Clinical Practice Guideline: Use of positive airway pressure adjucts to bronchial hygiene therapy," *Respiratory Care* 38 no. 5 (1993): 516–521.
4. Eubanks, D. H., and Bone, R. C., *Comprehensive Respiratory Care*, 2nd ed., Mosby, 1990.

Assessment Questions

1. You are summoned to the ER to evaluate a patient with atelectasis in both lung bases. You would recommend:
   I. IPPB
   II. Deep coughing
   III. Incentive spirometry
   IV. Low-flow oxygen therapy

   A. I only
   B. I and II only
   C. II and III only
   D. III and IV only

2. The preceding patient with atelectasis has incentive spirometry orders changed from

a flow displacement device to a volume displacement spirometer. You would set the therapeutic goal by:

A. Measuring inspiratory capacity
B. Measuring forced vital capacity
C. Measuring peak expiratory flow
D. Measuring inspiratory reserve volume

3. Complications of IPPB would include which of the following?

   I. Barotrauma
   II. Decreased cardiac output
   III. Nosocomial infection
   IV. Gastric distension

   A. I only
   B. I, II and III only
   C. I, II, III and IV
   D. I and IV only

4. Hyperinflation therapy aids in lung expansion by:

   A. Increasing transpulmonary pressure
   B. Decreasing transthoracic pressure
   C. Decreasing alveolar pressure
   D. Decreasing transpulmonary pressure

5. IPPB could easily cause barotrauma in a patient with:

   A. Bacterial pneumonia
   B. Bullous emphysema
   C. Cardiac insufficiency
   D. Pulmonary fibrosis

6. The safest way to clear the airway of a newborn infant is to:

   A. Insert an endotracheal tube
   B. Perform a Heimlich maneuver
   C. Use a bulb suction device
   D. Turn the infant over and deliver a sharp blow to the back

7. You are called to a skilled nursing facility to help with a patient regaining consciousness from a deep coma. The physician informs you that the upper airway reflexes have not yet recovered. Which reflex would you expect to return first?

   A. Moro
   B. Gag
   C. Carinal
   D. Tracheal

8. You would set a patient's initial sustained maximal inspiration value at:

   A. Whatever the patient's measured vital capacity is
   B. Twice their measured tidal volume
   C. One-half of their peak expiratory flow rate
   D. Just less than the patient's residual volume

9. When instructing a patient on how to use an incentive spirometer, you would tell them to sustain the breath for at least:

   A. 1 second
   B. 3 seconds
   C. 5 seconds
   D. 8 seconds

Chapter 21

Mechanical Ventilation of Adults

I. Indications[1]

A. Severely altered lung mechanics
   1. Tidal volume—less than 500 ml
   2. Vital capacity—less than 10–15 ml/Kg of ideal body weight
   3. FEV_1—less than 10 ml/Kg of ideal body weight
   4. FRC—less than 50% of the predicted value
   5. Respiratory rate—greater than 35 breaths per minute
   6. Maximum inspiratory force—less than 20–30 cmH_2O
   7. Minute ventilation—greater than 10 L/min at rest
   8. MVV—less than 20 L/min or the inability to double the resting minute volume
B. Severely altered gas exchange
   1. $PaCO_2$—greater than 50–55 mmHg
   2. PaO_2—less than 50 mmHg on room air
   3. A-a DO_2—greater than 350–450 mmHg with an FIO_2 of 1.0
   4. a/A ratio—less than 0.15
   5. PaO_2/FIO_2 ratio—less than 200
   6. V_D/VT_T—greater than 0.60
   7. $\dot{Q}s/\dot{Q}t$—greater than 20–30%

II. Tidal volume, rate, and/or minute ventilation

A. Tidal volume's appropriate levels for any patient requiring ventilatory support is widely variable.
   1. If ventilating a patient whose lung function is presumed to be normal, a tidal volume of 5–7 ml/Kg ideal body weight is appropriate. When volumes of this size are used, sigh breaths are necessary.

a. This volume assumes a normal V_D/V_T ratio, airway configuration, and cardiac output.
b. Drug overdose patients without aspiration often fall in this category.
2. Starting V_t is usually 7–10 ml/Kg of ideal body weight.[2]

B. Respiratory rate
1. At a tidal volume of 10 ml/Kg ideal body weight, a rate of 10–15 per minute is usually appropriate to maintain adequate minute ventilation.
2. With tidal volumes in the 15 ml/Kg ideal body weight range, rates of less than 12 per minute are usually required to minimize adverse effects of positive pressure ventilation.
3. In the patient with clinically normal pulmonary function, in whom a tidal volume of 5–7 ml/Kg ideal body weight is selected, a respiratory rate of 12 per minute is standard.
4. Determinants of effective ventilation include control of $PaCO_2$, which will depend on the actual amount of effective alveolar ventilation that occurs compared to the amount of CO_2 being produced by the tissue and transported to the lung for excretion.

C. Calculation of required minute ventilation
1. Calculation allows accurate determination of alveolar tidal volume when the other variables in the equation are measured or assumed. Refer to Equation 21-1.
2. Calculation of the tidal volume, as measured at the exhalation valve of the mechanical ventilator, is illustrated by Equation 21-2.
3. Once the alveolar tidal volume has been calculated, using a desired respiratory rate, the required minute volume may then be determined.

$$V_t = Vt_{alv} + Vd_a + Vd_m + V_{comp}$$

a. V_t = tidal volume measured at the ventilator exhalation valve.
b. Vt_{alv} = calculated alveolar tidal volume.
c. Vd_a = anatomical dead space, usually the volume of the conducting airways.
(1) It is referred to as dead space because this gas does not participate in any exchange of CO_2 or O_2 in conventional forms of mechanical ventilation.
(2) The dead space volume is normally equal to 1 ml/lb. of ideal body weight, with 50% of this value being eliminated by either endotracheal intubation or tracheostomy.
d. Vd_m = the amount of tubing volume between the patient "wye" and the airway connector in a mechanical ventilator circuit.
(1) Mechanical dead space causes the patient to rebreathe some of their exhaled air.

Chapter 21: Mechanical Ventilation of Adults

EQUATION 21-1: Calculation of Alveolar Tidal Volume

$$Vt_{alv} = \frac{(Pb - PH_2O)BSA \times CO_2 \text{ production}}{f \times PaCO_2}$$

where
- Vt_{alv} = alveolar tidal volume
- Pb = barometric pressure in mmHg
- PH_2O = partial pressure of water vapor in the respiratory tract (constant at 47 mmHg)
- BSA = body surface area in M^2
- CO_2 prod = CO_2 produced by the tissue in ml/min/M^2
- f = desired respiratory rate
- $PaCO_2$ = desired $PaCO_2$

Example: Given a patient, at sea level, with a body surface area of 1.7M^2, a CO_2 production of 131 ml/min, and a $PaCO_2$ of 40, calculate the alveolar tidal volume if the rate desired is 12 breaths/min.

$$Vt_{alv} = \frac{(760 - 47)1.7 \times 131}{12 \times 40} = \frac{(713)222.7}{480} = 330.8 \text{ or } 331 \text{ ml}$$

EQUATION 21-2: Calculation of Exhaled Tidal Volume

$$V_t = Vt_{alv} + Vd_a + Vd_m + V_{comp}$$

Example: You have calculated that the required alveolar tidal volume is 331 ml when using a respiratory rate of 12 breaths per minute. Given that you are using 60 ml (6") of mechanical dead space, a patient weight of 150 lbs. (ideal body weight), a peak pressure of 27 cmH_2O, and a tubing compliance factor of 3.7 ml/cmH_2O, calculate the required tidal volume.

$$V_t = 331 + (150/2) + 60 + (27 \times 3.7)$$
$$= 331 + 75 + 60 + 99.9 = 565.9 \text{ or } 566 \text{ ml}$$

(2) Increased mechanical dead space causes a direct reduction in effective alveolar volume, and in the controlled ventilator patient, will result in an increased $PaCO_2$.

(3) As a rule, the use of significant volumes of mechanical dead space (more than 60 ml) is useful only in controlled patients who require large tidal volumes for the relief of dyspnea, such as Guillain-Barrè patients.

(4) Up to 60 ml of mechanical dead space is clinically useful for the mobility of the patient and to minimize ventilator tubing traction on the airway.

(5) Generally there are 10 ml of dead space per inch of large-bore ventilator tubing.

e. Vcomp = volume of compressed gas remaining in the ventilator tubing at the end of inspiration, in ml/cmH$_2$O pressure.

D. Minute volume[4]

1. A normal inverse relationship exists between arterial $PaCO_2$ and minute alveolar ventilation.

2. Because normal kidneys take 24–36 hours to compensate for a respiratory alkalosis, mechanical hyperventilation (a $PaCO_2$ less than 35 mmHg, pH greater than 7.45) will result in an alkalemic environment with associated electrolyte changes for the cardiovascular, hepatorenal, and central nervous systems.

3. Respiratory alkalosis is associated with electrophysiologic instability and altered autonomic nervous system response to administered drugs.

   a. Serum potassium (K+) decreases an average of 0.5 mEq/L for each 0.1 rise in the arterial pH.

   b. Serum calcium (Ca++) decreases an average of 0.17 mg% for each 0.1 rise in arterial pH.

4. Eucapnic ventilation with $PaCO_2$ values of 35–45 mmHg allows optimal acid-base and electrolyte balance.

5. Intentional mechanical hyperventilation ($PaCO_2$ 25–30 mmHg) is sometimes used.

   a. This induced hyperventilation is desirable for limited periods to reduce cerebral blood flow, blood volume, and intracranial pressure.

   b. The resulting proportional decrease in cerebral blood flow is potentially detrimental in critically ill patients without cerebral edema.

III. **Flow rates (pattern), I:E ratio, inspiratory hold, expiratory retard, sighs, and sensitivity**

A. Inspiratory flow patterns[3]

1. No significant difference is noted between any of the patterns, whether sinusoidal, accelerating, or decelerating for PaO_2, $PaCO_2$, or cardiac output.

2. The V_D/V_T ratio is highest using the accelerating flow pattern, probably secondary to high peak inspiratory pressures, which possibly overdistend some lung units and cause compression of the capillary flow in those units.

Chapter 21: Mechanical Ventilation of Adults

B. Flow rates and I:E ratio
  1. High flow rates of greater than 40 L/min will shorten inspiratory time, but will also result in higher peak airway pressures and will reduce the evenness of gas distribution in the tracheobronchial tree.
  2. Low inspiratory flow rates will prolong inspiration and improve gas distribution, but will increase the I:E ratio (i.e., 1:3 to 1:1), may increase the mean airway pressure, and may cause greater cardiovascular side effects.
  3. The flow rate should be set to achieve an I:E ratio of about 1:2. Refer to Equation 21-3.
  4. Predicted inspiratory flow rate requirement can be found by multiplying the minute volume $\times$ 4 (minute ventilation of 15 L/min $\times$ 4 = inspiratory flow rate of 60 L/min).
C. Inspiratory hold is defined as breath holding, or preventing exhalation for a preset time, after the tidal volume is delivered.
  1. Gas distribution will be improved and may improve the matching of blood and ventilation and reduce V_D/V_T.
  2. Plateau inspiratory pressures may be used to calculate static effective compliance.
  3. Inspiratory hold will increase the mean airway pressure, increase the I:E ratio, and could cause increased cardiovascular side effects in the susceptible patient.
D. Expiratory retard may benefit those patients with chronic airway disease (asthma/COPD) that promotes airway collapse on expiration.
  1. By increasing resistance at the exhalation port, the airway may be kept open for a longer period of time, thereby allowing more air to exit the lung. The back pressure created keeps the smallest airways from collapsing during exhalation.
  2. Mean airway pressure will be increased with this adjustment, and the patient must be observed for increased heart rate, blood pressure changes, and any arrhythmias.
  3. Monitoring inspiratory and expiratory tidal volume is essential to determine effectiveness of the retard maneuver.
     a. When the inspired volume is greater than expired volume, air trapping is the reason.
     b. Adjust the amount of retard until the inspiratory and expiratory volumes are equal.
     c. Wheezing should become less bilateral on auscultation due to small airways opening up as retard becomes effective.
E. Sighs may be used to prevent cumulative atelectasis in the mechanically ventilated patient.
  1. Patients managed on volume-cycled ventilators with large tidal volumes (10–15 ml/Kg) do not require sigh breaths, but should be observed carefully for the occurrence of atelectasis.
  2. Patients managed on volume-cycled ventilators with tidal volumes of less than 10 ml/Kg should have several sigh breaths (2–5) given every 10–15 minutes at

EQUATION 21-3: Calculation of Inspiratory Flow Rate

$$\text{Flow rate (L/sec)} = \frac{\text{Tidal volume (L)}}{\text{Inspiratory time (sec)}}$$

Example: If you know the required tidal volume, I:E ratio, and respiratory rate, you can calculate what inspiratory flow rate to use. You desire to deliver a 500 ml tidal volume, with an I:E ratio of 1:4, and a respiratory rate of 12 per minute. Determine the necessary inspiratory flow rate.

Step 1: Determine total respiratory cycle time (T_T). Because tidal volume is already known (500 ml), the inspiratory time must be calculated before the flow rate equation can be solved. At a respiratory frequency (f) of 12/minute, the total respiratory cycle time, which is the sum of inspiratory and expiratory time, can be calculated.

$$T_T = \frac{60 \text{ seconds}}{f} = \frac{60}{12} = 5 \text{ seconds for both inspiration and expiration}$$

Step 2: Determine inspiratory time in seconds (T_I). By adding together the two parts of the I:E ratio (i.e., 1:4 ratio has 5 parts), the respiratory cycle time can be divided by these parts to give the inspiratory time.

$$T_I = \frac{T_T}{\text{I:E}} = \frac{5}{1+4} = \frac{5}{5} = 1 \text{ second inspiratory time}$$

Step 3: Flow rate can now be calculated.

$$\text{Flow rate (L/sec)} = \frac{\text{Tidal volume (500 ml)}}{\text{Inspiratory time (1 sec)}} = 0.5 \text{ L/second}$$

Step 4: To convert to a more conventional value such as L/min, the answer in L/sec must be multiplied by 60.

$$\text{Flow rate (L/min)} = 0.5 \times 60 = 30 \text{ L/min}$$

      1.5–2.0 times the set tidal volume. Minute ventilation and CO_2 elimination will be altered during these maneuvers.
  3. Patients managed on pressure cycled ventilators should be "sighed" at 1.5–2.0 times their delivered tidal volume by either increasing cycling pressure or using a manual ventilation bag of sufficient capacity, at least every 30 minutes.
F. Sensitivity is defined as the normal amount of pressure drop the patient must create in their airway in order to "trigger" the ventilator.

Chapter 21: Mechanical Ventilation of Adults

1. The normal sensitivity setting for most patients is -2 cmH$_2$O. This level creates an appropriate amount of work for patients in respiratory failure.
2. At times, it may be desirable to make the ventilator less sensitive to the patient's inspiratory effort. It may be an advantage in building inspiratory muscle strength in the long-term ventilator patient on assist-control. The use of -5 cmH$_2$O sensitivity mimics the normal effort required in normal individuals at rest.
3. Setting the sensitivity higher than -1 cmH$_2$O will often cause the mechanical ventilator to begin "self-cycling" at a much faster rate.
4. If the sensitivity is set so that it takes more than -5 cmH$_2$O to "trigger" the ventilator, excessive inspiratory work may be required of the patient.
5. Work of breathing increases greatly with high airway resistance patients (asthma) and low lung compliance patients (ARDS). Control, assist-control, IMV, and SIMV are all ways to help decrease the work of breathing. Pressure support ventilation is a popular method of relieving the increased effort of breathing.

IV. IMV, SIMV[5]

A. Theoretical support for intermittent mandatory ventilation (IMV) is based on the following:
   1. Mechanical ventilation should provide only the amount of support in a spontaneously breathing patient required to ensure normal alveolar ventilation.
   2. IMV decreases the adverse pressure-related side effects associated with conventional assist-control or controlled ventilation.
B. Selecting settings for the ventilator during IMV
   1. The initial IMV rate for a patient requiring full support is set at 6–8 breaths per minute. The criteria for required rate are:
      a. Whatever is required to maintain arterial pH at greater than 7.35.
      b. Whatever is required to allow the patient to maintain a PaCO$_2$ of less than 60 mmHg.
      c. Whatever is required to maintain a spontaneous respiratory rate of less than 35/minute.
      d. Some patients who are experiencing primary difficulties in oxygenation, despite adequate alveolar ventilation and normal to low PaCO$_2$, may require only 1–2 breaths per minute.
   2. IMV rates are usually decreased in increments of 1–2 breaths per minute.
   3. Tidal volumes for IMV are in the same range as for controlled or assisted ventilation.
      a. In general, an average tidal volume of 15 ml/Kg ideal body weight is desirable with IMV.
      b. Inspiratory flow rates should be adjusted to deliver the volume in 0.5–1.5 seconds.[4]

C. IMV versus synchronized IMV (SIMV)
  1. IMV delivers the preset volume at predetermined intervals whether the patient is breathing in, out, or not at all.
  2. Synchronized IMV delivers the mechanical breath in response to the patient's inspiratory effort, and therefore avoids the discoordination of the ventilator with the patient's spontaneous effort.
  3. It has been assumed that SIMV has inherent advantages over IMV in the following areas:
     a. Pressure trauma
     b. Altered pulmonary blood flow and ventilation match-up
  4. While it is true that SIMV may result in slightly lower mean intrathoracic pressures, there does not appear to be any clinical advantage of SIMV over IMV.
D. Possible disadvantages of IMV include the following:
  1. It cannot respond to changes in clinical status; close monitoring is required.
  2. It increases work of breathing and O_2 consumption.
  3. It may prolong weaning from the ventilator if used improperly.
  4. In patients with poor left ventricular reserve, IMV may cause clinical worsening by enhancing blood return to the thorax, when spontaneous ventilation is allowed.
     a. Ventricular wall tension and therefore "afterload" is increased during contraction when the ventricle has negative pressure surrounding it, as with spontaneous ventilation.
     b. The use of PEEP or the move to controlled mechanical ventilation is necessary to reduce this effect.

V. Pressure support ventilation[6]

A. Pressure support ventilation (PSV) is a form of mechanical ventilation in which the patient's spontaneous inspiratory effort is augmented with clinician-selected level of positive airway pressure.
  1. PSV is similar to IPPB but differs in that airway pressure is held constant throughout the inspiratory period.
  2. Inspiratory pressure during PSV can range from 1 to 100 cmH_2O.
  3. A PSV breath is terminated when a certain minimum inspiratory flow is reached.
B. The differences between PSV and conventional volume-cycled ventilation are that the clinician selects only the inspiratory pressure, with the inspiratory time, size of breath, and respiratory pattern determined by the patient.
C. PSV is based on the same goals as for any form of mechanical ventilatory support:
  1. To supply adequate ventilation and oxygenation

Chapter 21: Mechanical Ventilation of Adults 361

2. To reduce dyspnea, which is especially important to the usefulness of PSV because it allows the patient to have better control over those factors that may lend to dyspnea. Dyspnea (respiratory sensation) is contributed to by effort, inspiratory time, and rate. Equation 21-4 illustrates the relationship between these factors.
3. To promote rest and conditioning of fatigued ventilatory muscles.

D. Proposed physiologic effects of PSV
   1. The lungs and thoracic cage have mechano-receptors that supply important input to the central nervous system regarding the mechanical aspects of ventilation. These receptors include:
      a. Diaphragmatic tendon receptors
      b. Intercostal muscle spindle receptors
      c. Intrapulmonary stretch receptors
      d. C fibers
   2. The ventilatory control center in the central nervous system uses mechanical input data and blood gas data to set the ventilatory pattern (including rate, tidal volume, and inspiratory flow) that results in the best gas exchange for the least amount of muscle work.
   3. PSV allows the patient more control over inspiratory flow, inspiratory time, and tidal volume than does conventional volume-cycled ventilation and so ought to minimize dyspnea.

EQUATION 21-4: Respiratory Sensation (Dyspnea)

$$\text{Respiratory sensation} = K \times Pm^{1.4} \times Ti^{0.5} \times f^{0.2}$$

where Pm = pressure generated at the mouth in order for the patient to take a breath. This factor contributes most to the patient's dyspnea. Pressure support can be especially effective in reducing this factor.

Ti = inspiratory time. This factor contributes the least overall to the sensation of breathing. It can, however, be controlled by the patient during the use of pressure support, so that its influence as a cause of dyspnea may be minimized.

f = breathing frequency. This factor is second in importance to mouth pressure. Because pressure support can enlarge the tidal volume, it will also reduce the respiratory rate.

4. Better synchronization between the ventilator and patient should result (therefore reducing dyspnea and lessening work), because during PSV constant muscle work, intrapulmonary stretch, and gas exchange result from every effort to breathe.

E. Pressure support and ventilatory muscle function
   1. Ventilatory muscle function in respiratory failure
      a. The diaphragm is the primary muscle of ventilation and normally accounts for about 60% of the tidal volume at a workload of 0.5 kg $\times$ m (this force times distance relationship can be clinically expressed as change in pressure times change in volume).
         (1) About 65% of the work is done to overcome elasticity of the pulmonary tissue.
         (2) About 35% of the work is nonelastic work used to overcome friction. About 80% of this nonelastic work is used to overcome airway resistance, and about 20% is used to overcome viscous resistance of the lung.
      b. Workload on the diaphragm increases when disease increases minute ventilation needs.
      c. Diaphragm fatigue and failure will result when the workload reaches 2–3 kg $\times$ m/min and will be characterized by tachypnea, paradoxical abdominal motion, and hypercarbia.
      d. Fatigued muscles require absolute rest, but if they are allowed complete rest for more than 72–96 hours, they will begin to atrophy. Muscle strength will be lost at a rate of 15% after 72 hours and 15% daily thereafter.
      e. Appropriate workloads must be placed on respiratory muscles to prevent atrophy and to provide reconditioning during the weaning process.
   2. The benefits of the type of conditioning need to be considered during reconditioning of the respiratory muscles.
      a. High-pressure, low-volume change work tends to stimulate strength conditioning through development of increased sarcomeres (the contractile unit of muscle fibers).
      b. Low-pressure, high-volume change work tends to stimulate endurance conditioning through development of increased mitochondrial density. PSV works in this manner because the patients can be required to generate very little pressure on their own.
   3. Comparison of conventional methods of weaning to PSV.
      a. Ideally, mechanical ventilation should initially rest fatigued muscles and then provide appropriate conditioning workloads, both in quantity of the work and the pressure-volume change characteristics of that work.
      b. With conventional weaning techniques, the patient takes unsupported spontaneous breaths (T-tube or IMV) that are alternated with volume-assisted or controlled breaths.

(1) The amount of work the patient does is clinician-controlled through adjustment of the mandatory breath rate with IMV.

(2) The pressure-volume change characteristics of the spontaneous breathing are fixed in a high pattern because of high airway resistance (ET tube plus airways) and/or poor lung compliance.

c. Pressure supporting a spontaneous breath should have the following advantages:

(1) The clinician adjusts the total amount of work that the patient must do each breath.

(2) The pressure-volume change work characteristics of each breath can be adjusted.

d. The diaphragm is an endurance-oriented muscle with a capacity for high power output. Pressure support is especially appropriate here, because it uses pressure to achieve the desired volume change, helping with endurance and conditioning work.

F. Recommendations for use of pressure support
1. Determine that the patient is ready to move to a lower level of ventilatory support. This is accomplished by assessing the weaning parameters.
2. Begin with Pmax. Pmax is whatever level of pressure it takes to achieve the tidal volume the patient is presently receiving. Conventional volumes are in the 10–12 ml/Kg ideal body weight range.
3. Slowly reduce the pressure each shift, based on clinical assessment of the patient. Pressure is usually reduced in 2 cmH_2O increments.

G. Using pressure support to overcome imposed work from ventilators and artificial airways.[10]
1. The imposed work of breathing from the ventilator tubing, demand flow system, and artificial airway should be reduced to zero, so that total work of breathing is determined by the patient's pulmonary mechanics.
2. The imposed work of breathing varies directly with the patient's peak inspiratory flow rate demand and resistance and response time of the ventilator's demand flow system.
3. Imposed work of breathing varies inversely with the internal diameter of the artificial airway and the triggering sensitivity of the demand flow system.
4. A broad range of pressure support will be needed, based on the amount of imposed work plus the patient's own altered pulmonary mechanics.
5. A portable bedside monitor should be used to measure work of breathing (Bicore) and pressure support levels adjusted accordingly.
6. Arbitrary adjustment (i.e., using 10 cmH_2O pressure support) may result in too little or too much support. Evaluating the patient's breathing pattern as an indicator of work may be inaccurate, although a rule of thumb may be to use as much pressure support as necessary to reduce the patient's spontaneous respiratory rate to 15–25/minute.

VI. Pressure-controlled inverse-ratio ventilation (PC-IRV)[7]

A. Indication: critically ill patients who have diffuse lung disease that causes increased stiffness of the lungs, without airway obstruction or significant secretions, and who fail to oxygenate adequately at high levels of PEEP. One suggested set of guidelines are as follows, assuming these criteria exist at the same time in the same patient.
  1. PaO_2/FIO_2 less than 80
  2. Peak pressure higher than 35 cmH_2O
  3. PEEP greater than 8 cmH_2O
  4. I:E ratio of 1:1
B. Strategies
  1. PC-IRV is a strictly controlled mode of ventilation, and patients need to be sedated and/or paralyzed so as to have no spontaneous respiration.
  2. With volume-controlled breathing, the inspiratory flow rate can be slowed until inspiratory time begins to encroach on expiration time.
     a. This method tends to waste the early portion of inspiration because the volume is still very low.
     b. Unstable lung units can continue to empty to the point of collapse during early inspiration.
  3. With volume-controlled breathing, an inspiratory pause can be adjusted, which allows total inspiratory time to be prolonged beyond expiratory time.
     a. Higher peak pressures may overventilate and damage the more compliant areas of lung.
     b. The plateau pressure established during the pause time may not be sufficient to keep unstable lung units open.
  4. Pressure-controlled ventilation delivers inspiratory pressure rapidly until the desired preset pressure is reached. A pressure plateau is then created and maintained for the rest of the inspiratory phase.
     a. Appropriate selection of respiratory rate I:E ratio results in an "auto-PEEP" effect.
     b. Auto-PEEP is confirmed when each new breath begins just before terminal flow returns to baseline from the previous breath.
     c. Gas is effectively trapped and functional residual capacity (FRC) increased.
     d. The decelerating flow pattern may provide better gas distribution on inspiration.
C. Proposed mechanisms of function
  1. Mean airway pressure and average lung volumes rise as inspiratory time is prolonged and gas trapping (auto-PEEP) is created.
  2. Prolonged inspiratory times expose the lungs to longer periods of maximum inspiratory pressure leading to improved collateral ventilation and increased traction to recruit adjacent collapsed alveolar units.

Chapter 21: Mechanical Ventilation of Adults

3. Lower mean and end-inspiratory flow allows lung units with longer time constants (higher resistance or compliance) to participate in gas exchange.

D. Method
1. A ventilator must be selected that has pressure-control inverse-ratio with pressure and flow graphics capability.
2. The typical patient would be one with ARDS where:
    a. Hemodynamic stability is present (no vasopressor drugs).
    b. The patient does not have copious secretions.
    c. The patient is already being ventilated with parameters similar to PEEP = 15 cmH$_2$O, FIO$_2$ = 0.7, PIP = 65–70 cmH$_2$O, in spite of full sedation.
    d. Radiographic infiltrates are progressing.
    e. Lung compliance and PaO$_2$ are dropping.
3. It is important to begin this mode of ventilation before you have reached FIO$_2$ = 1.0.
    a. "Onset hypoxemia" may occur when switching modes of ventilation.
    b. It may take up to an hour for any improvement to be seen if this mode of ventilation is going to show improvement.
4. Disposable ventilator tubing is replaced with stiff, noncompliant tubing to reduce gas compressibility and reduction in delivered tidal volume.
5. If not already being done, graphics monitoring of pressure and flow waves is begun.
6. If there is still spontaneous breathing by the patient, sedation and/or neuromuscular blocking drugs are added to achieve patient apnea.
7. The ventilator is switched to pressure-control mode after an FIO$_2$ of 1.0 has been delivered for several minutes.
8. Inspiratory time is increased to 67% for a 2:1 I:E ratio.
9. The pressure-control level is adjusted to 1/2 to 2/3 of the PIP when the patient was in the volume-cycled mode.
10. A target tidal volume is 400–600 ml.
11. The respiratory rate is arbitrarily set at 25/minute and then adjusted up or down by watching the terminal flow curve and starting the next breath just before the previous breath has ended.
12. PEEP is reduced to no more than 5–7 cmH$_2$O, and the FIO$_2$ is reduced to the value it was at before deciding to switch to PC-IRV.
13. Patient data is then gathered from the ventilator, pulmonary artery catheter, oximetry, capnography, cardiac output, etc.
14. Effective PEEP (adjusted PEEP + auto-PEEP) is then measured by using an expiratory pause.
15. Arterial blood gases are obtained 15–30 minutes later.

16. Pressure-control level and rate are adjusted to maintain desired $PaCO_2$.
17. I:E ratio and rate are adjusted to regulate effective PEEP of adequate oxygenation.
18. Total inspiratory time can be increased in 5% increments by adding inspiratory pause.
19. As inspiratory time becomes more prolonged, then set PEEP on the ventilator needs to be reduced, often to zero.
    a. As more gas trapping is produced (auto-PEEP) by increasing inspiratory time, the end-expiratory pressure in the lungs continues to increase, even though no adjustment has been made in the PEEP set on the ventilator.
    b. As end-expiratory pressure rises, the pressure difference between beginning inspiration (PEEP + auto-PEEP and end-inspiration (pressure-control setting) falls and the resulting tidal volumes get smaller and smaller, leading to CO_2 retention.
    c. The pressure-control setting can be increased, but this usually results in an undesirable increase in mean airway pressure.
20. It is important to monitor oxygen delivery (cardiac output × oxygen content).
    a. As the ratio moves from 2:1 towards 4:1, cardiac output may fall, reducing tissue oxygen delivery.
    b. If cardiac output falls, intravenous fluids should be increased to improve right ventricular preload and maintain adequate cardiac output and oxygen delivery.

VII. Airway pressure release ventilation (APRV)[7]

A. Description
   1. APRV is designed to allow unrestricted spontaneous breathing with CPAP that can also augment ventilation.
   2. APRV is a CPAP system that allows brief interruption of the CPAP and then returns to the adjusted CPAP level.
B. Equipment
   1. A high-flow CPAP system is used with a release valve in the expiratory limb of the circuit.
   2. Flows from 90–100 L/min through the circuit are required in order to ensure unrestricted spontaneous ventilation.
   3. Rapid changes in airway pressure are required and the humidifier, circuit, tubing, and connections must, as a unit, offer low flow resistance of ≤2 cmH_2O/100 L/minute.
   4. The release valve in the expiratory limb must be able to open or close in 10 milliseconds so that airway pressure can rise or fall rapidly.

Chapter 21: Mechanical Ventilation of Adults 367

5. The switch controlling the release valve must allow it to stay open for 1–2 seconds.
    a. This results in a short expiratory phase.
    b. This determines the length of the ventilatory cycle (inspiration + expiration).
    c. This determines the mechanical ventilatory rate achieved per minute.
6. The valve in the expiratory limb that creates the CPAP must be a threshold resistor so that widely varying flow through the valve does not cause airway pressure to fluctuate widely.
    a. If the circuitry or the CPAP valve creates resistance to airflow, then airway pressure will vary with gas flow through the circuit.
    b. If flow through the circuit varies widely during the spontaneous ventilatory efforts of the patient, work of breathing will increase.
    c. If the CPAP valve is not low resistance, coughing by the patient could result in transient pressures as high as 200–300 mmHg, causing barotrauma.

C. Advantages
   1. Spontaneous ventilation is often more efficient than mechanical ventilation in achieving alveolar ventilation and ventilation/perfusion matching.
   2. Spontaneous breathing helps to avoid the hemodynamic side effects associated with assisted or controlled mechanical ventilation.
   3. Lower peak and mean alveolar pressures help to avoid barotrauma.
   4. The potential for overdistention is less since peak inspiratory pressure is limited to the CPAP level set.

D. Disadvantages and potential problems
   1. A vigorously breathing patient might intermittently expose the peripheral lung to high peak stretching pressures, because stretching pressure is the absolute sum of the CPAP and intrapleural pressures.
   2. In order to assist ventilation significantly, substantial CPAP pressures need to be used to create the pressure difference between CPAP and release pressure.
       a. If chest compliance is high, the respiratory muscles will be stretched (hyperinflation) to a length that will cause a mechanical disadvantage.
       b. Dyspnea may result, even though it is one of the problems this therapy is designed to overcome.
       c. As the mechanical rate for APRV rises, the mean airway pressure falls, resulting in hypoxemia and necessitating an increase in the CPAP pressure.

E. Clinical application
   1. Patients with relatively normal lung compliance
       a. Most critically ill patients in the recumbent position have total thoracic compliance values of 70–80 ml/cmH$_2$O.
       b. In these patients, airway pressure changes of 10–12 cmH$_2$O will produce tidal volumes of 800–900 ml.

- c. A CPAP pressure of 10–12 cmH$_2$O should be used with a release pressure of no greater than 2 cmH$_2$O.
- d. Expiratory release time should not be greater than 1.5–2.0 seconds and can start at 1.5 seconds.
- e. Inspiratory time can start at 2.5 seconds, giving a mechanical respiratory rate of 15/minute. (Insp. time = 2.5 sec. + Exp. time = 1.5 sec. = 4 sec. total respiratory cycle time. 60 sec./4 sec. = 15 breaths/minute.)
- f. If greater minute ventilation is necessary, raise the CPAP level in 2–3 cmH$_2$O increments until adequate tidal volumes and minute ventilation is generated.
- g. An FIO$_2$ should be chosen that results in SaO$_2$ ≥92% (usually ≤40% O$_2$ in these patients).

2. Patients with moderately to severely decreased lung compliance
   - a. First establish an optimal CPAP level that reduces the FIO$_2$ to ≤0.5 and decreases the elastic work of breathing as much as possible.
   - b. Then start APRV with an inspiratory time of 4.5 seconds and an expiratory (release) time of 1.5 seconds, resulting in a mechanical rate of 10/minute.
   - c. The CPAP level should now be set at 10 cmH$_2$O higher than the determined optimal CPAP level for this patient.
   - d. The release pressure level should be at least 10 cmH$_2$O, and the difference between the release pressure and the CPAP pressure should be at least equal to the optimal CPAP level.
     - (1) If the patient's optimal CPAP level is 15 cmH$_2$O, and the release pressure is 10 cmH$_2$O, then the CPAP level set with now should be at least 25 cmH$_2$O.
   - e. If the PaCO$_2$ is normal or low and the patient's spontaneous respiratory rate is ≤30/minute, the mechanical rate can be decreased by increasing the inspiratory time using the following guidelines.
     - (1) Decrease mechanical rate until the patient's spontaneous rate begins to rise.
     - (2) Decrease the mechanical rate until respiratory acidosis occurs.
     - (3) Return to the next highest mechanical rate that avoided further tachypnea or respiratory acidosis.
     - (4) If tachypnea or respiratory acidosis persist, the mechanical rate can be increased to a maximum of 15/minute by decreasing inspiratory time.
     - (5) If a mechanical rate of 15/minute is reached and greater minute ventilation is needed, increase the CPAP level in 2–3 cmH$_2$O increments until adequate minute ventilation is achieved.

F. Weaning
1. The CPAP and pressure release levels should be kept constant, and the mechanical rate reduced (by prolonging inspiratory time) until the mechanical rate is zero.

Chapter 21: Mechanical Ventilation of Adults

2. Weaning should be stopped, and the mechanical rate returned to its previous value if a reduction in mechanical rate results in one or more of the following:
   a. Increased spontaneous ventilatory rate.
   b. Respiratory acidosis.
   c. Use of inspiratory accessory muscles, particularly the sternocleidomastoid group.
3. As long as no complications occur when the mechanical rate has reached zero, continue to wean from CPAP in 3–5 cmH$_2$O increments as long as adequate oxygenation is maintained.
   a. When a CPAP of 5 cmH$_2$O is reached, consider extubation as long as other criteria for extubation have been met.

VIII. Noninvasive positive pressure ventilation (NPPV)[8]

A. Indications for in-hospital use
   1. Weaning critical care patients from conventional mechanical ventilation.
   2. Treatment of acute hypercapnic exacerbation of chronic obstructive lung disease in patients who would otherwise require intubation and who meet the following criteria:
      a. Refuse intubation but are willing to accept the mask for 1–7 days if recovery is possible.
      b. Respiratory status is marginal, but treatment is likely to reverse the condition in 24–48 hours, as an alternative to intubation.
      c. Post-extubation where the clinical status is marginal, but likely to improve in 48 hours.
      d. A recent study found NPPV noninvasive (no endotracheal tube) but somewhat intrusive to patient toleration. Data appears promising when used as an alternative to post-extubation weaning.[9]
   3. Providing temporary ventilatory support for patients scheduled for heart/lung transplantation.
   4. Providing ventilatory support for postoperative patients following extubation.
   5. Treating atelectasis.
   6. Treating stable patients admitted to the hospital for another reason than respiratory failure, who are already using the device at home.
B. Indications for home treatment of chronic hypercapnic respiratory failure include patients with:
   1. Chest wall defects
   2. Neuromuscular disorders
   3. Chronic obstructive pulmonary disease
   4. Selected patients with obstructive sleep apnea/hypopnea syndrome

C. Criteria for use
   1. The patient must be alert, oriented, and cooperative.
   2. The patient must be able to protect their airway from aspiration.
   3. The hemodynamic status must be stable.
   4. No active process, such as seizures, which would require intravenous sedation to control.
   5. No evidence of significant gastric retention or emesis likely to result in aspiration.
   6. Drug overdose not present.
D. Contraindications (absolute and relative)
   1. Patients who are incapable of maintaining life sustaining ventilation in the event of malposition of the mask.
   2. Caution should be exercised when applying a snug-fitting full face mask in patients who may be prone to vomiting. A nasogastric tube may be inserted to maintain a patient airway.
   3. Patients with bullous lung disease.
   4. A history of allergy or hypersensitivity to the mask material, where the allergic reaction outweighs the benefit of ventilatory assistance.
E. Application
   1. It is important to understand that BiPAP differs from airway pressure release ventilation (APRV) in that with BiPAP every patient breath receives the higher CPAP during inspiration and the lower CPAP during expiration.
   2. Establish baseline patient data.
      a. Systemic arterial blood pressure
      b. Pulse and respiratory rate
      c. Skin color, temperature, and perfusion
      d. Use of accessory muscles of ventilation
      e. Paradoxical movement of the chest wall or abdomen, which may reflect respiratory muscle fatigue
      f. Breath sounds
      g. ABGs
      h. Chest X-ray
   3. Carefully fit the nasal or full-face mask.
      a. Proper mask sizing is crucial to successful ventilation.
      b. Mask comfort is often the limiting factor in successful use of this form of ventilation.
      c. Select the smallest mask size to comfortably fit the patient. When using the nasal mask, observe the following.
         (1) The mask should fit from the end of the nasal bone to just below the nares.

Chapter 21: Mechanical Ventilation of Adults 371

   (2) Ensure that the mask rests above the upper lip.
   (3) If a mask rests on the lip or in the area immediately above the lip, one of the following may occur.
      (a) Increased likelihood for leaks
      (b) Discomfort for the patient
      (c) Irritation to the gums
   (4) Place the mask over the patient's nose and select the proper spacer size. Attach the spacer to the mask.
   d. Attach the headstrap to the mask.
   e. Apply the mask and headstrap to the patient.
   f. Adjust the headstrap until all significant leaks are eliminated.
      (1) Avoid overtightening, which will cause patient discomfort.
      (2) Overtightening may also cause leaks due to distortion of the mask cushion.
      (3) If possible, have the patient move his head around after the mask is applied so that you can confirm a good mask seal with normal range of motion.
   g. Be careful not to cause excessive stress in an anxious patient when applying the mask. If the patient does not tolerate the mask and is continuing to fail in their ventilatory efforts, another mode of support should be considered.
   h. Advise the patient to immediately report any unusual chest discomfort, shortness of breath, or severe headache when using the BiPAP system.
   i. If using a full face mask, advise the patient not to eat or drink 2–3 hours before bedtime.
4. When clinically appropriate, periodic chest X-rays should be taken to monitor for the development of barotrauma.
5. Initial ventilation is begun with an inspiratory pressure of 8–10 cmH$_2$O and an expiratory pressure of 3–5 cmH$_2$O.
6. Adjustments are made in 2 cmH$_2$O increments while maintaining an inspiratory pressure at least 3–5 cmH$_2$O above expiratory pressure. Adjustments are made to achieve maximum patient comfort indicated by:
   a. Greater relaxation
   b. Slowed cardiac and respiratory rates
   c. Improved skin color and breath sounds
   d. Reduced accessory muscle use
   e. Adequate arterial blood gases 30 minutes after stabilization
7. Continue to monitor data collected prior to starting BiPAP.
8. Monitor patient for mask leaks or any discomfort.
9. If patient discomfort occurs, evaluate the following.
   a. Check the inspiratory and expiratory pressure settings.

b. Check the mask size and fit.
    (1) Consider changing the mask from nasal to full face or vice versa as appropriate.
    (2) Place a patch of wound care dressing on the bridge of the nose to provide a cushion between the nose and mask.
    (3) If there appears to be a skin reaction to the mask, consider using a skin barrier such as Duoderm or Micropore tape.
  c. Check headstrap adjustment.
  d. Observe the patient for development of ear discomfort and conjunctivitis.
  e. Consider adding humidification.
F. Complications
  1. Barotrauma can occur with any form of positive pressure ventilation.
  2. Aerophagia and gastric distention can occur because this method is delivered via nasal mask.
    a. Having the patient assume a lateral position may control this problem.
    b. The patient can wear an abdominal strap to help alleviate this problem.
    c. The incidence of gastric distention decreases with continued use.
  3. Hypoventilation because of airleaks through the mouth.
  4. Nasal dryness because of high gas flow through the nasal mask.
  5. Eye irritation secondary to leaks from the nasal mask.
  6. Patient discomfort from wearing head straps to secure the mask in place.
G. Contraindications to noninvasive ventilation
  1. Acute GI bleed
  2. Allergy or hypersensitivity to the mask material
  3. Coma score < 11
  4. Excessive airway secretions
  5. Facial or neck trauma
  6. Hemodynamic instability
  7. High risk of aspiration
  8. Inability to cooperate
  9. Marked cardiac dysrhythmias

IX. Independent lung ventilation (ILV) or differential lung ventilation (DLV)[9]

A. Rationale
  1. Unilateral lung injury alters the homogenous distribution of ventilation and perfusion throughout both lungs.
  2. The presence of unilateral lung injury also interferes with effective use of mechanical ventilation and PEEP.

Chapter 21: Mechanical Ventilation of Adults

      a. A disproportionate amount of ventilation will be delivered to the undamaged lung, and PEEP will increase functional residual capacity to a significantly greater extent in the normal lung.

      b. Damage may occur by overdistending and providing excessive stretching forces to the good lung.

      c. Compression of intraalveolar capillaries will result in reduced perfusion and increased dead space in the good lung, and increased perfusion to the bad lung with worsening blood gases.

    3. ILV has also been shown to improve oxygenation in diffuse bilateral lung disease with or without differential PEEP.

      a. The patient is placed in the lateral decubitus position to establish regional mismatch of ventilation and blood flow.

      b. Higher PEEP is then applied to the dependent lung, creating higher vascular resistance and redirecting more blood flow to the upper more distended lung, which may then improve gas exchange.

B. Indications

    1. A chest X-ray that shows unilateral lung damage is neither a clear indication nor a prerequisite.

      a. The chest radiograph may not reveal any lung damage.

      b. Once PEEP is applied to the lungs, the good lung will appear to be overdistended.

    2. A more clear indication is a paradoxical response to PEEP therapy in the presence of a positive chest radiograph for unilateral lung damage.

      a. PaO_2 falls because of increased perfusion to the bad lung.

      b. The measured intrapulmonary shunt fraction increases.

    3. Placing the patient with the good lung down, following the paradoxical response to PEEP is useful to determine if the PaO_2 and shunt fraction improve. If so, then a trial of independent lung ventilation is warranted.

    4. If hyperexpansion of the normal lung is present, demonstrating two different static compliance curves, a clear indication for ILV exists.

    5. The most common causes of unilateral lung injury include pulmonary contusion, aspiration pneumonia, lobar pneumonia, refractory atelectasis, pulmonary edema, bronchopleural fistula, pulmonary embolus, and postoperative thoracic surgery.

C. Preparing the patient for ILV

    1. The first step required is the placement of an endobronchial tube with double-lumen and high-volume, low-pressure cuffs.

      a. A flexible bronchoscope is recommended for assisting in tube placement.

      b. It is preferable to place the bronchial lumen in the mainstem bronchus going to the injured lung.

- c. As long as these tubes are large (39–41 Fr), periodic topical anesthetic sprays and appropriate sedation may be required to improve patient tolerance.
- d. Because the individual bronchial lumens are small in size, suctioning is more difficult than with conventional ET tubes.
    - (1) Patients with copious secretions may not tolerate endobronchial intubation.
    - (2) These airways will impose an increased workload for any spontaneous breathing by the patient.
- e. Once the tube is placed, careful monitoring for position must done.
- f. The most frequent cause of changed tube position is a change in the patient's position and can be detected by the following.
    - (1) Sudden deterioration in patient status from the tube starting to come out and loss of isolation of each lung.
    - (2) Loss of volume returning from each bronchial lumen.
    - (3) Distal migration of the tube can be detected by a rise in pressure on the bronchial side.
        - (a) Collapse of the right upper lobe may be seen secondary to occlusion of the bronchus feeding that area of lung.
- g. Inspired and expired tidal volumes should be checked every two hours and after every position change (X-ray, bath, linen change, etc.).

D. Techniques for ILV
  1. Differential CPAP
     a. Two separate CPAP systems are used and the level to each lung is titrated to accomplish optimal pulmonary function.
     b. The disadvantage of this technique is that spontaneous breathing through the narrow bronchial lumens is required of the patient.
  2. A single ventilator can be used with modified distribution circuits.
     a. A "wye" is placed in the inspiratory limb of the ventilator circuit and two separate ventilator circuits are run from the wye to each endobronchial tube connector.
     b. In most cases, a variable flow resistance device is placed in the inspiratory limb of the circuit going to the uninjured lung.
        (1) A large-bore stopcock such as that used with pulmonary function equipment will work adequately.
        (2) The disadvantage of such a device is that the increased resistance used to reduce the volume to the good lung increases the time needed for the lung to fill and empty, so that only relatively slow respiratory rates can be used.
     c. Each circuit is equipped with a separate PEEP device.
     d. Disadvantages

Chapter 21: Mechanical Ventilation of Adults

      (1) There are larger numbers of connections that may be prone to disconnection or leakage. This can be avoided with proper attention to the circuit integrity.

      (2) The number of variables that can be adjusted for each lung are limited to tidal volume and PEEP.

  3. Separate ventilation devices for each lung

    a. Two separate ventilators are most ideal because all variables—flow, pressure, volume, PEEP, FIO_2, etc.—can be regulated for each lung.

      (1) Synchronization of the separate ventilators for each lung is shown to be unnecessary.

      (2) In animal studies, asynchronous ventilation that is 180 degrees out of phase (one ventilator is starting inspiration while the other is starting expiration) has been shown to improve cardiac output and reduce pulmonary vascular resistance.

    b. Two ventilators can also be used where one is conventional and the other high-frequency.

    c. A single ventilator can be used for one lung, while the other (contralateral) lung is placed on CPAP.

E. Ventilator settings

  1. Using two ventilators is the preferred method for ILV.[7]

    a. Using differential CPAP or contralateral CPAP may represent excessive work of breathing for intensive care patients due to the small endobronchial lumens.

  2. Tidal volume can be adjusted in two ways.

    a. Take the conventional mechanical tidal volume (10ml/kg ideal body weight) and cut it in half, delivering volumes of 5ml/kg ideal body weight to each lung.

    b. Construct static compliance curves for each lung and adjust tidal volume for each lung to the point where a flattening of the curve occurs, suggesting overdistention. The previous volume is then selected as being optimal for that lung.

  3. PEEP adjustment

    a. Whenever possible, PEEP levels to each lung should be set at the lowest possible level (5 cmH_2O is suggested).

    b. PEEP to the bad lung is then increased in increments to achieve optimal arterial blood gases and static compliance for that lung.

    c. Optimum PEEP for the good lung should be determined in the same fashion as for the bad lung.

    d. Ideally, measurement of cardiac output and shunt fraction with accompany PEEP adjustment.

F. Discontinuation of ILV
   1. The majority of cases can be discontinued and returned to conventional ventilation within 48 hours.
   2. The most widely used method is to compare compliance for each lung.
      a. When the peak airway pressure and PEEP requirement for each lung are similar, the suggestion is that the bad lung has improved substantially and the transition from ILV can be made.

X. **Permissive hypercapnic ventilation**[11]

A. The goal is to avoid pulmonary damage associated with conventional mechanical ventilation with excessive tidal volumes (10–15 ml/kg) and excessive peak inspiratory pressures.
B. Rationale
   1. Allowing $PaCO_2$ to rise above baseline is a simple technique that provides for:
      a. Reducing the ventilatory workload.
      b. Reducing the pressure cost of breathing.
      c. Reducing the total number of machine cycles needed per minute.
      d. Allowing smaller tidal volumes to lower the peak and mean inflation pressures.
      e. Reduced work of breathing in the spontaneously breathing patient.
         (1) Ventilatory power varies as the second power of minute ventilation.
         (2) A small reduction in minute ventilation can result in a significant reduction in effort and transpulmonary pressure.
      f. Gradual increases in $PaCO_2$ are accompanied by only minimal shifts in arterial pH because of metabolic compensation and are usually well tolerated, even at high levels.
      g. Abrupt changes in $PaCO_2$ and resultant acidosis can be managed by infused buffer.
   2. ARDS, a disease previously thought to be homogeneous, has now been shown to be a heterogeneous lung disease.
      a. Consolidated areas of lung are mixed with normal areas of lung and other areas that are overdistended.
      b. Infiltrates are seen to gravitate to dependent portions of lung.
      c. The use of conventional tidal volumes of 10–15ml/kg and high minute ventilation may lead to overdistention and damage to normal areas and rupture of those areas already overdistended.
   3. Acute severe asthma
      a. Conventional ventilation frequently results in unusually high peak inspiratory pressures and overdistention.

Chapter 21: Mechanical Ventilation of Adults

      b. Auto-PEEP easily occurs and leads to hypotension, alveolar rupture, pneumothorax, and other forms of lung trauma.

C. Guidelines for permissive hypercapnic ventilation
1. Peak alveolar pressure of ≤35 cmH_2O.
2. Tidal of appropriate size to maintain desired peak alveolar pressure, often 5–7 ml/kg.
3. PEEP of 10–15 cmH_2O.
4. When monitoring pressure-volume curves, set tidal volume to a level where the curve does not plateau.
5. Avoid air-trapping and Auto-PEEP.
6. The respiratory rate is set at ≤20–25/minute and is limited by the development of Auto-PEEP.
7. Inspiratory time is limited by the development of Auto-PEEP.
8. I:E ratio usually ≤1:1 but is limited by the development of Auto-PEEP.
9. Keep arterial pH ≥7.25 using appropriate buffer therapy.
10. Use this form of ventilation from the onset of management so that as $PaCO_2$ does increase, pH is naturally compensated.

XI. Mandatory minute volume ventilation (MMV)[12]

A. Description
1. Exhaled minute ventilation of the patient is monitored, and a preset target level of exhaled minute ventilation is guaranteed to the patient.
2. If the patient is unable to meet the targeted minute ventilation, the ventilator provides the difference between the patient's spontaneous contribution and the target exhaled minute ventilation.
3. If the patient exceeds the targeted minute ventilation, no ventilation is forthcoming from the mechanical ventilator.
4. MMV provides a mode of mechanical ventilation that automatically adjusts itself according to the patient's spontaneous exhaled minute volume.

B. Advantages
1. The built-in safety of allowing the patient to receive a stable minute volume despite changes in their ability to provide that minute volume.
2. Acute reductions in the patient's breathing will not allow acute severe respiratory acidosis.
3. $PaCO_2$ may be easier to control in some patients.
4. The transition from spontaneous to mechanical to spontaneous, as in patients who are anesthetized or heavily sedated with respiratory depression, is automatic and does not allow acute respiratory acidosis.

5. MMV can provide the most stable level of support in patients with unstable respiratory drive or variable chest mechanics.
6. MMV may be the optimal method for weaning from mechanical ventilation.

C. Application
1. MMV can be used in earlier ventilator models to add a variable number of fixed volume machine breaths, which can present a hazard in that:
   a. The targeted minute volume can be met by rapid yet ineffective tidal volumes on the part of the patient.
   b. Lobar atelectasis and overall hypoventilation could occur.
2. Current ventilators that combine MMV with pressure support and vary the amount of pressure support with each breath are preferable.

D. Initiation of MMV
1. If MMV is used in patients with unstable ventilatory drive, then target minute ventilation should be set at a level that will provide acceptable $PaCO_2$ and pH.
2. If MMV is being used for weaning, target minute ventilation should be set at a level that will allow mild hypoventilation as a stimulus for breathing.

XII. High-frequency ventilation[13]

A. High-frequency positive pressure ventilation (HFPPV) may be achieved with a conventional ventilator system at tidal volumes of 1–3 ml/Kg and breathing rates greater than 150 breaths per minute.
B. High-frequency jet ventilation (HFJV) uses a pneumatically powered entrainment device to achieve low peak airway pressures with breathing rates of 100–600 cycles per minute.
C. High-frequency oscillation (HFO) uses various devices to achieve sinusoidal flow oscillations at the airway at frequencies of 500–3000 cycles per minute.
D. Peak airway pressures will be reduced during high-frequency ventilation when compared to conventional mechanical ventilation, as will the mean intrathoracic pressure.[1] This will lead to:
1. Less interference with cardiac output.
2. Less pressure trauma in the form of pneumothorax, etc.
3. A reduction in intracranial pressure changes in the neurosurgical or head trauma patient.
4. Increased mucociliary clearance with the potential for the prevention of aspiration.
E. Possible clinical applications for high-frequency ventilation include:
1. Situations where cardiovascular instability exists.
2. Microneurosurgery for prevention of "brain bounce."

Chapter 21: Mechanical Ventilation of Adults

3. Thoracic and laryngeal surgery for less interference with the operative field.
4. Rigid bronchoscopy and laryngoscopy for the maintenance of adequate ventilation during these procedures.
5. Unmanageable bronchopleural fistula and large air leaks appears to be most useful for bedside application.

F. Clinical application of high-frequency jet ventilation (HFJV)
   1. A rate of 100 breaths per minute appears to allow sufficient time for the rise and fall of pressure in the airway, with an I:E of 1:2.
      a. Rates faster than 100 may still allow control of I:E ratio, but may not allow return of airway pressure to baseline.
      b. Inadvertent PEEP may occur with the use of higher rates.
   2. When converting from conventional ventilation, the minute ventilation required to maintain the same blood gases is about three times normal.
   3. Because the "jet" functions by entrainment of gases secondary to small volumes of gas through the jet itself, ventilation may not be stable. If the patient's abdominal, chest wall, or lung compliance worsens, ventilation will drop. The same is true if airway resistance worsens.
   4. Conventional analysis of expired gases for CO_2 does not appear feasible with high-frequency ventilation because of the following:
      a. Small exhaled volumes do not reflect alveolar gas.
      b. Current CO_2 analyzers are incapable of maintaining the response time necessary to deal with the high rates.

G. The following information has been gained from the experimental evaluation of high-frequency jet ventilation.
   1. Tidal volume—at constant driving pressures for the jet, tidal volume is directly proportional to injector cannula diameter and duration of inspiration (duty cycle). Tidal volumes are normally in the range of 3–5 ml/Kg.
   2. Respiratory rate—rates of 100 breaths/minute appear to work well in most studies. Increasing the rate may actually cause a fall in tidal volume because of turbulent gas flow. Higher rates may also cause higher alveolar pressure because of gas trapping, as well as causing reduced air entrainment.
   3. Airway pressure—with tidal volumes as high as 20 ml/Kg (even though 3–5 ml/Kg is normally used) the peak airway pressure does not exceed the set PEEP value by more than 6–10 cmH$_2$O. This value is independent of respiratory rate or injector cannula size. Mean airway pressure does increase as the PEEP value or rate goes up.
   4. Gas entrainment—gas velocity at the jet nozzle is of primary importance, because the gas velocity is inversely proportional to the injector cannula diameter. Therefore, gas entrainment is higher with a smaller injector. In addition PEEP and higher rates increase downstream pressure reducing entrainment.

5. Humidification of inspired gases—this is accomplished by the delivery of small drops of fluid in front of the jet nozzle. It allows the jet itself to act as a nebulizer, and a continuous saline drip of 15–20 ml/hour appears to work well.
6. Adequate ventilation is always achieved with injector driving pressures of 45 PSI or less. At increasing I:E ratio (i.e., changing from 1:2 to 1:1), lower driving pressure will maintain the same tidal volume. Regardless of the driving pressure used to start with, it will need to increase if:
    a. The cannula size is reduced.
    b. PEEP is increased.
    c. Ventilator rates are increased.
7. The ventilator parameters during high-frequency jet ventilation that create the best gas exchange are:
    a. Ventilator rates of about 100 per minute.
    b. I:E ratios of 1:2 or 1:3.
    c. Injector cannula diameter of 1.5 to 2.0 mm.
8. Weaning from high-frequency jet ventilation is done by decreasing the driving pressure in 5 PSI increments at Q4 hour intervals, as long as blood gases are stable.
    a. Weaning continues until the driving pressure is 15 PSI, with stable blood gases, and then the patient is removed from the jet ventilator.
    b. An alternative method is to place the patient on CPAP following a decrease of driving pressure to 10 PSI, provided there is an adequate spontaneous respiratory rate and PCO_2.[21]

XIII. Complications of positive pressure ventilation[14]

A. Auto-PEEP. Although PEEP therapy is normally indicated for helping to "splint" stiff and collapse-prone lungs open and to improve oxygenation, it is often a complication of mechanical ventilation.[15]
1. Auto-PEEP is the positive difference between alveolar pressure and set airway pressure (PEEP) at end exhalation. It is a function of:
    a. Expiratory resistance to airflow.
    b. The compliance of the respiratory system.
    c. The time allowed for expiration.
    d. The volume from which exhalation begins.
2. Auto-PEEP can be divided into three categories.
    a. Auto-PEEP without dynamic hyperinflation
        (1) If exhalation is active, positive intrapleural and alveolar pressure may be produced but no hyperinflation.

Chapter 21: Mechanical Ventilation of Adults

   (2) This form of Auto-PEEP is not associated with undesirable consequences.
  b. Auto-PEEP with dynamic hyperinflation, but without airflow obstruction, during tidal breathing
     (1) It occurs in patients who do not have airway obstruction, but do have inadequate expiratory times to allow emptying of the tidal volume and equilibration of alveolar and ventilator system end-expiratory pressure.
     (2) When high levels of ventilation (large tidal volumes and/or high rates) are used, much of the Auto-PEEP effect may be caused by the expiratory resistance of the ventilator tubing and endotracheal tube.
  c. Auto-PEEP with dynamic hyperinflation and airflow obstruction.
     (1) Auto-PEEP occurs most often in this group, which includes patients with COPD and/or severe acute asthma.
     (2) Minute ventilation may not be very high, but expiratory airway resistance is several times greater than inspiratory resistance.
     (3) Dynamic airway compression and obstruction frequently occur during exhalation.
3. Consequences of Auto-PEEP
   a. Cardiovascular effects include:
      (1) Increased right ventricular afterload.
      (2) Increased intrapleural pressure.
      (3) Decreased venous return, left ventricular filling, and cardiac output.
   b. Work of breathing
      (1) Dynamic hyperinflation increases the work of breathing in both spontaneous and mechanical ventilation.
         (a) When inspiration begins, an alveolar pressure exists, which must be reduced to atmospheric or ventilator system pressure before any airflow begins.
         (b) During machine assisted breaths, Auto-PEEP depresses triggering sensitivity.
         (c) During spontaneous breaths, because the higher lung volume has reduced compliance, the patient has to overcome this added elasticity in addition to the elastic and frictional work of tidal breathing.
      (2) The function of the thoracic pump is compromised secondary to:
         (a) Increased inward movement of the rib cage.
         (b) Horizontally placed ribs.
         (c) Flattened diaphragm, which means less force generated.
         (d) Decreased zone of apposition between the diaphragm and rib cage.
         (e) Shortened respiratory muscle fiber length prior to contraction.

4. Measurement of Auto-PEEP
   a. During passive mechanical ventilation (controlled ventilation):
      (1) The expiratory limb of the ventilator is occluded at end-expiration and the resulting pressure difference between end-expiratory pressure set on the ventilator (PEEP) and the pressure now seen on the manometer is an estimate of the amount of Auto-PEEP.
      (2) The amount of pressure required to initiate inspiratory flow is an estimate of Auto-PEEP.
      (3) Tidal volume can be subtracted from the total volume exhaled during a prolonged period of apnea (about 20 seconds).
         (a) The difference between total exhaled volume and set tidal volume is the trapped gas volume.
         (b) Dividing the trapped gas volume by compliance gives an estimate of Auto-PEEP.
      (4) When Auto-PEEP is caused by dynamic airway compression, the amount of PEEP added that results in increased lung volume of peak cycling pressure is thought to be the amount equal to the Auto-PEEP.
   b. In spontaneously breathing patients, Auto-PEEP can be estimated with an esophageal catheter system where the amount of negative pressure required by the patient to initiate inspiration is an estimate of the Auto-PEEP.
5. Treatment of Auto-PEEP
   a. Medical strategies (bronchodilation, diuresis, etc.) are used to improve airway resistance.
   b. Ventilator strategies
      (1) Set lower tidal volumes to reduce the volume that must be exhaled in a given time.
      (2) Reduce the respiratory rate to reduce minute ventilation and increase expiratory time.
      (3) Use a higher inspiratory flow rate to shorten inspiration and provide longer expiratory time.
      (4) Use a square wave flow pattern because it has a higher average flow rate, decreasing inspiratory time, and prolonging expiration.
      (5) Add PEEP to treat Auto-PEEP.
         (a) If PEEP is added to an already hyperinflated patient without expiratory muscle activity or airway obstruction, it will further inflate already overinflated lungs.
            i) This will further increase the work of breathing.
            ii) The thorax and respiratory muscles will be at further disadvantage.
         (b) In some patients, PEEP or CPAP may preload the expiratory muscles so that they boost the beginning of inspiration.

Chapter 21: Mechanical Ventilation of Adults

      (c) In patients with airway obstruction, adding PEEP less than the level of Auto-PEEP will reduce the difference between alveolar pressure (Auto-PEEP) and end-expiratory pressure set on the ventilator.
          i) The inspiratory threshold is reduced.
          ii) Triggering sensitivity is improved.
          iii) The high ventilatory workload is partially reduced.

B. "Fighting" the ventilator[16]
1. When confronted with sudden distress in the mechanically ventilated patient, the following sequence is recommended.
   a. Remove the patient from the ventilator and begin manual ventilation with 100% O_2.
      (1) This quickly eliminates any problem caused by the ventilator itself.
      (2) It allows for rapid assessment of lung mechanics by "feeling" the resistance to inflation.
   b. Rapidly examine the patient and note monitoring parameters available (systemic and pulmonary arterial pressures, pulse oximetry, capnography, ECG, etc.).
   c. Check the patency of the airway and pass a suction catheter.
   d. If death appears imminent, consider and treat the most likely causes.
      (1) If airway obstruction cannot be alleviated with suctioning, the airway must be promptly removed and another inserted.
      (2) Pneumothorax: should be detected during the physical exam.
   e. Once the patient is stabilized, a more detailed assessment may be done, which may reveal other contributing causes.
2. Causes of the patient "fighting" the ventilator
   a. Mainstem bronchial intubation
      (1) It may occur in as many as 10% of intubated and mechanically ventilated patients.
      (2) It occurs more often in women than men, likely because of the shorter distance from the lips to the carina.
      (3) It occurs most often into the right mainstem bronchus because the less acute bronchial angle facilitates this.
      (4) If bronchial intubation occurs, atelectasis of the opposite lung will occur with shunting and hypoxemia.
      (5) With all of the mechanical tidal volume delivered into one lung, pneumothorax can easily result.
      (6) If it is detected, the tube must be retracted to bring the tip 3–4 cm above the carina and confirmed with chest X-ray.
      (7) Generally, the endotracheal tube should be secured so that the centimeter markings at the teeth or gums is 23 cm for men and 21 cm for women.

b. Movement of the endotracheal tube to above the vocal cords
   (1) A gross air leak quickly occurs and the patient is able to phonate.
   (2) The tube must be reinserted and verified by chest X-ray.
c. Cuff herniation over the end of the tube
   (1) It most commonly occurs with changes in the patient's head and neck position or with changes in the position of the tube.
   (2) An increase in airway pressure, increased resistance to bagging, difficulty in passing a suction catheter, and an abnormal musical sound during inspiration are all indications.
   (3) Relief can be realized immediately upon deflation of the cuff.
d. Cuff rupture
   (1) Decreases in delivered tidal volume, gross air leak around the airway, inability to deliver set PEEP may indicate this problem.
   (2) Aspiration of saliva, food, or vomitus may result and be an indication of cuff problems.
   (3) Failure to withdraw the same volume of gas used to inflate the cuff is an indicator.
   (4) Management usually consists of replacing the tube.
   (5) An alternative form of management is as follows.[17]
      (a) Blended gas is supplied with a pressure-compensated flowmeter through a vented, pressure-monitored O_2 line to the pilot balloon valve of the defective cuff.
      (b) The flow is increased to the pilot balloon valve in 1 L/min increments until the leak disappears.
      (c) Flow rates of 4–6 L/min are usually necessary to control the leak and maintain safe intracuff pressures ≤ 25 mmHg.
e. Endotracheal tube kinking
   (1) This problem is relatively uncommon, but can occur with soft rubber nasotracheal tubes and results from changes in position of the head and neck.
   (2) Correction is accomplished with repositioning of the head and neck.
f. Tracheoesophageal fistula most often occurs in patients who have had a nasogastric tube and an endotracheal tube in place for a long time.
g. Innominate artery rupture
   (1) Causes
      (a) Tracheostomy done at too low a site (below the third tracheal ring)
      (b) Use of excessively long tube so that the tip impinges on the tracheal wall and causes erosion.
      (c) Pressure necrosis and erosion from an improperly managed cuff.
      (d) Infection of the tracheal wall.

Chapter 21: Mechanical Ventilation of Adults

(2) Presentation may be dramatic with blood gushing from the airway, or a small bleed may occur as a signal of a greater problem.

(3) Management

  (a) Overinflate the cuff to attempt tamponade of the eroded artery.

  (b) Insert a gloved finger into the stoma, passing it as far as possible toward the carina, and then pulling it back in an attempt to compress the artery against the forward part of the sternum.

  (c) If successful, transfuse the patient on the way to the operating room.

h. Pneumothorax

  (1) 60–90% of pneumothoraces in mechanically ventilated patients are under tension.

  (2) A 14–16 gauge needle attached to a liquid-filled syringe should be inserted into the second intercostal space.

  (3) If the patient is stable, get a chest X-ray prior to inserting a chest tube.

i. Bronchospasm

  (1) Dyspnea, wheezing, and increased work of breathing will be evident.

  (2) Treatment is with inhaled bronchodilators, which may need to be supplemented with systemic medication.

j. Secretions

  (1) Copious or thick secretions may cause airway plugging, atelectasis, and increased shunt with hypoxemia.

  (2) If routine suctioning is unsuccessful in management, therapeutic flexible bronchoscopy should be performed.

k. Pulmonary edema may occur suddenly, and will require medical management.

  (1) Temporary increases in FIO_2 and PEEP may reduce the patient's acute distress.

l. Acute pulmonary embolism

  (1) Dyspnea, tachypnea, chest pain, hemoptysis, pleural rub, and fever are all possible clues.

  (2) When the patient has a normal static compliance on the ventilator (60–100 ml/cmH$_2$O) in the face of sudden distress with hypoxemia, the likely cause is pulmonary embolism.

m. Auto-PEEP, or dynamic hyperinflation

n. Increased respiratory demand can result from a single or combined cause secondary to pain, anxiety, hypoxic stimulation, hypercapnic stimulation, peripheral sensory receptor stimulation, medications, or inappropriate ventilator settings.

o. Alteration in body position leading to hypoxemia

p. Drug-induced distress

(1) Aminoglycoside antibiotics can provoke or aggravate neuromuscular blockade.
(2) Vasodilators (B_2 adrenergic bronchodilators, nitroglycerine, nitroprusside) can alter pulmonary perfusion, leading to worsening ventilation perfusion mismatch and hypoxemia.
(3) Intravenous lipid infusions can produce hypoxemia.

q. Abdominal distention
   (1) The diaphragm may be pushed upward, leading to atelectasis, V/Q mismatch, and hypoxemia.
   (2) Gastric distention can be caused by:
      (a) Elevated mouth pressure above lower esophageal sphincter pressure during manual ventilation.
      (b) Elevation of tracheal pressure above airway cuff pressure and lower esophageal sphincter pressure in the mechanically ventilated patient with mouth closed.
      (c) Prolonged and difficult intubation.

r. Improper adjustment of the ventilator include system leaks, inadequate FIO_2, inadequate levels of support, improperly set sensitivity, and inadequate flow settings.

C. Pulmonary barotrauma is the most significant complication of mechanical ventilation. The various types include:
1. Pulmonary interstitial emphysema
2. Pneumomediastinum
3. Pneumopericardium
4. Pneumoperitoneum
5. Tension pneumothorax
6. Venous and arterial air embolism

D. Cardiovascular complications also may occur as a result of increased intrathoracic pressure. The following are undesirable side effects of raised intrathoracic pressure.
1. Decreased venous return
   a. Tachycardia
   b. Decreased urinary output
   c. Neck vein distension with central venous pressure change
   d. Hypoxemia
   e. Decreased pulmonary blood flow
2. Decreased blood return to the left atrium with subsequent increased stimulation of antidiuretic hormone secretion
3. Decreased cardiac output resulting in decreased perfusion to the vital organs
4. Increased intracranial pressure

Chapter 21: Mechanical Ventilation of Adults

E. Miscellaneous complications, although not necessarily cause-effect related, include:
  1. Pulmonary infection
  2. Airway obstruction
  3. Tracheal damage

XIV. Weaning procedures[14]

A. Several general factors are worth optimizing before initiating ventilator weaning.
  1. Acid-base abnormalities (particularly metabolic alkalosis)
     a. A normal compensatory mechanism for metabolic alkalosis is hypoventilation, which may lead to hypoxemia, atelectasis, and worsening $\dot{V}/\dot{Q}$ matchup.
     b. Alkalemia also causes a leftward shift in the oxyhemoglobin dissociation curve (decreased P_{50}), thus decreasing the release of oxygen to the tissue.
     c. If respiratory alkalosis exists and renal compensation has occurred, resumption of spontaneous breathing may result in acidosis, as the patient is unable to spontaneously maintain the hyperventilation.
  2. Anemia
     a. This condition may result in a detrimental decrease in the oxygen-carrying capacity.
     b. A hemoglobin concentration of at least 10 g/100 ml is recommended for weaning.
  3. Electrolytes[18]
     a. Hypokalemia may result in myocardial irritability and skeletal muscle weakness, as well as metabolic alkalosis.
     b. Hypomagnesemia may impair muscle performance and create chronic respiratory failure.
     c. Hypophosphatemia may result in respiratory failure secondary to poor respiratory muscle function.
  4. Caloric and protein depletion
     a. This condition may occur over a long period of mechanical ventilation in patients who are being sustained only by IV fluids.
     b. Muscle wasting due to inactivity significantly reduces the patient's ability to tolerate spontaneous breathing.
     c. Patients who do not respond to intensive nutritional regimes with increased protein synthesis are not likely to be weaned.
     d. When hyperalimentation is used for nutritional support, the high carbohydrate load may result in greater CO_2 production than the patient can successfully eliminate during weaning. This condition can be corrected by:
        (1) Switching to a parenteral solution that provides the number of calories that correspond to measured resting energy expenditure.

(2) Giving a solution that provides 50% of nonprotein calories as fat instead of carbohydrates.
5. Fever needs to be controlled because it increases oxygen demands as well as CO_2 production, and usually signifies infection.
6. Fluid balance must be optimized to promote good mucociliary clearance and avoid fluid overload pulmonary edema.
7. Sleep deprivation and pain
   a. These factors are common in ICU patients and directly interfere with the patient's ability to wean.
   b. Narcotics and tranquilizers should be discontinued prior to weaning in order to ensure alertness and to avoid respiratory center depression. A minimal analgesic dose may be helpful.
8. Level of consciousness
   a. In general it is advantageous to have the patient alert and cooperative to begin weaning.
   b. In patients with severe head injuries and cerebral vascular accidents, the return of consciousness may follow successful weaning by weeks or even months.

B. Determine the presence of adequate pulmonary function prior to weaning.
  1. Tests of mechanical ability should be carefully explained to the patient prior to measurement; the patient should be allowed to practice; and they should be performed a total of three times if possible, with the best of the three values being recorded.
     a. Peak inspiratory pressure
        (1) This parameter is a useful index of neuromuscular strength and requires less cooperation than other tests of mechanical ability.
        (2) The ability to create subatmospheric pressure less than -20 cmH_2O (i.e., -30 cmH_2O or -40 cmH_2O) suggests adequate inspiratory muscle strength for weaning. This measure is the same for infants and children.
     b. Vital capacity
        (1) VC can be measured using any bedside spirometer with the patient being instructed to inhale maximally and then exhale maximally.
        (2) Vital capacity should be greater than 10–15 ml/Kg ideal body weight to allow the patient to sigh deeply enough to avoid the complication of atelectasis.
           (a) A value of at least 10 ml/Kg should be seen in children.
     c. Forced expired volume in 1 second (FEV_1)
        (1) This value may have great significance in weaning COPD patients who would exhale an adequate vital capacity, given enough time, but whose reserve is still inadequate for weaning.
        (2) This value should be at least 10 ml/Kg ideal body weight.

Chapter 21: Mechanical Ventilation of Adults

      d. Maximum voluntary ventilation (MVV)
- (1) The ability to sustain muscular effort while off the ventilator is critical to weaning.
- (2) The MVV, while greatly effort dependent, is reflective of this ability.
- (3) The patient can be extubated and considered weaned if resting minute ventilation is less than 10 L/min and can be doubled with an MVV effort.

2. Tests of oxygenation capability
   a. Alveolar-arterial oxygen gradient (A-a DO_2)
      - (1) It provides an index of the extent of $\dot{V}/\dot{Q}$ mismatch, diffusion defect, and/or shunt.
      - (2) It is usually performed while on the ventilator and breathing 100% oxygen. If the resulting value is less than 300–350 mmHg, the patient is considered to have adequate oxygenation capacity for weaning.
   b. $\dot{Q}s/\dot{Q}t$ (shunt fraction)
      - (1) The shunting of blood past unventilated or poorly ventilated alveoli severely interferes with the ability to oxygenate the blood.
      - (2) A computed shunt fraction of less than 15% is desirable.
      - (3) Post-cardiac surgery patients with large intra-cardiac shunts may need to be weaned with values much higher than 15%.
   c. V_D/V_T ratio—less than 55–60% of the ventilation should be wasted. A greater amount than this may not permit adequate oxygenation.
3. These pulmonary function tests should be performed daily, with both absolute values and trend values being observed and recorded. While some patients will never receive a "passing score" in all areas, a positive trend is a helpful indicator of the ability to wean.
4. Nitrogen balance[19]
   a. Nitrogen balance relates to nutritional protein requirements.
      - (1) All proteins are made up of various kinds and amounts of amino acids that contain an acid group (COOH) and an amino group (NH_2).
      - (2) Nitrogen is readily measured in the blood as blood urea nitrogen (BUN) or in the urine as urinary urea nitrogen (UUN).
   b. Every 100 grams of protein contains 6.25 grams of nitrogen.
      - (1) Grams of nitrogen can be converted to grams of protein by multiplying the nitrogen value by 6.25.
      - (2) To find how many grams of nitrogen are present in a given amount of protein, divide the amount of protein by 6.25.
   c. Patients who excrete the same amount of nitrogen that they take in through dietary protein are said to be in nitrogen balance.
   d. Patients who excrete more nitrogen than they take in are said to be in negative nitrogen balance.

(1) This is bad because the nitrogen being excreted is not coming from dietary sources but from the patient's own body protein.

(2) Negative nitrogen balance is an ominous sign in patients who are being considered for weaning from mechanical ventilation since this catabolic state is reducing muscle mass (respiratory muscles included).

(3) Patients with deficiency of protein intake will suffer other negative effects as well.[20]

(a) Decreased ventilatory response to hypoxemia.

(b) Decreased cell-mediated immunity.

(c) Altered immunoglobin G (IgG) turnover.

(d) Impaired macrophage function.

e. Patients who excrete less nitrogen than they take in through dietary protein are said to be in positive nitrogen balance.

(1) Patients who are nutritionally depleted need to be in positive nitrogen balance to build up body tissues.

(2) This is a good sign in patients being considered for weaning since it indicates laying down of new muscle and improving strength potential.

C. Preparing the patient for weaning

1. There must be an established trust. The patient will trust the health care worker when they recognize competence and caring.

2. The patient must have an established feeling or goal of wanting to get off the ventilator.

a. Pick an optimum time to explain the plan for weaning. This is best done when the patient feels "good" and his spirits are high.

b. Diet changes, ambulating, and other changes in routine are best accomplished before starting to wean from the ventilator. Patients will usually cooperate with the weaning program better when they have positive feedback from progress in other areas.

3. Proper and adequate information can help eliminate problems of insecurity during the weaning process.

a. Explain to the patient that he is going to hear the term "weaning" and this means that he has improved to the point that he can be without the ventilator for gradually increasing periods of time or can begin reducing the backup rate in the case of IMV. Assure the patient that you will work with him to achieve the weaning goal.

b. Explain to the patient that it is normal to have plateaus and set-backs during the weaning process, and when and if this happens, he should not get discouraged.

c. Tell the patient what to expect when he is taken off the ventilator. They should know that it will be harder to breathe at first, but it will get gradually easier. Make certain you check the patient's volumes closely.

Chapter 21: Mechanical Ventilation of Adults

    d. Tell the patient that the weaning will be done progressively and not abruptly. Assure him that you will be watching closely and checking heart rate, blood pressure, and respirations on a frequent basis as clues to the degree of tolerance.

    e. Assure the patient that he will never be left alone if you have him on T-tube trials, and keep your promise. The patient's trust can either be built or shattered by this.

    f. The patient's family should be informed and involved during the weaning process. They should be told how the patient may look, or react, and that it is important that the patient not be upset during the time he is off the respirator. If the family is unable to be appropriately supportive, visiting hours may need to be adjusted so as not to interfere with the weaning process.

D. Weaning methods
1. Progressive weaning by removing the patient from the ventilator.
   a. As much as possible, the same nurse and therapist should be assigned to the patient until long periods of weaning are established, taking into account the patient's preference.
   b. Weaning should initially be done only during the hours of the day and evening shifts. The rare exception is the patient whose established living habits require a different sleep schedule, and then weaning may be done at night if the patient receives adequate rest during other hours.
   c. Work and supplies ideally should be organized so there is minimal need to leave the room during weaning.
   d. Patient observation is essential when the patient is off the ventilator or first having the backup rate reduced.
   e. Organize the patient's schedule so the patient is not exhausted before weaning. Allow for rest periods before taking the patient off the ventilator.
   f. Make weaning the number 1 priority in the patient's daily schedule and allow other activities to be done at another time. Bathing and bed changes can be done at night when the patient is not being weaned.
   g. Be sure to obtain a baseline pulse, BP, respiratory rate, and tidal volume before taking the patient off the ventilator or reducing the backup rate. These measurements provide a baseline to compare with when assessing the patient's ability to tolerate the weaning process.
   h. Try to avoid other energy-requiring activities during the weaning process.
   i. If suctioning is required while the patient is off the ventilator, be sure to provide hyperoxygenation and manual ventilation so as not to upset the weaning process.
   j. Taking the patient off the ventilator
      (1) The patient is removed from the ventilator and given supplemental oxygen 10% higher than when on the ventilator (usually via "T"-piece).

(2) Weaning is begun with the patient off the ventilator for five minutes or less each hour. Each hour, the time period is increased by five minutes, as tolerated.

k. Observation checklist when the patient is off the ventilator
  (1) Note the patient's level of consciousness, apprehension, or diaphoresis.
  (2) Note the blood pressure, pulse, and cardiac rhythm every five minutes until the patient can tolerate 15–30 minutes off the ventilator and then every 10–15 minutes after that. The patient should be on a cardiac monitor for arrhythmia detection.
  (3) The respiratory rate and tidal volume should be checked every five minutes initially and then every 10–15 minutes as weaning tolerance increases.
    (a) An increase in respiratory rate without other accompanying signs of respiratory effort suggests that the patient is anxious and will benefit from assurance and encouragement.
    (b) An increase in respiratory rate accompanied by nasal flaring and use of accessory muscles of respiration, along with a progressive fall in tidal volume, indicate the need for assisted ventilation.

l. Time limits
  (1) The patient should be placed back on the ventilator at the end of the pre-designated time period, even if they are doing great. Don't push it.
  (2) If the time limit has not been reached, and the patient asks to be put back on the ventilator, don't argue with the patient just return the patient to the ventilator.
  (3) When the patient is connected back to the ventilator, whether it is because the patient is unable to tolerate being off the ventilator or because the time period is up, you should:
    (a) Reassure the patient. It is important to apply behavior modification techniques by reinforcing good behavior and ignoring undesirable behavior. Praise the patient if he tolerates weaning. If he hasn't, be honest, but don't scold or censure the patient.
    (b) Tell the patient what the plans for the day are, how long she will be allowed to rest, and when she will be taken off again.

m. Weaning aids
  (1) Breathing simulators can mimic breath sounds and a variety of breathing patterns, and just as it is tempting to tap your foot to a rhythm, patients can sometimes do much better off the ventilator when they breathe along with a simulator.
  (2) Soothing music or whatever music is pleasing to the patient and establishes a feeling of well being and low anxiety is appropriate.
  (3) A "caring" touch for human beings in anxious moments often stimulates a positive response to this form of reassurance.

Chapter 21: Mechanical Ventilation of Adults

        (4) Fenestrated tracheostomy tubes have a hole cut into the main body of the tube. During weaning, the inner cannula can be removed and the resistance to breathing is reduced. The patient can now breathe through the main orifice of the tube, and through the hole in the body of the tube. This hole in the body also allows air to pass through the patient's own natural airway, helping to reestablish the feeling of normal breathing, and permitting the patient to talk.

    n. Several factors indicate the need to reconnect the patient to the ventilator, or to increase the level of support, in the case of IMV as a weaning technique:

        (1) Blood pressure rise or fall—generally a change of 20 mmHg systolic or 10 mmHg diastolic.

        (2) Pulse increase—20/minute or rate greater than 110.

        (3) Respiratory rate increase—greater than 10/minute or a total respiratory rate greater than 30/minute.

        (4) Tidal volume—less than 250–300 ml in adults.

        (5) Significant ECG changes—due to dangerous arrhythmias such as premature ventricular contractions (PVCs), or a distinct change in the rhythm or configuration of the ECG complex.

        (6) PaO_2 less than 60 mmHg—except in COPD patients.

        (7) $PaCO_2$ greater than 55 mmHg—except in COPD patients.

        (8) pH less than 7.35—except in COPD patients.

2. Keeping the patient on the ventilator and using ventilator modes for weaning[2]

    a. Argument can be made that all bedridden, mechanically ventilated patients can benefit from low level PEEP (3–5 cmH_2O) and sufficient pressure support to overcome the resistance of the ventilator-tubing-artificial airway system (about 10 cmH_2O).

    b. While no one weaning technique has been shown to be clearly superior to another, keeping the patient on the ventilator does require increased caregiver time during the weaning process.

    c. Use of intermittent mandatory ventilation (IMV), synchronized intermittent mandatory ventilation (SIMV), pressure support ventilation (PSV), mandatory minute ventilation (MMV), or a combination of these modes can all facilitate the weaning process.

    d. A proposed method of weaning using IMV and Pressure support[10]

        (1) Set pressure support value to keep total respiratory rate ≤20/minute.

        (2) Wean IMV to CPAP.

        (3) When tolerating CPAP + PSV for ≥2 hours, gradually reduce PSV with each weaning period.

        (4) When tolerating CPAP + 5 cmH_2O PSV, gradually lengthen time until only nighttime ventilation is required.

(5) Decrease tracheostomy tube size.

(6) Use fenestrated tracheostomy tube to facilitate plugging and speech.

(7) Consider following the first night completely removed from the ventilator with a night of ventilator support.

(8) When removed from the ventilator for 48 hours straight, remove tracheostomy and insert stoma button.

(9) When the patient is coughing well, secretions are minimal, and has been removed from the ventilator for seven days, remove the button and allow the stoma to close.

e. In addition to monitoring physiologic parameters previously mentioned, it is useful to monitor respiratory mechanics.[20]

(1) Pressure-time product

   (a) Normal is ≤100 cmH$_2$O/sec.

   (b) A value of ≤250 cmH$_2$O/sec is sustainable by the patient and indicates an ability to continue the weaning process.

   (c) A value of ≥300 cmH$_2$O/sec is not sustainable and is an indication that the patient will fail to maintain their present work of breathing.

(2) Work of breathing (P × V expressed in joules/L)

   (a) Normal is 0.45–0.65 joules/L.

   (b) Successful weaning can be done at ≤0.75 joules/L.

   (c) Work of breathing ≥0.75 joules/L is unsustainable and will result in weaning failure.

   (d) Work of breathing can also be calculated in joules/min where a value greater than 20 joules/min indicates unsuitability for weaning. (See Equation 21-5.)

(3) Tracheal occlusion pressure for the first 1/10 of a second of inspiration (P 0.1)

EQUATION 21-5: Work of Breathing (WOB) in Joules/minute

$$\text{WOB (joules/min.)} = \frac{(P_{peak} - PEEP) - 1/2(P_{plat} - PEEP) \times \dot{V}_E}{10}$$

where P_{peak} = peak airway pressure
        P_{plat} = plateau pressure
        PEEP = positive end-expiratory pressure
        $\dot{V}_E$ = exhaled minute volume

Chapter 21: Mechanical Ventilation of Adults 395

      (a) Normal is 2–4 cmH$_2$O.
      (b) Greater than 6 cmH$_2$O is not sustainable and will indicate weaning failure.

XV. Special tests during mechanical ventilation[21]

A. Establishing brain death
  1. The etiology of the coma must be known with reasonable certainty.
    a. Hypothermia, drug overdose, neuromuscular blockade, and shock must NOT be present.
    b. No sedative or narcotic drugs can be present in the circulation.
  2. The patient must be observed over at least 24 hours to document the absence of seizures, decorticate, or decerebrate posturing.
  3. Cerebral function must be absent at the hemispheric, midbrain, pontine, and medullary levels.
    a. A totally unresponsive and unreceptive state is evidence of loss of cortical function.
    b. Loss of midbrain function is seen by absence of pupillary activity.
    c. Complete loss of the ability to evoke eye movements is evidence of loss of pontine function.
    d. Loss of medullary function is confirmed by apnea testing.
      (1) The patient is removed from the mechanical ventilator after preoxygenation with FIO$_2$ of 1.0.
      (2) An O$_2$ catheter (or O$_2$ line) is introduced into the end of the endotracheal/tracheostomy tube and run at a flow rate of 5 L/min.
      (3) The patient is observed throughout the test for any respiratory activity.
      (4) The patient is allowed to be apneic until the PaCO$_2$ reaches at least 60 mmHg, which is adequate stimulation of the medullary centers.
        (a) With a functioning circulation, PaCO$_2$ usually rises 3–5 mmHg/minute.
        (b) In general, with a normal baseline PaCO$_2$ of 40 mmHg, 4–6 minutes are sufficient to obtain the necessary PaCO$_2$.
      (5) An ABG is drawn to confirm the PaCO$_2$.
    e. A confirmatory electroencephalogram (EEG) may be required. A flat EEG is prognostic in the absence of other evidence that may cause such a tracing (drug-induced coma or loss of cortical activity with retention of brainstem activity).
    f. Loss of cerebral blood flow that is documented by radiological study is evidence of brain death.[4]

References

1. Pilbeam, S. P., *Mechanical Ventilation Physiological and Clinical Applications 3rd ed.*, Mosby, 1998.
2. Bone, R., et al., *Pulmonary and Critical Care Medicine, Vol. 2*, Mosby-Yearbook, 1993.
3. Branson, R. D., and Hurst, J. M., "Effects of Inspiratory Flow Pattern on Airway Pressure, Ventilation, and Hemodynamics," *Respiratory Care* 32, no. 10, October 1987.
4. Shoemaker, W. C., et al., *The Society of Critical Care Medicine Textbook of Critical Care, 3rd ed.*, W. B. Saunders Co., 1999.
5. Kirby and Graybar, "Intermittent Mandatory Ventilation," *International Anesthesia Clinics* 18, no. 2, Little-Brown, 1980.
6. MacIntyre, N. R., "Respiratory Function During Pressure Support Ventilation," *Chest* 89, no. 5, 1986.
7. Perel, A., and Stock, M., *Handbook of Mechanical Ventilatory Support, 2nd ed.*, Lippincott, Williams & Wilkins, 1998.
8. Day, S., et al., "Selection of Initial Pressure Settings for Patients Using the BiPAP S/FD Ventilatory Support System," *Interventions, Respironics, Inc.* 93, no. 2, June 1993.
9. Nicholson, D., Tiep, B., Jones, R., Sadana, G., Sandhu, R., Aldworth, C., and Robles, M., "Noninvasive positive-pressure ventilation in chronic obstructive pulmonary disease," *Current Opinion in Pulmonary Medicine* 4, (1998): 66–75.
10. Pierson, D., and Kacmarek, R., *Foundations of Respiratory Care*, Churchill-Livingston, 1992.
11. Kacmarek, R., and Hickling, K., "Permissive Hypercapnia," *Respiratory Care* 38, no. 4, April 1993.
12. Quan, S., et al., "Mandatory Minute Volume (MMV) Ventilation: An Overview," *Respiratory Care* 35, no. 9, September 1990.
13. Alone, C. A., and Hill, T. V., *Respiratory Care of the Newborn and Child, 2nd ed.*, Lippincott, 1997.
14. Burton, G. G., Hodgkin, J. E., and Ward, J. J., *Respiratory Care: A Guide to Clinical Practice, 4th ed.*, Lippincott, 1997.
15. Tobin, M., "Respiratory Monitoring During Mechanical Ventilation," *Critical Care Clinics* 6, no. 3, July 1990.
16. Tobin, M., "What Should the Clinician Do When a Patient Fights the Ventilator?" *Respiratory Care* 36, no. 5, May 1991.
17. Tinkoff, G., et al., "A Continuous Flow Apparatus for Temporary Inflation of Damaged Endotracheal Tube Cuffs," *Respiratory Care* 35, no. 5, May 1990.
18. Guyton, A. C., *Textbook of Medical Physiology, 9th ed.*, W. B. Saunders, 1999.
19. Wilkins, R. L., Sheldon, R. L., and Krider, S. J., *Clinical Assessment in Respiratory Care, 3rd Ed*, Mosby, 1995.

Chapter 21: Mechanical Ventilation of Adults

20. Belamy, P., "Respiratory Mechanics and Ventilatory Waveform Analysis: Clinical Value in Decision Making," 25th Annual California Society for Respiratory Care Convention, Monterey, CA, June 1993.

21. Marini, J., and Wheeler, A., *Critical Care Medicine: The Essentials,* Lippincott, Williams & Wilkins, 1997.

Assessment Questions

1. Pressure control ventilation is a positive pressure ventilation mode in which:

   I. The ventilator delivers a breath until a set pressure is reached
   II. The ventilator delivers a breath until a set inspiratory time is reached
   III. The tidal volume varies with each breath

   A. I only
   B. I and II only
   C. I, II and III
   D. II and III only

2. A patient in respiratory failure due to inadequate alveolar ventilation secondary to poor lung expansion is in need of ventilatory support. Which of the following modes of ventilation would you choose?

   A. IMV with PEEP, Vt = 5–7 ml/Kg
   B. CMV with PEEP, Vt = 5–7 ml/Kg
   C. PSV at 15 cm H_2O
   D. CMV with PEEP, Vt = 10–15ml/Kg

3. An inverse I:E ratio alarm alerts you during a ventilator check. Which of the following would you choose to correct the problem?

   A. Increase the frequency
   B. Increase the flowrate
   C. Increase the tidal volume
   D. Silence the alarm

4. A patient with which of the following blood gases would you identify as needing ventilatory support?

	pH	$PaCO_2$	HCO_3
A.	7.34	62 mmHg	32 mEq/L
B.	7.21	64 mmHg	25 mEq/L
C.	7.39	58 mmHg	34 mEq/L
D.	7.36	51 mmHg	27 mEq/L

5. A patient being weaned by "T"-piece has become diaphoretic and distraught, to the point of disconnecting the aerosol tubing from the "T"-piece. ABG data is as follows:

pH	7.42
$PaCO_2$	40 mmHg
HCO_3	26 mEq/L
PaO_2	56 mmHg
SO_2	87%

   Based on the preceding blood gas values, which of the following interventions would you choose?

   A. Administer Alupent/Atrovent aerosol mixture immediately
   B. Change mode of ventilation to pressure support
   C. Extubate and put on 40% entrainment mask
   D. Administer 10 mg IV diazepam

6. Flow cycling has been incorporated as the mechanism that terminates inspiration in which of the following modes?

   A. IMV
   B. CMV
   C. PSV
   D. MMV

7. Deliberate hyperventilation via CMV may sometimes be applied to patients with closed head injuries in order to

   A. Depress the central chemoreceptors
   B. Provoke dilation of the cerebral vasculature
   C. Reduce brain swelling and decrease intercrainal pressure
   D. Increase oxygen consumption of the brain

8. Which of the following are true regarding time-cycled ventilation?

   I. Time-cycled ventilators are not used on adults
   II. The device cycles off when a preset time interval ends
   III. The delivered pressure, flow, and volume may vary
   IV. Inspiratory time is constant breath to breath

   A. I, II and III only
   B. II, III and IV only
   C. III and IV only
   D. IV only

9. When using pressure ventilation, how is volume delivery influenced as lung characteristics change?

   A. Volume delivery is not influenced when lung characteristics change
   B. Volume delivery increases when lung characteristics improve
   C. Volume delivery decreases when lung characteristics deteriorate
   D. Volume delivery increases when lung characteristics deteriorate

Chapter 22

Mechanical Ventilation of Neonates

I. Indications (See Table 22-1.)[1]

TABLE 22-1: Indications for Assisted Ventilation of the Neonate

Pulmonary
IRDS (30–85%)[68]
Aspiration syndromes
Pneumonia
Pulmonary hemorrhage
Pulmonary edema
Wilson-Mikity Syndrome
Bronchopulmonary dysplasia
Pulmonary insufficiency
  of immaturity

Loss of Lung Volume
Pneumothorax
Tumor
Diaphragmatic hernia
REM sleep
Atelectasis

Airway
Choanal atresia
Pierre-Robin
Micrognathia
Nasopharyngeal
  tumor

Miscellaneous
PDA with CHF
Postoperative
Asphyxia neonatorum
Tetanus neonatorum
Extreme immaturity
Shock
Sepsis

Central Problems
Apnea of prematurity
Drugs (i.e., morphine)
Seizures
Birth asphyxia
Hypoxic encephalopathy
CNS hemorrhage
Ondine's Curse
REM sleep

Abnormalities of Respiratory Muscles
Phrenic nerve palsy
Spinal cord injury
Myasthenia Gravis

Source: J. P. Goldsmith and E. H. Karotin, *Assisted Ventilation of the Neonate*, 3rd ed., W. B. Saunders, 1996.

II. Application

A. Choice of ventilator
1. Constant pressure generators that are time-triggered and pressure limited are preferable. Continuous or demand flow, in which gas flows through the circuit during expiration as well as inspiration, is desirable because it facilitates the use of IMV with PEEP/CPAP.
2. Barotrauma and bronchopulmonary dysplasia are major complications of mechanical ventilation in neonates, which require carefully regulated peak inspiratory pressures. This regulated pressure is easily accomplished with the time-cycled, pressure-limited ventilators.
3. With the use of time-triggered pressure-limited ventilators, a high I:E ratio (i.e., 1:1, 1.5:1, 2:1, etc.) can be used with a lower peak inspiratory pressure to achieve the same degree of ventilation.
4. The square pressure wave achieved with constant pressure generators provides the highest pressure gradients, and may provide better expansion of low $\dot{V}/\dot{Q}$ compartments. During the pressure plateau, gas continues to enter areas of high resistance.
5. Complications of square wave ventilation are associated with a prolonged inspiratory time.
   a. When considering the ventilatory parameters of mean airway pressure, inspiratory time, peak inspiratory pressure, and PEEP, prolonged inspiratory time is the factor most often associated with lung rupture.[2]
   b. A study of ventilator variables and arterial oxygenation showed that at comparable mean airway pressures, oxygenation improved most by increasing PEEP and least by increasing inspiratory time.
6. Patient-triggered ventilation[3]
   a. Airflow, chest wall movement, airway pressure, or esophageal pressure are used by various brands of machines to achieve patient triggering.
   b. Once the ventilator detects an effort, the breath is delivered according to the predetermined settings for peak inspiratory pressure, inspiratory time, and flow rate.
   c. A flow-triggering device has been shown to be effective in a small group of very low birth-weight infants.
      (1) An increase in respiratory rate and minute ventilation was seen when compared to conventional IMV.
      (2) Oxygenation improved but $PaCO_2$ remained the same.
   d. Very small infants with poor respiratory effort may not be able to effectively trigger the ventilator on a continuing basis, so any machine incorporating this mode should be able to provide a preset mandatory rate if the infant fails to maintain an adequate minute volume.

Chapter 22: Mechanical Ventilation of Neonates

7. Because conventional ventilation applied to neonates is by pressure-limited, time-triggered ventilation, the following apply when adjusting the inspiratory time:
   a. Shortening the inspiratory time will increase expiratory time.
   b. Because the pressure limit is established separately, peak airway pressure will not increase, but may decrease if insufficient time is allowed due to short inspiratory times.
   c. Shortening the inspiratory time will decrease tidal volume.
   d. Shortening the inspiratory time will decrease the length of time the pressure is applied to the airway, thereby causing the mean airway pressure to decrease.
   e. Increasing the inspiratory time will increase the time that positive pressure is applied to the airway, thus increasing mean airway pressure.
   f. Increasing the pressure limits will allow an increase in positive pressure, thus increasing the mean airway pressure.

B. Setting up the ventilator[4]
   1. Peak inspiratory pressure (PIP) in normal lungs is 12–18 cmH$_2$O, in stiff lungs (RDS) 20–25 cmH$_2$O.
   2. Positive-end expiratory pressure (PEEP) in normal lungs is 2–3 cmH$_2$O, in stiff lungs (RDS) 4–5 cmH$_2$O.
   3. Respiratory rate in normal lungs is 10–20/min., in stiff lungs (RDS) 20–60/min.
   4. I:E ratio in normal lungs is 1:2–1:10, in stiff lungs (RDS) 1:1–1:2.

C. Adjustment of ventilator parameters
   1. Effecting oxygenation
      a. Mean airway pressure (MAP) correlates best in determining PaO$_2$.
      b. There are four ways of altering the MAP.
         (1) Respiratory rate
         (2) Peak airway pressure
         (3) PEEP
         (4) I:E ratio
      c. Time constants of the lung are a product of resistance and compliance and are measured in seconds. The shorter the time constant, the quicker proximal airway and alveolar pressures become equal.
      d. In IRDS, the time constant may be extremely short, but in a disease like meconium aspiration, the time constant secondary to the airway obstruction may be so long that proximal airway and alveolar pressure never approach the same value.
      e. When adjusting the I:E ratio initially, it is useful to use an equation to determine just how long the inspiratory time should be. This calculation avoids wasting time in establishing the proper I:E ratio when making changes in ventilator settings or when setting up the ventilator. Refer to Equation 22-1.
      f. Refer to Equation 22-2 for the computation of mean airway pressure.

EQUATION 22-1: Calculation of Inspiratory Time

Example: You have an ordered respiratory rate of 30 breaths/min. with a 1:1.5 I:E ratio. Calculate the inspiratory time.

$$X + 1.5X = 2 \text{ seconds}$$

where
- X = the inspiratory time
- $1.5X$ = the right-hand term of the ratio
- 2.0 sec = the total time available for the respiratory cycle (60 ÷ 30)

$$X + 1.5X = 2 \qquad X = 2/2.5$$
$$2.5X = 2 \qquad X = 0.8 \text{ sec available for inspiration}$$
$$1.5X = 1.2 \text{ sec available for expiration}$$

EQUATION 22-2: Calculation of Mean Airway Pressure

$$\text{MAP} = \frac{f \times T_I}{60} \times (\text{PIP} - \text{PEEP}) + \text{PEEP}$$

where
- f = respiratory rate (frequency)
- T_I = inspiratory time in seconds
- PIP = peak inspiratory pressure in cmH_2O
- PEEP = positive-end expiratory pressure in cmH_2O

Example: Orders for neonatal mechanical ventilation are given for a frequency of 30, I:E ratio of 1:1.5, peak pressure of 25 cmH_2O, and PEEP of 5 cmH_2O. (Note Equation 22-1 for T_I.)

$$\text{MAP} = \frac{30 \times 0.8}{60} \times (25 - 5) + 5 = \frac{24}{60} \times (20) + 5$$

$$\text{MAP} = 0.4\,(20) + 5 = 8 + 5 = \text{MAP of 13 } cmH_2O$$

Chapter 22: Mechanical Ventilation of Neonates

2. Effecting ventilation and CO_2 excretion
   a. CO_2 elimination is determined by minute ventilation, or tidal volume times frequency.
   b. The size of the tidal volume and therefore the minute ventilation when the frequency is held constant is effected by other adjustments.
      (1) The duration of positive pressure (DPP), from when inspiratory pressure leaves baseline until it returns to baseline, has been shown to correlate with alveolar ventilation, with a longer DPP resulting in better ventilation.
      (2) When all other ventilator parameters are held constant, increasing the PEEP levels appears to reduce alveolar tidal volume, perhaps due to a reduction in the inspiratory pressure change when PEEP has not yet improved compliance. It lowers tidal volume, and PEEP worsens compliance, in addition to lowering the inspiratory pressure change.
3. Guidelines for adjustment of pressure-limited ventilation of neonates with RDS[5]
   a. When adjusting for a low $PaCO_2$, if PaO_2 is relatively high (80 mmHg) and PIP is ≥ 18 cmH_2O, reduce ventilation by reducing peak inspiratory pressure (PIP), because it will reduce tidal volume, raise $PaCO_2$, and help lower FIO_2 while maintaining PaO_2 in an acceptable range.
      (1) If PaO_2 is at the lower limits of acceptablity (50 mmHg), it is better to raise $PaCO_2$ by reducing ventilator rate (if it is greater than 10/min.), thus maintaining the same mechanical tidal volume and helping to preserve PaO_2. Because of overall reduction in minute ventilation, FIO_2 will need to be increased.
         (a) If a toxic level of FIO_2 is in use (≥ 0.6), and PEEP is ≤ 6 cmH_2O, increasing PEEP and therefore mean airway pressure will lower both tidal volume and minute ventilation, and assist in preserving oxygenation while reducing minute ventilation.
      (2) If PIP and rate are already low, a CPAP trial may be appropriate.
   b. When adjusting for a high $PaCO_2$ consider the following.
      (1) If expiratory time is ≤ 0.5 seconds and/or mechanical rate is ≥ 45/min., use PIP to adjust minute volume and adjust FIO_2 as needed.
      (2) If PIP is already ≥ 25 cmH_2O and expiratory time is ≥ 0.5 seconds and/or mechanical rate is ≤ 45/min., increase the respiratory rate.
   c. When adjusting PaO_2 in the presence of normal $PaCO_2$, consider the following.
      (1) When PaO_2 is ≥ 100 mmHg and FIO_2 is ≤ 0.4 with PEEP ≤ 3 cmH_2O, and inspiratory time is ≥ 0.5, reduce inspiratory time (T_I) to reduce mean airway pressure and therefore PaO_2. Keep T_I at 0.5 to ensure adequate delivery of tidal volume.
      (2) If FIO_2 is ≥ 0.4 while PEEP is ≥ 3 and T_I is ≤ 0.5, then reduce PaO_2 by reducing FIO_2.

(3) If FIO_2 is already ≤0.4 and PEEP is ≥3, then adjust PaO_2 by reducing PEEP.

(4) When PaO_2 is low, adjust the parameter that has not reached its acceptable limit, such as FIO_2, PEEP, Ti, or PIP.

4. Permissive hypercapnic ventilation in low birthweight infants (500–1500 grams)
   a. Early treatment is begun with nasal CPAP at 5 cmH_2O in the presence of tachypnea, inspiratory retractions, and grunting.
      (1) FIO_2 is adjusted to keep PaO_2 at 50–70 mmHg.
   b. Mechanical ventilation is indicated by the following situations.
      (1) Marked retractions on CPAP.
      (2) Frequent apnea while on CPAP.
      (3) PaO_2 ≤ 50 mmHg with an FIO_2 of 0.8–1.0.
      (4) $PaCO_2$ ≥ 65 mmHg.
      (5) Intractable metabolic acidosis.
   c. Modes of ventilation
      (1) Conventional mode
         (a) Flow rate of 5–7 L/min.
         (b) FIO_2 to maintain PaO_2 at 50–70 mmHg.
         (c) IMV rate of ≤40/min., usually started at 20–30/min. and adjusted to maintain $PaCO_2$ at 50–60 mmHg.
         (d) Inspiratory time adjusted to 0.5–0.6 seconds.
         (e) Peak inspiratory pressure adjusted so that chest excursions are adequate, usually 20–30 cmH_2O.
         (f) PEEP of 5 cmH_2O.
      (2) High-frequency positive pressure ventilation
         (a) IMV rate set at 100/min.
         (b) Inspiratory time set at 0.3 seconds.
         (c) Flow rate set at 10–20 L/min.
         (d) Peak inspiratory pressure is decreased by 5 cmH_2O from conventional settings.
         (e) PEEP set at zero.
      (3) Prolonged inspiration time mode
         (a) All settings are the same as for the conventional mode except inspiratory time.
         (b) Inspiratory time is set at 0.8–1.0 seconds.
      (4) Synchronized mode
         (a) The IMV rate is set at the infant's spontaneous breathing rate.
   d. Weaning
      (1) Attempts to wean are made as soon as the infant is stable.

Chapter 22: Mechanical Ventilation of Neonates

(2) If ventilating in the conventional mode:
  (a) FIO_2 is lowered to maintain a PaO_2 50–70 mmHg.
  (b) IMV rate is decreased to keep $PaCO_2$ 50–60 mmHg.
  (c) Peak inspiratory pressure is lowered as chest excursions become excessive.
  (d) Extubation is accomplished when IMV rate is at 6/min.
  (e) Nasal CPAP of 5 cmH_2O is started following extubation.
  (f) Weaning from nasal CPAP is done as tolerated.
(3) When using high-frequency, prolonged inspiratory time, or synchronized mode, the patient is weaned to the conventional mode as the condition improves and then weaned as in the conventional mode.

III. Weaning in infants is generally done via trial-and-error method, because they are unable to cooperate in the effort.

A. Tests before weaning
  1. Chest X-ray certifies that there is no advancing disease.
  2. Arterial blood gases should optimally yield:
     a. PaO_2 of at least 50 mmHg
     b. $PaCO_2$ of at least 55 mmHg
     c. pH of at least 7.3
  3. Hemoglobin should be at least 12–15 gms/100 ml or hematocrit of 36–45 vol%.
  4. For accurate assessments of fluids, the following categories should be compared.
     a. Intake
     b. Output
     c. Daily body weights to assess hydration and thriving
B. A suggested sequence in weaning:
  1. Reduce the PIP to below 30 cmH_2O
  2. Reduce the FIO_2 to below 0.6
  3. Further reduce PIP to below 20 cmH_2O
  4. Further reduce FIO_2 to below 0.4
  5. Reduce ventilator rate

IV. Hazards and side effects

A. Barotrauma occurs in about 15% of ventilated infants.
  1. Pneumothorax
     a. Stimulation of lung reflexes that cause the preterm infant to actively exhale against mechanical inspiration may predispose them to pneumothorax.

b. One factor associated with an increased incidence of pulmonary air leak is a prolonged inspiratory time of between 1 and 2 seconds.
  2. Pneumomediastinum
  3. Pulmonary interstitial emphysema (PIE) frequently precedes formation of pneumothorax. The highest risk group includes neonates that are under 1000 gms.
  4. Pneumoperitoneum with pneumoscrotum
  5. Pneumopericardium
  6. Air embolism
B. Blood gas abnormalities
  1. Hypocapnia or severe respiratory alkalosis may reduce cerebral blood flow to a harmful extent, and the intracellular alkalosis created by loss of the readily diffusible CO_2 may interfere with cellular metabolism.
     a. Hypocapnia also causes an increase in airway resistance and may interfere with good inspired gas distribution.
     b. Low CO_2 increases oxygen consumption and causes a leftward shift in the oxyhemoglobin dissociation curve, worsening tissue oxygenation.
     c. Hypocapnia decreases cardiac output and potassium depletion may occur.
  2. Hypercapnia
     a. Increased pulmonary vascular resistance with alveolar hypercarbia or systemic acidosis may impair oxygenation.
     b. There is concern that increased cerebral perfusion may cause intraventricular hemorrhage and some evidence suggests that prolonged hypercarbia is associated with decreased intelligence.
  3. Hyperoxia increases risk of retrolental fibroplasia in low birthweight infants.
C. Intracranial pressure changes[7]
  1. One study showed that in a series of ten infants receiving mechanical inspiration, intracranial blood volume increased an average of 8.3% and a consistent relationship was demonstrated between clinical estimation of lung compliance and the amount of cranial volume expansion.
  2. Intracranial hemorrhage is present in about one-half of infants who die with IRDS.
  3. Neurological impairment is estimated to occur in about 15% of all survivors of respiratory therapy for IRDS.
D. Altered circulation
  1. High MAP may obstruct the circulation and cause redistribution of blood flow, particularly if pulmonary perfusion pressure is low. Overdistention of the lungs may cause obstruction of the pulmonary circulation and increase right-to-left extrapulmonary shunting through the ductus arteriosus and foramen ovale.
  2. The atria and vena cava may be compressed, resulting in a decreased cardiac output and subsequent fluid retention from decreased renal function. The decreased

renal function is likely due to both decreased perfusion and stimulation of left atrial pressure receptors that sense a diminished blood volume.
3. Worsening hypoxemia may result from the increased extrapulmonary shunting as well as an alteration of regional pulmonary blood flow. To determine whether the pressure being used is excessive, a chest film is helpful. If the chest film reveals atelectasis, then more pressure would be helpful. If the film reveals good expansion, then a reduction of pressure would be necessary.

E. Gastrointestinal complications
1. Complications seen during positive pressure ventilation include ileus, gastric dilatation, and gastrointestinal bleeding.
2. These complications do not appear to be a direct result of positive pressure ventilation. Positive airway pressure has been shown to reduce portal and splanchnic blood flow and increase splanchnic vascular resistance. These changes could cause the gastrointestinal tract to be more susceptible to ischemia should the arterial supply be compromised.

V. High-frequency ventilation[6]

A. Common uses of high-frequency ventilation include the following:
1. Respiratory failure that does not respond to conventional mechanical ventilation.
2. Pulmonary interstitial emphysema (PIE) and other air leak syndromes.
3. Persistent pulmonary hypertension (PPHN) where hyperventilation is desirable.
4. Congenital diaphragmatic hernia (CDH) where pulmonary hypoplasia is present.

B. High-frequency jet ventilation (HFJV)
1. The Bunnell Life-Pulse is a pressure-driven, servo-controlled, solenoid-based device that is used in conjunction with a conventional ventilator.
   a. A triple-lumen High-Lo endotracheal tube must be inserted before starting jet ventilation.
      (1) The main port is for connection to the conventional ventilator.
      (2) The distal port is for monitoring airway pressure at the tip of the endotracheal tube.
      (3) The middle port is connected to the jet ventilator and delivers the gas pulse in the midportion of the tube.
2. Adjustment
   a. HFJV is usually started at a rate of 420 breaths/min. Adjustment is by controlling the time the high-frequency breath is off, which when used in combination with a fixed-breath, determines the I:E ratio.
      (1) In infants with air leaks, jet ventilation is started without any IMV breaths from the conventional ventilator.

(2) A time period of 6–24 hours is allowed to lapse until conventional breaths are added in the presence of air leaks.
   b. Background conventional IMV ventilation is provided at 5–10 breaths/minute to avoid atelectasis.
   c. PEEP is provided through the main port of the triple-lumen ET tube, which is connected to the conventional ventilator.
   d. For RDS infants, use a peak inspiratory pressure (PIP) with the jet of 80% of that previously used with the conventional ventilator. Pressure amplitude is the result of the end-expiratory pressure and the mean airway pressure delivered by the ventilator.
   e. For non-RDS, infants or in the presence of pulmonary hypertension, the same PIP is used as was used for conventional ventilator breaths.
   f. The "jet valve on-time" (inspiratory time) is set at the minimum of 0.02 seconds.
   g. If oxygenation is a problem, do one or all of the following:
      (1) Increase the FIO_2.
      (2) Increase the PEEP.
      (3) Increase the background IMV rate to 15–20 breaths/min. or higher if necessary.
   h. If undesirable hyperventilation occurs after initiating jet ventilation, adjust one of the following parameters to elevate the $PaCO_2$.
      (1) Increase the PEEP to decrease the pressure change during inspiration and reduce tidal volume.
      (2) Decrease the conventional ventilator rate.
      (3) Decrease the conventional ventilator peak inspiratory pressure.
      (4) Decrease the jet peak inspiratory pressure.
3. Weaning
   a. FIO_2 and peak inspiratory pressure should be alternately reduced.
   b. Changes should be made only every 1–2 hours to avoid delayed deterioration with a reduction in settings.

C. High-frequency oscillatory ventilation (using Sensormedics 3100)
1. Perform patient circuit calibration and ventilator performance check.
2. Setting up the ventilator
   a. Flowrate should be set at 20 L/min.
      (1) The flowrate may need to be reduced when using low mean airway pressure (MAP) and high amplitude settings.
   b. Set the % inspiratory time at 33%.
   c. Set the frequency at 10 Hz.

Chapter 22: Mechanical Ventilation of Neonates

    d. Set the amplitude at 15.
       (1) As soon as the ventilator is connected to the patient, increase the amplitude if necessary until you see good chest vibrations.
       (2) Further adjustment of amplitude should be made using transcutaneous or directly measured PCO_2.
    e. Setting mean airway pressure (MAP)
       (1) The MAP for infants with RDS should be set 1–2 cmH_2O above what it was during conventional ventilation.
       (2) In infants with pulmonary interstitial emphysema (PIE), the MAP should be set at the lowest possible level that achieves adequate PaO_2.
    f. FIO_2
       (1) It should be set to achieve prescribed PaO_2.
       (2) In patients with PIE, the MAP should be lowered prior to lowering the $FIO_2 \leq 0.7$.
    g. The piston should be centered after both the MAP and amplitude have been set.
    h. An adult humidifier device should be used and set at 36.5–37° centigrade.
       (1) The oscillator has high water consumption and rainout.
       (2) The exhaled side of the circuit should be positioned lower to facilitate drainage.
    i. Alarm limits should be set 2 above and below the MAP setting.
3. Weaning from high-frequency oscillation
    a. Weaning applies to all patients who are placed on the oscillator ventilator except those with persistent pulmonary hypertension (PPHN).
    b. Decrease the MAP by 0.5–1.0 cmH_2O.
       (1) If SaO_2 increases, leave MAP the same for one hour, then decrease by 0.5–1.0.
       (2) If SaO_2 remains the same after a 0.5–1.0 cmH_2O decrease, do the following:
          (a) If $FIO_2 \geq 0.6$, return to the previous MAP setting.
          (b) If $FIO_2 \leq 0.6$, leave at the present MAP setting and attempt another 0.5–1.0 cmH_2O decrease in 4–8 hours.
       (3) If SaO_2 decreases after the MAP change, return the patient to the previous MAP setting.
          (a) Reassess the patient in 4–8 hours.
          (b) If the patient is stable, attempt a 0.5–1.0 cmH_2O reduction in the MAP.

References

1. Goldsmith, J. P., and Karotkin, E. H., *Assisted Ventilation of the Neonate*, 3rd ed., W. B. Saunders, 1996.
2. Merenstein, G. B., and Gardner, S. L., *Handbook of Neonatal Intensive Care*, 4th ed., Mosby, 1997.
3. Koff, P., et al., *Neonatal and Pediatric Respiratory Care*, 2nd ed., Mosby-Yearbook, 1993.
4. Polin, R., et al., *Practical Neonatology*, 2nd ed., W. B. Saunders, 1993.
5. Cloherty, J. P., and Stark, A. R., *Manual of Neonatal Care*, 4th ed., Lippincott Raven, 1998.
6. Gerstmann, D., et al., "High-Frequency Ventilation: Issues of Strategy," *Clinics in Perinatology* 18, no. 3, September 1991.
7. Leaky, F. A. N., et al., "Cranial Blood Volume Changes During Mechanical Ventilation and Spontaneous Breathing in Newborn Infants," *The Journal of Pediatrics*, 101, no. 6, December 1982.

Assessment Questions

1. During time-triggered, pressure-limited ventilation, if the pressure limit is reached prior to completion of the inspiratory time cycle, which of the following will occur?

    I. Excess flow will vent to the atmosphere
    II. The ventilator will cycle and begin expiration
    III. The pressure will be maintained at the pressure limit setting

    A. I only
    B. II only
    C. III only
    D. I and II only

2. When trying to influence the $PaCO_2$ of a newborn receiving HFOV ventilation, which of the following controls need to be adjusted?

    I. MAP
    II. CPAP
    III. Rate
    IV. Amplitude

    A. I and II only
    B. II and III only
    C. III and IV only
    D. IV only

3. It has been determined that your neonate on mechanical ventilation has developed some auto-PEEP. Which of the following maneuvers will reduce the auto-PEEP?

    I. Decrease the flowrate
    II. Decrease tidal volume
    III. Increase expiratory time
    IV. Decrease the PEEP level

    A. I only
    B. II only
    C. III only
    D. II and IV only

4. While ventilating a newborn infant with a time-triggered, pressure-limited ventilator, you record the peak airway pressure as 36 cmH_2O, and the mean airway pressure as 21 cmH_2O. If you shorten the inspiratory time, which of the following would you expect to occur?

Chapter 22: Mechanical Ventilation of Neonates

A. The peak pressure will increase
B. The expiratory time will decrease
C. The mean airway pressure will decrease
D. The tidal volume will increase

5. A neonate receiving mechanical ventilation has their PaO_2 decrease from 68 torr to 50 torr. Which of the following would you recommend?

   I. Increase the expiratory time
   II. Increase the inspiratory time
   III. Increase the pressure limit

   A. I only
   B. I and III only
   C. II only
   D. II and III only

6. Which of the following techniques are currently used for delivery of high-frequency ventilation?

   I. High-frequency flow interruption (HFFI)
   II. High-frequency jet ventilation (HFJV)
   III. High-frequency positive pressure ventilation (HFPPV)
   IV. High-frequency oscillation ventilation (HFOV)

   A. I only
   B. I and II only
   C. I, II and III only
   D. I, II, III and IV

7. Potential problems associated with HFPPV include which of the following?

   I. Pulmonary hyperinflation
   II. Breath stacking
   III. Inadequate tidal volume delivery

   A. I only
   B. I and II only
   C. I, II and III
   D. II and III only

8. A newborn infant has been intubated and placed on a time-triggered, pressure-limited ventilator with the following settings and umbilical artery blood gases.

   $PIP = 27\ cmH_2O$
   Itime = 0.3 sec.
   Rate = 25 BPM
   $FIO_2 = 0.60$
   $PEEP = 5\ cmH_2O$
   $pH = 7.22$
   $PaCO_2 = 62$ torr
   $PaO_2 = 50$ torr
   $HCO^3 = 22$ mEq/L

   Which ventilator adjustment would you recommend?

   A. Increase rate
   B. Increase PEEP
   C. Increase PIP
   D. Increase FIO_2

9. A newborn infant has been intubated and placed on a time-triggered, pressure-limited ventilator with the following settings and umbilical artery blood gases.

   $PIP = 25\ cmH_2O$
   Itime = 0.35 sec.
   Rate = 32 BPM
   $FIO_2 = 0.80$
   $PEEP = 5\ cmH_2O$
   $pH = 7.34$
   $PaCO_2 = 44$ torr
   $PaO_2 = 57$ torr
   $HCO^3 = 22$ mEq/L

   Which ventilator adjustment would you recommend?

   A. Increase rate
   B. Increase PEEP
   C. Increase PIP
   D. Increase FIO_2

Chapter 23

Monitoring of Blood Gases

I. Transcutaneous oxygen monitoring[1]

A. Measuring technique
1. There is a two degree drop between electrode core temperature of 45° centigrade and skin temperature that equals 43° centigrade.
   a. T_cPO_2 appears to plateau at 43° centigrade skin temperature, suggesting no further increase in blood flow (hyperemia).
   b. Accuracy of T_cPO_2 values is good when the arterial PO_2 is not high, but may not be reliable under conditions of hyperoxia.
2. The weight of the standard electrode is approximately 3.3 grams, which produces a pressure of about 1 mmHg.
   a. A 15-fold increase in pressure is necessary to begin to effect the heat induced hyperemia and reduce perfusion of the superficial capillary layer.
   b. Even where conditions of slight reduction of blood flow and capillary pressure occur, the weight of the standard electrode is considered acceptable.
3. The use of a double-sided, self-adhesive ring that extends beyond the electrode by 8 mm is used.
   a. If the electrode is properly attached, then diffusion of external gas is impossible, even after many hours.
   b. The pathway for diffusion of ambient air is long enough that accurate measurement for several hours is possible in 100% O_2 or even under hyperbaric conditions.
   c. To ensure good contact between the skin and electrode at its measuring surface, it is necessary to wet the skin by placing a drop of distilled H_2O exactly where the center of the electrode will be located.
   d. Other mediums for improving contact (i.e., gel) have been shown to increase response time.
4. There are several factors to consider in choosing the electrode skin location.

Chapter 23: Monitoring of Blood Gases

a. The skin at the measurement site should preferably be thin and situated over a large capillary bed.
b. The highest capillary density is over the face, but this site is irritating to both infants and adults.
c. Acceptable locations
   (1) Chest recommended as the routine location in newborns because the area is supplied from both sides by branches of the internal thoracic artery that stems from the innominate brachiocephalic artery arising from the aortic arch prior to the ductus arteriosus.
   (2) The neck in the region of the carotid arteries.
   (3) The abdomen of premature infants.
   (4) The back of newborns and premature infants lying in the prone position.
   (5) Ear lobes with a large surface area.
5. Preparation of hairless skin is neither necessary or advisable, because skin breakdown could occur secondary to preparation.
   a. Hairy skin must be shaved.
   b. Fine lanugo hair does not adversely affect measurements.
6. Experience shows that the electrode can remain in the same location for a two-hour measurement without any permanent skin damage. This time period is recommended for routine monitoring.
   a. The skin of patients with good circulation remains undamaged when in place for six hours with a core temperature of 45 degrees centigrade.
   b. In cases of severe illness, shock, and hypothermia, the electrode position should be changed every hour as a precautionary measure. The skin should be checked at least every hour for abnormal redness.
   c. A suggested alternative method to avoid frequent repositioning of the electrode is to reduce the core temperature to 42–43° centigrade. When an arterial check is desired, the core temperature is increased for a few minutes until sufficient hyperemia is achieved. Even with the decreased temperatures, a trend indication is still possible.

B. The recording of "relative local perfusion"
   1. The first phase of recording
      a. The heating power of the electrode is initially high after immediately attaching the electrode, in order to increase the skin temperature to the desired level.
      b. As skin temperature is increased, the heating power of the electrode is decreased and it eventually plateaus.
      c. The amount of time required for the plateau, like the $TcPO_2$, is variable and dependent on the following:

(1) Patient circulation
(2) Heat conductivity of the skin
(3) Local blood flow conditions
(4) The thermal environment
   2. Characteristic behavior of "relative local perfusion"
      a. Skin blood flow
         (1) Vasodilatation and skin blood flow during thermoregulation may show an overall twentyfold increase in blood flow.
         (2) Vasodilatation after heating of the skin is brought about independently of nervous control. It is hypothesized that the increase may be due to vessel smooth muscle relaxation and resultant hyperemia.
      b. Changes in blood flow will be reflected in the record of the transducer heating power if the vessel diameters are constant.
      c. The signal is useful only in terms of relative blood flow or blood pressure if all other parameters such as blood temperature are under steady state and strict thermoinsulation is used.
      d. The heating power recording can be helpful in demonstrating physiologic changes in blood flow and in the diagnosis of progressive cardiovascular collapse.
C. Quantifying right-to-left shunting requires using two $TcPO_2$ monitors.
   1. In the newborn infant, one electrode is placed at a preductal site for circulation such as the right upper chest wall, and the other is placed at a postductal site such as the abdomen.
   2. The infant is placed on an FIO_2 of 1.0 and a comparison of the two electrode values is made.
      a. If the preductal electrode value rises rapidly, there is indication of extrapulmonary right-to-left shunt through the ductus arteriosus and/or foramen ovale.
      b. If there is no dramatic response of the preductal electrode, it is suggestive of significant intrapulmonary right-to-left shunting secondary to atelectasis.
D. Conditions associated with poor correlation between PaO_2 and $TcPO_2$:
   1. Shock—when the blood pressure is 2–3 standard deviations from normal.
   2. Acidosis—pH of less than 7.05.
   3. Hypothermia—body core temperature less than 35° centigrade.
   4. Congenital cyanotic heart disease—PaO_2 is less than 30 mmHg.
   5. Post cardiac surgery—likely due to a combination of shock, acidosis, and hypothermia.
   6. Severe anemia.

Chapter 23: Monitoring of Blood Gases

7. High doses of a vasodilator such as tolazoline.
8. Dying infants.
9. Skin edema.

II. Measuring arterial oxygen saturation with pulse oximetry[1]

A. Defining functional oxygen saturation
   1. Oxyhemoglobin is a hemoglobin molecule bound completely with four molecules of oxygen.
   2. Deoxyhemoglobin is a hemoglobin molecule that is unbound with any substance.
   3. A dyshemoglobin is a hemoglobin molecule bound to something other than oxygen, such as carbon monoxide, sulfur, or cyanide.
   4. Functional saturation is simply the ratio (expressed as a percentage) of oxyhemoglobin to the total hemoglobin (including oxyhemoglobin) available for binding to oxygen.
   5. Dyshemoglobins are not factored into the measurement of functional saturation because they are not immediately available for transporting oxygen.
   6. Available hemoglobin is thus the sum of oxyhemoglobin and deoxyhemoglobin.
   7. For example, if a person has 15 grams of hemoglobin for each 100 ml of whole blood, and if 2 grams were dyshemoglobin, only the remaining 13 grams would be counted in the calculation of functional saturation. If 11 of the 13 grams available of hemoglobin are oxyhemoglobin, the functional saturation would be 11/13 or 85%.

B. Fractional saturation
   1. This measurement is reported from a laboratory-based instrument rather than by a bedside instrument.
   2. The standard instrument is the Instrumentation Laboratories IL 282 Co-oximeter.
   3. Oxygen saturation is reported as the ratio of oxyhemoglobin to total hemoglobin, or the sum of available hemoglobin plus dyshemoglobins.
   4. In the example of a person with 15 grams of hemoglobin for each 100 ml of blood, the laboratory oximeter would calculate saturation on the ratio of 11/15 rather than 11/13.
      a. The 15 is the sum of available hemoglobin (11 grams of oxyhemoglobin plus 2 grams of deoxyhemoglobin) plus dyshemoglobins (i.e., 2 grams of carboxyhemoglobins and methemoglobin).
      b. Fractional saturation would be reported as 73% compared to the functional saturation of 85%.

C. Precautions must be taken with clinical measurement of arterial saturation with pulse oximetry.

1. If oxygen saturation is calculated in the laboratory, instead of being measured, a difference may exist between the calculated data and the bedside saturation indicated by the pulse oximeter.
    a. A calculated saturation uses the variables of pH and PaO_2 and assumes that the hemoglobin has a normal affinity for oxygen.
    b. If the affinity of the hemoglobin for oxygen were increased or decreased compared to normal, then the pulse oximeter value would be more accurate because of the direct measurement being made.
2. In the emergency setting, without the benefit of a baseline measurement of an arterial blood gas with fractional saturation measurement, the pulse oximeter may be seriously misleading by failing to recognize carboxyhemoglobin or methemoglobin fractions. Once it is established that adequate amounts of functional hemoglobin are present, the pulse oximeter is then a safe and useful monitoring tool.
3. In the neonatal intensive care unit, where high fractions of fetal hemoglobin may be present in the patient population, pulse oximetry can be seriously misleading when used to estimate PaO_2. Fetal hemoglobin saturates much more easily at a lower PaO_2 than adult hemoglobin.[2]
    a. Pulse oximetry saturations and their derived PaO_2 values correlate well with measured arterial saturation and PaO_2 in neonates with chronic lung disease and prolonged oxygen dependence. These infants have small fractions of fetal hemoglobin.
    b. In infants with acute cardiorespiratory problems, pulse oximetry does not reliably reflect PaO_2, but may be useful in detecting clinical deterioration.

D. Technical limitations of pulse oximetry
1. Motion artifact
    a. Excessive motion of the digit being monitored by an oximetry probe can cause the instrument to see a fluctuation in transmitted light and signal strength and intensity of received light.
        (1) False arterial waveforms can be produced that the oximeter cannot tell from genuine signals.
    b. Some venous blood may be included in the instrument's calculation of SaO_2.
        (1) Arterial pulse pressure may compress and empty the venous bed being measured.
        (2) Subsequent opening and filling of venous vessels may mimic an arterial filling.
2. Intravascular dyes can be read by the oximeter as desaturated hemoglobin.
    a. Methylene produces the greatest falsely low value for SaO_2.
    b. Indocyanine green produces the next greatest falsely low value for SaO_2.

Chapter 23: Monitoring of Blood Gases

3. Fingernail polish
   a. Dark colors such as blue or black interfere by absorbing the red light transmitted by the pulse oximeter.
   b. Dark fingernail polish may cause light shunting around the periphery of the finger.
4. Serum bilirubin: pulse oximetry does not appear to be affected by high bilirubin values.
5. Low perfusion states
   a. Poor blood pressure interferes with the pulse oximeter's ability to process a good arterial signal.
   b. The earlobe is less affected by vasoconstriction than the finger and may be the site of choice in compromised patients.
6. Increased venous pressures may alter pulse volume amplitude, thus reducing the accuracy of the signal.
7. Ambient light and external light
   a. Fluorescent lights, operating room lights, and infrared heat lamps have been seen to cause falsely high values.
   b. Direct sunlight has been reported to cause high readings.
   c. Fiberoptic lights have caused falsely high readings.
8. Skin pigmentation
   a. Dark skin pigmentation may affect the accuracy of the oximeter.
   b. Shunting of the light signal may occur around the periphery of the monitoring site.
9. Pulse oximetry maintains an accuracy range within 2–3% of the oxyhemoglobin levels measured in-vitro with multiwavelength oximeters. Commercial oximeters maintain this degree of accuracy over a range of 70–100% oxygen saturation.

III. Performing arterial puncture[3]

A. Prior to beginning the procedure, carefully check the patient's chart for data (coagulation studies, anticoagulant therapy, and history) concerning the patient's ability to clot blood.
B. Necessary equipment includes
   1. Alcohol or disinfectant swabs
   2. Sterile 3–5 ml glass syringe or prepackaged disposable kit
   3. Sterile 1 1/2 inch, 21 gauge, short bevel needle
   4. Sodium heparin (1:1000)
   5. Sterile gauze pads (4 × 4s)

6. Stopper to seal the needle
7. Container of ice

C. Puncture site—any arterial site may be used, but the safest and most accessible is the radial artery in the wrist. The wrist has the advantage of two arterial supplies, the ulnar and radial arteries.

D. The Allen's test should be done to establish that ulnar artery blood supply is present, in the event of trauma to the radial.
   1. Compress the patient's wrist so there is no blood flow past the radial or ulnar arteries.
   2. Require the patient make a tight fist.
   3. Release pressure on the ulnar artery while still holding pressure on the radial artery.
   4. If the hand immediately "pinks up," it suggests that ulnar blood flow is good. If the hand does not "pink up," try the opposite wrist.

E. Drawing the blood sample
   1. Having washed your hands, place the patient's wrist on a rolled towel so that the hand is hyperextended and supinated.
   2. Thoroughly clean the site to be used by using 2–3 alcohol swabs, one right after the other.
   3. A small skin wheal of 2% lidocaine (without epinephrine) may be used to prevent pain and reduce hyperventilation during the blood sampling. If the lidocaine is injected around the artery, it may help to prevent arterial spasm.
   4. Prepare the sampling syringe by drawing about 0.5 ml of 1:1000 heparin into the syringe and working the plunger back and forth in the barrel. Expel all excess heparin.
      a. The PO_2 and PCO_2 of heparin are virtually the same as that of ambient air (approximately 150 mmHg and 0 mmHg).
      b. High concentrations of heparin are acidic (<7.0) and will lower the pH.
   5. While palpating the arterial pulse with one hand, the free hand holds the syringe at its base (similar to holding a pencil), keeping it at about a 45 degree angle, with the needle bevel pointing up and against the flow of blood.
   6. Enter the skin in one smooth motion and advance the tip of the needle to where the pulse is felt.
   7. Having punctured the artery, blood will freely begin to enter the syringe in a pulsating manner. Hold the syringe very still until 2–3 ml of blood is collected.
   8. Smoothly withdraw the needle and immediately compress the site for 5 minutes.
   9. With your free hand, stick the needle into the stopper, rapidly rotating the syringe several times to mix the heparin with the blood, and place the syringe into the container of ice. Ideally, air bubbles are removed from the syringe. If there are bubbles, they must be evacuated prior to insertion into the ice.

Chapter 23: Monitoring of Blood Gases

a. At sea level, air has a PO_2 of about 150 torr, and a PCO_2 of about 0 torr. Should a sample be contaminated with air, the measured PO_2 of the sample increases, provided the actual blood value is less than 150 torr.
b. For the same reason the measured value of the $PaCO_2$ decreases, changing the pH.
c. This requires removal of any air bubbles entering the sample immediately.

10. Having carefully determined that bleeding has completely stopped, an elastic bandage may be placed over the gauze pad and wrapped 3/4 of the way around the wrist. This bandage should remain in place for 2 hours.

IV. Monitoring of exhaled CO_2[4]

A. The source of end-tidal CO_2 ($PetCO_2$)
 1. Regional alveolar CO_2 tension will vary directly with the ratio of ventilation to perfusion ($\dot{V}/\dot{Q}$).
 2. The time constant of a lung region, which is determined by the product of its compliance and resistance, is a major determinant of both regional $\dot{V}/\dot{Q}$ and the timing of regional deflation.
    a. Areas of high $\dot{V}/\dot{Q}$ will have low alveolar PCO_2.
    b. Clinically, patients with large areas of high $\dot{V}/\dot{Q}$ are those with hypovolemia, high PEEP levels, or pulmonary embolism.
    c. The V_D/Vt ratio is higher when high $\dot{V}/\dot{Q}$ areas contribute the most to exhaled gas and $PaCO_2$ is usually greater than $PetCO_2$.
    d. Exhalation from low $\dot{V}/\dot{Q}$ (high $PACO_2$) areas may be delayed because of local airway obstruction. Gas from these areas might be exhaled after the high $\dot{V}/\dot{Q}$ areas have emptied. This may cause $PetCO_2$ to be greater than arterial.

B. Uses for exhaled CO_2 monitoring
 1. In spontaneously breathing patients, hypoventilation, hyperventilation, apnea, and periodic breathing can all be rapidly detected.
 2. The capnogram is useful for selection of the optimal combination of settings to produce a desired $PaCO_2$. It might prevent the lowering of $PaCO_2$ too rapidly when mechanical ventilation is initiated.
 3. Sudden changes in $PetCO_2$ may indicate a disconnection, leak, obstruction in the circuit, or ventilator malfunction.
 4. Capnography may signal recurrent respiratory failure during weaning. Patients who maintain a stable $PetCO_2$ during weaning usually do well. Those whose $PetCO_2$ has a progressive rise or fall often have difficulty weaning.
 5. It is useful for calculating the arterial-to-alveolar carbon difference ($P[a-A]CO_2$). An increase in this value is one of the most sensitive indications of acute pulmonary embolism.

6. Changes in CO_2 production may be detected by $PetCO_2$ and can occur secondary to seizures, altered body temperature, shivering, carbohydrate loading, or $NaHCO_3$ loading.
7. Changes in transport of CO_2 from the periphery to elimination in the lungs may be detected and can occur in impairment of tissue perfusion in shock and during restoration of the circulation following cardiac arrest.
8. Assessment of endotracheal tube placement[5]

C. Interpretation of exhaled CO_2 values
   1. A positive arterial-alveolar tension difference, where the $PaCO_2$ is greater than the $PetCO_2$, can result from:
      a. Any cause of increased regional $\dot{V}/\dot{Q}$, such as an upright rather than supine position.
      b. Hypovolemia with decreased pulmonary artery pressure.
      c. Increased alveolar pressure from large mechanical tidal volumes or high PEEP.
         (1) With positive pressure breaths during mechanical ventilation, a lower regional PCO_2 may occur in nondependent portions of lung.
         (2) Mechanical compression of capillaries occurs with large tidal volumes and/or PEEP. Smaller tidal volumes may minimize the cyclic changes in exhaled CO_2.
         (3) Because of the variable influence of regional time constants, the $PaCO_2$-$PetCO_2$ difference does not necessarily reflect the degree of $\dot{V}/\dot{Q}$ mismatch.
      d. The ratio of $PetCO_2$-$PaCO_2$ is sometimes used rather than the difference when the gradient between $PaCO_2$-$PetCO_2$ is a small fraction of the $PaCO_2$.
         (1) A $PaCO_2$-$PetCO_2$ gradient of 10 is much more meaningful if the $PaCO_2$ is 25 than if it is 75.
         (2) A significant correlation of $PetCO_2$-$PaCO_2$ with the fraction of perfused lung has been shown in patients with pulmonary embolism.
         (3) The lower the numerical value, the lower the percentage of lung perfusion.
   2. Negative arterial-alveolar CO_2 differences
      a. Rebreathing CO_2 may occur from the anatomical dead space into the most compliant alveoli at the beginning of inspiration.
      b. Equilibration of alveolar gas occurs with $P\bar{v}CO_2$ in low $\dot{V}/\dot{Q}$ areas of the lung where alveolar expansion occurs early in inspiration and perfusion is maintained throughout inspiration and expiration.
      c. The Haldane effect occurs where binding of oxygen to hemoglobin causes the release of chemically bound CO_2 and increases end-capillary and alveolar PCO_2.

Chapter 23: Monitoring of Blood Gases

      d. $PaCO_2$ represents average arterial CO_2 tension and $PetCO_2$ refers to CO_2 in expired gas at a specific point in time. A high proportion of low $\dot{V}/\dot{Q}$ areas contributing to exhaled gas will increase $PetCO_2$ above arterial.

      e. Clinically, the $PaCO_2$-$PetCO_2$ difference is likely to be negative when:

         (1) High $\dot{V}/\dot{Q}$ areas are minimized (patient supine rather than upright), large tidal volumes are avoided, and intravascular volume is adequate.

         (2) High FIO_2 is administered (Haldane effect).

         (3) A longer equilibration time is provided through a prolonged inspiratory phase, use of inspiratory plateau, or increased I:E ratio (longer inspiration).

         (4) An increased venous-arterial CO_2 content difference may occur with increased metabolic rate, or decreased cardiac output (decreased transport from the periphery).

V. Gastric tonometry to assess tissue oxygenation[1]

A. Rationale
1. Perfusion of the gut is affected early in the development of tissue hypoxia.
2. Tissue hypoxia should result in a decrease in the pH of the gastric mucosa as anaerobic metabolism begins in that tissue.

B. Technique
1. A nasogastric tube with an distally attached CO_2 permeable balloon is inserted so that the balloon is in the stomach.
2. The balloon is filled with 2.5–3.0 ml of 0.9% NaCl.
3. A period of 1–2 hours is allowed for the CO_2 in the stomach to equilibrate with the saline in the balloon.
4. The saline is then withdrawn from the balloon, discarding the first 1.5 ml (dead space volume) and analyzing the remaining 1.5 ml for PCO_2, using a blood gas analyzer.
5. An arterial blood sample is drawn at the same time as the gastric sample to allow computation of plasma HCO_3^-.
6. Gastric pH is then calculated using the Henderson-Hasselbach equation and the PCO_2 from the gastric sample along with the serum HCO_3^- from the arterial blood sample.
7. A gastric mucosal pH of ≤ 7.32 is diagnostic of tissue hypoxia and may be an early predictor of mortality.

References

    1. Kacmarek, R., et al., *Monitoring in Respiratory Care,* Mosby-Yearbook, 1993.
    2. Walsh, M. C., et al., "Relationship of Pulse Oximetry to Arterial Oxygen Tension in Infants," *Critical Care Medicine* 15, no. 12, December 1987.

3. Eubanks, D. H., and Bone, R. C., *Comprehensive Respiratory Care*, 2nd ed., Mosby, 1990.

4. Alone, C. A., and Hill, T. V., *Respiratory Care of the Newborn and Child*, 2nd ed., Lippincott, 1997.

5. Day, S., et al., "Rapid Analysis of Exhaled CO_2 to Assess Endotracheal Tube Placement," *Respiratory Care* 37, no. 10, October 1992.

Assessment Questions

1. When placing a patient on capnography, the therapist is evaluating the patient's ability to:
   A. Oxygenate the tissues
   B. Ventilate the lungs
   C. Perfuse the tissues
   D. Exhale a complete tidal volume

2. Transcutaneous monitoring is used to evaluate:
   I. Oxygen diffusion
   II. Tissue perfusion
   III. Carbon dioxide diffusion

   A. I only
   B. I and II only
   C. I, II and III
   D. I and III only

3. Common complications associated with transcutaneous monitoring are:
   I. Necrosis
   II. Bruising
   III. Erythemia

   A. I only
   B. II only
   C. III only
   D. I, II and III

4. Why are blood gas samples transported packed in ice?
   A. To keep the sample PO_2 from increasing
   B. To keep the sample PCO_2 from increasing
   C. To keep the sample PO_2 from decreasing
   D. To keep the pH from increasing

5. Which of the following will *NOT* affect the accuracy of a pulse oximeter?
   A. Pigmented skin
   B. Vascular lipid infusion
   C. Carboxyhemoglobin
   D. Methemoglobin

6. Common complications of arterial puncture include:
   I. Nerve damage
   II. Arteriospasm
   III. Hematoma formation
   IV. Infection

   A. I and II only
   B. I, II, and III only
   C. I, II, III and IV
   D. III and IV only

7. Multiple wavelength co-oximetry that measures oxygen saturation by light absorption is capable of measuring:
   I. HbO_2
   II. metHb
   III. COHb

   A. I only
   B. I and II only
   C. I, II and III
   D. II and III only

8. Prior to performing an arterial puncture you perform the Allen's Test. You observe

that hand color returns within 30 seconds after releasing pressure from the ulnar artery. This would indicate:

A. The ulnar circulation is adequate
B. The radial circulation is adequate
C. The ulnar circulation is inadequate
D. A 30-second return time is normal

9. Pulse oximetry calibration values are within _____% of oxyhemglobin levels measured invitro.

A. 1–2
B. 2–3
C. 3–4
D. 4–5

Chapter 24

Achieving Adequate Oxygenation

I. Position the patient[1]

A. Elevation of the head and chest decreases the pressure of the abdominal viscera against the diaphragm. This more upright position produces the best overall $\dot{V}/\dot{Q}$ ratios in the lung and, as a rule, the best oxygenation.

B. Proper positioning of obese patients is particularly important. When lying flat, the weight of the anterior chest and the pressure of the abdominal viscera against the diaphragm may greatly increase the work of breathing, decrease tidal volume, and worsen $\dot{V}/\dot{Q}$ match up.

C. Critically ill patients should have frequent position changes. This maneuver significantly reduces the tendency towards atelectasis.

D. If a patient has unilateral lung dysfunction, the patient should not lay with the bad lung in the down position as this will cause blood flow to gravitate to the bad lung and may result in severe hypoxemia and even precipitate cardiopulmonary arrest.

E. Exceptions to always positioning the patient with the bad lung in the "up" position occur in the following instances.
   1. A completely or partially filled abscess in the "up" lung may suddenly drain large volumes of purulent material and result in sudden cardiac arrest.
   2. Pulmonary interstitial emphysema (PIE) is a case where it is preferable to place the effected lung down in order to reduce the FRC in that lung.
   3. In infants with a congenital diaphragmatic hernia, the hemi-thorax with the bowel segment present should be placed downward to avoid any compression of the unaffected lung.

II. Oxygen therapy

A. PaO_2 values
   1. Based on clinical research, a PaO_2 of 70 mmHg is associated with increased survival in critically ill patients when:

Chapter 24: Achieving Adequate Oxygenation

a. Hemoglobin > 10 gm/100 ml of blood.
b. $SaO_2 > 90\%$.
c. Cardiac output and oxygen uptake combine to keep mixed venous values ($P\bar{v}O_2$) at 30 mmHg or greater.
d. P_{50} is at least 30 mmHg.

2. The PaO_2 in COPD patients must be adjusted according to their disease.
   a. A resting PaO_2 of less than 50 mmHg in these patients promotes pulmonary hypertension and right ventricular hypertrophy and failure. These patients are candidates for continuous low flow (2 L/min or less) oxygen therapy.
   b. Patients whose $PaCO_2$ levels are chronically 55–60 mmHg or greater have lost their normal ability to adjust ventilation according to CO_2 levels.
      (1) Their primary respiratory drive arises from chronic hypoxic stimulation of carotid and aortic chemoreceptors.
      (2) Elevation of PaO_2 above 60 mmHg in this group may promote further hypoventilation, respiratory decompensation, and a worsening of respiratory acidosis.
3. In the infant population, an arterial PO_2 of 50–80 mmHg, measured at a preductal arterial site, is satisfactory. It is unlikely that brain damage may occur until a PaO_2 is well below 50 mmHg and retrolental fibroplasia (RLF) is unlikely to occur at PaO_2 less than 80 mmHg.
4. In noncritically ill patients without chronic disease, other guidelines should be chosen to determine what appropriate PaO_2 must be maintained. The "normal" PaO_2 is based on age, position, and altitude.
5. Predicted normals at sea level:
   a. PaO_2 decreases with age secondary to altered pulmonary function. Refer to Table 4-10.
   b. PaO_2 is highest in the seated or upright position because ventilation and perfusion are both occurring predominantly in the bases of the lung, resulting in the best $\dot{V}/\dot{Q}$ match up. Refer to Equation 24-1.
6. Predicted PaO_2 at altitude
   a. The ambient PO_2 decreases with altitude and results in a lower normal PAO_2 and consequently a lower normal PaO_2.
   b. Refer to Equation 4-2 for calculation of the gradient between alveolar and arterial O_2. This gradient may be referred to as $P(A-a)O_2$ or A-a DO_2.
   c. The a/A O_2 ratio is useful to determine the relationship between arterial and alveolar O_2. Refer to Equation 24-2.
   d. The normal PaO_2 at altitude can be determined by applying the a/A O_2 ratio equation. Refer to Equation 24-3.

> **EQUATION 24-1: Predicting PaO$_2$ in the Supine and Seated Positions**
>
> $$\text{Predicted PaO}_2 \text{ (supine)} = 103.5 - (0.42 \times \text{age}) \pm 4$$
> $$\text{Predicted PaO}_2 \text{ (seated)} = 104.2 - (0.27 \times \text{age})$$
>
> **Example:** A 62-year-old patient is seen for his biannual outpatient clinic visit at San Diego Bay Community Hospital. Calculate his PaO$_2$ in both the supine and seated position.
>
> $$\begin{aligned}\text{Predicted PaO}_2 \text{ (supine)} &= 103.5 - (0.42 \times 62) \pm 4 \\ &= 103.5 - 26.04 \pm 4 \\ &= 77.46 \pm 4 \\ &= 77 \pm 4 \text{ mmHg}\end{aligned}$$
>
> $$\begin{aligned}\text{Predicted PaO}_2 \text{ (seated)} &= 104.2 - (0.27 \times 62) \\ &= 104.2 - 16.74 \\ &= 87.46 \\ &= 87 \text{ mmHg}\end{aligned}$$
>
> The PaO$_2$ might normally be as low as 73 mmHg when the patient is lying down and as high as 87 mmHg when sitting. These equations then yield a predicted normal range of PaO$_2$ for this 62-year-old patient at sea level of 73–87 mmHg.

7. Predicting the required FIO$_2$ in stable patients is demonstrated in Equation 24-4.
    a. The A-a DO$_2$ has been clinically popular for many years as a trend indicator for severity of lung dysfunction. Problems with using A-a DO$_2$ as a predictor include:
        (1) The A-a DO$_2$ changes with any change in FIO$_2$ as a function of the shape of the oxyhemoglobin dissociation curve.
        (2) As the FIO$_2$ increases, so does the A-a DO$_2$.
        (3) As the FIO$_2$ decreases, so does the A-a DO$_2$.
    b. Applying the a/A ratio as a predictor
        (1) The patient must be stable in the following areas:
            (a) Cardiovascular dynamics
            (b) $\dot{V}/\dot{Q}$ match up (the patient must be kept in the same position)

Chapter 24: Achieving Adequate Oxygenation

EQUATION 24-2: Determining a/A Ratio

$$\text{a/A ratio} = \frac{\text{measured } PaO_2{}^*}{\text{calculated } PAO_2}$$

Example: An ICU patient at San Diego Bay Community Hospital** has had one blood gas analysis and is hypoxemic with a PaO_2 of 50 mmHg on 40% oxygen. His $PaCO_2$ is 40 mmHg. Compute the a/A O_2 ratio from this initial blood gas data.

Step 1: Compute the PAO_2 (refer to Equation 4-2)

$$PAO_2 = FIO_2\,(P_B - P_{H_2O}) - PaCO_2 \times 1.25$$
$$= 0.4(760 - 47) - 40 \times 1.25$$
$$= 0.4(713) - 50$$
$$= 285.2 - 50$$
$$= 235.2 \text{ or } 235 \text{ mmHg}$$

Step 2: Compute the a/A ratio

$$\text{a/A ratio} = \frac{50}{235} = 0.2127$$

Note: The a/A ratio is a more stable value when FIO_2 is changed, making it useful for (1) comparing gas exchange in patients receiving different levels of FIO_2, (2) following gas exchange in the same patient as FIO_2 is changed, (3) calculating PaO_2 expected at a given FIO_2 from blood gas data for different FIO_2, and (4) predicting the PaO_2 following changes in altitude.

*The predicted PaO_2 may also be inserted here as determined in Equation 24-1.
**P_B at sea level is 760 mmHg.

- (c) Respiratory quotient (the CO_2 production and oxygen uptake must remain stable)
- (2) The a/A ratio is most accurate when the FIO_2 is between 0.3 and 0.7 and the PaO_2 is less than 100 mmHg.
8. Adjusting FIO_2 in unstable patients is a guess at best, but there are standard approaches that have been used clinically for many years. The following is recorded in one well-known source.[3]
   - a. Initiate ventilation with an FIO_2 of 1.0. Wait the customary 20 minutes for blood gas stability, and then draw and measure blood gases.

> **EQUATION 24-3: Predicting the PaO$_2$ Following Changes in Altitude**
>
> $$\text{PaO}_2 \text{ (new)} = \text{PAO}_2 \text{ (new)} \times \text{a/A ratio (old)}$$
>
> **Example:** The 62-year-old outpatient presented in Equation 24-1 desires to travel to Denver to visit some friends. His room air blood gases are as follows: PaO$_2$ is 87 mmHg, PaCO$_2$ is 40 mmHg. Predict his PaO$_2$ in Denver (P$_B$ at 5000 feet is 632 mmHg).
>
> **Step 1:** Determine PAO$_2$ at sea level.
>
> $$\text{PAO}_2 \text{ (old)} = \text{FIO}_2 (P_B - P_{H_2O}) - \text{PaCO}_2 \times 1.25$$
> $$= 0.21(760 - 47) - 40 \times 1.25$$
> $$= 99.7 \text{ or } 100 \text{ mmHg}$$
>
> **Step 2:** Determine the a/A ratio at sea level.
>
> $$\text{a/A ratio (old)} = \text{PaO}_2/\text{PAO}_2$$
> $$= 87/100 \text{ or } 0.87$$
>
> **Step 3:** Determine PAO$_2$ at 5000 feet.
>
> $$\text{PAO}_2 \text{ (new)} = 0.21(632 - 47) - 40 \times 1.25$$
> $$= 72.9 \text{ or } 73 \text{ mmHg}$$
>
> **Step 4:** Predict PaO$_2$ at 5000 feet.
>
> $$\text{PaO}_2 \text{ (new)} = 73 \text{ mmHg} \times 0.87$$
> $$= 63.5 \text{ or } 64 \text{ mmHg}$$

    b. Adjust the FIO$_2$ according to the following rules.
       (1) If the PaO$_2$ is greater than 300 mmHg, then decrease the FIO$_2$ in increments of 0.20.
       (2) If the PaO$_2$ is 150–300 mmHg, then decrease the FIO$_2$ in increments of 0.10.
       (3) If the PaO$_2$ is 100–150 mmHg, then decrease the FIO$_2$ in increments of 0.05.
    c. Recheck the PaO$_2$ a minimum of 20 minutes after each step change.
    d. If the patient is very unstable, with fluctuating blood pressure and pulse, it is advisable to NOT adjust FIO$_2$ until better clinical stability is achieved. In the

Chapter 24: Achieving Adequate Oxygenation

EQUATION 24-4: Predicting Required FIO_2 in Stable Patients

$$FIO_2 \text{ (required)}* = \frac{PAO_2** + PaCO_2 \times 1.25}{P_B - P_{H_2O}}$$

Example: Utilizing the data regarding the ICU patient discussed in Equation 24-2, determine the required FIO_2 in order to bring the PaO_2 up to 70 mmHg.

Step 1: Compute the current PAO_2.

$$PAO_2 = FIO_2 (P_B - P_{H_2O}) - PaCO_2 \times 1.25 = 235 \text{ mmHg}$$

Step 2: Determine the a/A O_2 ratio.

$$\text{a/A ratio} = \text{measured } PaO_2/\text{calculated } PAO_2$$

$$50/235 = 0.2127$$

Step 3: Compute the required PAO_2.

$$PAO_2 \text{ (required)} = \frac{\text{Desired } PaO_2}{\text{a/A ratio}}$$

$$= 70 \text{ mmHg}/0.2127$$

$$= 329.1 \text{ or } 329 \text{ mmHg}$$

Step 4: Determine the required FIO_2 to increase PaO_2.

$$FIO_2 = \frac{329 + (40 \times 1.25)}{760 - 47}$$

$$= \frac{329 + 50}{713} = \frac{379}{713} = 0.53$$

Therefore, in this generally stable patient, by increasing the FIO_2 from 0.40 to 0.53, the PaO_2 should rise from 50 to 70 mmHg.
*This a rearrangement of Equation 4-2 to solve for FIO_2.
**The new required PAO_2 necessary for the new desired PaO_2.

---

very unstable patient, it may be best to go to an FIO_2 of 1.0 until further improvement is noted and then decrease gradually.
- B. Complications of oxygen therapy[4]
    1. Oxygen-induced hypoventilation
    2. Absorption atelectasis

3. Oxygen toxicity
    a. Inhibition of tissue cultures
    b. Inactivation of enzymes
    c. Damage to capillaries and pneumocytes
    d. Reduced mucociliary action
    e. Interference with pulmonary surfactant
    f. Reduction of alveolar macrophage activity
        (1) Random migration is inhibited at an FIO_2 of 0.6.
        (2) Phagocytic activity is inhibited at an FIO_2 of 1.0.
    g. Oxygen pneumonia
    h. Bronchopulmonary dysplasia
    i. Alteration of lung repair capabilities
    j. Retrolental fibroplasia
C. Oxygen combined with helium[4]
    1. When mixed with oxygen, helium-oxygen (HeO_2), acts as a transport agent to carry oxygen more easily through obstructed airways. This occurs secondary to the low density of helium. Helium reduces the pressure needed to move air in and out of areas where turbulent flow is present, especially the large airways.
        a. These mixtures are most useful when used in patients with status asthmaticus or other forms of severely increased airway resistance. With less pressure required to move air, the patient's work of breathing is substantially reduced.
        b. Therapeutic concentrations are either comprised of 80% helium and 20% O_2, or 70% He and 30% O_2. Oxygen must be combined with helium because the gas is inert and cannot support life.
        c. Helium mixtures should always be given with a tightly sealed system because the high diffusibility of helium will allow it to readily escape.
            (1) Cannulas, catheters, or tents are not satisfactory.
            (2) Tightly fitting nonrebreathing masks, or cuffed airways are most suitable. The gas mixture can also be given via positive pressure ventilator.
            (3) Standard oxygen flowmeters will not be accurate in the presence of such a low density gas. Refer to Equation 14–6.
        d. Because helium possesses such low gas density, it is a poor medium in which to attempt to administer therapeutic aerosols.
D. Oxygen combined with carbon dioxide[4]
    1. A mixture of 95% oxygen-5% carbon dioxide or 93% oxygen-7% carbon dioxide can be used.
    2. Indications for use
        a. Improvement of cerebral blood flow is sometimes desirable in dilation of the vessels of the eye when thromboses have impaired the blood flow.

Chapter 24: Achieving Adequate Oxygenation 431

      b. In overcoming hypoventilation, it can be used for stimulation of deep breathing in aged and debilitated patients, although more current methods are considered safer.
      c. Prevention of postoperative atelectasis is possible but better techniques are now available, such as incentive spirometry.
      d. To assist coughing the increased respiratory activity caused by the carbon dioxide stimulation of respiration can also stimulate increased cough in the presence of retained secretions. Present methods are safer.
      e. With singulation (hiccup), O_2/CO_2 therapy may be very successful in this case secondary to strong stimulation of central respiratory discharge that will override the spasmodic diaphragm.
  3. Potential side effects include headache, dizziness, drop in blood pressure, dyspnea, nasal irritation, palpitation, dimming of vision, muscle tremor, paresthesia, sensation of cold, and/or mental depression.
  4. Toxicity is indicated by the presence of severe dyspnea, nausea, vomiting, disorientation, and blood pressure elevation.

III. Continuous positive airway pressure (CPAP) by mask[8]

A. CPAP masks should possess the following qualities.
  1. Transparency allows monitoring of the oral airway for the presence of secretions or vomitus.
  2. Light weight to aid in the ease of application.
  3. Soft and pliable material with an adjustable seal reduces facial trauma and provides for a comfortable fit. It has been suggested that a water-soluble jelly be used on the inner side of the mask to give a good seal.
  4. An effective seal does not require a tight seal. An effective seal is achieved using a standard four-tailed anesthesia head strap. Leaks are okay as long as the pressure in the system is maintained.

B. Choice of circuitry
  1. Valve design can reduce the work of breathing and maintain constant pressures regardless of changes in expiratory flow; a threshold resistor is the CPAP valve of choice.
      a. The threshold resistor provides variable resistance to gas flow.
      b. $P = (R)(F)$, where the pressure in the CPAP circuit will be equal to resistance (R) times flow (F).
      c. If flow increases because of cough or forced exhalation, the resistance can decrease, thus keeping pressure constant.
      d. The Emerson water column PEEP valve is the most stable of available threshold resistors. Any mask device containing a spring-loaded valve may behave as a threshold resistor to a degree.

2. Adequate flow should be provided so that system pressure does not fluctuate more than 2 cmH$_2$O either direction from the set value. A flow setting of four times the initial minute volume of the patient is usually sufficient.
3. A five-liter elastic reservoir bag provides additional gas volume to meet changing inspired volume needs.
4. A high-low pressure alarm with pressure manometer lines should be placed in the circuit as close to the patient as possible.

C. Nasogastric tubes are recommended as a routine part of mask CPAP by some, but are probably not needed if CPAP values are less than 10 cmH$_2$O.

D. Goals of mask CPAP are similar to the general goals for any PEEP/CPAP therapy.
1. Increase the functional residual capacity, resulting in an increased pulmonary compliance, decreased work of breathing, and increased oxygen uptake.
2. Decrease the intrapulmonary shunt, resulting in an increased PaO$_2$.
3. Avoid tracheal intubation and mechanical ventilation.

E. Indications for mask CPAP
1. Patient criteria include:
    a. The patient should be breathing spontaneously.
    b. The patient should be able to adequately protect their airway by having functional airway reflexes.
    c. The patient's PaCO$_2$ should be normal or may be low secondary to hypoxemia.
    d. There should be a functioning nasogastric tube inserted for any pressures used greater than 10 cmH$_2$O.
2. Physiologic criteria
    a. PaO$_2$/FIO$_2$ ratio of less than 250 or shunt fraction of greater than 15%
    b. An A-a DO$_2$ of greater than 400 mmHg, or an a/A ratio of less than 0.4.
3. Pathologic criteria
    a. Acute respiratory failure—continuous application should be used.
    b. Pulmonary contusion and flail chest—continuous application should be used.
    c. Cardiogenic pulmonary edema—continuous application should be used.
    d. Asthma and COPD—continuous application of low levels (4–9 cmH$_2$O) should be used.
    e. Postoperative atelectasis—intermittent application for a period of 10–12 hours may be used. Intermittent application may, however, allow recollapse following removal of the therapy. Assessment of clinical indicators of decreasing lung compliance will be useful to dictate the need for continuous versus intermittent application.

F. Potential complications of mask CPAP
1. Aerophagia, gastric distention, which is avoidable with the use of a nasogastric tube
2. Aspiration of gastric contents, which is avoidable with a functioning nasogastric tube
3. Decreased cardiac output

Chapter 24: Achieving Adequate Oxygenation 433

4. Pulmonary barotrauma
5. Hypoventilation, CO_2 retention secondary to decreased pulmonary compliance and altered pulmonary perfusion (as a result of excessive CPAP pressures)
6. Facial skin erosion and/or erythema with patient discomfort

IV. PEEP or CPAP in adults during mechanical ventilation

A. Positive effects of PEEP or CPAP[4]
  1. The primary physical change seen with PEEP is an enlargement of the functional residual capacity (FRC) secondary to two factors:
     a. Increased alveolar volumes when alveoli are already patent
        (1) Volumes increase linearly from 1–10 cmH_2O pressure PEEP.
        (2) Alveolar diameters at end-expiration, increase more than end-inspiratory diameters.
        (3) With the application of greater than 10 cmH_2O pressure PEEP, the response in alveolar diameter becomes less linear and plateaus at a pressure of 15 cmH_2O.
        (4) At greater than 15 cmH_2O, alveolar pressure increases without a measurable increase in alveolar volume.
     b. The occurrence of alveolar recruitment (reexpansion of previously collapsed alveoli)
  2. Improvement of arterial oxygenation occurs secondary to:
     a. Increased surface area for diffusion through enlargement of already patent alveoli.
     b. A reduction of intrapulmonary right-to-left shunting through reexpansion of collapsed alveoli.
        (1) Dramatic improvement in PaO_2 may occur at PEEP levels above critical opening pressures, which is anywhere between 7–20 cmH_2O pressure.
        (2) Once collapsed alveoli are expanded, an FIO_2 of 0.4 or less will result in adequate PaO_2.
     c. A decreased airway closure at low lung volumes with PEEP levels of 5–10 cmH_2O pressure.
  3. Decrease in work of breathing
     a. If FRC can be increased toward normal, then the lung can function at a more advantageous point on the compliance curve.
     b. This improved compliance results in less energy being required to move the same tidal or minute volume.
  4. Improvement in $\dot{V}/\dot{Q}$ inequality secondary to:
     a. Increased alveolar volume and alveolar recruitment.
     b. Shifting of net pulmonary perfusion to the nongravity dependent lung, thus increasing blood flow to the well ventilated lung.

B. Suggested application of PEEP
 1. In therapeutic ranges (10–30 cmH$_2$O pressure) PEEP should be increased or decreased in 5 cmH$_2$O pressure increments.
 2. Adequate fluid status for the patient must be assured for proper ventricular filling when using PEEP.
 3. Evidence of decreased cardiac output (hypotension, decreased $P\bar{v}O_2$) requires that PEEP be adjusted downward.
 4. FIO$_2$ changes must be accomplished independently of PEEP changes.
 5. The optimal PEEP level for a given patient is achieved when the following criteria are met.
    a. Adequate arterial oxygenation is provided while acceptable cardiac output is maintained at an FIO$_2$ of 0.4 or less.
    b. Serial measurements of static effective compliance demonstrate increasing improvement of lung compliance when collapsed alveoli are being reexpanded.
       (1) Because PEEP can reduce cardiac output, static effective compliance correlates well with the "best PEEP" value only in those patients with excellent cardiovascular reserve who are able to maintain adequate cardiac output.
       (2) Because both chest wall and lung compliance are measured with this technique, chest wall compliance must remain stable for this value to accurately reflect changes in lung compliance.
       (3) Static effective compliance is most accurately measured as demonstrated in Equation 24-5.
    c. Measured $\dot{Q}s/\dot{Q}t$ decreases to 15%.
    d. $\dot{Q}s/\dot{Q}t$ increases from a previously lower level.
    e. V_D/V_T ratios increase from a previously lower level.
C. Classification and clinical approaches to the use of PEEP in ARDS
 1. Minimal PEEP: less than 10–15 cmH$_2$O
    a. The goal is to achieve a nontoxic level of FIO$_2$ (less than 0.4) while achieving adequate oxygenation (PaO$_2$ = 70, SaO$_2$ = 90%) without significant cardiovascular side effects.
    b. Vasopressors and/or transfusion are not usually needed when this level of pressure is applied.
    c. No beneficial effect on the course of ARDS is assumed at this level of pressure application.
 2. Moderate PEEP: 10–20 cmH$_2$O
    a. The goal is to improve O$_2$ transport as judged by the following criteria.
       (1) PaO$_2$/FIO$_2$ ratio of less than 200, while avoiding any harmful effects of PEEP
       (2) An intrapulmonary shunt fraction ($\dot{Q}s/\dot{Q}t$) of less than 20%, while avoiding any harmful effects of PEEP

Chapter 24: Achieving Adequate Oxygenation

EQUATION 24-5: Calculation of Static Effective Compliance

$$Cst = \frac{V_t - (C_{vent})(P_{pl} - PEEP)}{P_{pl} - PEEP}$$

where
- Cst = static effective compliance.
- Vt = tidal volume.
- $Cvent$ = the amount of gas that is compressed in the ventilator tubing circuit at end inspiration and does not enter the patient, expressed in ml/cmH$_2$O pressure.
- Ppl = plateau pressure, achieved by an inspiratory hold maneuver.
- $PEEP$ = positive-end expiratory pressure.

Example: A patient has a measured exhaled tidal volume of 500 ml, is on 10 cmH$_2$O PEEP, and has a plateau pressure of 32 cmH$_2$O. The gas compressibility factor for the ventilator tubing system is 4 ml/cmH$_2$O. Determine the static effective compliance.

$$Cst = \frac{500 - (4)(32 - 10)}{32 - 10}$$

$$= \frac{500 - (4)(22)}{22}$$

$$= \frac{500 - 88}{22} = \frac{412}{22}$$

$$= 18.7 \text{ ml/cmH}_2\text{O}$$

    b. Vasopressors and/or transfusion are not usually needed with this level of pressure application.

    c. No beneficial effect on the outcome of ARDS is assumed at this level of pressure application.

3. Maximum PEEP: 25 to 40+ cmH$_2$O

    a. The goal is to "normalize" pulmonary function and reverse the pathophysiologic defect in ARDS by reducing the intrapulmonary shunt to less than 15%.

    b. Vasopressors and/or transfusion are needed at this level of pressure application in order to maintain cardiac output.

    c. A beneficial effect on the course of ARDS is assumed at this level of pressure application.

D. Clinical guidelines in PEEP reduction[6]
   1. Successful weaning from PEEP has been defined as PaO_2 remaining equal to or greater than 65 mmHg following a 5 cmH_2O reduction in pressure.
   2. A 90% success rate has been shown when using the following criteria.
      a. The patient is stable and nonseptic.
      b. FIO_2 is less than or equal to 0.4.
      c. PaO_2 is greater than 80 mmHg and has been stable or increased for greater than 12 hours.
      d. After a successful 3-minute trial of PEEP reduction has occurred, the following procedure is used.
         (1) PEEP is lowered by 5 cmH_2O for 3 minutes and then increased by 5 cmH_2O back to the previous baseline.
         (2) Arterial blood gas analysis is done just prior to the reduction of PEEP and again after 3 minutes, just prior to the return to the baseline PEEP value.
         (3) PaO_2 should fall less than 20% of the original value. A fall of 20% or more indicates the patient is not yet ready to be managed on reduced PEEP levels.
E. Adverse effects of raised intrathoracic pressure (includes mechanical tidal volumes, PEEP, or CPAP)[1]
   1. Decreased cardiac output from:
      a. Decreased right and left ventricular filling (preload)
      b. Increased right ventricular afterload, which may cause:
         (1) A shift of the intraventricular septum to the left, causing a reduction in left ventricular compliance.
         (2) Right ventricular dysfunction.
      c. High PEEP levels (greater than 15 cmH_2O pressure) may decrease endocardial blood flow and decrease ventricular function secondary to ischemia.
      d. It is believed that overstretching of the lung, as may occur with excessive pressure, causes release of chemicals from the lung, which have a vasodilating effect on the systemic vascular bed. The exact structure of these chemicals is unknown.
   2. Pulmonary barotrauma resulting in pneumothorax, pneumomediastinum, subcutaneous emphysema, pneumopericardium, and pneumoperitoneum
   3. Increased intracranial pressure
      a. It occurs in patients with decreased intracranial compliance secondary to head trauma.
      b. In some patients, this effect may be reduced by maintaining a 30 degree head-up angle.

4. Decreased urine output secondary to:
   a. Decreased renal blood flow
   b. Decreased glomerular flow rate
   c. Increased antidiuretic hormone secretion from:
      (1) Reduction of left atrial filling
      (2) Stimulation of left atrial pressure receptors
5. Increased extravascular lung water may occur. Present evidence indicates that when PEEP is applied, lung water either increases or remains the same.
   a. As PEEP increases, the relative size on zone "1" (high ventilation/low perfusion = high $\dot{V}/\dot{Q}$), fluid movement from extra-alveolar vessels increases, thus slowly increasing lung water.
   b. PEEP applied to lung zones "2" and "3" (the lower 2/3 of the lung) increases fluid movement into the pulmonary interstitial space from both intra- and extra-alveolar vessels.
   c. Fluid movement from pulmonary vessels into the interstitial space depends on:
      (1) Increased blood flow, which is enhanced by alveolar inflation that increases the distending forces on extra-alveolar vessels, causing increased blood flow.
      (2) Pleural pressure changes that influence both pulmonary vascular pressures and interstitial pressure.

V. Application of PEEP or CPAP in Infants[7]

A. Application
   1. In intubated infants with normal lungs, PEEP should be started at 2–3 cmH$_2$O.
   2. In intubated infants with RDS, PEEP should be started at 4–5 cmH$_2$O.
   3. In gas-trapping syndromes (meconium) PEEP should be kept to a minimum.
B. Pulmonary effects
   1. Increased functional residual capacity is achieved through an increase in alveolar size.
   2. Increased PaO$_2$ results from a decrease in physiological shunting as noted by decreased atelectasis and fluid redistribution within the lung.
   3. Increased lung compliance
      a. Dynamic compliance in infants with respiratory distress syndrome (IRDS) or after cardiac surgery, the value is 0.5–0.8 ml/cmH$_2$O pressure and remains unchanged for several days.
      b. Static compliance is in the low normal range initially and increases daily thereafter.

c. The differences in improvement between dynamic and static compliance are due to differences in time constants in various parts of the lung. It allows for volume and pressure equilibrium during inspiration in some parts of the lung, while not in others. Static lung compliance shows improvement, because it is measured after all areas have come to equilibrium. Dynamic compliance, in spite of improvement in $\dot{V}/\dot{Q}$, is still low even when CPAP is being reduced on clinical grounds.
4. Esophageal pressure (pleural pressure)
   a. These changes normally occur with spontaneous respiration, but the pressure swings are greater with increased effort secondary to respiratory distress. CPAP reduces the magnitude of the pressure swings because it reduces airway resistance and therefore the respiratory effort necessary to exchange adequate volume.
   b. Only 25–75% of the applied pressure is transmitted to the esophagus during treatment of hyaline membrane disease, with the remainder being dissipated in the airways and lung.
   c. As lung compliance improves, approximately 90% of the applied pressure is transmitted to the esophagus.
5. Respiratory rate
   a. The rate in infants with hyaline membrane disease is initially between 60–100 per minute and is significantly reduced by CPAP.
   b. Respiratory work is usually 2–4 times normal in infants with respiratory distress syndrome, and the combination of decreased rate and pleural pressure swings reduces respiratory work.
   c. The respiratory rate decreases to a normal level of about 40/minute after 2–4 days despite a continuous need for CPAP.

C. Effects of CPAP on other organ systems
 1. Cardiovascular
    a. $P\bar{v}O_2$ and metabolic acidosis are unchanged or decreased when the lowest CPAP value possible is used to increase PaO_2 above 50 mmHg.
    b. A reduction in peripheral blood flow may be expected if CPAP decreases cardiac output.
    c. CPAP reduces peripheral pulses blood flow and blood pressure if blood volume is inadequate.
 2. Cerebral blood flow
    a. Blood flow from any cerebral vein to the right atrium is determined by the pressure gradient between the two points. Elevating intrathoracic pressure will decrease this gradient, and therefore blood flow.
    b. The following clinical observations support the contention that the veins and capillaries of newborn brain tend to expand and are prone to rupture when overdistended.

(1) Superior vena cava obstruction in infants is associated with dramatic increases in head circumference, but little or no change in ventricular volume.

(2) Increased sagittal sinus pressure, with inadvertent jugular venous obstruction, during CPAP results in cerebral venous hypertension, which is associated with a high incidence of intracranial bleeding and post hemorrhagic hydrocephalus.

(3) Development of tension pneumothoraces in infants receiving assisted ventilation are often associated with increases in head circumference and fontanel pressure.

c. CPAP will decrease venous return from the head in proportion to the amount of pressure transmitted to the pleural space. Continual pleural or esophageal pressure monitoring is recommended to guide the optimal use of CPAP.

References

1. Burton, G. G., Hodgkin, J. E., and Ward, J. J., *Respiratory Care: A Guide to Clinical Practice, 4th ed.*, Lippincott, 1997.

2. Demers, R., "Down With The Good Lung (Usually)," *Respiratory Care* 32, no. 10, October 1987.

3. Avery, G., *Neonatology, 3rd ed.*, Lippincott Raven, 1987.

4. Scanlon, C. L., Wilkins, R. L., and Stoller, J. K., *Egan's Fundamentals of Respiratory Therapy, 7th ed.*, Mosby, 1999.

5. Pilbeam, S. P., *Mechanical Ventilation Physiological and Clinical Applications, 3rd ed.*, Mosby, 1998.

6. Craig, K. C., et al., "The Clinical Application of Positive End-Expiratory Pressure (PEEP) in the Adult Respiratory Distress Syndrome (ARDS)," *Respiratory Care* 30 no. 3, March 1985.

7. Klaus, M. and Fanaroff, A., *Care of the High-Risk Neonate, 4th ed.*, W. B. Saunders, 1993.

8. Alone, C. A., and Hill, T. A., *Respiratory Care of the Newborn and Child, 2nd ed.*, Lippincott, 1997.

Assessment Questions

1. When administering oxygen to a neonate, disadvantages of nasal prongs include:

   I. Gastric distension
   II. Prong obstruction
   III. Easy dislodgment

   A. I only
   B. II only
   C. I and II only
   D. I, II and III

2. Helium/oxygen mixtures are indicated:

   A. In patients prone to air trapping
   B. In patients with increased work of breathing

C. When aerosol administration is needed
D. For management of an acute restrictive disorder

3. Calculate the A/a gradient for a patient with the following values:

   Pb: 735 mmHg
   $PaCO_2$: 44 mmHg
   PaO_2: 222 mmHg
   FIO_2: 0.45

   A. 254 mmHg
   B. 212 mmHg
   C. 106 mmHg
   D. 32 mmHg

4. A patient with severe hiccups secondary to a sarcoma applying pressure to the central nervous system arrives on your service. To cure the hiccups you would:

   A. Administer 100% oxygen
   B. Administer 2% lidocaine with epinephrine by aerosol
   C. Administer a 80% helium, 20% oxygen mixture
   D. Administer a 95% oxygen, 5% carbon dioxide mixture

5. The term "Ideal PEEP" would occur with:

   I. PaO_2 increases
   II. % shunt decreases
   III. Pulmonary compliance increases
   IV. Pulmonary vascular resistance decreases

   A. I only
   B. I and II only
   C. I, II and III only
   D. I, II, III and IV

6. Complications associated with PEEP therapy include:

   I. Barotrauma
   II. Decreased venous return
   III. Decreased cardiac output
   IV. Increased intercranial pressure

   A. I only
   B. I and II only
   C. I, II and III only
   D. I, II, III and IV

7. Determine the static effective compliance for a patient with the following values:

   Exhaled tidal volume: 0.5 L
   PEEP: 10 cmH_2O
   Plateau pressure: 23 cmH_2O
   Tubing compressible factor: 4 ml/cmH_2O

   A. 32 cmH_2O
   B. 22 cmH_2O
   C. 19 cmH_2O
   D. 13 cmH_2O

8. Which of the following clinical disorders would benefit from PEEP/CPAP therapy?

   I. Diffuse, bilateral pneumonia
   II. IRDS
   III. ARDS
   IV. Cardiogenic pulmonary edema

   A. I only
   B. I and II only
   C. I, II and III only
   D. I, II, III and IV

9. One of the main mechanisms by which PEEP helps reduce physiological shunting and improve oxygenation is by:

   A. Increasing lung compliance
   B. Increasing tissue perfusion
   C. Recruiting collapsed alveoli
   D. Decreasing airway resistance

Chapter 25

Cardiovascular Monitoring

I. Measurement of cardiac output[1]

A. Dye-dilution cardiac output
 1. The patient must have a catheter placed in a central vein or the pulmonary artery for injection of the dye sample.
 2. An arterial line must be inserted for withdrawal of a blood sample following dye injection.
 3. A bolus of dye (usually 5 ml of cardiogreen) is injected through the venous line.
 4. Arterial blood is withdrawn at a steady rate (usually 10 ml/minute) during dye injection.
    a. The blood is withdrawn through a densitometer cuvette by a syringe withdrawal pump.
    b. The densitometer sends a light beam through the blood to a photocell in the cuvette.
 5. When the bolus of dye crosses the light source, the amount of light that can pass through the blood decreases, and a curve is printed out or appears on the cardiac output computer screen.
    a. As the concentration of dye in the blood increases, the light transmission decreases and the curve rises.
    b. When the concentration of dye decreases, the curve falls.
 6. Cardiac output is inversely proportional to the area under the printed curve.
 7. The measurement should be repeated a total of three times with each measurement within 5% of the others.
 8. The cardiac output should be recorded as the average of the set of three.

B. Thermodilution cardiac output
 1. This technique requires the placement of a thermodilution pulmonary artery catheter and the appropriate thermodilution cardiac output computer for the

catheter used. A thermistor is attached to the catheter to measure fluid temperature and provide continuous monitoring of pulmonary artery blood temperature (core temperature).
2. A bolus of iced or room temperature sterile dextrose in water or normal saline (at least 2° centigrade cooler than blood temperature) is injected into the proximal port (right atrial) of the pulmonary artery catheter.
3. The cool injectate causes a decrease in PA blood temperature and is detected by a thermistor bead just behind the balloon of the catheter in the pulmonary artery.
4. A temperature-time curve is then recorded by the computer.
   a. When the blood flow is moving rapidly, the PA blood temperature quickly returns to baseline.
   b. Slow blood flow makes the PA blood temperature take more time to return to baseline.
5. Thermodilution cardiac output measurement can be done as frequently as every 60 seconds because the blood rewarms in one pass through the circulatory system.
6. Measurement should be repeated a total of three times with each measurement within 5% of the others.
7. The cardiac output recorded should be the mean of three individual measurements.

C. Cardiac index (CI) is a calculated value that compares the oxygen demands of different-sized people. This calculation indexes the cardiac output to the individual's body surface area (BSA), and eliminates the effect of body build.[2]
1. Normal CI values range from 2.4–4.2 liters/minute/m^2, and verifies that they are receiving all the blood and oxygen they need to meet the body's metabolic demands.
2. A CI less than 2.4 indicates that they are not receiving all the blood and oxygen they need to meet the body's metabolic demands.
3. A CI of greater than 4.2 liters indicates they are pumping much more blood than they need to meet the body's metabolic demands.
4. Diuresis and third-space shifting are capable of changing weight dramatically on a day-to-day basis, which will impair accuracy of the value since BSA is derived from a nomogram.

II. Measurement of vascular pressures[1]

A. Central venous pressure (CVP) is a numerical value that represents right atrial pressure or right ventricular filling pressure. This numerical value is affected by cardiac performance, blood volume, vasopressor therapy, vascular tone, and increased intrathoracic pressure.

1. Water manometer method
    a. The manometer is filled with IV fluid to a pressure value above the expected CVP value.
        (1) With the patient supine, the zero level of the manometer is placed at the level of the patient's right atrium, and the manometer is opened to the patient's venous pressure.
        (2) The fluid level in the manometer should fall rapidly until the patient's CVP is reached, and then should oscillate with respirations.
        (3) The pressure should be read at the end of expiration, because that is the point at which lung volumes most closely approximate FRC.
            (a) Spontaneous inspiration causes the pressure to fall.
            (b) Mechanical ventilation causes the pressure to rise.
        (4) Criteria for interpretation of CVP by water manometer measurement include:
            (a) X-ray verification that the tip of the catheter is in the central vein.
            (b) Free-flowing IV fluid.
            (c) Easy aspiration of a blood sample from the CVP catheter.
            (d) A rapidly falling water column when the pressure is measured.
            (e) Small oscillations at the top of the water column, indicating changes in CVP throughout a cardiac cycle.
            (f) Larger oscillations occur with respiration.
        (5) Water manometer measurements usually overestimate transducer-determined mean right atrial pressure.
    2. With the transducer method, careful attention to technique must be given before a pressure reading is taken, including the following:
        a. The catheter must be patent.
        b. The waveform seen on the oscilloscope display must be clear and nondamped.
        c. The patient must be in the supine position.
        d. The transducer must be zero balanced at the level of the patient's right atrium.
        e. The pressure must be recorded at end-expiration, as the numerical value is least affected by the transmitted pleural pressure.
B. Pulmonary artery and capillary wedge pressures
    1. Placement of a pulmonary artery catheter is indicated for the following reasons:
        a. Measurement of left ventricular preload through monitoring pulmonary artery diastolic pressure and pulmonary capillary wedge pressure.
        b. Monitoring of pulmonary vascular resistance by continuous measurement of pulmonary artery systolic pressure and mean pulmonary artery pressure.
        c. Monitoring of cardiac output by either thermodilution of dye-dilution methods.

d. Measurement of the arteriovenous oxygen difference.
e. Measurement of right ventricular preload by monitoring right atrial pressure.
2. Placement of the pulmonary artery catheter
    a. The catheter may be placed using fluoroscopy, but is most often placed by "floating" the catheter with the balloon inflated.
        (1) The catheter is introduced into a central vessel such as the internal or external jugular or subclavian veins.
        (2) The balloon is inflated when the tip of the catheter is in the right atrium and the force of the blood flow carries the catheter through into the right ventricle, out of the ventricle through the pulmonary valve, and on into the pulmonary artery.
        (3) The location of the catheter tip is judged by reading the pressure waveform that is transmitted through the catheter back to the transducer and monitoring unit.
        (4) The catheter is connected by plastic tubing to a pressurized bag to maintain positive fluid pressure, and then to a transducer that converts the fluid pressure to an electrical signal
        (5) Insertion is particularly difficult in patients with chronic pulmonary disease and altered pulmonary circulation.
        (6) The catheter may fail to "float" into position.
        (7) In most adults, for catheters inserted into the subclavian or jugular veins, the tip of the catheter is in the pulmonary artery when 50 cm of catheter have been advanced beyond the skin surface.
            (a) When more than 50 cm of catheter have been inserted into the patient and no pulmonary artery waveform can be seen, it is assumed that the catheter has become kinked or curled up inside the atrium or ventricle.
            (b) The catheter is withdrawn until the tip is in the atrium (demonstrated by a venous pressure value and waveform) and is then reinserted.
    b. "Wedging" the catheter
        (1) When the catheter reaches a "wedged" position in the pulmonary circulation by reaching an arterial branch too small to allow further progress, the arterial blood flow becomes occluded and the monitoring waveform appears similar to the venous waveform with left atrial pressure values.
        (2) When the balloon is deflated, the pulmonary artery waveform should return.
        (3) Thereafter, the balloon is wedged by inserting 1.25–1.5 ml of air to obtain a "wedged" pressure tracing. Should a pressure tracing be obtained with less than 1 ml of air, the assumption is that the catheter tip has slipped too far into the periphery of the pulmonary circulation and needs to be pulled back.

(4) The balloon is left inflated only long enough to obtain the pressure tracing and value, and is then allowed to empty to room pressure, without aspirating the air out of the balloon.
(5) Overinflation of the balloon will result in distortion of the pressure waveform.
(6) The exact position of the catheter tip in the pulmonary circulation must be verified by chest X-ray.
   (a) With the patient in the supine position, the tip of the catheter should be in the lower one-third of the lung at about the level of the left atrium.
   (b) If the catheter tip is located in the upper half of the lung, pulmonary circulation downstream from the tip will be collapsed, and wedge pressure readings will be inaccurate.
   (c) Improperly placed catheters must be withdrawn and reinserted.
(7) PEEP increases intrathoracic pressure and artifactually raises the vascular pressure measured by the catheter. The artifact does not become clinically important unless the PEEP is >10 cmH_2O.

c. Mixed venous sampling is guaranteed because the device allows sampling of blood from the distal tip of the catheter.
   (1) The sample is a mixture of blood from all the systemic veins prior to it entering the pulmonary capillaries.
   (2) Blood is sampled with the balloon deflated, and aspirated at a rate of less that 3 ml/min.
   (3) False PaO_2 values can arise from blood aspirated faster than 3 ml/min., as the blood will come from the pulmonary capillary, thus giving a false reading.

C. Systemic arterial pressure
   1. The radial artery is most frequently used for measuring arterial pressure with a catheter because there is excellent collateral circulation for the hand through the ulnar artery, and the site provides for easy maintenance and access. Alternative sites include brachial, axillary, femoral, and dorsalis pedis arteries. The umbilical artery is commonly used in the newborn.
   2. Indications
      a. To avoid multiple arterial punctures for blood gases.
      b. Continuous arterial pressure monitoring.
      c. Determination of cardiac output by the dye-dilution method.
   3. Normally a 5–20 mmHg systolic pressure difference is found between invasively monitored arterial pressure and pressure measured via a standard blood pressure cuff.
      a. This difference is acceptable as long as the systolic pressure via the catheter is the higher value.

b. If cuff measured pressure is higher, the patient's position in relation to the transducer level should be checked.
   (1) If the vent port of the transducer is above the patient's right atrial level, the weight of the water in the tubing will pull away from the transducer and decrease the pressure.
   (2) By moving the transducer up and down while the patient stays in one place, the numbers can be made to change values.

III. Hemodynamic changes with altered cardiac output[3]

A. Changes in vascular volume or "preload" (the amount of filling or stretch of the myocardial muscle prior to ventricular contraction) are indicated by the following pressures:
   1. Right heart
      a. Right atrial pressure (RAP)
      b. Central venous pressure (CVP)
   2. Left heart
      a. Left atrial pressure (LAP)
      b. Pulmonary artery diastolic pressure (PADP)
      c. Pulmonary capillary wedge pressure (PCWP)
B. Causes of altered "preload" can be divided into two categories: those that cause pressures to rise, and those that cause pressures to fall.
   1. Causes of low preload pressures include:
      a. Not enough vascular volume
      b. Decreased systemic vascular resistance from:
         (1) Drugs
         (2) Spinal anesthesia
         (3) Fever
         (4) Sepsis
      c. Systemic vascular resistance may increase to maintain MAP and cardiac output if significant hypovolemia has developed.
   2. Causes of high preload pressures are determined by interpretation of both right and left heart preload pressures. In general, high preload pressures are caused by an inadequate myocardial pump, or too much vascular volume.
      a. The combination of increased CVP and increased LAP may be caused by the following:
         (1) Cardiac failure
         (2) Cardiac tamponade

Chapter 25: Cardiovascular Monitoring 447

   b. The combination of decreased CVP and increased LAP may be caused by the following:
      (1) Left heart failure
      (2) Intra-operative myocardial infarction
      (3) Left heart valve malfunction
   c. The combination of increased CVP and decreased LAP may be caused by the following:
      (1) Right heart failure
      (2) Right heart valve malfunction
      (3) Pulmonary embolism
C. Treatment of altered preload
   1. The following interventions are used when low preload pressures are found.
      a. Not enough volume—give volume in the form of IV fluids, blood, or albumin.
      b. Decreased systemic vascular resistance
         (1) Stop vasodilators.
         (2) Give volume.
         (3) Give vasoconstrictors.
      c. Increased systemic vascular resistance
         (1) Give volume.
         (2) If resistance does not decrease, use vasodilators and additional volume.
   2. The following interventions are used when high preload pressures are found:
      a. When both the CVP and LAP are increased:
         (1) The patient is in cardiac failure—give inotropes and diuretics.
         (2) When cardiac tamponade is the cause—give volume and isoproterenol until correction of the tamponade is made.
      b. When the CVP is decreased, but the LAP is increased, give inotropes and vasodilate to decrease systemic vascular resistance.
      c. When the CVP is increased and the LAP is decreased, do the following:
         (1) Right valve failure/valve malfunction—give inotropic agents.
         (2) If pulmonary embolism is the suspected cause, heparin, inotropes, vasopressors, and surgery may all be indicated.
D. Adequate pump effectiveness or contractility of the myocardium is indicated when the following clinical values exist:
   1. Mean arterial pressure (MAP) of 70–100 mmHg.
   2. Diastolic pressure of 60 mmHg.
   3. Cardiac index (CI) of 2.5–4.0 L/min/M^2.
   4. Systemic vascular resistance and preload pressures within the normal ranges.

E. Causes of decreased contractility
   1. Decreased volume is the most important determinant of contractility.
      a. Circulating blood volume may be reduced secondary to fluid loss, and indicated by low preload pressure (CVP).
      b. Venous return may be poor because of dilation of arterial and venous vessels, which then may result in hypotension.
      c. Venous return may be poor because of the application of positive pressure in the thorax, increased right atrial pressure, and a decreased pressure gradient for blood return to the thorax.
   2. Inadequate coronary perfusion occurs with an inadequate diastolic pressure, myocardial infarction and/or ischemia, aneurysm, congenital defects, or surgery.
   3. Heart rate is less than 60 or greater than 110.
   4. Atrial and ventricular arrhythmias.
   5. Drugs: beta blockers (Inderal), antiarrhythmic agents, barbiturates.
   6. Increased systemic vascular resistance.
   7. Altered blood chemistries including decreased PaO_2, pH, K+, Ca++, or increased $PaCO_2$.

F. Treatment of decreased contractility
   1. When the cause is decreased volume, administer volume until adequate pump effectiveness is achieved. In some failing hearts, the LAP must be maintained at 15–18 mmHg or higher in order to maintain adequate contractility.
   2. When there is inadequate coronary perfusion:
      a. Maintain the mean arterial pressure at greater than 60 mmHg.
      b. Maintain the arterial diastolic pressure at greater than 50 mmHg.
      c. When volume is adequate, inotropic drugs are used to support the weakened myocardium.
         (1) Driving the heart with inotropes when volume is inadequate causes myocardial infarction.
         (2) Low dose inotropic support may be used continuously for 24–48 hours postsurgery to support a weakened myocardium.
   3. When alterations in pulse rate cause decreased contractility, the following interventions are used:
      a. When the heart rate is less than 60/min:
         (1) Administer Isuprel and watch for a decrease in systemic vascular resistance from the B_2 effect.
         (2) A pacemaker may be necessary for stimulation of atrial contraction as cardiac output will decrease from loss of "atrial kick."

Chapter 25: Cardiovascular Monitoring 449

      b. When the heart rate is greater than 110:
- (1) Make sure that vascular volume is adequate because the tachycardia may be compensatory.
- (2) Administer adequate pain medication.
- (3) Administer digitalis.
- (4) Administer Inderal.

4. When ventricular arrhythmias are the cause of decreased contractility they should be controlled with lidocaine.
5. When drug therapy is the cause of decreased contractility, inotropes should be administered to counteract the depressant effects.
6. When systemic vascular resistance is too high and is causing a decrease in contractility, due to extreme workloads on the left ventricle, the following interventions are needed.
   a. Administer vasodilators and also volume if necessary.
   b. Administer inotropic agents.
7. When blood chemistries are altered and appear to be a cause of decreased contractility, the oxygen deficit, electrolytes, and acid-base balance should all be corrected.

G. Afterload (resistance the ventricles have to pump against) can be determined individually for the right and left ventricles. Refer to Equations 25-1 and 25-2.
   1. Alterations in perfusion or afterload
      a. Causes
         (1) Increased systemic vascular resistance
            (a) It may be a natural compensatory response to maintain perfusion to vital organs when blood pressure drops.
            (b) Vasoconstriction may occur in an attempt to maintain body temperature.
         (2) Decreased systemic vascular resistance or vasodilation may occur for the following reasons:
            (a) Spinal anesthesia and blockage of sympathetic nerves
            (b) Increased body temperature
            (c) A vaso-vagal response
            (d) Sepsis leading to shock
         (3) Increased pulmonary vascular resistance will occur secondary to hypoxemia, hypercarbia, acidosis, and excessive intrapulmonary pressures.
      b. Treatment
         (1) Increased systemic vascular resistance
            (a) When CVP and LAP are decreased, add vascular volume.

EQUATION 25-1: **Calculation of Pulmonary Vascular Resistance**

$$PVR = \frac{MPAP - PCWP}{CO}$$

PVR = pulmonary vascular resistance in units (normal is less than 2 units).
MPAP = mean pulmonary artery pressure in mmHg.
PCWP = pulmonary capillary wedge pressure in mmHg.
CO = cardiac output in L/min.

Example: Given a MPAP of 15 mmHg, a PCWP of 10 mmHg, and a cardiac output of 3 L/min, calculate the PVR.

$$PVR = \frac{(15 - 10)}{3} = \frac{5}{3}$$

$$= 1.66 \text{ units}$$

EQUATION 25-2: **Calculation of Systemic Vascular Resistance**

$$SVR = \frac{MAP - MVP}{CO}$$

SVR = systemic vascular resistance in units (normal is 15 to 20 units).
MAP = mean arterial pressure in mmHg.
MVP = mean venous pressure in mmHg.
CO = cardiac output in L/min.

Example: Given a MAP of 80 mmHg, and MVP of 6 mmHg, and a CO of 4 L/min, calculate the systemic vascular resistance.

$$SVR = \frac{80 - 6}{4}$$

$$= \frac{74}{4}$$

$$= 18.6 \text{ units}$$

Chapter 25: Cardiovascular Monitoring

(b) When LAP is elevated, administer:
   i) vasodilators
   ii) diuretics
   iii) inotropic agents
(c) When LAP is elevated with decreased MAP, use vasodilators that also affect the venous bed and give diuretics.

(2) Decreased systemic vascular resistance
   (a) Stop vasodilators and diuretics if they are being used.
   (b) Consider giving volume, vasoconstrictors, and inotropes.

(3) Increased pulmonary vascular resistance
   (a) Administer oxygen to keep PaO_2 above 60 mmHg.
   (b) Establish normal acid-base balance.
   (c) Reduce excessive mechanical tidal volumes or PEEP.

References

1. Wilkins, R. L., Sheldon, R. L., and Krider, S. J., *Clinical Assessment in Respiratory Care*, 3rd ed., Mosby, 1995.
2. Darovic, G. O., *Hemodynamic Monitoring: Invasive and Noninvasive Clinical Application*, 2nd ed., W. B. Saunders, 1995.
3. Shoemaker, W. C., et al., *The Society of Critical Care Medicine Textbook of Critical Care*, 3rd ed., W. B. Saunders, 1999.

Assessment Questions

1. Factors that affect the CVP reading are:
   I. Cardiac performance
   II. Blood volume
   III. Vasopressor therapy
   IV. Intrathoracic pressure

   A. I only
   B. I and II only
   C. I, II, III and IV
   D. III and IV only

2. The pulmonary artery wedge pressure measurement is always performed:
   A. During a pressure plateau maneuver
   B. At the end of expiration
   C. At the beginning of inspiration
   D. When the cardiac cycle is in diastole

3. Complications unique to pulmonary artery catheterization include:
   I. Ventricular rupture
   II. Bundle branch block
   III. Balloon rupture
   IV. Kinking of the catheter

   A. I and II only
   B. I, II, III and IV
   C. II, III and IV only
   D. III and IV only

4. PEEP affects the accuracy of pressures recorded by the pulmonary artery catheter by:
   A. Falsely increasing the values the catheter measures

B. Falsely decreasing the values the catheter measures
C. Falsely increasing end-expiratory pressure
D. Falsely approximating FRC

5. You would not consider the PWP to be elevated unless the numerical value was greater than:

   A. 4 cm H_2O
   B. 8 cm H_2O
   C. 12 cm H_2O
   D. 16 cm H_2O

6. The standard for defining coronary artery anatomy is:

   A. A Technetium (Tc99m) scan
   B. A Thallium scan
   C. Coronary angiography
   D. Echocardiography

7. Why is the rate of aspiration of mixed venous blood from the pulmonary artery so important?

   A. Fast aspiration of bloods causes leaks to develop within the system
   B. The value represents left ventricular function
   C. Fast aspiration risks contamination of the sample with venous blood
   D. Fast aspiration risks removing air from the balloon

8. While checking the PCWP, you notice that the pressure tracing appears once you get 0.5 ml of air into the balloon. You can assume that:

   A. The balloon has ruptured
   B. The balloon has an obstruction
   C. It represents the normal amount of air needed to fill the balloon
   D. The catheter tip has slipped into the pulmonary circulation

9. The principal function of the pressure transducer used with a pulmonary artery catheter is to :

   A. Amplify the generated electrical signal
   B. Convert the pressure signal into an electrical waveform
   C. Filter emboli from the system
   D. Dampen the electrical signal so it can be transmitted to the recorder

Chapter 26

Cardiopulmonary Resuscitation

I. **Emergency resuscitation of adults**[1]

A. Recognition
   1. The clinical picture is that of sudden cessation of circulation in a patient who was not expected to die at that time. Most sudden deaths of cardiac origin are secondary to arrhythmias
      a. There is an absence of pulse in the large arteries.
      b. The pupils become dilated.
   2. Complete airway obstruction is recognized when one cannot hear or feel airflow at the nose or mouth.
      a. Noisy airflow may occur due to a partially obstructed airway.
      b. Hypercarbia and hypoxemia rapidly result with acute airway obstruction.
B. A rescuer who encounters a victim of cardiopulmonary arrest should immediately yell for help.
C. Creating a patent airway
   1. With the neck extended, the mandible usually moves forward and the tongue is drawn forward.
   2. The chin lift–head tilt method is the most effective technique in patients without cervical spine injury.
   3. The jaw thrust maneuver is necessary in situations where it is not feasible or desirable to hyperextend the head, such as with cervical neck injury.
D. Ventilation
   1. After establishing unresponsiveness, and calling for help, apply 1–2 rapid deep lung inflations.
   2. In mouth-to-mouth ventilation, the rescuer maintains a head tilt and pinches the victim's nostrils.

a. Two inflations for each fifteen chest compressions are used if there is only one rescuer.
   b. One inflation for each five chest compressions is used if there are two rescuers.
  3. A bag-valve-mask combination is most effective in the intubated patient and somewhat difficult in the nonintubated patient.
   a. Insert a pharyngeal tube if possible.
   b. The bag permits delivery of oxygen during spontaneous and artificial ventilation.
   c. Mold the mask over the patient's nose and mouth.
E. Cardiac compressions must be initiated if a pulse is absent or if cardiac output is inadequate to maintain consciousness.
  1. The patient should be placed in the supine position.
  2. The heel of the hand should be placed two-finger widths above the xiphoid process.
   a. The fingers should not touch the chest wall during compressions.
   b. The hands should remain in contact with the patient's chest during release of the compression.
   c. The sternum should be compressed about 1½ to 2 inches.
F. Check the pulse for effective compressions or the return of spontaneous cardiac function.
  1. The carotid pulse should be checked one minute after compressions have begun.
  2. An alternate site for checking pulse is the femoral artery.
  3. The pulse should be checked every 3–4 minutes.
  4. Compressions should not be halted for more than five seconds to check the pulse.
G. ECG monitoring
  1. This is indicated in acute myocardial infarction, serious arrhythmias, or incidence of ventricular fibrillation.
  2. Arrhythmias are monitored by rhythm strip or amplified on a oscilloscope.
H. Assessing the pupils
  1. The pupils can provide an evaluation of cerebral circulation and oxygenation.
  2. Constricted and light-reactive pupils indicate that the resuscitation effort is ineffective.
  3. Dilated pupils that are nonreactive to light indicate that cerebral oxygenation is inadequate.
  4. Narcotics constrict pupils.
I. Chest excursion
  1. The visible rise and fall of the chest indicates adequate ventilation. If rise and fall is absent, the airway should be reestablished by repositioning the head and neck.

Chapter 26: Cardiopulmonary Resuscitation 455

2. Observation of chest rise and fall should be done without interrupting compressions.

J. Defibrillation
  1. Delivery of electrical stimulus during CPR to treat ventricular tachycardia or fibrillation.
  2. Initial defibrillation should use 200 joules and should not exceed 360 joules.

K. Endotracheal intubation
  1. Position the patient in the supine position with the neck flexed and the head hyperextended to align the airway for best visualization of the vocal cords.
  2. Standing at the head of the patient, you should hold the patient's mouth open with your right hand, and by grasping the laryngoscope handle in your left hand, insert the laryngoscope blade into the right side of the patient's mouth.
  3. The blade should then be centered by pushing the tongue to the left, while the blade is held firmly against the tongue and lower jaw so as to avoid using the upper row of teeth as a fulcrum.
  4. The blade should be advanced to the level of the epiglottis and the epiglottis lifted to expose the vocal cords.
  5. Insert the endotracheal tube into the right side of the mouth and advance the tip past the epiglottis and through the vertical opening of the larynx and then through the vocal cords.
  6. Advance the tube to the point where the cuff is just past the level of the vocal cords and withdraw the stylet at this time, if one is in use.
  7. Inflate the endotracheal tube cuff to seal the airway and tape the tube in place. The cuff should be inflated to seal the airway during resuscitation to avoid aspiration of gastric contents and permit ventilation. The airway may be readjusted following successful resuscitation and stabilization.
      a. The endotracheal tube should have a high-compliance, low-pressure cuff.
      b. Cuff pressure and volume should be measured and charted every four hours following resuscitation and stabilization of the patient.
          (1) Cuff volume measurement is made with a syringe.
          (2) Cuff pressure can be measured by attaching one side of a three-way stopcock to the mercury column of a sphygmomanometer and another side to the pilot tube of the endotracheal tube.
          (3) Cuff pressure should not exceed 25 mmHg during the expiratory phase for patients on mechanical ventilation. If the patient is not mechanically ventilated, the pressure should not exceed 25 mmHg at any time.
  8. Confirming tube placement with $ETCO_2$ detectors.
      a. Adequate perfusion with spontaneous heartbeat
          (1) Connect colorimetric (EASY CAP) detector to the endotracheal tube and after six full breaths, evaluate the cap color.

(2) If the color is purple there is 0.03–0.5% $ETCO_2$.
  (a) The ET tube is NOT in the trachea.
  (b) Reinsert tube.
  (c) Recheck with colorimetric detector.
(3) If the color is tan there is 0.5–2% $ETCO_2$.
  (a) There may be retained CO_2 in the esophagus or low perfusion or hypocarbia.
  (b) Deliver six more breaths.
  (c) If color remains tan, the ET tube is in the trachea with low perfusion or hypocarbia.
(4) If the color is yellow there is 2–5% $ETCO_2$.
  (a) The ET tube is in the trachea.
  (b) Secure the ET tube.
  (c) Continue to observe color change.
b. Poor perfusion cardiac arrest
  (1) Connect detector to the ET tube and after six full breaths, evaluate detector cap color.
  (2) If the color is purple there is 0.03–0.5% $ETCO_2$.
    (a) The ET tube is NOT in the trachea or there is inadequate perfusion secondary to ineffective CPR.
    (b) Check to see whether ET tube is through the vocal cords.
    (c) If tube is NOT through cords, reinsert tube and recheck with detector.
    (d) If ET tube is through vocal cords, there is inadequate perfusion, and appropriate clinical action should be taken to improve perfusion.
  (3) If the color is tan, there is 0.5–2% $ETCO_2$.
    (a) There is retained CO2 in esophagus or low perfusion.
    (b) Deliver six more breaths.
    (c) If color remains tan, the ET tube is in the trachea with low perfusion.
  (4) If the color is yellow, there is 2–5% $ETCO_2$.
    (a) The ET tube is in the trachea.
    (b) Secure the ET tube.
    (c) Continue to observe the color of detector cap.
c. An esophageal detection device (EDD) incorporates an aspirator squeeze bulb that attaches to the standard 15 mm adapter on the endotracheal tube.
  (1) Squeezing the aspirator bulb creates negative pressure (−80 to −90).
  (2) The EDD is attached to the positioned endotracheal tube inserted in the patient's airway.

Chapter 26: Cardiopulmonary Resuscitation 457

      (3) Because the trachea is held open by cartilaginous rings, the bulb quickly reexpands on release, indicating successful intubation.

      (4) The bulb will not release if the tube entered the esophagus, because the cartilage rings are absent. This causes the soft esophagus to collapse around the tube preventing the bulb from reinflating.

L. Technique for endotracheal drug administration[2]
  1. The total volume of fluid per dose should be 5–10 ml. Any greater volume may wash surfactant from alveoli and cause atelectasis and pulmonary damage.
  2. The medication should be rapidly instilled with a syringe through the opening of the endotracheal tube.
  3. Following instillation, 5–10 rapid hyperinflations with a manual ventilation bag should be given.
     a. With entry of the medication into the airway, reflex coughing can cause the medication to "shoot" back out of the opening of the endotracheal tube.
     b. Immediately following instillation of medication, the endotracheal tube opening should be briefly covered with a finger, until the manual ventilation bag can be attached and hyperinflation given.

M. Extubation[3]
  1. The decision to extubate is based on the following criteria:
     a. Completed weaning from mechanical ventilation
     b. Recovery of consciousness following anesthesia
     c. Resolution of the initial indications for intubation
  2. Technique of extubation
     a. With the patient supine, place the head of the bed at a 45 degree angle (semi-Fowlers).
     b. The patient should be alert if possible.
     c. Suction the posterior pharynx for removal of any pooled secretions.
     d. Preoxygenate the patient for at least one minute with 100% O_2 and a manual ventilation bag.
     e. Explain the procedure to the patient.
     f. Deflate the endotracheal tube cuff completely.
     g. Have the patient take as deep a breath as possible and smoothly remove the tube as the patient nears the peak of inspiration.
        (1) The vocal cords will be further apart, which will help to avoid any damage from removal of the tube.
        (2) The patient will be able to cough immediately upon removal of the tube and evacuate any secretions that move down into the trachea.
     h. Place the patient on an aerosol mask or face tent with bland aerosol and 40% O_2.

N. Esophageal obturator airway (EOA)[4]
1. The EOA is indicated as an alternative to intubation in the following situations:
   a. Rescuer cannot or is not permitted to intubate trachea.
   b. When equipment for intubation is not available or is not working properly.
   c. Tracheal intubation is not technically possible or desirable.
2. Advantages
   a. Visualization is not required for insertion, so it can be introduced more quickly and easily than an ET tube.
   b. Because there is no need for hyperextension of the head and flexion of the neck during insertion, it is an attractive technique for trauma victims with suspected neck injury.
3. Insertion
   a. The tube should first be attached to the airway and the cuff inflated to test for a leak.
   b. The cuff is then deflated prior to insertion and the tube lubricated.
   c. With the head in mid-position, or slight flexion, the rescuer elevates the tongue and jaw with one hand and with the other hand inserts the tube through the mouth and into the esophagus. The tube is advanced until the mask is seated on the face.
   d. Because the EOA can inadvertently enter the trachea, positive pressure ventilation should be delivered prior to inflating the cuff.
      (1) If the chest rises with positive pressure inflation, 35 ml of air should be put in the cuff.
      (2) After inflation of the cuff, breath sounds are listened for bilaterally at the midaxillary line.
      (3) The epigastrium should also be auscultated. If the tube is improperly placed in the trachea, gurgling sounds will be heard.
   e. If there is difficulty in advancing the tube during insertion, it should be withdrawn slightly, the tongue-jaw lift improved, and the tube readvanced.
   f. If the patient remains unconscious 2 hours after the insertion of the EOA, the trachea should be intubated with a cuffed endotracheal tube and the EOA removed.
      (1) This will reduce the incidence of pressure necrosis of the esophageal mucosa.
      (2) Before removal, the patient should be turned to the side and suction provided, as regurgitation frequently follows removal.

O. Patient transport[4]
1. The major objective of transport is that the patient arrives in the same or better condition than when he started the transport.
2. The transport team and vehicle should be able to provide for emergency care.

Chapter 26: Cardiopulmonary Resuscitation

3. The patient should be stabilized prior to beginning the transport.
4. If the patient must be moved before the restoration of spontaneous circulation, CPR must be continued without interruption during the transport process.
5. When moving with a stretcher and continuing resuscitation:
   a. The person ventilating works from the head of the stretcher while the person compressing works from the side.
   b. Three or more bystanders should carry the stretcher while the most experienced person present should act as the team leader and coach the others.
6. In the case where there are exceptions to stabilization at the scene of cardiopulmonary arrest, transportation must be accomplished as rapidly as possible and life support administered as feasible enroute. Exceptions may include:
   a. Airway closure by laryngeal edema
   b. Tension pneumothorax
   c. Pericardial tamponade
   d. Intractable heart block requiring pacemaker
   e. Hypothermic cardiac arrest, requiring rewarming
   f. Internal hemorrhage requiring surgery

II. Resuscitation of infants at the time of delivery[5]

A. Intrauterine assessment
   1. Fetal scalp blood pH of less than 7.20, or one that is falling with successive measurement, signals an infant that will likely be depressed at birth and require medical care.
   2. Fetal heart rate monitoring indicates distress when the following patterns exist.
      a. There is a persistent tachycardia of greater than 160 beats per minute, and there is no maternal fever that could account for the elevated fetal heart rate.
      b. There is persistent bradycardia of less than 120 beats per minute.
      c. There is loss of the beat-to-beat variation in the ECG that is usually present in normal newborns.
         (1) Short-term variability is the averaged difference in the R wave to R wave interval, measured in milliseconds.
         (2) Long-term variability is the averaged difference between the slowest and fastest heart rate each minute and is measured in beats per minute.
         (3) Variability must be interpreted with the knowledge of any maternal medication that may lead to this loss of variability. Stimulation of the fetus does not reverse the problem.
      d. There is a pattern of late deceleration of the fetal heart following uterine contraction when fetal heart slowing should occur right after the contraction. This pattern signals uteroplacental insufficiency.

B. Extrauterine assessment utilizes the Apgar scoring system in which points are assigned in the assessed areas of vital function (refer to Table 9-1).
   1. Heart rate—absence = 0, less than 100 = 1, greater than 100 = 2
   2. Respiratory effort—none = 0, weak with no crying or an irregular gasping effort = 1, strong effort with strong crying = 2
   3. Muscle tone—none = 0, some movement of the extremities = 1, strong active movement = 2
   4. Reflex—easily elicited by performing bulb suctioning, No response = 0, grimacing = 1, and coughing or sneezing = 2
   5. Color—blue and pale = 0, pink body with blue extremities or hands and feet = 1, completely pink = 2
C. Management by Apgar score
   1. If the initial score is 3 or less:
      a. Immediate drying is necessary.
      b. The upper airway should be suctioned with a bulb syringe.
      c. Bag and mask ventilation with oxygen should be started.
      d. when there is not a quick response to these methods, the airway needs to be cleared and oral intubation considered.
   2. If the initial Apgar score is 4–6:
      a. Immediate drying is necessary.
      b. the upper airway should be suctioned with a bulb syringe.
      c. "Whiffs" of warmed and humidified oxygen should be given by directing a large bore tubing from a heated humidifier at the infant's face.
      d. When there is no improvement within one minute, bag and mask ventilation with oxygen should be started before the rate begins to drop
   3. If the initial Apgar score is greater than 6:
      a. Immediate drying is necessary.
      b. "Whiffs" of oxygen may be given if there is cyanosis.
      c. If respirations are absent or weak then tactile stimulation through drying, rubbing the back, or pinching the extremities should be used for 20–30 seconds.
      d. If the pulse rate begins to fall, bag and mask ventilation with oxygen should be started.
D. General management
   1. Clearing the airway is often done partially by the obstetrician while the fetus is still in the birth canal with just the head clear.
      a. It is performed usually with a bulb syringe rather than a suction catheter, because inserting a suction catheter through the mouth or nose of a depressed infant may promote bradycardia.
      b. It is a critical procedure when intrauterine aspiration of meconium is suspected.

Chapter 26: Cardiopulmonary Resuscitation

2. Drying the infant quickly is very important to avoid loss of body heat secondary to convective and evaporative heat loss. Cold stress will increase the infant's metabolic demands and may promote apnea and bradycardia.
3. The tactile stimulation of drying and handling, and the thermal stimulation of the extrauterine environment are both important factors in the onset of normal respiration in the newborn.
4. Warming is initially desirable to place the infant in a warmed environment such as a radiant warmer. It facilitates maintenance of body heat and allows an open area so that the resuscitation team may be able to physically perform their various tasks.

E. Specific management[6]
  1. If there is no spontaneous breathing, apply bag/mask ventilation for 15–30 seconds, and if drug depression is suspected, give narcan. Evaluate heart rate.
     a. If heart rate is below 60, continue ventilation and start chest compressions.
        (1) This is done in severely depressed infants whose heart beats remain below 60 per minute after one to two minutes of effective ventilation.
        (2) Compressions should be done at a rate of 120 per minute to the mid-sternum with a depression of 1–2 centimeters with each compression.
        (3) The resuscitator's hands should encircle the chest to stabilize the infant, with the thumbs overlapping and compressing the sternum.
     b. If heart rate is 60–100/min.:
        (1) And not increasing, continue ventilation and continue compressions if heart rate remains below 80/min.
           (a) Initiate medications if heart rate is below 80/min. after 30 seconds of bagging with 100% O_2 and chest compressions.
        (2) If heart rate is increasing, continue ventilation.
     c. If heart rate is above 100/min.:
        (1) Watch for spontaneous ventilation.
        (2) Discontinue mechanical ventilation.
  2. If there is spontaneous breathing, evaluate heart rate.
     a. If heart rate is less than 100/min., follow the procedure for when there is no spontaneous breathing.
     b. If heart rate is above 100/min., evaluate color.
        (1) If blue, provide O_2.
        (2) If the infant is pink or acrocyanosis is present, observe and monitor.

III. Treatment of cardiovascular collapse/ACLS[1]

For many years the American Heart Association has used the algorithm as an educational tool to help deal with emergency cardiac care. The symbol shapes represent specific steps that require action as you move through the algorithm. Refer to Figs. 26-1–26-5.

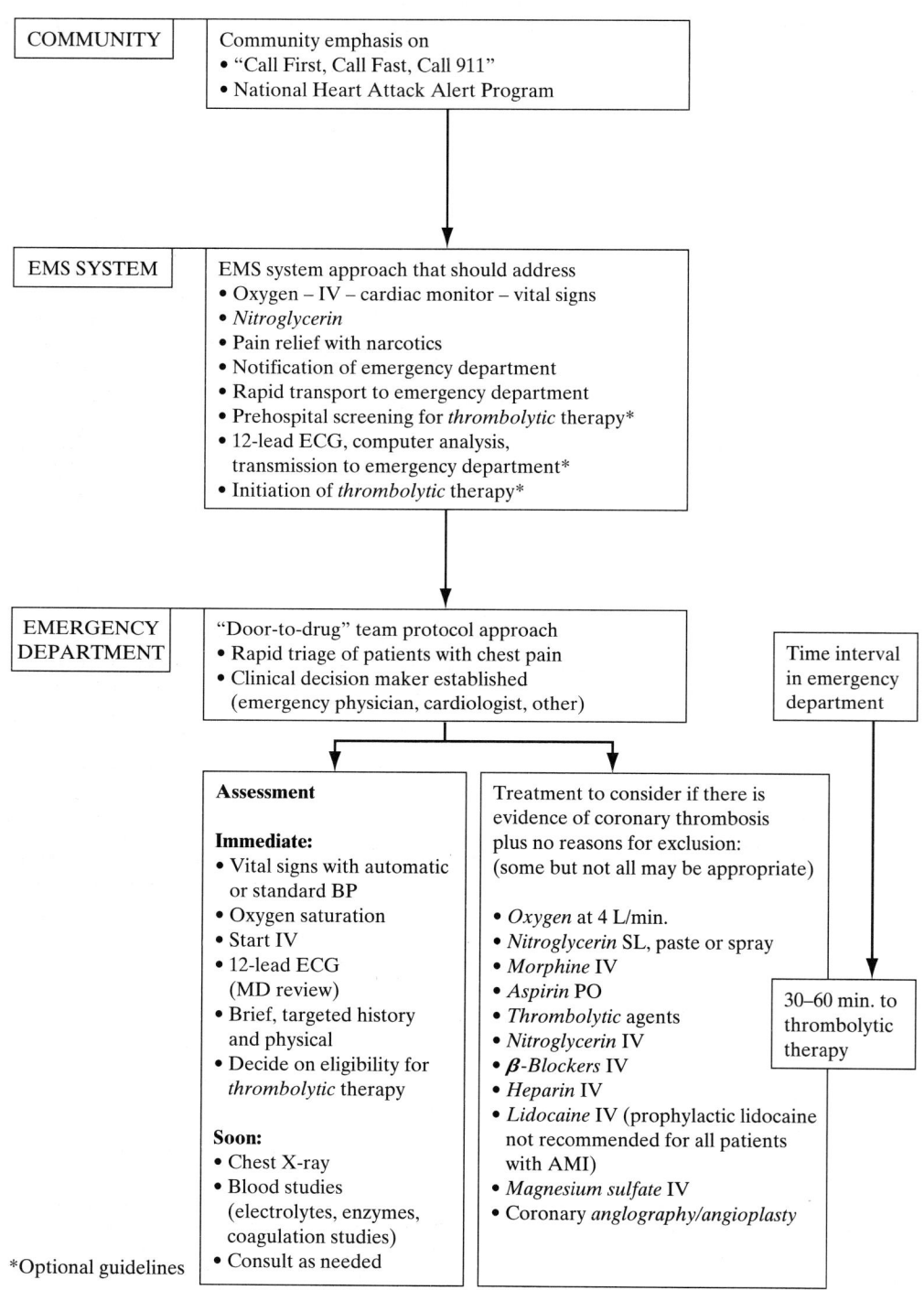

FIGURE 26-1: Acute Myocardial Infarction Algorithm. Recommendations for early management of patients with chest pain and possible AMI. Reproduced with permission. © *Advanced Cardiac Life Support,* 1997. Copyright American Heart Association.

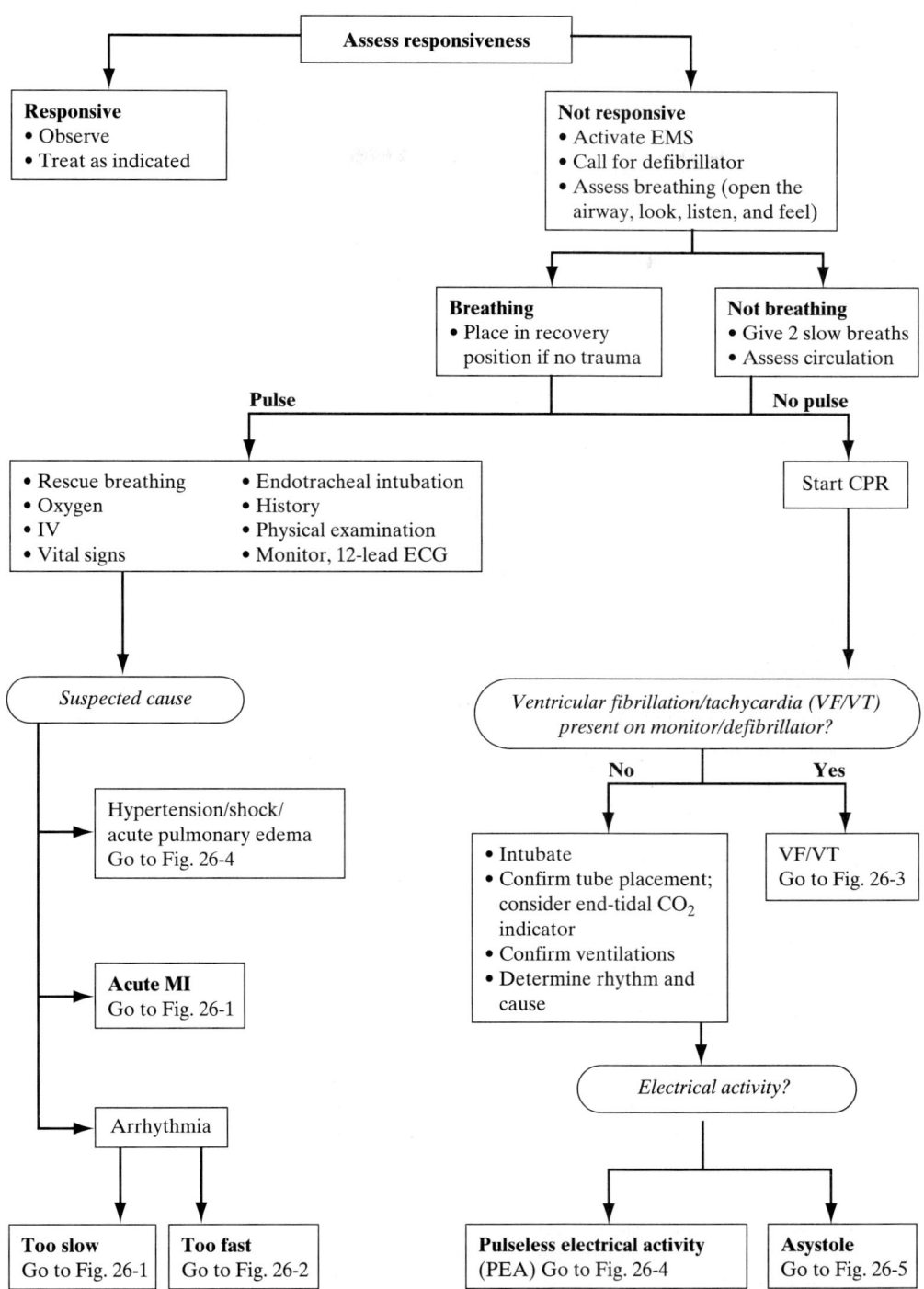

FIGURE 26-2: Universal Algorithm for Adult. Emergency Cardiac Care. Reproduced with permission. © *Advanced Cardiac Life Support,* 1997. Copyright American Heart Association.

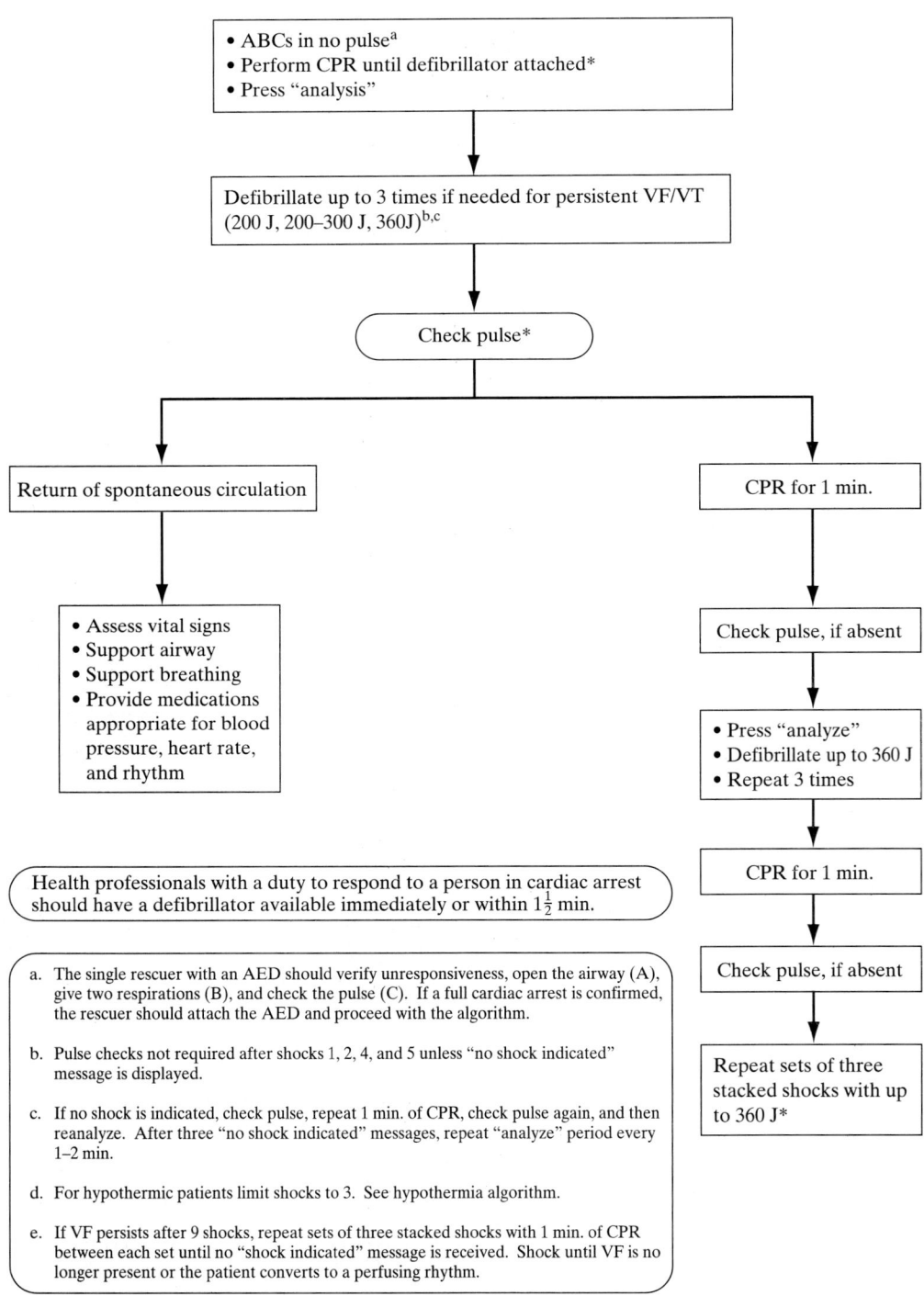

FIGURE 26-3: Automated External Defibrillation Treatment Algorithm. Emergency cardiac care pending arrival of ACLS personnel. Reproduced with permission. © *Advanced Cardiac Life Support,* 1997. Copyright American Heart Association.

Includes
- Electromechanical dissociation (EMD)
- Pseudo-EMD
- Idioventricular rhythms
- Ventricular escape rhythms
- Bradyasystolic rhythms
- Postdefibrillation idioventricular rhythms

- Continue CPR
- Intubate at once
- Obtain IV access
- Assess blood flow using Doppler ultrasound, end-tidal CO_2, echocardiograhy, or arterial line

---

Consider possible causes
(parentheses = possible therapies and reatments)

- Hypovolemia (volume infusion)
- Hypoxia (ventilation)
- Cardiac tamponade (pericardiocentesis)
- Tension pneumothorax (needle decompression)
- Hypothermia (see hypothermia algorithm)
- Massive pulmonary embolism (surgery, *thrombolytics*)
- Drug overdoses such as tricyclics, digitalis β-blockers, calcium channel blockers
- Hyperkalemia[a]
- Acidosis[b]
- Massive acute myocardial infarction (go to Fig. 26-2)

- ***Epinephrine*** 1 mg IV push[a,c] repeat every 3–5 min.

- If absolute bradycardia (<60 BPM) or relative bradycardia, give ***atropine*** 1 mg IV
- Repeat every 3–5 min. to a total of 0.03–0.04 mg/kg[d]

Class I: definitely helpful
Class IIa: acceptable, probably helpful
Class IIb: acceptable, possibly helpful
Class III: not indicated, may be harmful

a. *Sodium bicarbonate* 1 mEq/kg is Class I if patient has known preexisting hyperkalemia.

b. *Sodium bicarbonate* 1 mEq/kg:
   Class IIa
   - If known preexisting bicarbonate-responsive acidosis
   - If overdose with tricyclic antidepressants
   - To alkanlinize the urine in drug overdoses
   Class IIb
   - If intubated and continued long arrest interval
   - Upon return of sponaneous circulation after long arrest interval
   Class III
   - Hypoxic lactic acidosis

c. The recommended dose of epinephrine is 1 mg IV push every 3–5 min. If this approach fails, several Class IIb dosing regimens can be considered.
   - Intermediate: *epinephrine* 2–5 mg IV push, every 3–5 min.
   - Escalating: *epinephrine* 1 mg-3 mg-5 mg IV push, 3 min. apart
   - High: *epiephrine* 0.1 mg IV push, every 3–5 min.

d. The shorter atropine dosing interval (3 min.) is possibly helpful in cardiac arrest (class IIb).

FIGURE 26-4: Pulseless Electrical Activity Algorithm. (Electromechanical Dissociation [EMD]. Reproduced with permission. © *Advanced Cardiac Life Support,* 1997. Copyright American Heart Association.)

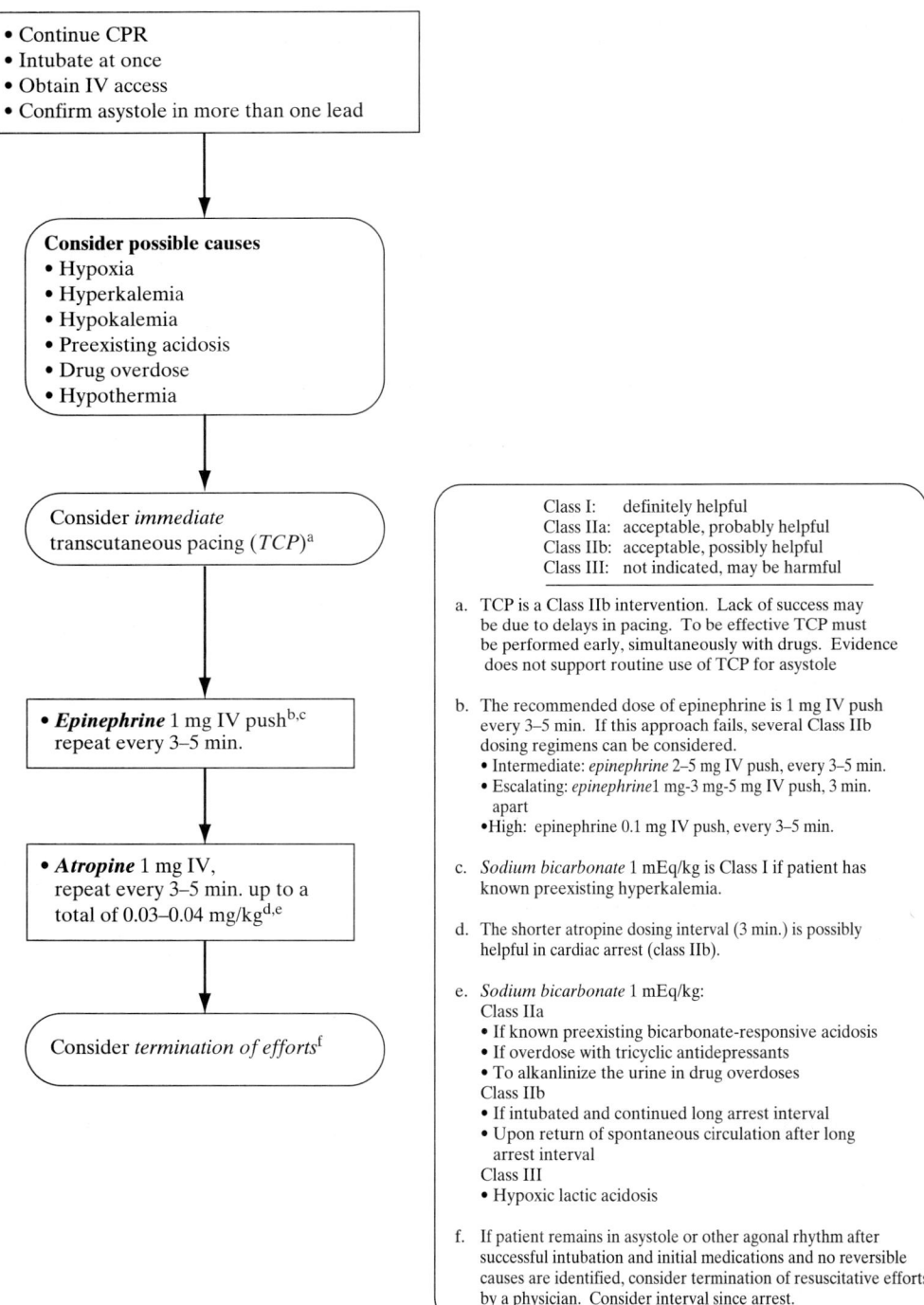

FIGURE 26-5: Asystole Treatment Algorithm. Reproduced with permission. © *Advanced Cardiac Life Support,* 1997. Copyright American Heart Association.

Chapter 26: Cardiopulmonary Resuscitation

References

1. *Advanced Cardiac Life Support,* American Heart Association, 1997.
2. Greenberg, M. I., et al., *Advanced Techniques in Resuscitation,* Williams and Wilkins, 1985.
3. Ripe, J. M., et al, *Procedures and Techniques in Intensive Care Medicine,* Little Brown and Co., 1995.
4. Scanlon, C. L., Wilkins, R. L., and Stoller, J. K., *Egan's Fundamentals of Respiratory Therapy, 7th ed.,* Mosby, 1999.
5. Burton, G. G., Hodgkin, J. E., and Ward, J. J., *Respiratory Care: A Guide to Clinical Practice, 4th ed.,* Lippincott, 1997.
6. Whitaker, K., *Comprehensive Perinatal and Pediatric Care, 2nd ed.,* Delmar, 1996.

Assessment Questions

1. The recommended treatment for ventricular fibrillation is:
   A. Bolus lidocaine administration
   B. Defibrillation
   C. Bolus administration of epinephrine
   D. Cardioversion at 200 watt seconds

2. When intubating a newborn for resuscitation, the infant's head should be placed in which of the following positions?
   A. The head flat on the bed
   B. The head hyperextended 55 degrees
   C. The head placed in the sniffing position
   D. Tilted to the side to prevent aspiration

3. According to the American Heart Association, the appropriate rate for external cardiac compressions of the newborn is:
   A. 80 beats/minute
   B. 90 beats/minute
   C. 100 beats/minute
   D. 110 beats/minute

4. When resuscitating a patient with a pneumatic demand valve resuscitator, which of the following limitations are expected?
   I. Incapability of the device to respond to changes in the patient's respiratory rate
   II. Incapability of being able to detect changes in patient lung characteristics
   III. Premature termination of inspiration during chest compression

   A. I only
   B. I and II only
   C. I and III only
   D. II and III only

5. Which of the following blood gases would reflect the need for cardiopulmonary resuscitation?

   A. $PaO_2 = 57$ $pH = 7.48$
      $PaCO_2: 32$ $HCO_3 = 26$
   B. $PaO_2 = 51$ $pH = 7.32$
      $PaCO_2: 52$ $HCO_3 = 26$
   C. $PaO_2 = 57$ $pH = 7.48$
      $PaCO_2: 22$ $HCO_3 = 16$
   D. $PaO_2 = 32$ $pH = 7.21$
      $PaCO_2: 86$ $HCO_3 = 6$

6. Most sudden deaths of cardiac origin are due to:
   A. Cardiac arrhythmias
   B. Air embolism
   C. Congestive heart failure
   D. Cardiac tamponade

7. Which of the following will help confirm proper tube placement during an emergency resuscitation attempt?

   I. Colorimetric analysis
   II. Bilateral auscultation
   III. Capnometry
   IV. Endotracheal detection device

   A. I, II, III and IV
   B. II, III and IV only
   C. III only
   D. III and IV only

8. Which of the following is used to assess the circulatory status of an adult patient undergoing cardiopulmonary resuscitation?

   A. Radial pulse
   B. Brachial pulse
   C. Ulnar pulse
   D. Carotid pulse

9. According to the American Heart Association, properly performed cardiac compressions will result in a carotid blood flow rate that is approximately _____ % of normal.

   A. 5–15 %
   B. 15–25%
   C. 25–30%
   D. 30–35%

Chapter 27

Pulmonary Rehabilitation and Home Care

I. Pulmonary rehabilitation[1]

A. Physical therapy training for the patient and family includes effective coughing, clapping, and postural drainage. Pursed-lip breathing, diaphragmatic breathing, and relaxation techniques are also included.

B. Exercise conditioning begins with selection of a safe program determined by measuring workloads, gas exchange behavior, heart rate, and ECG.

C. Respiratory therapy may include supplemental oxygen on a PRN or continuous basis (continuous O_2 therapy is indicated when resting PaO_2 on room air is 55 mmHg or less), or aerosolization of medications such as bronchodilators or corticosteroids.

D. Education for the patient and family includes instruction in the use and purpose of any mode of care to be applied in the home care setting. Side effects should also be explained.
   1. Adequate nutrition must be emphasized.
   2. The importance of smoking cessation should be emphasized, and an appropriate program instituted where needed.
   3. Environmental factors such as temperature, humidity, inhaled irritants, and altitude should be explained, along with methods for their control and/or avoidance.
   4. Immunization with influenza and pneumococcal vaccines is recommended.

E. Assessment of the patient's progress prior to the treatment plan being developed is essential.

F. Long-term follow-up will generally be the responsibility of the primary care physician.

II. Home care[2]

A. IPPB—the patient is instructed in the following areas:
   1. Assembly and disassembly of the patient manifold

2. The method of attaching the patient circuit to the machine
3. Operation of the machine's controls
4. How to measure the medication properly
5. Proper cleaning of the equipment
6. Frequency and duration of therapy, usually TID or QID, but if the patient finds it necessary to use more often, they should contact their physician
7. How to take the treatment

B. Compressor nebulizer—instruct the patient in the following areas:
   1. Frequency and duration of therapy
   2. Assembly and disassembly of the parts of the equipment
   3. Measuring the prescribed medication
   4. Procedure for performing the therapy
   5. Cleaning the equipment

C. Hand-bulb nebulizer—the patient should be taught in the same areas as for IPPB and compressor nebulizer.

D. Oxygen therapy—instruct the patient in the following areas:
   1. Frequency and duration
      a. Determination of these factors should be done at rest and during exercise testing by blood gas data, and whether signs of cor pulmonale are present.
      b. Patients must be carefully instructed to use only the amount of oxygen prescribed by their physician.
      c. Costs of home oxygen can create a considerable financial burden for the patient, even with insurance coverage.
         (1) The therapist and physician should determine the lowest possible liter flow that will maintain adequate blood gas levels of oxygen.
         (2) A one-liter reduction for a patient using oxygen 24 hours a day represents a substantial saving to both the patient and third party payers.
   2. Cleaning procedure for the oxygen humidifier (if used)
   3. Humidifier bottle
      a. It is important to use only boiled distilled water in the humidifier bottle because tap water contains minerals. In addition, *Pseudomonas* is an organism frequently found in tap water.
      b. Change the humidifier bottle water daily.
   4. Oxygen concentrators[2]
      a. The O_2 tubing length used should not exceed 50 feet unless authorized by the manufacturer.
      b. The concentrator should be placed in the home in such a way as to avoid heat sources and covering of air intakes.

Chapter 27: Pulmonary Rehabilitation and Home Care

    c. When placed in the home, both the oxygen concentration and flow from the concentrator should be verified.

    d. All filters, alarms, and batteries should be checked according to manufacturers recommendations.

    e. A backup source of O_2 (cylinder) should be available in the event of an electrical failure.

    f. The family and patient should be trained in all aspects of safety and care of the concentrator.

E. Apnea monitoring[3]
  1. Indications
     a. Siblings of infants who have died suddenly, or sudden infant death syndrome (SIDS).
     b. Infants who have had one or more episodes of prolonged apnea, especially premature infants.
  2. All apnea monitors have a primary and secondary method of monitoring physiologic change (i.e., respiration and ECG).
  3. Instructions for parents and other caregivers in the home should include the following:
     a. How the monitor is to be used and how it monitors and displays parameters, and the risks and hazards common to this type of equipment.
     b. Warnings about electromagnetic interference causing monitor malfunction.
     c. Battery care and maintenance procedures.
     d. Precautions about skin irritation and breakdown from the electrodes if the infant is constantly kept on the monitor. Time-off periods need to be established in order to relax the skin from the pressure exerted by the electrodes.
     e. Responding appropriately to the monitor's alarms conditions, and ensuring the audio part of the alarm can be heard throughout the home.
     f. False alarms and loose leads are common in the home environment. Do the caregivers understand proper lead placement, and are they capable of preventing the infant from loosening the electrodes?
     g. How to keep an event log, and when and what action needs to be taken.
     h. Basic CPR instructions.
  4. Discontinuation
     a. Monitor infants at risk for SIDS until 6 months of age or until they have gone 3 months without any documented episodes and have had at least one normal pneumogram.
     b. Infants who are apnea prone from disease states or prematurity should be apnea free (no significant episodes) for at least 3 months before monitoring is discontinued.

c. The infant is able to tolerate the external stress associated with immunization and common childhood illness without episode.

F. Home assessment is the first process that needs to be performed prior to the patient's discharge.[3]
   1. Is the home really the most appropriate place for the patient after discharge from the hospital? Is there financial and family support available to care for the patient upon release from the hospital? On many occasions, patients are released to overburdened families and the support just isn't there.
   2. Preparation of the home is essential prior to release of the patient. Issues to be answered prior to release include:
      a. Is there adequate space for storage?
      b. Is the electrical system safe for the new equipment used at home?
      c. Are the environmental conditions within the home appropriate to living there?
      d. Is the family capable of dealing with the task of support?
      e. Is the educational level of the patient and family capable of dealing with the equipment and procedures required for the patient's care?
      f. Are police, utility companies, and insurance people aware of how this patient is able to cope at home?
      g. Is there adequate insurance to maintain the home?

III. **Progress evaluation: In general, rehabilitation effectiveness is best monitored by reviewing before and after baseline data regarding the patient's physical status upon examination. However, alternative methods to assessing progress can be any of the following:**

A. Reduction in hospitalizations
B. Reduction in mortality
C. Reduction in morbidity
D. Reduction in costs due to medical services
E. Reduction in time lost from work

IV. **Family instruction should be done in the following areas so that family members have a clear understanding of the goals of the prescribed therapy.**

A. IPPB goals:
   1. To improve alveolar ventilation
   2. To improve mucociliary activity and mucus clearance

Chapter 27: Pulmonary Rehabilitation and Home Care 473

3. To relieve bronchospasm and decrease the work of breathing
4. To decrease mucosal congestion
5. To prevent or correct atelectasis

B. Compressor nebulizer or hand-bulb nebulizer goals:
1. To improve alveolar ventilation
2. To relieve bronchospasm
3. To improve mucociliary clearance
4. To decrease mucosal congestion

C. Oxygen therapy goals:
1. To treat hypoxemia
2. To reduce the work of breathing
3. To reduce myocardial work

V. Continuum treatment of the patient with COPD

A. Identify and select patient, and explain program and objectives to patient.
B. Initiate therapy.
   1. Patient is instructed in proper use of MDI with spacer.
   2. Q4H & PRN MDI Proventil and Atrovent.
   3. Mobilize patient a minimum of twice daily post use of MDI.
   4. Instruct on pursed-lip breathing, cough techniques, and oxygen training as needed.
C. Patient mobilization
   1. Exercises are to be directed in mobilizing the patient to prevent deconditioning.
   2. Direct range of motion and walking exercises.
   3. At the end of the mobilization session the patient performs a Shortness of Breath (SOB) level.
      a. Have the patient count to twenty.
      b. The SOB level is equal to the number of breaths that it took to count to twenty.
      c. Keep track of the SOB level.
D. Treatment progression
   1. Change MDI to PRN.
   2. Continue mobilization.
   3. Subjective factors indicating improvement:
      a. Patient is less SOB
      b. Improved SOB level
      c. Decreased level of oxygen

d. Improved walk time
e. Improved breath sounds
f. Improved ABG

References

1. Hodgkin, J., et al., *Pulmonary Rehabilitation: Guidelines to Success, 2nd ed.,* Lippincott, 1993.
2. Scanlon, C. L., Wilkins, R. L., and Stoller, J. K., *Egan's Fundamentals of Respiratory Therapy, 7th ed.,* Mosby, 1999.
3. Alone, C. A., and Hill, T. V., *Respiratory Care of the Newborn and Child, 2nd ed.,* Lippincott, 1997.

Assessment Questions

1. Which of the following should the therapist recommend as part of the home care plan for a patient with cor pulmonale and COPD?
   I. Chest physical therapy
   II. Oxygen therapy
   III. Adequate hydration
   IV. Mask CPAP therapy
   A. I and II only
   B. I, II and III only
   C. II, III and IV only
   D. II and IV only

2. You are setting up a home care plan for a patient who is being discharged with a permanent tracheostomy. You would recommend:
   I. Teaching the patient how to suction themselves
   II. Teach the patient's family pulmonary drainage techniques
   III. Instructing the patient in breathing retraining techniques
   IV. Instruct the patient on how to use incentive spirometry
   A. I and II only
   B. I, II and III only
   C. II and III only
   D. III and IV only

3. Which of the following characteristics of respiratory care equipment are important when operating in the home care/rehabilitation environment?
   I. Apparatus should have loud alarms
   II. Equipment should be easy to operate
   III. Electrical devices must have an internal battery
   A. I only
   B. I and II only
   C. I, II and III
   D. II and III only

4. When considering when to discharge a patient to the home environment, which of the following needs evaluation?
   I. The patient's ability to cope with being home
   II. What support the family can provide
   III. Environmental conditions within the home
   A. I only
   B. II only
   C. I and II only
   D. I, II and III

5. In reviewing the case of a homebound COPD patient, you notice that each time

Chapter 27: Pulmonary Rehabilitation and Home Care

the patient uses the peak flowmeter the meter invariably reads the peak flow as 100 L/min. The action you would take would be to:

- **A.** Recommend the patient start an exercise program
- **B.** Recommend the patient for a pulmonary function exam
- **C.** Provide the patient with a new peak flowmeter
- **D.** Recommend a change in the patient's MDI medication

6. The primary goal of a rehabilitation program is:

- **A.** Overall increase in functional ability
- **B.** Improvement in oxygenation ability
- **C.** Overall improvement in arterial blood gases
- **D.** Improved results on pulmonary function

7. While visiting a 62-year-old patient in her home, the patient informs you she has been having severe chest pain that comes and goes for the past two days. After connecting the patient to her oxygen source, you would inform the hospital a patient was being delivered to the emergency room for:

- **A.** An immediate stress test
- **B.** An immediate pulmonary function
- **C.** Immediate insertion of a test tube
- **D.** Immediate ECG monitoring

8. You would recommend discontinuing an apnea monitor on a child when:

- **A.** No alarm situations have occurred during the past six months
- **B.** ABGs have been normal for past three months
- **C.** No apnea episodes have occurred during the past three months
- **D.** Once the child reaches 18 months no further need for a monitor is indicated

9. Pulmonary rehabilitation helps a patient to recondition his inspiratory muscles by:

- **A.** Performing breathing exercises
- **B.** Incorporating an aerobic walking routine
- **C.** Using biofeedback
- **D.** Pedaling on a stationary bicycle

Chapter 28

Assistance with Special Procedures

I. Bronchoscopy[1]

A. Assure that the equipment is in proper working order.

B. The cleanliness and/or sterilization of the equipment should be certified.

C. The light source should be checked for proper operation.

D. If a flexible scope is being used, response of the scope tip should be inspected by manipulating the thumb control.

E. Visualization through the scope should be checked when using the flexible fiberoptic scope.

F. With the flexible scope, patency of the suction and biopsy channels should be checked, along with the condition of the biopsy brush and forceps and their ability to pass through the necessary channel.

G. Check that adequate supplies are present for the procedure.
   1. Sterile gloves, clean cover gowns, masks, and goggles, all in the correct size.
   2. Preoperative medications consist of benzodiazepines, anticholinergic agents, and narcotics.
   3. 2% lidocaine is given through the suction channel of the scope to anesthetize the hypopharynx, larynx, and vocal cords.
   4. 2% viscous lidocaine may be used to anesthetize the nares.
   5. A solution of normal saline in prepared syringes for irrigation through the bronchoscope during the procedure.
   6. Labeled containers for sputum and biopsy specimens.
   7. Appropriate emergency drugs and defibrillator in the event of arrhythmias or cardiac arrest.
   8. An oxygen setup for provision of O_2 during the procedure.

H. A pulse oximeter and cardiac monitor should be present and connected to patient prior to beginning the procedure.

Chapter 28: Assistance with Special Procedures

I. Indications for bronchoscopy include:
  1. Chest roentgenographic abnormalities
  2. Suspicion of airway or lung malignancy
  3. Pulmonary infections
  4. Hemoptysis
  5. Airway trauma
  6. Refractory cough
J. Contraindications associated with bronchoscopy include:
  1. Uncooperative patient
  2. Hemodynamic instability
  3. Status asthmaticus
  4. Unstable angina
  5. Life-threatening arrhythmias

II. Thoracentesis[2]

A. Positioning the patient
  1. The patient should be sitting upright to ensure that the diaphragm is in the most dependent position.
  2. The patient can sit on the edge of the bed and rest his arms on a pillow placed on an over-the-bed table.
  3. An alternative is to have the patient straddle a chair backwards and rest his head on a pillow on the back of the chair.
  4. In the rare instance the patient may need to be reclining, the position of the diaphragm needs to be checked with fluoroscopy or ultrasound.
B. Skin disinfection
  1. First stage: the skin is scrubbed with a povidone-iodine solution plus a detergent, and then rinsed and blotted dry.
  2. Second stage: the skin needs to be swabbed with a povidone-iodine solution that is allowed to dry on the skin.
C. Anesthesia
  1. The skin and subcutaneous tissue above the upper border of the first rib above the fluid level is infiltrated with 2% lidocaine with a 25-gauge needle.
  2. Deep anesthesia is then performed with a 2-inch, 22-gauge needle and lidocaine to the interspace above the rib and carried through to the pleural cavity.
D. Procedure
  1. With the patient in the upright position, an 18- or 19-gauge needle with a three-way stopcock is attached to a heparinized 20–50 ml syringe, and inserted into the pleural space.

2. Twenty-five mls of fluid are removed and collected for appropriate studies, which may include:
   a. Bacterial or fungal smears
   b. Cultures
   c. Cytology
   d. Protein concentration
   e. Lactic dehydrogenase (LDH)
   f. Glucose
   g. Amylase
   h. Hemoglobin, hematocrit, RBCs
   i. White cell count with differential count
   j. Fat staining
   k. Lipid concentration
   l. PH
3. A biopsy may be performed at this time.
4. The remaining fluid is then drained with no more than 1500 ml being drained at one time.
5. Following completion of fluid removal, the skin is then cleaned and a small sterile dressing applied.

E. The only real clinical indication for a thoracentesis is when a pleural effusion of unknown cause is present. This procedure will definitively or presumptively establish the cause of the effusion.

F. There are no absolute contraindications to the procedure if clinical judgement dictates the information gained from pleural fluid analysis will assist in diagnosis and therapy.

III. Tracheostomy[3]

A. Necessary equipment includes spotlights, sterile gowns, gloves, and drapes.

B. The tracheostomy tray includes appropriate surgical instruments, local anesthetic, sutures, and the common various types and sizes of tracheostomy tubes.

C. Ancillary supplies include suction equipment and an electrocautery device.

D. Preparation
   1. The patient is placed in the supine position with the neck hyperextended and supported.
   2. Prior to the tracheotomy, an endotracheal tube or bronchoscope should be passed into the trachea to maintain the airway and to facilitate palpation of the trachea during dissection.
   3. Povidone-iodine solution is used to prep the neck and upper chest.

Chapter 28: Assistance with Special Procedures

4. Local anesthetic is used, usually with epinephrine.
    a. Epinephrine with lidocaine helps to control bleeding during the procedure.
    b. The local anesthetic may also reduce undesirable reflex response to surgical stimulation of the airway.
5. If a cuffed tube is being used, the cuff should be tested in a pan of sterile water to be sure that no leaks are present.

E. As the surgeon proceeds with the operation to the point where a tracheal window has been created, the endotracheal tube is retracted to a level just above the tracheal orifice.

F. When the tracheostomy tube is ready for insertion, the endotracheal tube is withdrawn at the same time that the tracheostomy tube is inserted.

G. Common indications for tracheostomy include removal of airway secretions, access for long-term mechanical ventilation, prevention of aspiration, and relief of upper airway obstruction. There basically are no contraindications to this procedure.

IV. Chest tubes[3]

A. Equipment
    1. Applicators for antiseptic
    2. Antiseptic (povidone-iodine)
    3. Sterile gloves
    4. Lidocaine, 1% without epinephrine
    5. Syringes, 10 ml and 30 ml
    6. Needles: 1/2 inch, 25 gauge; 1 1/2 inch, 22 gauge
    7. Scalpel with No. 11 and No. 15 blades
    8. Suture, 2-0 silk or synthetic with cutting skin needle
    9. Hemostats, one sharp pointed "mosquito," one Kelly or Mayo clamp
    10. Scissors, preferably pointed
    11. Connectors, two "five-in-one" double tapered
    12. Test tubes for laboratory specimens
    13. Dressings, four 4 X 4 inch
    14. Chest tubes (usually kept separately) 12 Fr trocarcath; 20 or 36 Fr multi-fenestrated vinyl tube
    15. Pleurevac
    16. Tubing, to connect apparatus to vacuum source

B. Procedure
    1. Prepare and drape the patient and inject the local anesthetic.
    2. Insert the trocar catheter after first aspirating through the 22-gauge needle to certify that fluid or air exists at the site for insertion.

3. An incision is made with a No. 11 scalpel blade.
4. A "mosquito" clamp is inserted through the small incision.
5. A 12 Fr trocarcath is inserted along the same path as the clamp, using carefully controlled force to avoid impaling the lung.
6. The stylet in the trocar is then withdrawn a few millimeters into the end of the tube, and the tube is inserted all the way to the flared end.
7. The stylet is withdrawn all the way, and the tube is clamped.
8. Once the tube is sutured in place, it is connected to the suction apparatus.

C. Estimation of volume loss through the chest tube(s) can be done in mechanically ventilated patients by subtracting the measured exhaled volume from the measured inspired volume in a patient on continuous volume ventilation. The difference between the two volumes is what is lost from the pleura through the chest tube(s).

D. The main indications for chest tube placement are pneumothorax, hemothorax, symptomatic pleural effusion, empyema, and chylothorax.

E. Chest tubes are not always required for pneumothorax. If the pneumothorax is less than 20% of the lung volume on the chest X-ray, and the patient is hemodynamically stable, a strategy of waiting and watching is appropriate. Chest tubes can always be inserted if needed.

V. Vascular monitoring

A. Central venous pressure (CVP)[4]
   1. Indications
      a. Monitoring of blood volume and adequate central venous return
      b. Monitoring left heart function when pulmonary artery pressure monitoring is not possible
   2. Equipment
      a. Plastic disposable or glass manometer with three-way stopcock
      b. IV pole to hold the manometer
      c. IV tubing for infusion of fluid through the CVP catheter
      d. CVP catheter
         (1) Large 15-gauge catheter with a 14-gauge needle
         (2) Medium 18-gauge catheter with a 17-gauge needle
      e. Disposable razor for site preparation
      f. Povidone-iodine solution
      g. 70% alcohol solution
      h. Sterile gloves and drape
   3. Preparation

a. The catheter insertion site should be shaved and scrubbed in the standard fashion with iodine solution and allowed to dry.
b. 70% alcohol should then be applied to the skin.

B. Pulmonary artery catheterization
1. Indications
   a. Measurement of right atrial, pulmonary arterial, and pulmonary capillary wedge pressures
   b. Measurement of cardiac output using either thermodilution or dye dilution technique
   c. Sampling of pulmonary arterial blood for mixed venous PO_2 values
2. Equipment
   a. Pulmonary artery catheter
   b. Two three-way stopcocks to allow connection of the proximal right atrial and distal pulmonary arterial catheter ports to the pressure monitoring lines
   c. The pressure monitoring lines that must be used to connect to the transducers
   d. A syringe for inflation of the catheter balloon
   e. The equipment necessary for either percutaneous catheter insertion or cut-down technique
   f. Sterile gowns, drapes, gloves, masks, and hair covers
   g. Transducers and oscilloscope equipment
3. Preparation
   a. If the patient is on mechanical ventilation, settings and alarms should be checked, tubing emptied of water, and the patient suctioned.
   b. An IV line should be in place in the event that the patient requires treatment for arrhythmias during catheter insertion.
   c. Lidocaine, atropine, and a defibrillator should be available at the bedside for treatment of arrhythmias.
   d. The patient should be monitored with a continuous ECG.
   e. The transducers and connecting tubing should be set up with transducers properly leveled and the oscilloscope tested, zeroed, and calibrated.
   f. A sterile solution of 0.9% saline with 2–4 units of heparin per milliliter must be available to flush the catheter.
   g. The area of insertion should be properly scrubbed with povidone-iodine solution.
   h. Once the area for insertion is properly scrubbed, the largest area possible should be covered with a sterile drape.
   i. All assistants and the physician should be gowned, gloved, capped, and masked, to avoid any possible contamination.
   j. The physician will then proceed with the catheter insertion.

C. Cannulation of the radial artery
  1. Indications
     a. The need for continuous arterial pressure monitoring as opposed to intermittent monitoring with a cuff system
        (1) There may be a variance of 5–20 mmHg between direct measurement and indirect measurement of arterial blood pressure.
        (2) Direct reads higher.
     b. To avoid discomfort and injury when a large number of arterial punctures would be expected for blood gas assessment
     c. To allow arterial blood sampling without disturbing the patient's steady state
     d. For dye dilution cardiac output determination
     e. To provide a site for rapid phlebotomy in the case of fluid overload
  2. Equipment
     a. 20-gauge teflon, catheter over the needle with a nontapered shaft, 1¼–2 inches in length
     b. A short arm board with a roll of gauze
     c. Povidone-iodine solution
     d. 1% lidocaine without epinephrine and a 3 ml syringe with a 25-gauge needle
     e. Sterile gloves, masks, hair covers, and drapes
     f. Fluid-filled connecting tubing for the transducer
     g. Transducer and oscilloscope, properly checked and prepared prior to cannulation

VI. Transtracheal aspiration[5]

A. Before performing the procedure, coagulation studies should be drawn to be sure the procedure is not contraindicated.

B. The procedure is described to the patient and then the expected discomfort is demonstrated by pressing firmly on the patient's trachea. The patient often feels a choking sensation, plus moderately severe coughing.

C. Hand-nebulize 3 ml of 1% methylene blue into the oropharynx in order to mark the upper respiratory tract. In this way, any oropharyngeal contamination that might occur during the procedure can be detected.

D. Administer nasal oxygen during the procedure because the patient may become significantly hypoxemic due to paroxysmal coughing. Maintain SaO_2 of at least 90% by oximetry measurement.

E. Position the patient so that the neck is hyperextended. A pillow under the shoulders is usually sufficient.

F. Cleanse the anterior neck with an iodophor gauze or pad.

G. After putting on sterile gloves, place a sterile drape on the patient's chest and prepare a 10 cm intracath. A large (14 gauge) CVP needle and catheter (16 gauge) are cut to 10 cm in length.

H. Fill a 2 ml syringe with 2% lidocaine and draw up 5 ml of sterile saline into a 5 ml syringe. The saline must not contain any bacteriostatic preservative. Have on hand another 10 ml syringe without saline.

I. Hand the patient a sputum cup so he may expectorate if necessary. He only need turn his head to the side.

J. Have an assistant hold the patient's forehead so that the patient will not lurch forward during the procedure. Ask the patient not to swallow, which would make the cricothyroid membrane move up and down.

K. After the catheter is inserted through the cricothyroid membrane, the assistant should put gentle pressure on the insertion site with a 3×3 sterile gauze pad.

L. The inserted catheter is then connected to a collection device that is already set up.

M. Once the specimen has been obtained, the catheter is pulled out of the trachea and firm pressure applied to the percutaneous puncture site for at least 5 minutes.

N. Coughing should not be encouraged for at least 12 hours, and IPPB, chest percussion, and postural drainage should not be done.

O. The specimen obtained is sent to the lab only if there is no contamination by methylene blue.

VII. Cardioversion[6]

A. The patient should be comfortable and lying on a hard surface in case CPR is required.

B. An intravenous catheter should be in place.

C. The patient is anesthetized 5–10 minutes before the procedure with 50–100 mg of IV phenobarbital or 25–50 mg of Brevital.

D. Blood pressure is monitored constantly during the anesthesia.

E. The airway is maintained in a patent position and the patient ventilated with a manual ventilation bag and mask with 100% O_2.

F. Just prior to cardioversion, 5 mg of valium (sedative) is given IV, followed by 2.5 mg IV every 2–3 minutes until appropriate sedation occur.

G. The cardioverting equipment should be set on "synchronous" mode and adequate synchronization demonstrated.

H. To facilitate synchronization, the ECG lead with the biggest R wave should be selected.

I. Both electrodes are completely covered with gel to prevent skin burns.
J. The paddles are applied firmly to the chest wall, and the monitor is inspected to ensure that proper synchronization is occurring.
K. The shock is delivered only after the operator is certain that no assisting personnel are in contact with the patient or the bed.

VIII. Transtracheal oxygen catheter placement[7]

A. Preprocedure preparation
   1. The patient arrives one hour before the procedure and should not have taken food or drink by mouth after midnight (medications can be taken with small sips of water).
   2. If the patient's $PaCO_2$ is ≤50 torr, a single dose of antitussive, analgesic, and sedative medication may be given (Tylox or Percocet).
   3. In patients whose $PaCO_2$ is ≥50 torr, 25–50 mg of Benadryl can be given one hour prior to the procedure.
   4. A prophylactic antibiotic effective against *Staphylococcus aureus* is given.
   5. Patients at risk for bronchospasm are given a bronchodilator treatment about 30 minutes prior to the procedure.
   6. Patient removes upper body clothing and dons a hospital gown.
   7. The patient is positioned in an ENT (ear, nose, and throat) examination chair, which is angled backward about 10 degrees with slight extension of the patient's neck.
   8. Nasal prongs are positioned for the O_2 tubing to arrive from behind the patient's head. If an O_2 mask is used, it is inverted and taped to the patient's head.
   9. The procedure is best done in an open room with a window, with patient-preferred music playing, with a confident and organized team.
B. Insertion of the stent (SCOOP)
   1. The puncture site is selected by passing the necklace around the patient's neck and noting where the necklace crosses the tracheal midline.
      a. This should be below the cricoid membrane.
      b. Puncture through the cricoid membrane will result in hoarseness and potential induration and discomfort.
   2. Local anesthesia of the pretracheal tissues is performed, followed by transtracheal anesthesia with lidocaine.
   3. The skin is prepared with a chlorhexidine scrub from the jaw to the clavicles and laterally to include the sternocleidomastoid muscles.
   4. The patient is draped appropriately and a vertical 1 centimeter incision is made over the chosen site.

Chapter 28: Assistance with Special Procedures 485

5. A 7 centimeter needle is inserted in the midline and perpendicular to the trachea through the interspace of the tracheal cartilages.
6. The atraumatic end of the wire guide is inserted through the needle to the 11 centimeter mark.
7. The dilator is passed over the wire guide with a firm and steady push to a point 2 centimeters into the trachea and left in place for one minute.
8. The stent is inserted immediately after removal of the dilator to help tamponade any venous seepage and is twirled 360 degrees so that the flange rests against the skin.
9. The stent is secured with sutures.
10. Observe the patient for at least one hour after the procedure.
11. Following one week with the stent in place to form a tract, the SCOOP catheter is inserted and catheter cleaning supplies and instructions given to the patient.

IX. Sleep apnea studies (Polysomnography)[8]

A. An electrocardiogram is monitored with a standard Lead II electrode arrangement.
B. The electroencephalogram and electro-oculogram are used to prove that the patient actually sleeps and are applied in the standard way. The chin, leg, or intercostal electromyelogram can also be used to recognize sleep.
C. Oxygen saturation is measured continuously during the study using ear or pulse oximetry.
D. Nasal and oral airflow measurements are made by placing thermistor tips into the nose and mouth.
E. Measurement of ventilatory effort is made by placement of respiratory magnetometers on both the chest wall and abdomen.
F. Identification of type of apnea
   1. Loss of flow at the mouth and nose demonstrates apnea.
   2. If apnea occurs during continued effort to breathe, as seen by documented movement of the thorax and abdomen, the apnea is a result of obstruction.
      a. SaO_2 decreases in proportion to the length of apnea.
      b. Slow wave (delta) sleep is typically absent due to frequent arousals from repeated episodes of apnea.
      c. Onset of rapid-eye-movement (REM) sleep is often delayed or absent.
   3. Central apnea has occurred if there is simultaneous absence of thoracic or abdominal movement.
      a. Hypercapnic central apnea
         (1) A gradual reduction in ventilation is seen until the apnea occurs with the onset of sleep.

(2) SaO_2 decreases as hypopneas and apnea persist.
(3) The amount and distribution of stages of sleep may be normal in this group.
  b. Nonhypercapnic central apnea
    (1) Recurrent episodes of hypopneas and apneas are seen in the transition from wakefulness to sleep.
    (2) Hyperpnea occurs during arousal and minimal or no periods of falling SaO_2 are seen in this group.

X. Stress testing[9]

A. Purposes
  1. To confirm or establish a tentative diagnosis.
  2. To exclude a specific diagnosis.
  3. To establish whether the patient is impaired.
  4. To identify the most limiting disorder the patient has.
  5. To evaluate the need for or response to treatment.
B. Exercise testing outside of the laboratory
  1. Climbing one or two flights of stairs with the patient directly shows the patient's ability to perform this level of exercise and allows direct assessment of the level of dyspnea.
  2. In severely limited patients, slow walking in a hallway for evaluation for the need for supplemental O_2 may be safer than using a treadmill.
  3. Running out-of-doors is a better test for exercise-induced bronchospasm than the treadmill.
    a. Forced expiratory maneuvers should be performed immediately prior to the exercise and at 1, 3, 5, and 10 minutes following exercise.
  4. In patients with known respiratory disease, reports of the time it takes the patient to walk a fixed distance can be used to assess progress.
C. Exercise testing inside the laboratory
  1. Treadmill versus cycle ergometer
    a. A slightly higher VO_2max is seen with the treadmill compared to the cycle.
    b. Maximum values for heart rate, ventilation, and lactate are similar for both apparatus.
    c. ST segment abnormalities on the ECG are more easily induced on the treadmill in some patients.
    d. Quantifying workload is more difficult on the treadmill due to the following reasons:
      (1) A training effect commonly occurs with treadmill exercise.

(2) A change in the patient's gait from walking to running, while treadmill speed remains constant, may affect metabolic demand and therefore alter those indicators during the test.

(3) Physical attachment of the patient to a fixed object such as a railing may significantly reduce the work performed at a given treadmill speed and grade.

2. Advantages of the cycle ergometer
   a. Patient movement is lessened and results in less artifact in measurements being performed.
   b. There is a more accurate measurement of actual work performed.
   c. Lower work levels can be used than with the treadmill.
3. Final decisions to use treadmill or cycle ergometer are based on:
   a. The patient's physical ability to use one or the other.
   b. The patient's coordination.
   c. The availability of the equipment.
   d. The experience of the laboratory staff.

D. Measurements performed
   1. Work rate is recorded as the speed and grade or revolutions/minute.
   2. Gas exchange
      a. Using computers and rapid gas analyzers, $\dot{V}O_2$, $\dot{V}CO_2$, $\dot{V}E$, $\dot{V}E/\dot{V}O_2$, $\dot{V}E/\dot{V}CO_2$, respiratory rate, and tidal volume can be measured before, during, and after exercise.
      b. In addition, heart rate and arterial blood gas data allow calculation of O_2 pulse, $P(A\text{-}a)DO_2$, and $P(a\text{-}ET)CO_2$.
      c. With serial measurements of the data, $\dot{V}O_2$max, anaerobic threshold, and change in $\dot{V}O_2$/change in work rate can be calculated.
   3. Electrocardiogram and blood pressure
      a. For safety reasons, these should be measured before, during, and after testing.
      b. Monitoring intra-arterial pressure during monitoring is more accurate and allows identification of pulsus paradoxus in patients with severe pulmonary disease.
   4. Blood gases, pH, and lactate
      a. Blood is ideally drawn from an indwelling arterial catheter over a period of 10–20 seconds and analyzed promptly.
      b. Samples are typically drawn at the following times:
         (1) At rest, before and after insertion of the mouthpiece.
         (2) During unloaded cycling or walking.
         (3) Every 2 minutes during each change in work increment, at maximum exercise, and 2 minutes into recovery.

c. Pulse oximetry can be used for surveillance, but may not be reliable during high intensity exercise because of compromise of perfusion or very low saturations.

d. Transcutaneous measurements during exercise in the adult are not considered reliable.

E. Constant work rate protocols
1. This approach is useful to define the anaerobic threshold or response to drug or rehabilitation therapy.
2. Moderate intensity work at a constant rate may be helpful to define the need for supplemental O_2 in the pulmonary patient.

F. Incremental work rate protocols
1. Metabolic and cardiovascular measurements are made for 3 minutes at rest, 3 minutes of unloaded cycling or walking, during incremental work rate change until the patient's symptom-related maximum work rate is reached, and during 2 minutes of recovery.
    a. When the cycle is used, the work rate is changed in 10–30 watts/minute in most patients.
    b. When the treadmill is used, the work rate is increased by maintaining the original walking speed and increasing the grade 1–3%/minute.
2. The work rate increments needed should be determined in order to reach maximal exercise in 8–10 minutes of incremental cycle exercise. Guidelines are:
    a. Respiratory patients to increase 5 watts/minute.
    b. Healthy sedentary persons to increase 17 watts/minute.
    c. Athletes to increase 23 watts/minute.
3. Any indication of chest pain terminates the stress test immediately.

XI. Percutaneous needle (pleural) biopsy[10]

A. Pleural biopsy is considered in patients with undiagnosed exudative effusion, most commonly malignancy or tuberculosis.

B. Common contraindications include
1. Uncooperative patient
2. Hemodynamic instability
3. Status asthmaticus
4. Unstable angina
5. Life-threatening arrhythmias

C. Procedure for pleural biopsy is essentially the same as for thoracentesis.

D. The most common complication associated with the procedure is pneumothorax. Refer to Ch. 28, II, A.

Chapter 28: Assistance with Special Procedures

XII. Venipuncture[11]

A. Indications include access to the patient's veins for laboratory testing as well as point of entry for IVs and blood transfusions.

B. Equipment
   1. Tourniquet
   2. 70% alcohol prep pads
   3. Dry gauze pads
   4. Appropriate evacuation tubes
   5. Blood collection system holder
   6. Adhesive pressure strip

C. Procedure
   1. Verify order and wash hands.
   2. Identify and confirm patient.
   3. Inform patient of the procedure.
   4. Reassure the patient.
   5. Properly position the patient.
      a. Have bed patients lie on their back with a support (pillow) under the arm.
      b. Have ambulatory patients seated comfortably in a chair with the arm slanting in a straight line from the shoulder to the wrist.
      c. Never perform venipuncture on a patient when they are standing upright.
   6. Assemble equipment.
   7. Select proper size needle (21-gauge, 1 inch).
   8. Select site for venipuncture.
   9. Do not draw blood above an intravenous line.
   10. Apply the tourniquet 3–4 inches above the site you selected, never leaving it on longer than one minute.
   11. Select the appropriate vein:
      a. Basilic
      b. Cephalic
      c. Median cubital
   12. Ask the patient make a fist to prominately display the veins.
   13. Using the index finger palpate the vein.
   14. Clean the venipuncture site.
   15. Grasp the patient's arm two inches below the puncture site and pull the skin tight with your thumb to prevent the vein from rolling.
   16. Perform the ventipuncture.
   17. The evacuation tube should be below the puncture site to prevent backflow.

18. Release the tourniquet.
19. Ask the patient to open their hand.
20. Place sterile gauze over the puncture site and remove the needle.
21. Apply pressure until the bleeding stops.
22. Apply adhesive pressure strip over the puncture site.
23. Label the tubes.
24. Wash your hands.

References

1. Burton, G. G., Hodgkin, J. E., and Ward, J. J., *Respiratory Care: A Guide to Clinical Practice*, 4th ed., Lippincott, 1997.
2. Jay, S. I., and Stonehill, R. B., *Manual of Pulmonary Procedures*, W. B. Saunders, 1980.
3. Scanlon, C. L., Wilkins, R. L., and Stoller, J. K., *Egan's Fundamentals of Respiratory Therapy*, 7th ed., Mosby, 1999.
4. Darovic, G. O., *Hemodynamic Monitoring: Invasive and Noninvasive Clinical Application*, 2nd ed., W. B. Saunders, 1995.
5. Shoemaker, W. C., et al., *The Society of Critical Care Medicine Textbook of Critical Care*, 3rd ed., W. B. Saunders, 1999.
6. *Advanced Cardiac Life Support*, American Heart Association, 1997.
7. Spofford, B., et al., "Transtracheal Oxygen Therapy," *Problems in Respiratory Care* 3, no. 4, December 1990.
8. Wilkins, R. L., Sheldon, R. L., and Krider, S. J., *Clinical Assessment in Respiratory Care*, 3rd ed., Mosby, 1995.
9. Hansen, J., "Exercise Testing for the Pulmonologist," *Current Pulmonology* 14, Mosby-Yearbook, 1993.
10. Parsons, P. E., and Heffner, J. E., *Pulmonary/Respiratory Therapy Secrets*, Hanley & Belfus Inc., 1997.
11. Pendergraph, G. E., *Handbook of PHLEBOTOMY*, 3rd ed., Lea & Febiger, 1992.

Assessment Questions

1. A chest tube is not necessarily indicated for pneumothorax until the collapsed lung volume becomes greater than _____% of the total lung volume.
    A. 20
    B. 25
    C. 30
    D. 40

2. The hypopharynx is normally anesthetized with:
    A. 2% ketamine
    B. 2% epinephrine
    C. 2% atropine
    D. 2% lidocaine

3. The main indication for performing a thoracentesis is:
    A. Pneumothorax
    B. Pleural effusion
    C. Air embolism
    D. Hemoptysis

Chapter 28: Assistance with Special Procedures

4. The most common complication to performing percutaneous needle biopsy of the chest is:
   A. Pneumothorax
   B. Unstable angina
   C. Pleural effusion
   D. Hemorrhage

5. You would stop a stress test from proceeding when:
   A. The patient complains of chest pain
   B. The patient's heart rate increases >20 bpm
   C. The patient's respiratory rate increases
   D. The patient's systolic blood pressure increases by 20 mmHg over normal

6. Which of the following are common sites for venipuncture?
   I. Radial
   II. Basilic
   III. Cephalic
   IV. Median cubital

   A. I, II, III and IV
   B. I, III and IV only
   C. II only
   D. II, III and IV only

7. The popular procedure for obtaining an anaerobic sputum sample in a nonintubated patient would be:
   A. Nasotracheal suction
   B. Percutaneous needle biopsy
   C. Transtracheal aspirate
   D. Thoracentesis

8. Which of the following positions are appropriate for performing venipuncture?
   I. Sitting in a chair
   II. Standing upright
   III. Lying in bed

   A. I only
   B. I, II and III
   C. I and III only
   D. III only

9. Which drugs are indicated when assisting the physician with a patient who requires cardioversion?
   I. Phenobarbital
   II. Diazepam
   III. Sodium Brevital

   A. I and II only
   B. I, II and III
   C. II only
   D. II and III only

Chapter 29

Record Maintenance and Documentation

I. **General care includes IPPB, aerosol, oxygen, and chest physical therapy. The following areas should have data recorded when general care is performed.**[1]

A. Patient identification, including name, hospital ID number, and room number

B. Identifying time factors, including date, specific time, how long the therapist spent from beginning to end of the entire procedure, and how long the patient was actually receiving therapy

C. Documenting the specific therapy will include a varying number of parameters to record depending upon the specific type of therapy. For example, when setting up oxygen therapy, it may not be practical to record breath sounds before, during, and after because it will be continuous therapy. With IPPB, however, it is practical to record before, during, and after data.
  1. Mode of therapy includes oxygen, IPPB, aerosol, etc.
  2. Description of the therapy includes oxygen via trach "T," etc.
  3. Breath sounds are noted before, during, and after the therapy.
     a. Region for the breath sounds is best described by:
        (1) Specifying the major bronchopulmonary segment, such as over the anterior segment of the upper lobe.
        (2) Diffuse lung sounds may be described in a more general manner (i.e., lobe, lung, or bilateral).
     b. Types of breath sounds
        (1) Absent or reduced
        (2) Normal
        (3) Wheezes or rhonchi
        (4) Crackles or rales
     c. Inspiratory or expiratory sounds
  4. Pulse rate before, during, and after when appropriate.

Chapter 29: Record Maintenance and Documentation 493

5. Blood pressure before, during, and after when appropriate.
6. Respiratory rate before, during, and after when appropriate.
7. Patient's general condition may be noted in a single descriptive term such as alert, quiet, confused, restless, apprehensive, fatigued, fully conscious, semi-conscious, comatose, asleep, or medicated.
8. Patient's attitude may be described using terms such as cooperative, uncooperative, not responding.
9. Does the patient feel that the therapy is helpful?
10. Are there any adverse reactions to the therapy?
11. Types of cough may be noted with such descriptive terms as frequent, infrequent, when encouraged, none, strong, moderate, weak, loose or moist, nonproductive, or dry.
12. Sputum description.
    a. Quantity in milliliters
    b. How it was obtained
       (1) Spontaneously produced by coughing
       (2) Suctioned—stipulate whether it was through the patient's natural airway or through an artificial airway
       (3) Induced
       (4) Sterile procedure—such as transtracheal or via flexible bronchoscope
    c. Color and consistency
13. Patient interface.
    a. Oro-nasotracheal tube or tracheostomy tube
    b. Mask or mouthpiece
    c. Cushion seal with mouthpiece
14. Mode of breathing may be described as spontaneous, assisted, controlled, IMV, pressure support, manual ventilation bag
15. Patient position.
16. Tidal volume or vital capacity.
17. Pressure or flowrate or both, depending on the mode of therapy.
18. Inspired oxygen concentration.
19. Medication name and dosage if appropriate.

II. For critical care (adult), the same general data should be recorded that is recorded in the general care category. Additional critical care data may include any or all of the following:

A. Spontaneous or physiological data
   1. Pulse and respiratory rate
   2. Blood pressure (systolic, diastolic, and mean)

3. Urine output
4. Patient temperature
B. Lung mechanics
1. Tidal volume and vital capacity
2. Maximum inspiratory and expiratory force
C. Hemodynamic data
1. Cardiac output
2. Central venous pressure
3. Pulmonary artery pressure (systolic, diastolic, mean)
4. Pulmonary capillary wedge pressure
5. Left atrial pressure
D. Mechanical data
1. End-tidal CO_2
2. Mechanical rate and tidal volume
3. Minute ventilation
4. Peak and static pressures, including pressure support level
5. Static/dynamic compliance
6. FIO_2
7. Peak inspiratory flowrate
8. PEEP/CPAP value
9. Mechanical deadspace
10. Inspiratory:expiratory time and ratio
11. Sigh volume and rate per hour
12. Artificial airway cuff volume and pressure
13. Inspired gas temperature
E. Arterial blood gas data
1. Acid-base: pH, $PaCO_2$, Plasma HCO_3, standard HCO_3, base excess, T_{40} HCO_3
2. Oxygenation: PaO_2, SaO_2, O_2 content, P_{50}, PO_2

III. Pediatric/neonatal care

A. Many of the data categories recorded are the same ones used for adults.
1. Patient identification data
2. Ventilator parameters
3. Breath sounds
4. Vital signs: pulse, BP, respiratory rate
5. Sputum data

Chapter 29: Record Maintenance and Documentation 495

B. Values generally unique to neonatal/pediatric care
   1. Monitoring data
      a. $TcPO_2$
      b. $TcPCO_2$
      c. Mean airway pressure
      d. Transpulmonary pressure
      e. Duration of positive pressure
      f. I:E ratio, inspiratory and expiratory times
   2. Patient interface
      a. Orotracheal tube
      b. Tracheostomy tube
      c. Nasal prongs
   3. Mechanical airway size and length
   4. Patient condition may include awake/quiet, awake/active, quiet/sleep, active/sleep, medicated

IV. Legal/ethical implications in charting and documentation[1]

A. A seemingly reciprocal relationship characterizes patients' rights and the rights of health care providers. This relationship revolves around certain ethical principles.
   1. Autonomy acknowledges the patient's right to decide her own course of treatment. Prior to any procedure being performed or medication administered a signed consent for treatment must be part of the patient's record making the patient part of an agreed-upon treatment plan.
   2. Veracity binds a relationship to truthfulness. To effectively treat the patient, the health care giver relies on subjective and objective data. The result being that patient and caregiver benefit from mutual trust and sharing of information. This part of the relationship is essential and helps create accurate profiles and records on the patient.
   3. Nonmaleficence requires the caregiver to actively prevent putting the patient in harm's way. A large dose of a physician-ordered drug that is not commonly ordered would not be administered, because data was insufficient to indicate the treatment was warranted. Conferring with the physician and documenting the discussion help prevent an incident that could potentially have an adverse effect on the patient.
   4. Beneficence is a higher standard than "no harm," and although some controversy exists, the reference is generally regarded to mean that the caregiver will contribute to the health and well-being of the patient. The quality of life issue resides here and requires the caregiver to do everything possible to promote the patient's life, regardless of cause.

B. Confidentiality is founded in the Hippocratic Oath, and must be in harmony with the other principles.
  1. The "Harm Principle" is where controversy arises. Is more harm caused by maintaining confidentiality, or by harmful disclosure? A patient you are treating is being reimbursed for a disability due to a disease, and you are well aware there is no trace of any disease process. This principle requires restraint from acts of omission.
  2. The AMA Code of Ethics, Section 9, makes this statement: "A physician may not reveal the confidences entrusted to him in the course of medical attendance or the deficiencies he may observe in the character of patients, unless he is required to do so by law, or unless it becomes necessary in order to protect the welfare of the community or a vulnerable individual."

References

1. Scanlon, C. L., Wilkins, R. L., and Stoller, J. K., *Egan's Fundamentals of Respiratory Therapy*, 7th ed., Mosby, 1999.

Assessment Questions

1. The single most important event to document when providing oxygen therapy to a COPD patient who has developed cor pulmonale is:
   A. Decreased respiratory rate
   B. Decreased work of breathing
   C. Decreased right ventricular preload
   D. Increased left ventricular afterload

2. After obtaining a sputum sample from a patient, you would want to chart which of the following?
   I. Sputum color
   II. Sputum odor
   III. Sputum quantity
   IV. Sputum viscosity

   A. I and II only
   B. I, II, III and IV
   C. II, III and IV only
   D. III and IV only

3. During a patient's initial interview, which of the following are important?
   I. Privacy
   II. Minimal interruptions
   III. Comfortable environment
   IV. Making sure the patient listens to the interviewer

   A. I and II only
   B. I, II and III only
   C. II, III and IV only
   D. IV only

4. You have just finished administering an aerosol treatment to a patient, and they start complaining of severe dyspnea. You would do which of the following?
   I. Review the patient's medical record
   II. Immediately give another treatment
   III. Question patient regarding nature of dyspnea
   IV. Notify physician for recommendations for therapy

   A. I only
   B. I and IV only
   C. II and III only
   D. III and IV only

Chapter 29: Record Maintenance and Documentation

5. Which of the following principles apply to a patient's rights associated with informed consent?
   A. Confidentiality
   B. Autonomy
   C. Beneficence
   D. Veracity

6. Communicating patient information to the other members of the health care team is accomplished through:
   A. Giving report at shift change
   B. Giving report to the shift supervisor
   C. Informing the unit manager of all patient changes
   D. Recording the information in the patient's chart

7. Which of the following principles apply to a patient's right to pursue her own course of treatment?
   A. Confidentiality
   B. Autonomy
   C. Beneficence
   D. Veracity

8. While reviewing a patient's progress notes you realize changes have been made in the respiratory care plan. Your first response would be to:
   A. Consider the new plan as an alternative to current therapy
   B. Implement the new plan changes immediately
   C. Check the chart for a corresponding order
   D. Carefully assess the patient prior to implementing changes

9. Which of the following principles require caregivers to contribute to a patient's health and well-being?
   A. Confidentiality
   B. Autonomy
   C. Beneficence
   D. Veracity

Section IV:

Self-Assessment

Setting

In any testing or evaluation setting, the respiratory therapist is able to demonstrate the mastery of key clinical skills and their underlying theoretical foundations.

As mentioned in Chapter 1, the self-assessment examinations should only be taken following a thorough review of the content in Chapters 2 through 29. An appropriate understanding of content, along with a basic understanding of test-taking tips, will provide a sound base for successful completion of the credentialing exams.

Because the credentialing exams are timed (three hours for the CRT, two hours for the RRT, and four hours for the Csim), it is advisable to limit the following individual exams to their corresponding time length. Completing the self-assessment exam within this self-imposed time frame will help you adapt to some of the pressures of timed exams. Once the exams start being administered by computer (January 2000), a visible on-screen clock will continually count down the remaining examination time.

Chapters within this section include self-assessments for:

30. Certified Respiratory Therapist (CRT) Self-Assessment Examination

31. Registered Respiratory Therapist (RRT) Self-Assessment Examination

Clinical Simulation Examinations are contained on the CD inside the back cover.

Based on results from the 1998 job analysis conducted by the NBRC, examination matrices were again developed for both the entry level and advanced practitioner exams. These matrices identify the number of questions and the complexity level (recall, application, and analysis) assessed for the major content areas.[1]

The 140-question CRT examination consists of 36 questions at the recall level, 72 questions related to application, and 32 questions at the analysis level of complexity. Refer to Table IV-1 for a more detailed account of the CRT examination matrix.

The 100-question RRT examination consists of 12 questions at the recall level, 15 questions related to application, and 73 questions at the analysis level of complexity. Refer to Table IV-2 for a more detailed account of the written registry examination matrix.

TABLE IV-1: Entry Level (CRT) Examination Content Outline

Content Area	Cognitive Level			Number of Items
	Recall	Application	Analysis	
I. Clinical Data	—	17	4	25
A. Review patient records; recommend diagnostic procedures	2	3	0	5
B. Collect and evaluate clinical information	3	7	0	10
C. Perform procedures and interpret results	2	3	0	5
D. Assess therapeutic plan	0	1	4	5
II. Equipment	14	22	0	36
A. Select, obtain, and assure cleanliness	5	8	0	13
B. Assemble and check malfunctions; perform quality control	9	14	0	23
III. Therapeutic Procedures	15	36	28	79
A. Educate patients; maintain records and communication; implement infection control	2	3	0	5
B. Maintain airway; mobilize and remove secretions	2	3	0	5
C. Achieve adequate ventilation and oxygenation	2	5	9	16
D. Assess patient response	2	6	2	10
E. Recommend and modify therapeutics; recommend pharmacologic agents	3	12	17	32
F. Treat cardiopulmonary collapse by protocol	2	4	0	6
G. Assist physician; conduct pulmonary rehabilitation and home care	2	3	0	5
Totals	36	72	32	140

Source: Used with permission granted from NBRC. Revised content outlines, the National Board for Respiratory Care, Inc. July 1998.

Section IV: Self-Assessment

TABLE IV-2: RRT Written Examination Content Outline

Content Area	Cognitive Level			Number of Items
	Recall	Application	Analysis	
I. Clinical Data	3	3	11	17
A. Review patient records; recommend diagnostic procedures	1	1	3	5
B. Collect and evaluate additional clinical information	1	1	5	7
C. Perform diagnostic procedures, interpret results, and assist in care plan	1	1	3	5
II. Equipment	3	4	13	20
A. Select, obtain, and assure cleanliness	1	2	5	8
B. Assemble, check for proper function, identify and/or correct malfunctions, and perform quality control	2	2	8	12
III. Therapeutic Procedures	6	8	49	63
A. Evaluate, monitor, and record patient's response	2	3	13	18
B. Maintain airway, remove secretions, and assure ventilation and tissue oxygenation	1	1	10	12
C. Modify therapy	0	1	10	11
D. Perform emergency procedures	1	1	10	12
E. Assist physician and conduct pulmonary rehabilitation home care	2	2	6	10
Totals	12	15	73	100

Source: Used with permission granted from NBRC. Revised content outlines, the National Board for Respiratory Care, Inc. July 1998.

TABLE IV-3: RRT Clinical Simulation Examination Content Outline

Clinical Simulation Examination Matrix

I. **Data**
   A. Review patient information
   B. Collect clinical information
   C. Perform diagnostic procedures

II. **Equipment**
   A. Select, obtain, assure cleanliness
   B. Assemble, check function correct malfunctions

III. **Therapeutic Procedures**
   A. Explain therapy, protect patient
   B. Evaluate, monitor, record responses
   C. Conduct therapeutic procedures
   D. Modify procedures or care plan
   E. Modify care in emergency setting
   F. Assist physician, conduct rehabilitation, and home care

Source: Used with permission granted from NBRC. Revised content outlines, the National Board for Respiratory Care, Inc. July 1998.

Teaching and testing clinical scenarios are supplied in simulation format within the CD. Refer to Table IV-3 for a more detailed account of the clinical simulation examination matrix.

The correct answers, corresponding reference page numbers, and individual chapter keys follow the examinations.

Reference

"Revised Content Outlines, The National Board for Respiratory Care, Inc., July 1998.

Chapter 30

Certified Respiratory Therapist (CRT) Self-Assessment Examination

Directions: Select the one best answer or completion for each of the following questions or incomplete statements. The correct response along with the corresponding MASTER GUIDE reference may be found following Chapter 31.

1. Clinical lab evaluation of a patient with known allergic reactions would most likely reveal

   A. decreased neutrophils.
   B. increased eosinophils.
   C. decreased basophils.
   D. decreased monocytes.

2. From a forced vital capacity maneuver, which of the following pulmonary function values may be obtained?

   I. FVC
   II. FEV_1
   III. FRC
   IV. IRV
   V. ERV

   A. I, II, III, IV, and V
   B. I, II, III, and V only
   C. I, II, IV, and V only
   D. I, III, and V only

3. An elderly patient has received bronchodilator therapy and has coarse crackles in the major airways. The patient's cough in the semi-Fowler's position is weak and ineffective. Which position may lead to improved cough effectiveness?

   A. Semi-prone
   B. High-Fowler's
   C. Trendelenburg
   D. Supine

4. Which combination of air and oxygen will produce an FIO_2 of 35%?

O_2 (L/min)	Room Air (L/min)
I. 2 L/min	8 L/min
II. 4 L/min	18 L/min
III. 6 L/min	24 L/min
IV. 8 L/min	32 L/min

   A. I, II, III, and IV
   B. I, III, and IV only
   C. II, III, and IV only
   D. II and IV only

5. When sampling the atmosphere of an incubator or oxygen hood, the gas sample intake tubing or sensor needs to be

   A. near the face of the patient.
   B. at the farthest point from the patient.

C. near the oxygen outlet.
D. at the top of the enclosure to reduce humidity interference.

6. Following a FVC maneuver, the flowrate that is considered the least effort dependent is the
   A. FEV_1.
   B. $FEF_{200-1200}$.
   C. FEF_{25-75}.
   D. MVV.

7. Given a VO_2 of 250 ml/min with $C_{(a-v)}O_2$ of 5 vol%, calculate the cardiac output.
   A. 1.25 L/min
   B. 5.0 L/min
   C. 12.5 L/min
   D. 50.0 L/min

8. During a thoracentesis, the patient suddenly becomes bradycardic with a rapid onset of pulmonary edema leading to cardiac arrest. Most likely this is due to
   A. a rapid loss of fluid.
   B. pericardial puncture.
   C. insertion of air into pleural space.
   D. hypoxemia.

9. An adult asthmatic patient is admitted to the emergency room in severe distress. Consciousness is impaired and the chest is silent. Peak expiratory flow is 25% baseline and $PaCO_2$ is 49 torr. You would recommend:
   I. nebulized B_2 agonists Q30–60 minutes.
   II. IV steroids.
   III. IV aminophylline.
   IV. intubation and mechanical ventilation.
   V. supplemental O_2.

   A. I, II, and III only
   B. II, III, and V only
   C. I and V only
   D. I, II, III, IV, and V

10. A respiratory therapist receives a physician's order to deliver a 7% carbon dioxide, 93% oxygen mixture. The therapist would look for a cylinder that is colored coded
    A. green.
    B. grey.
    C. gray top and green body.
    D. green top and grey body.

11. Which of the following are considerations of an ineffective cough?
    I. Usually is high pitched.
    II. Usually is low pitched.
    III. Originates high in the airway.
    IV. Huff coughing with COPD.

    A. I and III only
    B. I and IV only
    C. II and III only
    D. II and IV only

12. Successful entry of the trachea during nasotracheal suctioning is best judged by
    A. gagging by the patient.
    B. sounds of airflow at the proximal end of the catheter.
    C. the use of auscultation.
    D. the patient being unable to speak in a normal tone.

13. Important factors in the deposition of aerosols within the respiratory tract include
    I. gravity.
    II. kinetic activity of gas molecules.
    III. inertial impaction.
    IV. ventilatory pattern.

    A. I and II only
    B. I, II, III, and IV
    C. I, III, and IV only
    D. II and IV only

14. All of the following may be considered correct statements regarding the administration of a nitrogen washout test EXCEPT

Chapter 30: CRT Self-Assessment Examination

   A. test is used to obtain FRC, RV, and TLC.
   B. the normal lung can generally be washed out in 3 minutes.
   C. incomplete washout may occur in COPD patients.
   D. inhalation of 100% O_2 may satisfy the hypoxic drive mechanism.

15. During a chest physical exam, it is noted that there is increased tactile fremitus on the right side. This is most likely due to
   A. lung consolidation on the right side.
   B. lung consolidation on the left side.
   C. a pneumothorax on the right side.
   D. a pleural effusion bilaterally.

16. A patient is admitted through the emergency room as a result of auto versus tree. The patient has sustained multiple injuries to the skeleton including skull fracture. Following surgical intervention, the patient is transferred to the ICU and orders given for mechanical ventilation to achieve hyperventilation. From this action, you draw the conclusion that you are trying to:
   A. control the patient by removing respiratory drive.
   B. control intracranial blood volume and pressure.
   C. combat metabolic acidosis.
   D. improve myocardial contractility.

17. A oxygen entrainment mask will deliver a higher FIO_2 than expected if
   I. the internal diameter of the jet is increased.
   II. the external diameter of the jet is decreased.
   III. the entrainment ports have been blocked.
   IV. the flowrate on the flowmeter has been increased.

   A. I and II only
   B. I and III only
   C. II only
   D. III and IV only

18. Given a plasma bicarbonate (HCO_3^-) of 48 mEq/L and a PCO_2 of 80 mmHg, the pH would be
   A. equal to 7.40.
   B. greater than 7.40.
   C. less than 7.40.
   D. impossible to calculate.

19. In order to prevent excess pressure from building up inside humidifiers and nebulizers, a pop off device is utilized. Pressure pop offs are usually set at
   I. 40 mmHg.
   II. 80 mmHg.
   III. 2 PSIG.
   IV. 50 PSIG.

   A. I and III only
   B. I and IV only
   C. II and III only
   D. III only

20. Which of the following devices will provide positive end expiratory pressure?
   I. Threshold resistors
   II. Orifice resistors
   III. Flow resistors
   IV. Opposing flow devices

   A. I, II, III, and IV
   B. II and III only
   C. III only
   D. III and IV only

21. What toxic by-product may result when previously gamma-irradiated items are exposed to ETO sterilization?
   A. Propylene glycol
   B. Ethylene chlorohydrin
   C. Ethylene oxide
   D. Ethylene glycol

22. Coughing against an open glottis has been shown to be most effective in patients with
    A. polio.
    B. kyphosis.
    C. COPD.
    D. croup.

23. Upon finding a patient unresponsive, having tapped and shouted at the patient, having created an airway to find no spontaneous respiration with no discernible pulse, you would immediately
    A. pull the patient to the floor.
    B. look for a back board.
    C. run to find someone.
    D. yell for help.

24. The $P_{(A-a)}O_2$ normally increases with age because normally with age
    A. the PAO_2 increases.
    B. the PAO_2 decreases.
    C. the PaO_2 increases.
    D. the PaO_2 decreases.

25. Which of the following statements apply to the Coanda effect?
    A. Retard caps
    B. Hyperbaric oxygen therapy
    C. PEEP
    D. Fluidic control

26. The recommended maximum range of negative pressure that can be applied to the adult airway during suctioning is
    A. 50–60 mmHg.
    B. 60–80 mmHg.
    C. 80–100 mmHg.
    D. 100–120 mmHg.

27. Over the course of one year, a 48-year-old male developed progressive weakness of his right arm, with beginning involvement of his respiratory muscles. As compared with previous chest X-rays, there was a slight elevation of the hemidiaphragms. The patient had no known viral infections.

    Based on the observations, you would suspect which one of the following neuromuscular disorders?
    A. Amyotrophic lateral sclerosis
    B. Tetanus
    C. Guillain-Barre Syndrome
    D. Myasthenia gravis

28. As the disorder progresses, what should the therapeutic goals for the patient identified in the preceding question include?
    I. Airway maintenance
    II. Supportive ventilation
    III. Prevention of infection
    IV. Use of anticholinesterase therapy
    V. Adequate nutrition and hydration

    A. I and II only
    B. I, II, III, IV, and V
    C. I, II, III, and V only
    D. I, III, and V only

29. When performing cardiopulmonary resuscitation, if visible rise and fall of the chest is absent, the first move should be to:
    A. suction.
    B. ventilate more forcefully.
    C. reposition the airway.
    D. auscultate.

30. During metabolic studies, a respiratory quotient of 1.0 is obtained. This most likely would indicate that the main type of food being metabolized for energy is
    A. fats.
    B. carbohydrates.
    C. proteins.
    D. both A & B.

31. The suction device of choice when suctioning large food particles or vomitus from the mouth is the

Chapter 30: CRT Self-Assessment Examination

A. Murphy eye.
B. Carlens suction device.
C. Lukens tube.
D. Yankauer tonsil sucker.

32. A patient leaving the hospital has a 2-hour ride before arriving home. An "E" cylinder containing 1750 psig is providing the patient with continuous oxygen. What is the maximum liter flow that can be utilized and still allow the patient to arrive home with oxygen remaining?

   A. 1 L/min
   B. 2 L/min
   C. 3 L/min
   D. 4 L/min

33. Initial signs and symptoms of patients with pulmonary burns and smoke inhalation may include all of the following EXCEPT

   A. singed nasal hairs.
   B. tachypnea.
   C. carbon tinted sputum.
   D. low $PaCO_2$.

34. Which of the following statements regarding compliance is or are correct?

   I. Average adult lung compliance is 0.2 L/cmH_2O.
   II. Average neonate lung compliance is 0.006 L/cmH_2O.
   III. Lung compliance varies with volume of lungs at FRC.
   IV. Specific compliance of the neonate is 0.8 L/cmH_2O/L.
   V. Specific compliance of the adult is 0.8 L/cmH_2O/L.

   A. I only
   B. I, II, III, IV, and V
   C. I and III only
   D. I, III, and V only

35. The need for home oxygen therapy in the adult should be determined by the presence of

   A. PaO_2 less than 55 mmHg on room air.
   B. PaO_2 60–70 on room air.
   C. $PaCO_2$ greater than 60.
   D. systemic hypertension.

36. Chest physical therapy and postural drainage are being performed in a patient admitted with chronic bronchitis and pneumonia. After five minutes of therapy, the patient's distress has increased markedly. The probable cause is

   A. pain.
   B. pneumothorax.
   C. worsening V/Q mismatch.
   D. myocardial infarction.

37. You receive a physician's order to provide 28% oxygen via a mainstream nebulizer to a spontaneously breathing patient with a peak inspiratory flowrate of 48 L/min. What flowmeter setting must be utilized in order to provide a total flowrate of gas delivery that is greater than the patients inspiratory flowrate?

   A. 2 L/min
   B. 3 L/min
   C. 4 L/min
   D. 5 L/min

38. An arterial blood analysis reveals pH = 7.36; PCO_2 = 33 mmHg; HCO_3 = 18 mEq/L; base = -8 mEq/L. The most likely interpretation would be a(n)

   A. normal blood gas.
   B. fully compensated metabolic acidosis.
   C. respiratory alkalosis.
   D. uncompensated metabolic acidosis.

39. Which of the following conditions will appear radiopaque on chest X-ray?

   I. Atelectasis
   II. Pneumothorax
   III. Pneumonia
   IV. Emphysema
   V. Pleural effusion

A. I only
B. I, II, III, IV, and V
C. I, II, III, and V only
D. I, III, and V only

40. A normal spontaneous tidal volume, in ml/unit of ideal body weight, for a 150-pound person would be

   A. 3 ml/kg.
   B. 6–7 ml/LB.
   C. 6–7 ml/kg.
   D. 10–15 ml/LB.

41. The water content (absolute humidity) of a patient's inspired gas at normal body temperature is exerting a pressure of 28 mmHg. What is the % relative humidity?

   A. 56%
   B. 60%
   C. 64%
   D. 68%

42. Areas of lung requiring postural drainage are best identified by

   A. chest X-ray.
   B. tactile fremitus.
   C. inspection.
   D. percussion.

43. You are caring for a mechanically ventilated patient on SIMV = 4/min., Vt = 10 ml/Kg, PEEP = 5, inspiratory time = 2 sec., FIO_2 = 0.40. The patient's spontaneous rate is 35/min, and labored. You would now recommend

   A. increasing SIMV to 8/min.
   B. increasing PEEP to 10 cmH$_2$O.
   C. increasing FIO_2 to 0.5.
   D. maintain the same parameters.

44. Water is lying in the wide-bore tubing connected to a jet nebulizer that is powered by 100% oxygen and entraining air. Which of the following statements apply?

   I. Total flow remains the same.
   II. Total flow increases.
   III. Total flow decreases.
   IV. Oxygen concentration decreases.
   V. Oxygen concentration increases.

   A. I and IV only
   B. II and IV only
   C. II and V only
   D. III and V only

45. During physical exam, a patient is noted to be tachypneic. What are the possible causes?

   I. Pulmonary edema
   II. Brain trauma
   III. Pneumonia
   IV. Collagen vascular disease
   V. Methemoglobinemia

   A. I, II, and III only
   B. I, II, III, IV, and V
   C. I and III only
   D. II, III, and V only

46. An H-cylinder of oxygen was placed in service with 2,000 psig and has been used for 5 hours at a flowrate of 10 L/min. It can be used for how many additional hours?

   A. 4
   B. 5
   C. 6
   D. 7

47. Volume incentive spirometers are designed to

   A. require a minimum inspiratory flowrate in order to display the patient's inspiratory volume.
   B. display the patient's maximum voluntary ventilation.
   C. display the patient's maximum inspiratory volume regardless of the peak inspiratory flowrate.
   D. display the patient's vital capacity.

48. A normal healthy person is capable of generating an inspiratory force in excess of _____ in 10 seconds.

A. −80 cmH$_2$O
B. −40 cmH$_2$O
C. −20 cmH$_2$O
D. +20 cmH$_2$O

49. Assessing an infant for Apgar score includes which of the following?

   I. Color
   II. Heart rate
   III. Reflexes
   IV. Muscle tone

   A. I only
   B. I and II only
   C. I, II, and III only
   D. I, II, III, and IV only

50. You receive a written order to perform nasotracheal suctioning on a patient who is congested and has an ineffective cough. Which of the following would make this a hazardous procedure?

   I. Low platelet count
   II. Spastic airways
   III. Upper respiratory tract infection
   IV. Retained secretions
   V. Presence of a cardiac pacemaker

   A. II and IV only
   B. I, II, and III only
   C. III and IV only
   D. I, III, IV, and V only

51. You are administering a B$_2$ adrenergic bronchodilator treatment to a 23-year-old female patient with a history of asthma. After 10 minutes of therapy, the patient complains of shakiness and being "antsy." The pulse and blood pressure are only slightly above pretreatment values. You would

   A. discontinue therapy and contact the physician.
   B. stop the treatment and run to get the nurse.
   C. inform the patient that this is a normal side effect for this type of drug and not harmful.
   D. inform the nurse and physician and recommend discontinuing therapy.

52. Which of the following is the best overall indicator of the cardiopulmonary health and physical fitness of a patient?

   A. VO$_2$MAX
   B. Pulse
   C. PaO$_2$
   D. PvO$_2$

53. The Miller laryngoscope blade is placed

   A. under the uvula to expose the vocal cords.
   B. on top of the epiglottis to expose the glottis.
   C. under the epiglottis in order to expose the glottis.
   D. between the tongue and the tonsils.

54. The actual device used to measure end-tidal CO$_2$ is referred to as

   A. a capnometer.
   B. capnometry.
   C. a capnogram.
   D. capnography.

55. Fetal heart monitoring shows distress when there exists

   I. heart rate over 120/minute.
   II. loss of beat-to-beat variability.
   III. late deceleration.
   IV. early deceleration.
   V. constant beat-to-beat variability.

   A. I, II, and III only
   B. I, IV, and V only
   C. II and III only
   D. III and V only

56. You receive an order to do breathing technique training for a patient recently diagnosed with moderate chronic obstructive pulmonary disease. Which of the following is NOT an appropriate goal to share with the patient?

- A. To promote greater use of the diaphragm instead of accessory muscles
- B. To decrease hurried and gasping respiration via increased sensory awareness
- C. To better handle the feeling of dyspnea
- D. To restore the patient to having only mild instead of moderate disease

57. During the normal aging process, the chest takes on which of the following shapes?
    - A. Barrel
    - B. Funnel
    - C. Pigeon
    - D. Kyphosis

58. How many liters of gas are contained in one cubic foot of gas?
    - A. 14.3 L
    - B. 18.3 L
    - C. 24.3 L
    - D. 28.3 L

59. The best site to check for effective pulse during cardiac compressions is the _____ artery.
    - A. radial
    - B. brachial
    - C. femoral
    - D. carotid

60. When training a patient to perform incentive spirometry, the patient must taught that a common adverse effect is
    - A. hyperventilation.
    - B. infection.
    - C. arrhythmia.
    - D. gastroesophageal reflux.

61. The gross appearance of sputum in bronchiectasis is often
    - I. mucoid.
    - II. purulent.
    - III. fetid.
    - IV. bloody.
    - V. frothy.
    - A. I only
    - B. I and II only
    - C. I, II, III, IV, and V
    - D. II, III, and IV only

62. In order for an oxygen blender (controlling device) to provide precise oxygen concentrations it must
    - I. use a heated thermistor bead to measure the incoming gases.
    - II. use a proportioning valve that closes one side as it proportionally opens the other side.
    - III. use some method of pressure reduction in order to equalize the two incoming gas pressures.
    - A. I only
    - B. II only
    - C. I, II, and III
    - D. II and III only

63. The "best" PEEP value for any adult patient is reflected by which of the following?
    - I. Qs/Qt decreases to 15%
    - II. PvO_2 decreases with a further increase in PEEP
    - III. Qs/Qt increases from a previously lower level with a further increase in PEEP
    - IV. Vd/Vt decreases with a further increase in PEEP
    - A. I and II only
    - B. I, II, and III only
    - C. II and III only
    - D. II, III, and IV only

64. The lowest acceptable PaO_2 at sea level in adults without chronic pulmonary disease is
    - A. 50.
    - B. 60.
    - C. 70.
    - D. 80.

65. A 10-year-old asthmatic boy is being treated by you and is improving to the

point where he can be discharged. This patient has periodic attacks and several known allergies. At present, he is using only a B2 adrenergic metered-dose inhaler outside the hospital. Your recommendation to his physician would be

A. to add cromolyn sodium.
B. to add oral steroids.
C. to double the MDI dose.
D. to add theophylline.

66. A 50-year-old patient has the following blood gas values obtained while breathing room air:

$$pH = 7.31; PO_2 = 60 \text{ mmHg};$$
$$\text{and a } PCO_2 = 55 \text{ mmHg}$$

What is the cause of his hypoxemia?

I. Overall hypoventilation
II. Ventilation to perfusion mismatching
III. Diffusion defect
IV. Shunting

A. I only
B. I, II, III, and IV
C. I and III only
D. II, III, and IV only

67. A patient fills her portable oxygen walker to 900 liters prior to going out. As long as the flowrate is kept at 3 L/min the patient can stay out for

A. 4 hr 28 min.
B. 5 hr.
C. 5 hr 30 min.
D. 6 hr.

68. Aerosol output of an ultrasonic nebulizer is dependent upon

A. the speed of the blower motor.
B. the pressure in the couplant chamber.
C. the setting on the amplitude control.
D. the setting on the frequency control.

69. Mechanical percussors

I. can traumatize the patient's soft tissues and chest wall.
II. have an output range of 20–60 cycles per second.
III. are contraindicated in fragile patients.

A. I only
B. I and II only
C. I, II, and III
D. II only

70. The reading of the Beckman D-2 oxygen analyzer is most closely related to

A. polarographic readouts.
B. the quantity of oxygen molecules present in a magnetic field.
C. thermoconductivity passing through a twisted quartz fiber.
D. heating and cooling within a nitrogen-filled glass dumbbell.

71. In patients with large amounts of secretions, postural drainage should be done

A. two times per day for ten minutes.
B. three times per day for ten minutes.
C. three times per day for thirty minutes.
D. four times per day for thirty minutes.

72. Asymmetrical chest movement is noted on a 6-year-old boy during a scheduled preschool physical exam. The most likely cause is

A. the presence of a flail chest.
B. improper endotracheal tube placement.
C. congenital rib deformities.
D. unilateral pneumothorax.

73. A 27-year-old female patient is admitted with right lower lobe pneumonia acquired in the community. Following two days of Q4H bronchodilator therapy and clapping and postural drainage, the patient complains of feeling worse following the physical therapy. Considering the diagnosis, your recommendation would be to

A. discontinue the physical therapy.
B. change to vibration with posturing.
C. continue the same therapy.
D. change bronchodilators.

74. Two flowmeters are needed to supply an FIO_2 of 0.6. What flowrate needs to be set on the oxygen flowmeter, and what flowrate needs to be set on the air flowmeter to deliver 0.6 FIO_2 and keep the total flowrate at 10 L/min?
    A. 2 L O_2 and 8 L air
    B. 5 L O_2 and 5 L air
    C. 1 L O_2 and 9 L air
    D. 3 L O_2 and 7 L air

75. The audible alarm on an oxygen blender is sounding continuously, signaling that
    I. recalibration of the proportioning valve is required.
    II. recalibration of the step-down regulator is required.
    III. the compressed air line pressure is too low.
    IV. the oxygen line pressure is too low.
    V. a high flow blender is being used on the low flow setting.
    A. I, II, III, IV, and V
    B. II, III, IV, and V only
    C. III and IV only
    D. III, IV, and V only

76. Statements that describe how the venturi affects flow and pressure of a pneumatic pressure limited ventilator include which of the following?
    I. Flowrate decreases as inspiratory pressure rises.
    II. Throughout inspiration, flow and airway pressure rise synchronously.
    III. As the entrained flow of room air decreases during inspiration, source gas flow increases.
    IV. Inspiratory flow is the greatest at the beginning of inspiration.
    A. I and II only
    B. I and III only
    C. I and IV only
    D. IV only

77. The proper use of PEEP is reflected in an FIO_2 that is equal to or less than
    A. 0.4.
    B. 0.5.
    C. 0.6.
    D. 0.7.

78. The safest and most accessible site for arterial puncture is the _____ artery.
    A. brachial
    B. radial
    C. femoral
    D. brachiocephalic

79. The cuff pressure of an artificial airway should not exceed the value of _____ torr.
    A. 25
    B. 30
    C. 35
    D. 40

80. A patient admitted to the emergency room with a known history of diabetic ketoacidosis most likely will present with which type of breathing pattern?
    A. Cheyne-Stokes
    B. Biots
    C. Oligopnea
    D. Kussmauls

81. Setting the pressure control on a pressure preset ventilator will determine
    A. how much volume is required to inflate the patient's lungs.
    B. how much line pressure is available to drive the ventilator.
    C. the pressure gradient needed to reach alveolar critical opening pressure.
    D. when the ventilator will cycle into the expiratory phase.

82. You just finished analyzing an arterial blood sample in the laboratory and the co-oximeter shows a total hemoglobin of 15 grams/100ml with a carboxyhemoglobin or 2 grams and a methemoglobin of 2 grams. The amount of functional hemoglobin in this sample would be _____ grams.

    A. 15
    B. 13
    C. 11
    D. 9

83. The attending physician asks you to obtain a sterile sputum specimen from an intubated patient. The equipment you will need to obtain the sample includes

    I. a sputum sample collecting (Lukens) tube.
    II. a suction catheter with an external diameter that is ideally less than one-half the inner diameter of the patient's airway.
    III. a Yankauer tonsil sucker.
    IV. a fenestrated obturator.

    A. I only
    B. I and II only
    C. I, II, and IV only
    D. II and IV only

84. Conditions with severe hypoxemia that may exist without the presence of cyanosis include all of the following EXCEPT

    A. pulmonary arteriovenous fistula.
    B. anemia.
    C. carboxyhemoglobin.
    D. systemic vasodilatation with rapid blood flow.

85. Which of the following oxygen delivery devices may have their FIO_2s vary due to changes in a patient's ventilatory pattern?

    I. Nasal catheter
    II. Nasal cannula
    III. Entrainment (venturi) mask
    IV. Simple oxygen mask

    A. I, II, and III only
    B. I, II, III, and IV
    C. I, II, and IV only
    D. II, III, and IV only

86. All of the following are conditions where bronchial and bronchovesicular breath sounds may be heard over consolidated areas with a patent bronchial tree EXCEPT

    A. pneumonia.
    B. emphysema.
    C. pulmonary edema.
    D. atelectasis.

87. Respiratory acidosis may be caused by

    A. severe pulmonary edema.
    B. interstitial disease.
    C. pulmonary embolism.
    D. acute asthma.

88. A pneumatic nebulizer that delivers 70% oxygen would have an air-to-oxygen ratio of

    A. 1:1.
    B. 1:0.6.
    C. 1:1.6.
    D. 1:2.4.

89. You are caring for a mechanically ventilated patient on A/C = 14/min., Vt = 8ml/Kg, PEEP = 5, inspiratory time = 1.5 sec., FIO_2 = 35%. ABGs are within the normal range and the chest X-ray and breath sounds have cleared. The physician would like to wean the patient, but the patient has no spontaneous breathing even though he is awake. You recommend

    A. giving respiratory stimulants.
    B. reducing the FIO_2 to induce hypoxemia.
    C. switching to SIMV at a lower rate.
    D. cerebral blood flow studies.

90. Which of the following statements concerning particle size and deposition are correct?

I. Particles 100 microns in size are too large to enter the respiratory tract.
II. Increased alveolar deposition occurs with 5–7 micron size.
III. Particles 2–3 microns in size are most desirable for peripheral airway deposition.

A. I only
B. I and II only
C. I, II, and III
D. I and III only

91. You have received an order for bronchodilator therapy that requires 2.0mg of drug to be given Q4H. Your department stocks only unit dose medications and this drug comes prepared as 2.5mg in 3ml of solution. How much of this prepared solution will you draw up to get the required 2.0mg?

A. 2.0ml
B. 2.4ml
C. 1.8ml
D. 2.8ml

92. A patient is admitted in moderate to severe distress with pneumonia involving the right lower and middle lobes. You wish to position the patient to optimize $\dot{V}/\dot{Q}$ relationships. The position you would use is

A. Trendelenburg.
B. right decubitus.
C. left decubitus.
D. Semi-Fowler's.

93. You are caring for a mechanically ventilated patient on SIMV = 12/min., Vt = 10 ml/Kg, PEEP = 0, FIO_2 = 0.60. The patient is hemodynamically stable. The most recent blood gas shows a PaO_2 = 53, SaO_2 = 85%, Hb = 12 grams/100ml. Your recommendation would be to

A. add 10 CmH_2O PEEP.
B. increase FIO_2 to 0.80.
C. increase SIMV to 14/min.
D. increase Vt to 12ml/Kg.

94. Which of the following statements are true concerning pressure support ventilation (PSV)?

I. Inspiratory pressure during PSV can range from 1 to 100 cmH_2O.
II. Pressure is held constant through servo-control of delivered flow.
III. A PSV breath is terminated when a certain minimum inspiratory flow is reached.
IV. PSV can be delivered every breath, every other breath, or every fourth breath.
V. PSV is a method of ventilation designed to increase the strength, rather than the endurance, of the respiratory muscles.

A. I, II, and III only
B. I, II, III, IV, and V
C. I, II, and IV only
D. II, III, IV, and V only

95. Patients with significant air-trapping disease may benefit during mechanical ventilation from the use of

A. inspiratory hold.
B. accelerating flowrates.
C. sighs.
D. expiratory retard.

96. Which of the following statements are true of intermittent mandatory ventilation (IMV)?

I. It helps restore or maintain patient respiratory muscle strength and coordination.
II. It is a combination of controlled (or assisted) ventilator rate and spontaneous patient breathing.
III. Rates may not be sufficient to maintain the patient's blood gases, especially if apnea occurs near the end of the weaning period.

IV. It is a static positive pressure held at the airway following active expiration and prior to the next inspiration.

A. I only
B. I and II only
C. I, II, and III only
D. II, III, and IV only

97. What is the V_D/V_T of a patient with a P_ECO_2 of 25 mmHg and a $PaCO_2$ of 55 mmHg?

A. 0.25
B. 0.35
C. 0.45
D. 0.55

98. You are caring for a mechanically ventilated patient on IMV = 6/min., Vt = 10 ml/Kg, PEEP = 5, inspiratory time = 2 sec., FIO_2 = 0.45. ABGs reveal pH = 7.39, $PaCO_2$ = 42, PaO_2 = 54. You would now recommend to

A. increase FIO_2 to 0.55.
B. increase IMV to 8/min.
C. increase Vt to 12 ml/Kg.
D. increase PEEP to 10 cmH_2O.

99. An oxygen flowmeter is running at 3 L/min and an air flowmeter is running at 7 L/min. What is the FIO_2 the being delivered?

A. 0.40
B. 0.42
C. 0.44
D. 0.46

100. A pressure-limited pneumatic-driven ventilator would be considered appropriate for which of the following patients?

I. A patient with neuromuscular disease
II. A patient with chronic obstructive pulmonary disease
III. A very obese patient
IV. An overdose patient without aspiration

A. I and II only
B. I, II, III, and IV

C. I and IV only
D. II and III only

101. During positive expiratory pressure PEP therapy, the target pressure during expiration should be _____ cmH_2O.

A. 10–20
B. 15–25
C. 20–30
D. 25–35

102. Which of the following controls, when adjusted independently, will change the length of the expiratory phase of a volume ventilator incorporating a rate control?

I. Volume
II. Respiratory rate
III. Flow rate

A. I only
B. I, II, and III
C. II only
D. II and III only

103. When administering a strong B_2 adrenergic bronchodilator, anticipated effects would NOT include

A. pulmonary vasodilatation.
B. peripheral venous dilation.
C. increased blood sugar.
D. increased intestinal motility.

104. A patient with known mild COPD has returned from abdominal surgery and has orders for mask CPAP at 10 cmH_2O. ABGs prior to application of CPAP show pH = 7.37, $PaCO_2$ = 45, PaO_2 = 49, FIO_2 = 0.6. Following application of CPAP, ABGs show pH = 7.34, $PaCO_2$ = 54, PaO_2 = 51, FIO_2 = 0.6. Your recommendation is to

A. lower CPAP to 5 cmH_2O.
B. raise CPAP to 15 cmH_2O.
C. raise FIO_2 to 0.8.
D. maintain present settings.

105. Therapeutic goals for treatment of pulmonary edema due to noxious gas inhalation may include all of the following EXCEPT

   A. adequate oxygenation.
   B. ventilatory assistance (if indicated).
   C. improving cardiac output.
   D. elimination of excess fluids.

106. When observing your mechanically ventilated patient at the bedside, you notice that the patient appears to be trying to continue to exhale when the next ventilator breath begins. You suspect that auto-PEEP is occurring. Which of the following would NOT be recommended to treat auto-PEEP?

   A. Lower the tidal volume
   B. Reduce the mechanical respiratory rate
   C. Increase inspiratory time
   D. Increase inspiratory flowrate

107. Therapeutic goals for treatment of pulmonary burns with smoke inhalation may include all of the following EXCEPT

   A. adequate oxygenation.
   B. prevention of bacterial infection.
   C. fluid and electrolyte balance.
   D. PEEP.

108. A patient is admitted to the emergency room in respiratory distress with respiratory rate = 40/min., Vt = 280ml, $PaCO_2$ = 50, PaO_2 = 45, FIO_2 = 0.21. You would recommend

   A. mask CPAP.
   B. mechanical ventilation.
   C. oxygen therapy.
   D. bronchodilator therapy.

109. A patient has been placed on a mechanical ventilator with a FIO_2 of 1.0 and orders for blood gases in 20 minutes. The PaO_2 obtained was 202 mmHg. Approximate the amount of this patient's cardiac output that is shunted.

   A. 5%
   B. 10%
   C. 15%
   D. 20%

110. A volume ventilator is set to cycle on at a respiratory rate of 12 BPM. The I:E ratio is 1:1.5. Which of the following inspiratory and expiratory times are correct?

	Inspiratory	Expiratory
A.	1.0 seconds	2.5 seconds
B.	1.5 seconds	3.0 seconds
C.	2.0 seconds	3.0 seconds
D.	2.5 seconds	2.5 seconds

111. A spirometer is reading 850 ml and represents the volume delivered from the ventilator. The ventilator compliance factor is 4.5 ml per cmH_2O, and the peak pressure is 45 cmH_2O. The approximate delivered volume to the patient is

   A. 850 ml.
   B. 750 ml.
   C. 650 ml.
   D. 550 ml.

112. The mechanically ventilated patient you are caring for has failed to progress in an attempt to wean him from the ventilator. Negative inspiratory force is 15 cmH_2O, vital capacity is 6 ml/Kg and laboratory data are normal except for hypokalemia and hypophosphatemia. You conclude that the problem is

   A. renal failure.
   B. infection.
   C. fluid overload.
   D. respiratory muscle weakness.

113. A patient with diffuse wheezing and pneumonia is placed on mechanical ventilation. The initial SIMV rate is 8/min,

Chapter 30: CRT Self-Assessment Examination

$Vt = 8ml/Kg$, $PEEP = 5$ cmH_2O, $FIO_2 = 0.5$. Inspiratory flowrate should be set to achieve which of the following?

A. Long inspiration and short expiration 2:1
B. Equal inspiration and expiration 1:1
C. Short inspiration and long expiration 1:4
D. Very long inspiration and very short expiration 4:1

114. Recommendations for the clinical application of pressure support ventilation (PSV) include

   I. determine that the patient is ready to move to a lower level of ventilatory support.
   II. begin with whatever level of pressure it takes to achieve the tidal volume the patient is presently receiving.
   III. slowly reduce the pressure each hospital shift based on clinical assessment of the patient.
   IV. reduce the pressure in increments of 5–10 cmH_2O.

   A. I and II only
   B. I, II, and III only
   C. I, II, III, and IV
   D. II and IV only

115. You are in the intensive care unit assisting in repositioning a mechanically ventilated patient with pneumonia occupying most of the left lung. As you move the patient from her back to her left side, the patient becomes very agitated, dusky, and arrhythmic. Your next action would be to

   A. suction.
   B. increase the FIO_2.
   C. move to supine.
   D. move to Trendelenburg.

116. When suctioning a tracheostomy tube, the suction catheter should remain in the airway NOT MORE than _____ seconds.

   A. 5
   B. 10
   C. 15
   D. 20

117. Which of the following statements are true concerning helium-oxygen ($He-O_2$) therapy?

   I. $He-O_2$ passes through constricted airways more easily than air or oxygen because of its low density.
   II. Therapeutic concentrations of $He-O_2$ are usually 50% helium and 50% oxygen.
   III. $He-O_2$ must be administered with a tightly sealed system.
   IV. $He-O_2$ mixtures are a poor medium in which to administer therapeutic aerosols.

   A. I and II only
   B. I, III, and IV only
   C. II and III only
   D. II, III, and IV only

118. Criteria for the application of mask CPAP include

   I. a spontaneously breathing patient.
   II. functional airway reflexes.
   III. a normal or low $PaCO_2$.
   IV. a functional nasogastric tube in place for pressures greater than 10 cmH_2O.

   A. I, II, and III only
   B. I, II, III, and IV
   C. II and III only
   D. II, III, and IV only
   E. II and IV only

119. You are caring for a mechanically ventilated patient in the coronary care unit who was admitted 24 hours ago for acute myocardial infarction. The ventilator settings include $IMV = 10/min.$, $Vt = 10ml/Kg$, $FIO_2 = 0.60$, and $PEEP = 0$. Spontaneous breathing rate is 30. The patient's hemodynamic status is worsening, indicating

increasing left ventricular failure. You would recommend

A. reducing IMV to 8/min.
B. adding 10 cmH$_2$O PEEP.
C. switching to T-tube.
D. increasing FIO$_2$ to 1.0.

120. A patient is being ventilated with a volume-cycled machine that has a 3 ml/cmH$_2$O compressible tubing volume. Which of the following parameters would provide the greatest potential change in the patient's PaCO$_2$?

A. Machine pressure 18 cmH$_2$O, rate 22, tidal volume 250 ml
B. Machine pressure 33 cmH$_2$O, rate 12, tidal volume 500 ml
C. Machine pressure 22 cmH$_2$O, rate 15, tidal volume 300 ml
D. Machine pressure 25 cmH$_2$O, rate 18, tidal volume 400 ml

121. The optimal procedure for the use of a therapeutic aerosol metered-dose inhaler (MDI) includes

I. holding the inhaler with the mouthpiece down.
II. shaking the container vigorously several times.
III. breathing out in the normal passive fashion.
IV. opening the mouth widely and letting the mouthpiece touch the lips.
V. starting to inhale slowly and then squeezing the cartridge to release the spray.
VI. inhaling as deeply as possible and then holding the breath for ten seconds, if possible.

A. I, II, III, and V only
B. II, IV, V, and VI only
C. I, IV, V, and VI only
D. I, II, III, IV, V, and VI

122. You are in the intensive care unit, and a nurse calls out to have you quickly come to the bedside of a mechanically ventilated patient. The patient is agitated and "fighting" the ventilator. Possible causes include

I. main-stem bronchial intubation.
II. kinking of the endotracheal tube.
III. pneumothorax.
IV. bronchospasm.
V. acute pulmonary embolism.

A. I, II, III, IV, and V
B. III and V only
C. I and II only
D. II, III, and V only

123. Special precautions should be taken when doing chest percussion in someone with

A. cystic fibrosis.
B. bronchitis.
C. carcinoma.
D. acute inflammatory disease.

124. A patient is being mechanically ventilated with a volume-cycled machine with a measured tidal volume of 900 ml, a respiratory rate of 10/minute, a peak inspiratory pressure of 25 cmH$_2$O, and an ideal body weight of 150 pounds. The mechanical dead space is 60 ml and the tubing compliance factor is 4 ml/cmH$_2$O. What is this patient's alveolar minute ventilation?

A. 9.0 L
B. 8.5 L
C. 7.25 L
D. 6.65 L

125. Which of the following volumes is NOT included in the mechanical tidal volume measured at the exhalation valve?

A. Alveolar tidal volume
B. Anatomical dead space volume
C. Nasopharyngeal volume
D. Mechanical dead space volume

Chapter 30: CRT Self-Assessment Examination

126. A Co-oximeter will simultaneously analyze _____ and report the sum as total hemoglobin.

    I. reduced hemoglobin
    II. oxyhemoglobin
    III. carboxyhemoglobin
    IV. methemoglobin
    V. carbon monoxide

    A. I only
    B. I and II only
    C. I, II, III, and IV only
    D. I, II, III, IV, and V

127. Oxygen therapy is always indicated when

    A. hemoglobin is less than 90% saturated.
    B. hemoglobin is less than normal.
    C. hemoglobin is greater than normal.
    D. there is a decrease in compliance.

128. Positive end-expiratory pressure (PEEP) is used in order to

    I. maintain adequate oxygenation by increasing the FRC.
    II. decrease pulmonary blood flow in order to compensate for a low $\dot{V}/\dot{Q}$.
    III. increase pulmonary blood flow in order to increase the rate of diffusion across the alveolar capillary membrane.
    IV. stimulate surfactant production.

    A. I only
    B. I and II only
    C. I, II, and III only
    D. I and IV only

129. You are preparing to perform a right radial arterial puncture on a patient and are doing the Allen's test prior to the puncture. The response to the test is for the patient's hand to "pink up" upon pressure being released. The results are consistent with

    A. occluded radial artery.
    B. patent ulnar artery.
    C. occluded ulnar artery.
    D. patent brachial artery.

130. When an inspiratory hold maneuver is used during mechanical ventilation, which of the following statements are true?

    I. Gas distribution will be improved.
    II. Plateau inspiratory pressures may be used to calculate static effective compliance.
    III. Vd/Vt ratio may be reduced.
    IV. Cardiovascular side effects may be increased in the susceptible patient.

    A. I and II only
    B. I, II, III, and IV
    C. II, III, and IV only
    D. II and IV only

131. When setting an initial mechanical tidal volume for a patient in acute respiratory failure, the standard range is

    A. 20–25 ml/Kg.
    B. 15–20 ml/Kg.
    C. 10–15 ml/Kg.
    D. 5–10 ml/Kg.

132. If metabolic alkalosis exists at the time of ventilator weaning, compensatory hypoventilation may result in

    I. hypoxemia.
    II. atelectasis.
    III. worsening $\dot{V}/\dot{Q}$ matchup.

    A. I only
    B. I and II only
    C. I, II, and III
    D. II only

133. For postural drainage, with the patient sitting upright and slightly forward, the bronchus most effectively drained is

    A. upper lobe—apical bronchus.
    B. lingula—superior bronchus.
    C. lower lobe—anterior bronchus.
    D. middle lobe—medial bronchus.

134. Which of the following parameters may show that a mechanically ventilated adult patient is ready to begin the weaning process?
    I. Negative inspiratory force of -30 cmH_2O
    II. Vital capacity of 13 ml/Kg/ideal body weight
    III. FEV_1 of 10 ml/Kg/ideal body weight
    IV. A-aDO_2 of 200 torr
    A. I and III only
    B. II only
    C. III and IV only
    D. I, II, III, and IV

135. The standard respiratory rate for mechanical ventilation to begin adult patients on is
    A. 8.
    B. 10.
    C. 12.
    D. 14.

136. If a patient is being ventilated with an FIO_2 of 1.0, and the ABG showed a PaO_2 of 367 mmHg, the best "rule of thumb" adjustment would be to decrease the FIO_2 by _____ and repeat the ABG in 20 minutes.
    A. 0.05
    B. 0.10
    C. 0.15
    D. 0.20

137. The patient position that usually produces the best PaO_2 is
    A. prone.
    B. upright.
    C. supine.
    D. left side.

138. Continuous positive airway pressure (CPAP)
    I. holds a preset inspiratory pressure for a certain period of time.
    II. promotes improvement of oxygenation by preventing alveolar collapse.
    III. refers to a patient spontaneously breathing at an elevated baseline pressure.
    IV. may or may not be combined with an IMV system.
    A. I and II only
    B. I, II, and III only
    C. II, III, and IV only
    D. III and IV only

139. Adequate psychological preparation of the patient to be weaned from mechanical ventilation includes
    I. warning about plateaus and setbacks.
    II. telling the patient what to expect.
    III. assuring him you'll stay with him.
    IV. involving the family.
    A. I and II only
    B. I, II, and III only
    C. I, II, III, and IV
    D. II, and III only

140. A patient on a volume ventilator in the assist control mode has a change in the I:E ratio. The ratio has changed from 1:4 to 1:2.5. Which of the following are responsible for this change?
    I. The patient's breathing rate has changed.
    II. A change in the preset tidal volume
    III. A change in the preset flowrate
    IV. A change in the preset ventilator rate
    A. I only
    B. I and II only
    C. I, II, and III only
    D. I, II, III, and IV

STOP—REFER TO ANSWER KEY

Chapter 31

Registered Respiratory Therapist (RRT) Self-Assessment Examination

Directions: Select the one best answer or completion for each of the following questions or incomplete statements. The correct response along with the corresponding MASTER GUIDE reference may be found following this chapter.

1. Adequate myocardial contractility is indicated by a mean arterial pressure of at least _____ torr.
   - A. 70
   - B. 80
   - C. 90
   - D. 100

2. When selecting an endotracheal tube, a larger diameter is better because resistance is inversely proportional to the radius to the _____ power.
   - A. 2nd
   - B. 4th
   - C. 5th
   - D. 7th

3. You would recommend initiation of airway pressure release ventilation (APRV) based on which of the following advantages?
   - I. Ventilation-perfusion match-up is improved with spontaneous breathing.
   - II. Spontaneous breathing helps to avoid the hemodynamic compromise seen with other forms of mechanical ventilation.
   - III. APRV results in lower peak and mean airway pressures than other forms of mechanical ventilation.
   - IV. The potential for alveolar overdistension and barotrauma is less with APRV.
   - A. I, II, III, and IV
   - B. II and III only
   - C. IV only
   - D. I and II only

4. An oxygen concentrator in a patient's home has the oxygen alarm sounding on a continuous basis. This suggests that
   - A. the O_2 tubing connections are not tight.
   - B. the air inlet filter is clogged with dirt.
   - C. the relief valve on the humidifier is faulty.
   - D. a fuse has blown in the concentrator's electrical system.

5. On physical exam, a patient exhibits the following findings: malnourished with poor body development; foul smelling stools; clubbing; hyperresonance to percussion;

productive cough; and use of accessory muscles for ventilation. You would suspect

A. ARDS.
B. CHF.
C. cystic fibrosis.
D. chronic bronchitis.

6. Which of the following would be expected benefits of quitting smoking?
   I. Improved health
   II. Reduced risks to others in the environment
   III. Reduced risk of cancer
   IV. Reduced risk of cardiovascular and peripheral vascular disease.

   A. I only
   B. II and III only
   C. I, II, III, and IV
   D. III only

7. Given a mean pulmonary artery pressure (MPAP) of 30 mmHg, a pulmonary capillary wedge pressure (PCWP) of 10 mmHg, and a cardiac output of 4 L/M, the pulmonary vascular resistance (PVR) in units would be

   A. 1.
   B. 2.
   C. 3.5.
   D. 5.

8. A normal cardiac index is _____ L/min./M².

   A. 1.5–2.0
   B. 2.0–3.5
   C. 2.5–4.0
   D. 3.0–6.0

9. When a hemodynamically monitored patient displays increased right atrial pressure (RAP), and reduced pulmonary capillary wedge pressure (PCWP), the possible causes could include
   I. right heart failure.
   II. left heart failure.
   III. pulmonary embolism.
   IV. hypovolemia.
   V. cardiac tamponade.

   A. I and IV only
   B. I and III only
   C. II, III, and IV only
   D. IV only

10. You set the flowrate on a volume ventilator to 40 L/min and an inspiratory time of 1 second. The tidal volume being delivered by the ventilator is approximately

    A. 400 ml.
    B. 550 ml.
    C. 660 ml.
    D. 730 ml.

11. The pulmonary function values of a 35-year-old female are listed here:

Value		
Observed		Predicted
FVC L	2.61	1.79
FEV_1 L	1.96	1.45
FEV_1/FVC %	75	81
FEF_{25-75} L/sec.	2.3	2.0
TLC L	4.02	2.68
RV/TLC %	25–40	33
MVV L/min.	78	70
D_LCO ml/mmHg/min	24	23
D_LCO ml/mmHg/min	25–40	2.68

    This patient would most likely have which of the following pulmonary conditions?
    I. Obstructive lung disease
    II. Intrapulmonic restrictive lung disease
    III. Diffusion defect

    A. I only
    B. I and III only
    C. II only
    D. III only

12. With an exhaled tidal volume of 600 ml, a compressible gas factor of 4 ml/cmH_2O, plateau pressure of 20 cmH_2O, and a PEEP of 5 cmH_2O, the static effective compliance value would be _____ ml/cmH_2O.

A. 24
B. 36
C. 48
D. 56

13. A patient is being continuously ventilated on a volume ventilator and the pressure limit alarm is activated. This is consistent with

    A. a tear in the exhalation valve creating a leak.
    B. inspiration ending immediately with the delivered tidal volume being less than what was set on the volume control.
    C. inspiration being longer than expiration.
    D. maximum pressure being reached within the system and held at the patient's airway.

14. A patient is being given ventilatory support with a BiPAP device. The EPAP is 10 cmH$_2$O, and the BiPAP is assisting the patient 12 times per minute. The RCP finds the patient extremely agitated, using accessory muscles to breathe, and in acute distress. The most likely cause of this problem is

    I. not enough flow to meet patient's inspiratory demand.
    II. malfunction of the EPAP/PEEP valve.
    III. the patient is in ventilatory failure.
    IV. a leak in the system.

    A. I and II only
    B. I, II and III only
    C. II and III only
    D. II and IV only

15. When placing the leads for a 12-lead ECG, Lead I is set up as:

    A. left arm +, right arm −
    B. left leg +, right arm −
    C. right arm +, left leg −
    D. left foot −, right leg +

16. Due to a heroin overdose, a patient is admitted to the ER with the following signs and symptoms: labored breathing; bronchial breath sounds; refractory hypoxemia with metabolic acidosis; diffuse, bilateral alveolar infiltrates on X-ray; tachycardia; and increased serum miscellaneous anions. You would suspect

    A. asthma.
    B. ARDS.
    C. CHF.
    D. carcinoma.

17. You are managing an acute respiratory failure patient on mechanical ventilation and a Swan-Ganz catheter is in place. Right atrial pressure (RAP) is increased, pulmonary vascular resistance (PVR) is markedly increased, and pulmonary capillary wedge pressure (PCWP) is decreased. Which therapeutic guidelines would help to treat this clinical problem?

    I. Keep PaO$_2$ above 60 mmHg.
    II. Start diuretics.
    III. Maintain normal acid-base balance.
    IV. Begin vasopressors.
    V. Avoid excessive intrapulmonary pressures.

    A. I, III, and V only
    B. II and IV only
    C. I, IV, and V only
    D. III only

18. When counseling a patient on the application of nicotine gum, you should recommend a starting routine of

    A. one piece of nicotine gum every waking hour.
    B. one piece of nicotine gum for every two cigarettes.
    C. nicotine gum only when the craving for a cigarette is very strong.
    D. nicotine gum after each meal.

19. Mechanical ventilation has been initiated on a 35-year-old male patient with acute

left ventricular decompensation and pulmonary edema. Initial ABGs show PaO$_2$ to be 355 mmHg. You would recommend reducing the F$_I$O$_2$ by

   A. 0.05.
   B. 0.10.
   C. 0.20.
   D. 0.30.

20. Your patient is being monitored with a Swan-Ganz catheter and displays a decreased right atrial pressure (RAP), decreased pulmonary capillary wedge pressure, and increased systemic vascular resistance. The treatment would be to

   A. start diuretics.
   B. give inotropic agents.
   C. add vascular volume.
   D. begin vasodilators.

21. Of the following electrolytes, all are cations EXCEPT

   A. sodium.
   B. potassium.
   C. calcium.
   D. chloride.

22. You are managing a patient on mechanical ventilation in the assist/control mode with a tidal volume of 15 ml/Kg ideal body weight, rate of 12/min., I:E ratio of 1:2, PEEP of 5 cmH$_2$O, and F$_I$O$_2$ of 0.6. ABGs reveal a pH of 7.34, PaCO$_2$ = 54, BE = +2, PaO$_2$ = 52, SaO$_2$ = 84, P$_{et}$CO$_2$ = 26. Your recommended response to this data would be to

   A. increase the PEEP.
   B. start chest physical therapy.
   C. administer diuretics.
   D. reduce the tidal volume.

23. You would recommend the use of Doxapram in patients with:

   I. ARDS.
   II. acute respiratory insufficiency.
   III. sedative-hypnotic intoxication.
   IV. status asthmaticus.
   V. left ventricular failure.

   A. I and IV only
   B. II and III only
   C. III, IV, and V only
   D. V only

24. Symmetrically inverted "T" waves represent

   A. a normal occurrence in the neonate.
   B. left ventricular hypertrophy.
   C. myocardial ischemia.
   D. myocardial infarction.

25. You are caring for a mechanically ventilated patient in the ICU who has consolidation of the right middle and lower lobes, with the rest of the lung fields clear. You assist the nurse in turning the patient to her right side and note sudden deterioration in your patient. What is likely to have occurred?

   A. Increased pulmonary shunt
   B. Pneumothorax
   C. Pulmonary embolism
   D. Increased $\dot{V}/\dot{Q}$ in the right lung

26. The best radiographic view for differentiating between the presence of parenchymal and mediastinal lesions is the

   A. posterior-anterior view.
   B. anterior-posterior view.
   C. apical lordotic view.
   D. anterior or posterior oblique view.

27. You are monitoring your mechanically ventilated patient in the ICU for the readiness to wean and note that the patient appears to have poor respiratory muscle strength. A primary cause of this problem could be

   A. hyperkalemia.
   B. hypermagnesemia.
   C. hypophosphatemia.
   D. hyponatremia.

28. You are reviewing the chest X-ray done 20 minutes ago on your mechanically ventilated patient in the ICU. When comparing this X-ray to previous films from this admission, you notice that 9 ribs are showing above the diaphragm and peripheral vascular markings are absent in both lung fields. Your conclusion is that this film shows

    A. pneumothorax.
    B. pulmonary edema.
    C. congestive heart failure.
    D. hyperinflation.

29. A flowmeter has popped out of its DISS quick-disconnect outlet creating a massive leak. Reinserting the flowmeter does not correct the leak. Which of the following is the appropriate action?

    A. Reinsert a different flowmeter.
    B. Locate and shut off the main regulator at the bulk system.
    C. Shut off oxygen to that floor only.
    D. Locate and shut off zone-valve to that area only.

30. Which of the following drugs could be recommended for prolonged skeletal muscle relaxation?

    A. Pentamidine
    B. Succinylcholine
    C. Pancuronium
    D. Flurazepam

31. You have just completed an ABG analysis on your mechanically ventilated patient in the ICU. A mixed venous sample was also analyzed. Arterial PO_2 is at 85 mmHg, while mixed venous PO_2 is at 32. Possible causes of these results may include

    I. low cardiac output.
    II. cyanide poisoning.
    III. deptic shock.
    IV. anemia.

    A. I and II only
    B. III only
    C. III and IV only
    D. I and IV only

32. The application of diuretic therapy would most benefit the patient with

    A. left-to-right cardiac shunt.
    B. acute hypovolemia.
    C. left ventricular failure.
    D. open foramen ovale.

33. SIMV refers to a mode of ventilation where

    A. a deeper than normal ventilator breath is delivered.
    B. the breath volume and the initiation of the breath are under patient control.
    C. the patient controls the ventilatory rate and inspires a tidal volume with which they feel comfortable.
    D. the ventilator senses the patient assist efforts and synchronizes the ventilator breath accordingly.

34. When designing a program for respiratory muscle training for a COPD patient, which of the following is likely to give positive results?

    I. Strength training
    II. Nonspecific total body exercise
    III. Voluntary isocapnic hyperpnea
    IV. Inspiratory resistive loading
    V. Inspiratory threshold loading

    A. I, II, and IV only
    B. IV and V only
    C. II only
    D. I, III, IV, and V only

35. Vocal fremitus may be increased when

    A. consolidation with an open airway exists.
    B. the voice is decreased.
    C. there is an obstructed bronchus.
    D. a pneumothorax exists.

36. Which of the following patient conditions would make positive expiratory pressure (PEP) mask therapy inappropriate?

   I. Atelectasis
   II. Acute sinusitis
   III. Hemodynamic instability
   IV. Middle ear pathology
   V. Retained secretions

   A. I and V only
   B. II, III, and IV only
   C. III, IV, and V only
   D. I and IV only

37. A RCP notices fluid underneath a molded plastic chest drainage system. The RCP finds a leak in the plastic housing exposing the chest tube to atmosphere. The RCP should immediately

   A. increase the ventilator volume.
   B. clamp the chest tube.
   C. attach the chest tube to wall suction 20 mmHg.
   D. submerge the chest tube in a cup of water.

38. When initiating BiPAP therapy, adjustments in inspiratory and expiratory pressure are made to achieve

   I. patient relaxation.
   II. slowed cardiac and respiratory rates.
   III. reduced accessory muscle use.
   IV. PaO_2 of 70 on F_IO_2 of 0.3.

   A. I, II, and III only
   B. IV only
   C. II and IV only
   D. I and III only

39. The occurrence of peripheral edema may be caused by all of the following EXCEPT

   A. CHF.
   B. venous thrombosis.
   C. corticosteroid administration.
   D. an increased oncotic pressure in the vascular space.

40. You are initiating mechanical ventilation in a patient whose arterial mean pressure is at 72 mmHg with a right atrial pressure of 3 mmHg. Your mechanical ventilation protocol allows adjustment of tidal volume within a range of values. It would be best at this time to adjust the tidal volume to _____ ml/Kg of ideal body weight.

   A. 15
   B. 13
   C. 11
   D. 7

41. Exosurf administration would be recommended for

   A. diuresis.
   B. surfactant deficiency.
   C. inotropic support.
   D. sedation.

42. You would recommend use of an inspiratory plateau in a mechanically ventilated patient to accomplish

   A. lower peak inspiratory pressure.
   B. greater tidal volume.
   C. a reduction in intrapleural pressure.
   D. improved gas distribution.

43. The best overall indicator of the adequacy of tissue oxygenation is considered the

   A. PaO_2.
   B. P_EO_2.
   C. P_VO_2.
   D. $P_{A-a}O_2$.

44. Assessment of progress in pulmonary rehabilitation can be done by seeing a reduction in

   I. hospitalizations.
   II. mortality.
   III. morbidity.
   IV. costs due to medical services.
   V. time lost from work.

Chapter 31: RRT Self-Assessment Examination

A. II and III only
B. I, II, III, IV, and V
C. III, IV, and V only
D. II and V only

45. A patient is being ventilated by a pressure-limited cycled ventilator in the control mode. Which of the following will occur if the patient's lung compliance decreases?

    A. Decreased tidal volume
    B. Increased inspiratory time
    C. Increased flowrate
    D. Increased tidal volume

46. Ribavirin is typically recommended for
    A. staphylococcal pneumonia.
    B. cystic fibrosis.
    C. laryngotracheobronchitis.
    D. respiratory syncytial virus.

47. Following X-ray examination for endotracheal tube placement in the adult, it is important for the radiopaque marking on the tube tip to be approximately
    A. 2 cm below the carina.
    B. at the carina.
    C. 2 cm above the carina.
    D. 5 cm above the carina.

48. A method of determining proper placement of the endotracheal tube immediately after intubation would include
    A. an end tidal CO_2 monitor.
    B. a catharometer.
    C. an easy-cap CO_2 detector.
    D. a mass spectrometer.

49. When initiating BiPAP therapy, initial inspiratory pressure should be _____ cmH_2O.
    A. 8–10
    B. 12–14
    C. 18–20
    D. 24–26

50. When recommending use of pressure-controlled inverse-ratio ventilation, which of the following should be considered?
    I. The patient should be hemodynamically stable without the use of vasopressors.
    II. Copious secretions cannot be present.
    III. The patient is already being ventilated with high PEEP, F_IO_2, and peak inspiratory pressure in spite of full sedation.
    IV. I:E ratio is already 1:1.

    A. I only
    B. II and III only
    C. IV only
    D. I, II, III and IV

51. In each of the following, the D_LCO may be decreased, EXCEPT
    A. polycythemia.
    B. pulmonary emboli.
    C. emphysema.
    D. pulmonary fibrosis.

52. When switching a patient from SIMV to a pressure-support only mode, the beginning pressure-support level should be set at
    A. one-half the previously required peak inspiratory pressure.
    B. the same peak inspiratory pressure used to assure adequate tidal volume.
    C. 10% higher pressure than achieved on SIMV.
    D. whatever pressure keeps the patient's spontaneous respiratory rate at <40/min.

53. A capnometer with a mainstream sensor is experiencing erratic $ETCO_2$ readings. You would expect the cause of this problem to be related to
    I. secretions obstructing the sample tubing.
    II. the unit being out of calibration.
    III. the length of sample tubing dampening the reading.
    IV. a leak in the circuit.

A. I only
B. I and II only
C. I, II, and III only
D. I, II, III, and IV

54. A 12-year-old female, well known to the hospital, is admitted in mild acute respiratory distress. Two hours prior to admission she had been helping her grandmother with "spring cleaning." What is the most likely underlying problem causing the respiratory distress?

    A. Respiratory distress syndrome
    B. Extrinsic asthma
    C. Intrinsic asthma
    D. Refractory asthma

55. The ABGs of the patient listed in #54 would most likely reveal which of the following?

    A. Normal arterial blood gas values
    B. Normal oxygenation with hypercapnia
    C. Normal oxygenation with hypocapnia
    D. Hypoxemia with hypocapnia

56. You are monitoring a patient on mechanical ventilation whose static effective compliance has changed from 64 ml/cmH$_2$O to 44 cmH$_2$O in the last six hours. Peak inspiratory pressure has risen from 13 cmH$_2$O to 19 cmH$_2$O during the same period. Arterial CO$_2$ has risen by 5 mmHg also. The change in alveolar ventilation appears to be due to

    A. increased dead space ventilation.
    B. increased compressed gas volume.
    C. increased intrapulmonary shunt.
    D. changes in anatomical dead space.

57. When assisting with sputum collection by transtracheal aspiration, the method used to identify oropharyngeal contamination of the sample is to look for

    A. frothy saliva.
    B. food particles.
    C. methylene blue dye.
    D. purulence.

58. All of the following may indicate pulmonary edema of cardiac origin on chest X-ray EXCEPT

    A. fluffy alveolar pattern.
    B. air bronchograms.
    C. cardiac enlargement.
    D. absence of Kerly "B" lines.

59. You have begun a patient on pressure-control, inverse ratio (PCIRV) ventilation. You have started the patient on a 2:1 ratio with a Vt of 400 ml, rate of 25/min., pressure control of 1/2 the PIP in the volume cycled mode, and 7 cmH$_2$O PEEP. As you continue to increase the inspiratory time, holding all other parameters stable, the PaCO$_2$ begins to rise. You would now

    A. reduce the PEEP.
    B. increase the tidal volume.
    C. increase the respiratory rate.
    D. increase the pressure control level.

60. When recommending sigh volume settings, the sigh volume should be _____ times greater than the set tidal volume.

    A. 1–1.5
    B. 1.5–2.0
    C. 2–3
    D. 3–4

61. An electric volume ventilator is set up with the following values: V_t = 850 ml, compression factor = 4.5 ml/cmH$_2$O, peak pressure = 46 cmH$_2$O. If 850 ml is returning on the expiration spirometer, what volume does the patient actually receive?

    A. 850 ml
    B. 805 ml
    C. 745 ml
    D. 645 ml

62. When using pressure-controlled, inverse ratio ventilation (PCIRV) the inspiratory-expiratory ratio can be adjusted to a maximum of

A. 1.5:1.
B. 2.0:1.
C. 3.0:1.
D. 4.0:1.

63. Retractions of the chest wall are prominent in the neonate with RDS due to the presence of
    A. decreased chest wall compliance.
    B. increased chest wall compliance.
    C. increased lung compliance.
    D. decreased airway resistance.

64. Volume measurement calibration of a rolling-seal spirometer requires
    A. a two-liter manual resuscitator bag.
    B. a high-volume flowmeter.
    C. a high-volume pressure transducer.
    D. a super syringe.

65. Arterial blood gases performed on an obese patient in the supine position indicate hypoxemia. Which of the following maneuvers would likely improve the hypoxemia?
    A. Place the patient in the prone position.
    B. Position the patient with the head and chest elevated.
    C. Perform chest physical therapy in the Trendelenburg position.
    D. Place the patient in the right lateral decubitus position.

66. A self-inflating manual resuscitator bag expands very slowly after the bag is squeezed. Which of the following would cause this to occur?
    I. The patient is unable to exhale through the exhalation valve, thus causing resistance to bag filling.
    II. Oxygen flow is inadequate to allow the bag to fill properly.
    III. Oxygen flowrate is too high pressurizing the bag.
    IV. The intake valve is only opening partway.
    A. I only
    B. I and III only
    C. II and III only
    D. II and IV only

67. Recommendation of expiratory retard to mechanical ventilation would best be made in patients with
    A. COPD.
    B. pneumonia.
    C. asthma.
    D. pneumothorax.

68. You would recommend initiation of BiPAP therapy in which of the following patients?
    I. Those being weaned from conventional mechanical ventilation.
    II. COPD patients with acute hypercapnic exacerbation.
    III. Temporary support for patients scheduled for heart/lung transplant.
    IV. Postoperative patients following extubation.
    V. Selected patients with obstructive sleep apnea.
    A. II and IV only
    B. III, IV, and V only
    C. I and III only
    D. I, II, III, IV, and V

69. You are attempting to wean a patient to a lower level of mechanical ventilatory support by lowering the SIMV rate and instituting pressure support. The patient is on 5 cmH$_2$O PEEP. The SIMV is reduced from 10 to 6/min. and pressure support begun at 10 cmH$_2$O. The patient complains of difficulty in getting a spontaneous breath in between SIMV breaths. Which adjustment would you make?
    A. Increase SIMV
    B. Increase PEEP
    C. Increase pressure support
    D. Increase F$_I$O$_2$

70. When checking for a pulse in a potential cardiac arrest victim, the best site to use is the _____ artery.

    A. radial
    B. brachial
    C. femoral
    D. carotid

71. You are starting a patient on mechanical ventilation who just returned from the operating room following thoracotomy. The patient is still sedated and skeletal muscle relaxation has not been reversed. You wish to establish a 1:3 I:E ratio with a set rate of 12/min. and a tidal volume of 600 ml. You recommend setting the inspiratory flowrate at approximately _____ L/M.

    A. 20
    B. 30
    C. 40
    D. 50

72. In the application of airway pressure-release ventilation (APRV) in patients with moderately to severely decreased lung compliance, the initial step is to

    A. determine minute ventilation adequate to maintain $PaCO_2$ at 40–50 mmHg.
    B. establish a mechanical respiratory rate of 20/min.
    C. determine optimal CPAP level that reduces F_IO_2 to <0.5.
    D. determine the distending pressure level that gives a static effective compliance of 0.05 L/cmH_2O.

73. Quality control and diagnostic standards for pulmonary function tests are established by the

    A. Department of Transportation.
    B. American Medical Association.
    C. Center for Disease Control.
    D. American Thoracic Society.

74. Predominantly a CNS disorder, central sleep apnea may be associated with which of the following?

    I. Narcolepsy
    II. "Ondine's curse"
    III. Obesity
    IV. Respiratory center damage
    V. Upper airway deformity

    A. I only
    B. I, II, III, IV, and V
    C. I, II, and IV only
    D. I, III, and V only

75. You are asked to evaluate a patient who has been started on BiPAP therapy. The patient is demonstrating marked use of accessory muscles, tachypnea, and tachycardia. The inspiratory pressure is set at 10 cmH_2O and the expiratory pressure at 5 cmH_2O. Your recommendation would be to

    A. reduce the pressures to 8 and 2 respectively.
    B. lightly sedate the patient.
    C. insert a nasogastric tube.
    D. increase pressures by 2 cmH_2O increments until clinical improvement is seen.

76. You are asked to evaluate a bronchitic patient who has a secretion retention problem in spite of a forceful cough and is becoming fatigued. You observe that the patient takes a deep breath, bears down against a closed glottis, and creates an explosive cough with very little productivity. Which technique would you instruct the patient in to improve secretion removal?

    A. Huff coughing
    B. Abdominal breathing
    C. Inspiratory muscle training
    D. Pursed-lip breathing

77. A microprocessor volume ventilator is supporting a patient in the assist-control mode. Which of the following conditions

will prevent the preset volume from being delivered?

I. A system leak
II. A patient with decreased compliance
III. A preset pressure limit that prematurely ends inspiration
IV. A patient with increased airway resistance

A. I only
B. I and III only
C. II and III only
D. II and IV only

78. When measuring exhaled tidal volume during mechanical ventilation, the volume measured includes all of the following EXCEPT

A. intrapulmonary loculated volume.
B. volume of anatomical dead space.
C. volume of mechanical dead space.
D. ventilator circuit compressed gas volume.

79. Flattened diaphragms with more than seven anterior ribs showing, the presence of retrosternal airspace, the loss of peripheral vascular markings, and a proportionally narrower mediastinum are all radiographic evidence of

A. an uncomplicated pneumothorax.
B. lung hyperinflation.
C. asthma.
D. a normal posterior-anterior chest X-ray.

80. You are monitoring a mechanically ventilated patient who demonstrates increased right atrial and pulmonary artery wedge pressures, with falling oxygenation. You would recommend

A. inotropic support with diuresis.
B. volume loading with systemic vasodilation.
C. diuresis with systemic vasoconstriction.
D. volume loading with systemic vasoconstriction.

81. You are monitoring a patient on controlled mechanical ventilation and the physician requests that you add six inches of mechanical dead space for the convenience of positioning the ventilator circuit. After adding the dead space, what would be your next response?

A. Decrease the respiratory rate
B. Increase the PEEP level
C. Increase the F_IO_2
D. Increase the tidal volume

82. A patient being managed on airway pressure release ventilation (APRV) is continuing to show improving oxygenation on 40% O_2. You are asked for a recommendation for which parameters to change and you suggest

A. decreasing the pressure release level.
B. increasing CPAP level and reducing F_IO_2.
C. reducing respiratory rate by increasing inspiratory time.
D. reducing CPAP and pressure release levels and increasing F_IO_2.

83. The oropharyngeal airway is designed to

I. be used in spontaneously breathing patients.
II. provide an artificial air passage by exposing the glottis.
III. allow for direct visualization of the larynx.
IV. be utilized in conscious patients only.

A. I only
B. I and III only
C. I, III, and IV only
D. II, III, and IV only

84. When considering changes in mean airway pressure during conventional mechanical ventilation, the variable that will most influence mean airway pressure is

A. inspiratory time.
B. positive end-expiratory pressure.

C. respiratory rate.
D. inspiratory flowrate.

85. You are treating a patient with ARDS with nebulized surfactant. Temporary problems that you would anticipate during nebulization of a 300 ml dose would include

   I. increased shunt fraction.
   II. increased airway pressures.
   III. bronchial obstruction.
   IV. desaturation.

   A. II only
   B. III and IV only
   C. I, II, III, and IV
   D. IV only

86. When administering endotracheal drugs during resuscitation, which of the following procedural steps should be performed?

   I. Use a total fluid volume of 5–10 ml.
   II. The medication should be rapidly instilled with a syringe through the opening of the ET tube.
   III. Following instillation, give 5–10 rapid hyperinflations with a manual ventilation bag.

   A. I, II, and III
   B. II only
   C. III only
   D. I and II only

87. When managing the patient in cardiopulmonary arrest, which of the following types of problems should be stabilized prior to transport?

   A. Airway closure by laryngeal edema
   B. Cardiac arrest with ventricular fibrillation
   C. Pericardial tamponade
   D. Hypothermic cardiac arrest

88. The QRS complex is an electrical representation of which phase of the cardiac cycle?

   A. Atrial depolarization
   B. Atrial repolarization
   C. Ventricular depolarization
   D. Ventricular repolarization

89. An infant who presented at delivery with a heart rate greater than 100/min., irregular respiratory effort, some movement of the extremities, grimace with bulb suction of the nose, and blue hands and feet would have an Apgar score of

   A. 6.
   B. 7.
   C. 8.
   D. 9.

90. A molecular sieve oxygen concentrator will provide an oxygen concentration of _____ percent with flowrates of 2–4 L/min.

   A. 100%
   B. 85–95%
   C. 75–85%
   D. 65–75%

91. The pilot balloon on a tracheostomy tube is used to

   A. prevent aspiration.
   B. monitor cuff volume.
   C. maintain proper placement of the tracheostomy tube.
   D. monitor intracuff pressure.

92. Which of the following factors are signals that an infant is likely to be depressed at birth?

   I. Fetal scalp pH of 7.30
   II. Fetal heart rate >160/min.
   III. Fetal heart rate <120 min.
   IV. Loss of beat-to-beat variability in the fetal heart rate

   A. I and II only
   B. III and IV only
   C. II, III, and IV only
   D. I only

93. When applying an inflation hold pressure plateau maneuver, the following would be true.

   I. Total inspiratory time becomes longer.
   II. Expiratory time becomes longer.
   III. During this maneuver the exhalation valve remains closed.
   IV. This maneuver occurs following a ventilator breath.

   A. I, II, III, and IV
   B. I, II, and III only
   C. I, III, and IV only
   D. II, III, and IV only

94. When performing a sleep study, which of the following would not be continuously monitored?

   A. Electrocardiogram
   B. Pulmonary artery pressure
   C. Electroencephalogram
   D. Electro-oculogram

95. A galvanic oxygen analyzer is being used to measure continuous oxygen percentage within a ventilator circuit. Which of the following statements apply to the analyzer reading incorrectly?

   I. The fuel cell is exhausted.
   II. The battery is exhausted.
   III. Water has accumulated upon the sensor membrane.
   IV. High pressures are occurring within the circuit on inspiration.
   V. The oxygen concentration is being measured on the expiratory side of the circuit.

   A. I, III, and IV only
   B. I, III, and V only
   C. II, III, and IV only
   D. II, III, and V only

96. A newborn's right radial ABG sample has a PaO_2 of 68 mmHg. The newborn's umbilical artery sample has a Pa_2O of 55 mmHg. Which of the following answers best explains this difference between the radial and umbilical artery results?

   A. A left-to-right shunt through a patent foramen ovale
   B. A right-to-left shunt through a patent ductus arteriosus
   C. The increased temperature in the umbilical sample
   D. Blood allowed to flow from the right atrium to the left atrium

97. Which of the following would not be routine management in neonatal resuscitation?

   A. Clearing the airway
   B. Drying the infant
   C. Tactile stimulation
   D. Cardiac compressions

98. For patients on home oxygen therapy who are using a humidifier bottle, the water in the bottle should be changed

   A. twice a week.
   B. every day.
   C. once a week.
   D. every four days.

99. Pathologic conditions that exhibit a water-type density on chest X-ray include all of the following EXCEPT

   A. CHF.
   B. pneumothorax.
   C. pneumonia.
   D. fibrosis.

100. When assisting the physician in a cardioversion procedure, which of the following should be performed?

   I. The patient should be comfortable and lying on a hard surface.
   II. Anesthesia should be given 5–10 minutes before the procedure.
   III. The cardioverting equipment should be set in "synchronous" mode.

IV. Once sedated, the patient should be manually ventilated with 100% O_2.

A. I and II only
B. III and IV only
C. I, II, III, and IV
D. I, III, and IV only

STOP—REFER TO ANSWER KEY

Self-Assessment Answer Key

Following are the answers and corresponding MASTER GUIDE reference pages for each of the respective self-assessment examinations.

CRT Self-Assessment

1.	B	80	26.	D	219	51.	C	314	76.	C	228
2.	C	58	27.	A	140	52.	A	119	77.	A	434
3.	A	289	28.	C	141	53.	C	163	78.	B	418
4.	B	188	29.	C	454	54.	A	270	79.	A	455
5.	A	191	30.	B	117	55.	C	459	80.	D	23
6.	C	59	31.	D	174	56.	D	344	81.	D	229
7.	B	93	32.	D	178	57.	A	22	82.	C	79
8.	A	87	33.	C	147	58.	D	178	83.	B	174
9.	D	320	34.	B	63	59.	D	454	84.	A	22
10.	D	179	35.	A	469	60.	A	345	85.	C	185
11.	A	27	36.	C	292	61.	D	28	86.	B	31
12.	D	300	37.	D	189	62.	D	215	87.	A	76
13.	B	302	38.	B	72	63.	B	434	88.	B	189
14.	B	56	39.	D	106	64.	C	425	89.	C	360
15.	A	29	40.	C	42	65.	A	322	90.	D	304
16.	B	327	41.	B	198	66.	A	76	91.	B	309
17.	B	188	42.	A	291	67.	B	182	92.	C	424
18.	A	65	43.	A	359	68.	C	201	93.	A	434
19.	A	202	44.	D	188	69.	C	224	94.	A	361
20.	A	283	45.	B	41	70.	B	264	95.	D	357
21.	B	283	46.	B	180	71.	D	292	96.	C	359
22.	C	290	47.	C	225	72.	C	24	97.	D	434
23.	D	461	48.	A	44	73.	A	295	98.	A	434
24.	D	69	49.	D	460	74.	B	214	99.	C	211
25.	D	230	50.	B	300	75.	C	215	100.	C	228

101.	A	295	111.	C	233	121.	D	303	131.	C	353
102.	B	208	112.	D	387	122.	A	383	132.	C	387
103.	A	213	113.	C	358	123.	D	296	133.	A	293
104.	D	433	114.	B	363	124.	D	43	134.	D	387
105.	B	147	115.	C	426	125.	C	355	135.	C	353
106.	C	381	116.	C	299	126.	C	121	136.	D	429
107.	C	147	117.	B	430	127.	A	425	137.	B	424
108.	B	353	118.	B	431	128.	A	433	138.	C	433
109.	D	95	119.	B	433	129.	B	418	139.	B	390
110.	C	233	120.	D	233	130.	B	357	140.	D	232

RRT Self-Assessment

1.	A	447	26.	D	108	51.	A	63	76.	A	289
2.	B	298	27.	C	387	52.	B	363	77.	B	232
3.	A	366	28.	D	112	53.	C	270	78.	A	354
4.	B	181	29.	D	177	54.	B	135	79.	B	112
5.	C	137	30.	C	335	55.	D	135	80.	A	446
6.	C	325	31.	D	100	56.	B	435	81.	D	353
7.	D	450	32.	C	451	57.	C	482	82.	C	367
8.	B	450	33.	D	243	58.	D	112	83.	A	165
9.	C	446	34.	D	347	59.	A	433	84.	B	433
10.	C	236	35.	A	32	60.	B	357	85.	C	339
11.	D	60	36.	B	294	61.	D	233	86.	A	457
12.	B	435	37.	D	222	62.	D	364	87.	B	459
13.	B	246	38.	A	370	63.	B	25	88.	C	101
14.	A	239	39.	D	21	64.	D	273	89.	A	460
15.	A	255	40.	D	353	65.	B	424	90.	B	181
16.	B	134	41.	B	336	66.	D	159	91.	C	173
17.	A	446	42.	D	357	67.	A	357	92.	C	460
18.	A	327	43.	C	100	68.	D	370	93.	C	241
19.	C	428	44.	B	469	69.	C	363	94.	B	485
20.	C	448	45.	A	229	70.	D	454	95.	A	265
21.	D	82	46.	D	327	71.	B	358	96.	B	414
22.	D	398	47.	C	110	72.	C	366	97.	C	460
23.	B	333	48.	C	271	73.	D	273	98.	B	470
24.	C	102	49.	A	370	74.	C	152	99.	B	108
25.	A	424	50.	D	364	75.	D	370	100.	C	483

Assessment Questions

Chapter 2
1. B
2. B
3. D
4. D
5. A
6. B
7. A
8. C
9. A

Chapter 3
1. A
2. B
3. D
4. B
5. B
6. D
7. A
8. B
9. B

Chapter 4
1. C
2. C
3. B
4. C
5. A
6. B
7. B
8. B
9. B

Chapter 5
1. B
2. A
3. C
4. C
5. D
6. B
7. B
8. A
9. C

Chapter 6
1. D
2. B
3. B
4. B
5. D
6. D
7. C
8. B
9. C

Chapter 7
1. B
2. B
3. C
4. B
5. A
6. B
7. B
8. C
9. C

Chapter 8
1. D
2. B
3. B
4. B
5. C
6. A
7. D
8. D
9. C

Chapter 9
1. B
2. C
3. C
4. B
5. C
6. C
7. B
8. C
9. C

Chapter 10
1. B
2. D
3. D
4. C
5. B
6. A
7. C
8. C
9. A

Chapter 11
1. A
2. C
3. B
4. C
5. B
6. A
7. D
8. B
9. B

Chapter 12
1. B
2. B
3. C
4. D
5. C
6. A
7. D
8. A
9. C

Chapter 13
1. B
2. C
3. D
4. D
5. A
6. D
7. B
8. D
9. A

Chapter 14
1. A
2. A
3. C
4. A
5. A
6. D
7. D
8. B
9. A

Chapter 15
1. B
2. B
3. C
4. B
5. A
6. B
7. D
8. C
9. A

Assessment Questions

Chapter 16
1. B
2. B
3. C
4. C
5. A
6. C
7. B
8. B
9. D

Chapter 17
1. C
2. B
3. D
4. A
5. C
6. A
7. D
8. D
9. D

Chapter 18
1. D
2. A
3. C
4. D
5. B
6. C
7. A
8. B
9. C

Chapter 19
1. C
2. D
3. C
4. A
5. B
6. B
7. B
8. D
9. C

Chapter 20
1. C
2. A
3. C
4. D
5. B
6. C
7. C
8. B
9. C

Chapter 21
1. C
2. D
3. B
4. B
5. B
6. C
7. C
8. B
9. B

Chapter 22
1. D
2. C
3. C
4. C
5. D
6. D
7. C
8. A
9. D

Chapter 23
1. B
2. D
3. C
4. A
5. B
6. C
7. C
8. C
9. B

Chapter 24
1. D
2. B
3. D
4. D
5. D
6. D
7. C
8. D
9. C

Chapter 25
1. C
2. B
3. B
4. A
5. D
6. C
7. C
8. D
9. B

Chapter 26
1. B
2. C
3. C
4. D
5. D
6. A
7. A
8. D
9. C

Chapter 27
1. B
2. B
3. C
4. D
5. C
6. A
7. D
8. C
9. A

Chapter 28
1. A
2. D
3. B
4. A
5. A
6. D
7. C
8. C
9. B

Chapter 29
1. B
2. B
3. B
4. D
5. B
6. D
7. B
8. C
9. C

Index

In this index, *italic* page numbers designate figures; page numbers followed by "t" designate tables; *See also* refers to related topics or more detailed topic breakdowns.

A-aDO$_2$ (alveolar-arterial oxygen gradient), 72, 72t, 389, 420–421
Abdominal distention, 386
Abscess, lung, 290, 424
Absolute humidity, 197
Absorption atelectasis, 429
Accessory muscle activity, 24
Acetic acid, 282
Acetylcysteine (Mucomyst), 315
Acid/alkaline aqueous solutions, 283
Acid–base disturbances, 74t, 75t, 76t. *See also* Acid–base tests
Acid–base tests, 68, 69t
  base excess/deficit (BE), 70
  interpretation of, 73t–76t, 73–76
Acid fast stain, 85
Acidosis
  metabolic, 74t–76t
  respiratory, 74t–76t
ACLS algorithms (American Heart Association), 461–463, *463–467*
Acquired immune deficiency syndrome (AIDS). *See* AIDS/HIV
Acrocyanosis (peripheral cyanosis), 22
Activities of daily living (ADLs), 37
Acute myocardial infarction, algorithm for, *463*
Acute polyneuritis (Guillain-Barré syndrome), 140
ADH (antidiuretic hormone), 103
ADLs (activities of daily living), 37
Adult cardiac care, universal algorithm for, *464*
Adult respiratory distress syndrome (ARDS), 101, 134–135, 339
Adventitious breath sounds, 32–34
Aerobid (flunisolide), 317

Aerophagia, 432
Aerosol generators, 197–207. *See also* Nebulizers
  metered-dose inhalers (MDIs), 200–201, 303–305
  nebulizers, 197–199, 200t, 302–303, 311t, 312t, 472
    ultrasonic, 201–202, 202t
  small particle (SPAG-2), 199–200
Aerosol therapy, 301–304. *See also* Aerosol generators
  bland, 304
  with metered dose inhaler (MDI), 303–304
  with small volume nebulizer, 302–303
Afterload (alterations in perfusion), 449–451
Age, gestational, 129
AIDS/HIV, 86, 88, 144, 145t
Air bronchogram sign, 108
Air entrainment oxygen masks, 187–188
Air-mixture control, 228–229
Air-oxygen blenders, 215–216
Air/oxygen ratio, 189t
Air-trapping, 108
Airway(s)
  artificial, 46, 47, 166t
    Brook/Safar, 165
    esophageal obturator airway (EOA), 164–165, 165t, 458
    esophago-tracheal combination tube (ETC)/pharyngotracheal lumen airway (PTL), 167–168
    Guidel, 165
    laryngeal mask (LMA), 166–167
    nasopharyngeal, 166
    oral pharyngeal, 165–166
    oronasal, 350–351
    radiographic appearance of, 109–111
Airway inflammation, upper, 139–140

Airway management, emergency, 453
Airway pressure release (APRV) ventilation, 238, 366–369
Airway resistance, 46–47
Airway resistance (raw) test, 62
Airway secretions, 29
Airway X-rays, upper, 114
Alarm systems, ventilator, 245–247, 246t
Albuterol, 311t
Alcohols, for antisepsis, 283
Alkalosis
    metabolic, 74t–76t
    respiratory, 74t–76t
Allen's test, 418
Allergic asthma, 135–136
Allergic reactions, 142t
ALS (amyotrophic lateral sclerosis), 140
Altered resonance, 30
Altitudes, PaO_2 at, 425–427
Alveolar/arterial (a/A) ratio, 426–427
Alveolar-arterial oxygen gradient (A-aDO_2), 72, 72t, 420–421
Alveolar atelectasis, 96
Alveolar dead space, 55
Alveolar phase of physical maturity, 129
Alveolar ventilation ($\dot{V}_A$), 23, 43–44
AMA Code of Ethics, 496
Amantadine, 327
Ambulatory electrocardiography (Holter monitor), 274, 275
American Heart Association, ACLS algorithms, 461–463, 463–467
American Society for Testing and Materials (ASTM), 159
American Standard Safety System, 208
Ammonium compounds, quaternary, 283
Amniotic fluid testing, lecithin-sphingomyelin (L/S) ratios, 130
Amyotrophic lateral sclerosis (ALS), 140
Analgesic/anesthetic drugs, 340, 340t, 341t
Analysis, blood gas. *See* Analyzers: blood gas; Blood gas analysis
Analysis level items, 6–7
Analyzers. *See also* Monitoring devices
    blood gas, 260–264, 262t. *See also* Blood gas analysis
    helium, 272–273
    oxygen, 264–265, 266t, 267t
Anatomic dead space, 54
Anatomic differences between infants and adults, 127–128
Anatomic positions, of lung segments (lobes), 107t
Anemia, 80, 387
Anenometers, 259–260
Anesthetics/analgesics, 340, 340t, 341t
Anger, 35
Angiography, 109
Anion gap, 83
Anterior-posterior (AP) view, 108

Antibiotics, 336
Antidiuretic hormone (ADH), 103
Antihistamines, 334t, 334–335
Antiseptics, 281t
Antivirals, 327–328
Apgar scores, 128t, 128–129, 450
Apical lordotic view, 108
Apnea, 23
    sleep, 121–123, 151–153, 485–486
Apnea monitoring, 123
    home, 471–472
Appearance, general, 19
Application items, 6
APRV (airway pressure release ventilation), in adults, 366–369
ARDS (adult respiratory distress syndrome), 101, 134–135, 339
Arrest
    cardiac, 162–163, 456
    sinus, 102
Arrhythmias, cardiac. *See* Dysrhythmias; *specific arrythmias*
Arterial catheters, 255–256
Arterial line insertion, 99–100
Arterial oxygen saturation, 415–416. *See also* Oxygen *entries;* Pulse oximetry
Arterial pressure
    systemic, 445–446
Arterial puncture, 417–419
Arterial/venous O_2 difference, 93
Arteriosclerosis, 84, 325
Artificial airways, 166t. *See also* Endotracheal intubation; Intubation
    Brook/Safar, 165
    esophageal obturator airway (EOA), 164–165, 165t, 458
    esophago-tracheal combination tube (ETC)/pharyngotracheal lumen airway (PTL), 167–168
    Guidel, 165
    laryngeal mask (LMA), 166–167
    nasopharyngeal, 166
    oral pharyngeal, 165–166
    oronasal, 350–351
Artificial surfactants, 336–338
Asbestosis, 141–144, 142t
Asepsis defined, 281t
Aspergillosis, 145t
Aspiration
    of gastric contents, 432
    transtracheal, 85, 482–483
Aspiration pneumonia, 145t
Assessment, 17–40. *See also* Bedside monitoring; Monitoring
    by auscultation, 31t, 31–34
    bronchoscopy, 123–124, 124t

Index

Assessment (*cont.*)
    cardiopulmonary status, 18t, 19–34, 21t, 31t
    co-oximetry, 120–121
    exercise stress testing, 118–120
    history, 17
    home, 472
    by inspection, 19–28, 28t
    intrauterine, 459–460
    metabolic studies, 117–118
    by palpation, 28–30
    patient interview, 34–38
    by percussion, 30
    perinatal/neonatal, 127–132. *See also* Perinatal/neonatal monitoring
    progress notes, 18
    sleep studies, 121–123
    ventilation/perfusion scans, 118
    vital signs, 17–18
Assistance with special procedures, 476–491
    bronchoscopy, 476–477
    cardioversion, 483–484
    chest tubes, 479–480
    percutaneous needle (pleural) biopsy, 488
    sleep apnea studies (polysomnography), 485–486
    stress testing, 486–488
    thoracentesis, 477–478
    tracheostomy, 478–479
    transtracheal aspiration, 482–483
    transtracheal oxygen catheter placement, 484–485
    vascular monitoring, 480–482
    venipuncture, 489–492
Asthma, 135, 317–324
    in adults, 317–320
    in children, 320–324
Asymmetrical chest movement, 24–25, 28–29
Asystole, algorithm for, *467*
Atarac (hydroxyzine), 334t, 334–335
Atelectasis, 25, 26, 108, 112
    absorption, 429
    alveolar, 96
ATM (American Society for Testing and Materials), 159
Atrial flutter, 102
Atrophy, muscle, 19–20
Atropine, 311t, 331, 333
Attitude, 11
Auscultation, 31t, 31–34
Autoclave, 284. *See also* Sterilization
Autogenic drainage, 295
Automatic external defibrillators (AEDs), 163
Automatic pneumatic chest compressors, 161–162
Autonomy, 495
Auto-PEEP. *See under* Positive end-expiratory pressure (PEEP)

Babbington hydronamic nebulizers, 199
Bacteria
    drug-resistant, 285
    filters, 249
    resident flora, 281t
    transient flora, 281t
Bacterial causes of pneumonia, 145t
Bacterial colonization, 281t
Bactericide, defined, 281t
Bacteriostatic, defined, 281t
Bagassosis, 141–144, 142t
Ballard gestational age scale, 129
Banks, oxygen cylinder, 177–178
Barbiturates, 333, 334t
Baritosis, 141–144, 142t
Barking cough, 26
Barotrauma
    in neonates, 405–406
    pulmonary, 386, 433, 436
Barrel chest, 22
Base excess/deficit (BE), 70
Basophils, 80, 81t
Beclomethasone dipropionate (Vanceril), 317
Bed, rocking, 248
Bedside monitoring
    hemodynamic, 91–105
        blood pressure, 91, *92*
            mean arterial pressure (MAP), 91–92
        cardiac output, 92–94
            Fick equation for, 93
        central venous pressure (CVP), 98–99, 481
        clinical conditions related to, 100, 101t
        electrocardiography (ECG), 101t, 101–103
        fluid balance (intake/output), 103
        insertion of lines
            arterial, 99–100
            central venous, 98–99
        mixed venous sampling (P–O_2), 100
        pulmonary artery pressure (PAP), 96–97
        pulmonary capillary wedge pressure (PCWP), 97–98
        shunt studies (Qs/Qt)[5], 94–96, 389
            classic (Fick) equation, 95
            modified equation, 96
    respiratory. *See also specific methods and indices*
        airway resistance, 46–47
        alveolar ventilation, 43–44
        capnography, 54
        dead space:tidal volume ratio ($V_{CD}C/V_{CT}C^2$), 54–55
        forced vital capacity, 45
        I:E ratio, 43–44
        lung compliance, 47–48
        lung mechanics (mechanics of breathing), 48–49, 49t

Bedside monitoring (cont.)
    maximum expiratory pressure, 44
    maximum inspiratory pressure, 44
    minute volume, 42t, 42–43
    peak flow, 45–46
    pressure, flow, volume wave forms, 49–51, *50–51*
    pulse oximetry, 51–53, *52–53*
    respiratory rate, 41
    tidal volume, 41–42
    timed forced expiratory vokume, 45
    transcutaneous O_2/CO_{2B}, 53–54, 412–415
    vital capacity, 45
Beer's law, 121
Beneficence, 495
Berman airway, 165
Bernoulli effect, 187, 189
Berylliosis, 141–144, 142t
β_2 agonists, 311–312
Bicarbonate (HCO_{3-}), 70, 82t, 83
Bicycle ergometry, 118–120
Bilevel positive airway pressure (BiPAP) ventilation, 238–239, *240*
Biopsy, percutaneous needle (pleural), 488
Biot's breathing, 23–24
Bitolterol, 311
Blades, laryngoscopic, 163–164, 164t
Blastomycosis, 145t
Blenders/controllers, 215–216, 217t
Blood and fluid culture/sensitivity tests, 86–89, 87t
Blood cells
    red (RBCs, erythrocytes), 79
    white (WBCs, leukocytes), 80–81, 81t
Blood cell types, 79
Blood chemistry tests, 83–84
Blood count, complete (CBC), 79–81, 81t
Blood flow, cerebral, CPAP and, 438
Blood gas analysis. *See also specific gases and parameters*
    electrodes for, 261–262, 262t
        calibration of, 263–264
        Clark polarographic (PO_2), 261–262, 265, 269
        indwelling optical biosensor, 262
        Sanz (pH electrode), 261
        Stowe-Severinghaus (PCO_2), 261
    for monitoring during mechanical ventilation, 412–423
    in neonates, 405
    sampling for, 417–418
    systems for, 260–264, 262t
    tests used in, 67–76
        A-aDO_2 (alveolar-arterial oxygen gradient), 72, 72t, 389, 420–421
        HCO_{3-} (plasma bicarbonate), 70, 82t, 83
        interpretation of, 72t, 72–74, 73t
        normal values, 68t
        O_2 content, 71t, 71–72

        O_2–Hb (oxygen–hemoglobin) saturation curve, 71t, 415
        $PaCO_2$ (partial pressure of carbon dioxide), 68
        PaO_2 (partial pressure of oxygen), 68–70, 69t
        $SAaO_2$ (hemoglobin saturation), 70–71
Blood pressure, 34, 91, *92*. *See also* Hypertension; Hypotension
    central venous pressure (CVP), 98–99, 442–443, 481
    mean arterial pressure (MAP), 91–92
    in preload abnormality, 446
    pulmonary artery pressure (PAP), 96–97, 443–445, 481–482
    pulmonary capillary wedge pressure (PCWP), 97–98
    systemic arterial, 445–446
    types of, 91
Blood tests, coagulation studies, 88–89
Blood urea nitrogen (BUN), 83
"Blue bloaters," 136–137
Blue skin, 22
Body-fluid precautions, 88
Body fluids, contaminated, 278, 279t
Body plethysmography, 59–62, 62t
Body temperature and pressure under saturated conditions (BTPS), 59
Bohr effect, 80
Bohr equation, 54–55
Botulism, 140–141
Bourdon flowmeter, 210, 258
Boyle's Gas Law, 62t
Bradycardia, 102
Bradypnea, 23
Brain death, 395
Breath, sigh, 233
Breath sounds, 31t, 31–33
Breathing
    Biot's, 23–24
    Cheyne-Stokes, 23
    diaphragmatic, 344
    intermittent positive pressure (IPPB), 47, 348–350, 469–470, 472
    Kussmaul's, 23
    pursed-lip, 344
    types of abnormal, 36–37
    work of, 394, 433
Breathing pattern, 23–24
Breathing techniques, 344
Bretylium tosylate, 331–332
Briggs "T" adaptor, 188
Bronchial occlusion, 25
Bronchitis, chronic, 136–137. *See also* Chronic obstructive pulmonary disease (COPD)
Bronchodilator drugs, 28, 58, 310–315, 311t, 312t, 313t, 314t
    for adult nebulizers, 311t
    β_2 agonists, 312–313

Bronchodilator drugs (cont.)
    for metered-dose inhaler, 311–312
    for neonate nebulizers, 312t
    oral, 313–315
        sympathomimetics, 313–314
        theophylline, 314–315
Bronchogenic carcinoma, 136
Bronchography, 109
Bronchophony, 32
Bronchoprovocation, 66
Bronchopulmonary secretions, removal of, 289–307. See also Secretion removal
Bronchoscopes, 223–224
    flexible fiberoptic (FFB), 223
    rigid, 223–224
Bronchoscopy, 123–125
    assistance with, 476–477
    complications of, 124t
    flexible fiber (FFB), 123
Bronchospasm, 135–136. See also Asthma
    as complication of mechanical ventilation, 385
Brook/Safar airway, 165
Bruits, 33
BTPS (body temperature and pressure under saturated conditions), 59
Bubble humidifiers, 202–203
Buffer base value, 70
Bulk oxygen systems, 177
BUN (blood urea nitrogen), 83
Burns, smoke inhalation, 147–148
Buttons, tracheostomy, 170

Calcium (Ca^{2+}), 82t, 83
Caloric and protein depletion, in mechanical ventilation, 387–388
Canalicular phase, of physical maturity, 129
Cannulas, oxygen, 183
Cannulation. See also Catheterization
    of radial artery, 482
    umbilical, 131
Capacity
    diffusing, 63–65, 64t
    forced vital (FVC), 45, 49t, 60–61
    functional residual (FRC), 59t, 60–61, 296, 433
    residual (RV), 59t, 60–61
    total lung (TLC), 61–62
    vital (VC), 45, 59t, 60–61
Capillary refill, 20–21
Capillary wedge pressure, 443–445
Capnography, 54, 419–421
Capnometers, 270–271, 272t
Carbon dioxide (CO_2)
    exhaled, 419–421
        detection device for, 272–273
    glucose metabolism and, 117

    with oxygen (Carbogen), 430–431
    partial pressure of ($PaCO_2$), 68
Carbon dioxide monitors
    capnometers, 270–271, 272
    transcutaneous, 267–269
Carboxyhemoglobin, 121
Carboxyhemoglobinemia, 80
Carcinoma, bronchogenic, 136
Cardiac arrest, 162–163, 456. See also Cardiopulmonary resuscitation (CPR)
Cardiac arrhythmias. See Dysrhythmias
Cardiac care algorithms, 461–462, 463–467
Cardiac compression, 454
Cardiac cycle, 101
Cardiac index, 94, 442, 447
Cardiac output, 92–94
    dye-dilution method, 441
    Fick equation for, 93
    hemodynamic changes related to, 446–451
    indicator-dilution method, 92
    monitoring of, 441–442
    thermodilution method, 93, 441–442
Cardiac versus pulmonary conditions, 98
Cardiopulmonary resuscitation (CPR), 453–468. See also Resuscitation devices
    ACLS algorithms for, 461–463, 463–467
    emergency of adults, 453–459
    of infants at delivery, 459–461
Cardiopulmonary status assessment, 18t, 19–34, 21t, 31t
Cardiovascular complications, of intrathoracic pressure increase, 386
Cardiovascular disease, 325
Cardiovascular drugs, 329, 329t, 330t
Cardiovascular effects, of CPAP, 438
Cardiovascular monitoring, 441–451
    cardiac output, 441–442
    central venous pressure (CVP), 98–99, 442–443
    hemodynamic changes, 446–451
    pulmonary artery and capillary wedge pressure, 96–97, 443–445, 481–482
    systemic arterial pressure, 445–446
Cardiovascular testing, 118–120
Cardioversion. See also Cardiopulmonary resuscitation (CPR); Defibrillation
    assistance with, 483–484
Care plan, respiratory, 133–155. See also Respiratory care plan
Carlens tube, 169
Cascade-type humidifiers, 203
Catharometer (helium aznalyzer), 273–274
Catheter(s)
    arterial, 255–256
    oxygen delivery, 184–185
    radiographic appearance, 113
    suction, 173–174, 174t, 175t

Catheter(s) (cont.)
   Swan-Ganz, 96–97, 113, 256–257
   transtracheal oxygen (TTO), 184–185
   "wedging" of, 444–445
   Yankauer tonsillectomy, 175
Catheterization
   arterial, 99–100
   central venous, 98–99
   lung puncture and, 113
   pulmonary artery, 96–97, 443–445, 481–482
   transtracheal oxygen, 484–485
   umbilical, 130
CBC (complete blood count), 79–81, 81t
CDC-Tubocurarine (curare), 335
Central sleep apnea (Ondine's Curse), 122, 151–153
Central venous line insertions, 98–99
Central venous pressure (CVP), 98–99, 442–443, 481
   transducer method, 443
Cerebral blood flow, CPAP and, 438
Challenge testing, bronchial (bronchoprovocation), 66
Charting. *See* Recordkeeping
Chest
   flail, 24–25
   transillumination of, 25
Chest compressors, automatic pneumatic, 161–162
Chest configuration, 22
Chest cuirass, 248
Chest excursion, assessment of, 454–455
Chest movements, asymmetrical, 24–25, 28–29
Chest percussors, 224
Chest physical therapy
   autogenic drainage, 295–297
   contraindications to, 291
   indications for
      adults and older children, 290
      infants and young children, 291
   percussion, 293
   positive airway pressure adjuncts (PEP and EPAP), 294–295
   postural drainage, 291–292
   precautions and complications, 292–293
   vibration, 294
Chest trauma, 153–154
Chest tubes, 111, 221–223
   assistance with, 479–480
Chest vibrators, 224–225
Chest wall retractions, gestational age and, 130
Chest X-rays, 106–114, 107t
   inspection of, 109–114
Cheyne-Stokes breathing, 23
Children. *See also* Infants; Neonates
   CT scan in, 115
   indications/contraindications for chest physical therapy, 290–291
   respiratory rate in, 18

Chlamydia, 145t
Chloral hydrate, 333
Chloride (Cl^-), 82t, 83
Cholesterol, 84
Chronic bronchitis, 136–137. *See also* Chronic obstructive pulmonary disease (COPD)
Chronic obstructive pulmonary disease (COPD), 22, 32, 43, 67t, 108–109, 136–139, 312–313
   continuum home care treatments for, 473–474. *See also* Home care
   coughing techniques in, 290
   PaO_2 in, 425
Cidex, 283
Cigarette smoking. *See* Smoking
Circulatory alterations in neonates, 406–407
Cl^- (chloride), 82t, 83
Clark polarographic (PO_2) electrode, 261–262, 265, 269
Clinical laboratory tests, 79–90. *See also specific tests*
   blood and fluid culture/sensitivity, 86–89, 87t
   blood chemistries, 83–84
   complete blood count (CBC), 79–81, 81t
   electrolytes, 81–83, 82t
   sputum, 84–86
Clinical simulation questions, strategies for, 8–11, 9t
Closing volume (CV), 63
Clostridium sp., 85, 140–141
Clubbing, digital, 21–22
CMV (controlled mechanical ventilation), 48–51, 50–51
Coagulation studies, 88–89
Coal Miner's Lung, 141–144, 142t
Cobalt 60, 284
Coccidiodiodomycosis, 145t
Cole style tubes, 166–167
Colonization, bacterial, 281t
Colors, for $ETCO_2$ detectors, 456
Coma, 34–35
Commitment to excellence, 12–13
Complete blood count (CBC), 79–81, 81t
Compliance, lung, 47–48, 62–63, 63t
   in infants, 437–438
   static effective, 47, 434–435, 435
Compression, cardiac, 454
Compressors, 220–221, 221t
Computed tomography (CT scan, "CAT" scan), 109
Concentration equation, 310t
Concentrators, 180
Confidentiality, 496
Confusion, 34
Congenital diaphragmatic hernia, 424
Congestive heart failure (CHF), 101
Consciousness, level of, 34–35
Consolidation of lungs, 112, 144–146, 145t
Contamination, defined, 281t

Index

Continuous positive airway pressure (CPAP), 51, *53*, 235, 238–239
    by mask, 431–433
    masks for, 190, 191t
    during mechanical ventilation
        in adults, 433–437
        in infants, 437–439
        organ-system effects of, 438–439
Contractility, myocardial, 447–449
Controlled mechanical ventilation (CMV), 48–51, *50–51*
Cooperate, ability to, 35–36
Co-oximeters, 265
Co-oximetry, 120–121
COPD. *See* Chronic obstructive pulmonary disease (COPD)
Correct or keyed options, 4
Corticosteroid drugs, 316–317
Coughing, 26–27
    directed, 27
    huff (forced expiratory technique, FET), 26–27, 290, 296
    nonproductive, 28
    techniques for assisted, 289–290
CPAP. *See* Continuous positive airway pressure
CPAP (PEP) oxygen masks, 190, 191t
CPK (creatine phosphokinase), 84
CPR (cardiopulmonary resuscitation), 453–468. *See also* Cardiopulmonary resuscitation
Crackles, 32, 296
Creatine phosphokinase (CPK), 84
Creatinine, 84
Credentialing examination, 1–13
    advanced practitioner, 1
    clinical simulation questions, 2t, 2–3, 8–11, 9t
    entry-level, 1
    familiarization with, 2
    5-percent margin in, 8–11, 9t
    multiple-choice questions, 1, 2–8
    validation of, 2
Crepitus, 29
Cromolyn sodium, 315–316
Croup, 139
CT scan (computed tomography, "CAT" scan), 109
Cuff inflation devices, 173
Cuff rupture, 385
Cuffs
    complications related to, 383–385
    endotracheal tube, 172–173, 455
    sphygmomanometer, 217–218
Cuirass, chest, 248
Culture, sputum, 84–87
Culture and sensitivity tests, blood and body fluids, 86–89

Curare (CDC-tubocurarine), 335
Curshmann's spirals, 28
CV (closing volume), 63
CVP (central venous pressure). *See* Central venous pressure (CVP)
Cyanosis, 22
    peripheral (acrocyanosis), 22
Cylinder banks, 177–178
Cystic fibrosis, 137–138
Cytomegalovirus, 144, 145t

Dalmane (flurazepam), 334, 334t
Data, 15
    bedside monitoring. *See also* Bedside monitoring
        hemodynamic, 91–105.
        respiratory, 41–57
    clinical laboratory, 79–90
    patient assessment, 2–40
    pulmonary laboratory, 58–78
Data analysis and plan determination, 133–155
Dead space
    alveolar, 55
    anatomic, 54
Dead space:tidal volume ratio ($V_{CD}C/V_{CT}C^2$), 54–55
Death
    brain, 395
    tissue (necrosis), 84
Decision-making section, 10–11
Decontamination, 281t
Deep breathing, 289–290
Defibrillation, 455, 483–484
    algorithm for, *465*
Defibrillators, 162–163
    automatic external (AED), 163
Dehydration, 101, 103
Delirium, 35
Denaturing, 281t
Denial, 35
Density on X-rays, 106–107
Depression, 35
Detection device, esophageal (EDD), 456–457
Detectors, $ETCO_2$, 455–456
Deviation, tracheal, 29
Diagnosis. *See* Monitoring; *specific modalities*
Diameter Index Safety System (DISS), 208
Diaphoresis (sweating), 21
Diaphragm, 22
    hemi-, 113
Diaphragm compressors, 220, 221t
Diaphragmatic breathing, 344
Diaphragmatic excursion, 30
Diaphragmatic hernia, congenital, 424
Diaphragmatic movement, 22–23
Diastolic blood pressure, 91
Diazepam (Valium), 334, 334t

Differential/independent lung ventilation (IPV/DLV), in adults, 372–376
Difficulty levels, 6
Diffusing capacity, 63–65, 64t
Digital clubbing, 21–22
Dilution equation, 309t
Diplococcus sp., 85
"Dirty" lung, 109
Disinfectant, 281t
DISS (Diameter Index Safety System), 208
Distention
    abdominal, 386
    venous, 20
Distractor options, 5
Diuretics, 330t
Documentation. *See also* Recordkeeping
    legal definition of, 19
    of sterilization processes, 279
Dosage calculation, 308–310, 309t, 310t
Doxapram, 333
Drainage
    autogenic, 295–297
    postural, 291–292
Drug administration, endotracheal, 457
Drug expressions, 309t
Drug-resistant bacteria, 285
Drugs, respiratory, 308–343. *See also* Pharmacologic agents; *specific drugs; drug classes*
Dry heat sterilization, 283
Dubowitz gestational age scale, 129–130
Dullness to percussion, 30
Dye-dilution method. for cardiac output, 441
Dynamic compliance, 47
Dynamic hyperinflation (auto-PEEP). *See under* Positive end-expiratory pressure (PEEP)
Dyspnea, 36–37, 361
    paroxysmal nocturnal (PND), 37
Dysrhythmias, 34, 83, 102. *See also* Electrocardiography (ECG); *specific dysrhythmias*

Easy Cap carbon dioxide detector, 272–273
ECG (electrocardiography), 101t, 101–103
Edema
    glottic and subglottic, 114
    peripheral, 20, 21t
    pulmonary, 112–113, 148, 385
Effective compliance, 47, 434
Effusion, pleural, 87t
Egophony, 32
Ejection fraction (EF), 94
Electric ventilators, 231–237, 234t, 236t, 237t, 245t
Electrocardiography (ECG), 101t, 101–103, 254, 255t
    ambulatory (Holter monitor), 274, 275
    emergency, 454
Electrochemical oxygen analyzers, 264–265

Electrodes, for blood gas analysis, 261–262, 262t
    calibration of, 263–264
    Clark polarographic (PO_2), 261–262, 265, 269
    indwelling optical biosensor, 262
    Sanz (pH electrode), 261
    Stowe-Severinghaus (PCO_2), 261
Electrolyte abnormalities, in mechanical ventilation, 387
Electrolyte tests, 81–83, 82t
Electromechanical dissociation, algorithm for, *466*
Embolism, pulmonary, 149–150, 385
Emergency transport, 458–459
Emotional state, 35
Emphysema, 138–139. *See also* Chronic obstructive pulmonary disease (COPD)
    subcutaneous, 111–112
Empyema, 292
End-diastolic/end-systolic volume, 93–94
End-inspiratory pause (inspiratory plateau) ventilation, 241
Endotracheal drugs, 332
Endotracheal intubation, 29–30, 110–111, 455–457
Endotracheal tubes
    nasal, 167
    oral, 166–167
    suctioning of, 85
Entrainment masks, 188
Entrainment nebulizers, 199
Environment, physical, assessment of, 37–38
Enzyme chemistries, 84
EOA (esophageal obturator airway), 458
Eosinophils, 80, 81t
EPAP (expiratory positive airway pressure), 239
Epiglottitis, 114
Epinephrine, 311t, 331, 332
Equations
    air/oxygen ratio, 189
    Bohr for dead space calculation, 55
    Boyle's gas law, 63
    concentration, 310
    cylinder gas flow duration, 180
    dilution, 309
    Fick
        for cardiac output, 93
        for shunting, 95
        modified, 96
    FIO_2, 211
        predicted in stable patients, 428
        from two flowmeters, 214
    flow, total, 211
    flow rate
        gas with two flowmeters, 213
        helium/oxygen mixtures, 214
        inspiratory, 358
        oxygen, 212
        ventilator, 236

Index

Equations (*cont.*)
  humidity, relative, 198
  humidity deficit, 198
  I:E ratio, 233
  inspiratory flow rate, 358
  inspiratory time, 236, 402
  mean airway pressure (MAP), 402
  mean arterial pressure (MAP), 94
  minute volume, 43
  O_2 content, 71
  oxygen flow rate, 212
  $P(A-a)CO_2$, 72
  PaO_2 values
    a/A ratio, 426–427
    predicted normals
      at altitude, 425, 427, 428
      at sea-level, 425, 426
      in supine and seated positions, 426
  pH, 69
  Poiseuille's, 288, 298
  portable oxygen system time estimates, 182
  relative humidity, 198
  respiratory quotient, 117
  respiratory sensation (dyspnea), 361
  shunt
    classic (Fick derivation), 95
    modified, 96
  static effective compliance, 435
  tidal volume
    alveolar, 355
    exhaled, 355
    ventilator, 236
  total flow, 211
  tubing compliance corrections, 234
  vascular resistance
    pulmonary, 444, 450
    systemic, 444, 450
  ventilator flow rate, 236
  ventilator tidal volume, 236
  work of breathing in joules/min, 394
Equipment, 157–286. *See also* Trouble shooting; *individual subtopics*
  aerosol generators and humidification equipment, 197–206, 305
  contaminated, 278–282, 279t
  for home care, 469–472
  monitoring, analyzing, and testing devices, 254–276
  oxygen delivery devices, 177–196
  record maintenance and documentation, 492–502
  respiratory support equipment, 208–227
  resuscitation devices, 159–176
  sterilization, 277–307
  ventilator systems and support accessories, 228–253
Ergometry, 118–120
Escherichia coli, 85

Esophageal detection device (EDD), 456–457
Esophageal obturator airway (EOA), 164–165, 165t, 458
Esophago-tracheal combination tube (ETC)/pharyngotracheal lumen airway (PTL), 167–168
$ETCO_2$ detectors, 455–456
Ethical issues, in recordkeeping and documentation, 495–496
Ethylene oxide, 283
Euphoria, 35
Eupnea, 23
Examination, credentialing, 1–13. *See also* Credentialing examination
Excellence, commitment to, 12–13
Excursion, diaphragmatic, 30
Exercise/stress testing, 118–120, 486–488
Exercise tolerance, 37
Exercise training, 37
Exhalation valves, 249
Exhaled carbon dioxide (CO_2), 271–273, 419–421
Exosurf, 336–338
Expansion, chest, 28–29
Expiratory flow
  forced (FEF), 59t
  peak (PEF), 59t
Expiratory muscles, 24
Expiratory positive airway pressure (EPAP), 239, 295
Expiratory pressure, maximum, 44
Expiratory retard/resistance ventilation, 239, 359
Expiratory volume, timed forced, 45
Extubation, 457

Family interaction, in home care, 472–473
Farmer's lung, 141–144, 142t
Fat density, 106
Fear, 35
FEF (forced expiratory flow), 59t
Fenoterol, 311
FET (forced expiratory technique, huff coughing), 26–27, 290, 296
Fetal hemoglobin, 80
Fetal maturity, 130
Fetal scalp blood pH, 460
FEV (forced expiratory volume), 45
Fiberoptic transillumination of chest, 25
Fibrillation, ventricular, 102, 162–163. *See also* Cardiopulmonary resuscitation (CPR)
Fick equation
  for cardiac output, 93
  for shunting, 95
    modified, 96
FIO_2
  calculation of, 211t, 212t
  predicted in stable patients, 428

Fistula(e)
    tracheoesophageal, 111
    tracheoinnominate, 111
Fixed-performance oxygen devices, 188
Flail chest, 24–25
Flaring, nasal, 25
Flexible fiber bronchoscopy (FFB), 123, 223
Flora
    resident, 281t
    transient, 281t
Flow. *See also* Flow rate
    oxygen, 181t, 182t, 278, 279t
    peak, 45–46, 229
Flow interrupter high-frequency ventilation, 240–241
Flow rate
    definitions, 59t
    of gases (FIO_2), 211t, 212t
    inspiratory, 356–357, 358t
    for mechanical ventilation in adults, 356–359
    ventilator, 236
Flow restrictors, 213–214
Flow volume loops (V/V), 65–66
Flowmeters, 209–212, 210t–215t
Fluid, pleural, 86–89, 114
Fluid balance (intake/output), 103
Fluid culture/sensitivity tests, 86–89, 87t
Fluid movement, in tissues, 21t
Flunisolide (Aerobid), 317
Fluoroscopy, 109, 124
Flurazepam (Dalmane), 334, 334t
Flushing, 20
Flutter, atrial, 102
Flutter valve therapy, 225
Forced expiratory flow (FEF), 59t
Forced expiratory technique (FET, huff coughing), 26–27, 290, 296
Forced vital capacity, 45
Foreign bodies
    radiographic appearance, 113
    tracheal, 110
Fowler's method of breath analysis, 55
FRC (functional residual capacity), 296, 433
    by helium dilution, 60
    by nitrogen washout, 61
Fremitus, 32
    tactile, 29
French (Fr) sizing, 174t
Friction rub, 33
Functional residual capacity (FRC), 296, 433
    by helium dilution, 60
    by nitrogen washout, 61
Fungal infections, 141–144, 142t, 145t
Fungicide defined, 281t
Funnel chest (pectus excavatum), 22
FVC (forced vital capacity), 45

Galvanization, 141–144, 142t
Gap, anion, 83
Garments, 277–278
Gas cylinders, oxygen, 178–180, 179t, 180t
Gas density, 106
Gas law, Boyle's, 62t
Gastric tonometry, 421
Gastrointestinal complications, in neonates, 407
Gauges, pressure, 216–218
General appearance, 19
Germicide, 281t
Gestational age, 129
Gestational age scales, 129–130
    Ballard, 129
    Dubowitz, 129–130
    Silverman/Anderson, 130
Glandular phase of physical maturity, 129
Gloves, 277
Glucose, 83
Glucose metabolism, 117
Glycopyrrolate, 311t
Glycosuria, 88
Gowns, 277–278
Gram negative/gram positive bacilli, 85
Gram's stain, 85
Granulocytes, 80, 81, 81t
Granuloma, pulmonary, 141–144, 142t
Grunting, 25
Guessing, 5
Guidel airway, 165
Guillain-Barré syndrome (acute polyneuritis), 140

Haemophilus sp., 85, 139
Haldane effect, 80
Halo sign, 25
Handwashing, 277
Harm principle, 496
HCO_{3-} (plasma bicarbonate), 70, 82t, 83
HDLs (high-density lipoproteins), 84
Heart failure, 101
Heart rate, 28, 449
    fetal, 459–460
    neonatal, 461
Heart sounds, 33–34
Heat
    dry, 283
    moist, 284
Heat-moisture exchangers (HMEs), 205, 206t, 305
Helium analyzer, 272–273
Helium dilution test, 60
Helium with oxygen, 430
Hematocrit, 79
Hematuria, 88
Hemidiaphragm, 113
Hemodynamic monitoring, bedside, 91–105. *See also*
    Bedside monitoring: hemodynamic

Index

Hemoglobin (Hb), 79–80, 120–121, 266, 267. *See also* Blood gas analysis
    fetal, 128
Hemoglobin saturation (SaO$_2$), 70–71, 415
Hemoglobinemias, 80
Hemolysis, 79
Hepatitis, 86, 88
Hernia, congenital diaphragmatic, 424
High-frequency ventilation (HFV), 239–241
    in adults, 378–380
    flow interrupter (HFFIV), 240–241
    jet, 239–240
    of neonates, 407–409
        oscillatory with Sensormedics 2100, 408–409
    positive-pressure (HPPFV), 190
Histoplasmosis, 145t
History, 17
    perinatal, 127–128
HIV (human immune deficiency virus). *See* AIDS/HIV
Hoarseness, 26
Holter monitors, 274, 275
Home assessment, 472
Home care, 212, 469–475
    common treatments for COPD, 473–474
    family interaction, 472–473
    progress evaluation, 472
    treatment methods and equipment, 469–472
Hoods, oxygen, 190–191
    infant, 305
Hormone, antidiuretic (ADH), 103
HPO$_4$– (phosphate), 82t, 83
Huff coughing (forced expiratory technique, FET), 26–27, 290, 296
Human immune deficiency virus (HIV). *See* AIDS/HIV
Humidifiers, 202–204, 204t, 305
    bubble, 202–203
    cascade-type, 203
    heated tubes, 205
    heat-moisture exchangers (HMEs), 205, 206t
    vapor-phase, 204
    wick-type, 203
Humidity, absolute, 197
Humidity, relative, 197, 198t
Humidity deficit, 198t
Hyaline membrane disease (respiratory distress syndrome of newborn, surfactant deficiency disease), 150–151, 336–339, 437
Hydroxyzine (Atarax, Vistaril), 334, 334t
Hyperbaric, 194
Hypercapnia, 124, 406
Hypercapnic central apnea, 485–486
Hypercapnic ventilation, permissive
    in adults, 376–377
    in neonates, 404

Hyperglycemia, 83
Hyperinflation, 108
    pulmonary, 112
    tube cuff, 110–111
Hyperkalemia, 82t, 102, 387
Hypernatremia, 82t
Hyperoxia, 406
Hyperpnea, voluntary isocapnic, 347
Hyperresonance, 30
Hypersensitivity pneumonia, 141–144, 142t
Hypertension, 91
    pulmonary, 101
Hyperventilation, 23
Hypocapnia, 406
Hypodermic needles, 261
Hypokalemia, 82t, 103, 387
Hyponatremia, 82t
Hypophosphatemia, 387
Hypopnea, 42
Hypotension, 91–92
Hypoventilation, 431, 433
    oxygen-induced, 429
Hypoxemia, 18, 47–48, 72, 76t, 123, 292. *See also* Blood gas analysis; Ventilation
    lipids and, 117
    in neonates, 406–407
Hypoxia, 22

I:E ratio, 43–44, 232, 233, 356–359
Impedance pneumography, 123
IMV (intermittent mandatory mechanical ventilation),
    in adults, 359–360
Incentive breathing devices (spirometers), 42, 225–226, 273–275
Incentive spirometry, 345–346
Increased intrathoracic pressure, 386, 436
Incremental work rate, 488
Incubators/warmers, 192
Independent/differential lung ventilation (IPV/DLV),
    in adults, 372–376
Index, cardiac, 94
Indicator-dilution method for cardiac output, 92
Indwelling optical biosensor, 262
Infant(s). *See also* Neonates
    anatomic differences from adults, 127–128
    chest configuration, 22
    gestational age scales, 129
    grunting in, 25
    home apnea monitoring of, 471–472
    hyaline membrane disease (respiratory distress syndrome of newborn, surfactant deficiency disease), 150–151, 336–339, 437
    indications/contraindications for chest physical therapy, 291
    lung compliance in, 437–438

Infants (*cont.*)
  neonatal/perinatal monitoring, 127–132. *See also* Perinatal/neonatal monitoring
  PaO_2 in, 425
  respiratory rate in, 18
  resuscitation of, 459–460
  suctioning in, 301
  tension pneumothorax and CPAP in, 439
  vena caval obstruction in, 439
Infant hoods, 305
Infant mortality, 127–128. *See also* Perinatal/neonatal monitoring
Infection, 137, 139–140. *See also* Pneumonia
  defined, 281t
  fungal, 141–144, 142t, 145t
  medical device–related, 284
Inflation devices, for endotracheal tubes, 173
Inflation hold (inspiratory plateau) ventilation, 241, 357
Information gathering section, 9–10
Innominate artery rupture, 384–385
Inotropes, 329t
Insertion of lines. *See also* Catheterization
  arterial, 99–100
  central venous, 98–99
Inspection, 19–28, 28t
Inspiration, sustained maximal (SMI), 225
Inspiratory/expiratory (I:E) ratio, 43–44, 232, 233, 356–359
Inspiratory flow, peak (PIF), 59t
Inspiratory flow rate, 356–357, 358t
Inspiratory hold (inspiratory plateau) ventilation, 241, 357
Inspiratory positive airway pressure (IPAP), 239
Inspiratory pressure, maximum, 44
Inspiratory time, 237, 402
  calculations of, 237
Inspiratory training, resistive, 347–348
Insulin, 83
Intake/output monitoring, 103
Intercostal retractions, 25
Intermittent mandatory (IMV) ventilation, 51, 52, 241
Intermittent mandatory (IMV) mechanical ventilation, in adults, 359–360
Intermittent positive pressure breathing (IPPB), 47, 348–350, 469–470, 492
Interview, patient, 34–38
Intracranial pressure (ICP) elevation, 291, 406, 436
Intracranial pressure (ICP) monitoring, 124–125
Intrathoracic pressure increase, 386, 436
Intrinsic asthma, 135–136
Intubation, endotracheal, 29–30, 110–111, 455–457
Inverse ratio (IRV) ventilation, 241–242
Ionizing radiation, 284
Ions, 81–83. *See also* Electrolytes; *specific ions*
IPAP (inspiratory positive airway pressure), 239

IPPB (intermittent positive pressure breathing), 47, 348–350, 469–470, 492
Iprapropium bromide (Atrovent), 311, 312
IPV/DLV (independent/differential lung ventilation), in adults, 372–376
Iron lung, 247–248
Isoetharine, 311t
Isoflow volume point (VisoV), 66
Isolation, types of, 278
Isolation precautions (universal precautions), 280t
Isoproterenol, 311t
Isotropic cardiovascular agents, 329, 329t
Item responses, 7–8
Items, types of test, 6–7

Jet high-frequency ventilation (HFJV), 239–240
  of neonates, 407–408
Joule seconds, 162
Jugular venous obstruction, 439
Jugular venous pressure, 20

K^+ (potassium), 81, 82t. *See also* Hyperkalemia; Hypokalemia
Kenalog (triamcinolone acetonide), 316
Keyed or correct options, 4
Kinking, cuff, 384
Klebsiella sp., 85
Kronig's isthmus, 30
Kussmaul's breathing, 23
Kyphoscoliosis, thoracic, 22

Laboratory tests. *See also specific tests; parameters*
  clinical, 79–90
  pulmonary, 58–78
Lactic dehydrogenase (LDH), 84
LAP (left atrial pressure), 446–447
Large for Gestational Age, 129
Laryngoscopes, 163–164, 164t
Lasers, YAG, 223–224
Lateral decubitus view, 108
Lateral neck X-rays, 114–115
Lateral view, 108
Laws. *See also* Equations
  Beer's, 121
  Boyle's Gas, 62t
  Poiseuille's, 46, 298
LDH (lactic dehydrogenase), 84
LDLs (low density lipoproteins), 84
Leads, electrocardiographic, 255t
Learning needs assessment, 38
Lecithin-sphingomyelin (L/S) ratios, 130
Left atrial pressure (LAP), 446–447
Legal issues, in recordkeeping and documentation, 19, 495–496
Legionnaire's disease, 145t

Index

Leukocyte count (WBC), 80–81, 81t
Leukocytes (WBCs, white blood cells), 80–81, 81t
Level of consciousness, 34–35
Lidocaine, 331
Linde Walker system, 181–182
Lines, insertion of
    arterial, 99–100
    central venous, 98–99
    umbilical, 130–131
Lobes, lung, anatomic positions of, 107t
Low birth weight, 129
Lukens traps, 85, 175
Lung(s)
    anatomic positions of segments (lobes), 107t
    consolidation of, 112, 144–146, 145t
    "dirty," 109
    iron, 247–248
    puncture of, 113
Lung abscess, 290, 424
Lung compliance, 47–48, 62–63, 63t
    in infants, 437–438
Lung disease, occupational (pneumoconiosis), 141–144, 142t
Lung mechanics (mechanics of breathing), 48–49, 49t
Lung volumes and capacities, 59t
Lung water, with PEEP, 437
Lymphocytes, 81, 81t

Macintosh blade, 163–164, 164t
Magnesium (Mg^{++}), 82t, 83
Magnetic resonance imaging (MRI), 109
Mainstream nebulizers, 198
Malt worker's lung, 141–144, 142t
Malnutrition/nutrition, 118, 387–388
Mandatory minute volume ventilation (MMV), 242, 377–378
Maneuver, Sellick, 29
Manometers and gauges, 216–218
Manual resuscitators, 159–160, 160t
MAP (mean airway pressure), 402
MAP (mean arterial pressure), 91–92, 447
Masks
    CPAP, 431–433
    oxygen, 185–190, 189t
        air entrainment, 188–188
        Briggs "L" adaptor, 188
        CPAP (PEP), 190, 191t
        nonrebreathing, 187–188
        partial rebreathing, 187
        simple, 186–187
        tracheostomy, 188
    for sterilization, 277
Mass median aerodynamic diameter (MMAD), 302
Mass spectrometers, 269–270
Master Guide, 1, 12

Maturity, fetal, 130
Maximum breathing capacity (MBC), 65. *See also* Maximum voluntary ventilation (MVV)
Maximum expiratory pressure, 44
Maximum inspiratory pressure, 44
Maximum voluntary ventilation (MVV), 59t, 65
MBR-TB (multiple-drug resistant tuberculosis), 284
Mean airway pressure (MAP), 402, 402t
Mean arterial pressure (MAP), 91–92, 447
Measures, drug, 309t
Mechanical ventilation
    of adults, 353–398. *See also* Weaning
        airway pressure release (APRV), 366–369
        complications of PEEP (auto-PEEP), 380–383, 385. *See also under* Positive end-expiratory pressure (PEEP)
        flow rates (pattern), 356–359
        high-frequency, 378–380
        independent/differential lung ventilation (IPV/DLV), 372–376
        indications for, 353–356
        intermittent mandatory (IMV), 359–360
        mandatory minute volume (MMV), 377–378
        noninvasive positive pressure (NPPV), 369–372
        permissive hypercapnic ventilation, 376–377
        pressure-controlled inverse-ratio (PC-IRV), 364–366
        pressure support (PSV), 360–364
        special tests during, 395
        synchronized intermittent mandatory (SIMV), 360
        weaning procedures, 387–395
    complications of, 381–387
    continuous positive airway pressure (CPAP) with
        in adults, 433–437
        in infants, 437–439
    of neonates, 399–412
        application of, 400–404
        hazards and effects of, 403–407
        high-frequency ventilation (HFV), 407–409
            jet (HFJV, Bunnell Life-Pulse), 407–408
            oscillatory with Sensormedics 2100, 408–409
        indications for, 399t
        inspiratory time calculation, 402t
        mean airway pressure (MAP) calculation, 402t
        patient-triggered, 400
        permissive hypercapnic ventilation, 404
        weaning from, 403, 407, 409
    positive end-expiratory pressure (PEEP) with
        in adults, 433–437
        in infants, 433–437
Mechanical ventilators. *See* Ventilation; Ventilators
Mechanics of breathing (lung mechanics), 48–49, 49t
Mediastinal shift, 108, 114
Medical device–related infections, 284

Medication nebulizers, 199
Medications, respiratory, 308–343. *See also* Pharmacologic agents; *specific drugs and drug classes*
MEO (maximum expiratory pressure), 44
Metabolic acidosis, 74t–76t
Metabolic alkalosis, 74t–76t
Metabolic rate, 117
Metabolic studies, 117–118
Metal density, 106
Metal fume fever, 141–144, 142t
Metaprotereno, 311t
Metered-dose inhalers (MDIs), 200–201, 303–304
Metering devices (turbinometers), 257–258, 258t
    inspiratory/expiratory force meters, 258
    respirometers, 257–258
Methemoglobinemia, 80
Mg^{++} (magnesium), 82t, 83
Microprocessor-controlled ventilators, 237–239
Miller blade, 163–164, 164t
Minimal pass level (MPL), 1–2
Minute ventilation, 354–356
Minute volume, 42t, 42–43, 356
MIP (maximum inspiratory pressure), 44
Mist therapy. *See* Aerosol generators; Nebulizers
Mistakes, in recordkeeping, 19
Mixed venous sampling ($P-O_2$), 100, 445
MMAD (mass median aerodynamic diameter), 302
MMV (mandatory minute volume ventilation), 377–378
Monitoring
    apnea, home, 471–472
    bedside hemodynamic, 91–105. *See also* Bedside monitoring: hemodynamic
    bedside respiratory, 41–57. *See also* Bedside monitoring: respiratory
    of blood gases in neonates, 412–423. *See also* Blood gas analysis
    cardiovascular, 441–451
        cardiac output, 441–442
        central venous pressure (CVP), 98–99, 442–443, 481
        hemodynamic changes, 446–451
        pulmonary artery and capillary wedge pressure, 96–97, 443–445, 481–482
        systemic arterial pressure, 445–446
    co-oximetry, 120–121
    exercise stress testing, 118–120, 486–488
    intracranial pressure (ICP), 124–125
    metabolic studies, 117–118
    perinatal/neonatal, 127–132. *See also* Perinatal/neonatal monitoring
    radiographic, 106–116. *See also* Radiographic monitoring
    sleep studies, 121–123
    ventilation/perfusion scans, 118

Monitoring devices, 254–275
    blood gas analysis systems, 260–264, 262t
    capnometers, 270–271, 272t
    catheters
        arterial, 255–256
        Swan-Ganz, 256–257
    electrocardiography (ECG), 254, 255t
        ambulatory (Holter monitor), 274, 275
    exhaled CO_2 device, 271–272
    helium analyzer, 272–273
    mass spectrometers, 269–270
    metering devices, 257–258, 258t
    oximeters, 266–267, 268t
    oxygen analyzers, 264–265, 266t, 267t
    pneumotachometers, 259–260
    pressure transducers, 258–259
    spirometers, 42, 225–226, 273–275
    transcutaneous O_2 and CO_2 monitors, 53–54, 267–269, 412–415
Monocytes, 81, 81t
Morphine, 332
Mortality, infant, 127–128. *See also* Perinatal/neonatal monitoring
MRI (magnetic resonance imaging), 109
MRSA (methicillin-resistant *Staphylococcus aureus*), 284
Mucolytic drugs, 315
Mucomyst (acetylcysteine), 315
Multiple-choice questions, strategies for, 2–8
Multiple-drug resistant bacteria, 284
Multiple-drug resistant mycobacterium tuberculosis (MDR-TB), 284
Multiple true-false items, 7–8
Murmurs, 33
Murphy eye, 168
Muscle activity, accessory, 24
Muscle relaxants, 335–336
Muscle training, respiratory, 346–348
Muscle wasting, 19–20
Muscle weakness, 19–20
Muscles
    accessory, 24
    expiratory, 24
    respiratory, 24
Mushroom handler's lung, 141–144, 142t
MVV (maximum voluntary ventilation), 65
Myasthenia gravis, 140
Mycobacterium sp., 85, 150
Mycoplasma pneumoniae, 145t
Myocardial contractility, 447–449

Na^+ (sodium), 81, 82t
Nasal airways, 350–351
Nasal CPAP, 190
Nasal endotracheal tubes, 167
Nasal flaring, 25

Index

Nasopharyngeal airway, 166
Nasotracheal suctioning, 299–301
Nebulizers, 197–199, 200t
    Babbington hydronamic, 199
    drugs for use in, 310–315, 311t, 312t
    entrainment, 199
    for home care, 470
    medication, 199
    small volume, 302–303
    ultrasonic, 201–202, 202t
NebuPent® (pentamidine isethionate), 328–329
Neck vein distention, 20
Neck X-rays, lateral, 114–115
Necrosis (tissue death), 84
Needles, hypodermic, 261
Neisseria gonorrhoeae, penicillin-resisting, 284
Neisseria sp., 85
Neonatal care, recordkeeping in, 494–495
Neonatal/perinatal monitoring, 127–132. *See also* Perinatal/neonatal monitoring
Neonates. *See also* Infants
    Apgar scores, 128t, 128–129
    blood gas monitoring in, 413–414
    endotracheal tubes for, 166–167
    heart rate in, 461
    mechanical ventilation in, 399–410. *See also under* Mechanical ventilation
    resuscitation of, 459–460
Neuromuscular disorders, 140–141
Neutrophils, 81
Newborn, respiratory distress syndrome of (hyaline membrane disease, surfactant deficiency disease), 150–151, 336–339, 437
Nicotine therapy, 324–327
Nitrogen balance, 389–390
Nitrogen shunt, 96
Nitrogen washout test, 61
Noninvasive positive pressure ventilation (NPPV), 369–372
Noninvasive ventilation support systems, 247–249
    chest cuirass, 248
    iron lung, 247–248
    rocking bed, 248
Nonmaleficence, 495
Nonproductive cough, 28
Nonsteroidal anti-inflammatory agents (NSAIDs), 341t
Notes, progress, 18
NPPV (noninvasive positive pressure ventilation), 369–372
NREM sleep, 122–123
NSAIDs (nonsteroidal anti-inflammatory agents), 341t
Nutrition/malnutrition, 118
Nutritional status, 37–38

Obesity, sleep apnea and, 121–122
Oblique view, 108

Obstruction
    jugular venous, 439
    vena caval, 439
Obstructive sleep apnea, 121–123, 151–153
Obturator airway, esophageal (EOA), 164–165, 165t, 458
Occlusion, bronchial, 25
Occupational lung disease (pneumoconiosis), 141–144, 142t
O_2/CO_2, transcutaneous, 53–54, 267–269, 412–415
O_2 content, 71t, 71–72
O_2–Hb (oxygen–hemoglobin) saturation curve, 71t, 415
Oligopnea, 24
Ondine's Curse (central sleep apnea), 122, 151–153
One-response items, 7
Opioid agonists, 341t
Opposing-flow devices, 252
Optical biosensors, indwelling, 262
Options
    correct or keyed, 4
    distractor, 5
Oral endotracheal tubes, 166–167
Oral pharyngeal airways, 165
Orientation to time, place, and person, 35
Ornithosis, 141–144, 142t, 145t
Oronasal airway insertion, 350–351
Orthopnea, 36–37
Oscillatory high-frequency ventilation (HFV) of neonates, 408–409
Output, urinary, 103
Oximeters, 266t, 266–267, 268t
    co-, 265
    pulse, 265–267
Oximetry
    co-, 120–121
    pulse, 51–53, *52–53*, 415–416
Oxygen analyzers, 264–265, 266t, 267t
    electrochemical, 264–265
    paramagnetic (Beckman), 264
    polarographic (Clark) electrode, 261–262, 265, 267
    thermal conductivity, 264
Oxygenation-enhancing techniques, 424–439
    continuous positive airway pressure (CPAP)
        by mask, 431–433
        during mechanical ventilation
            in adults, 433–437
            in infants, 437–439
    oxygen therapy, 424–431
        with carbon dioxide (Carbogen), 430–431
        complications of, 429–430
        with helium, 430
        at home, 470
        PaO_2 values, 424–429. *See also* PaO_2 values
    patient positioning, 424
    positive end-expiratory pressure (PEEP)
        in adults, 433–437
        in infants, 437–439

Oxygenation tests, 67–76. *See also* Acid–base tests; Blood gas tests
Oxygen (O$_2$)
   content, 71t, 71–72
   flow rate calculation (FIO$_2$), 211t, 212t
   partial pressure of (PaO$_2$), 68–70, 69t
Oxygen conservation systems, 183–184
Oxygen delivery devices, 177–196
   bulk oxygen systems, 177–178
   cannulas, 183
   catheters, 184–185
   environmental scavenging systems (ESVS), 193–194
   gas cylinders, 178–180, 179t, 180t
   hoods, 190
   hyperbaric oxygen (HBO), 194
   incubators/warmers, 192
   masks, 185–190, 189t
      air entrainment, 187–188
      Briggs "L" adaptor, 188
      CPAP (PEP), 190, 191t
      nonrebreathing, 187–188
      partial rebreathing, 187
      simple, 186–187
      tracheostomy, 188
   oxygen conservation systems, 183–184
   oxygen extraction devices, 180–181, 181t
   oxygen tents, 192–193
   portable systems, 181–183, 182t, 183t
   transtracheal catheter, 184–185
Oxygen enrichers, 181
Oxygen extraction devices, 180–181, 181t
Oxygen–hemoglobin saturation curve (O$_2$–Hb), 71t, 415
Oxygen monitors, transcutaneous, 53–54, 267–269, 412–415
Oxygen pneumonia, 430
Oxygen therapy, 424–431
   with carbon dioxide (Carbogen), 430–431
   complications of, 429–430
   with helium, 430
   at home, 470
   PaO$_2$ values, 424–429. *See also* PaO$_2$ values
   side effects of, 96
Oxygen toxicity, 430
Oxymizer, 183–184

P$_{50}$, 71
PaCO$_2$ (partial pressure of carbon dioxide), 68
   in neonates, 403–404
PADP (pulmonary artery diastolic pressure), 446–447
Palpation, 28–30
Pancuronium (Pavulon), 335
PaO$_2$ (partial pressure of oxygen), 68–70, 69t
PaO$_2$ values
   a/A ratio, 427
   in COPD, 425
   in infants, 425
   predicted normals
      at altitude, 425, 427, 428
      at sea-level, 425, 426
      in supine and seated positions, 426
PAP (pulmonary artery pressure), 96–97
Paramagnetic (Beckman) oxygen analyzers, 264
Paroxysmal atrial tachycardia (PAT), 102
Paroxysmal nocturnal dyspnea (PND), 37
Paroxysmal ventricular tachycardia (PVT), 102
Partial rebreathing mask, 186
Particle sizes, of aerosols, 304
Pasteurization, 284
PAT (paroxysmal atrial tachycardia), 102
Pathogen, defined, 281t
Patient assessment, 17–40. *See also* Assessment
Patient interview, 34–38
Patient rights, 495–496
Patient transport, emergency, 458–459
Pauling's principle, 264
PC-IRV (pressure-controlled inverse-ratio ventilation), 364–366
PCO$_2$, 43
PCWP (pulmonary capillary wedge pressure), 97–98, 446–447
Peak expiratory flow (PEF), 59t
Peak flow, 45–46, 229
Peak inspiratory flow (PIF), 59t
Pectus carinatum (pigeon chest), 22
Pectus excavatum (funnel chest), 22
PEEP. *See* Positive end-expiratory pressure (PEEP)
Penicillin-resisting *Neisseria gonorrhoeae*, 284
Pentamidine isethionate (NebuPent®), 328–329
PEP (positive expiratory pressure), 190, 295. *See also* Continuous positive airway pressure (CPAP)
Percussion
   diagnostic, 30
   therapeutic, 293
Percussors, 224
Percutaneous needle (pleural) biopsy, assistance with, 488
Perfusion, relative local, 413–414
Perfusion alterations (afterload), 449–451
Perinatal/neonatal monitoring, 127–132
   Apgar scores, 128t, 128–129
   gestational age, 129
   history and data, 127–128
   lecithin-sphingomyelin (L/S) ratios, 130
   umbilical line insertion, 130–131
Peripheral cyanosis (acrocyanosis), 22
Peripheral edema, 20, 21t
Permissive hypercapnic ventilation
   in adults, 376–377
   in neonates, 404
Perspiration, excessive (diaphoresis), 21
PET (peak expiratory flow), 45–46

Index

pH, 68, 69t, 70, 73t–76t, 73–76
    fetal scalp blood, 460
    pleural, 88
Pharmacologic agents, 308–343. *See also specific drugs and drug classes*
    analgesic/anesthetics, 340, 340t, 341t
    antibiotics, 336
    antivirals, 327–328
    artificial surfactants, 336–338
    in asthma, 317–324
        adults, 317–320
        children, 320–324
    bronchodilators, 310–315, 311t, 312t, 313t, 314t
    cardiovascular agents, 329, 329t, 330t
    cromolyn sodium, 315–316
    endotracheal drugs, 332
    mucolytics, 315
    muscle relaxants, 335–336
    pentamidine isethionate (NebuPent®), 328–329
    respiratory stimulants, 333
    respiratory suppressants, 335
    resuscitation drugs, 330–331
    sedatives, 333–335, 334t
    smoking cessation and nicotine therapy, 324–327
    solutions and dosages, 308–310, 309t, 310t
    steroids, 316–317
Pharyngotracheal lumen airway (PTL), 167–168
Phosphate (HPO_{4-}), 82t, 83
Photoelectric pneumotachometers, 260
Photosensors, 262
Physical environment, assessment of, 37–38
Physical therapy, chest, 290–297. *See also* Chest physical therapy
Pickwickian syndrome (sleep apnea), 121–123, 151–153
PIE (pulmonary interstitial emphysema), 424
Pin Index Safety System (PISS), 208, 209t
Pirbuterol, 311
PISS (Pin Index Safety System), 208, 209t
Plasma bicarbonate (HCO_{3-}), 70, 82t, 83
Platelet count, 89
Platelets, 81, 81t
Platypnea, 37
Plethysmography, 274
    body, 59–62, 62t
Pleural (percutaneous needle) biopsy, 488
Pleural drainage devices (chest tubes), 221–223
Pleural effusion, 87t
Pleural fluid, 114
Pleural fluid tests, 86–88
PND (paroxysmal nocturnal dyspnea), 37
Pneumatic chest compressors, automatic, 161–162
Pneumatic resuscitation, 160–161, 161t
Pneumatic (pressure) ventilators, 228–230, 231t
Pneumoconiosis, 141–144, 142t
Pneumocystis carinii, 144

Pneumography, impedance, 123
Pneumonia, 108, 144–146, 145t
    aspiration, 145t
    hypersensitivity, 141–144, 142t
    oxygen, 430
Pneumotachometers, 259–260
    anenometers, 259–260
    photoelectric, 260
    vortex-shedding, 260
Pneumothorax, 24–25, 108, 111
    as complication of bronchoscopy, 123–124, 124t
    as complication of mechanical ventilation, 385
    in neonates, 405–406
    tension, 439
PO_2, 53–54
Poiseuille's law, 46, 298
Polarographic (Clark) electrode, 261–262, 265, 269
Poliomyelitis, 140
Polycythemia, 80
Polyneuritis, acute (Guillain-Barré syndrome), 140
Polysomnography, 123, 152–153, 485–486
$P-O_2$ (mixed venous sampling), 100, 445
POMR (problem-oriented medical record), 19
Portex style tubes, 166–167
Position, Trendelenburg, contraindications to, 291
Positioning
    for effective coughing, 289
    to enhance oxygenation, 424
    for postural drainage, 293
Positive end-expiratory pressure (PEEP), 100, 235, 245–246, 250–252. *See also* Mechanical ventilation; Ventilation; Ventilators
    in adults, 433–437
    complications of (auto-PEEP), 380–387. *See also under* Positive end-expiratory pressure (PEEP)
        cardiovascular, 381–382
        "fighting" the ventilator, 383–384
    in infants, 437–439
    in neonates, 403–404
Positive expiratory pressure (PEP), 190, 295. *See also* Continuous positive airway pressure (CPAP)
Positive-pressure high-frequency ventilation (HFPPV), 190
Posterior-anterior (PA) view, 108
Post-inspiratory hold (inspiratory plateau) ventilation, 241, 357
Postoperative pulmonary complications, 146–147
Postural drainage, 291–292
Potassium (K^+), 81, 82t. *See also* Hyperkalemia; Hypokalemia
PPNG (penicillin-resisting *Neisseria gonorrhoeae*), 284
Precautions
    body-fluid, 88
    isolation (universal), 280t
Prednisone, 316

Preload alterations, 446–447
Premature ventricular contraction (PVC), 102
Prematurity, 129
Pressure
    blood. See Blood pressure; Hypertension; Hypotension
    central venous, 442–443
    continuous positive airway pressure (CPAP), 51, *53*, 235, 238–239
        masks for, 190, 191t
    expiratory positive airway (EPAP), 239
    increased intrathoracic, 386, 436
    inspiratory positive airway (IPAP), 239
    intracranial, 124–125
    pulmonary artery and capillary wedge, 96–97, 443–445, 481–482
Pressure, flow, volume wave forms, 49–51, *50–51*
Pressure-control (PCV) ventilation, 242–243, *244*
Pressure-controlled inverse-ratio ventilation (PC-IRV), 364–366
Pressure support ventilation (PSV), 263, 360–364
Pressure transducers, 258–259
Procainamide, 331
Progress evaluation, for home care, 472
Progress notes, 18
Proportional assist (PAV) ventilation, 243
Proteins, blood, 82t, 83
Proteinuria, 88
Prothrombin time (PT), 88
Protozoal pneumonias, 145t
Pseudomonas sp., 85
    in tap water, 470
PT (prothrombin time), 88
Pulmonary artery catheterization, 481–482
Pulmonary artery diastolic pressure (PADP), 446–447
Pulmonary artery pressure (PAP), 96–97, 443–445, 481–482
Pulmonary artery wedge pressure, 96–97, 443–445, 481–482
Pulmonary barotrauma, 386, 433, 436
Pulmonary capillary wedge pressure (PCWP), 97–98, 446–447, 481–482
Pulmonary diseases, 67, 67t
Pulmonary edema, 112–113, 148, 385
Pulmonary embolism, 149–150
Pulmonary function tests, 58–66. See also Respiratory care plan
    bronchoprovocation, 66
    closing volume (CV), 63
    diffusing capacity, 63–65, 64t
    effort dependence of, 36
    flow rate definitions, 59t
    flow volume loops (V/V), 65–66
    functional residual capacity (FRC)
        by helium dilution, 60
        by nitrogen washout, 61
    isoflow volume point (VisoV), 66
    lung compliance, 62–63, 63t
    lung volumes and capacities, 59t
    maximum voluntary ventilation (MVV), 65
    normal and abnormal values, 60t
    prior to weaning, 389
    raw (airway resistance), 62
    spirometry, 69
    total lung capacity (TLC), 61–62
Pulmonary hyperinflation, 112
Pulmonary hypertension, 101
Pulmonary interstitial emphysema (PIE), 424
Pulmonary laboratory, 58–78
    blood gases, oxygenation, and acid–base determination, 67–76, 71t–76t
    pulmonary function values, 58–66
Pulmonary rehabilitation, 469. See also Home care
Pulmonary scanning, 118
Pulmonary *versus* cardiac conditions, 98
Pulse, 28
Pulse dose/demand oxygen controllers, 216
Pulseless electrical activity, algorithm for, *466*
Pulse oximeters, 265–267
Pulse oximetry, 51–53, *52–53*, 415–417
Pulse pressure, 91
Pulse rate, 18, 18t, 448
Puncture
    arterial, 417–419
    of lung, 113
Pupils, assessment of, 454
Pursed-lip breathing, 344
PVT (paroxysmal ventricular tachycardia), 102

QRS complexes, 102. see also Electrocardiography (ECG)
$\dot{Q}s/\dot{Q}t^s$ (shunt studies), 94–96, 389
Quadriplegia, 140
Quality control, 263
Quaternary ammonium compounds, 283
Questions
    clinical simulation, 8–11, 9t
    multiple-choice, 2–8

Radial artery, cannulization of, 482
Radiographic monitoring, 106–116
    chest X-rays, 106–114, 107t
    lateral neck X-rays, 114–115
    upper airway X-rays, 114
Radiographic views, 108
Rales, 32
RAP (right atrial pressure), 446–447
Raw (airway resistance), 62
Reconditioning exercise training, 37
Recordkeeping, 492–497
    critical care, 493–494
    general care, 492–493

Index

Recordkeeping (cont.)
    legal/ethical implications in, 495–496
    pediatric/neonatal care, 494–495
    progress evaluation, for home care, 472
    progress notes, 18
Red blood cells (RBCs, erythrocytes), 79
Refill, capillary, 20–21
Regulator/reducing valves, 208–209, 209t
Rehabilitation, pulmonary, 469. *See also* Home care
Relative humidity, 197, 198t
Relative local perfusion, 413–414
Relaxants, muscle, 335–336
Relief valves for resuscitators, 159
REM sleep, 122–123
R-epinephrine, 311t
Resident flora, 281t
Residual volume, 296
Resistance
    airway, 46–47, 52
    to antibiotics, 285
    vascular, 444
Resonance, altered, 30
Respiration. *See* Breathing
Respiratory acidosis, 74t–76t
Respiratory alkalosis, 74t–76t
Respiratory care plan, 133–155
    ARDS (adult respiratory distress syndrome), 101, 134–135, 339
    asthma, 135
    bronchogenic carcinoma, 136
    chronic bronchitis, 136–137
    COPD (chronic obstructive pulmonary disease), 138–139
    cystic fibrosis, 137–138
    emphysema, 138–139
    neuromuscular disorders, 140–141
    pneumoconiosis, 141–144, 142t
    pneumonia, 144–146, 145t
    postoperative pulmonary complications, 146–147
    pulmonary edema, 148
    pulmonary embolism, 149–150
    respiratory distress syndrome of newborn (hyaline membrane disease, surfactant deficiency), 150–151, 336–339, 437
    sleep apnea, 151–153
    smoke inhalation burns, 147–148
    thoracic trauma, 153–154
    tuberculosis, 150
    upper airway inflammation, 139–140
Respiratory distress syndrome of newborn (hyaline membrane disease, surfactant deficiency disease), 150–151, 336–339
Respiratory isolation, 278
Respiratory monitoring, bedside, 41–57. *See also* Bedside monitoring: respiratory
Respiratory muscle training, 346–348
Respiratory muscles, 24
Respiratory pharmacologic agents, 308–343. *See also* Pharmacologic agents; *specific drugs and drug classes*
Respiratory quotient (RQ), 117
Respiratory rate, 18, 41, 354
Respiratory sensation (dyspnea), 361
Respiratory stimulants, 333
Respiratory support equipment, 208–227
    blenders/controllers, 215–216, 217t
    bronchoscopes, 223–224
    compressors, 220–221, 221t
    flow restrictors, 213–214
    flowmeters, 209–212, 210t–215t
    incentive breathing devices (spirometers), 42, 225–226, 273–275
    manometers and gauges, 216–218
    pleural drainage devices (chest tubes), 221–223
    regulator/reducing valve, 208–209, 209t
    safety systems, 208
    stethoscopes, 224–225
    vacuum systems, 218–219, 219t
Respiratory suppressants, 335
Respirometer, 42. *See also* Spirometer; Spirometry
Responses, types of, 7–8
Restrictive pulmonary diseases, 67t. *See also* Chronic obstructive pulmonary disease (COPD)
Resuscitation, cardiopulmonary (CPR), 453–468. *See also* Cardiopulmonary resuscitation; Resuscitation devices
Resuscitation devices, 159–176
    airways, 166t. *See also* Artificial airways
        esophageal obturator airway, 164–165, 165t
        oral pharyngeal, 165–166
    automatic pneumatic chest compressors, 161–162
    cuff inflation devices, 173
    defibrillators, 162–163
    esophago-tracheal combination tube (ETC)/pharyngotracheal lumen airway (PTL), 167–168
    laryngeal mask (LMA), 166–167
    laryngoscopes, 163–164, 164t
    manual resuscitators, 159–160, 160t
    nasopharyngeal, 166
    pneumatic resuscitation, 160–161, 161t
    suction catheters, 173–174, 174t, 175t
    tracheostomy buttons, 168
    tube cuffs, 172–173
    tubes, 166–172. *See also* Endotracheal intubation
        nasal endotracheal, 167
        oral endotracheal, 166–167
        tracheostomy, 170t, 170–173, 171t, 172t

Resuscitation drugs, 330–331
Retard, expiratory, 357
Retractions
    chest wall, gestational age and, 130
    intercostal or sternal, 25
Reverse isolation, 278
Reynolds Number, 46
Rhonchi, 32
Rib deformities, 25
Ribavarin (virazole), 199, 327–328
Rickettsia, 145t
Right atrial pressure (RAP), 446–447
Rights, patient, 495–496
Right-to-left shunting, 95
Riker valve, 200
Rocking bed, 248
Roentgenography, 109. *See also* Radiographic monitoring
Rotary compressors, 220, 221t
Rub, friction, 33
Rupture
    cuff, 384
    innominate artery, 384–385

Safety systems, for ventilators, 208
Sampling, for blood gas analysis, 260–261, 417–418. *See also* Venipuncture
Sanitizer defined, 281t
Sanz (pH) electrode, 261
SaO_2 (hemoglobin saturation), 70–71, 415
Scale, gestational age, 129–130
    Ballard, 129
    Dubowitz, 129–130
    Silverman/Anderson, 130
Scans. *See* Radiographic imaging; *specific types*
Scintigraphic (radionuclide) scans, 109
Sclerosis, amyotrophic lateral (ALS), 140
Secretion removal, 289–307. *See also individual subtopics*
    aerosol/humidity therapy, 303–305
    chest physical therapy, 290–297
    coughing techniques, 289–290
    suctioning, 297–303
Secretions
    airway, 29
    as complication of mechanical ventilation, 385
Sedatives, 333–335, 334t
Self-assessment, 499–540
    answer keys
        chapter self-assessments, 537–540
        CRT self-assessment, 535
        RRT self-assessment, 536
    outlines
        Entry Level (CRT) Examination, 500t
        RRT Clinical Simulation Examination, 502t
        RRT Written Examination, 501t
    sample examinations
        Certified Respiratory Therapist (CRT), 503–519
        Registered Respiratory Therapist (RRT), 521–534
    setting, 499
Sellick maneuver, 29
Sensitivity controls, for ventilators, 229–230
Septic shock, 101
Serratia sp., 85
Serum glutamic oxaloacetic transaminase (SGOT), 84
Setting, 15
Severinghouse electrode, 261
SGOT (serum glutamic oxaloacetic transaminase), 84
Shaver's disease, 141–144, 142t
Shift, mediastinal, 108, 114
Shock, septic, 101
Shunt, nitrogen, 96
Shunt studies ($\dot{Q}s/\dot{Q}t$)[5], 94–96
    classic (Fick) equation, 95
    modified equation, 96
Siderosis, 141–144, 142t
SIDS (sudden infant death syndrome, crib death), 471–472
Sigh breath, 233
Sighs, 357–359
Signs
    air bronchogram, 108
    halo, 25
    silhouette, 107
    steeple, 114
Silicosis, 141–144, 142t
Silo filler's disease, 141–144, 142t
Silverman/Anderson gestational age scale, 130
SIMV (synchronized intermittent mechanical ventilation), 360
Sinus arrest, 102
Sinus arrhythmia, 102
Situational set items, 8
Sizing, French (Fr), 167, 174t
Skin, clammy, 21
Skin signs, 21–22
Sleep, types of, 122–123
Sleep apnea, 121–123, 151–153
    central (Ondine's Curse), 122, 151–153
Sleep apnea studies (polysomnography), assistance with, 485–486
Small for gestational age, 129
Small particle (SPAG-2) aerosol generators, 199–200
SMI (sustained maximal inspiration), 225
Smoke inhalation, 147–148
Smoking, 121, 136–137, 325
Smoking cessation and nicotine therapy, 324–327
Smoking history, 38
SOAP formula, 19
Social support systems, 37–38

Index

Sodium (Na$^+$), 81, 82t
Sodium bicarbonate (HCO$_3{}^-$), 70, 82t, 83
    in resuscitation, 330–331
Sodium hypochloride, 282
Solutions and dosages, 308–310, 309t, 310t
Somnolence, 34
Sonacide, 283
SO$_4{}^-$ (sulfate), 82t, 83
Sounds
    breath, 31t, 31–33
    heart, 33–34
SPAG-2 aerosol generator, 199
Spectrometer, mass, 269–270
Sphygmomanometer, 217–218
Spinal cord injury, 140
Spinous processes, of airway, 110
Spirals, Curshmann's, 28
Spirometers, 42, 225–226, 273–275
    calibration of, 273
    plethysmography, 274
    rolling-end, 273
    water seal, 273–274
    wedge, 274
Spirometry, 69
    effort dependence of, 36
    incentive, 345–346
Sporicide, 281t
Sputum, visual examination of, 27, 28t
Sputum tests, 84–89, 87t
Stains, types of, 85
Staphylococcus sp., 85
Static effective compliance, 47, 434, 435
Status asthmaticus, 135–136, 430
Steeple sign, 114
Stem statement, 4
Stenosis, tracheal, 110
Sterile, defined, 281t
Sterilization, 277–285
    categories and techniques of, 277–278
    defined, 281t
    definitions of, 281t
    handling contaminated equipment, 278–282, 279t
    isolation precautions, 280t
    methods of, 282t, 282–285
    multiple-drug resistant bacteria, 285
Sternal retractions, 25
Steroid drugs, 316–317
Stethoscopes, 224–225
Stimulants, respiratory, 333
Stop-Think-Act technique, 326
Stowe-Severinghaus (PCO$_2$) electrode, 261, 269
Streptococcus sp., 85
Stress testing, 118–120, 486–488
Strict isolation, 278
Stridor, 26, 33

Stroke volume (SV), 93–94
"ST" segment dysrhythmias, 102
Study skills, 3
Stupor, 34
Stylet, 168
Subcutaneous emphysema, 111–112
Succinylcholine (Anectine), 335–336
Suction catheters, 173–174, 174t, 175t
Suction specimen collectors (Lukens traps), 85, 175
Suctioning
    endotracheal tube, 85
    in infants, 301
    nasotracheal, 299–301
    tracheostomy, 297–299
Sudden infant death syndrome (SIDS), 471–472
Sulfate (SO$_4{}^-$), 82t, 83
Sulfhemoglobinemia, 80
Synchronized intermittent mandatory (SIMV) ventilation, 243
Suppressants, respiratory, 335
Supraclavicular retractions, 25
Surfactant deficiency disease (hyaline membrane disease, respiratory distress of newborn), 150–151, 336–339
Surfactants, artificial, 336–338
Survanta, 338–339
Sustained maximal inspiration (SMI), 225
SV (stroke volume), 93–94
Swan-Ganz catheters, 96–98, 113, 256–257
Sweating, excessive (diaphoresis), 21
Sympathomimetic brochodilators, 313t, 313–314
Synchronized intermittent mechanical ventilation (SIMV), 360
Syringes, for blood gas sampling, 260–261
Systemic arterial pressure, 445–446
Systolic blood pressure, 91

T$_{40}$, 70
Tachycardia, 18, 74, 102
    paroxysmal atrial (PAT), 102
    paroxysmal ventricular (PVT), 102
Tachypnea, 23, 41
Tactile fremitus, 29
Talcosis, 141–144, 142t
Tap water, contamination of, 470
Temperature, 17
Tension pneumothorax, 439
Tents, oxygen, 192–193
Terbutaline, 311t
Test, Allen's, 418. *See also* Blood gas analysis; Pulmonary laboratory
Test-taking strategies, 1–13. *See also* Credentialing examination
Tetanus, 140–141
Theophylline, 314t, 314–315

Therapy. *See also individual subtopics*
  assistance with special procedures, 476–491
  blood gas monitoring, 412–423
  cardiopulmonary resuscitation (CPR), 453–468
  cardiovascular monitoring, 441–452
  mechanical ventilation
    adults, 353–398
    neonates, 399–412
  oxygenation-enhancing techniques, 424–440
  pharmacologic agents, 308–344
  rehabilitation and home care, 469–475
  removal of secretions, 289–307
  ventilation-enhancing techniques, 345
Thermal conductivity oxygen analyzers, 264
Thermodilution method, for cardiac output, 93, 441–442
Thoracentesis, 87–88
  assistance with, 477–478
Thoracic kyphoscoliosis, 22
Thoracic trauma, 153–154
Thoracotomy/thoracostomy. *See* Chest tubes
Thorpe tubes, 210
Tidal volume, 41–42, 235–236, 354–355
Time, inspiratory, 237
Timed forced expiratory volume, 45
Tissue death (necrosis), 84
Tissues, fluid movement in, 21t
TLC (total lung capacity), 61–62
Tobacco use. *See* Smoking *entries*
Tomography, 109. *See also* Radiographic monitoring
  computed (CT scan, "CAT" scan), 109
Tonometry, 263
Total body water, 103
Total lung capacity (TLC), 61–62
Toxicity
  oxygen, 430
  of sterilants, 284
Trach mates, 170
Trachea
  bifurcation of, 110
  radiographic appearance, 109–110
Tracheal deviation, 29
Tracheal stenosis, 110
Tracheoesophageal fistula, 111
Tracheoinnominate fistula, 111
Tracheomalacia, 110
Tracheostomy, 110
  assistance with, 478–479
Tracheostomy buttons, 168
Tracheostomy mask, 188
Tracheostomy suctioning, 297–299
Tracheostomy tubes, 170–173
Transcutaneous O_2 and CO_2 monitors, 53–54, 267–269, 412–415
Transducer method, for central venous pressure (CVP), 443
Transducers, pressure, 258–259
Transient flora, 281t
Transillumination of chest, 25
Transport, emergency, 458–459
Transtracheal aspiration, 85
  assistance with, 482–483
Transtracheal oxygen catheter (TTO), 184–185
  assistance with placement, 484–485
Trauma, thoracic, 153–154
Treadmill testing, 118–120
Trendelenburg position, contraindications to, 291
Triamcinolone acetonide (Kenalog), 316
Triglycerides, 84
Trouble shooting guides
  aerosol generators, 200
  airways, oral/nasal pharyngeal, 167
  arterial catheters, 257
  blending and controlling devices, 217
  blood gas electrodes, 262
  bottled gas systems, 180
  capnographs, 272
  catheters, arterial, 257
  compressors, 221
  CPAP devices, 191
  electrodes
    blood gas, 262
    transcutaneous, 269
  endotracheal tubes, oral/nasal, 171
  flowmeters, 214
  heat/moisture exchangers, 206
  humidifiers, 204
  nebulizers, ultrasonic, 202
  oximeters, 267
  oxygen analyzers, 266
  oxygen enclosures, 193
  oxygen extraction devices, 182
  oxygen masks, variable performance, 186
  oxygen systems
    fixed performance, 189
    portable, 183
    variable performance, 185
  regulators, 210
  resuscitators
    manual, 160
    pneumatic, 161
  suction catheters, 175
  tracheostomy tubes, 172
  transcutaneous electrodes, 269
  turbinometer, gas-driven, 258
  ultrasonic nebulizers, 202
  vacuum systems, 219
  ventilators
    electric, 245
    pressure, 231
T-tube (Briggs adaptor), 187
Tube cuff hyperinflation, 110–111
Tube cuffs, 172–173, 455
  complications related to, 383–385

Index

Tuberculosis, 150
    multiple-drug resistant (MDR-TB), 284
    pulmonary, 150
Tubes/tubing, 166–172, 170t, 171t, 172t
    chest, 111, 221–223, 479–480
    endotracheal, 110–111
        nasal, 167
        oral, 166–167
        placement of, 29–30
    heated humidification, 205, 305
    Thorpe, 210
    tracheostomy, 170–173
Tubing compliance correction equation, 234
Turbinometers, 257–258, 258t
"T" wave dysrhythmias, 102

Ultrasonic nebulizers, 201–202, 202t
Ultrasonography, 109
Umbilical lines, 130–131
Underwater Medical Society (UMS), 194
Universal precautions, 280t
Upper airway inflammation, 139–140
Upper airway X-rays, 114
Urinary output, 103
Urine abnormalities, 88
Urine tests, 88
"U" wave abnormalities, 103

Vacuum systems, 218–219, 219t
Validation, of examination, 2
Valium (diazepam), 334, 334t
Valves
    flutter, 225
    relief for resuscitators, 159
    Riker, 200
Vanceril (beclomethasone dipropionate), 317
Vapor-phase humidifiers, 204
Vascular monitoring, assistance with, 480–482
Vascular resistance equations
    pulmonary, 444
    systemic, 444
Vasoconstrictors, 329, 329t
Vasodilators, 329, 329t
V_D/V_T (dead space:tidal volume ratio), 54–55
Vena caval obstruction, CPAP and, 439
Venipuncture, assistance with, 489–492
Venous distention, 20
Venous sampling, mixed ($P-O_2$), 100, 445
Ventilation. *See also* Ventilators
    airway pressure release (APRV), 238
    alveolar, 43–44
    alveolar ($V_{CA}C$), 23. *See also* A-aDO$_2$ (alveolar-arterial oxygen gradient)
    bilevel positive airway pressure (BiPAP), 238–239, *240*
    controlled mechanical (CMV), 48–51, *50–51*
    emergency, 453–454
    expiratory retard/resistance, 239
    high-frequency, 239–241
        flow interrupter (HFFIV), 240–241
        positive-pressure (HFPPV), 190
    inspiratory plateau, 241
    intermittent mandatory (IMV), 51, *52,* 241
    inverse ratio (IRV), 241–242
    mandatory minute (MMV), 242
    maximum voluntary (MVV), 59t, 65
    mechanical. *See also* Mechanical ventilation
        of adults, 353–398
        of neonates, 399–412
    minute, 354–356
    noninvasive support systems, 247–249
        chest cuirass, 248
        iron lung, 247–248
        rocking bed, 248
    positive pressure, 103
    pressure-control (PCV), 242–243, *244*
    pressure-support (PSV), 243
    proportional assist (PAV), 243
    synchronized intermittent mandatory (SIMV), 243
Ventilation/perfusion (V/Q) scans, 118
Ventilation scans, radioactive, 109
Ventilator alarm systems, 245–247, 246t
Ventilator flow waveform, 234–235, *235*
Ventilator systems, 228–253
Ventilators. *See also* Ventilation
    electric, 231–237, 234t, 236t, 237t, 245t
    external circuitry for, 249–250
    humidification tubes, 205, 305
    microprocessor-controlled, 237–239
    modifications to, 238–245
    PEEP administrating devices, 250–252
    pneumatic (pressure), 228–230, 231t
Ventilatory therapy, 344–351. *See also* Mechanical ventilation
    breathing techniques, 344
    incentive spirometry, 345–346
    intermittent positive pressure breathing (IPPB), 47, 348–350, 469–470, 492
    oronasal airway insertion, 350–351
    respiratory muscle training, 346–348
Ventilometer, 42. *See also* Spirometer; Spirometry
Ventricular contraction, premature (PVC), 102
Ventricular fibrillation, 102, 162–163
Ventricular work, 93–94
Veracity, 495
Verpamil, 332
Vibration
    therapeutic, 294
Vibrators, chest, 224–225
Views, radiographic, 108
Viral pneumonias, 145t
Virazole (ribavirin), 199, 327–328

Viricide, 281t
VisoV (isoflow volume point), 66
Vistaril (hydroxyzine), 334t, 334–335
Vital capacity, 45
    forced, 45
Vital signs, 17–18, 492–493
VLDLs (very low density lipoproteins), 84
Vocal fremitus, 32
Volume. *See also* Tidal volume
    closing (CV), 63
    end-diastolic/end-systolic, 93–94
    minute, 42t, 42–43, 356
    residual, 296
    tidal, 41–42, 235–236
Volume testing, 65–66
Voluntary isocapnic hyperpnea, 347
Vortex-shedding pneumotachometers, 260
VO_2/VOC_2, 117
$\dot{V}/\dot{Q}$ inequality, 433
VRE (vancomycin-resistant enterococci), 284
V/V (flow volume loops), 65–66

Wasting, muscle, 19
Water
    contamination of, 470
    lung with PEEP, 437
    total body, 103

Water density, 106
Water manometer method, for central venous pressure (CVP), 443
Watt-seconds, 162
Waveforms
    pressure, flow, volume, 49–51, *50–51*
    ventilator flow, 234–235, *235*
Weakness, muscle, 19–20
Weaning, from mechanical ventilation, 55
    of adults, 387–395
    of neonates, 403, 407, 409
Weight training, 348
Wheezing, 26, 32–33. *See also* Asthma
White blood cells (WBCs, leukocytes), 80–81, 81t
Wick-type humidifiers, 203
Woods metal, 208
Work
    of breathing, 394, 433
    ventricular, 93–94
Work rate, incremental, 488
Wright respirometer, 257–258

Xenon inhalation, 118
X-rays. *See* Radiographic monitoring

YAG laser, 223–224
Yankauer tonsillectomy catheter, 175

Index

Equations

- 3-1: Calculation of Minute Volume, 42
- 3-2: The Bohr Equation for Dead Space Calculation, 55
- 4-1: Calculation of O_2 Content, 71
- 4-2: Calculation of A-a Gradient, 72
- 6-1: Calculation of Mean Arterial Pressure, 92
- 6-2: Fick Equation for Determining Cardiac Output, 93
- 6-3: The Classic Shunt Equation (Fick Derivation), 95
- 6-4: Modified Shunt Equation, 96
- 12-1: Duration of Cylinder Gas Flow, 180
- 12-2: Time Estimates for Portable Oxygen Systems, 182
- 12-3: Air/Oxygen Ratio, 189
- 13-1: Calculating % Relative Humidity, 198
- 13-2: Calculation of Humidity Deficit, 198
- 14-1: Calculating FIO_2, 211
- 14-2: Calculating Total Flow, 211
- 14-3: Calculating Oxygen Flow Rate, 212
- 14-4: Calculating Gas Flow Rates with Two Flowmeters, 213
- 14-5: Shortcut Equation to Determine FIO_2 from Two Flowmeters, 214
- 14-6: Calculating Flow Rate of Helium/Oxygen Mixtures, 214
- 15-1: Calculating I:E Ratio, 233
- 15-2: Correcting for Tubing Compliance, 234
- 15-3: Solving for Ventilator Tidal Volume, 236
- 15-4: Solving for Average Ventilator Flow Rate, 236
- 15-5: Solving for Inspiratory Time, 237
- 18-1: Application of Poiseuille's Law and Airway Resistance, 298
- 19-1: Dilution Equation, 309
- 19-2: Concentration Equation, 310
- 21-1: Calculation of Alveolar Tidal Volume, 355
- 21-2: Calculation of Exhaled Tidal Volume, 355
- 21-3: Calculation of Inspiratory Flow Rate, 358
- 21-4: Respiratory Sensation (Dyspnea), 361
- 21-5: Work of Breathing (WOB) in Joules/minute, 394
- 22-1: Calculation of Inspiratory Time, 402
- 22-2: Calculation of Mean Airway Pressure, 402
- 24-1: Predicting PaO_2 in the Supine and Seated Positions, 426
- 24-2: Determining a/A Ratio, 427
- 24-3: Predicting the PaO_2 Following Changes in Altitude, 428
- 24-4: Predicting Required FIO_2 in Stable Patients, 429
- 24-5: Calculation of Static Effective Compliance, 435
- 25-1: Calculation of Pulmonary Vascular Resistance, 450
- 25-2: Calculation of Systemic Vascular Resistance, 450

Tables

- 1-1: Scoring Rationale for Clinical Simulation Exams, 2
- 2-1: Causes of Change in Pulse Rate, 18
- 2-2: Fluid Movement in the Tissues, 21
- 2-3: Gross Appearance of Sputum, 28
- 2-4: Normal Breath Sounds, 31
- 3-1: Mechanics of Breathing Symbols, 49
- 4-1: Lung Volumes and Capacities, 59
- 4-2: Flow Rate Definitions, 59
- 4-3: Pulmonary Function Abnormalities, 60
- 4-4: Boyle's Gas Law, 62
- 4-5: Specific Compliance Comparisons, 63
- 4-6: Conditions That May Influence D_LCO, 64
- 4-7: Types of Pulmonary Disease, 67
- 4-8: Normal Blood Gas Values, 68
- 4-9: pH Relationships, 69
- 4-10: Predicted PaO_2 as a Function of Age, 69
- 4-11: Factors that Shift the O_2-Hb Dissociation Curve, 71
- 4-12: Classification of Hypoxemic Interpretation, 73
- 4-13: Acid-Base Interpretation Possibilities, 73
- 4-14: Acid-Base Compensation, 74
- 4-15: Acid-Base Interpretation Example, 75
- 4-16: Symptoms Associated with Acid-Base Disturbances, 75
- 4-17: Causes of Acid-Base Disturbances, 76
- 4-18: Causes of Hypoxemia, 76
- 5-1: Normal Values for Differential Leukocyte Count, 81
- 5-2: Normal Electrolyte Values, 82
- 5-3: Causes of Electrolyte Disturbances, 82
- 5-4: Specific Etiologies of Pleural Effusions, 87
- 6-1: Conditions Altering Cardiac Output, 94
- 6-2: Clinical Deviations from Normal CVP, 99
- 6-3: Hemodynamic Changes in Various Clinical Conditions, 101
- 6-4: Cardiac Cycle of the ECG, 101
- 7-1: Relative Anatomic Positions of Lung Segments, 107
- 8-1: Complications of bronchoscopy, 124
- 9-1: APGAR Scoring System, 128
- 10-1: Inhaled Substances That May Lead to Pneumoconiosis, 142
- 10-2: Causative Microorganisms of Pneumonia, 145
- 11-1: Laryngoscope Blade Dimensions, 164
- 11-2: Oral Airway Dimensions, 165
- 11-3: Endotracheal Tube Dimensions, 170
- 11-4: Suction Catheter Sizes, 174
- 12-1: Color Codes for Medical Gas Cylinders, 179
- 12-2: Factors for Calculating Duration of Oxygen Flow, 179
- 12-3: Percentage of O_2 at Varying Flow rates in Concentrators, 181
- 12-4: Air/Oxygen Entrainment Ratios, 169
- 14-1: Pin Index Connections, 209
- 14-2: Pressure Conversion Factors, 218
- 14-3: Optimal Pressure Range for Suction Catheters, 219
- 15-1: Ventilator Alarms, 246
- 16-1: ECG Leads, 255
- 16-2: Desaturation Event Response Time, 267
- 17-1: Human Body Fluids 279
- 17-2: Universal Precautions 280

17-3: Definitions of Sterilization, 281
17-4: Methods of Sterilization, 282
19-1: Drug Expressions, 309
19-2: Bronchodilator Drugs for Use in Nebulizers (adults), 311
19-3: Bronchodilator Drugs for Use in Nebulizers (neonates), 312
19-4: Response To Stimulation of Autonomic Drug Receptors, 313
19-5: Dosage Adjustments for Altered Metabolism of Theophylline, 314
19-6: Drugs for Altering Pump function, Preload, and Afterload, 329
19-7: Diuretics, 330
19-8: Sedative Drugs, 334
19-9: Local/Regional Analgesic Agents and Techniques, 340
19-10: Classification of Analgesic Agents, 341
22-1: Indications for Assisted Ventilation of the Neonate, 399
IV-1: CRT Examination Content Outline, 500
IV-2: RRT Written Examination Content Outline, 501
IV-3: RRT Clinical Simulation Examination Content Outline, 502

Trouble Shooting Guides

11-1: Manual Resuscitators, 160
11-2: Pneumatic Resuscitators, 161
11-3: Oral/Nasal Pharyngeal Airways, 167
11-4: Oral/Nasal Endotracheal Tubes, 171
11-5: Tracheostomy Tubes, 172
11-6: Suction Catheters, 175
12-1: Bottled Gas Systems, 180
12-2: Oxygen Extraction Systems, 182
12-3: Portable Oxygen Systems, 183
12-4: Variable Performance Oxygen Systems, 185
12-5: Variable Performance Oxygen Masks, 186
12-6: Fixed Performance Oxygen Systems, 189
12-7: CPAP Devices, 191
12-8: Oxygen Enclosures, 193
13-1: Aerosol Generators, 200
13-2: Ultrasonic Nebulizers, 202
13-3: Humidifiers, 204
13-4: Heat Moisture Exchangers, 206
14-1: Regulators, 210
14-2: Flowmeters, 215
14-3: Blending & Controlling Devices, 217
14-4: Vacuum Systems, 219
14-5: Compressors, 221
15-1: Pressure Ventilators, 231
15-2: Electric Ventilators, 245
16-1: Arterial Catheters, 256
16-2: Gas Driven Turbinometer, 258
16-3: Blood Gas Electrodes, 262
16-4: Oxygen Analyzers, 266
16-5: Oximetry, 268
16-6: Transcutaneous Electrodes, 269
16-7: Mainstream & Sidestream Capnographs, 272